16-bit Microprocessors

16-bit Microprocessors

IAN R. WHITWORTH

Royal Military College of Science, Shrivenham

COLLINS

8 Grafton Street, London W1

Collins Professional and Technical Books
William Collins Sons & Co. Ltd
8 Grafton Street, London W1X 3LA

First published in Great Britain by
Granada Publishing 1984 (Previous ISBN 0-246-11572-6)
Reprinted with amendments by
Collins Professional and Technical Books 1985

British Library Cataloguing in Publication Data
Whitworth, Ian R.
16-bit microprocessors.
1. Microprocessors
I. Title
001.64'04 QA76.5

ISBN 0-00-383113 2

Typeset by Columns of Reading
Printed and bound in Great Britain by
Richard Clay (The Chaucer Press) Ltd, Bungay, Suffolk

Contents

Preface

The world of the microprocessor is becoming increasingly complex, with new developments being announced every day. Despite this complexity, the microprocessor is becoming ever more pervasive, entering, in one form or another, all aspects of the lives of those fortunate to be resident in technologically advanced countries. Even underdeveloped nations are feeling the impact of the microprocessor. In the short space of twelve years, semiconductor companies have evolved through several generations of microprocessor designs; at first, their devices were looked upon as logic systems replacements, or microcontrollers, but now their most sophisticated products rival the upper end of the minicomputer spectrum in speed and power.

At the time of writing, nearly all microprocessor-based products have been designed around 4-bit or 8-bit microprocessor central processor units (CPUs), or single-chip computers with on-chip memories and interfaces. These devices have matured into well-proven designs, backed-up by a wealth of knowledge and applications experience. From the point of view of the professional engineer, a knowledge of 8-bit microprocessors – hardware and systems design, software design and maintenance, and applications – is almost mandatory. Indeed, a recently-graduated engineer is likely to have used 8-bit microprocessors in practical work during his College or University courses, whilst many older practising engineers will have become familiar with them through manufacturers' training courses, followed by the practical experience of designing devices into useful products. For anyone wanting to become familiar with the 8-bit microprocessor, there are numerous elementary textbooks available which will serve as a good introduction to the field. Accordingly, a knowledge of 8-bit microprocessors is assumed, and in the interests of space, this book does not start from scratch. A 'revision chapter', Chapter 1, serves to remind the reader of the concepts and terminology of the 8-bit processor. The rest of the book is devoted to the new, and perhaps unfamiliar, ideas of the 16-bit processor, and other relevant developments.

The 16-bit microprocessor is much more than an 8-bit design with twice the word length. Although some of the early 16-bit processors did not offer much more than the speed advantage gained by their word length, the modern processor is completely different from its 8-bit counterpart. Modern 16-bit designs have attempted to ease the systems designer's task by providing instruction sets of considerable sophistication, operating system support in hardware, good support of high-level languages, and ease of interfacing to the sort of bus structure which will form the basis of a multiple-processor installation. Whereas the first 8-bit designs embodied the view of what was needed in a processor from a hardware logic designer's standpoint, the modern 16-bit designs reflect the importance of software in overall systems design, and incorporate features requested by the systems designers who had soon uncovered the limitations of the 8-bit designs. Whilst many digital design engineers found the transition from logic design to 8-bit system design easy because of the similarities, the transition to 16-bit design may be thought more difficult, since the territory is less familiar. 16-bit terminology may seem strange, with its references to 'exceptions', 'privilege levels', 'memory management', 'virtual memory', 'coprocessors', 'semaphores', and many other new terms. The main objective of this book is to explore these new features, and give the reader an idea of how they work, how they are applied, and of their advantages and limitations. An appreciation is also given of the communications facilities which will become increasingly important as the new field of information technology expands, and with it the 16-bit processor, built into all types of information-processing equipment.

The author is indebted to various associates for their help and encouragement during preparation of the book. In particular, acknowledgement should be accorded to Professor C J Harris, Head of E and EE Department, RMCS, and Professor P C J Hill, Head of Electronics Branch, RMCS, for their tolerance and encouragement, to Graham Turner, for many helpful discussions, to Mrs A Hare, for typing parts of the manuscript, and to Dr F Hartley, Acting Dean, RMCS, for giving permission to publish this work.

CHAPTER 1
Introduction

The microprocessor, since its development in the early 1970s, has revolutionised not only electronics, but also many other fields, manufacturing industry, and even leisure and domestic products. The speed of evolution has been breathtaking; in little over a decade, the microprocessor has passed through several generations of devices, starting with the 4-bit 4004, and standing now on the threshold of minicomputer and mainframe domains. No semiconductor manufacturer with a product line encompassing digital integrated circuits has dared not compete with a microprocessor of his own, or a second-source device supporting another's design. The result has been to create a wide choice, in the current industry-standard 8-bit microprocessor field, and fierce competition to produce the next generation, 16-bit microprocessor which will attain industry-standard status. A rough chronology of microprocessor evolution might run:

1971	Introduction of first 4-bit microprocessor.
1972	First 8-bit microprocessor.
1973-5	Introduction of current industry-standard 8-bit CPUs and interfaces, ultraviolet-erasable PROM, 4K dynamic RAMs.
1976-7	First 8-bit single-chip computers.
1978-80	Introduction of modern 16-bit microprocessors, 16K static RAM, dynamic RAM to 64K, larger EPROM.
1980-date	Announcement of 32-bit microprocessor, second generation 8-bit microcontrollers, some second generation 16-bit microprocessors, electrically erasable PROM (E^2PROM).

Many engineers have become familiar with 8-bit microprocessors, either general purpose CPUs or single-chip microcontrollers, making the transition from electronic engineering to microprocessor applications fairly readily, assimilating the hardware techniques fairly readily, and perhaps taking a little longer to become fluent with (in most cases) assembly-code software. The degree of support provided by the semiconductor manufacturers for their devices, somewhat limited at first, has grown, with a vast investment in development system design and in software. As industry has woken up to the possibilities afforded by the 8-bit microprocessor, the average engineer is nowadays likely to have a good working knowledge of 8-bit microprocessors, but many feel overawed by the 'new' 16-bit CPUs, with their apparent complexity, and unfamiliar features. The problems of making the transition from 8-bit to 16-bit microprocessor applications are not trivial. Many new concepts in hardware, in software, in languages, in operating systems, and in networks, are necessary, and it is the intention of this book to introduce them.

The rest of this chapter will be devoted to a description of typical 8-bit microprocessors, their support devices, and their software, partly to refresh the reader's knowledge, and partly for comparison with the 16-bit systems which form the bulk of the book.

1.1 8-bit microprocessor hardware

The 8-bit microprocessor field is characterised by its relative uniformity – although many 8-bit devices are available, they differ in speed and in some features, but, with only one or two exceptions, they have similar structure and philosophy. Certainly the 'industry-standard' microprocessors are all register oriented, all have the same addressing range, and all have broadly similar instruction sets. The block diagram of a typical 8-bit microprocessor is shown in fig. 1.1.

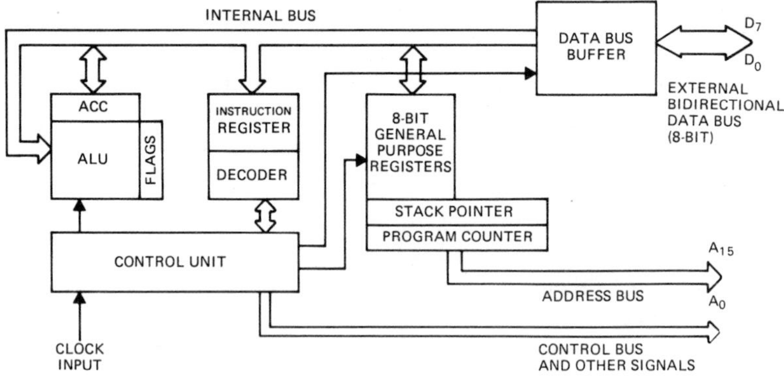

Fig. 1.1 8-bit CPU architecture.

An 8-bit arithmetic-and-logic unit (ALU) operates upon arguments held in programmer-accessible registers or accummulators, returning a result in a register and setting single-bit flags grouped into an 8-bit condition code register, in response to the result of an arithmetic or logical instruction. Timing is performed by a control unit driven by an externally-generated clock signal; the control unit takes signals from an instruction decoder, linked to an 8-bit instruction register. A block of programmer-accessible general-purpose registers for holding data and operands may be available. The microprocessor will certainly possess some 16-bit registers with dedicated functions, in particular, a program counter (or instruction pointer), automatically incremented by the control unit so as to keep track of instruction operation codes, a stack pointer, used as an address register to support the stack, a data structure in read-write memory which is controlled as a last-in, first-out (LIFO) buffer, indirect address registers, and possibly index registers. All these functional blocks communicate using an internal parallel

8-bit data bus, shared using time-division multiplexing.

The signals available at the pins of the microprocessor, which is usually in a 40-pin package, generally consist of separate parallel address and data buses, of width 16 bits and 8 bits, respectively. The 16-bit address bus width allows an addressing range of 64 kbytes, and conveniently, because an address is twice the width of a data word, any address values held in memory will, of course, occupy two bytes. To control data transfers over the bus, a set of control signals are generated by the CPU control unit. The bus control usually exercised is for *synchronous* transfers, controlled in timing exclusively by signals derived from the CPU system clock. Data transfers over the bus require two discrete pieces of information: directional information (transfers from memory or interfaces to the CPU are considered read operations, those in the reverse direction are write operations); and timing or 'strobe' information (to control the time when an addressed location or device should place its data on the bus, or accept data from the bus). Microprocessors may use bus control signals which combine direction and timing information, or may use discrete direction and timing signals. The two possibilities are illustrated in fig. 1.2. Those used by the general class of processors allied to the 8080, for both read and write operations, are shown in fig. 1.2(a). A read operation starts with the CPU issuing the address of the memory or input-output location, followed by the assertion of the $\overline{\text{RD}}$ control line. In response to the $\overline{\text{RD}}$ signal, the device will place data on the data bus, where it will be accepted by the CPU, followed by the release of $\overline{\text{RD}}$ and the removal of the address. The access time of the device must fit in with the CPU bus timing. The write operation starts, like the read, with the CPU issuing an address, followed by the CPU placing data on the data bus. When address and data are stable, the CPU asserts $\overline{\text{WR}}$, which the addressed device uses to latch the data from the bus.

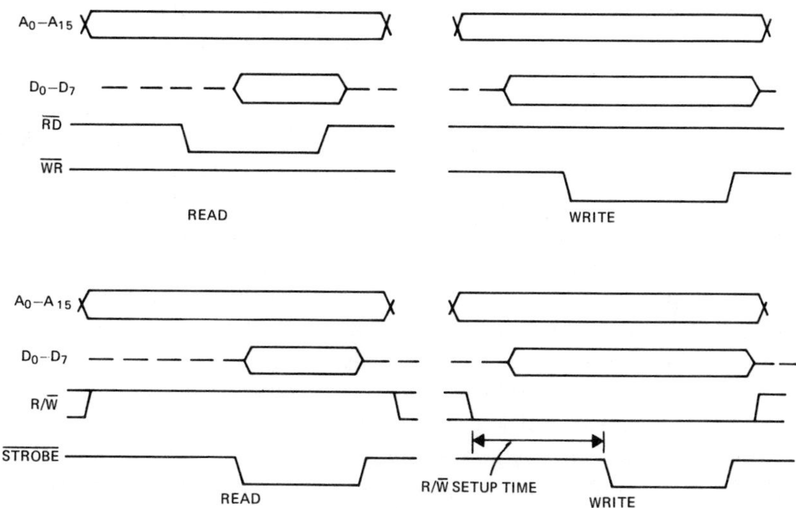

Fig. 1.2 (a) 8080-type bus control, (b) 6800-type bus control.

The second class of control signals, used by 6800-type microprocessors, is shown in fig. 1.2(b). The read operation starts with the CPU issuing an address, and simultaneously taking the R/$\overline{\text{W}}$ control signal high. When the address and R/$\overline{\text{W}}$ signals are stable, the CPU asserts the strobe signal E. The addressed device responds to the assertion of E by placing its data on the data bus, to be accepted by the CPU. The write operation starts with the CPU issuing an address, and simultaneously asserting the R/$\overline{\text{W}}$ line low and placing data on the data bus, followed by E, once address, data and R/$\overline{\text{W}}$ signals are stable. E may be used as a strobe signal by the addressed device, to latch data from the bus. For the 8080 class of microprocessors, any device must respond to directional information at the same time as it is responding to the timing strobe signal, whereas for the 6800 class, the directional information (R/$\overline{\text{W}}$) 'set-up' time with respect to the timing strobe signal is the same as that for the address information.

As well as these synchronous bus control signals, a negative-acknowledgement signal, READY (8080) or $\overline{\text{WAIT}}$ (Z80), may be available to allow memories or interface devices with longer access time than that implied by the CPU bus cycle timing. This signal is not a handshaking signal, since it is only asserted when the addressed device is unable to respond; no positive acknowledgement that a device has been able to respond in time is provided. The usual CPU response to this READY or $\overline{\text{WAIT}}$ signal is to insert 'idle' or wait state clock cycles into the read or write bus cycle, keeping address and control signals stable, and effectively stretching the bus cycle by an integral number of CPU clock cycles until the READY or $\overline{\text{WAIT}}$ signal is removed. To distinguish between memory and input-output operations, two alternatives are possible: the first, and conceptually possibly the 'cleanest', is to make no distinction at all, so that all input-output devices must occupy memory address space, and respond to all bus cycles generated by memory reference instructions. This memory-mapped input-output will also imply that the CPU instruction set need not include explicit input-output instructions. The second style of handling input-output is the provision of explicit input-output control signals, either IO/$\overline{\text{M}}$ (8085) or separate $\overline{\text{IORD}}$, $\overline{\text{IOW}}$ (8080). In this case, input-output devices have their own address space (I/O address space), distinguished from memory address space by the different control signals. I/O addresses can thus overlap memory addresses, and I/O devices require explicit instructions, usually given mnemonics IN and OUT.

All operations of the CPU are controlled by the CPU clock, and each elementary bus cycle or *machine cycle* (read, write, I/O write, instruction fetch, etc.) consists of a number of clock cycles. Each instruction consists of at least one machine cycle (instruction fetch), with memory reference instructions taking several machine cycles (instruction fetch, data read or write, etc.). Microprocessors such as the Z80 and 8080 take several clock cycles to perform each machine cycle, whereas in 6800-style microprocessors, clock cycles and machine cycles are much the same (a memory read, for example, takes just one clock cycle). To illustrate the sort of timing involved, a typical instruction cycle for the Z80 is shown in fig. 1.3 for an output (OUT) instruction. This takes three machine cycles (instruction fetch, read I/O port address [8-bit] from memory location following the location containing the OUT opcode [operation code],

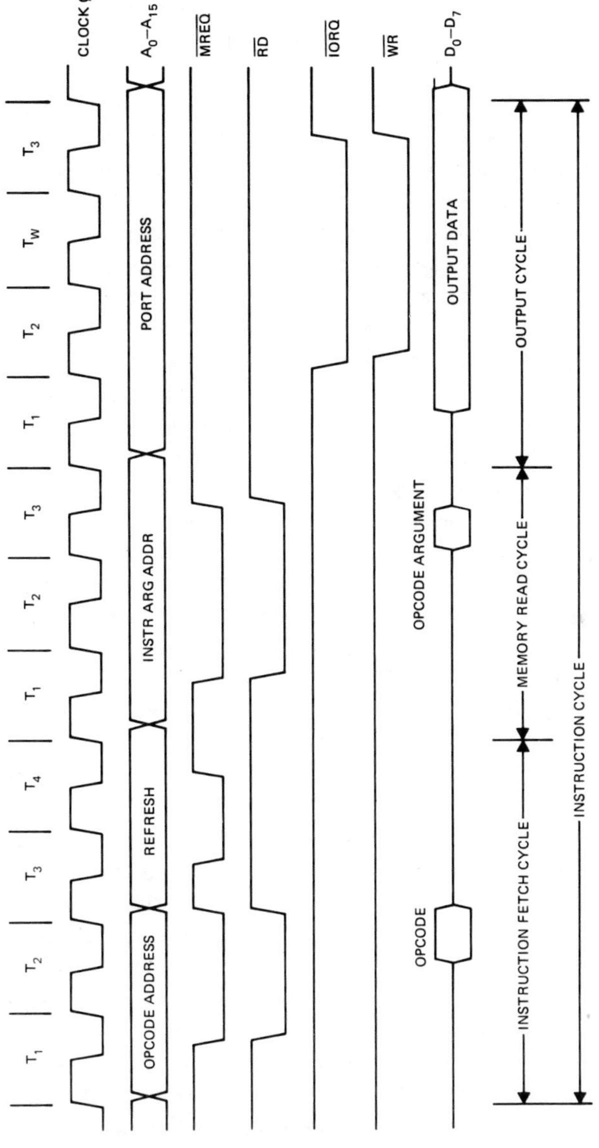

Fig. 1.3 Z80 output instruction execution.

and transfer the contents of the A [accumulator] register to the device). Note that this particular OUT instruction automatically inserts a WAIT state into the write machine cycle, a feature included so that slightly slower devices can be used without any external $\overline{\mathrm{WAIT}}$ signal generation logic. This automatic stretching of any I/O read or write cycles is unique to the Z80 microprocessor. In many 8-bit microprocessors, a hardware signal (possibly part of a coded status signal multiplexed with others) is provided to identify the instruction fetch cycle. It may be used for emulation, trace and debugging, and for special bus cycles (e.g. interrupt acknowledgement).

Bus request and grant signals are relatively simple and centred around use of the bus for direct memory access (DMA). Typically, a HOLD or $\overline{\mathrm{BUSREQ}}$ signal from a device (such as a DMA controller) will cause the CPU to complete its current machine cycle (or maybe instruction cycle) and to suspend its operation by entering an idle state where it simply keeps any internal data and status information refreshed. As soon as the CPU has completed the cycle, the external buses (address, data and control) may be relinquished, and floated to their tristate high-impedance mode (all CPU internal bus drivers have three logic states: the usual '0', approximately 0 V, '1', approximately 2.4 V minimum for a 5 V CPU, and an 'off' state, where the bus is not driven at all, and the only load on it is driver leakage current). Once the buses have achieved their high-impedance state, the CPU can issue an acknowledgement signal HOLDA, or $\overline{\mathrm{BUSAK}}$, which may be used by the requesting device to gain control of the bus. When a device requesting the bus has completed its data transfers, it can release HOLD or $\overline{\mathrm{BUSREQ}}$, and the CPU will regain control of its buses, continuing operation where it left off. This style of bus control is well suited to the requirements of a direct memory access (DMA) controller, which will transfer data to or from memory without CPU intervention, but less suited to multiprocessor shared-bus operation.

Other signals commonly available on an 8-bit CPU are interrupt inputs, which allow a logic signal which is not synchronised with the CPU clock to communicate with the synchronous logic of the CPU. Interrupts may be *maskable*, that is, they may be prevented from occurring by software control, programming a bit in a status or interrupt 'mask' register, or non-maskable, where they cannot be prevented from occurring. A separate hardware input for each type is usual. When a signal occurs on an enabled interrupt input, the CPU will latch it during a normal instruction cycle, so that the signal is remembered, and at the end of the instruction cycle a 'context switch' takes place. The CPU will stop executing its current program, and will begin executing a different program which is specific to the interrupt (and the device causing the interrupt). Usually, the CPU will be returned by software to where it left off in the original interrupted program when this special 'interrupt service routine' is complete, so some means of preserving and restoring the program counter value associated with the interrupted program are necessary. The virtually universal way of achieving this is by using the microprocessor stack. When an interrupt occurs, it is acknowledged, and during the acknowledgement process (which may invoke a read cycle on the data bus immediately following the instruction cycle during which the interrupt occurred) an interrupt code or 'vector' may be acquired. The CPU will then 'push' the program counter onto the stack (writing it in two bytes using the stack pointer as an address pointer, decremented between successive 8-bit writes) which grows from high to low addresses. Once the program counter contents have been saved in this way, it can be loaded with a new value, which points to the start of the interrupt service routine. This address value may be acquired in a number of ways:

(a) It may be the contents of an interrupt location, used as an indirect address location.
(b) It may be the address of the interrupt location itself, where the service routine (or unconditional jump to the service routine) must be placed.
(c) The interrupt input may be 'vectored', that is, the interrupting device will supply, during the interrupt acknowledge cycle, a number (or vector) which identifies it. The address of the interrupt location may be derived directly from the vector (the 8080, for example, has eight interrupt locations, each identified by a 3-bit vector N, and located at an absolute address 8*N) or may be used as an index to a table of interrupt routine addresses. Alternatively, the 8080 allows a 'CALL' instruction to be generated directly by the interrupting hardware, using three successive interrupt acknowledge cycles. The subroutine call may be to an address anywhere in the 64K memory address space of the CPU.

When the interrupt service routine has completed its execution, a RET statement will cause a return to the interrupted program, automatically 'POPping' the saved program counter value off the top of the stack (incrementing the stack pointer register between POPs) into the program counter register. All 8-bit microprocessors are provided with a non-maskable RESET input, which causes the CPU to start operation from a fixed location (usually absolute memory address 0) with an instruction fetch from that location, when RESET is released.

Various 8-bit microprocessors have additional features unique to their own family of microprocessors: multiplexed data bus and lower byte of address bus, with an address strobe signal ALE provided for off-chip demultiplexing (8085); separate tristate bus control (6800); software-testable single-bit inputs (8085); interrupts vectoring to single fixed locations (8085); refresh signals for dynamic memory (see chapter 5, section 5.3) $\overline{\text{RFRSH}}$, indicating, with refresh address, that dynamic memory can be refreshed in a distributed refresh manner during the instruction decode part of an instruction fetch cycle (Z80). This description, however, covers most of the general 8-bit CPU features.

1.2 8-bit microprocessor machine code software

The 8-bit microprocessor is limited in its instruction set compared with an average minicomputer. Its arithmetic is performed as 8-bit, two's complement binary, with single-bit flag registers set according to the results of an arithmetic or logical instruction. Arithmetic instructions are limited in scope too, with no hardware multiply-divide unit on-chip. Addressing modes and memory reference instructions reflect the fact that in most embedded applications (where the microprocessor is built into equipment and runs completely autonomously), program code will be in read-only memory (ROM), and changeable data in read-write random-access memory (RAM). Little provision is made for operating system support, error checking, or regularity in instruction sets or in internal registers to support those instruction sets.

1.2.1 8-BIT PROGRAMMING MODELS

A programming model of a microprocessor is one which shows none of the hardware detail, just the registers of the CPU which are accessible by the programmer. Typical programming models are shown in fig. 1.4. Arithmetic and logical instructions may be confined to one or more accumulator registers (A in fig. 1.4(a), the 8080/8085, A and B in fig. 1.4(b), the 6800). The other general-purpose registers may be used as address pointers (in pairs) as 8-bit or 16-bit counter registers (e.g. iteration counters), or for holding data. An index register (X in fig. 1.4(b)) is used, when its contents are combined with address information, to access arrays or tables of data by referring to an entry by its position in the array. The program counter (PC) is a 16-bit register which keeps track of the instruction stream of the program, and is automatically incremented during the last part of an instruction fetch cycle, ready to point to the next location. The stack pointer has already been commented upon earlier in this chapter. The flag register, or condition code register, contains a number of 1-bit flags, set automatically by the CPU in response to the result of an arithmetic or logical instruction (including perhaps increment and decrement); these are typically a selection from:

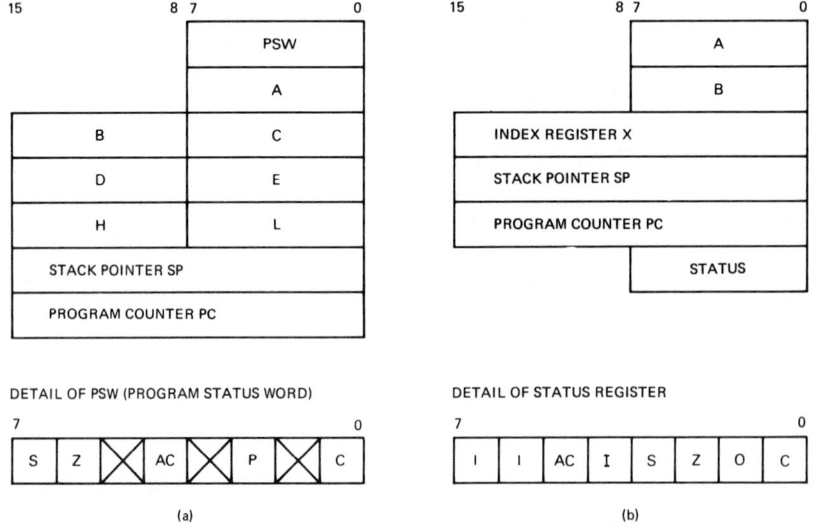

Fig. 1.4 8080, 6800 register models.

S sign (two's complement)
Z zero
CY carry
V overflow (arithmetic)
AC auxiliary (binary-coded decimal, BCD) carry, or half carry. Set when a carry, caused by a result greater than nine, occurs when two BCD numbers are used in an instruction execution. Used to restore a BCD result, represented as two 4-bit BCD numbers packed into an 8-bit word
P parity

1.2.2 ADDRESSING MODES

The 8-bit microprocessor addressing modes are appropriate to devices intended for applications which are relatively simple from a computing point of view. An 8-bit CPU cannot be considered an effective CPU for numerically intensive or multiuser applications (although 8-bit microprocessors have been used for both), and, as a consequence, addressing modes are unsophisticated. Usually a single addressing mode is used on its own, and not combined with others to form complex modes. In the context of addressing modes, the *effective address* is usually taken to mean the physical address formed as a result of the address computation implied by the mode. Typical modes are:

(a) Register: The operand is held in a register, identified by a field in the instruction operation code (opcode).
(b) Direct (or absolute): An absolute address is specified in the program (usually as two bytes following the opcode).
(c) Indirect: The effective address is the contents of a specified register or memory location.
(d) Indexed: The effective address is the sum of the contents of an index register (usually 16-bit register) and an offset (usually 8 bits) specified following the opcode.
(e) Relative (to PC): The effective address is the sum of the contents of the program counter (PC) register and (usually) an 8-bit signed two's complement offset, giving a range of addressing from −125 bytes to +127 bytes relative to PC, for the 6800. Usually reserved for jump instructions only.
(f) Immediate: The 8-bit operand follows the opcode immediately (i.e. is in the next memory location).
(g) Base page: As absolute, but with only one byte specified, giving an address in the range 0 to FFH.

Addressing modes are illustrated in fig. 1.5.

1.2.3 INSTRUCTION SETS

The instructions available in 8-bit microprocessors fall into a number of categories: arithmetic; logical; data moves; branches and calls, and CPU control. Taking each category at a time, typical instructions are shown:

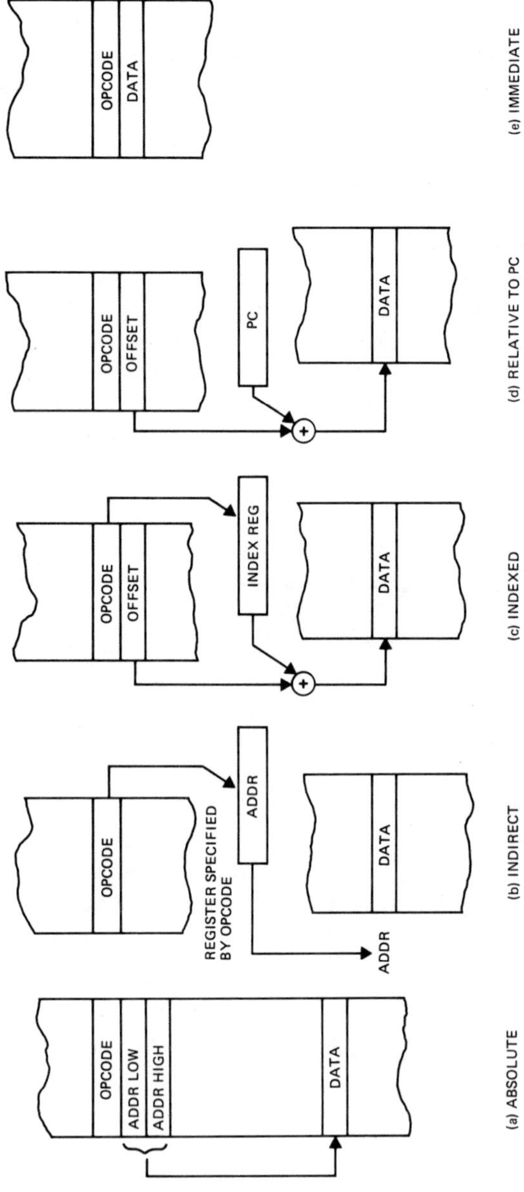

Fig. 1.5 Addressing modes: (a) absolute, (b) indirect, (c) Indexed, (d) relative to PC, (e) immediate.

(a) Arithmetic instructions

ADD	(two's complement)
ADC	Add with carry
SUB	Subtract
SBC	Subtract (using carry as borrow)
DAD	Double (16-bit) add
INC	Increment by one (8-bit register)
DEC	Decrement by one (8-bit register)
INX	Increment 16-bit register
DCX	Decrement 16-bit register
CMP	Compare (perform subtraction and set flags, but do not return result)
COM	1's complement (invert bits of word)
NEG	Negate (2's complement)
DAA	Adjust BCD result

(b) Logical instructions

AND	
OR	Inclusive OR
XOR	Exclusive OR
SET	Bit clear
TST	Bit test

(c) Moves

MOV	) Move or load memory or register
LD	) with 8-bit data
XCHG	Exchange register contents
Shifts:	arithmetic left, right one place (ASL, ASR) logical right one place (LSR)
Rotates:	Through carry (RAL, RAR) one place
	Just register (RLC, RRC) one place

Shifts and rotates are illustrated in fig. 1.6

Stack operations: Load stack pointer SP

PUSH onto stack

POP from stack

(d) Branches

JMP	Unconditional jump to absolute address
J	(condition) Jump to absolute (sometimes relative to PC) address if specified condition (flags) is met, e.g. Jump if zero, nonzero, carry, no carry, positive, negative, parity odd, parity even, overflow
CALL	Subroutine, PUSH current PC onto stack and unconditionally jump to absolute address
RET	Return by POPping PC from stack
SWI	Software interrupt. PUSH current PC onto stack and unconditionally jump to interrupt routine

(e) CPU control

NOP	No operation

HLT	Halt (wait for interrupt)
EI, DI	Enable/disable maskable interrupts
IN, OUT	I/O instructions
CLC, SEC	Clear, set carry

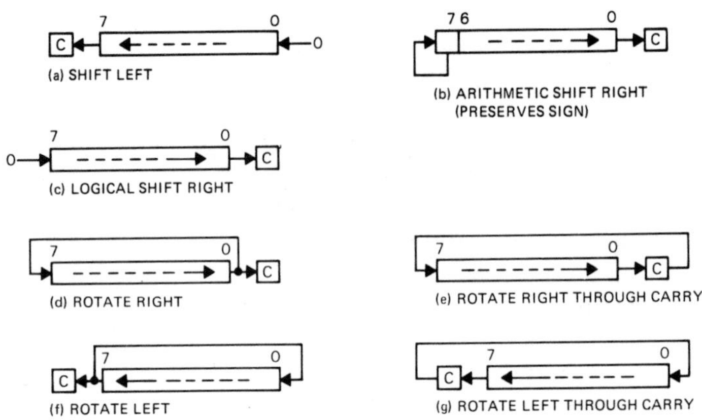

Fig. 1.6 Shifts and rotates: (a) shift left, (b) arithmetic shift right (preserves sign), (c) logical shift right, (d) rotate right, (e) rotate right through carry, (f) rotate left, (g) rotate left through carry.

Note that these instructions will generally not include multiply-divide instructions, multibit shifts and rotates, or any string primitives formed from compound instructions. The Z80 comes closest to including compound instructions with its DJNZ (decrement a register and jump if result is non-zero), useful for iteration control, its block data transfer and search instructions LDIR, LDDR (load location specified by DE register pair with the contents of the location specified by HL register pair, increment (decrement) both, and repeat the number of times specified by the BC register pair) and CPIR, CPDR (compare). Typically, only one stack is supported, and no provision is made for any operating system support or memory management. In some microprocessors, instructions are restricted in the addressing modes they can use, for instance, conditional branches may be limited to PC-relative addressing, and subroutine calls may be limited to absolute addressing. Invariably, most 8-bit microprocessors have some instructions which require absolute addressing, which implies that position-independent code is difficult to write. Invariably, then, any ROM-based code tends to be absolute, and cannot be relocated.

Despite these criticisms, the instruction sets of the present 8-bit microprocessors have proved remarkably effective. They do not, however, meet the requirements of some of the up and coming computer applications, such as office automation applications, local-area networks, and fast complex control systems. The former applications require multiuser operating systems, protection mechanisms, memory management, and, ultimately, virtual memory support, while control applications require fast, high-precision arithmetic and fast interrupt handling.

1.3 Memory devices

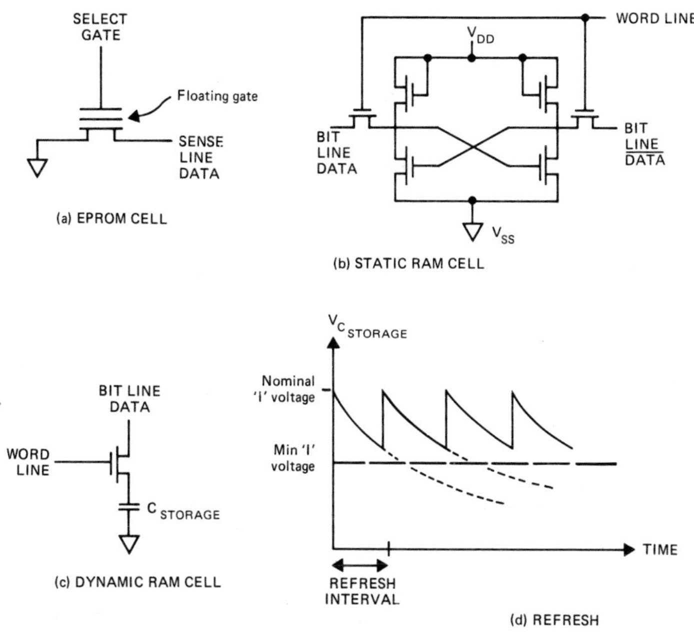

Fig. 1.7 Memory technology: (a) EPROM cell, (b) static RAM cell, (c) dynamic RAM cell, (d) refresh.

Memory devices for 8-bit microprocessors encompass the full spectrum of semiconductor memories, including read-only memory (ROM) in all its guises, for program and permanent data storage, and both static and dynamic read-write random-access memory (RAM). Read-only memory, programmed by the manufacturer, is only used in the highest-volume applications because of the expense of mask making. More often used is field-programmable ROM (PROM) and and erasable PROM (EPROM). The storage element or 'cell' of a typical EPROM is shown in fig. 1.7(a), which uses a single FET transistor with a 'floating gate', insulated from the transistor by oxide layers. Charge may be induced on the gate by applying high voltages to this cell, and will remain there for a long time, and is typically guaranteed to last at least ten years. The state of charge on the gate may be read non-destructively using the transistor itself. To erase the information, the most common EPROMs use ultraviolet light which causes ionisation in the chip and destroys any stored charge when the chip is illuminated through a quartz window built into the package. The process takes about twenty minutes. Naturally, parts of the EPROM chip cannot be selectively exposed to ultraviolet light, so every location is erased in one operation. Recently electrically-erasable PROMs (EEPROMs or E[2]PROMs) have become available, rivalling one of the most popular sizes of UV-EPROM, 2 kbytes. Charge in an EEPROM is induced and erased by an electron tunnelling process, so individual locations may be altered. Erasure and rewriting is faster than with the UV-EPROM, and although the first devices required externally-applied high programming voltages, the most recent ones use an on-chip voltage generator, and are five-volt only devices. Although EEPROMs are still significantly more expensive than UV-EPROMs, they are likely to become popular because of their convenience, and their possible use as 'read-mostly' (write sometimes) memories. Virtually all types of semiconductor ROM presently available are non-volatile, that is, they retain their information in the absence of power applied to them.

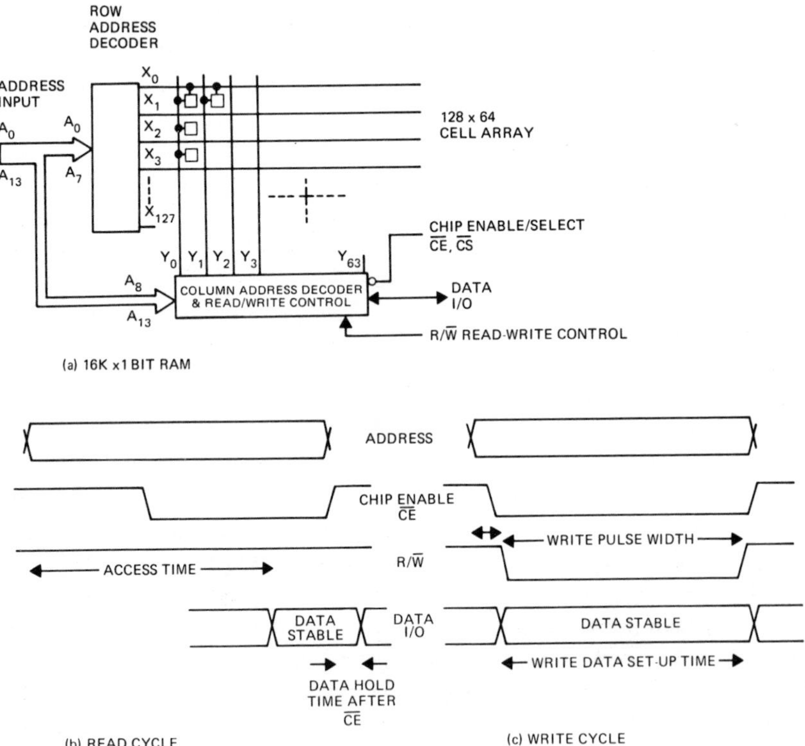

Fig. 1.8 Memory organisation and timing: (a) 16K × 1 bit RAM, (b) read cycle, (c) write cycle.

Static RAM has a cell similar to that illustrated in fig. 1.7(b), basically a bistable which can be set and reset at will by writing to the device, and read non-destructively. A single read-write (R/$\overline{W}$) control gives access to the cell. Unlike ROM, although static RAM holds its information indefinitely while power remains applied to the chip, that information is lost when power is removed, so the memory is volatile. Dynamic RAM (fig. 1.7(c)) works on a completely different principle, that of storing data as charge (or absence of charge) on the gate of an insulated-gate transistor (FET) which possesses a small capacitance. Unlike the UV-EPROM, there is a direct connection to the transistor gate, so that charge can be transferred directly, allowing 5 V operation without on-chip generators. Readout of information is similar to that of the UV-EPROM. One aspect of dynamic RAM behaviour worthy of note: since charge is stored on the FET gate capacitance, and there is a finite though very large leakage resistance, the charge does decay, and the voltage drops in an exponential discharge curve if no action is taken. Typically, the voltage at the storage FET gate will drop from an initial 'nominal logic 1' value, to the minimum acceptable value in a few milliseconds. To retain data, the cell must be periodically read and rewritten, at intervals shorter than the time taken for the gate voltage to decay below the minimum '1' value, a process called refreshing, illustrated in fig. 1.7(d). The provision of refresh circuitry implies that a dynamic RAM system will be more complex than its static counterpart, especially since most dynamic RAMs are packaged in dual-in-line 16-pin packages, which require a multiplexed address, so an address multiplexer must be provided, which splits an address into a 'row address' and a 'column address', and generates row and column address strobes ($\overline{\mathrm{RAS}}$ and $\overline{\mathrm{CAS}}$). Nevertheless, the dynamic RAM does possess many advantages: its cell size is small, so the number of cells (bits) in a memory can be made very large (routinely 64 kbits compared with static RAM 16 kbits); the dynamic RAM cell only consumes power when it is being read from, written to, or refreshed, so the average memory power consumption is low; despite the address multiplexing, the dynamic RAM access time (time from application of address to being able to read or write data) is low.

The overall organisation of a memory chip is as a rectangular array of cells, with row and column addressing, derived from a single parallel binary address using internal decoders. Typical organisation is shown in fig. 1.8(a). It is common practice nowadays to adopt a 'Bytewide' organisation (a Mostek tradename) for static RAM and ROM, so that eight memory locations may be read or written in parallel. If the device is a RAM, it will, in addition to address and bidirectional data pins, possess a chip select ($\overline{\mathrm{CS}}$) input, which enables access, and a read-write (R/$\overline{\mathrm{W}}$) input, which controls the operation. If the device is a ROM, or EPROM, it will not have a R/$\overline{\mathrm{W}}$ input, but may possess an 'output buffer enable' ($\overline{\mathrm{OE}}$) input besides its chip select. The timing of read and write signals for a typical static RAM is shown in fig. 1.8(b), which illustrates its access time requirements. It may be seen from fig. 1.8(b) that the timing is compatible with CPU bus control signals.

1.4 Interfaces for 8-bit CPUs

Interfaces for 8-bit microprocessors fall into two categories: simple interfaces, which perform basic functions for embedded microprocessor systems, such as programmable parallel digital I/O, serial asynchronous and simple synchronous communications, and counter-timers, and more complex interfaces for 'computer-like' peripheral devices, such as keyboard seven-segment display interfaces, VDU controllers (with or without graphics support), diskette and tape controllers and formatters, and direct memory access (DMA) controllers. All programmable interfaces, whether simple or complex, adhere to the general structure of fig. 1.9, based around an internal bidirectional data bus not unlike that of a microprocessor CPU. On the left of the bus, drawn vertically in the diagram, is logic which is common to all programmable interfaces, which buffers the internal data bus, allowing direct connection to the CPU bus, and which accepts control signals from the CPU. The control logic allows access to individual I/O locations or registers within the interface, both for handling data, and for configuring the programmable logic of the interface itself. It possibly includes some decoder logic which accepts one, two or more of the least significant bits of the address bus and applies unique selection signals to the internal registers. In response to external events, the interface control logic may generate interrupts at the CPU.

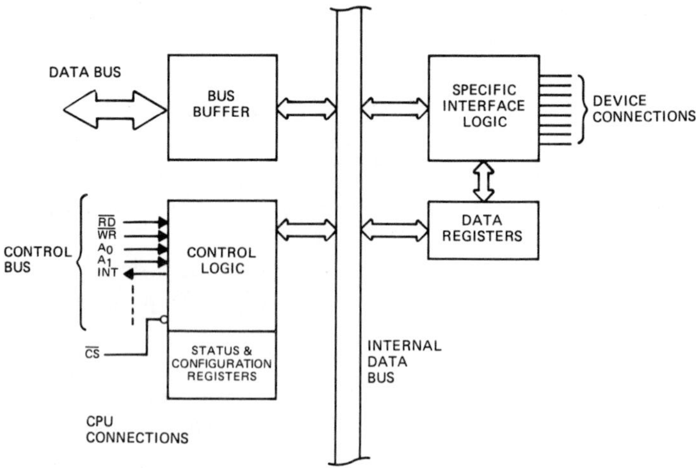

Fig. 1.9 Programmable interface structure.

On the right hand side of the internal data bus, the logic specific to a particular interface connects between the internal bus and the device being interfaced. It will usually include logic which can be configured in response to data written to a programmable device control register, and some data registers.

1.4.1 PARALLEL INTERFACES

A typical programmable parallel digital interface (the Motorola 6821 PIA) is shown in block diagram form in fig. 1.10. It supports two 8-bit digital 'ports' which may be programmed to operate in a variety of ways and which are each supported by a pair of strobe lines. Each port has associated with it a control register (CR), a data direction register (DDR), and a data or output register (OR), so there is a total of six registers, which must be addressed individually, using 'register select' inputs RS0 and RS1 which are usually connected to the two least significant CPU address bits A0 and A1. The control register of each 8-bit port has a unique address in the 4-address space occupied by the PIA, while the DDR and OR share an address, and a bit set or reset (bit2) in the associated control register determines which one is being accessed at a particular time. The data direction registers determine which pins of each port are inputs, and which are outputs; any mix is allowable. The control registers, besides controlling access to the DDRs and ORs, also determine how the PIA can generate interrupts, and how the two strobe lines associated with each port (CA1, CA2 and CB1, CB2) are used. By suitable programming, these strobe lines may be configured as pairs of handshaking lines (fig. 1.11) which will implement a 'data ready' and 'data accepted' exchange surrounding any transfer of parallel data via the associated port, giving control of transfer speed to match a peripheral device. Handshaking transfers can be implemented as either inputs or outputs, and the strobe lines can be linked to the CPU interrupt structure to notify the CPU that data is available, or has been accepted. To summarise, the PIA will support individual I/O pin programming, with latched outputs and unlatched inputs, or will support parallel byte transfers with handshaking.

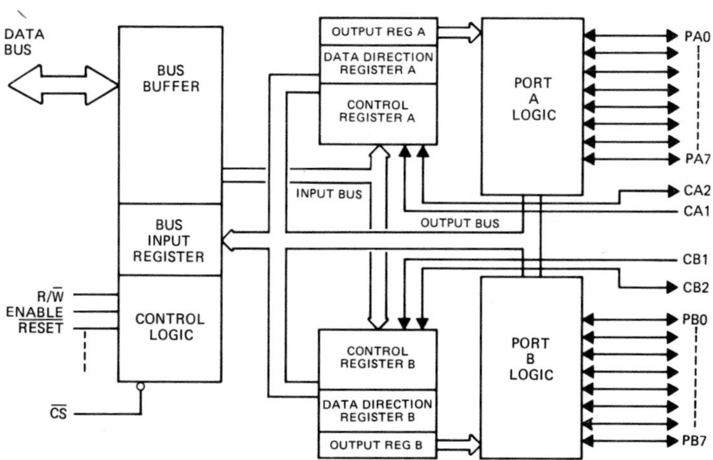

Fig. 1.10 6821 PIA.

1.4.2 SERIAL INTERFACES

A typical serial digital interface (USART) is shown in fig. 1.12(a), the Intel 8251A. It accepts separate transmit and receive clocks and may be programmed with a small number of prescaler division ratios to determine baud (symbol) rate. Transmission may be asynchronous or synchronous. In the asynchronous mode (fig. 1.12(b)) data from the transmit buffer is shifted serially out by the baud rate clock, preceded by a single start bit, and terminated by one, one-and-a-half, or two stop bits. A single parity bit may be added to the data, and the interface may be programmed to use between five and eight data bits, optional even or odd parity, and the requisite number of stop bits. The receiver will accept a similar format, but only ever requires a single stop bit, no matter how the transmitter has been programmed. Both the receipt of data and the end of transmission may invoke a CPU interrupt. A status register contains a number of error flags which may be set by the receiver: OVERRUN (previously received character has not been read from the data buffer before a new character has been received); PARITY ERROR, and FRAMING ERROR (no valid stop bit has been detected). The status register may also include flags which indicate that the transmitter buffer is empty, that the transmitter itself is ready, and that a received character may be read. This particular interface, the Intel 8251A, also supports the modern control signals data set ready (DSR), data terminal ready (DTR), request to send (RTS) and clear to send (CTS).

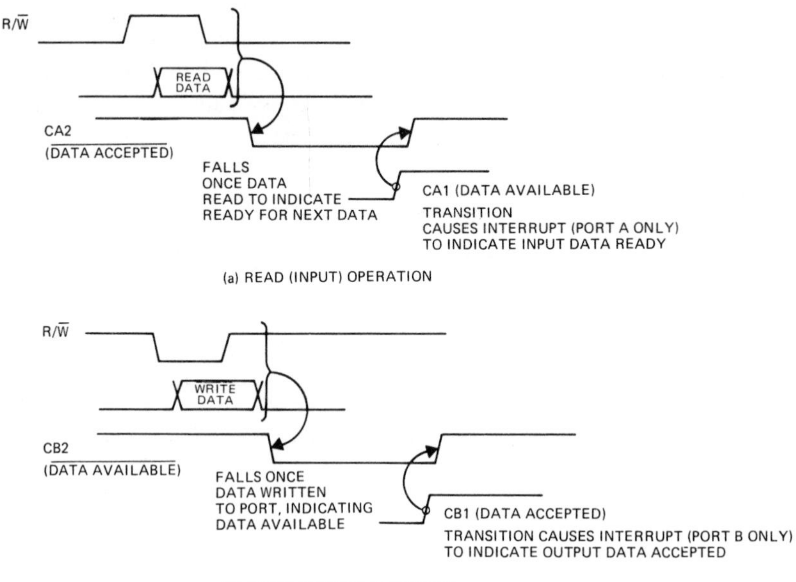

Fig. 1.11 Handshaking transfers: (a) read (input) operation, (b) write (output) operation.

In synchronous mode, the transmission format is shown in fig. 1.12(c). Transmission begins with one or two synchronisation characters, followed by unbroken data characters. Two separate synchronisation characters may be programmed, SYNC1 and SYNC2. In the receive mode, synchronisation with incoming data may be performed internally, using the ENTER HUNT command (a particular bit set in the command register of the USART). This command causes the synchronous receive clock to sample the incoming data on its rising edges. The content of the receive buffer is compared with the first of the internally stored SYNC characters at every bit boundary, until a match occurs. If two synchronisation characters are specified, the subsequent received character is also compared, and when both synchronisation characters have been detected, the USART is presumed to be synchronised, and terminates its hunt mode. Alternatively, an external synchronisation signal SYNDET may be used to force the USART out of its hunt mode. Characters can then be received, with checking for parity and overrun errors (but not for framing errors, which are only applicable to asynchronous reception).

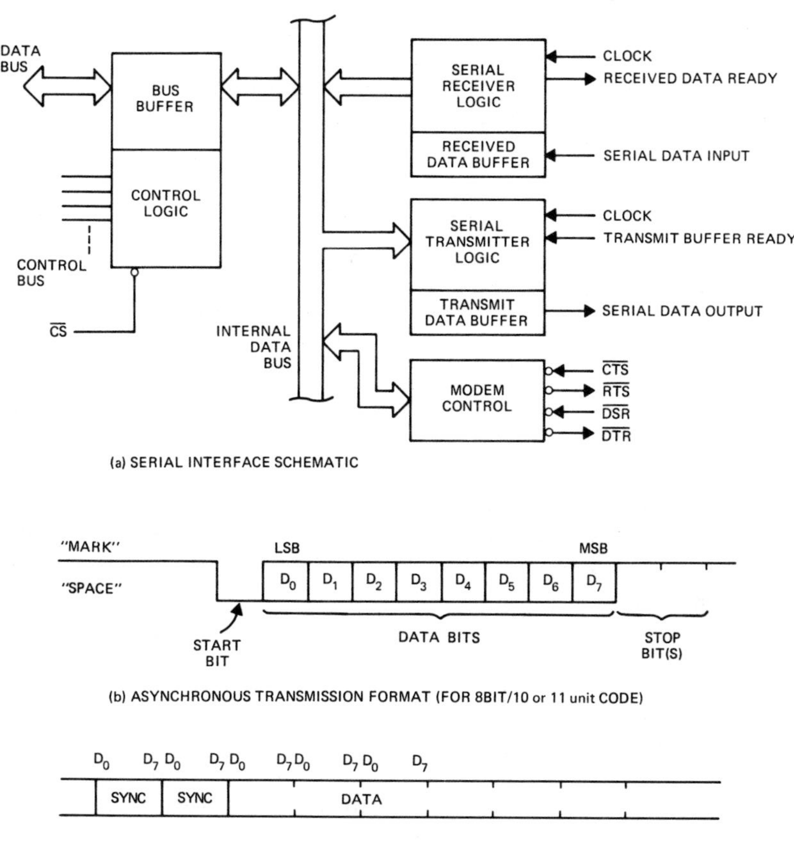

Fig. 1.12 Serial interface (8251A): (a) serial interface schematic, (b) asynchronous transmission format (for 8 bit/10 or 11 unit code), (c) synchronous transmission format.

Commands available for both modes (using a single bit in the control register for each command) are transmit and receive enable, signal data terminal ready (DTR), send a 'BREAK' character, reset error indication flags, signal request to send (RTS), force an internal reset, or enter synchronous reception HUNT mode. This particular USART has just one address pin C/$\overline{\text{D}}$, where a '1' will select the control register in a write operation, and the status register in a read operation, and a '0' will select the transmitter data buffer in a write operation, and the receiver data buffer in a read operation. Interrupts may be used to signal the CPU that received data is available, or that new transmitter data is required.

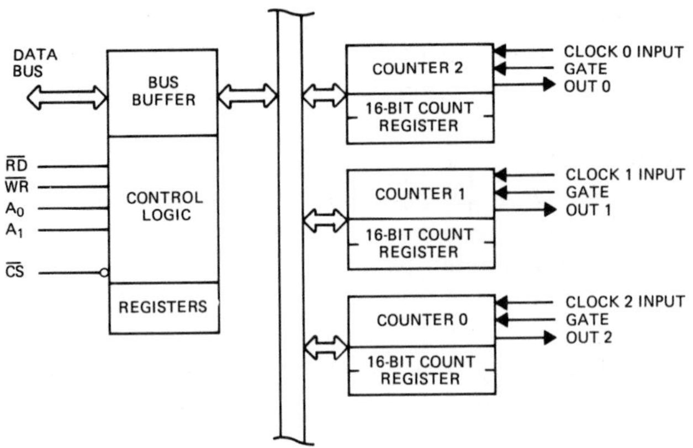

Fig. 1.13 Counter-timer (8253).

1.4.3 TIMER INTERFACES

A counter-timer device is shown schematically in fig. 1.13, which illustrates the Intel 8253. This device contains three independent timers, each with its own 16-bit count register, clock input, gate input, and output. The device occupies four consecutive addresses, one for each timer (shared between upper and lower byte of the counter register), and one for control. Using the control register, a number of modes of operation may be invoked, and methods of loading and reading the 16-bit count register may be specified, for each counter channel. Modes of operation include:

(a) Count down from a specified number loaded into the counter register, using the clock input, and interrupt when the counter reaches zero.
(b) Programmable monostable (one-shot), which, when triggered, will generate a pulse at the output whose length is set by the value in the counter register.
(c) Rate generator or divide-by-N counter, where the output will go low for one input clock period, every N pulses of the input clock, where N is the counter register value.
(d) Square wave generator. Equivalent to a rate generator with a square wave output. The output is high for $N/2$ counts and low for the next $N/2$ counts (N even) or high for $(N+1)/2$ counts and low for $(N-1)/2$ counts (N odd).
(e) Software or hardware triggered strobe, which generates a single clock pulse, N pulses after initiation.

The load method for the internal counters is an interesting one, since it is a technique used by more complex interfaces. Using the control register, it may be specified that the counter register may be loaded (or read 'on the fly') one byte at a time (specified high or low byte), or as a sequence (low byte followed by high byte) written to the counter address. This idea of saving I/O space addresses by specifying sequential access is a powerful one, so long as a different access to the device does not break the sequence, and microprocessor software must ensure that a load or read sequence is complete before another access is attempted. Both binary and binary-coded decimal (BCD) counting is supported, and use of a counter-timer hardware device unburdens the CPU considerably, removing any need for software delay generation, and similar timing operations.

1.4.4 OTHER INTERFACES

More complex interfaces allow not only peripheral interfacing (VDU, diskette, tape) which will not be discussed further here, but also allow extension of the limited 8-bit CPU interrupt structure, and provide for direct memory access. A typical priority interrupt controller (PICU) will provide a number of parallel interrupt inputs, and will automatically code a vector for transmission to the CPU during an interrupt acknowledgement cycle; most usually, this vector will consist of a full 16-bit address. In addition, interrupts will be capable of being masked individually (the interrupt controller will have an internal mask register accessible by software) and their relative priority altered by software. Interrupt priority schemes vary, and a typical interrupt controller may allow rotating priority (either an automatic rotation of one place in a circular interrupt priority hierarchy, or a specific rotation of a number of places) or fixed priority. Appropriate action changing the priority may be programmed to take place after interrupt acknowledgement ('end of interrupt'). A priority for the currently executing CPU program may be set in the controller, which will not then generate interrupts in response to lower priority requests; instead, these may be latched and cause an interrupt when the CPU priority is lowered. Any moderately complex real time application will usually benefit greatly from the addition of an interrupt controller to the system hardware, freeing the CPU from a (usually) restrictive internal interrupt structure.

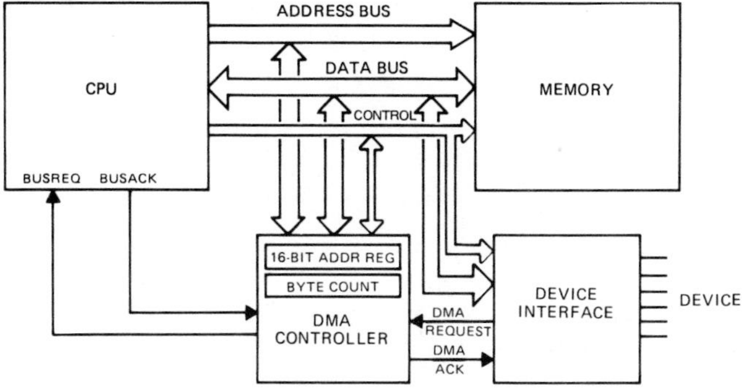

Fig. 1.14 Direct memory access (DMA).

Direct memory access (DMA) controllers are used between the CPU and a device interface, to handle data transfers in the system without involving the CPU. A typical block diagram is shown in fig. 1.14 of a controller supporting a number of DMA channels. A typical channel has two handshaking lines (data request, DRQ and data acknowledge, DACK) which control transfers to and from the device interface. When a request is received, the DMA controller issues a HOLD request to the CPU, which enters an idle state at the end of its current bus cycle, and then floats its address, data and control buses to their high-impedance ('OFF') state, and asserts an acknowledgement (HOLDA). Upon receipt of the acknowledgement, the DMA controller puts a memory address onto the address bus (from an internal 16-bit address register), and manipulates the bus control signals (memory read/write, I/O read/write) to effect a transfer over the data bus, and acknowledges the transfer. If the requesting device has no further request, the controller removes its address and control signals, and releases its HOLD request, allowing the CPU to regain control of the buses and continue its execution. Each channel will have its own registers which hold a 16-bit address, initialised to the start of the block of memory which participates in the transfer, and incremented at each DMA transfer, and a count register which specifies the number of bytes of data to be transferred without involving the CPU (and indeed, which will be completely transparent to CPU operation). These registers are set up by the CPU under program control. When the number of specified DMA transfers have taken place, the DMA controller may be programmed to interrupt the CPU to request further commands. As a further feature, DMA may be performed as 'burst DMA', where a number of transfers take place each time a HOLD request is asserted, and will usually require first-in, first-out (FIFO) buffering at the device interface, or 'distributed DMA', where only a single transfer takes place at each request.

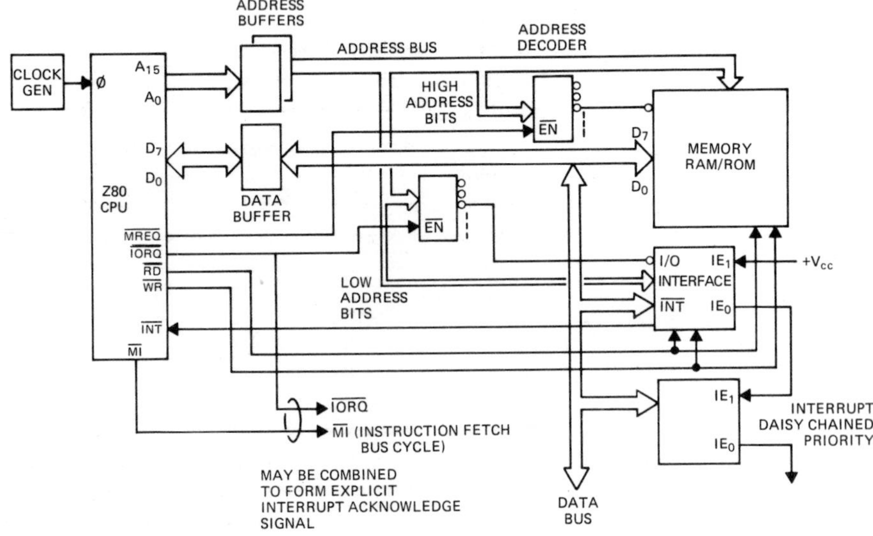

Fig. 1.15 Typical (Z80) 8-bit system.

1.4.5 COMPLETE SYSTEM

A complete microprocessor system, showing CPU, memory, address decoding and interfaces, is shown in fig. 1.15. The address decoders (usually 3-8 line, or 4-16 line), which apply unique signals to memory and interface chip select ($\overline{CS}$) inputs, may fully or only partly decode addresses to organise multiple memory chips in 'banks', and access several I/O devices. Partial address decoding, which allows only sufficient decoding to identify a device or location, while avoiding duplicate addressing, means that device address are not unique, and devices may be accessed at several addresses in the CPU address space. This description of interfacing is necessarily brief, but should serve to set the scene for the discussion of chapter 5.

1.5 8-bit microprocessor software

The 8-bit systems may be programmed in assembly code, or in a high-level applications language such as PL/M, using a microprocessor development system (MDS), and a large user base of software exists. For all the popular 8-bit microprocessors, in addition, where they are used in a 'personal computer' environment, and it is the 8-bit microprocessor which has created the personal computer market, the universal programming language is BASIC (an acronym of Beginners All-purpose Symbolic Instruction Code). A simple, interpreted language, looked upon scornfully by computer scientists, BASIC has the great virtue that it is extremely easy to use. It has its origins in minicomputer and mainframe programming teaching, and was enthusiastically adopted by the Commodore PET, one of the earliest and still one of the most popular personal machines. Other, compiled, high-level languages are available (Pascal, FORTH, and even COBOL and FORTRAN) but these are more suited to higher-performance CPUs, and are discussed in chapter 9.

Operating systems have appeared, some real-time systems (such as Intel's RMX/80 for the 8080) and some single-user disk operating systems. Most visible is one of the disk operating systems, which has become 'industry-standard', Digital Research's CP/M. CP/M (whose 16-bit version is described in chapter 8) is a disk file-handling system which provides an environment for manipulating file storage and running programs. As a simple system it is very effective, providing personal and small business microcomputer users with a file transfer 'standard', and nowadays, most machines based on the 8080, 8085, or Z80 microprocessors do offer it. It has, however, been severely criticised, and may not survive the transition to 16-bit microprocessors too well.

1.6 Transition to 16 bits

The 8-bit microprocessor is a mature product, well-established in many areas, with a vast pool of applications knowledge in many industries. As commented upon earlier, however, it does have limitations, and those of speed, operating system support, multi-user support and mutual protection, network support and provision of 'mainframe computer' facilities may be largely overcome by moving upwards to the newer ranges of 16-bit microprocessor. The learning process for 16-bit devices will have been eased by experience with 8-bit machines, but many new concepts have appeared in 16-bit designs, which are closer in some respects to data-processing mainframes and minicomputers than to electronics. By looking at a broad spectrum of 16-bit devices and applications, this book seeks to ease the learning process for the engineer wanting to get to grips with the modern 16-bit microprocessors.

CHAPTER 2
Intermediate microprocessors

2.1 Introduction

While some of the early 16-bit microprocessors have been introduced by companies opting for an immediate 16-bit solution, the newer 16-bit microprocessors are all associated with 8-bit bus microprocessors which possess strong 16-bit characteristics. These 'pseudo-16-bit' microprocessors have either been 'stepping stones' on the route to fully-fledged 16-bit CPUs, or they are versions of existing 16-bit microprocessor CPUs, reorganised around an 8-bit bus, and targetted at the upper end of 8-bit microprocessor applications. While the highest speed devices are the fully fledged 16-bit CPUs, the pseudo-16-bit microprocessors arranged with an 8-bit bus possess obvious advantages for small and medium sized systems. Board systems may possibly be made smaller when only an 8-bit wide bus has to be run around the printed circuit board. If source code and bus compatibility with existing 8-bit microprocessors is possible, the upgrade path towards higher performance is obvious; with very little modification in either hardware or software, an 8-bit product may be fitted with a pseudo-16-bit microprocessor.

An obvious advantage of an upgraded microprocessor with an 8-bit bus is the expansion of its instruction set; currently the 8080/5, 6800, Z80, 6502 and other popular 8-bit microprocessors all suffer deficiencies. Lack of hardware multiply-divide, poor choice of addressing modes, absolute (non-relocatable) code, and awkward and slow higher-precision arithmetic are just some of these, while in hardware, the restrictive interrupt structures and small (64 kbyte) addressing ranges are often liabilities to the 8-bit microprocessor's use. The pseudo-16-bit microprocessors meet many of these deficiencies, and provide higher clock and execution speeds, too. The most obvious example of a 'stepping-stone' microprocessor is the Motorola 6809, which is more closely associated with the 8-bit 6800/6802 than with the 68000. The examples of a 16-bit CPU with an 8-bit bus are the Intel 8088, the Motorola 68008 and the Texas 9980. In this chapter, only the 6809 is covered in detail – the other microprocessors have their parent CPUs covered in chapters 3 and 4, with only the major differences highlighted here. Eventually, no doubt, these microprocessors will oust the current industry-standard 8-bit CPUs; the costs of the 8088 and 6809 in particular are already very competitive.

2.2 Motorola 6809[1,2,3]

In 1979, the 6809 was termed in *Byte* magazine 'A microprocessor for the revolution',[2] and indeed, for price and performance, is to be highly recommended. Design of the CPU began with an analysis of its predecessor, the 6800, with the intention of highlighting deficiencies which could be made up in the new CPU. An analysis of 25 000 lines of typical 6800 source code revealed that data movement and subroutine calls were the most used instructions, closely followed by conditional and unconditional branches. Although arithmetic and logical instructions were not so widely used, detailed analysis of their use indicated a high proportion of double-precision (16-bit operations) involving 8-bit arithmetic instructions, and manipulation of carry and index registers. The statistics of addressing mode usage indicated equal use for all the modes: direct (8-bit absolute); extended (16-bit absolute); immediate; indexed; relative, and register. The amount of index register manipulation indicated that an expansion of index register facilities might be attempted. So long as only assembly source code compatibility is required (rather than full hexadecimal machine code compatibility), the instructions may be remapped onto the CPU opcode matrix – it is obviously sensible to map the most used source code statements to opcodes that occupy as few bytes as possible, and execute more quickly than less often used instructions. This has been done with the 6809.

2.2.1 6809 HARDWARE IMPROVEMENTS

One of the primary objectives of the 6809 designers was to create an advanced microprocessor which could be used directly with all the interface devices in the ageing 8-bit 6800 family. This constrained hardware design to a synchronous microprocessor bus like that of the 6800, including 16 address bits, 8 data bits, a single R/$\overline{W}$ line, timing strobe signal E (derived in the 6800 system from microprocessor signal Ø2 (clock)), BA, the bus available signal. IRQ maskable (interrupt request) and NMI (non-maskable interrupt request), HALT and RESET are also copied from the 6800, the bus access and switch to high-impedance (tristate off) mode are simplified, and the 6800 TSC (tristate bus control), DBE (data bus enable) and VMA (valid memory address) have been eliminated, their functions compressed into simpler signals.

A quadrature signal Q has been added to the strobe signal E. Q leads E, and indicates validity of address information on the microprocessor bus. It has no 6800 counterpart. Another added signal has been MRDY, which is the counterpart of the 8080/5, Z80 READY signal, a significant omission from the original 6800 design. MRDY is an input signal to the 6809 CPU which allows a slow memory or peripheral interface to stretch strobe signal E to extend data access time. When MRDY is high, E will operate normally as shown in fig. 2.1 in read and write operations. When MRDY is low, indicating that a device is not able to accept or generate data immediately, both E and Q are stretched by integral multiples of quarter bus cycles, to a maximum of 10 μs (with a CPU clock of 1, 1.5 or 2 MHz). Quarter cycles are possible because the 6809 has an on-chip crystal oscillator, which, with the addition of an external crystal, runs at four times the clock rate equal to the normal E and Q signals. Operation of MRDY is shown in fig. 2.2.

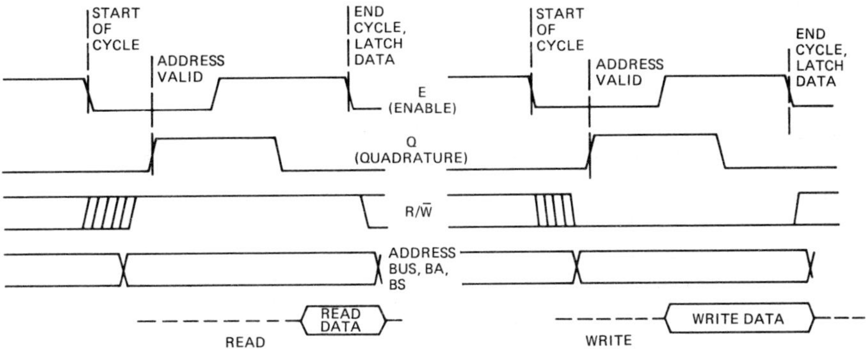

Fig. 2.1 6809 bus timing.

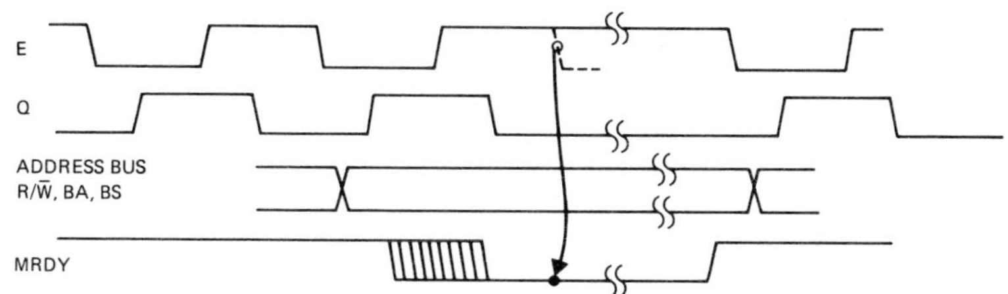

Fig. 2.2 Use of MRDY to stretch bus cycles.

Bus status (BS) is an output signal which has been added, and which, together with BA, may be decoded to give the current machine state:

BA	BS	State
0	0	Normal (running)
0	1	Interrupt acknowledge
1	0	SYNC acknowledge
1	1	HALT or bus grant

SYNC is a new function added to the CPU. The assembly source code command SYNC causes the CPU to enter a 'SYNC' state, where it stops processing instructions and waits for an interrupt to occur. If interrupts are enabled and unmasked (including NMI), the SYNC state is cleared, and a normal interrupt response (save registers as a fast interrupt FIRQ, or normal interrupt, IRQ, and jump to the interrupt service routine) occurs, with a return to the instruction following the SYNC opcode. If interrupts are disabled, the microprocessor, upon receipt of a signal at one of the interrupt pins, will clear the SYNC state and proceed with the next instruction. SYNC gives a convenient way of synchronising the microprocessor to external signals. While the microprocessor is in the SYNC state, it asserts BA = 1, BS = 0, the SYNC acknowledge combination.

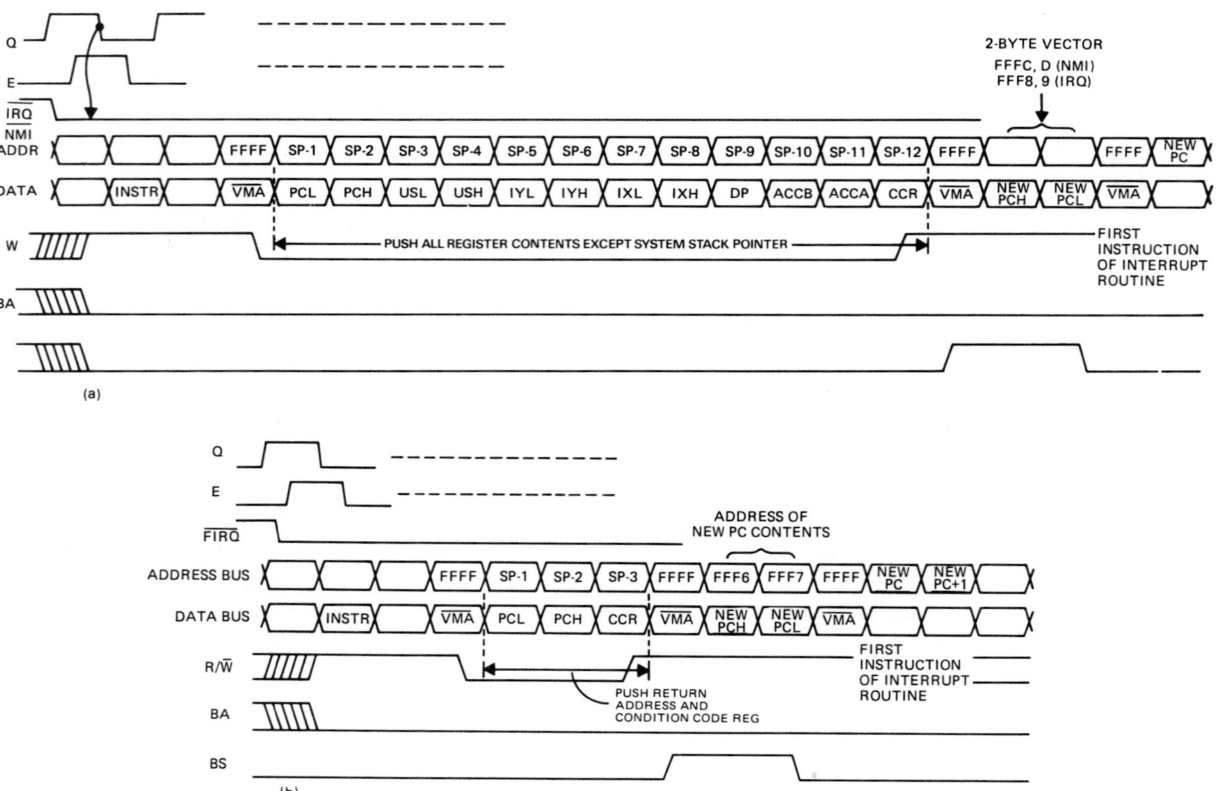

Fig. 2.3 (a) 6809 interrupt timing, (b) 6809 fast interrupt timing (FIRQ).

Interrupts have been expanded in the 6809. The non-maskable interrupt NMI and the maskable interrupt IRQ have their counterparts in the 6800, and may be requested by the interrupt outputs of the 6800 interface devices. Of course, timing of interrupt acknowledge and response is relative to Q and E, and there are additional registers present in the 6809, so the number of cycles of interrupt response is increased. All the CPU registers are automatically pushed onto the stack when NMI or IRQ occurs. FIRQ is an extra hardware interrupt input, where a maskable interrupt, of higher priority than IRQ, will push only the program counter and condition code (flag) register. Timing of both types of interrupt is shown in fig. 2.3.

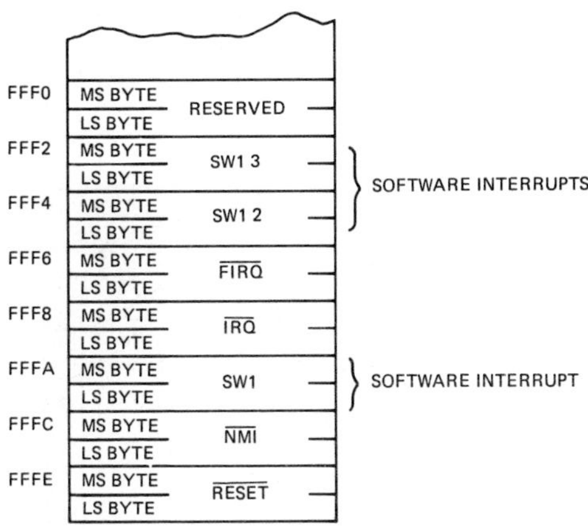

Fig. 2.4 6809 interrupt map.

A map of the 6809 interrupt vectors is shown in fig. 2.4. $\overline{\mathrm{RESET}}$, $\overline{\mathrm{NMI}}$, SWI and $\overline{\mathrm{IRQ}}$ occupy the same positions as they do in the 6800, and new vectors are added. SWI2 and SWI3 are software interrupt vectors, and with SWI they make three priority levels of software interrupt. Note that during the two cycles of the indirect address fetch, when the address bus contains the vector location addresses, interrupt acknowledge is indicated via BA and BS. This will allow the low four address lines to be decoded during interrupt acknowledge, and will provide an indication external to the CPU, identifying the interrupt that has occurred (and hence its priority), and allow 'vectoring by device' (i.e. each device supplies its own vector). The interrupt structure of the 6809 has been based heavily on the 6800 to maintain compatibility, but extends that structure considerably, and makes it all the more versatile by allowing external devices to decode the machine state and identify the interrupt acknowledgement cycles.

On-chip DMA control is added using another new CPU pin, $\overline{\mathrm{DMA/BREQ}}$. The pin may be used to request DMA cycles and dynamic memory refresh cycles by suspending execution and acquiring control of the microprocessor bus. When $\overline{\mathrm{DMA/BREQ}}$ is asserted, with the transition occurring during the quadrature signal Q, instruction execution will stop at the end of the bus cycle in progress, and the machine state HALT or bus grant will be indicated in acknowledgement. The CPU bus pins will be floated to their tristate high-impedance condition, and the requesting device can take over the bus. The bus timing signals E and Q continue to be generated, and may be used by the requesting device to clock its own signals onto the buses released by the CPU. The requesting device may take up to fifteen consecutive bus cycles for its transfers, and will then be forced by the CPU to relinquish the bus to allow the CPU to perform an internal refresh operation (the internal logic of the CPU is dynamic, and needs refreshing in the same way as a dynamic memory). Once the CPU asserts its DMA acknowledge signal (by setting both BA and BS equal to 1), a single 'dead' cycle occurs, during which bus control is transferred, before the first DMA cycle can occur. This dead cycle is one of the fifteen between internal CPU refreshes, so that in practice only fourteen consecutive DMA cycles can occur since false memory access must be prevented during the dead cycle. Timing is illustrated in fig. 2.5. An alternative way of acquiring the bus is to use $\overline{\text{HALT}}$; this input signal causes the CPU to complete its current instruction and then to remain halted without loss of data. Completion of the current instruction means a longer average latency (time to respond to $\overline{\text{HALT}}$) than use of $\overline{\text{DMA/BREQ}}$, but, in return, allows an indefinite period for any bus utilisation. A possible maximum delay of twenty-one bus cycles may occur before the buses become available to a requesting device asserting $\overline{\text{HALT}}$. In the halt state, the buses are floated by the CPU to their high-impedance state, and, as with the $\overline{\text{DMA/BREQ}}$ response, BA = BS = 1; a dead cycle will elapse before the bus is available.

A version of the 6809 is available (6809E) which requires an external clock generator rather than just a crystal, and which has some differences in its control signals to ease problems of multiprocessor operation (see chapter 10). XTAL and EXTAL inputs are now replaced by E_{in} and Q_{in} inputs from the external clock generator; TSC (tristate control) replaces $\overline{\text{DMA/BREQ}}$, and LIC (last instruction cycle) replaces E, and BUSY replaces Q (both outputs). Tristate control signal TSC will cause the microprocessor address bus and R/$\overline{\text{W}}$ line to be placed in high-impedance mode, allowing DMA or memory refresh. It is interesting to note that the data bus is floated to a high impedance state when E_{in} and Q_{in} are both low. LIC is an extremely useful signal which serves two purposes: first, by identifying the last cycle of an instruction, it gives advance warning of an impending HALT state, and secondly, it implicitly identifies each opcode fetch cycle of the CPU (the first low cycle after LIC is high). BUSY is another added signal useful in bus control; in particular, it makes the implementation of multiple microprocessor systems easier, by allowing semaphore manipulation to ensure mutual exclusion from shared resources. BUSY is asserted during read-modify-write instructions and may be used to make them indivisible, so that a semaphore location being accessed by one microprocessor may not be simultaneously altered by a second microprocessor. The BUSY signal is also asserted during execution of double-byte instructions (those with opcode and postbyte) and during execution of those which use indirect addressing modes.

The hardware features of the 6809 are clearly those of a microprocessor a generation ahead of the industry-standard 8-bit microprocessor, such as the 6800 or 8080. They provide for an elegant means of bus control for DMA and for multiple microprocessor systems, and for operating system support. Real time operation is improved by the SYNC and FIRQ signals, and by the extended interrupt system.

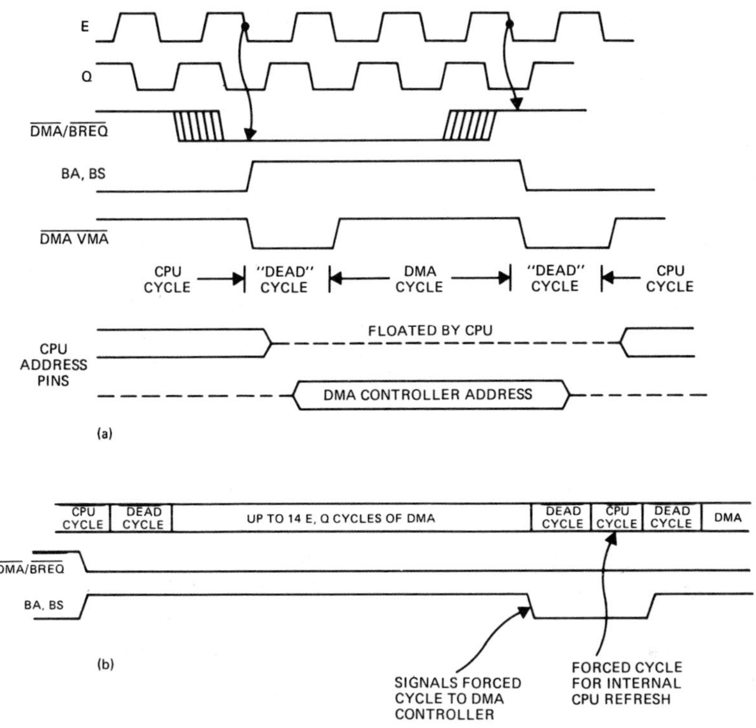

Fig. 2.5 (a) DMA timing, (b) auto-refresh DMA.

2.2.2 6809 INSTRUCTION SET IMPROVEMENTS

The original MC6800 registers really represented the minimum number of registers necessary for a successful 8-bit CPU. They consisted of two 8-bit accumulators, A and B, an index register IX (16 bits), a 16-bit stack pointer SP, a 16-bit program counter PC, and an 8-bit condition code register (with 6 bits actually used). The 6809 register set (fig. 2.6) adds a second index register Y, and a second user stack pointer U, both 16-bit, as well as an 8-bit direct page register, and uses all 8 bits of the condition code register. The two 8-bit accumulators A and B may be combined into one 16-bit accumulator, D, while all four of the 16-bit pointer registers X, Y, U and S may be used as index registers. The program counter PC may be used as an index register in certain instructions which reference data relative to PC. The two additional flags are the fast interrupt request (FIRQ) mask bit, and the E bit, set if the entire register set has been pushed onto the stack in response to non-maskable NMI or maskable IRQ interrupts.

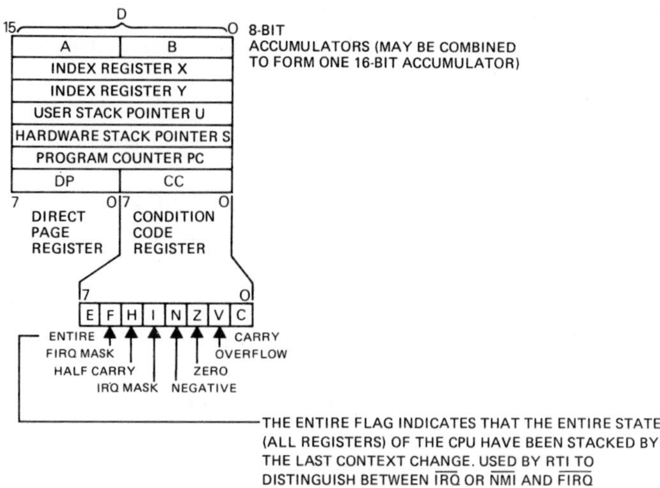

Fig. 2.6 6809 register set.

The really dramatic improvements made in the design of the 6809 are in its instruction set, and, in particular, its extensive range of addressing modes. The addressing modes are arranged to make writing position-independent code (PIC) easy – so easy, in fact, that writing PIC will become almost automatic. Combined with the register set of the 6809 (an expansion of the 6800 set, with two index registers rather than just one, a direct page register which extends single-byte offset direct addressing, and separate user and system stack pointers), the addressing mode capabilities make the 6809 a very attractive microprocessor. There are ten distinct addressing modes, upward compatible with the smaller 6800 set. They are:

(a) Inherent, where the opcode contains all the information (often a single register address).
(b) Immediate, where data follows the operation code in the next consecutive memory location, as one or two bytes.
(c) Extended, where an absolute 16-bit address value follows the instruction opcode (obviously not a position-independent mode).
(d) Extended indirect, where a single level of indirection is applied to the extended mode (i.e. the absolute address following the instruction opcode is a pointer to a location which contains the effective address for the instruction execution).
(e) Direct, a form of extended addressing where only one byte of address follows the opcode. The other (most significant) byte of the 16-bit address is contained in the 8-bit direct page register. The direct page register allows the zero-page (addresses 0000H to 00FFH) direct addressing of the 6800 to cover the complete memory space of 0000H to FFFFH, in 256 byte banks.

When the CPU is reset, the direct page register contains zero, so the direct addressing of the 6809 is equivalent to the zero-page addressing of the 6800. The direct page register may be manipulated under program control. Indirection is not allowed.

(f) Register, a mode which consists of an opcode followed by a second 'POSTBYTE' which defines a register or set of registers involved in the instruction execution.

(g) Indexed, a mode where one of the set of registers designated as 'pointer registers' is used as an index register. A postbyte is present, which specifies exactly how the indexing is to be applied. Legal modes are:
   (i) Zero-offset indexing – the pointer register contains the effective address.
   (ii) Constant-offset indexing – a two's complement offset of size 5, 8 or 16 bits (corresponding to decimal ranges –16 to +15, –128 to +127 or –32 768 to +32 767). The 5-bit offset is included in the postbyte, the 8-bit offset in a single byte following the postbyte, and the 16-bit offset in two bytes following the postbyte.
   (iii) Accumulator-offset indexed – the two's complement value in one of the accumulators A or B (8 bit) or D (16 bit) is added to the contents of one of the pointer registers to form a 16-bit address. A postbyte specifies which accumulator to use as the offset.
   (iv) Autoincrement indexed, autodecrement indexed. The pointer register contains the address of the operand and is post-incremented or pre-decremented by one or two (for byte or 16-bit word operations).

(h) Indexed indirect, a mode where most of the indexed modes of addressing may have a level of indirection specified (5-bit offset and autoincrement or autodecrement by one may not be used in indexed indirect mode), where the location addressed by the sum of the contents of the index register and any offset contains the effective address.

(i) Relative addressing, where an offset is added to the program counter to specify program branch destinations (the same as the 6800 branches). Both 8-bit (as 6800) and 16-bit signed offsets may be used.

(j) Program counter relative, an indexed mode using the program counter as the index register, and possessing the capability of indirection. Useful for writing position independent code, since all data may be referenced by its position relative to the PC.

Notice that within this array of addressing modes, the restriction that an 8-bit offset places on the number of available opcodes (256) has been overcome by the use of a second postbyte where necessary, bringing the instruction set more into line with that of a 16-bit microprocessor. The justification for regarding the 6809 as an intermediate microprocessor may be seen in its provision for 16-bit data accesses (autoincrement and autodecrement by two) and 16-bit register operations (treating the A and B accumulators as a single 16-bit accumulator, D). The actual instructions reflect the same thinking which has led to the 16-bit MC 68000 microprocessor, but with the constraint of 6800 compatibility at assembly

Table 2.1

Byte operations

Mnemonic	Description
ABX	Add B register to X register unsigned
ADCA, ADCB	Add memory to accumulator with carry
ADDA, ADDB	Add memory to accumulator
ANDA, ANDB	And memory with accumulator
ANDCC	And immediate with condition code register
ASLA, ASLB, ASL	Arithmetic shift left accumulator or memory
ASRA, ASRB, ARS	Arithmetic shift right accumulator or memory
BITA, BITB	Bit test memory with accumulator
CLRA, CLRB, CLR	Clear accumulator or memory
CMPA, CMPB	Compare memory with accumulator
COMA, COMB, COM	Complement accumulator or memory
DAA	Decimal Adjust A accumulator
DECA, DECB, DEC	Decrement accumulator or memory
EORA, EORB	Exclusive or memory with accumulator
EXG R1, R2	Exchange R1 with R2
INCA, INCB, INC	Increment accumulator or memory
LDA, LDB	Load accumulator from memory
LSLA, LSLB, LSL	Logical shift left accumulator or memory
LSRA, LSRB, LSR	Logical shift right accumulator or memory
MUL	Unsigned multiply (8 bit by 8 bit = 16 bit)
NEGA, NEGB, NEG	Negate accumulator or memory
ORA, ORB	Or memory with accumulator
ORCC	Or immediate with condition code register
PSHS (register)	Push register(s) on hardware stack
PSHU (register)	Push register(s) on user stack
PULS (register)	Pull register(s) from hardware stack
PULU (register)	Pull register(s) from user stack
ROLA, ROLB, ROL	Rotate accumulator or memory left
RORA, RORB, ROR	Rotate accumulator or memory right
SBCA, SBCB	Subtract memory from accumulator with borrow
STA, STB	Store accumulator to memory
SUBA, SUBB	Subtract memory from accumulator
TSTA, TSTB, TST	Test accumulator or memory
TFR R1, R2	Transfer register R1 to register R2

16-bit operations

Mnemonic	Description
ADDD	Add to D accumulator
SUBD	Subtract from D accumulator
LDD	Load D accumulator
STD	Store D accumulator
CMPD	Compare D accumulator
LDX, LDY, LDS, LDU	Load pointer register

Table 2.1 contd.

Mnemonic	Description
STX, STY, STS, STU	Store pointer register
CMPX, CMPY, CMPU, CMPS	Compare pointer register
LEAX, LEAY, LEAS, LEAU	Load effective address into pointer register
SEX	Sign extend (B register into A register)
TRR register, register	Transfer register to register
EXG register, register	Exchange register to register
PSHS (register)	Push register(s) onto hardware stack
PSHU (register)	Push register(s) onto user stack
PULS (register)	Pull register(s) from hardware stack
PULU (register)	Pull register(s) from user stack

Branch instructions

Mnemonic	Description
BCC, LBCC	Branch if carry clear
BCS, LBCS	Branch if carry set
BEQ, LBEQ	Branch if equal
BGE, LBGE	Branch if greater than or equal (signed)
BGT, LBGT	Branch if greater (signed)
BHI, LBHI	Branch if higher (unsigned)
BHS, LBHS	Branch if higher or same (unsigned)
BLE, LBLE	Branch if less than or equal (signed)
BLO, LBLO	Branch if lower (unsigned)
BLS, LBLS	Branch if lower or same (unsigned)
BLT, LBLT	Branch if less than (signed)
BMI, LBMI	Branch if minus
BNE, LBNE	Branch if not equal
BPL, LBPL	Branch if plus
BRA, LBRA	Branch always
BRN, LBRN	Branch never
BSR, LBSR	Branch to subroutine
BVC, LBVC	Branch if overflow clear
BVS, LBVS	Branch if overflow set

CPU control instructions

Mnemonic	Description
CWAI	Clear condition code register bits and wait for interrupt
NOP	No operation
JMP	Jump
JSR	Jump to subroutine
RTI	Return from interrupt
RTS	Return from subroutine
SWI, SWI2, SWI3	Software interrupts
SYNC	Synchronise with interrupt line

source code level. An acknowledged intention of the CPU designers was to make 'it easier to write good programs on the 6809 than bad ones!'. The full instruction set is shown in Table 2.1.

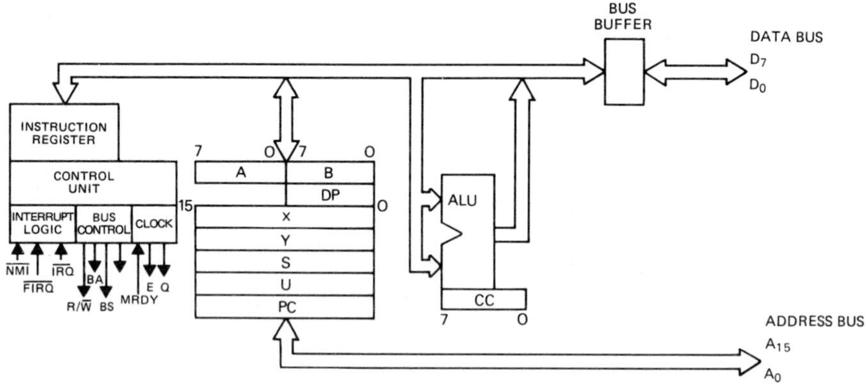

Fig. 2.7 6809 architecture.

Most of the arithmetic instructions have 16-bit counterparts (add, subtract, compare, sign extend) and a comprehensive set of 16-bit loads and stores are available. Multiply (MUL) is an unsigned 8 X 8 bit multiply giving a 16-bit product. Although this is an 8-bit instruction (indeed, the 6809 could not easily support a 16 X 16 bit multiply unless some of the pointer registers were used for data), it is relatively easy to extend its precision, and to make it signed, with software. The other important features are the branches, extended to allow 16-bit offsets, the register-register transfers, and the multiple-register stack operations. Part of the appeal of the 6809 for modern personal and desktop computer design will be its support in hardware of operating system software. Having both a user stack pointer and a hardware (system) stack pointer allows operating system software (with its associated interrupt service routines) to be kept separate from user software. The user stack remains free for use in passing parameters and for data storage. Pascal p-code interpreters may often be most efficiently realised using a stack machine architecture, and the dual stack pointers of the 6809, together with the autoincrement, autodecrement addressing modes, facilitate this.

2.3 Other intermediate processors[4,5,6,7,8]

The other intermediate processors available all have direct 16-bit counterparts, and differ from them only in the design of their bus control circuitry. The internal structure of such a processor's CPU will be identical to that of its 16-bit parent, but externally, only an 8-bit data bus will be supported, allowing perhaps, a smaller package size. Processors which fall into this category are the Texas TMS9980, the Intel 8088, and the Motorola 68008, which correspond to the 16-bit bus processor TMS9900, 8086, and 68000 respectively. Because these processors are dealt with separately elsewhere in this book, it is not proposed to repeat their description here. A possible exception is the TMS9980, since although it is functionally identical to the TMS9900, the fact that both processors are memory-oriented means that their architectures do differ somewhat. Fig. 2.8 shows the architecture of the 8-bit bus 9980 and may be compared with diagram of the 9900 elsewhere in this book.

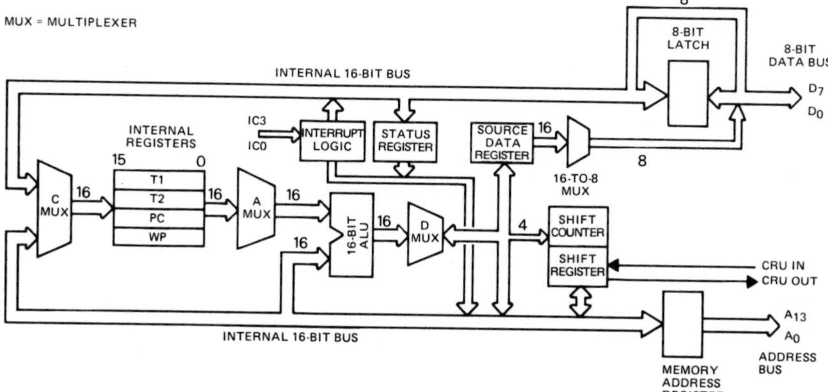

Fig. 2.8 TMS 9980 architecture.

So far as a requirement exists for such processors, suffice to say that for applications which require text (8-bit ASCII) handling, for personal computers and the like, such a processor may be more attractive than its 16-bit bus counterpart. Already, the 8088 has become the basis for the IBM Personal Computer, and for the Sirius One (Vector 9000 in the USA).

CHAPTER 3
Early 16-bit microprocessors

The modern 16-bit microprocessors which are covered in detail in the rest of this book are not the first 16-bit microprocessors to have been produced. Rather, they are the logical development of the mainstream 8-bit microprocessors, and their design makes up many of the deficiencies of their 8-bit predecessors, and makes use of the many valuable lessons learned from 8-bit systems design. A few bold companies took a gamble by leapfrogging the mainstream 8-bit microprocessor market, and going straight for 16 bits as a CPU wordlength. One of the earliest of these was National Semiconductor, with PACE, but others followed: General Instrument with the CP1600, Fairchild with the 9440, Data General with the Micro Nova, and Texas Instruments with the TMS9900. The attraction of this approach was obvious – to provide a CPU and perhaps board-based products which could compete with the low end of the minicomputer market, where chip-set based microprocessors, such as the Computer Automation Alpha-LS1, and DEC LS1-11, were already appearing on the horizon. These early microprocessors looked forward to an era of cheap semiconductor memory and applications large and complex enough to warrant the extra system cost and complexity. With the exception of the TMS9900 and its successors, these microprocessors failed to achieve an adequate customer base to ensure their survival as any sort of 'industry-standard' parts. Partly, they suffered from inadequate development tools (development systems, software support and an adequate range of peripheral interface chips), and partly, they may have been too sophisticated for the market at their time of launch. The more modern 16-bit CPUs have been aimed at a market with wide experience of 8-bit systems design, and with a considerable degree of software and development system sophistication, which has recognised the limitations of the 8-bit microprocessors of the 6800, 8080, Z80 and 6502 families, and is ready to move on to more complex microprocessors to overcome these limitations. When PACE was launched, no such market existed, and the commercial incentives to tackle a 16-bit system design were small.

The Micro Nova was an attempt by Data General to introduce a microprocessor of its own, before the lower end of its traditional minicomputer market was threatened, and which could capitalise on the user base of the highly successful Nova minicomputer. In addition, it would provide a supply of integrated CPUs for Data General's own in-house use. While it has enjoyed use in minicomputer-like systems, the Micro Nova has not penetrated the embedded microprocessor areas so essential to volume sales and industry-wide acceptance. It is likely to continue to support Data General's system production, and has been joined by the Micro Eclipse. The Fairchild 9440 is also based on the Nova instruction set, aiming at the same market as the Micro Nova.

The Texas Instruments' TMS 9900 is yet another microprocessor which retains compatibility with a parent minicomputer family, the 990 range. Unlike the other microprocessors mentioned, the 9900, and its board-based products, have been very successful. Before the launch of the 8086, they dominated the then small but expanding 16-bit applications area, and they still present stiff competition for the more modern microprocessors. Indeed, the product line is continuing with the 99000, and is likely to expand further. The 9900's success in the 16-bit area may be attributed to a number of factors: its architecture, memory-based rather than register-based, is almost unique, but neatly sidesteps many of the problems associated with context-switching. Its addressing modes, too, are more advanced and more flexible than those of the industry-standard 8-bit microprocessor, and its non-multiplexed bus pins (the standard 9900 has a 64-pin package, one of the first widely used 64-pin devices in the industry) allow relatively simple interfacing. The strong position of Texas Instruments in the field of bipolar logic, particularly the low-power Schottky TTL (LSTTL) devices often used for microprocessor buffering, ensured good hardware support, and the manufacturer's software and system support of the 9900, while perhaps not so comprehensive as the equivalent support of the leading 8-bit microprocessors, was certainly more than enough to allow the microprocessor's successful introduction into many systems. Quite apart from AMPL, the Texas development system for the 9900, support is available from many of the general-purpose development systems, such as the ones made by Tektronix and Philips. This combination of technical and commercial factors made the 9900 the leading 16-bit microprocessor in the pre-8086, Z8000, MC68000 era.

All of the early 16-bit microprocessors, built with die sizes and with densities appropriate to their time of introduction, are characterised by some common features: they all have limited linear addressing ranges; they all have a limited instruction set compared with more modern microprocessors (but nevertheless a useful one); they do not support sophisticated memory management or real time operating systems in their hardware facilities; they do not, in general, allow coprocessors (although the TMS9900 does have 'external instructions' which could perhaps allow them). A description of these early designs makes an interesting comparison with more recent microprocessors.

3.1 PACE

PACE[1] is a 16-bit PMOS microprocessor which was manufactured by National Semiconductor before the development of the 8-bit SC/MP or the second-source 8-bit INS8080. Like many of the early 8-bit microprocessors, PACE uses a two-phase clock of period 750 ns or 500 ns, generated externally (to call the clock two-phase in the case of PACE is really a misnomer, since one clock signal is actually the complement of the other). The device occupies a 40-pin package, which necessitates multiplexing the 16-bit address and 16-bit data lines, with an address strobe signal NADS present when the address is valid to allow demultiplexing. Compared with more modern 16-bit microprocessors, the PACE is rather slow, and, more importantly, many of its pins do not support standard TTL-level signals, necessitating some off-chip buffering for data and address lines, making up a multi-chip 'CPU group'. Its power requirements, too, are unusual, at +5 V, −12 V and +8 V substrate bias, although a card-based PACE system can run on +5 V and −12 V by deriving the low current substrate bias using an on-card d.c.-d.c. converter.

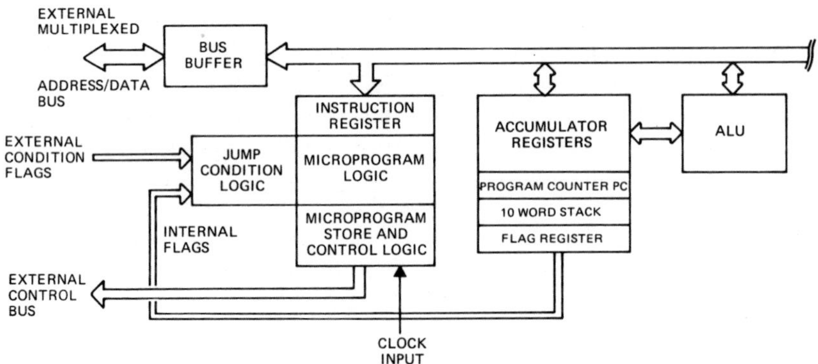

Fig. 3.1 PACE internal architecture.

The internal architecture of PACE is shown in fig. 3.1. Of the registers shown in the diagram, only AC0-AC3 and PC are accessible directly by the programmer, as well as the special-purpose status and control flag register. An internal 10-word stack is provided, with a stack pointer maintained internally by the control logic of the CPU. This restricted-length stack is used automatically for storing return addresses when an interrupt or subroutine call occurs, and may also be used for data storage using explicit PUSH or PULL instructions. The multiplexed data and address signals are demultiplexed using a ground-true signal NADS, and operations on the data bus are synchronous, using strobes $\overline{\text{IDS}}$ (input data strobe) and ODS (output data strobe) in a similar manner to $\overline{\text{RD}}$ and $\overline{\text{WR}}$. The CPU is microprogrammed, giving a typical instruction time of 12 μs, and possesses a number of control lines which interact with the control unit – for instance, four flag outputs F11-F14, which are settable, resettable or may be pulsed under program control. Three testable flag inputs, JC13, JC14 and JC15 are provided, each of which may invoke a program branch in response to a suitable branch-on-condition (BOC) instruction; an EXTEND input may be used to 'stretch' memory or input-output cycles to make them compatible with slow devices; a base-page control line BPS allows a continuous or split-address base page of 256 locations, and a reset line (negative-true initialise, or NINIT). NINIT sets program counter PC to zero, initialises the internal stack pointer, and clears all the flags and interrupt enables, except that of the highest priority (non-maskable interrupt

IRO). External interrupt requests are via four negative-true interrupt lines NIR2, 3, 4, 5 which may be individually enabled, and when so enabled, set corresponding bits in an internal interrupt-request latch obeying a hardware priority scheme with NIR5 lowest priority; if an overall enable (master interrupt enable) is set, the highest priority incoming interrupt is serviced after the current instruction is complete. Numbering of the external interrupts allows the incorporation into the interrupt scheme of two higher-priority interrupt requests, IR0, the highest priority, generated by NHALT, and IR1, generated by overflow or underflow of the internal stack (allowing stack error recovery). The NHALT and CONTIN signals are used together for a number of purposes, among them, generating level 0 interrupts. The microprocessor may be 'stalled', or forced into an internal HALT state, using NHALT to initiate the state, and CONTIN to terminate it. The CONTIN line is used, when an interrupt occurs, to output a pulse from the CPU, which forms an interrupt acknowledgement signal. If NHALT input and CONTIN output are synchronised correctly, a level 0 interrupt results. All six interrupt requests vector to fixed memory locations in the base page (which, depending on the BPS input, occupies addresses 0000-00FFH or 0000-007FH and FF80H-FFFFH). The memory locations associated with each interrupt are used as pointer locations, and contain the address of the relevant interrupt service routine. They are:

Interrupt level		Location
0	(NMI)	7, 8 (special function)
1	(Stack interrupt)	2
2	(NIR2)	3
3	(NIR3)	4
4	(NIR4)	5
5	(NIR5)	6

For interrupt level 0, location 7 is used to store the return address (rather than the stack), and location 8 contains the first executable instruction of the service routine (rather than a pointer).

Because of the signal levels at the pins of PACE, support circuits are needed to convert the system to TTL compatibility, and these are handled by the DP8302 system timing element (STE) and a number (usually three for 16-bit address/data lines and seven essential control outputs) of DP8300 8-bit bidirectional transceiver elements (BTEs). Also provided is an 8-bit parallel interface, the DP8301 MILE (microprocessor interface latch element). The CPU group for PACE consists of a minimum of five chips (CPU + STE + three BTEs). Interfacing, using standard logic, to this group is reasonably easy, but no really sophisticated programmable interfaces are available, and any system will have a high chip count.

From a programmer's viewpoint, PACE consists of the four general-purpose accumulator registers AC0-AC3, the program counter PC and the status and control flag register (fig. 3.2(a)). Detail of the status and control register is shown in fig. 3.2(b). Conventional flags, set by the results of arithmetic and logical operations, are OVF for arithmetic overflow, CRY for carry, and LINK, which is used in conjunction with shift and rotate instructions to give a single testable bit. BYTE is used to distinguish 16-bit and 8-bit data lengths and may be set and reset under program control. F14-F11 are the external flag outputs, while IE1-IE5 are interrupt enable bits in the status and control register. INTEN is the master interrupt enable bit. Instructions in PACE are all single word, with a general format shown in fig. 3.3. The 2-bit 'INDEX' (xr) field controls the addressing mode for a memory reference instruction, and the INDEX and part of the DISPLACEMENT field or OPERATION field are used when register operands are specified. 'Direct' memory addressing has three modes and is controlled using a paged memory scheme of three 256-word floating pages, and one fixed 'base page'; the three modes are base-page addressing, program-counter (PC) relative addressing, and indexed addressing. Each memory reference instruction contains an 8-bit displacement field (bits 0-7). Base page addressing (xr = 00) uses the displacement value as an absolute address in the range 0-FFH if BPS (base page select) input is low, and an absolute address formed by extending the sign (bit 7) of the displacement to set or reset all the bits of the high byte (bits 8-15), giving a split base page occupying absolute addresses 0000-007FH and FF80-FFFH. This feature allows the base page to be split between different memory types, for example, half in RAM, half in ROM. It also allows both memory and memory-mapped I/O devices to share the base page more easily. PC-relative addressing (xr = 01) uses the displacement field as a signed number in the range −128 to +127 (two's complement) which is added to the program counter value of the current instruction (before PC is automatically incremented). The indexed mode uses accumulator register AC2 (xr = 10) or AC3 (xr = 11) as a 16-bit address register, to which is added the signed 8-bit displacement to form the absolute address.

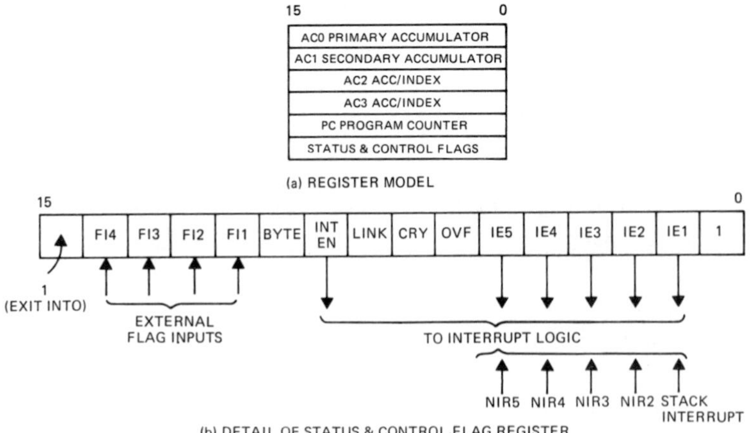

Fig. 3.2 PACE register set: (a) register model, (b) detail of status and control flag register.

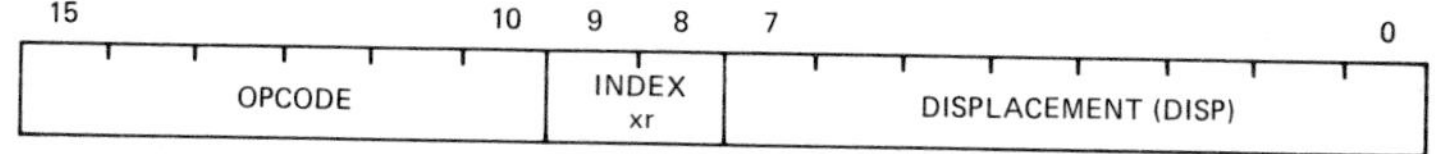

Fig. 3.3 PACE instruction format.

Table 3.1 PACE instruction set

Group	Assembler mnemonic	Description
Data transfer	LD r, <displacement>	Load AC0, 1, 2, 3 using direct or indexed addressing
	LD @ <displacement>	Load AC0 indirect
	LI r, <8-bit data>	Load immediate
	ST r, <displacement>	Store AC0, 1, 2, 3, addressing as load
	ST @ <displacement>	Store AC0 indirect
	LSEX <displacement>	Load AC0 with a signed byte, sign-extended into the upper byte
	RCPY dest, src	Copy source register into destination register
	RXCH dest, src	Exchange contents of source and destination registers
Arithmetic and logical	RADD dest, src	Register add
	RADC dest, src	Register add with carry
	ADD r, <displacement>	Add memory contents to register
	SUBB <displacement>	Add memory contents to AC0
	DECA <displacement>	Decimal add memory contents to AC0
	CAI r, <8-bit data>	Complement register, and add 8-bit sign-extended data
	RAND dest, src	Register AND
	AND <displacement>	AND memory with AC0
	OR <displacement>	OR memory with AC0
	RXOR dest, src	Register EXCLUSIVE-OR
Shift and rotate	SHL r, <count>, <L>	Shift left simply (L = 0) or through 1-bit link (L = 1)
	SHR r, <count>, <L>	Shift right
	ROL r, <count>, <L>	Rotate left
	ROR r, <count>, <L>	Rotate right
Branches	BOC cc, <displacement>	Branch on condition specified by cc
	JMP <displacement>	Unconditional jump
	JMP @ <displacement>	Unconditional indirect jump
	SKNE r, <displacement>	If register not equal to memory contents, skip the next instruction

Table 3.1 (contd.)

Group	Assembler mnemonic	Description
Branches (contd.)	SKG <displacement>	Skip if AC0 greater than memory
	SKAZ <displacement>	Skip if the result of AC0 AND memory is zero
	ISZ <displacement>	Increment memory, skip if zero
	DSZ <displacement>	Decrement memory, skip if zero
	AISZ r, <8-bit data>	Add immediate to register, skip if zero
Control and stack	JSR <displacement>	Jump to subroutine
	JSR @ <displacement>	Jump indirect to subroutine
	RTS	Return from subroutine
	RTI	Return from interrupt
	XCHRS r	Exchange register with the top of the stack
	CFR r	Copy flags into register
	CRF r	Copy register into flags
	PUSH r	Push register onto stack
	PULL r	Pull register from stack
	PUSHF	Push flags onto stack
	PULLF	Pull flags from stack
	SFLG <flag>	Set flag
	PFLG <flag>	Pulse flag
	HALT	Halt

Indirect addressing modes are allowed on a small number of instructions (load, store, indirect, jump to subroutine indirect). The direct addressing modes described above specify the location of the address pointer, which contains the absolute address required. The PACE instruction set is small by modern standards (table 3.1), but reflects the philosophy of the low-end minicomputer of the mid-1970s. In some respects, it is quite sophisticated – JRS @ (jump to subroutine indirect), for instance, allows easy creation of routing tables; increment/decrement-and-skip-on-zero (ISZ, DSZ) are similar to their counterparts on more modern microprocessors, and multibit shifts and rotates may be specified. The idea of a stack overflow/underflow interrupt is one that was ahead of its time – unfortunately its *raison d'être*, the small size of the internal stack of PACE, rather restricted stack operations.

The overall philosophy of the PACE instruction set is quite similar to that of the Data General Nova minicomputer, although the two microprocessors are not compatible, and to some extent PACE may be considered a direct predecessor to the Nova-compatible microprocessors discussed later in this chapter. The addition of a number of interrupt inputs direct to the CPU, and a simple form of interrupt control logic, together with flag outputs controlled by software, helped to bring PACE into competition with contemporary 8-bit microprocessors. Clearly, its architecture is much closer to the industry-standard 8-bit microprocessors than to the modern 16-bit ones, and the longer wordlength was insufficient to bring PACE into the very large volume use of the 8-bit machines.

3.2 General Instruments (GI) CP1600

Another early 16-bit microprocessor, the CP1600, is still available in quantity, and has been used in volume by GI itself and a small number of large customers. Although it has been a successful product, it is not well known by most of the applications industry, and has seen little use in small production runs. Like the PACE, the CP1600 has a 40-pin package, necessitating multiplexed 16-bit address and data signals, and requires multiple power supplies (+12 V, +5 V, –3 V), but has a faster clock (5 MHz), again with true and complementary inputs and is an NMOS device, allowing direct TTL compatibility. Buffering will still normally be necessary, however, to provide sufficient drive capability, and to demultiplex address and data signals, but standard TTL buffers may be used, rather than special MOS to TTL ones. The CP1600 block diagram is shown in fig. 3.4. Eight registers R0-R7 are available for the programmer to use in a general-purpose way, although most are also dedicated to specific uses. R7 is dedicated to be the program counter, R6 the stack pointer, R5 and R4 are data counters with autoincrement, and R1, R2 and R3 are general-purpose data counters. The feature that all the registers may be used generally is a very powerful one, and follows in the footsteps of the very successful PDP-11 mini-computer design. It also reduces the number of different instructions that are required. In its control signals, the CP1600 betrays its age. Three signals, BDIR, BC1, BC2 must be decoded externally to generate useful control signals (typically with a standard TTL 3-to-8 line decoder). The signals are illustrated in fig. 3.5. Strobed signals data write (DWS) and data read (DTB) take the place of $\overline{\text{WR}}$ and $\overline{\text{RD}}$, but the bus is still a synchronous one (no handshaking). Buffer control signal data write (DW) precedes DWS to allow some buffer set-up time.

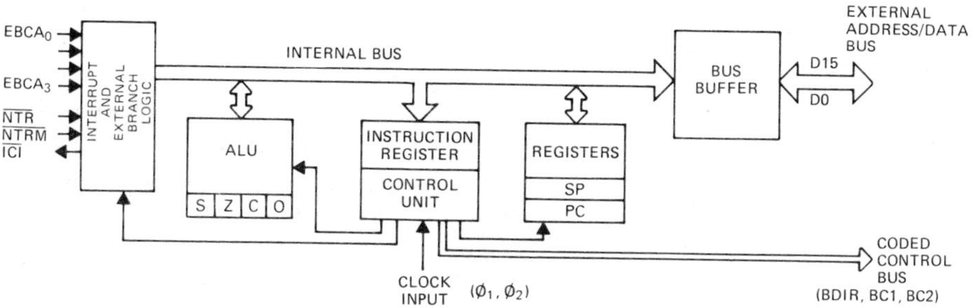

Fig. 3.4 CP1600 structure.

Reset for the CP1600 needs to be synchronised to its clock by internal logic so that $\overline{\text{MSYNC}}$, the equivalent to a reset signal when it is released, will cause

Ø1 and Ø2, the two phases of the clock, to start a new cycle. The effect of this cycle is to read the data bus, where an external device synchronised to MSYNC, must provide the address of the first executable instruction. The contents of the data bus are transferred to the program counter, R7, and execution begins. The request for this address may be decoded from the bus control signals (BAR in fig. 3.5). An unusual edge-triggered signal STPST causes the CPU to enter a HALT state; a second transition in the same sense on the STPST line will cause termination of the HALT state. The HALT state is signalled on a HALT output pin, which will also indicate when a HALT state is invoked by a HLT instruction. The CP1600 also possesses a 'ready' type of input BDRDY, which causes the CPU to execute wait states and stretch any instruction cycle to accommodate memory or I/O devices with long response times, although the dynamic nature of the CPU places a restriction of 40 μs on the maximum length of a wait period. Like PACE, the microprocessor has no explicit I/O operations, and treats peripheral interface ports as memory locations.

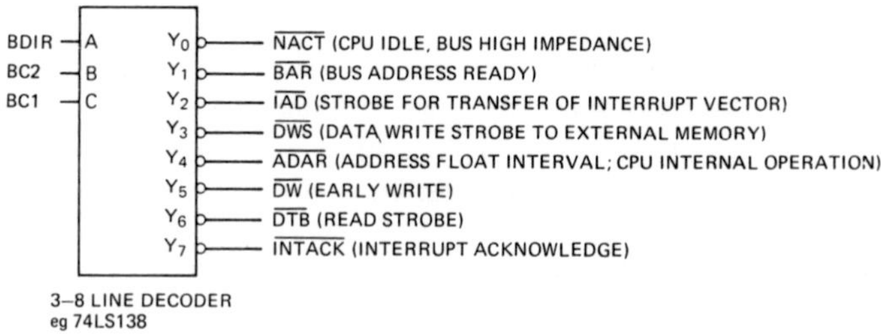

Fig. 3.5 CP1600 control signal decoding.

Bus control is an aspect of this microprocessor which fits in well with more modern thinking; BUSRQ is the bus request signal, BUSAK the corresponding acknowledgement; the coded bus control signal NACT also signifies that the CPU is inactive and the data/address bus is in a high impedance state. Interrupt requests in the CP1600 are versatile – for either INTR or INTRM (non-maskable and maskable interrupt pins, respectively), the CP1600 acknowledges the interrupt by pushing R7 (PC) contents onto the stack, followed by the INTAK control signal, itself followed by the IAD control signal, which causes external interrupt logic to respond by placing a 16-bit address on the address/data bus. This 16-bit address is loaded into R7, causing program execution to be transferred to an interrupt service routine. Return from an interrupt service routine may be effected by a terminate current interrupt (TCI) instruction, which generates an output on the TCI pin, to indicate that the routine is finished. An adjunct to the interrupt system is PCIT; this is activated when a software interrupt is invoked, but may also be used as an input to prevent the program counter from being incremented following an instruction fetch.

Like the PACE, the GI microprocessor has four output flag signals EBCA0-EBCA3, and an input signal EBC1. All five signals are used with the branch on external (BEXT) instruction, which outputs a pattern of bits on EBCA0-EBCA3, and then examines input EBC1. If EBC1 is high, BEXT will perform a branch instruction; if low, program execution will continue normally. The four output pins allow one of sixteen conditions to be signalled to external logic, which may then respond true or false on EBC1. A 4-to-16 line decoder will often form part of this logic.

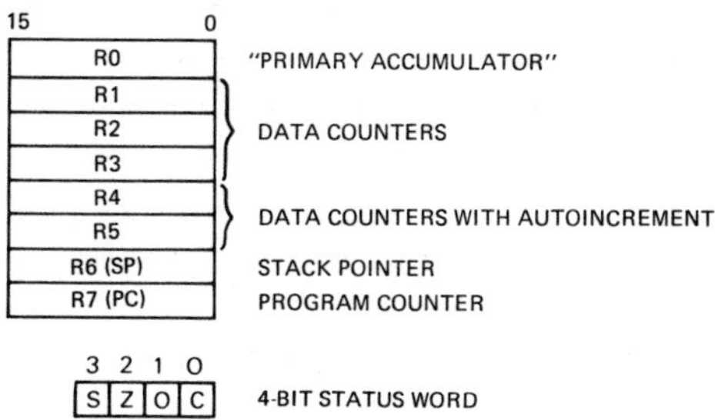

Fig. 3.6 CP1600 register model.

The instruction set of the CP1600 is typical of that of an early 1970s low-end minicomputer. It is relatively small, and the opcodes do not use the full 16 bits of the words they occupy. An opcode only takes the lower 10 bits, leaving the upper 6 bits unused, and available for future enhancement. Addressing modes may be direct, register-indirect (implied), register-indirect with autoincrement, or immediate (classified as immediate for loads, and immediate operate, for arithmetic actions). Direct addressing, as its name implies, uses a 16-bit absolute address which follows the instruction operation code. Implied, or register-indirect addressing uses the contents of one of the three data counter registers R1, 2 or 3 as the effective address. Implied addressing with autoincrement uses the contents of one of the two data counter registers R4 or R5, as the effective address, and these register contents are then incremented. Immediate and immediate operate instructions hold data in the word following the operation code. A programmer's model of the CP1600 registers is shown in fig. 3.6. The status word (or flag register) is only 4 bits long, indicating sign, zero, overflow and carry.

The CP1600 instruction set is summarised in table 3.2. Notice that data may be accessed either in 16-bit words or in bytes, using the SDBD instruction to switch mode for the duration of the following instruction. The same 16-bit address will be used, but the bytes accessed will be the low 8 bits of an addressed 16-bit word, with the upper 8 bits ignored. The rest of the instructions are predictable, although the omission of an inclusive-OR instruction seems odd. Shifts and rotates are interesting, allowing one or two place movements, and involving carry and overflow (two place movements) for logical shifts and rotates. Although R7, the PC, is automatically pushed onto the stack following an interrupt request, a jump-to-subroutine (JSR) instruction does not automatically use the stack, but saves the program counter in register R4 or R5, allowing a subroutine to manipulate the return address without involving stack operations. Thus a subroutine call (JSR) which is followed by a parameter list or a pointer to a parameter list, can have the subroutine code recover the parameters using register indirect-and-increment addressing, which will automatically adjust the return address ready to be pushed onto the stack. It does, however, imply that a simpler subroutine will have an extra explicit push instruction to store the return address on the stack. It also means that, to be absolutely safe, it may be necessary to disable interrupts until any manipulation of this sort is complete, and the return address safely stored on the stack. It would otherwise be possible for an interrupt to occur, and its service routine could itself call a subroutine, destroying the interrupted routine's return address. Note that JSRD will accomplish disabling interrupts in the same instruction as the subroutine call. Byte swapping in 16-bit registers is a useful facility of the CP1600.

Table 3.2 CP1600 instruction set

Group	Assembler mnemonics		Description
Data transfer	MVI <addr>, reg		Load register from memory (direct addressing)
	MVO reg, <addr>		Load memory from register (direct addressing)
	MVI @ <addr reg>, reg		Load register from memory (implied addressing)
	MVO reg, @ <addr reg>		Load memory from register (implied addressing)
	MVII <data>, reg		Load immediate
	MVOI reg, <data>		Store immediate (so long as program code is in RAM)
	MVOR src, dest		Move from source register to destination register
Arithmetic and logical	ADD		Add memory to register
	SUB		Subtract memory from register
	CMP	<addr>, reg	Compare memory and register
	AND		AND memory with register
	XOR		EXCLUSIVE-OR memory with register
	ADD		
	SUB		
	CMP	@ <addr reg>, reg	As above, implied addressing
	AND		
	XOR		
	ADDI		
	SUBI		
	CMPI	<data>, reg	As above, immediate
	ANDI		
	XORI		

Table 3.2 (contd.)

Group	Assembler mnemonics	Description
Arithmetic and logical	ADDR SUBR CMPR ANDR XORR } src, dest	As above, register
	CLRR TSTR INCR DECR COMR NEGR ADCR } reg	Clear Test for sign, zero Increment Decrement Ones complement Twos complement Add carry bit
Shift and rotate	SLL reg [,2]	Shift logical left 1 [or 2] places
	SLLC reg [,2]	Shift logical left through carry 1 [or 2] places
	SLR reg [,2]	Shift logical right 1 [or 2] places
	SAR reg [,2]	Shift arithmetic right 1 [or 2] places
	SARC reg [,2]	Shift arithmetic right 1 place into carry [or 2 places into carry and overflow]
	RLC reg [,2] RRC reg [,2]	Rotate left (right) 1 place through carry [or 2 places through carry and overflow]
	SWAP reg [,2]	Swap register bytes
Branches	B <displacement>	Unconditional branch relative to PC
	B <cond>, <displacement>	Branch relative to PC if condition <cond> true
	BEXT <displacement>	Branch relative to PC if external condition on EBCA0-3 true
	J <addr>	Unconditional jump
	JR <addr reg>	Indirect unconditional jump
Control and stack	JSR reg, <addr>	Jump to subroutine, saving return address in specified register
	PSHR reg	PUSH register onto stack
	PULR reg	PULL register from stack using R6 as SP
	SIN	Invoke software interrupt
	EIS, DIS	Enable, disable interrupts
	TCI	Terminate current interrupt
	JE <addr>	Jump and enable interrupts
	JD <addr>	Jump and disable interrupts
	JSRE reg, <addr> JSRD reg, <addr>	Jump to subroutine and enable, disable interrupts

Table 3.2 (contd.)

Group	Assembler mnemonics	Description
Control and stack	GSWD reg	Put status word in upper byte of register
	RSWD reg	Load status word from register
	CLRC, SETC	Clear, set carry
	SDBD	Set double byte mode for next instruction
	NOP	No operation
	HLT	Halt

The CP1600, although faster than PACE, is still firmly in the category of an 'extended-wordlength 8-bit CPU'. Its byte-addressing facilities are not very flexible, but its main advantages lie with its register set, and the regularity of its addressing modes. Its instruction set is adequate, but tends to be limited in some unexpected areas, such as the shift and rotate instructions, which only move one or two places, and in the lack of an inclusive-OR instruction, and possibly in its lack of indexed addressing. Nevertheless, the design has been very successful, and has enjoyed a long product life.

3.3 9440 Microflame

The 9440[2,3] from Fairchild is one of the microprocessors based on the Nova minicomputer. Unlike the Micro Nova, described in section 3.4, the 9440 does not enjoy direct Nova compatibility, but does execute the same instruction act as the Data General Nova line of minicomputers. Unlike the two previously described CPUs, the 9440 requires only a simple +5 V supply, and is a bipolar device, manufactured using Fairchild's isoplanar integrated injection logic (I^3L) process, in a 40-pin package with full TTL compatibility. Like the PACE, it is microprogrammed, and like some other microprocessors, it uses only fifteen of its sixteen address bits for word addressing (giving a total 16-bit address range of 0-32 K words). The address and data bits are multiplexed and carry ground-true information, and memory and explicit input-output operations are controlled using two groups of control signals, $\overline{\text{MO}}$-$\overline{\text{M2}}$ and $\overline{\text{MBSY}}$ for memory, and O0, O1, $\overline{\text{INTREQ}}$, $\overline{\text{DCHREQ}}$ for I/O devices. A block diagram of the 9440 CPU is shown in fig. 3.7. The microcode programmed logic array (PLA) controls both internal and external operations, and it generates a set of twenty-four signals for each of seventy-two different data-path operations specified by nineteen inputs. The multiplexed information bus (IB) which carries address and data is connected to a set of four general-purpose 16-bit accumulator registers, an instruction register, and a 15-bit program counter (the least significant bit of the address bus is used for upper and lower byte selection). Internally, buses are 4-bits wide, and the microcycles of the microcoded instruction set accommodate this by themselves consisting of nanocycles, or phases for each group of 4 bits (or nibbles) to build up a 16-bit operation.

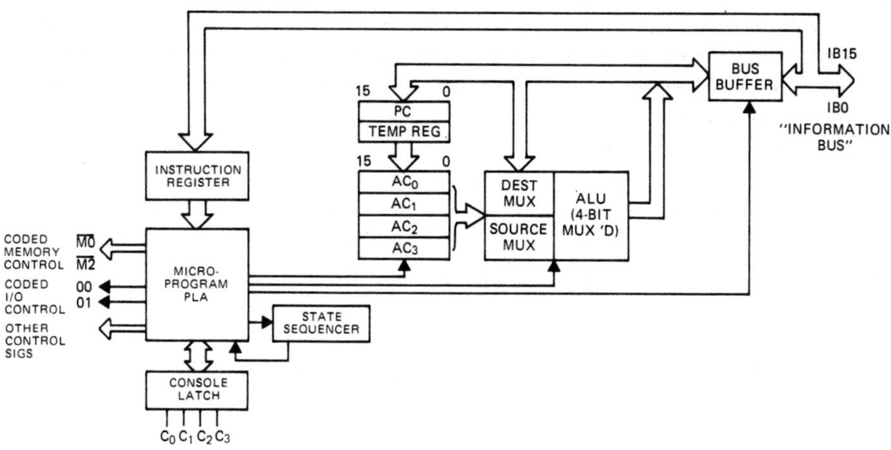

Fig. 3.7 9440 'Microflame'.

Table 3.3 9440 front panel support signals

C3	C2	C1	C0	Description
0	0	0	0	Display AC0 contents
0	0	0	1	Display AC1 contents
0	0	1	0	Display AC2 contents
0	0	1	1	Display AC3 contents
0	1	0	0	Display next
0	1	0	1	Display data memory contents
0	1	1	0	Load data memory
0	1	1	1	Halt
1	0	0	0	Load AC0 from panel switches
1	0	0	1	Load AC1 from panel switches
1	0	1	0	Load AC2 from panel switches
1	0	1	1	Load AC3 from panel switches
1	1	0	0	Load PC from panel switches
1	1	0	1	Continue
1	1	1	0	Load next from panel switches
1	1	1	1	No operation

The microprogram PLA has unique facilities provided in it to allow front panel console support by the 9440. The 'Nova-replacement' market for the 9440 will obviously make use of this facility, and field debugging at a machine code level becomes possible with a minimum of equipment. Using the $\overline{MR}$ (master reset) input to the CPU, the microprocessor may be halted immediately without completing the current instruction, with all registers unaffected, and interrupts disabled. Inputs C0-C3 are control lines for the CPU console, and allow memory and registers to be examined and changed, the program counter (PC) to be altered using console lights and switches, and a minimum of logic. The detailed operation of C0-C3 is shown in table 3.3. Timing for all operations is provided in the 9440 by an external clock connected to CP, or by a crystal connected between CP and XTL, which uses the on-chip oscillator, and the CPU provides a CLKOUT signal, and a $\overline{\text{SYN}}$ synchronisation signal for memory and I/O devices. Memory control uses $\overline{\text{M0}}$ to indicate memory read, $\overline{\text{M1}}$ to indicate memory write, and $\overline{\text{M2}}$ as a bidirectional signal which indicates that the memory address register must be loaded on or before the high-to-low transition of $\overline{\text{SYN}}$. While a read or instruction fetch operation will take just one machine cycle, write will require a 'load memory address' register cycle, followed by a write cycle. $\overline{\text{MBSY}}$ is an input from memory which indicates that a memory operation is in progress. For write, or load memory address register operations, the CPU asserts $\overline{\text{SYN}}$ only if $\overline{\text{MBSY}}$ is not asserted, and waits for the memory to respond by asserting $\overline{\text{MBSY}}$. For a read operation, the CPU asserts $\overline{\text{SYN}}$ only if $\overline{\text{MBSY}}$ is not asserted, and then waits for $\overline{\text{MBSY}}$ to be first asserted and then released before proceeding. Bus operations are thus asynchronous, and the microprocessor may be idled by holding $\overline{\text{MBSY}}$ permanently high.

Input-output control is performed via a specific set of signals, and distinguished from memory operations. O0 and O1 are valid during and before $\overline{\text{SYN}}$ is asserted, and distinguish between instruction fetch, data channel acknowledge, I/O execute and no operation. An I/O device can request direct memory access by using an input $\overline{\text{DCHREQ}}$ (data channel request); upon data channel acknowledge, the device can drive memory control $\overline{\text{M0}}$-$\overline{\text{M2}}$ lines. For I/O under program control, an interrupt input $\overline{\text{INTREQ}}$ is available, and it is assumed that like $\overline{\text{DCHREQ}}$, requests will be daisy-chained. The sixty-four I/O ports of the 9440 allow for movement of data between the CPU accumulators and one of three device data buffers (A, B or C), and allow for status indication on the low two information bus lines IB0 and IB1 (indicating 'busy' and 'available'). This brief description does not do justice to the sophistication of the input-output of the 9440, but does give some idea that the microprocessor is much more of a 'minicomputer look-alike' than PACE or CP1600, and that as such, it will require minicomputer-like hardware support in the form of a front panel or console, and complex I/O interfaces. Although sixty-four I/O ports are provided for, Port 1 is reserved for special functions such as hardware multiply/divide and stack manipulation, and Port 63 is reserved for the console logic associated with C0-C3.

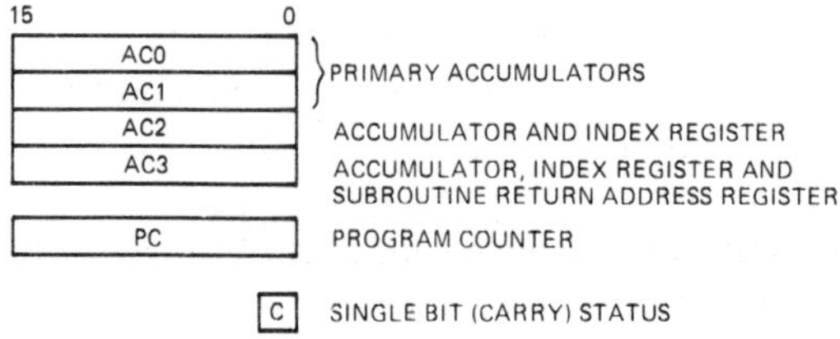

Fig. 3.8 9440 register model.

Status outputs are provided on the CPU pins, and indicate the state of the CPU, typically on the console supported by the internal PLA. RUN indicates that the CPU is executing instructions or console operations, CARRY, the state of the carry flag bistable, and INTON indicates when CPU interrupts are enabled. Only one more connection to the microprocessor needs some explanation – I_{INJ}. The integrated injection logic within the processor has no power supply as such, but is current operated, and will run at a speed appropriate to the current injected into pin I_{INJ}. In general, the higher the injected current up to the specified maximum, the faster the logic operation. Since the clock can be any speed between d.c. and 12 MHz (the internal CPU logic is static and does not need to be continuously clocked), the system designer can make a trade off between operating speed and power consumption, and can control I_{INJ} over a limited range with a single resistor.

The programmer's model of the 9440 is shown in fig. 3.8. Notice that there is no stack pointer register, and indeed, the 9440 in its basic form does not support a stack. Addressing modes, however, do allow the creation of stack-like data structures. The addressing modes of the 9440 are reasonably versatile. There are four addressing modes, and each may be used for direct or indirect addressing; the four are base-page addressing, PC-relative addressing, and indexed addressing using AC2 or AC3. Page-zero addressing uses the 8-bit opcode displacement to directly address memory in the range 0-255 (decimal). These memory addresses may contain data (direct addressing) or a pointer (indirect addressing) depending upon a single bit in the opcode field. Autoincrement and autodecrement may be achieved by base-page indirect addressing – when locations 20-27 octal (10-17H) are addressed, their contents are incremented and then used as an effective address (pre-increment). When locations 30-37 octal are accessed, their contents are decremented before being used as an effective address (predecrement). A unique feature which is a consequence of having 15-bit word addresses is the idea of using the most significant bit of an address held in memory to indicate whether this address is to be used for direct or indirect addressing, so indirection may be cascaded indefinitely! Thus an indirect addressing instruction may point to a memory location which itself may contain either a direct address, or an address pointer to another memory location, which again may contain either an address or a pointer, and so on.

PC-relative addressing simply adds the signed 8-bit offset of the opcode to the program counter, generating an address which may again be direct or indirect. Indexed addressing generates a similar direct or indirect address by adding the 8-bit displacement value of the opcode to the 16-bit contents of AC2 or AC3.

The instruction set for the 9440 is shown in table 3.4. Notice that instructions are quite complex – the memory reference instructions are straightforward, and include useful features such as increment/decrement-and-skip on zero result, but the arithmetic and logical functions, and the input-output instructions, are considerably more complicated. The arithmetic instructions, for instance, do not only perform the operation specified, but may also make a skip (of the next opcode) either unconditionally or on a specific result of the arithmetic operation (carry, no carry, zero, non-zero, both carry and zero, neither carry or zero), may choose to load the result into a destination accumulator, may shift or rotate the result through carry, or byte swap the result. Input-output operations allow a number of functions as well as basic data transfers, which allow control of a peripheral device as well as its initialisation. For CPU control and dealing with interrupts, a special device code of octal 77 (3FH) is used, and allows interrupt acknowledgement, allows masking device interrupts, skip-on-enable, CPU halt, and reading the front panel (console) switches.

Table 3.4 9940 and Micro Nova instruction set

Group	Assembler mnemonics	Description	
Data transfer	LDA reg, (@) <displacement>, <mode>	Load register from memory; @ denotes indirection, <mode> specifies one of zero page, PC-relative, indexed by AC2, indexed by AC3.	
	STA reg, (@) <displacement>, <mode>	Store register in memory	
	MOV src, dst, <condition>	Move contents of source register to destination register and skip on condition	
Arithmetic and logical	ADD } src, dest, <condition>	Add	Source register with dest'n, skip on condition
	SUB } src, dest, <condition>	Subtract	
	ADC } src, dest, <condition>	Add with carry	
	AND } src, dest, <condition>	And	
	NEG } src, dest, <condition>	2s complement	Source register put in dest'n, skip on cond'n
	COM } src, dest, <condition>	1s complement	
	INC } src, dest, <condition>	Increment	
	MUL	Multiply	Use AC0, AC1, and AC2
	DIV	Divide	
	ISZ (@) <displacement>, <mode>	Increment, Decrement memory contents, and skip if zero	
	DSZ (@) <displacement>, <mode>		
Branches	JMP (@) <displacement>, <mode>	Unconditional jump	
Control and stack	MFSP reg	Move SP to register	
	MFFP reg	Move FP to register	
	JMP @ <displacement>, <mode>	Branch to subroutine	
	RET	Return from subroutine	
	PSHA reg	PUSH register onto stack	
	POPA reg	POP register from stack	
	SAV	Save registers and flags on the stack	
	MTSP reg	Move register to SP	

Table 3.4 (contd.)

Group	Assembler mnemonics	Description
	MTFP reg	Move register to FP
	RTCEN, RTCDS	Enable, disable realtime clock
	INTEN, INTDS	Enable, disable interrupts
	INTA reg	Interrupt acknowledge; load register with the code of the interrupting device
	MSKO reg	Load mask register from data register
	SKP	Skip on power fail
	HALT	Halt
Input-output	NIO <dev>	Set device 'busy' and 'done' flags
	DIA, DIB, DIC reg, <dev>	Load register with contents of device A, B, or C buffer and set 'busy' and 'done' flags
	DOA, DOB, DOC reg, <dev>	Load device A, B or C buffer with contents of register, set 'busy' and 'done' flags
	SKP <dev>	Skip on I/O test
	IORST	Reset all devices' 'busy' and 'done' flags

The limitations of the instruction set are the limitations of the most basic Nova minicomputer – logic instructions and bit manipulation instructions are weak, I/O support is sophisticated but more suited to a minicomputer with computer-like peripheral devices than an embedded microcomputer. Interrupt processing is also limited. On assertion of $\overline{\text{INTREQ}}$, the 9440 CPU completes its current instruction, disables further interrupts, and acknowledges receipt of the interrupt request. The program counter contents are saved in location 0000H, and an indirect jump made via location 0001H to an interrupt service routine. Devices must then be polled to identify the interrupting one, or their requests daisy-chained. A return is affected by an indirect jump, JMP @ 0. Note that there is no stack, so any registers saved must be stored in some other reserved memory area. DMA is similarly simple, with little support given by the CPU. A DMA request on the $\overline{\text{DCHREQ}}$ input causes the CPU to suspend its operation and float the information bus; the external device must control memory via $\overline{\text{M0}}$-$\overline{\text{M2}}$ once it has recognised the data channel acknowledge code on O0 and O1. The lack of a stack makes support of modern high level languages such as Pascal difficult, and real time multitasking operation is possible only by severely compromising response times. Subroutine calls automatically store their return address in AC3, one of the general-purpose accumulators, and return with a register indirect jump. The lack of a stack means that nested subroutines require return addresses to be saved explicitly. In order to operate efficiently, the 9440 requires a small group of special integrated circuits which will control memory (9441), control input-output by creating a separate 64-port I/O bus (9442), and provide console logic and a front panel.

Despite the criticisms, the 9440 is fast, having a 10 MHz clock, and will benchmark well against microprocessors of more modern design. A successor, the 9445, is even faster, and features hardware multiply-divide on-chip. It has plenty of support, and can rely on the large user base of Data General customers. The demands of modern operating systems and languages, however, are not satisfied so well as with more modern CPU designs.

3.4 Data General Micro Nova

Not to be outdone by the semiconductor manufacturers, Data General has itself brought out a single-chip 40-pin CPU, the MN601, or Micro Nova,[4,5] which runs the Nova instruction set. The Micro Nova is an NMOS microprocessor which provides virtually direct compatibility with the Nova 3 minicomputer, but cannot, of course, provide the separate memory and I/O buses of that computer in a 40-pin package. The internal architecture is shown in fig. 3.9, and immediately a number of differences can be seen between it and the 9440. Two more 15-bit registers have been added, a stack pointer (SP) and a frame pointer (FP). In addition, as well as a 1-bit interrupt enable register, the MN601 has a stack-overflow request bit, which generates an interrupt when the stack overflows a 256-word memory address boundary, a real time clock enable bit, which allows the internal real time clock to generate interrupts (assuming interrupts are enabled) at a fixed interval of 1.8432 ms, and the real time clock request bit, set when the real time clock generates an interrupt. The real time clock addition is a useful one and is available partly as a result of providing on-chip memory refresh. The microprocessor contains a 6-bit refresh address counter, which is used to refresh dynamic RAM in the 32K address space, while maintaining normal CPU operation. The way in which this is done is controlled by the CPU, which may initiate any one of four memory cycles: read, write, read-modify-write, and refresh. Signals issued by the Micro Nova are considerably different to those of the 9440. The multiplexed address/data bus lines are given the designation MB (memory bus), and memory operations are controlled by signals P, WE and SAE. P signifies that a valid address is on MB0-MB14; WE is the write strobe signal, and SAE (sense amplifier enable) is the equivalent of a write strobe. Refresh is effectively a write operation, in which the contents of the refresh address counter have been issued as an address, WE has been asserted, but no data appears on the MB lines.

The MN601 also possesses on-chip DMA (direct memory access) control. A function called 'data channel break' allows the CPU to move information between I/O bus and memory without altering program operation. Power-up too, is somewhat different to normal, using a signal called $\overline{\text{CLAMP}}$, which is required to be held low for 100 μs after power has been first applied, whereupon the CPU is initialised, and enters the HALT state. In this state, the microprocessor generates a sequence of pulses, at a frequency of 0.417 MHz, at the HALT pin, and generates request enable (I/O synchronisation) signals, responds to interrupts and data channel requests, and generates refresh signals. Once the HALT state has been entered, the microprocessor can then be started by initiating a program interrupt, via input $\overline{\text{EXTINT}}$.

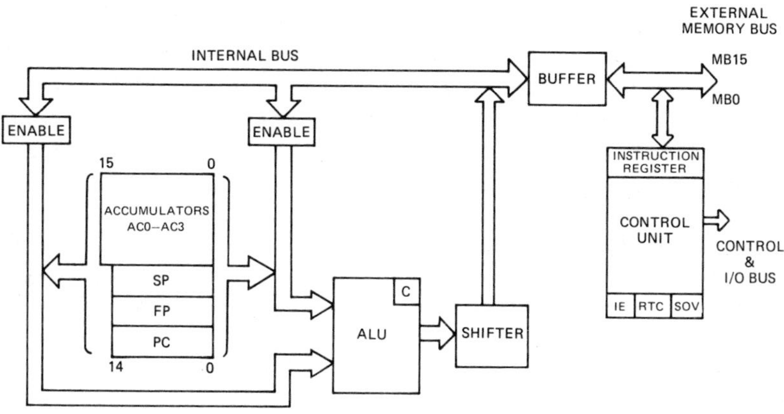

Fig. 3.9 Micro Nova architecture (mN601).

I/O operations are complex, consist largely of serial data signals, and a number of lines are dedicated to them. Two bidirectional data lines, I/O DATA1 and I/O DATA2, are provided, and carry all information (data, address and commands) between the CPU and its interfaces. Information is transmitted serially to MN603 I/O controllers over these two lines, at a bit rate of 8.3 MHz, twice that of the two-phase (Ø1, Ø2) microprocessor clock. For a 16-bit transfer, the most significant byte is transmitted over line I/O DATA1, and the least significant byte is transmitted simultaneously over I/O DATA2, giving an effective bit rate of 16.6 Mbits/s, approximately 1 Mword/s. Transfers are synchronised by an I/O clock signal, itself related to Ø1 of the two-phase CPU clock, and are identified by a pair of single code bits preceding the data bits on I/O DATA1 and I/O DATA2. These two code bits distinguish between request enable, data channel address request, data, and I/O command. Request enable is used by the CPU to enable individual I/O controllers to synchronise the assertion of program interrupt and data channel request lines ($\overline{\text{EXTINT}}$, $\overline{\text{DCHINT}}$). Data channel address request is a signal sent by the CPU in response to a data channel break request caused by a device asserting $\overline{\text{DCHINT}}$. The highest priority requesting device will respond with a 15-bit data channel address and mode (direction of transfer required) bit. Notice that the I/O DATA lines are bidirectional; a further signal, I/O INPUT, gives direction information for the other two lines.

I/O can be programmed, where the CPU transfers from one of its accumulator registers to a device, transmitting first a command, then data. Alternatively, $\overline{\text{DCHINT}}$ may be used by an I/O device to initiate a data channel break, where transfers are effected directly between device and memory. After the response to a data channel address request, the logic of the CPU commences a read-modify-write memory cycle and then examines the mode (direction) bit, and sets up a direct transfer between memory and I/O device. All I/O devices are connected to the pin described, which form a 6-wire I/O bus (I/O DATA1, I/O DATA2, I/O CLOCK, $\overline{\text{DCHINT}}$, $\overline{\text{EXTINT}}$, and I/O INPUT).

One further signal is available from the Micro Nova CPU. $\overline{\text{PAUSE}}$ is asserted when the CPU is not using memory and indicates periods when clocks Ø1 and Ø2 may be disabled, to allow multiport memory operation. Although both the Micro Nova and the 9440 are compatible to some degree with the Nova minicomputer instruction set, their electrical characteristics and signals at their pins are completely different. Power supplies, too, are different – for the Micro Nova, they are –4.25 V, +5 V, +10 V, and +14 V. Because of the unusual structure of the MN601, it is virtually mandatory to use the Data General support circuits, in particular, the MN603 input-output controller (IOC), which connects directly to the I/O bus of the CPU, and provides the device being interfaced with a 16-bit wide bidirectional data bus, and four function code control lines, allowing sixteen dedicated functions. Less complex, but still necessary for system architects, are the other support circuits, a range of bus sense amplifiers, memory bus transceivers, and memory address drivers.

In terms of its instruction set, the MN601 is similar to the 9940, and, of course, the Nova minicomputer. Naturally, the instruction set has been expanded over that of the 9440 to accommodate the additional facilities, and thus has DIV and MUL instructions for hardware divide and multiply, and stack instructions POPA, PSHA. The instructions are all one word long, and can access memory directly or indirectly, with the same multiple indirection technique (using the sixteenth memory address bit) as described earlier. Also as before, certain base page locations are autoincrementing and autodecrementing, and indexed addressing using an offset and accumulator AC2 or AC3 is available. Stack operations are interesting; the stack pointer register SP points to the top of the stack, and operates in the expected manner, but with the stack growing from low to high address. Thus, when a PUSH is executed, SP is incremented by one, and the 16-bit word to be pushed is stored in memory at the address pointed to by SP; when a POP is executed, the contents of the memory address indicated by SP are transferred to the specified accumulator, and SP is decremented by one. The contents of SP may be loaded into an accumulator, and SP may be loaded (initialised) from an accumulator. Also associated with the stack, however, is a frame pointer (FP), which is used in conjunction with block operations SAVE and RETURN. FP may be set up and examined by transferring data between FP and an accumulator, in a similar manner to SP. When a SAVE is performed, the contents of the CPU registers are stored on the stack addressed by SP in a structure called a return block. Each return block contains the contents of the four CPU accumulators, and the old value of the frame pointer. The purpose of the SAVE instruction is to provide subroutine calls with a suitable means of saving their environment, yet remain compatible with the Nova JSR instruction, which stores the return address in accumulator AC3. The format of the return block accommodates this by storing the registers in the order (of their removal from the stack) AC3 and the carry bit, old FP, AC2, AC1, AC0. The old frame pointer value provides a link to the previous return block (see fig. 3.10). When a RETURN is encountered, the return address is automatically loaded into PC, the carry bit, AC0, AC1, AC2, FP and SP are restored, with the restored value of FP in AC3. Notice too that FP is updated automatically on SAVE so that it always points to the most recent return block. Stack overflow (a condition where the stack crosses a 256-word address boundary) causes a stack overflow interrupt if CPU interrupts are enabled.

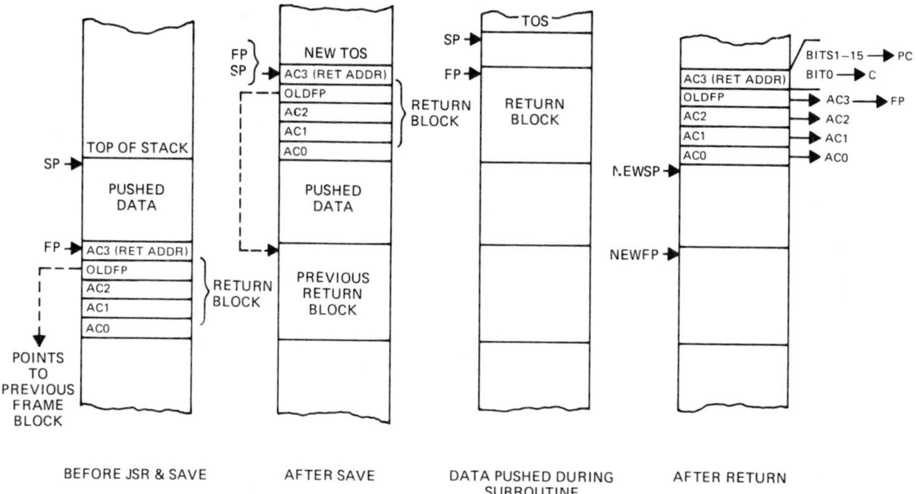

Fig. 3.10 Micro Nova subroutine call and return.

Multiply and divide are register operations, and use AC0, AC1 and AC2 to hold operands and results; both are unsigned. Both these and stack manipulation instructions are coded in Nova standard I/O instruction format. Other instructions in similar format control the real time clock interrupts, provide a TRAP (software interrupt, actually an arithmetic instruction format without arguments) and INTA (interrupt acknowledge). The occurrence of an enabled interrupt causes the microprocessor, at the end of its current cycle, to increment PC, store it in memory location 0, and jump indirect via the memory address appropriate to the interrupt:

Memory location	Type
0001	External I/O device interrupt (lowest priority)
0002	CPU real time clock
0003	Stack overflow (highest priority)

The interrupt enable flag will also be cleared (in the case of stack overflow and real time clock, the request flag will be cleared).

The MN601 is almost unique so far as microprocessors are concerned, in its handling of I/O devices, and its implementation of certain CPU operations as

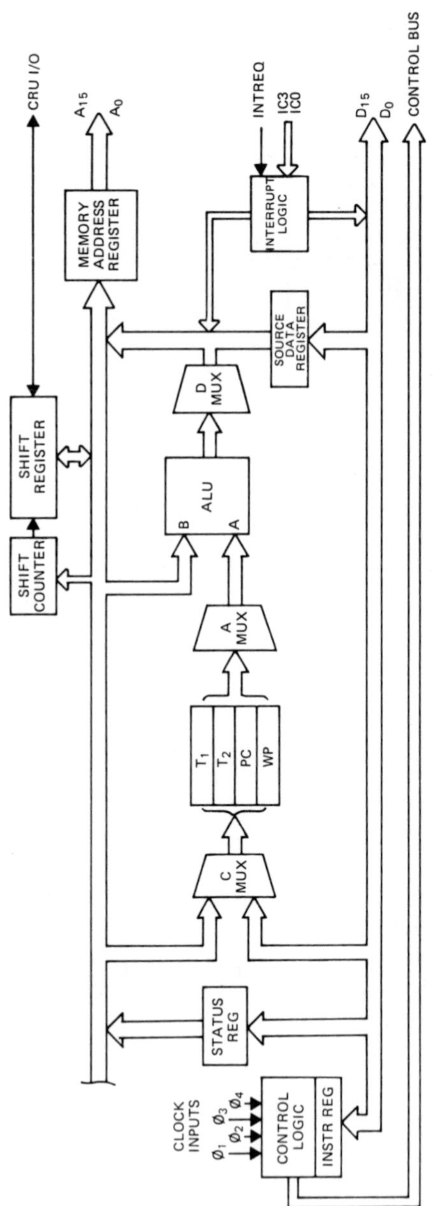

Fig. 3.11 TMS9900 architecture.

though they were I/O operations. It is oriented towards the minicomputer world, and possesses many facilities more appropriate to this world than to the embedded microprocessor one. Nevertheless, it is useful to examine in order to compare, for instance, its instruction set and addressing modes with more modern microprocessors. Its direct Nova compatibility means that the large body of existing Nova software will run on Micro Nova, and in hardware, Data General offer not only the chip set, but boards and packaged computers based around it.

3.5 TMS9900

The Texas Instruments TMS 9900[6–9] is the most widely used of the early 16-bit microprocessors, and, like many of the others, is based on a successful mini-computer design, the 990. The block diagram of the TMS9900 (fig. 3.11) shows at a glance how its architecture differs from most of the other popular 8-bit and 16-bit designs: it has no set of internal general-purpose registers. Its architecture is designed to operate on a memory-location to memory-location basis, and uses an area of memory, sixteen words long, as a workspace, that is, a block of locations which may be used for holding data, and used as a register file. The memory locations within the workspace may be used as accumulators, operand registers, address registers and index registers. Naturally, some CPU functions demand internal CPU storage, and three internal registers are present: the program counter (PC); workspace pointer (WP), and status register (ST). Two more registers, inaccessible to the programmer, are used for temporary storage during an instruction execution cycle. The basic TMS9900 runs from a four-phase clock signal at 3 MHz, is built in NMOS silicon-gate technology, and requires a triple (±5 V, +12 V) power supply. Significantly, it is packaged as a 64-pin device, which allows non-multiplexed address and data signals, so the two 16-bit buses are completely separate. Memory control is simplified, and consists of three signals, $\overline{\text{MEMEN}}$, memory enable, DBIN, which is asserted during a read operation to enable the addressed memory location to place data on the data bus, and $\overline{\text{WE}}$, write enable, which indicates that data from the CPU is available on the data bus and may be accepted by the addressed location. READY is available as an input which will extend memory reference cycles to accommodate slow devices. The 9900 will suspend operation and execute wait cycles until READY is indicated true, asserting the WAIT output to indicate wait cycle execution. Memory addressing uses a 16-bit address which assumes words start on even address boundaries, and where byte instructions can address either even or odd byte, as illustrated in fig. 3.12.

The interrupt facilities of the TMS9900 are very powerful, and consist of a single request line $\overline{\text{INTREQ}}$, and four interrupt codes IC0-IC3 (IC0 is the most significant). When $\overline{\text{INTREQ}}$ is asserted by an interrupting device, the micro-processor loads the interrupt code on IC0-IC3 into the interrupt-code storage register, compares it to the interrupt mask bits of the status register, and generates an interrupt sequence if the code is of higher or equal priority (IC0-IC3 = 0001 is the highest priority, 1111 the lowest). In real time operation, this allows a hardware decision, on the basis of priority, as to whether to pre-empt the running task. To accommodate DMA requests, HOLD and HOLDA (acknowledge) lines allow microprocessor operation to be suspended upon completion of the memory cycle in progress, and the address and data buses, as well as $\overline{\text{WE}}$, $\overline{\text{MEMEN}}$ and DBIN, are floated to a high-impedance state, followed by HOLDA being issued, in response to a HOLD request.

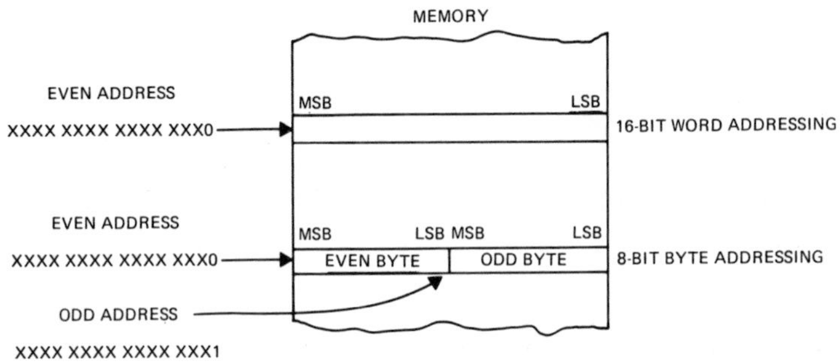

Fig. 3.12 TMS9900 word/byte addressing.

$\overline{\text{RESET}}$ causes the microprocessor to be reset and inhibits $\overline{\text{WE}}$ and the communications signal CRUCLK (see later); when released from $\overline{\text{RESET}}$, the CPU will initiate what Texas describe as a 'level-zero' interrupt sequence which loads the two registers WP and PC from locations 0000 and 0002, respectively, sets all status register bits to zero, and commences execution. $\overline{\text{LOAD}}$, another input, acts as a non-maskable interrupt which uses address FFFCH to load WP and PC. To assist illegal opcode detection, an instruction acquisition signal (IAQ) is asserted whenever the current memory cycle is an instruction fetch.

The final major hardware feature of the TMS9900 is its communications control unit (CRU). It is intended as a direct command-driven I/O device which can be considered to have access to 4096 input bits and 4096 output bits, using the memory address bus and three control pins CRUCLK, CRUIN, CRUOUT. The input pin, CRUIN, operates asynchronously, while the output pin, CRUOUT, is synchronised using pulses on CRUCLK. In single-bit CRU mode, the 9900 generates a CRU bit address and loads it onto the address bus lines A3 to A14, and for an output instruction, either set bit (SBO) or reset bit (SBZ), issues a CRUCLK pulse; the output instruction is distinguished by a '1' or a '0' at the CRUOUT pin at the time of this pulse. Input instructions, such as test bit (TB), do not generate any pulse on CRUCLK. Two multiple-bit operations, LDCR and STCR, allow load and store of any memory word from 1 to 16 bits in length. LDCR will fetch a word from memory and right-shift it to serially transfer its bits to the CRU output bits, so that when it is transferred to the CPU, each bit receives an address which is sequentially greater than the address for the previous bit (note that this address sequence coupled with right-shifting the original word implies that the least significant bit is assigned the lowest CRU address). STCR transfers serial data to a right-shifted form in the target memory

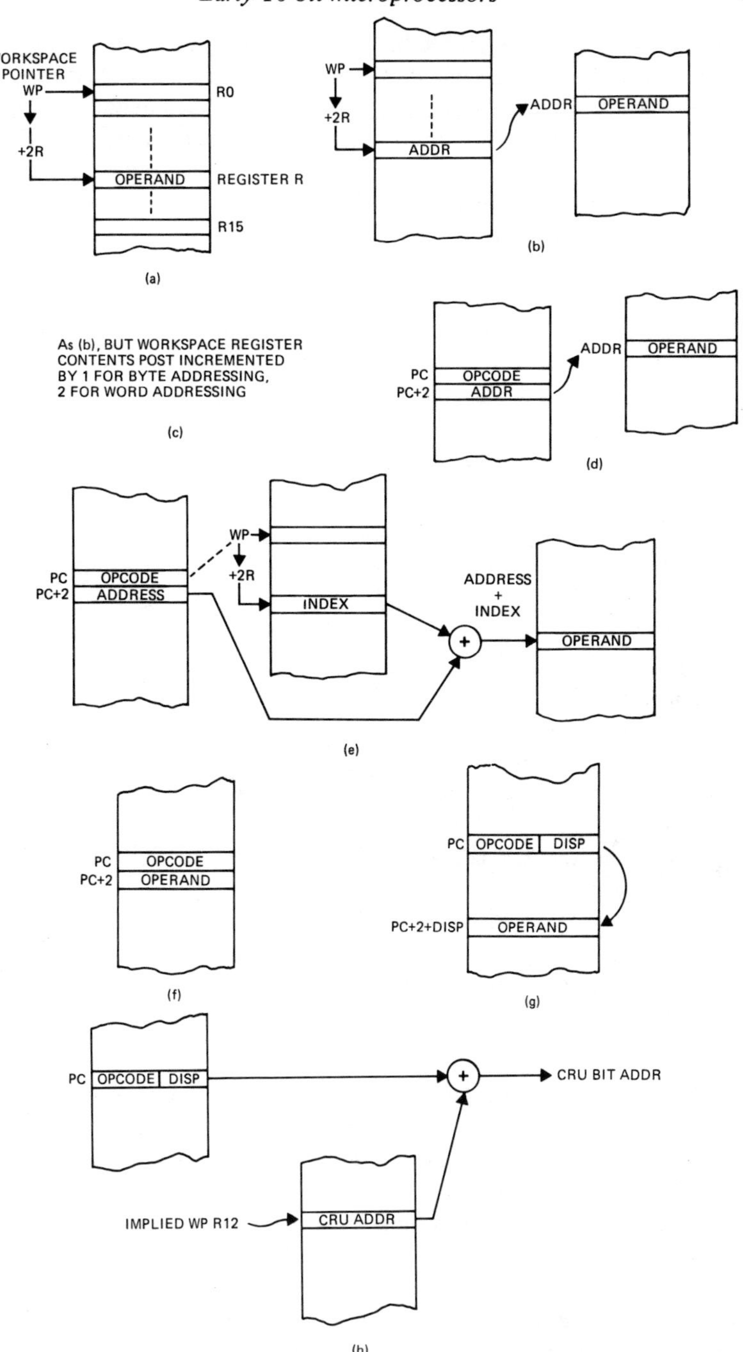

Fig. 3.13 TMS9900 addressing modes: (a) workspace register, (b) workspace register indirect, (c) workspace register indirect autoincrement, (d) direct addressing, (e) indexed addressing, (f) immediate addressing, (g) relative addressing, (h) CRU bit addressing.

location. The 9900 also uses CRUCLK to indicate the presence of an 'external instruction' on the most significant three lines of the address bus. Five of these external instructions allow user-defined functions to be initiated under program control (CKON, CKOFF, RSET, IDLE and LREX), and have unique address bus codes.

The instruction set of the TMS9900 is comprehensive, and possesses a versatility that was unrivalled before the launch of the modern 16-bit microprocessors. As might be expected for a memory-to-memory architecture machine, addressing is one of its strong features. The block of sixteen memory locations pointed to by the workspace pointer (WP), as mentioned previously, is treated as a register file, and the locations (the general, or workspace registers) are referred to by their position relative to the first workspace address (contents of WP). Because the address range is in bytes, the register number must be doubled before being added to WP, to get the actual memory address of the register. Addressing modes are:

(a) Absolute: address follows instruction code.
(b) Relative: displacement byte of the opcode (lower byte) is multiplied by two (to get byte addressing) and the address of the next sequential instruction added to it in two's complement form, giving a PC-relative address range of −128 to +127 of the current instruction.
(c) Immediate: operand word follows instruction word (only registers may be the destination of an immediate instruction).
(d) Register: operand is one of the contents of the general registers (accessed by adding the contents of the workspace pointer WP to twice the register number).
(e) Register indirect: the address of the operand is the contents of one of the general registers.
(f) Register indirect with autoincrement: register indirect addressing with post-increment.
(g) Indexed: the instruction is followed by an address which is added to the contents of a designated general register to form the effective address of the operand.

The CRU has its own addressing mode, which is relative to the CRU base address, contained in general register 12. All the modes are illustrated symbolically in fig. 3.13. The instruction set, table 3.5, has good arithmetic and bit manipulation facilities, including unsigned multiply and divide, multibit logical, circular, and arithmetic shifts, and a comprehensive set of conditional branch operations operating in conjunction with status bits ST0-ST5 (logical greater than, arithmetic greater than, equal, carry, overflow, and parity). The communications register has both the single bit and multiple bit instructions discussed earlier.

Subroutines and interrupts cause a context switch which obviates the need for a stack. A change of workspace pointer implies that a new set of general registers is made available, and that the old set is unchanged, and may be returned to via some sort of link. The equivalent of a subroutine call is branch and load workspace pointer (BLWP), which loads the workspace pointer with the contents of the source address and the program counter with the contents of the address following it. The old values are stored in the new general or workspace registers WR13 (old WP), WR14 (old PC), WR15 (old status ST). Thus program transfer is effected and the new workspace contains a link to the previous one, with the environment completely saved in just a few operations. Branch and link (BL) provides for a jump with return address stored in WR11, without change in workspace. A return from a subroutine (RTWP) restores the original environment by reverting to the old WP.

Table 3.5 TMS9900 instruction set

Group	Assembler mnemonics	Description	
Data transfer	MOV src, dest	16-bit move	direct, direct-indexed, implied or implied-with-autoincrement addressing
	MOVB src, dest	8-bit move	
	LI reg, <16-bit data>	Load immediate to workspace	
	SWPB dest	Swap bytes	
Arithmetic and logical	A src, dest	16-bit add	addressing modes as for MOV
	AB src, dest	8-bit add	
	S src, dest	16-bit subtract	
	SB src, dest	8-bit subtract	
	C src, dest	16-bit compare	
	CB src, dest	8-bit compare	
	XOR src, reg	Exclusive-OR with workspace register	
	MPY src, reg	Multiply	16-bit, unsigned
	DIV src, reg	Divide	
	INC (INCT) dest	Increment	by one or two
	DEC (DECT) dest	Decrement	
	CLR dest	Clear	
	SETO dest	Set to FFFF	
	INV dest	1's complement	
	NEG dest	2's complement	
	ABS dest	Absolute Value	
	AI reg, <16-bit data>	Immediate Add	with work-space register
	ANDI reg, <16-bit data>	Immediate AND	
	ORI reg, <16-bit data>	Immediate OR	
	CI reg, <16-bit data>	Immediate Compare	
Bit set	SOC src, dest	Set bits in 16-bit destination	
	SOCB src, dest	Set bits in 8-bit destination	
	SZC src, dest	Clear bits in 16-bit destination	
	SZB src, dest	Clear bits in 8-bit destination	
	COC src, dest	Compare bits	
	CZC src, dest		

Table 3.5 (contd.)

Group	Assembler mnemonics	Description
Branches	B src	Branch unconditional to address in source register
	BL src	Branch and Link
	BLWP src	Branch and load workspace pointer
	JMP <displacement>	Unconditional jump relative to PC
	JMP <cond>, <displacement>	Conditional jump relative to PC. Conditions are: arithmetic and logical equality, non-equality, greater than, less than, carry, no carry, overflow, no overflow, parity.
Shift and rotate	SLA	Arithmetic left shift
	SRA reg, <count>	Arithmetic right shift work-
	SRL	Logical right shift space
	SRC	Rotate right reg
Control	XOP src, dest	Context switch (software interrupt)
	X src	Execute the contents of the source as an instruction
	RTWP	Return from context switch
	STST reg	Store the contents of the status register in one of the workspace registers
	STWP reg	Store the contents of the workspace pointer register in one of the workspace registers
CRU operations	LDCR src, <count>	Load CRU with a number of bits
	STCR dest, <count>	Load destination from CRU
	SBO <displacement>	Set CRU bit
	SBZ <displacement>	Reset CRU bit
	TB <displacement>	Test CRU bit

Interrupts occur via the hardware priority comparison circuitry, and, upon interrupt acknowledgement, the microprocessor loads the new WP and PC values from fixed interrupt vector locations in memory (see memory map for the TMS9900, fig. 3.14). The old context is stored in general registers WR13, 14 and 15 in the same way as for a subroutine call. The CPU then automatically sets the interrupt mask to a priority value of one less than the interrupting priority, and inhibits interrupts until the first instruction of the interrupt service routine has been executed (this preserves program linkage should another interrupt occur immediately). Return from the interrupt service routine is via a RTWP.

An extended operation (XOP) instruction is provided, which transfers control while providing for multiple exits from the routine transferred to. It contains a source operand with a choice of addressing modes, and a 4-bit displacement value. When executed, it transfers the contents of location 40H + 4 (displacement) to the WP, and the contents of location 42H + 4 (displacement) to PC, while storing the source address in the new workspace register WR11 (as BL) and the old WP, PC and ST in WR13, 14 and 15 (as BLWP). This instruction was included to ensure compatibility with the 990 minicomputer, and can implement a software trap.

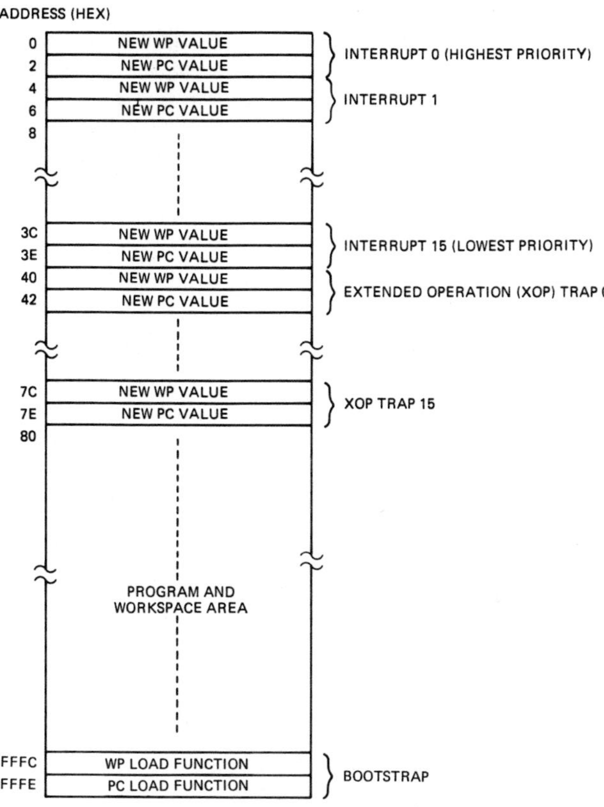

Fig. 3.14 TMS9900 memory map.

The TMS9900 is easily the most advanced of the older 16-bit microprocessors, and has good support (interface chips, boards, systems and software). In many ways it bridges the gap between the microprocessors with designs based on early low-end minicomputers and the newer, more capable, designs. It achieved a high degree of user acceptance and will still compare well with more modern microprocessors in many respects, but does not reflect the importance which is attached nowadays to large linear addressing ranges (32K words for the 9900), relocation of code, string operations, and operating system support.

3.6 Summary

A number of the earlier 16-bit microprocessors have been described with the aim of providing a yardstick with which to measure more recent machines. Naturally the list is not complete (it omits, for instance, the LSI-11, since, until very recently, it was not available in chip form, the F100L from Ferranti, a specialised mainly military microprocessor, and the HP MC^2, a microprocessor produced solely for in-house use by Hewlett-Packard). Nevertheless, a common thread runs through all the machines covered – they are all limited in address range, in addressing modes, in their register sets, in their instruction repertoires, treatment of interrupts, and support of operating systems. They have no 32-bit or other multiple-precision instructions, and will not (with the possible exception of the TMS9900) support multiple microprocessor or coprocessor operations, or resource sharing. Generally, they belong to the previous generation of devices, not to the current one.

CHAPTER 4
Modern 16-bit microprocessors

4.1 Introduction

This chapter concentrates on the architecture and hardware improvements that distinguish today's 16-bit microprocessors from their predecessors[1–4]. One of the most important aspects of the new generation of 16-bit microprocessors, typified by the 8086, Z8000 and MC68000, is the departure they represent from the concepts of their 8-bit predecessors – they are not simply more complicated CPUs with the same basic architecture and double-length registers, but have completely new internal designs. Some of the design changes have been made in response to criticisms of the earlier 8-bit microprocessors (such as the need for relocatability of code, regularity of register set, or increase in processing speed), others have been made to accommodate new requirements, such as the generation of standard bus signals and support of multiple microprocessor operation, and yet others have been made to enable the enhanced devices to fit in a standard size package and to remain compatible with existing interface devices, designed for 8-bit systems. The manufacturers' capabilities in fabrication increase rapidly year by year, and more and more devices can be integrated onto a single die. These advances alone can account for many of the new features common to all new 16-bit machines. On-chip hardware multiply and divide, and additional registers, are examples of new features which have been added simply because the density of gates and the area of the die were sufficient to allow such hardware to be included and would have required no major restructuring of CPU architecture.

The requirement to maintain compatibility with existing interface devices has led to interesting compromises; all of the 8-bit microprocessors possess a synchronous component-level bus structure (any device read from or written to on the bus must respond within a time determined by the microprocessor and its clock speed, and does not acknowledge the transfer positively) whereas most sophisticated backplane buses require a pair of handshake signals for each data transfer, making that transfer asynchronous. In addition, whereas the traditional method of bus control at the CPU pins using HALT or HOLD and the corresponding acknowledgement signal is adequate for a single microprocessor system with DMA, a bus request and grant system similar to those of the backplane buses (see chapter 11) may be desirable; multiple-microprocessor operation and implementation of semaphores may require bus locking from the CPU with a minimum of extra logic, and easy backplane bus interfacing may require CPU status information which a small single microprocessor component-level bus system may not. The approaches adopted by the main manufacturers have varied – Intel's 40-pin 8086, for instance, has two modes which use a group of CPU pins for different signals, selected by a single logic signal, minimum mode, which is designed for 8085 bus control signal compatibility, and maximum mode, which is designed for Multibus systems, and is inevitably of much higher complexity; the MC68000, with a 64-pin package, uses one set of pins for asynchronous bus control, and another set for MC6800 peripheral control. Obviously, the increased data bus width and additional control signals mean that the pin layouts of all the 16-pin CPUs differ considerably from their 8-bit counterparts. With a 40-pin package, invariably the data and address will be multiplexed onto the same set of pins; with a larger package, such as the 64-pin one used for the MC68000, non-multiplexed bus pins may be retained.

The number of internal CPU registers has been increased compared with the average 8-bit microprocessor, and for the 68000 and Z8000, the register set has been made much more uniform in that not many of the registers are dedicated, and most have no restrictions on their use (obviously stack pointers and the program counter are exceptions to this). In addition, they may be combined in pairs or quads for multiple-precision working. Additional dedicated registers may be included to facilitate memory management; both the Z8000 and the 8086 possess registers which provide a segment address. Unfortunately, the two manufacturers use the same name for a part of the address which is used in different ways. The 8086 possesses four segment address registers which provide location to any 16-byte address boundary in the 1 Mbyte address space, for code, stack, data and extra addresses. Thus memory management is internal to the 8086, but does not have the sophistication of valid address checking or protection. The Z8000, on the other hand, uses a segment number, 6 bits long, which must be related to a physical address within a separate memory management unit which has previously been loaded by software with the segment attributes (length, protection, start address) appropriate to that segment number.

Apart from specific individual additions, a split is evident in the philosophy of CPU design. The 8086 and MC68000 are both microcoded, that is, their instructions are each implemented as a sequence of even more elementary operations which occur on the edges of each microprocessor clock pulse; the microcode sequence is held in a fast internal read-only memory or programmed logic array, the microstore. The advantage of a microcoded approach lies in the ease with which parts of the CPU may be designed, and the design extended later on – it also allows easier design debugging. The penalty of a microcoded scheme for CPU design is speed: the minimum time for any elementary operation, or microcycle, will be the clock period (or the width of the '1' or '0' state of the clock). Since each actual machine instruction will consist of a number of microcycles, a microcoded CPU will either generally be slower than a CPU built with 'random' logic with the same clock speed, or will have to use a fast clock, and hence a more difficult fabrication process. The Z8000 is built with random logic and achieves respectable execution speeds with a relatively slow process. In common with bit-slice microprocessors, which are invariably microcoded, a microcoded monolithic 16-bit CPU may well use pipelining to speed up execution. The technique is simple in concept allowing memory instruction fetches to overlap execution of previous instructions. This overlapping, coupled with a fast internal CPU buffer store or cache memory, can allow the use of slow memory with a fast CPU without the microprocessor speed being limited by instruction fetches, and is employed in the 8086. All of the 16-bit microprocessors have been designed with the objective of fast execution speeds, but at the same time, easy interfacing with slow devices designed for the current 8-bit microprocessors, without having to slow down CPU operation. In particular, until recently, EPROM could not match the speed of static RAM (even now, the range of EPROM speeds available is not nearly so wide as that of other types of memory) and many interface devices, too, are considerably slower. Slowing the CPU down by generating wait states or stretching clock cycles is provided for on all the microprocessors, but obviously will waste some of the CPU performance, and may require additional circuitry.

Interrupt structures are features of the microprocessor CPU which have undergone considerable development; in order to group both hardware and software interrupts or traps with any event which is asynchronous with the CPU clock and which causes a context change (switch in program execution), all such events are now commonly referred to as 'exceptions'. Exception processing can be initiated in a uniform way, no matter what the cause of the exception, and all the new microprocessors reserve areas for vector tables. The 8086 and MC68000 have fixed areas for their vector tables, while the Z8000 will go to a fixed area after reset, but as part of the contents of its new program status area pointer (NPSAP) register, there is an 8-bit number interpreted as an upper byte of a 16-bit address (in the segmented version, the Z8001, the NPSAP also contains a 6-bit segment address) which is used, with a lower byte of zero, to point to the new program status area, which contains all the vectors. This means that each user in a Z8000-based multi-user system, or indeed, each process, can have its own vector table.

System support in hardware is present in the Z8000 and MC68000 in the form of operating modes: significantly both microprocessors have privileged or system modes, which allow the operating system or a privileged task to perform input-output, respond to interrupts, and other operations which could affect the integrity of the system. The alternative, or user mode, does not have access to such instructions. The 68000 also has a trace state controlled by a single bit in its status register; when set the bit causes the 68000 to generate a trace exception at the end of each instruction, which can be used to enter a suitable debugging routine.

While the three microprocessors (8086, Z8000, 68000) may enjoy the greater part of the market for newer design 16-bit microprocessors, they are not the only devices available, nor do they enjoy a monopoly of innovative features. Two more, rather more recently produced microprocessors, may well rise to prominence; they are the successor to the TMS9900 family, the TMS99000, and the National Semiconductor NS16000 family. The TMS99000 follows the previous Texas Instruments practice of using registers external to the CPU, defined in memory using a workspace pointer (see chapter 2) and hence creating a memory-to-memory architecture. A unique feature of the TMS99000 is the Macrostore; this consists basically of 1 kbytes of fast on-chip ROM and 32 bytes of on-chip RAM. The Macrostore may be addressed separately from the main memory, and is used to store frequently-used software functions (typically operating system primitives and real time functions) where they can be executed much faster than in normal memory. A prototype mode is available which allows the code needed for Macrostore to be debugged using external memory for the Macrostore accesses. Many microprocessors allow attached coprocessor operation, and the 99000 has an extended instruction set processor (XIP) capability. A given function may be implemented either in main memory, as a function in Macrostore, or as a function contained in an XIP. A new set of control signals control detection of Macrostore accesses and the XIP. Like the 8086, instruction overlapping is achieved using a prefetch technique.

The NS16000 design stresses memory management and the memory-management unit (MMU) will give virtual memory support which includes instruction abort and re-execution in the case of an address fault. The MMU provides debugging support for the CPU, and can activate breakpoints and memory access trace, providing debugging support for both high level and assembly code software operating within a virtual machine environment, as well as assisting hardware in-circuit emulation. Like those of the 68000, the general registers of the NS16000 CPU are 32 bits long, and, like the coprocessors of the 8086, the MMU and a floating-point unit are run as slave microprocessors and operate completely transparently to the system designer. Pipelining and an internal instruction queue are also featured.

This very brief overview highlights the current range of 16-bit microprocessors, many with 32-bit capability. Naturally, new members of each manufacturer's family are emerging all the time. Some will be featured in the final chapter of this book, which is devoted to future developments, and leaves this main chapter free to consider the original members of each family. The microprocessors will be considered in chronological order of release.

4.2 Intel 8086 family

First made available in 1978, the 8086[5–11] represents the first member of the new generation of 16-bit microprocessors. While it may lose out on execution speed and capabilities compared with more recent developments, it is nevertheless a very powerful microprocessor, and its architecture contains many features which have since become standard for almost any competitive 16-bit microprocessor. A block diagram of the 8086 internal architecture is shown in fig. 4.1. Organisation is based around internal buses like an 8-bit CPU, but memory control and the execution unit design are different. The execution unit uses a 6-byte instruction prefetch queue; while the buses and registers of the 8086 are all 16-bits wide, the CPU is still byte-oriented in many ways. Instructions are conceived as being a number of bytes long, and do not have to start on an even byte boundary; indeed, there are no constraints on instruction positioning. The bus interface unit (BIU) operates concurrently with the execution unit, and fetches 16-bit words from memory whenever there is space in the 6-byte queue. Note that the instruction queue is byte-oriented, and communicates with memory via the bus interface unit (BIU). The BIU is really a subdivision of fig. 4.1 which consists of a bus interface responsible for generating all the bus control signals (which may differ depending on the mode of the CPU: maximum or minimum mode), as well as the group of four 16-bit segment address registers, the instruction pointer (IP) register, and an addition unit which generates the 20-bit physical address. The 20-bit address is formed by extending the appropriate 16-bit segment address by adding four zero bits in the least significant part of the 20-bit word, and adding to it the 16-bit address contained in the instruction pointer, stack pointer, or one of the other 16-bit address registers. The process is illustrated in fig. 4.2, for instruction access, using the code segment (CS) register and the instruction pointer. The segment registers allow for separate access of the code segment (CS), stack segment (SS), data segment (DS) and extra segments (ES) within a maximum physical address space of 1 Mbyte (the least significant bit of the 20-bit physical address bus is used to select odd or even bytes of a 16-bit word). A physical segment must start on a 16-byte address boundary (low 4 bits of address zero) and can have a size of 64 kbytes.

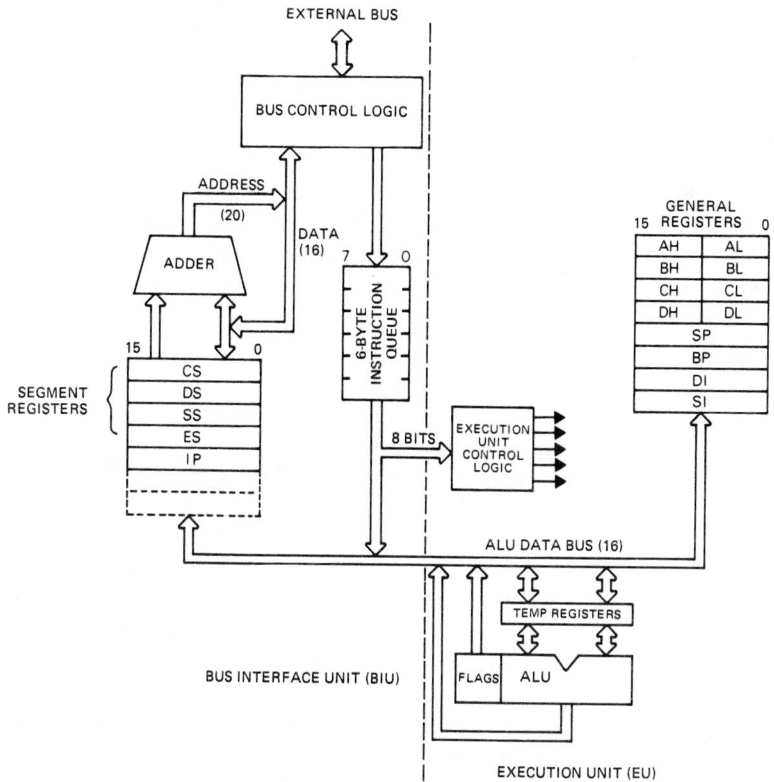

Fig. 4.1 8086 architecture.

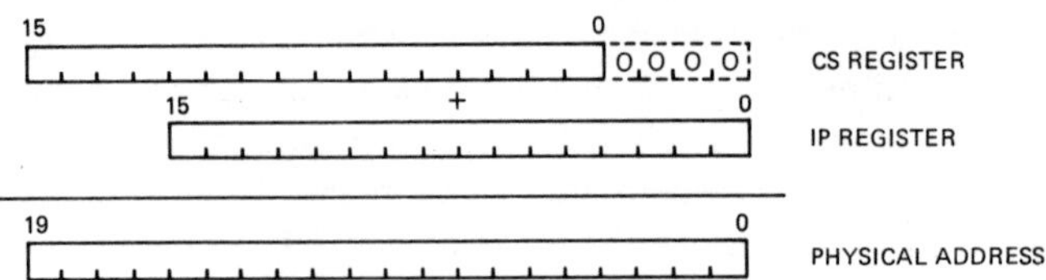

Fig. 4.2 8086 address calculation.

4.2.1 BUS INTERFACE UNIT OPERATION

The BIU can access memory either to read or write data requested by the execution unit (EU), or to fetch instructions. Instructions are fetched whenever the execution unit has not requested bus accesses, and whenever there are two or more bytes free in the instruction queue; a complete 16-bit word is fetched, and the two bytes of it are added in sequence of byte address to the queue. The execution unit takes instruction bytes as they are required from the queue, so that generally, bus accesses to fetch instruction bytes are asynchronous to instruction execution, and an instruction may be fetched while a previous one is being executed. The six bytes of the 8086 queue make the queue optimum length so that the queue is rarely empty, yet it is not so long that much of the queue will be wasted. If the queue is empty when the EU requires its next instruction, the EU must wait for the BIU to perform its next instruction fetch. The BIU will automatically adjust the instruction pointer. When a jump or other program transfer occurs, the instruction queue is re-initialised. Since instructions may possess an odd number of bytes, and therefore, by implication, may not be aligned on even-byte boundaries, the number of bus cycles required for an instruction fetch may not always be the same, but depend on the position of the instruction and the state of the queue. Whenever the instruction queue is full, and the EU has not requested any bus access, there will be clock periods where the bus is inactive; such clock periods are known as 'idle states', and may result from a long instruction (one requiring many clock cycles for execution, so that the queue has plenty of time to fill up), or coprocessor operation, for instance. The pipelining, or overlapping of instruction execution and next instruction fetch, afforded by an instruction queue such as the one described, means that the CPU bus accesses can be timed so as to require relaxed timing specifications for memory and input-output interfaces, and still achieve a fast execution time by using a fast microprocessor clock to drive the execution unit. From the point of view of any devices external to the CPU, the execution unit, which actually performs any instructions, is invisible, and communication only occurs through the BIU, whose bus cycles have the form shown in fig. 4.3.

4.2.2 MAXIMUM AND MINIMUM MODES

The BIU is controlled by a pin MN/$\overline{\text{MX}}$ which switches between minimum mode and maximum mode. Basically, the modes differ in their generation of control signals; the minimum mode control signals correspond roughly to those of the 8-bit 8085, they are:

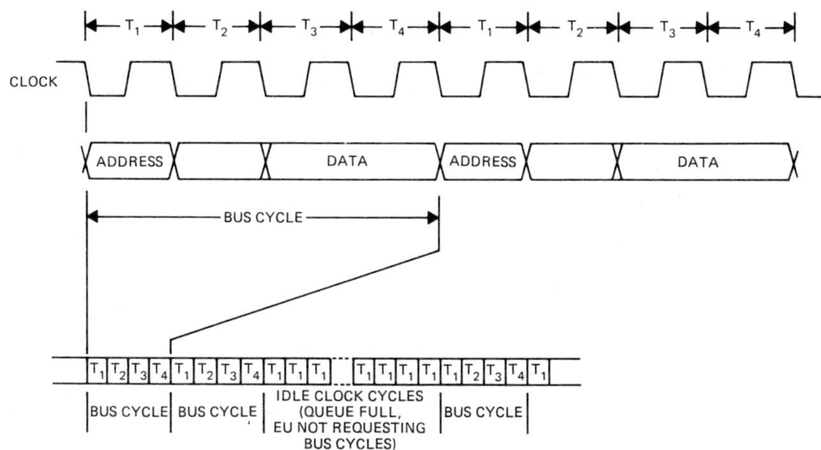

Fig. 4.3 8086 BIU clock cycles.

ALE — Address latch enable, which is asserted when there is a valid address on the multiplexed address and data bus
$M/\overline{IO}$ — Which distinguishes between input-output and memory signals
$\overline{WR}$ — Write control
$DT/\overline{R}$ — Data transmit-receive (data direction control for buffers)
$\overline{DEN}$ — Data enable
$\overline{INTA}$ — Interrupt acknowledge
HOLD — Hold request
HOLDA — Hold acknowledge

The 16-bit multiplexed bus handles the low 16 bits of address, and the 16 data bits, while the upper 4 bits of the address are multiplexed with status signals S3, S4, S5 and S6 (valid when ALE is asserted). These status signals allow external circuitry to decode the CPU status: S5 is the interrupt enable flag, S6 indicates that the CPU is on the bus and is always zero for the 8086; it can be used in a multiprocessor environment, such as with a coprocessor, to identify which type of microprocessor is using the bus (the 8089 input-output coprocessor, for instance, has 56 always '1'). S3 and S4 give an indication of the type of bus cycle in progress, distinguishing between code, data, stack and extra segment accesses (table 4.1). In fact, latching and decoding S3 and S4 gives a possible way of extending the addressing range of the 8086 by having separate memories for code and data, which overlap in address, but are enabled using the decoded status signals. The bus address, data and status signals just described are common to both maximum mode and minimum mode of the 8086. When maximum mode is selected, the eight minimum mode signals change their function, and provide coded outputs which may be used with a small amount of external circuitry to generate standard Intel Multibus signals (described in chapter 11). The normal control signals are replaced by three status signals

$\overline{\text{S0-S2}}$, called bus cycle status, which may be decoded into eight states, shown in table 4.2. This table also shows the equivalent Multibus signals generated by the 8086 bus controller, the 8288. This bus controller is a separate chip used by the 8086 CPU in maximum mode, which accepts the three status signals $\overline{\text{S0}}$ to $\overline{\text{S2}}$ and the CPU clock as inputs, and generates local bus buffer control signals DT/$\overline{\text{R}}$, DEN and ALE equivalent to those generated in minimum mode, and the Multibus control signals shown in table 4.2. In addition to the three status signals, the maximum mode of the 8086 provides for more sophisticated bus control and diagnostic signals. The bus control signals are $\overline{\text{RQ}}/\overline{\text{GTO}}$ and $\overline{\text{RQ}}/\overline{\text{GTI}}$, and $\overline{\text{LOCK}}$. The first two form a pair of bus request and grant signals which replace the previous HOLD/HOLDA signals and are specifically intended for multiprocessor and coprocessor. Each signal is bidirectional, and possesses three phases of operation, illustrated in fig. 4.4, for coprocessor operation. The request signal is a ground-true pulse persisting for one clock period and synchronised with the CPU clock as shown, and in response, the CPU after completing any bus cycle in progress, will issue a similarly synchronised ground-true bus grant pulse which indicates to the requesting device that the system buses have been floated to their high-impedance state, the bus controller will be disconnected on the next clock cycle, and that the CPU issuing the bus grant will enter its hold state. The execution unit (EU) of the microprocessor will continue to execute instructions in the queue until the queue is empty, or until an instruction is encountered which requires a bus access. When either of these circumstances arise, and the bus request is still being honoured, the EU will become idle. When the device or coprocessor which has taken over the bus has completed its bus operations, it will signify that the CPU can regain control of the bus by using a third and final ground-true pulse on the same $\overline{\text{RQ}}/\overline{\text{GTI}}$ line, again synchronised by the microprocessor clock. The two lines $\overline{\text{RQ}}/\overline{\text{GTO}}$ and $\overline{\text{RQ}}/\overline{\text{GTI}}$ will allow a CPU to support two other microprocessors (typically coprocessors 8089 for I/O channel control and 8087 for floating-point mathematics) without any external arbitration circuitry, with $\overline{\text{RQO}}$ having a higher priority than $\overline{\text{RQI}}$. Both request lines have higher priority than an interrupt request.

Table 4.1 Status lines S3 S4

S3	S4	Memory access
0	0	Alternate (using extra segment (ES) register)
1	0	Stack (using stack segment (SS) register)
0	1	Code or no access (using the code segment (CS) register, or a default of zero)
1	1	Data (using the data segment (DS) register)

The other bus control signal in maximum mode is $\overline{\text{LOCK}}$. Any instruction which requires multiple bus accesses may be made indivisible (i.e. no other requests for bus accesses from competing microprocessors in a multiple microprocessor system will be honoured until the locked instruction is complete). To make effective use of the $\overline{\text{LOCK}}$ facility, the CPU must be connected to a bus arbiter in the system. When an instruction prefixed by the mnemonic LOCK (so that the opcode starts with the corresponding single-byte prefix), $\overline{\text{LOCK}}$ output on the CPU is asserted in the first CPU clock cycle following execution of the prefix, and remains active until the clock cycle following completion of the lock-prefixed instruction. The bus arbiter, which will usually be an 8086-family compatible device, the 8289, must accept this LOCK output (as well as manipulating the $\overline{\text{RQ/GT}}$ lines), and ensure uninterrupted use of the bus for the duration of the prefixed instruction. Typically, the LOCK facility may be used to manipulate semaphores which control access to shared resources, and ensure mutual exclusion (thereby preventing possible data inconsistency caused by uncontrolled access). The technique, using the LOCK prefix in conjunction with the instruction XCHG, is detailed elsewhere in this book (notably chapter 6) and will not be repeated here. In order to ensure the indivisibility of interrupt acknowledgement cycles, the LOCK output is also asserted during such cycles; they are described in more detail in section 4.2.5, but basically all four types of interrupt cycle require stack access to save flags and possibly other registers, and vector access to acquire new code segment and instruction pointer values. To ensure reliable interrupt response, the same conditions prevail as with semaphore manipulation (i.e. any contention must be resolved) and bus requests from other multiprocessors (as well as other interrupts) must be prevented during the interrupt cycle.

Table 4.2 Maximum mode status lines $\overline{\text{S0}}$ to $\overline{\text{S2}}$

$\overline{\text{S2}}$	$\overline{\text{S1}}$	$\overline{\text{S0}}$	CPU cycle	Multibus signal (generated by 8288)
0	0	0	Interrupt Acknowledge	$\overline{\text{INTA}}$
0	0	1	Read I/O port	$\overline{\text{IORC}}$
0	1	0	Write I/O port	$\overline{\text{IOWC}}$, $\overline{\text{AIOWC}}$*
0	1	1	HALT	None
1	0	0	Instruction fetch (code access)	$\overline{\text{MRDC}}$
1	0	1	Read memory	$\overline{\text{MRDC}}$
1	1	0	Write memory	$\overline{\text{MWTC}}$, $\overline{\text{AMWC}}$*
1	1	1	Passive	None

*Note that signals prefixed with A are generated in advance of the command to allow the system to make an early preparation for command execution; although no longer a Multibus signal, the advanced write signal may be useful to enable local interface devices to avoid requiring wait states.

While the maximum mode 8086 possesses an explicit LOCK output signal to ease the implementation of LOCK in conjunction with a bus arbiter, the prefix may still be used when the microprocessor is operated in its minimum mode, where there is no explicit LOCK output signal. In the minimum mode, signals HOLD and HOLDA serve the bus control function instead of $\overline{\text{RQ/GT}}$, and the internal CPU logic does not allow HOLD request to be honoured until completion of the prefixed instruction, ensuring the instruction's indivisibility in the same way as before. Naturally, the latency of a HOLD request is affected by use of LOCK.

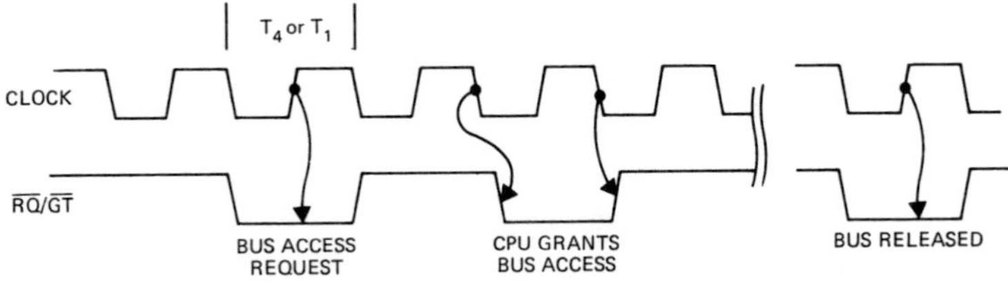

Fig. 4.4 $\overline{RQ}/\overline{GT}$ maximum mode signals.

The final exclusively maximum-mode feature of 8086 hardware signals consists of a pair of queue status outputs QS0 and QS1. Used in conjunction with the previously-described maximum-mode status signals $\overline{S0}$, $\overline{S1}$ and $\overline{S2}$, the queue status signals allow an external device to track CPU instruction execution, a facility which is necessary for coprocessor operation, and for diagnostic equipment, such as in-circuit emulators. The three status lines $\overline{S0}$-$\overline{S2}$ may be monitored for code accesses (0, 0, 1, respectively), indicating instructions entering the CPU instruction queue, and QS0, QS1 indicate instructions leaving the queue, in accordance with table 4.3.

Table 4.3 Queue status in maximum mode

QS1	QS0	
0	0	No operation (during the last clock cycle, nothing was taken from the queue)
0	1	First byte of opcode from queue
1	0	Empty the queue (queue reinitialised as a result of a transfer instruction)
1	1	Subsequent byte from queue (byte taken from the queue was a subsequent byte of the instruction)

Queue status is valid during the clock cycle following the queue operation. It is necessary to provide this information since the instructions which are executed come from the CPU queue, and the timing of their execution is independent of any external bus activity. The Intel coprocessors, described in detail in chapter 5, use the CPU to generate bus accesses for them, and detect execution of an ESCAPE instruction. The 8086 ESCAPE instruction possesses an effective address, and when executed, causes the CPU to perform no operation other than to access the memory location corresponding to its effective address, and to place the contents of the location on the bus. Using QS0 and QS1, a coprocessor can detect the occurrence of an ESCAPE instruction execution, and receive its instructions via the bus, making use of the CPU addressing modes and bus control signals.

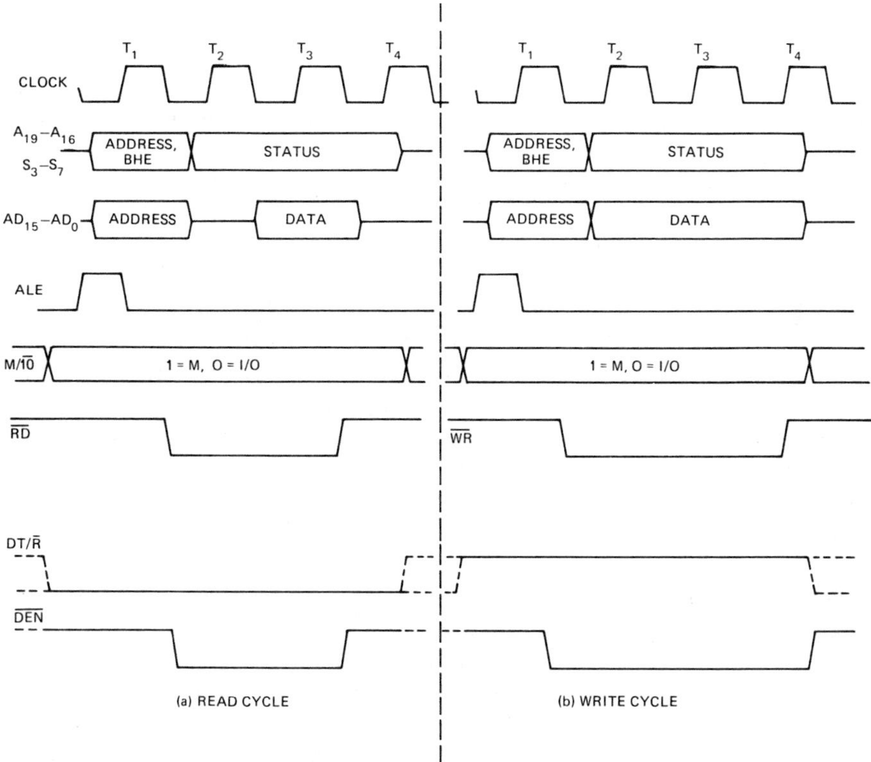

Fig. 4.5 8086 bus control signals: (a) read cycle, (b) write cycle.

The other use of QS0 and QS1 is to provide an in-circuit emulator with the means to track instruction execution, and hence to provide a trace facility. Up/down counters in the ICE circuitry monitor queue depth, and may be used to identify execution of the opcode at a given memory location, and trap on that execution.

Remember that from a program execution viewpoint, maximum and minimum modes are the same; they only vary in the hardware signals generated by the CPU in each mode. The internal states of the CPU are the same, and indeed, it is possible to devise external circuitry which will allow the CPU to operate in one mode, and convert its control signals to those of the other mode. The idea behind the two modes of operation, however, is to allow conflicting requirements to be fulfilled by a single CPU design. For simple 16-bit systems, low parts count, and a hardware (local bus) compatibility with interface devices designed for the 8086 family of 8-bit microprocessors require minimum mode signals. On the other hand, use of the CPU in a Multibus (see chapter 11) environment, with more sophisticated control and multiprocessor capabilities, requires maximum mode operation to give the best support. The solution of switching between modes using a single mode control pin is one economical way to give the hardware systems designer a choice of 16-bit implementation. Timing of the main bus control signals is shown in fig. 4.5.

4.2.3 EXECUTION UNIT

While the bus interface unit handles 8086 communication with the local microprocessor bus, actual CPU operations are performed by the execution unit (EU) part of fig. 4.1. The EU operates independently of the BIU; when it is ready to execute the next instruction it fetches the first byte of it from the BIU instruction queue, followed by subsequent bytes as required, and executes them accordingly. If the queue is empty when the execution unit requires an instruction byte, the EU will wait until the byte has been fetched by the BIU, and for memory reference or input-output instruction execution, the EU will request a bus cycle from the BIU. The execution unit maintains compatibility with Intel's 8080/8085 8-bit family of microprocessors by possessing a superset of 8080 registers. Referring to fig. 4.1, the seven general-purpose 8-bit registers of the 8080 have become eight equivalent 8-bit registers, grouped as four 16-bit ones, AX (AH + AL), BX (BH + BL), CX (CH + CL), DX (DH + DL). The flag register has been extended by the addition of an overflow flag (OF), which reflects a signed overflow condition, an interrupt flag (IF), which enables and disables external interrupts (but does not affect non-maskable and internal ones), a TRAP flag (TF), which controls execution – when the trap flag is set, the CPU is put into the single-step mode (discussed in the section on interrupt structure, section 4.2.5), and a direction flag (DF), which controls the direction of string operations (autodecrement or autoincrement). The single address pointer register of the 8080, the stack pointer, has been augmented by the addition of three more 16-bit registers, base pointer (BP), source index (SI) and destination index (DI) which support the greater range of addressing modes of the 8086. A comparison showing the equivalence of 8-bit 8085 registers and 8086 registers is shown in fig. 4.6.

Compared to other 16-bit microprocessors, more modern in their design, the 8086 register set stands out as being largely dedicated, rather than truly general. Indeed, even the registers designated 'general-purpose' are assigned uses in addition to their general ones. Thus, BX is also the base register, and may be used as a pointer register in the same way as BP, contributing to effective address calculation. CX is also a 16-bit 'count' register used for string operations (CL, the lower byte of CX, is used in multibit shifts and rotates), and DX is also a data register, used for indirect I/O port addressing throughout the 64K I/O address range. Operations which return a multiple-precision result (16-bit MUL and DIV) also require specific general registers, and certain other arithmetic operations are confined to the accumulator or its lower byte (AX or AL), for instance ASCII and decimal adjusts. Despite these limitations, the 8086 register set is a great improvement on the preceding 8-bit 8085 one. Arithmetic and logical operations are no longer confined to the accumulator, and with few exceptions, may be used directly on locations in memory. While many computer architects preach regularity of CPU facilities, such as register sets, and point out that writing high-level language compilers will be easier the more general and the larger the CPU register set is, it is nevertheless claimed that the 8086 comes close to having an optimum structure for support of structural high level languages and their operating systems. Where the 8086 obviously gains over its rivals is in the on-chip memory management of the BIU.

4.2.4 OTHER HARDWARE FEATURES

Apart from the interrupt structure of the 8086, covered in section 4.2.5, the other features of the CPU lie in the remaining signals at its pins, common to both maximum and minimum modes. Read control $\overline{\text{RD}}$ is similar to 8085 $\overline{\text{RD}}$, and READY acts as a 'wait state control', as before, synchronised to the CPU clock by the 8284 clock generator. An added signal is $\overline{\text{TEST}}$, which is a synchronising signal, allowing the CPU to synchronise itself with external devices. $\overline{\text{TEST}}$ is used in conjunction with an instruction WAIT. When WAIT is encountered, the microprocessor will enter a wait state if $\overline{\text{TEST}}$ is not asserted, and the microprocessor will resume operation when $\overline{\text{TEST}}$ is asserted. The wait state is interruptible, with a return to the same wait state from the interrupt routine (the saved return address is that of the WAIT instruction). It is obviously important to make the state interruptible to allow multiple task operation, and to avoid any lockout situation if $\overline{\text{TEST}}$ were to fail to be asserted.

RESET is a conventional type of initialisation signal (though active high rather than low) which is usually generated by the 8284 clock generator. When RESET is asserted (for at least 50 μs on power-up, or four clock cycles otherwise), the microprocessor will shut down operation for the duration of the RESET pulse. On the high-to-low transition which terminates the RESET pulse, an initialisation sequence is initiated internally which takes a small number of clock cycles (around ten), and which resets the instruction pointer (IP) register, the three segment registers DS, SS, ES to zero, and the flags to zero (to disable all external maskable interrupts and single-stepping) and which sets the code segment register (CS) to FFFFH. Once the sequence is complete, execution starts at the physical address FFFF0H (i.e. (CS) $\times$ 16 + (IP)).

$\overline{\text{BHE}}$/S7, a final output signal, multiplexes addressing and interrupt status information onto a single pin. $\overline{\text{BHE}}$ is used to enable byte information to be transferred on the upper half of the data bus (BHE stands for BUS High Enable), and is asserted when ALE is present. The 8086 20-bit address is a byte address, where the even byte (A0 = 0) of an addressed 16-bit word (identified by an address consisting of bits A19-A1) will appear on the lower 8-bits of the data bus (AD0-AD7) and the odd byte (A0 = 1) will appear on the upper 8 bits (AD8-AD15). To allow byte transfers on a 16-bit system, it is necessary to provide some means of disabling one byte of a 16-bit word while accessing the other byte (A0 alone will not accomplish this, since three, rather than two conditions distinguish a complete 16-bit word access, a lower (even) byte access, and an upper (odd) byte access). $\overline{BHE}$ may be used to disable an odd byte location (A0 = 0), while A0 = 1 may be used to disable an even byte location. Memory may physically be arranged in two banks, odd and even, with chip selects connected to $\overline{BHE}$ and A0, respectively. Transfers on the bus are illustrated in diagrammatic form in fig. 4.7. In addition to its use during memory read and write operations $\overline{BHE}$ is asserted during the first clock cycle (T1 cycle) of an interrupt acknowledge cycle. The status signal S7, multiplexed with $\overline{BHE}$ and valid during all but the first clock cycle of a bus cycle (its timing is like that of S3-S6, which are multiplexed with address bits A16-A19) is a 'spare' status signal, and carries no usable information.

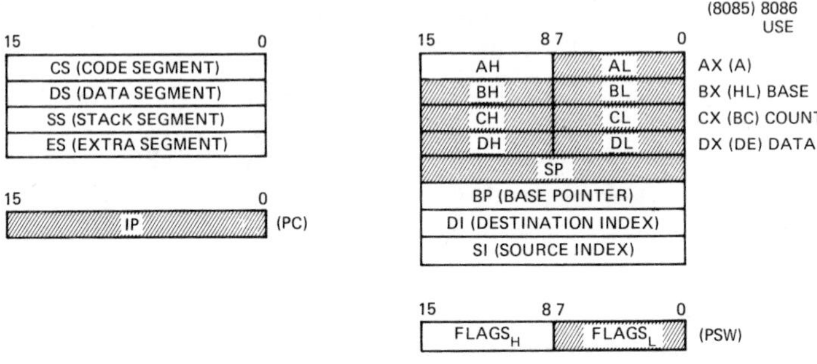

Fig. 4.6 8086 register set (8085 counterparts shaded).

4.2.5 INTERRUPT STRUCTURE

The interrupt structure of the any microprocessor is one of its most important features, and can fundamentally affect the microprocessor's suitability for a real time application. To take advantage of the sophistication present in other aspects of a 16-bit microprocessor's design, its interrupt structure should be as flexible as possible, and should impose minimum overheads on the system. The 8080/8085 8-bit microprocessors were limited but nevertheless effective in their interrupt structures – the 8080 had a hardware vectored structure which allowed eight discrete levels of interrupt (including reset, a special case of interrupt zero) but had no provision for non-maskable interrupts, and fixed interrupt locations. When used with an external interrupt controller, or a number of cascaded controllers, the number of interrupt locations could be increased, and their positions programmed anywhere in the 64K memory address space. The 8085 structure sought to overcome the limitations of blanket interrupt masking (through external masking via an interrupt controller) and lack of a non-maskable interrupt, by a 'kludge' – the addition of new interrupts, their locations interleaved with those of the 8080.

The 8086 is in a different class; compared with its predecessors, its allowed number of interrupts is large – 256 vector addresses are reserved in the CPU address space, and some new, predefined interrupts have been introduced. The interrupt map of the 8086 is shown in fig. 4.8. Each entry in the vector table consists of 4 bytes of information, corresponding to instruction pointer and code segment register addresses for the start of the interrupt service routine. The first thirty-two interrupt type numbers are reserved for future use, although only the first five are used in the 8086. Interrupts may be classified into three groups:

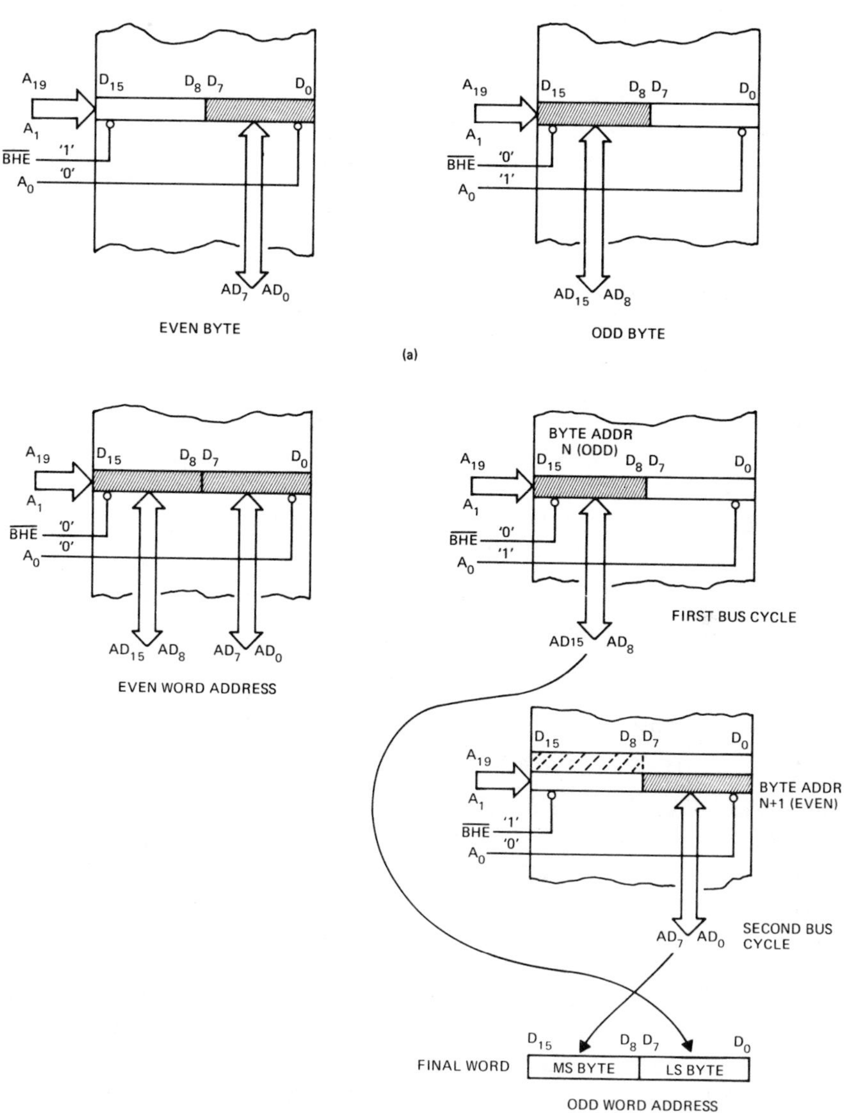

Fig. 4.7 (a) 8086 byte transfers, (b) 8086 word transfers.

(a) Predefined interrupts, fixed in location, and generated either by an internal CPU condition or a special external hardware signal.
(b) Software interrupts, invoked by program code which includes their type number.
(c) Hardware (vectored) interrupts, which are the only maskable ones.

Predefined interrupts are built-in by the CPU designer to facilitate good applications programming, and may be considered traps, particularly the type 0 interrupt which is invoked by a divide error caused by a division operation having its quotient exceed its maximum value (typically on divide-by-zero). Type 1 interrupts are invoked by the TF flag being set, and is used for microprocessor single-stepping. To allow debugging by single-stepping a piece of code in the 8086, the flags may be copied onto the stack, the TF bit set, and the flags popped from the stack, i.e.

```
PUSHF           Push flags onto the stack
POP AX          16 bit flags value in AX
OR AX, 0100H    Set bit position for TF
PUSH AX         Replace on stack
POPF            Load into flag register
```

The first type 1 interrupt will occur one instruction after the TF bit has been set. The vector locations for the type 1 interrupt, word addresses 00004 and 00006, contain IP and CS of the start of the interrupt (single step) routine, and the transfer of control to this routine is accomplished by the sequence of operations (common to all interrupt types):

(a) The contents of the flag register are saved on the stack.
(b) The values of CS and IP are saved on the stack (cf intersegment CALL).
(c) Further maskable interrupts are prevented by clearing the interrupt flag IF.
(d) The trap flag (TF) is cleared, so that if the CPU was in single-step mode, it reverts to normal operation for the duration of the interrupt service.
(e) The new values of CS and IP are loaded from the interrupt vector location.

Any other CPU registers must be saved on the stack by the code of an interrupt routine, if required. The single-step interrupt routine will execute normally. An interrupt return IRET executed at the end of the single-step service routine will restore CS and IP, and the flag register (which has TF set) and will execute the next instruction of the routine under test.

Type 2 interrupts are invoked by a signal on the microprocessor NMI input and is the 8086 non-maskable interrupt input. NMI is the highest priority external hardware interrupt. Type 3 interrupts are single-byte software interrupts, primarily used for software debugging as breakpoint interrupts. Type 4 interrupts are overflow interrupts, invoked by execution of the INTO instruction (interrupt-on-overflow) if the overflow flag (OF) is set when execution occurs. Use of the instruction can give a selective trap on overflow operation. General software interrupts, invoked by 2-byte instructions of the form INT type number can be used to invoke any of the 256 interrupts of the 8086. Like the predefined interrupts, they are non-maskable.

Maskable hardware interrupts are invoked via the INTR pin, and may be masked using the interrupt flag IF. The INTR pin is sampled during the last clock cycle of each instruction (except for a MOV or POP to a segment register, where the pin is sampled on the last clock cycle of the following instruction – this allows an uninterruptible 32-bit load of SS and SP registers) or continuously during a WAIT. The interrupt acknowledge sequence, invoked when IF is set, requires that the interrupting device supplies an 8-bit type vector which is used to point to the required location containing the new CS and IP values (address 4 × type vector). The CPU issues two consecutive interrupt acknowledge bus cycles. In the first one, the address/data bus is floated and $\overline{\text{LOCK}}$ asserted from the end of the T1 clock cycle, and with $\overline{\text{INTA}}$ asserted. $\overline{\text{LOCK}}$ is terminated after the first clock cycle T1 of the second acknowledge cycle, and $\overline{\text{INTA}}$ asserted a second time, to allow the interrupting device to supply the vector on the low byte of the address/data bus. Timing is shown in fig. 4.9. In the minimum mode of the 8086, $\overline{\text{LOCK}}$ is not available as an output, but HOLD requests will not be honoured until the interrupt acknowledge sequence is complete. In the maximum mode, it is up to the external bus arbiter to use $\overline{\text{LOCK}}$ to lock out any bus requests from other microprocessors. Once the vector has been received by the CPU, the rest of the interrupt sequence proceeds as before.

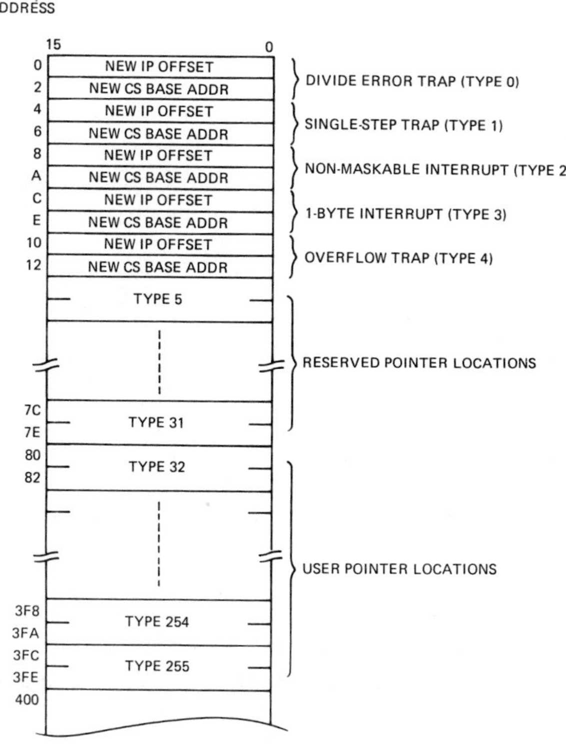

Fig. 4.8 8086 interrupt map.

4.2.6 GENERAL ASSESSMENT OF 8086 ARCHITECTURE

The 8086 architecture was designed with a number of constraints which more recent microprocessors have not had, those of compatibility with previous 8-bit microprocessors – the 68000 and Z8000 in particular, have been designed from scratch, without aiming for compatibility. Thus the register set of the 8086 is a superset of the register set of the 8080, and the bus signals reflect those of the 8085, to allow use of existing interface devices designed for the 8-bit microprocessor. However the new features introduced by the 8086 set a pattern for more modern microprocessors:

(a) Segmentation (i.e. memory management) and a large (1 Mbyte) addressing range.
(b) A large interrupt vector table.
(c) Bus locking capability to ensure mutual exclusion in multiple microprocessor systems.
(d) Pipelining via the instruction queue (overlapping of instruction fetch and execution).
(e) Hardware multiply-divide.
(f) ESCAPE to allow coprocessor operation (see chapter 5).
(g) Various fixed trap locations, notably those for overflow and divide error.
(h) Synchronisation input to the CPU, with supporting instruction opcode ($\overline{\text{TEST}}$, WAIT).
(i) Flexible byte operations over a 16-bit bus.

Most of these features will be found in competing 16-bit microprocessors introduced since the 8086 was launched. These and other facilities make up all of the deficiencies recognised in the older 8-bit microprocessors, and the 8086 has deservedly enjoyed a large degree of success. There are limitations to every design, however, and the 8086 suffers from a number of them:

(a) A clock generator (the 8284) is required, which will generate the single-phase clock signal required, from a crystal of frequency three times the clock frequency. The 8284 is also necessary to synchronise the READY input signal to the CPU with the clock, and to generate RESET from an asynchronous pushbutton or power-on *RC* circuit. The device has two READY inputs, with qualifying signals and as well as the microprocessor clock, generates a 1:1 (square wave) peripheral clock (PCLK) signal at half the microprocessor clock rate.
(b) In the maximum mode, a bus controller (the 8288) is required, to decode the status signals $\overline{\text{S0}}$-$\overline{\text{S2}}$, and generate from them the Multibus command signals. Thus a maximum mode 8086 is really a 3-chip CPU group.
(c) The on-chip segment registers may not be flexible enough for some applications, where, for instance, segment protection, size checking (i.e. out-of-segment checking) or where dynamic relocation demands much segment swapping. Originally, the 8086 was to have eight segment registers assigned by bits in the status word, so that at any one time, three would have been dedicated to CS, DS, SS duties, and the other five would have been dedicated

to ES duties. It is a pity that this scheme was simplified to the present one as a result of pressure to reduce the chip size – the more general scheme would have greatly reduced any segment swapping overheads.

(d) There is no distinction drawn between classes of instruction, which would have allowed operating system support in the form of privileged and user modes of operation, and support of separate system and user stacks.

It must be remembered, however, that many 16-bit microprocessor applications have emerged which were not envisaged when the 8086 was introduced in 1978, and to criticise the design in the light of later developments is a little unfair. The CPU fits well into a niche in the market, which can be considered small to medium-sized system applications, such as controllers, small desktop computer systems and some multiple microprocessor applications. It is particularly good in multiple microprocessor systems, having been designed with them in mind. It is also well-suited for high-level language programming, again, one of the design aims. Although the CPU requires a clock generator and bus controller, both are easily available.

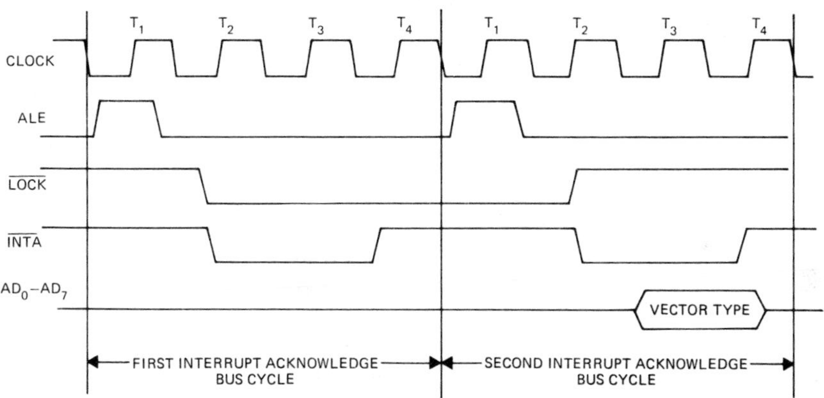

Fig. 4.9 8086 maximum mode vectored interrupt acknowledgement.

4.3 Zilog Z8000

Unlike the 8086, which is a microprogrammed CPU, the Z8000[12–15] is built with random logic, and, consequently, its architecture differs considerably from that of the 8086. The structure is shown in fig. 4.10. One of the major differences stems from the fact that the Z8000 instruction set is word, rather than byte, oriented in its opcode sizes, and uses off-chip segmentation, so is less suited to the instruction prefetch scheme used to great advantage by the 8086. It does, however, use a multiplexed address/data bus, and internally, it possesses a lookahead instruction decoder and accelerator which allows decoding to proceed at a speed independently of memory addressing mode (no more clock cycles are used to decode long offset instructions than are used to decode short offset ones). Like the 8086 strategy, that of the Z8000 is targetted at two applications areas – the minimum chip count one requiring 16-bit capability, and the more sophisticated minicomputer one, requiring memory management. The way the Z8000 tackles the conflict between these requirements is to split its functions rather differently from the 8086 and to produce two distinct devices in the CPU family, the Z8001 and the Z8002. The simplest applications are satisfied by the Z8002, a 40-pin device which has a limited addressing range (64 kbytes) and no memory management support, while the Z8001 possesses internal segment pointer registers which contain 7-bit unsigned segment numbers and a 48-pin package, allowing those segment numbers to be transferred to an external memory management unit (MMU) which will translate them to physical addresses and combine these physical segment base addresses with 16-bit offsets held in the CPU program counter, stack pointer, or general registers. The final 24-bit effective address will then be used as the physical address for the microprocessor memory. In all other respects, the Z8001 and Z8002 are identical.

A useful new feature emerged with the launch of the Z8000, copied from the minicomputer world, and to some extent pre-empted by the 6809, the idea of separating functions such as I/O operations, interrupt handling and CPU control instructions, which are often reserved solely for operating system use, from the more innocuous loads, stores, arithmetic, logical and conditional operations which make up the bulk of any application program. The instructions which dramatically affect CPU operation, and which, if invoked by a badly designed user program in a multi-user environment, possibly compromise the other concurrently executing programs, can be made accessible only when the CPU is in a privileged, or system mode, and not when it is in a normal operating or user mode. Privileged mode can only be invoked by an external interrupt or the operating system, and thus allows application programs to be made much more secure and less likely to interfere with one another if they contain erroneous code. This form of operating-system support, which has long been a feature of minicomputers and mainframes, will serve to increase the effectiveness of the Z8000 microprocessors at the upper end of the 16-bit application area.

Traps and interrupts are strong features of the Z8000 architecture, and the trap structure has important new features in the form of a privilege violation trap (attempt to use a privileged instruction in the non-privileged user mode) and a segment violation trap (attempt to access an area of memory outside the defined limits of the segment). Coprocessor support, too is provided in the form of 'extended instructions', which cause the Z8000 CPU to manipulate the buses in a similar way to an 8086 when it encounters ESCAPE. Although compatibility with its predecessor, the 8-bit Z80, is not maintained in the Z8000, the unique Z80 concept of providing dynamic RAM refresh using the CPU bus control logic during clock cycles where the microprocessor is executing only internal operations, is retained, and extended in its flexibility, no longer restricted to unused cycles immediately following opcode fetches.

Bus control in the Z8000 system is straightforward (simpler in implementation than the 8086), and reserved for DMA transfers, while a separate, dedicated set of signals handle requests in a multiple microprocessor environment. Following Z80 interrupt signal practice, interrupts, bus control signals, and multiple-microprocessor signals are all designed to be daisy-chained, removing the need for any on-chip prioritisation.

4.3.1 Z8000 BUS STRUCTURE

The address/data bus of either version of the Z8000 is a 16-bit bus AD0-AD15 with byte address multiplexed with data (most significant byte D8-D15 addressed by A0 = 0, least significant by A0 = 1). The control signals follow the Type 2 control signal philosophy for synchronous bus systems of chapter 1, possessing a single direction line R/$\overline{\text{W}}$ and a data strobe $\overline{\text{DS}}$. Like the 8086 multiplexed bus structure, that of the Z8000 provides an address demultiplexing signal $\overline{\text{AS}}$ (address strobe) to indicate the time when an address is valid. The machine cycles of the Z8000 are simpler than those of the 8086, since the Z8000 execution unit and the bus control unit are not so independent. Instructions are overlapped by pipelining, but there is no internal instruction queue. In the non-segmented CPU, the address range is limited to 64K, but in the 48-pin segmented Z8001, the 7-bit unsigned segment number is available on lines SN0-SN6. Unlike the 8086, where segmentation is internal and the segment address and pointer address combined in the BIU, the Z8000 in its segmented form requires the use of a memory management unit (MMU) which will generate the physical address of a memory location by combining a base address derived from an address table accessed using the segment number, and the pointer address (see chapter 5). Because the MMU will impose a propagation delay in the use of the segment information (particularly where segment checking is involved), the information on lines SN0-SN6 is made available one clock period earlier than the 16-bit offset address. $\overline{\text{WAIT}}$ input performs the READY function by allowing a slow addressed device to cause the CPU to generate wait states; during such states, the control outputs are held steady, and the $\overline{\text{WAIT}}$ input pin sampled every clock cycle.

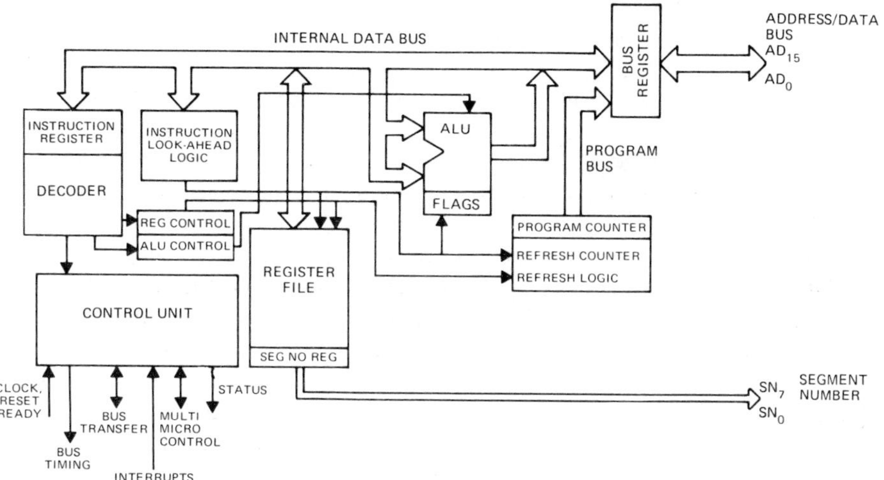

Fig. 4.10 Z8000 architecture.

Like its predecessor, the Z80, the Z8000 automatically inserts a single wait state into an input-output cycle (allowing interface devices to be manufactured to a slower specification than CPU or memory). Timing of Z8000 machine cycles is shown in fig. 4.11. The basic machine cycle (memory read or write, I/O read or write, interrupt acknowledge, or internal execution) needs between three and ten clock cycles to execute, three or four cycles for the external bus cycle and between one and five additional internal clock cycles, as required. Instructions require one or more machine cycles, in the same way as the 8-bit Z80 or 8080. Memory refresh cycles (see section 4.3.2) may be inserted after the completion of any first instruction fetch, or in some instructions which require a large number of internal operations (MULT, MULTL, DIV, DIVL, HALT, shifts, block moves and MREQ).

4.3.2 DYNAMIC MEMORY REFRESH

One of the useful features of the 8-bit Z80 was its provision of refresh counters on the CPU chip, with a refresh strobe. Because of internal decoding requirements immediately following an instruction fetch operation, the otherwise unused (for any bus operation) clock cycles were employed in the Z80 to place the refresh counter contents on the address bus, and issue a refresh strobe signal $\overline{\text{RFRSH}}$ to indicate that a refresh cycle was being generated. This feature reduced the external logic required for dynamic RAM interfacing to just the address multiplexing (it is usual to multiplex row and column addresses to allow a large capacity memory to use a standard 16-pin DIL package) and $\overline{\text{CAS}}$ and $\overline{\text{RAS}}$ (column and row strobe) generation, necessary for normal addressing anyway.

The Z8000 family also possesses RAM refresh capability, but it is more sophisticated than the simple Z80 facility. The basic refresh counter consists of a 6-bit prescaler, and a 9-bit address counter. The address counter is connected during a refresh cycle to address/data bus pins AD0-AD8; because A0 is only used during byte operations, it is always low, the refresh counter always incremented by two, and the 8 bits of the counter AD1-AD8 used to refresh a 16-bit word-organised memory. The presettable prescaler allows the refresh interval to be programmed; it behaves as a 6 bit modulo-n divider, where n may be programmed to be any value from 1 to 64. Using a 4 MHz microprocessor clock means that the prescaler will have a 1 MHz input, and the period between refreshes may be programmed to have any value between 1 μs and 64 μs. The counter and prescaler make up 15 bits of a 16-bit register which has the most significant bit reserved as an enable bit. Using the enable bit, refresh may be enabled and disabled under program control. The whole refresh register may be loaded from one of the CPU general-purpose registers, and the value of the refresh count may be read by software.

The way in which the refresh unit works is to detect the zero state of the prescaler (which occurs every $4n$ clock cycles if n is the preset prescaler division value) and when this state has been detected, the CPU will initiate a refresh cycle as soon as the bus may be accessed, at the end of the next first instruction fetch cycle, or immediately if the CPU is in the middle of one of the instructions mentioned in the previous section. Any delay imposed by the CPU having to wait for a cycle to finish before initiating its refresh cycle, is not cumulative, since the prescaler will continue to run after reaching its zero state, ensuring a constant period input to the refresh unit. After a refresh has been performed, the address counter is incremented ready for the next refresh. Note that with an 8-bit counter, 64- , 128- and 256-row refresh schemes can be implemented. When the CPU does not have control of the bus, an internal register records up to two missed refresh cycles, which are generated immediately the CPU regains control of the bus. This feature avoids the need for direct memory access (DMA) circuitry to avoid conflict with refresh, so long as any burst DMA is limited in the time it has possession of the bus, so that in the worst case, no more than two refresh cycles can be lost.

Of importance when refresh is considered is the CPU input signal $\overline{\text{STOP}}$, used by an extended instruction microprocessor (EPU) to hold up the normal CPU operation when required, so that EPU internal operations do not clash with a subsequent EPU instruction fetch. $\overline{\text{STOP}}$ is sampled by the CPU logic on the last clock falling edge preceding a first instruction fetch cycle. If $\overline{\text{STOP}}$ is asserted, the microprocessor will stop operations on the last clock cycle of the instruction fetch cycle, and will start generating a stream of memory refresh cycles, each taking three clock cycles. The usual prescaler and clock division by four are not used, so that while the CPU is held up by $\overline{\text{STOP}}$, a refresh cycle is generated every three clock cycles, with the refresh counter incremented by two each time. When $\overline{\text{STOP}}$ is released, the next refresh cycle is completed, and the broken first instruction fetch cycle completed, with the CPU resuming normal operation. This logic ensures that memory is still refreshed when the CPU is idle, waiting for a coprocessor (EPU) to complete its internal operations. $\overline{\text{STOP}}$ may also be used to implement single step operation.

4.3.3 Z8000 INTERNAL REGISTERS AND CPU STATUS

Register organisation in the Z8000 is much more general than in the 8086. The CPU possesses sixteen general-purpose 16-bit registers which may all be used as accummulators and all but one as index registers or memory address pointers. Register 0 is the odd register out, so that a particular addressing mode feature may be used. Register 15 has a duplicate image R15′, and is used as a 16-bit stack pointer (NSP) in normal (user) mode with R15′ used as a system mode stack pointer (SSP). With the unsegmented Z8002, only one 16-bit register is needed in each mode to indicate stack addresses, but in the segmented Z8001 a second register is needed in each mode to hold segment number information. Register R14 and its duplicate R14′ fulfil this function. The registers may be operated as individual 16-bit ones, as 32-bit pairs, or 64-bit quads, a facility more fully explained in chapter 6.

Of the remaining CPU registers, the refresh register has already been covered in the last section, the program counter is a single 16-bit register in the unsegmented CPU, and has a second offset register associated with it in the segmented CPU. The new program status area pointer (PSAP) is similarly a single 16-bit pointer register, and a second segment register associated with the pointer for the non-segmented and segmented versions, respectively, of the CPU. The flag and control word (FCW) register is a single 16-bit register which controls interrupt masks, a system and normal mode switch, and a segmented mode enable bit (only the Z8001), as well as the flags set as a result of arithmetic and other instructions (carry, zero, sign, even parity or overflow, decimal adjust and half carry). The flag and control word and program counter registers are designated the program status (PS) registers.

Table 4.4 Z8000 status signals

ST3	ST2	ST1	ST0	Definition
0	0	0	0	Internal operation
0	0	0	1	Memory refresh
0	0	1	0	I/O operation
0	0	1	1	I/O special operation
0	1	0	0	Segment trap acknowledge
0	1	0	1	NMI acknowledge
0	1	1	0	NVI acknowledge
0	1	1	1	Vectored interrupt acknowledge
1	0	0	0	Data memory access
1	0	0	1	Stack memory access
1	0	1	0	EPU data access
1	0	1	1	EPU stack access
1	1	0	0	Instruction code access
1	1	0	1	First word instruction fetch
1	1	1	0	EPU transfer
1	1	1	1	Reserved

The status outputs of the CPU occupy four pins, ST0-ST3, and an additional pin ($S/\overline{N}$) giving system/normal mode information. They are more comprehensive than the status lines of the 8086, but serve a similar purpose; they may be used for extending the effective addressing range and to protect certain memory accesses. They are shown in table 4.4. By suitable decoding of these status signals, physically separate memory may be allocated for program, data or stack, and physical addresses overlapped, so that the 64 kbyte address limit of the Z8002 may be exceeded. The memory management unit (MMU) available for use with segmented CPUs uses the status signals to check memory access and to generate address violation traps if address and operation are not compatible. Obviously, any in-circuit emulation and hardware debugging equipment can also use the status signals, getting its synchronisation information from the first word of instruction fetch status code.

4.3.4 COPROCESSOR SUPPORT

Like the 8086, the Z8000 CPU family has facilities for connection of a closely-coupled coprocessor. Zilog call such coprocessors 'extended processing units' or EPUs, and rather than invokving EPU operation by a single ESC instruction, the

Z8000 family has six otherwise unused opcodes reserved for EPU operations, provided that an EPU control bit is set in the status of the combination of CPU and EPU. If this bit is not set, an EPU instruction trap will be executed, allowing the equivalent EPU instruction to be implemented in software by an appropriate trap handler.

The extended instruction opcodes carry address and data transfer information, and have fields reserved for defining the EPU instruction required. Generally, EPU operations may be classified as follows:

(a) EPU internal operations, not requiring bus or memory access.
(b) Data transfers between memory and EPU internal registers.
(c) Data transfers between CPU registers and EPU registers.
(d) Flag and status information transfers between CPU and EPU.

Described in detail in chapter 5, the coprocessor EPU generally performs operations upon information held in its internal registers, transferred there using the CPU bus control signals, and defined by the EPU instruction field. When the Z8000 CPU encounters any extended instruction set opcodes, it computes the addresses of operands residing in memory, and generates any appropriate bus control signals to implement the required data movements on the bus. The internal logic of the CPU does not operate on any of the data, but merely manipulates the buses. The EPU monitors the bus activity and the CPU status lines ST0-ST3, and identifies the instructions intended for EPU operation, and latches them internally as they appear on the address/data bus. For internal EPU operations, the CPU is free to continue normal processing in parallel with EPU execution. If a second EPU instruction is encountered by the CPU while the EPU is busy, the EPU can suspend CPU operation until it is ready to accept the second instruction, using the $\overline{\text{STOP}}$ input pin on the CPU.

If the extended instruction indicates a transfer of data between the EPU internal registers and memory, the CPU will calculate the effective address and generate a machine cycle with appropriate timing ($\overline{\text{AS}}$, $\overline{\text{DS}}$, $\overline{\text{MREQ}}$) which is used by the EPU to effect the transfer. A CPU register-EPU register transfer is implemented by the originator of data or status signals placing them on the address/data bus for the recipient to accept on the next clock cycle. The six EPU codes recognised by the CPU occupy the upper byte of a 16-bit word, while the lower byte may specify one of a possible 256 EPU operations.

Although detailed operations differ from those of the 8086, the coprocessor and extended processing unit (EPU) are conceptually very similar. Both are coupled to the local bus of their parent microprocessor, and both use the CPU bus timing signals and addressing logic. Providing a microprocessor EPU present/absent switch and an instruction trap allows a smooth transition between (say) a system using software floating point operations implemented via a trap handler, and one implementing such operations using floating point EPU hardware.

4.3.5 BUS TRANSFERS

Like all the other 16-bit microprocessors, the Z8000 family allows straightforward bus request and grant signals, and, indeed, it must be remembered that, following Zilog's philosophy with Z80 parts, all external requests (bus requests, interrupt requests and multimicro requests) are designed to use a simple and inexpensive serial priority scheme, daisy-chaining from one device to the next. It is, of course, not necessary to implement a daisy-chained bus request, and, at the expense of additional hardware, request contention may be resolved by a parallel arbiter, but basically, the internal logic in all Zilog devices, is appropriate to a daisy-chained arbitration. Thus for bus transfers, the CPU possesses just two signals, $\overline{\text{BUSRQ}}$ and $\overline{\text{BUSAK}}$. $\overline{\text{BUSRQ}}$ is sampled at the beginning of any machine cycle, and, if low, is acknowledged at the end of that machine cycle, by taking $\overline{\text{BUSAK}}$ low. At this point, all the CPU buses (address/data, status, address and data strobes, segment number and control lines) are all at high impedance. Timing is shown in fig. 4.12. As soon as $\overline{\text{BUSAK}}$ is asserted, the requesting device (usually a DMA controller associated with a peripheral interface) can take over the bus. When $\overline{\text{BUSRQ}}$ is released, $\overline{\text{BUSAK}}$ is released. A clock cycle later, all buses resume being driven from the CPU, and the next machine cycle will commence. This is a similar sequence to the minimum mode 8086 signals HOLD and HOLDA. Typical daisy-chaining using DMA controllers is shown in fig. 4.13.

4.3.6 INTERRUPTS AND TRAPS

The Z8000 recognises four hardware inputs which invoke exception processing. Three are interrupts present on all CPUs, corresponding to non-maskable interrupt ($\overline{\text{NMI}}$), non-vectored interrupt ($\overline{\text{NVI}}$) and vectored interrupt ($\overline{\text{VI}}$). The fourth input is a segmentation trap $\overline{\text{SEGT}}$, present only on the Z8001 segmented CPU, and used when a memory management unit (MMU) is present, to trap on segment violation. $\overline{\text{NMI}}$ is internally latched asynchronously, and the internal NMI latch and the other inputs are sampled by the third clock cycle of the last machine cycle of any instruction. If any input is asserted, the subsequent instruction fetch cycle is generated, but not acted upon (and the program counter is not incremented). The interrupt acknowledge machine cycle which follows has five automatic wait states, and after these have been completed, a read operation is generated by the CPU, and information on the address/data bus (interpreted as an interrupt/trap identifier) is read and temporarily stored internally. This word, supplied by the interrupting device, may convey different information depending upon the type of interrupt:

(a) $\overline{\text{VI}}$: Low byte is the jump vector, high byte may be extra user status.
(b) $\overline{\text{NVI}}$, $\overline{\text{NMI}}$: Peripheral device status information.
(c) $\overline{\text{SEGT}}$: High byte is MMU identifier, low byte is undefined.

When this word has been read from the address/data bus, the acknowledge cycle is terminated, and the mode of the Z8000 is automatically changed to system mode, any change being reflected in the state of the normal/system ($\text{N}/\overline{\text{S}}$) output from the CPU. Following the acknowledge cycle, the CPU initiates a status saving sequence which pushes information onto the system stack in the following order:

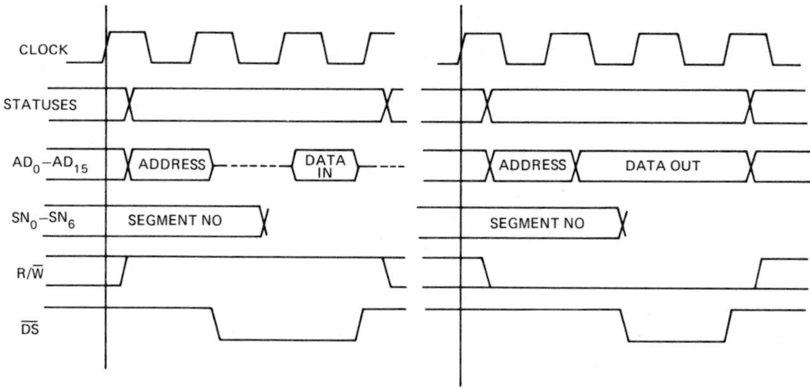

Fig. 4.11 Z8000 bus timing.

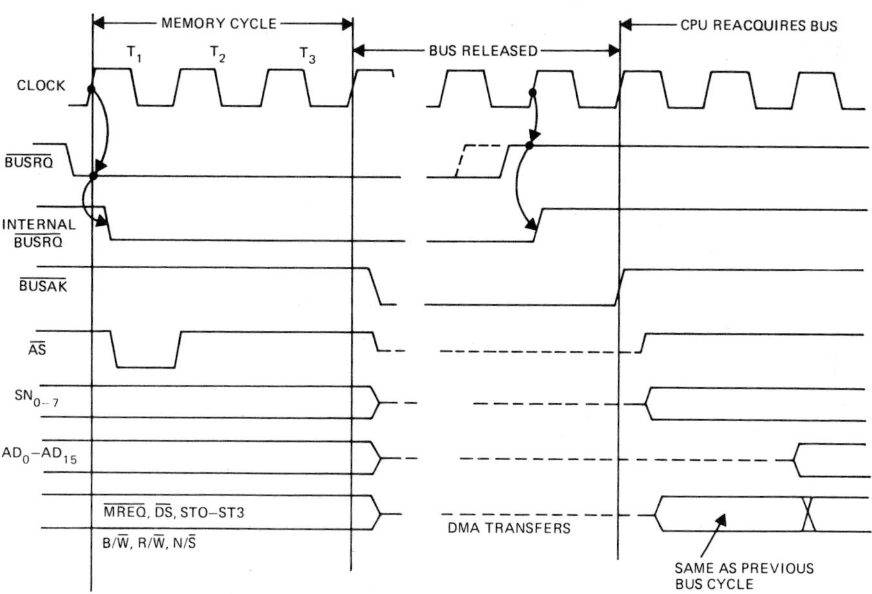

Fig. 4.12 Bus transfer for Z8000 DMA.

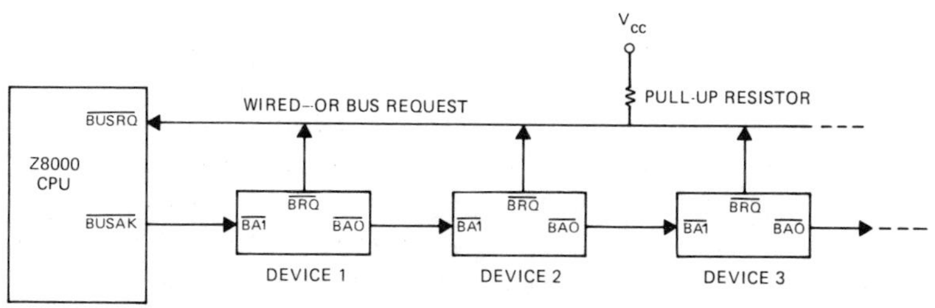

Fig. 4.13 Daisy-chained bus request.

16-bit program counter
Segment number (segmented Z8001 only)
Flag and control word (FCW)
Interrupt/trap identifier (from temporary storage)

The CPU then fetches the new program status using the pointer register(s) for the program status area (PSAP) using the interrupt/trap identifier; an index may be generated, which, when used with the address pointed to by PSAP, will access the appropriate information in the new program status area. The program status area is shown in fig. 4.14. The PSAP address defines the start of the status area; the low byte of the 16-bit address pointer is zero, so a program status area must start at a 256-byte boundary. In the Z8001, a segment number is also provided. Each entry in the table consists of 4 bytes (two words) in the non-segmented Z8002, and 8 bytes (four words) in the segmented Z8001, and contains new PC and new FCW (in short, new PS) register values. Up to location ICH (Z8002) or 38H (Z8001) are the trap locations (including internal ones such as privileged instruction violation), and the table entries above this are the vectored interrupt jump table – all vectored interrupts have the same FCW, held at the top of the vectored interrupt entries, and the individual entries consist just of new PC values. In a non-segmented CPU, the 8-bit vector (value 0-FFH) is doubled, and added to PSAP+IEH, and there are 256 possible vectors, the last being at 21CH. In the segmented version, only even vectors must be used, and these are doubled, and added to PSAP+3CH, giving 128 possible vectors, the last being at 238H.

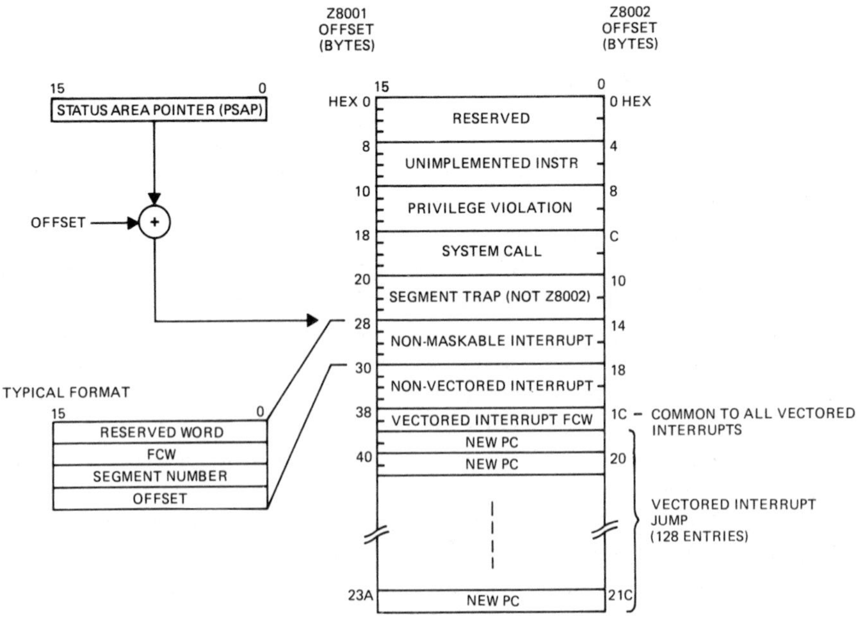

Fig. 4.14 Program status area.

Note that there are two internal traps (unimplemented instruction and privilege violation) and a supervisor (system) call (SVC) instruction within the first part of the PSA. The SVC instruction is the only way in which a user (non-privileged) program may invoke privileged system mode, and is essentially a user entry to the operating system. Reset, invoked by a low on the RESET pin when that low is released, gets its new FCW and PC from low memory (0002H and 0004H or 0002H and 0006H (depending on whether non-segmented or segmented, respectively). While RESET is asserted (for at least five clock cycles) the buses are high-impedance, control signals are high, status signals are low, and refresh is disabled. As soon as the PS information is read, the next machine cycle will be a first instruction, fetch cycle, using the loaded PC value.

Associated with interrupts is a HALT (wait for interrupt) state, invoked by a HALT instruction. The CPU will idle in this state, performing no operations, but executing refresh operations with a frequency determined by the programmed prescaler value. Only reset, segmentation trap, or an interrupt will cause the microprocessor to exit from the HALT condition.

4.3.7 MULTIPLE MICROPROCESSOR FACILITIES

Like the bus request signals, the signals Multimicro In MI and Multimicro Out MO form a daisy-chained request system. Using the resource request instructions, a microprocessor may gain exclusive access to a resource shared with other microprocessors. The operation is described in chapter 10.

4.3.8 ASSESSING THE Z8000 ARCHITECTURE

The philosophy of the Z8000 family is to adopt a regular register set, a 'clean' instruction set, and a segmented approach to addressing, which is implemented using a memory management unit separate from the CPU. The design is a good one, but falls between the 8086 and the MC68000 in power, and may suffer commercially as a result. The basic microprocessor benefits from the use of a clock generator, such as the Am Z8127, which provides not only the CPU clock, but also correctly synchronised RESET, WAIT and single step facilities. It does not generally need a system controller like the maximum mode 8086, though logic may be required to decode the status information. Since all the status conditions are mutually exclusive and are valid for the duration of each machine cycle, a simple 4-to-16 line decoder will usually suffice. Although the refresh capabilities are useful, a dynamic RAM address multiplexer is still required, as well as logic to correctly time RAS and CAS (see chapter 5) and there are now available some very sophisticated single-chip dynamic memory controllers which could bring more flexibility, and freedom from the CPU.

The Z8000 really scores on its dual (normal/system) mode operation. Privileged instructions, and the hardware mode signal, make for a much more secure and higher integrity software system, an aim of every real time system designer. The external MMU adds to this integrity by allowing segment attributes (which the basic 8086 does not do) and a trap if these attributes are violated. The operating-system support shown in the trap and interrupt structure further enhances the Z8000: automatic switch to system mode on interrupt or trap, system-call facilities and an unimplemented instruction trap allowing software implementation of EPU functions. In short, the Z8000 may be viewed as the 'minicomputer engineer's micro'.

4.4 Motorola MC68000

The launch of the MC68000[16–22] advanced the 16-bit microprocessor even further, since, internally, this Motorola microprocessor is a 32-bit machine, with all its registers and all its internal data paths 32-bits wide, but with a 16-bit wide arithmetic and logic unit (ALU) and a 16-bit wide external data bus. Moreover, the 24-bit address bus and 16-bit data bus are not multiplexed – the 68000 occupies a 64-pin package, allowing all bus signals to be brought out separately. Another noticeable feature of the 68000 is its use of asynchronous bus transfers. Unlike most microprocessors, its bus signals do not merely strobe data and address – an acknowledge signal is required for data transfers on the bus, giving a positive indication of a device or memory operation, replacing the negative one used by the 8086 and Z8000, where READY or $\overline{\text{WAIT}}$ serve to stretch machine cycles for slow memory or I/O devices. The bus transfer signals, too, are more complex, with not only bus request and bus grant, but also bus grant acknowledge. Like the Z8000, the 68000 has user and supervisor (system) modes for normal operation, and a further trace mode, invoked by setting a status register bit similar to the 8086 trap flag (TF), which will generate an exception (trap) every time an instruction is executed.

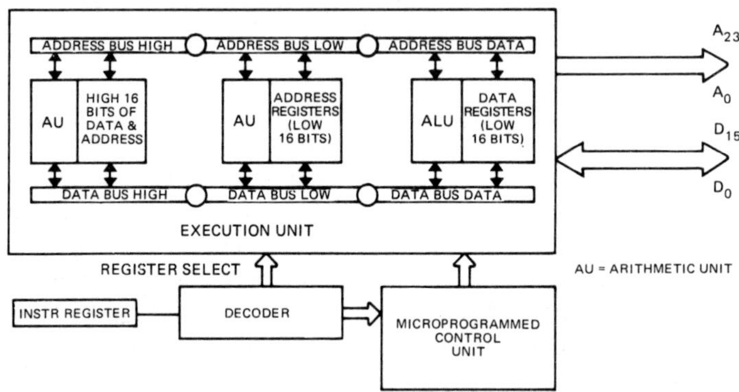

Fig. 4.15 68000 schematic.

The 68000 interrupt or exception processing structure of the 68000 is extremely versatile, with a much greater range of internally raised exceptions, including the 8086, Z8000 ones of zero divide, illegal instruction, privilege violation and trace, but also including new ones of bus error, address error and others. The external interrupts are prioritised into seven levels, with a coded interrupt request signal, which is compared with the priority of the currently executing task, and can only interrupt that task if the task's priority level is lower than that of the interrupting device. Reset is considered the highest level exception, and attempts to use uninitialised interrupt vectors and spurious interrupts are trapped to specific locations. The integrity of program operation is enhanced considerably by such features.

The internal structure of the 68000 is shown in fig. 4.15. Like the 8086, it is microcoded, with the execution unit controlled by a two-level structure which combines 'horizontal' and 'vertical' microcode. Horizontal microcode provides almost fully decoded fields which can drive the execution unit with a minimum of extra logic but requires a large control store and uses very wide instruction words. Vertical microcode, on the other hand, requires more clock cycles than horizontal microcode (and so may be slower), is more highly encoded, and requires extra decoding logic, but may use a smaller control store. The way in which the combination works is interesting: the first level of microcode consists of small micro-instructions in a sequence which emulates each macro-instruction, and which are basically address pointers for words in a second control store. These 'nano-instructions' occur individually, not in sequence, and are basically responsible for decoding the micro-instructions in the sequence generated by the first level. This means that the wide words controlling the execution unit need not be duplicated in the control store, as they would be if just horizontal micro-code had been used. Instruction pipelining, rather than an instruction queue, is used. As may be seen from fig. 4.15, the internal register files are connected by two buses; the files are divided into three sections which may be isolated or concatenated using bidirectional bus switches between each section. The arithmetic units in each section allow simultaneous address and data computation. This unique arrangement makes for a particularly concise and elegant control unit.

4.4.1 68000 BUS STRUCTURE

The non-multiplexed buses are of width 16 bits (data) and 24 bits (byte address, allowing 16 Mbytes of linear address). The bus timing signals are arranged to implement an asynchronous bus, while retaining compatibility with MC6800 family interface devices. Two modes of bus timing may be used, one for normal transfers (asynchronous), and the other a '6800 peripheral cycle' mode, which is synchronous, invoked by using a hardware input signal to signify the presence of a 6800 device at the address being accessed.

Asynchronous timing is shown in fig. 4.16. The direction of transfer is controlled by a single R/$\overline{W}$ line, as in the 6800, which becomes valid as the 24-bits of address, together with three status signals FL0-2 ('function codes') are placed on the appropriate buses. Shortly afterwards, the address and data strobes $\overline{AS}$, $\overline{UDS}$, and $\overline{LDS}$ may be asserted. The upper and lower bytes of the data bus are controlled by separate strobe signals $\overline{UDS}$ and $\overline{LDS}$, respectively, according to table 4.5.

The transfer acknowledge signal $\overline{DTACK}$ will be taken low by the addressed device, and the bus cycle can proceed. If no wait states are required by the addressed device, $\overline{DTACK}$ may be asserted using a simple gate to combine the address decoder output with the address strobe $\overline{AS}$ and one or both of the data

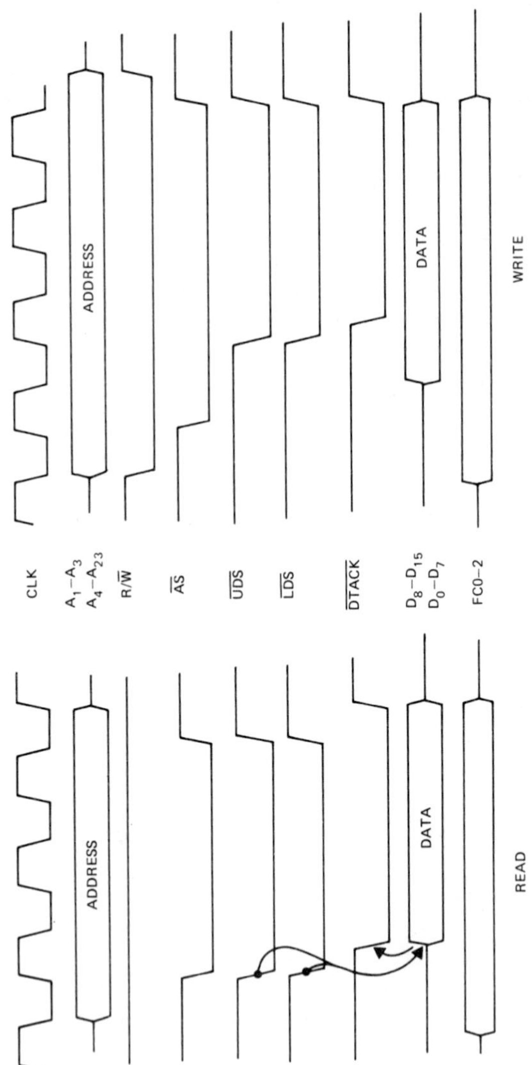

Fig. 4.16 68000 asynchronous bus timing.

strobes. If wait states are required by a slower device, $\overline{\text{DTACK}}$ must be delayed in its assertion to give the device time to respond to A0-A23 and the strobes. Typically a shift register may be used to delay $\overline{\text{DTACK}}$ and lengthen the cycle in one clock cycle increments, as much as may be required. The 68000, like its 8-bit predecessor, does not use explicit I/O instructions or control signals and all I/O devices are memory-mapped, so this technique is ideal for the possible mixture of access times that may result. $\overline{\text{DTACK}}$ may also be used to implement single-step (by bus cycle) operation, illustrated in fig. 4.17.

Table 4.5 Byte control

$\overline{\text{UDS}}$	$\overline{\text{LDS}}$	R/$\overline{\text{W}}$	D8-D15 (MS byte)	D7-D0 (LS byte)	Operation
High	High	x	Invalid	Invalid	None
Low	Low	High	Valid	Valid	Read
High	Low	High	Invalid	Valid	Read
Low	High	High	Valid	Invalid	Read
Low	Low	Low	Valid	Valid	Write
High	Low	Low	D7-D0*	Valid	Write
Low	High	Low	Valid	D8-D15*	Write

*Not part of MC68000 specification, merely a result of current implementation.

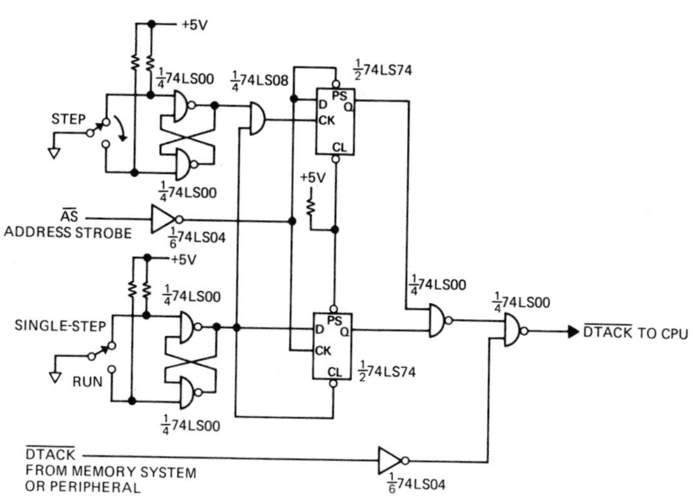

Fig. 4.17 68000 single-step using $\overline{\text{DTACK}}$.

Standard MC6800 interface devices do not have the facilities on-chip to generate $\overline{\text{DTACK}}$, and in any case, they are designed to use the synchronising signal E, a strobe generated directly from Ø2 of the 6800 clock (E is usually

VMA.Ø2): to use such devices effectively with the 68000, the signals E, $\overline{VMA}$ and a new one, $\overline{VPA}$ are available. $\overline{VPA}$ is an input signal which indicates to the CPU that the addressed device or region is a 6800 compatible one, and that data transfer should be synchronous, and coincide with the E strobe signal (it is also used during interrupt acknowledge). E is a constant clock signal derived internally from the CPU clock, and one-tenth of its frequency, with a 60/40 duty cycle (low for six clocks, high for four). When $\overline{VPA}$ has been received as a result of an address having been placed on the bus, and E is low, the CPU asserts $\overline{VMA}$ to be used as part of the device chip select, so it is issued with the correct timing to ensure no contention in device selection and deselection. Operation of the 68000 bus with 6800 devices is shown in fig. 4.18.

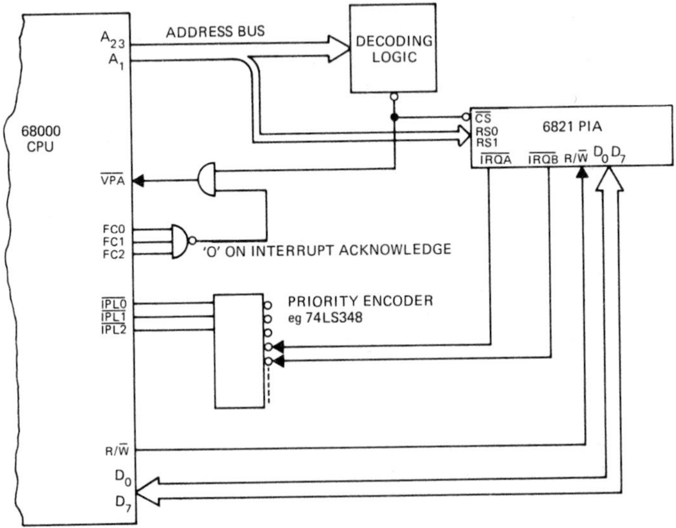

Fig. 4.18 Interfacing to 6800 devices.

The function codes FC0-FC2 serve to identify the class of operation being performed on the bus, and may be decoded to distinguish data and program code accesses and the CPU mode. They are shown in table 4.6, and are used particularly by the 68000 memory management unit.

As well as MMU use to control access, these codes may also be used to define separate address spaces, increasing the effective microprocessor addressing range to 64 Mbytes.

Both $\overline{DTACK}$ and the use of $\overline{VPA}$ cause bus cycles to be executed to completion. Such cycles may also be terminated by $\overline{BERR}$, an input line used by an external device to indicate a bus error. The memory-management unit may use this input to indicate an invalid access attempt, or a watchdog timer may use it to terminate a bus cycle involving a device which fails to respond within a preset time. An exception will be raised which may invoke a routine which recovers from such a potentially bad situation.

Table 4.6 68000 function codes

FC2	FC1	FC0	Reference
0	0	0	(Reserved)
0	0	1	User data
0	1	0	User program
0	1	1	(Reserved)
1	0	0	(Reserved)
1	0	1	Supervisor data
1	1	0	Supervisor program
1	1	1	Interrupt acknowledge

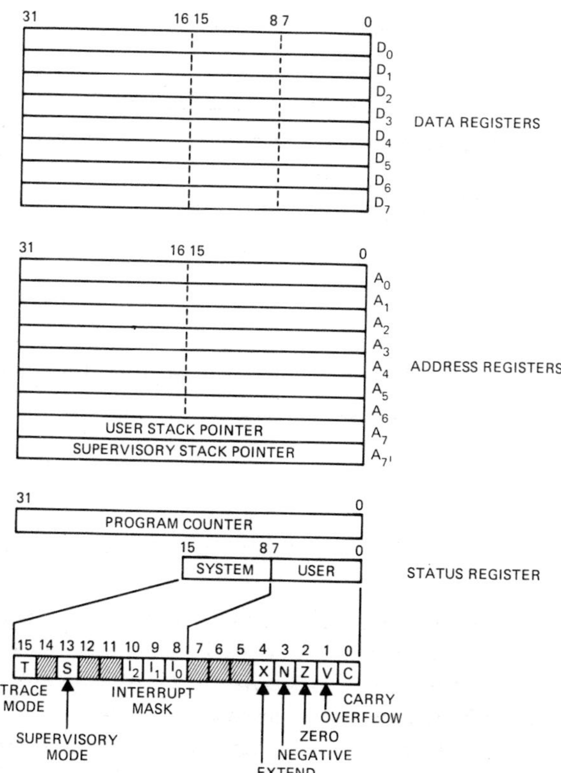

Fig. 4.19 68000 register set.

4.4.2 68000 INTERNAL REGISTERS

The arrangement of registers internally is shown in fig. 4.19, and, as has been noted previously, the general-purpose registers are all 32 bits in length, to allow for upward compatibility with future microprocessors. No segmentation is used, so the 24 bits of address available at the CPU pins represent a linear addressing range of 16 Mbytes. In the same way as the Z8000 possesses duplicate registers (stack pointer and stack segment register) to allow for user and system modes, so the 68000 has a duplicated address register A7, called A7', used as user and supervisory stack pointer, respectively. Notice that the register set is divided into eight data and seven address registers (plus the two stack pointers). This arrangement suits the internal twin bus structure of fig. 4.15. The program counter is also 32 bits in length, but only 24 of the 32 address bits are used.

The status register is only 16 bits in length, with the lower byte indicating user status, and the upper byte system status. While the user byte indicates the condition codes, the upper byte is of more interest from the viewpoint of system architecture. A bit is reserved to indicate trace mode (the single instruction trap mode of the 68000) and another bit is used as a user/supervisor mode bit. The three lower bits are used to indicate the coded interrupt mask which is the priority of the current executing microprocessor code.

4.4.3 BUS TRANSFERS

The bus control signals of the 68000 provide for the same type of DMA and other autonomous bus transfers as the grant and request signals of the previously described microprocessors. Since the package size of the 68000 does not put any serious restriction on the number of control signals, a bus arbitration sequence is used which requires three lines ($\overline{BR}$, $\overline{BG}$, $\overline{BGACK}$) for handshaking. Used with an external arbitration device, the lines allow a bus request-grant-acknowledge sequence of the form:

(a) Device makes a request to become bus master ($\overline{BR}$).
(b) If the bus can be relinquished to the requesting device, $\overline{BG}$ is asserted, indicating that the bus is available at the end of the current cycle.
(c) Bus mastership is acknowledged ($\overline{BGACK}$).

A flowchart of bus arbitration procedure is shown in fig. 4.20. $\overline{BR}$ may be wired-OR and indicates that some other device requires control of the bus. Since the current bus master is automatically assumed to possess a lower bus priority than the requesting device, it will relinquish the bus after completion of the current bus cycle. The microprocessor (default bus master) will issue bus grant $\overline{BG}$ in response to $\overline{BR}$ immediately after internal synchronisation provided address strobe $\overline{AS}$ for the current bus cycle has been asserted, otherwise $\overline{BG}$ will be delayed until assertion of $\overline{AS}$ has occurred. $\overline{BG}$ may be daisy-chained, forming a serial priority chain, or be used in conjunction with some other arbitration scheme.

Receipt of $\overline{BG}$ causes the requesting device to wait until $\overline{AS}$, $\overline{DTACK}$ are terminated and bus grant acknowledge is negated, and the device then issues its own $\overline{BGACK}$. While address strobe $\overline{AS}$ is asserted, no device can break the cycle, and termination of this signal indicates that the bus master has completed its cycle; termination of $\overline{DTACK}$ indicates that the slave or peripheral interface has completed its operation with the master, and the removal or negation of bus grant acknowledge $\overline{BGACK}$, indicates that the master has released the bus. $\overline{BR}$ may then be removed by the requesting device, and subsequently $\overline{BG}$ is negated by the relinquishing master to indicate that arbitration is complete, and the requesting device has control of the bus. The device can then perform its own bus cycles, keeping $\overline{\text{BGACK}}$ asserted until it has finished. When $\overline{\text{BGACK}}$ is removed, the device's bus mastership is terminated.

To avoid obvious pitfalls, the following default actions occur:

(a) If no acknowledgement ($\overline{\text{BGACK}}$) is received before $\overline{\text{BR}}$ is removed, the microprocessor will not relinquish the bus, and will continue processing as soon as $\overline{\text{BR}}$ becomes inactive.
(b) If $\overline{\text{BR}}$ persists after $\overline{\text{BGACK}}$ is removed, an immediate arbitration sequence is performed and another BG issued.

Bus timing is shown in fig. 4.21.

It is worthwhile to notice one condition governing the assertion of $\overline{\text{BGACK}}$ and subsequent transfer of bus control, namely that the fact that after $\overline{\text{BG}}$ has been asserted, $\overline{\text{AS}}$ must be removed before $\overline{\text{BGACK}}$ can be issued, may be used to create an indivisible semaphore manipulation signal. The read-modify-write cycle of the 68000 test-and-set instruction (TAS) keeps $\overline{\text{AS}}$ asserted throughout the cycle, so that the cycle cannot be interrupted.

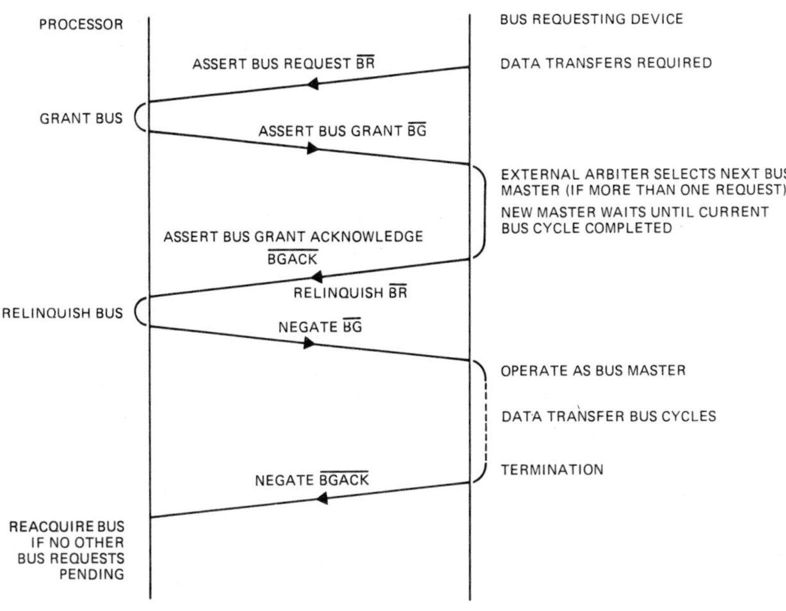

Fig. 4.20 68000 bus arbitration.

4.4.4 EXCEPTIONS

The 68000 groups traps, interrupts and system calls under the general heading of exceptions. Exception processing consists basically of fetching an address from an exception vector, saving machine context, and switching to a new context. Four steps outline the operations invoked by any exception:

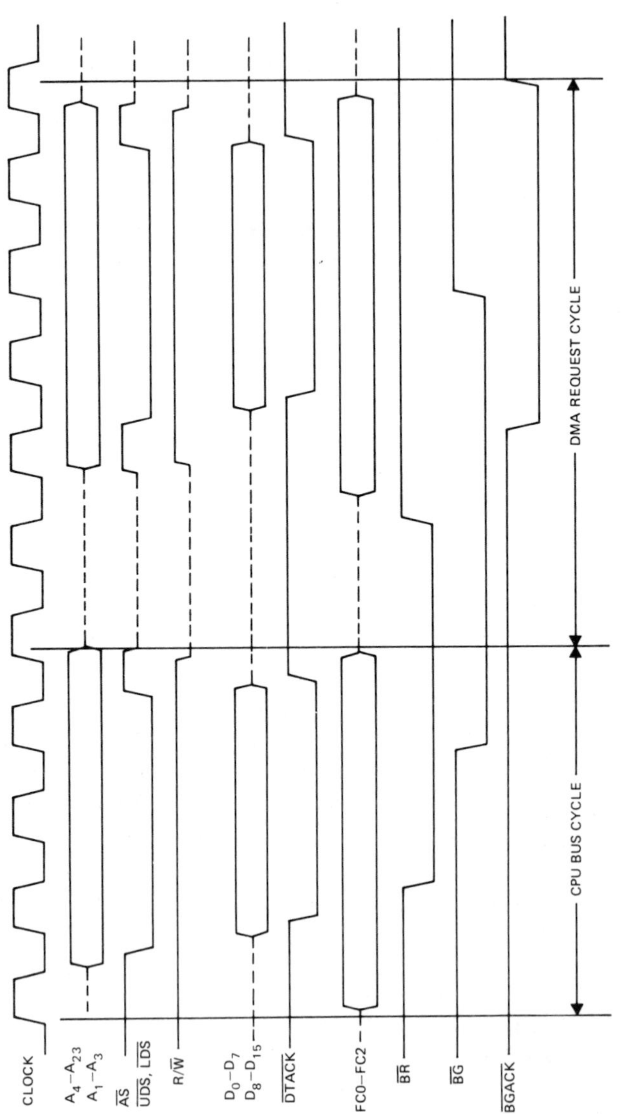

Fig. 4.21 68000 bus transfer.

(a) A temporary copy of the status register is made, and the status register then altered for exception processing (basically, the status register privilege bit is set to indicate supervisor mode, and the trace bit cleared so that the exception can be processed without hindrance).
(b) The exception vector is determined. This is the address of a memory location which will contain the address of the relevant handling routine.
(c) The current microprocessor context is saved on the supervisor stack, consisting of the contents of the program counter, and the previous status register (bus and address error exceptions also stack instruction register values, and access address together with information about the bus cycle in which the error occurred, such as the CPU function code, whether the cycle was read or write and whether it was an instruction cycle or not). The reset exception is the only one that does not perform this step.
(d) The new program counter (PC) value is fetched from the exception vector, and instruction execution is resumed.

For priority reasons, and because of the way in which they occur, exceptions can be grouped into one of three main groups, shown in table 4.7.

Table 4.7 Exception groups

Group	Exceptions	Action
0 (Highest priority)	Reset Bus error Address error	Instruction currently being executed is aborted, and exception processing commences immediately
1	Trace External interrupts Privilege violation trap Illegal instruction trap	Current instruction is allowed to complete, but subsequent instructions are pre-empted by exception processing
2 (Lowest priority)	TRAP TRAPV CHK Zero divide	Exception processing invoked by normal instruction execution

The exception vectors are stored in a fixed block of 256, occupying 1024 locations in memory (addresses 0 to 3FFH). Table 4.8 gives their order.

Reset, a special case of the exception vectors, does not reside in supervisor data space (defined by function codes FC0-FC2, table 4.6), but supervisor program space. Reset is a bidirectional signal – as in input, it is invoked by taking both $\overline{\text{RESET}}$ and $\overline{\text{HALT}}$ lines on the CPU low (for a minimum of 100 ms on power-on), whereupon the CPU will initialise the supervisor stack pointer (SSP) and the program counter, from memory locations 0000H and 0004H, respectively. The status register is loaded with an interrupt level of seven. The RESET instruction of the CPU, when executed, causes the microprocessor to drive the RESET pin (which is connected to the RESET inputs of all other devices in the system, as well as to the external reset circuitry) for 124 clock pulses, so that the rest of the system devices will be reset, while the CPU continues to operate with all internal registers unaffected.

Table 4.8 Exception vectors

Vector number	Address (hex)	Use
0	0	Initial SSP) In supervisor
	4	Initial PC) program space
2	8	Bus error
3	C	Address error
4	10	Illegal instruction
5	14	Zero divide
6	18	CHK instruction
7	1C	TRAPV instruction
8	20	Privilege violation
9	24	Trace
10	28	1010) unimplemented
11	2C	1111) instruction
12-23	30- 5F	(Reserved)
24	60	Spurious interrupt
25	64	Level 1 autovector
26	68	Level 2 autovector
27	6C	Level 3 autovector
28	70	Level 4 autovector
29	74	Level 5 autovector
30	78	Level 6 autovector
31	7C	Level 7 autovector
32-47	80- BF	TRAP vectors
48-63	C0- FF	(Reserved)
64-255	100-3FF	User interrupts

Bus error is the highest priority exception below reset, and is important in an asynchronous system to allow recovery from a potential deadlock situation where a bus cycle is frozen in the middle of its operation, waiting for an acknowledge signal $\overline{\text{DTACK}}$, which does not occur, owing, for example, to device failure. In such a situation, the only way to recover microprocessor operation is with an interrupt. While a normal external interrupt will cause an exit from the deadlock, it will not identify the problem, so it is usual instead to use a 'watchdog' timer in real time computer systems, which will generate a timeout interrupt if the handshake acknowledgement fails to occur within some preset maximum time. The timeout interrupt should be given a high priority (since it affects system integrity) and the input pin $\overline{\text{BERR}}$ is reserved for this function.

$\overline{\text{BERR}}$ invokes a bus error exception, which is another special exception, since its exception sequence is somewhat longer than the normal 68000 exception sequence. The sequence is as follows:

(a) PC and status register pushed to SSP.
(b) Error information (address information, function code of bus cycle, whether R/$\overline{\text{W}}$, whether instruction cycle or not) pushed onto SSP.
(c) The bus error vector table entry is read.
(d) The bus error routine is executed.

The address error exception is generated when the microprocessor attempts to access a word (16 bit), long word (32 bit) or instruction at an odd byte address (the 68000 requires its instructions to be aligned on even address boundaries). It behaves like an internally generated bus error signal, and the $\overline{\text{HALT}}$ pin is low, the microprocessor will enter a 're-run sequence' which will restart the bus cycle when $\overline{\text{HALT}}$ is removed (this does not apply to test-and-set, TAS, since it would violate the indivisible nature of this read-modify-write instruction).

Interrupts are normally invoked by applying a 3-bit priority code onto CPU pins $\overline{\text{IPLP}}$-$\overline{\text{IPL2}}$, which give seven levels of interrupt priority; devices may be daisy-chained externally on each of these priority levels (level 1 is the lowest priority, level 7 is the highest, and zero on the three lines indicates no interrupt request). When a request occurs, it is treated as a pending interrupt, and its priority is compared with the CPU priority encoded in the status register. If the priority of the pending interrupt is lower than or equal to that of the CPU, the exception processing is postponed, and normal CPU processing continues. If the priority of the pending interrupt is higher than that of the CPU, it is recognised at the end of the current CPU instruction, and an exception processing sequence is commenced. The following sequence of operations then occur:

(a) A copy of the status register is saved, supervisor mode is entered, trace exceptions are disabled, and the status register is altered to reflect the priority of the new exception.
(b) The microprocessor generates an interrupt acknowledge cycle (FCO-FC2 = III) to acquire the vector number of the interrupting device (during this cycle, the priority level of the interrupt being acknowledged appears on address lines A1-A3, and data is read on the lower byte of the data bus using AS and LDS, with handshake signal DTACK). The interrupt vector is computed by multiplying the vector number by four.
(c) The program counter and status register are pushed onto the supervisor stack.
(d) The program counter is loaded with the contents of the interrupt vector location, and processing proceeds from there.

A special interrupt technique, called 'autovectoring', is provided to allow compatibility with MC6800 interface devices. An interrupting device, which needs to use autovectoring, signals this requirement by asserting $\overline{\text{VPA}}$ when the interrupt acknowledge cycle commences. In this event, the CPU generates a normal 6800 read cycle, asserting $\overline{\text{VMA}}$, and uses the priority level of the interrupting device to compute the interrupt vector. The seven autovector locations 1-7 occupy addresses in the interrupt vector space of 064H-07CH, respectively. A flowchart detailing interrupt sequences is shown in fig. 4.22.

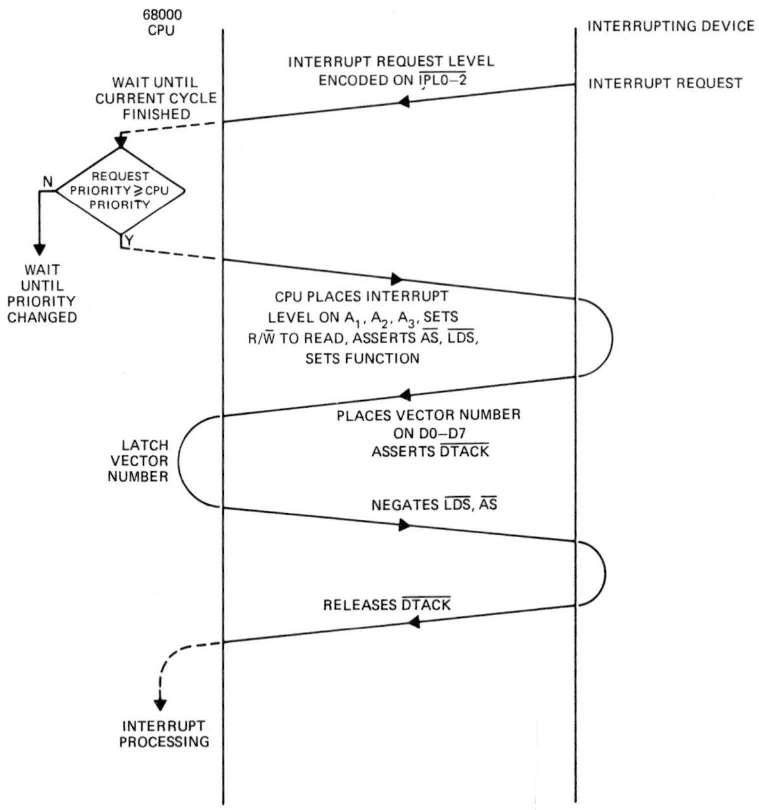

Fig. 4.22 68000 interrupt response.

Traps are internally generated exceptions invoked by privilege violation (attempting to execute certain instructions in user mode: STOP RESET, RTE (return from exception), any operation affecting the upper byte (supervisor byte) of the status register, or the user stack pointer USP), by abnormal processing conditions (zero divide) or similar events. TRAP (trap number) is a software interrupt which specifies one of sixteen vectors, TRAPV is an instruction which causes a trap if the overflow flag is set, CHK is an instruction which generates a trap if a register exceeds an upper bound specified by the contents of the effective address specified by the instruction. Trace will cause a trap on each instruction execution if the T-bit of the status register is set, useful for program debugging at machine code level. Illegal instructions will cause a trap exception, and so will a class of instructions designated 'unimplemented', rumoured to be floating point instructions which were to have been implemented internally in the CPU, but omitted to reduce CPU complexity, the opcodes of the unimplemented instructions with either 1010 or 1111 in bits 15-12. The traps provided allow software implementation while retaining code compatibility with any future hardware implementation of this class of instructions.

4.4.5 $\overline{\text{HALT}}$

The $\overline{\text{HALT}}$ input has already been mentioned in connection with bus error exceptions, but in normal operation (when there is no bus error), it provides a halt/run/single-step function. When $\overline{\text{HALT}}$ is asserted, the microprocessor completes its bus cycle, and then places the address, data and function-code lines in a high-impedance state, and does nothing until $\overline{\text{HALT}}$ is removed. $\overline{\text{AS}}$ may be used in conjunction with HALT to provide single-step operation, as shown in fig. 4.23.

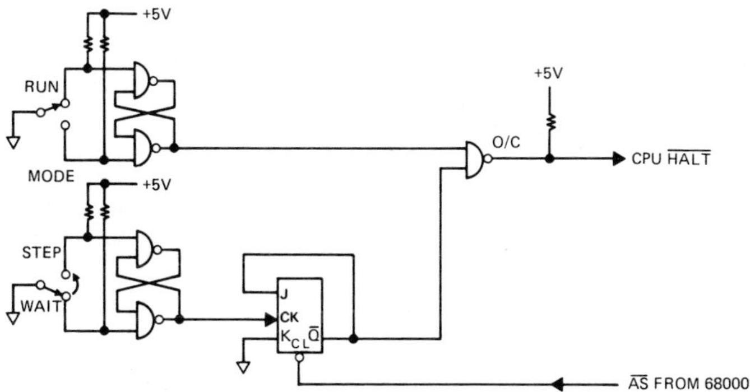

Fig. 4.23 Alternative single-step circuit.

4.4.6 ASSESSING MC68000 ARCHITECTURE

The 68000 stands out from its rivals in having a large linear address range, rather than using a segmented approach. This does not preclude use of a memory management unit, and makes operation of low complexity systems straightforward. The adoption by Motorola of a 64-pin package which allows the inclusion of non-multiplexed data and address buses is a forward looking one, as is the internal use of 32-bit paths and registers. Asynchronous bus operation and the exception processing structure both give credence to the view that this microprocessor is the low end of a range of future CPUs which will extend to 32 bits and maintain compatibility with 16-bit predecessors; the only concession made by the designers of the 68000 towards compatibility with previous devices has been the provision of compatible bus control signals and interrupts. These have been provided, not as part of the main structure of the 68000, but as additional features which may be ignored if they are not required, and need not compromise normal operation at all. The 64-pin package allows these extra control signals to coexist with the main ones, without multiplexing.

Conceptually, the internal register structure of the 68000 could not be simpler, with no compromise of generality by the division into address and data registers. Likewise, the exception vector structure is easy to appreciate, and allows 192 user interrupts. In terms of speed, too, the 68000 appears to have the edge on its rivals (see chapter 7). The only real criticism of the device is its currently rather high price. When its likely applications are considered (minicomputer look-alike, numeric applications, etc.) they are mainly at the upper end of the 16-bit spectrum, so perhaps cost is less important than the very impressive capabilities of the device. In any case, as the 16-bit market matures, and larger quantities of the device are produced, the price will soon drop to very low levels, repeating the experience of the 8-bit microprocessors.

4.5 Other 16-bit microprocessors

The microprocessors already covered currently enjoy the majority of sales in the 16-bit market-place, sharing it with one or two older designs like the TMS9900. There are some special microprocessors like the Western Digital MicroEngine, a 16-bit microprocessor designed to execute Pascal p-code directly, the Hewlett-Packard internally produced (and not for sale at chip level) MC^2 and the recently announced Digital Equipment Corporation PDP-11 compatible T-11. Two recent introductions look likely to wrest some of the market share from the current leaders, but have not yet appeared in commercial equipment to any great extent. They are the Texas Instruments' successor to the TMS9900, the TMS99000, and the National Semiconductor's NS16032. Both contain a considerable number of innovative features, and are discussed in less detail only because of their current scarcity.

4.5.1 TMS99000

This microprocessor is really a family of microprocessors:

(a) TMS99105 Basically an upgraded 9995.
(b) TMS99110 On-chip ROM gives floating-point capability.
(c) TMS99120 On-chip ROM gives operating system primitives to support the TI Realtime Executive and Micro Pascal.

All microprocessors in the family are 16-bit devices with an internal structure shown in fig. 4.24. Like the TMS9900[23–26], they retain the memory-memory architecture, with a workspace pointer (WP) register which locates sixteen contiguous machine registers in memory space. The microprocessors are microcoded but are nevertheless far from sluggish, with an 'intelligent prefetch' pipeline structure which is not compromised in its speed advantage by branch instructions. The microcode operating the pipeline automatically uses the correct next address, and since only one instruction ahead is prefetched, no complex queue management is necessary. The TM99000 uses an extremely wide (162 bits) control word in a horizontal microcode scheme, which makes it extremely fast. The manufacturer's benchmarks show its speed to be higher than any of its rivals, and compatibility with the 9900 is retained, but with the highly optimised microcode already hinted at. Amazingly, the functions of the 9900, which occupies a 64-pin package, have been greatly enhanced and squeezed into a 40-pin package, with address and data multiplexed. The bus timing is synchronous, using ALATCH to demultiplex the address, MEM to signify a memory cycle, DEN as the equivalent of $\overline{RD}$, WE as the equivalent of $\overline{WR}$ (fig. 4.25). Status lines are valid for the duration of the cycle (BST1-BST3, table 4.9).

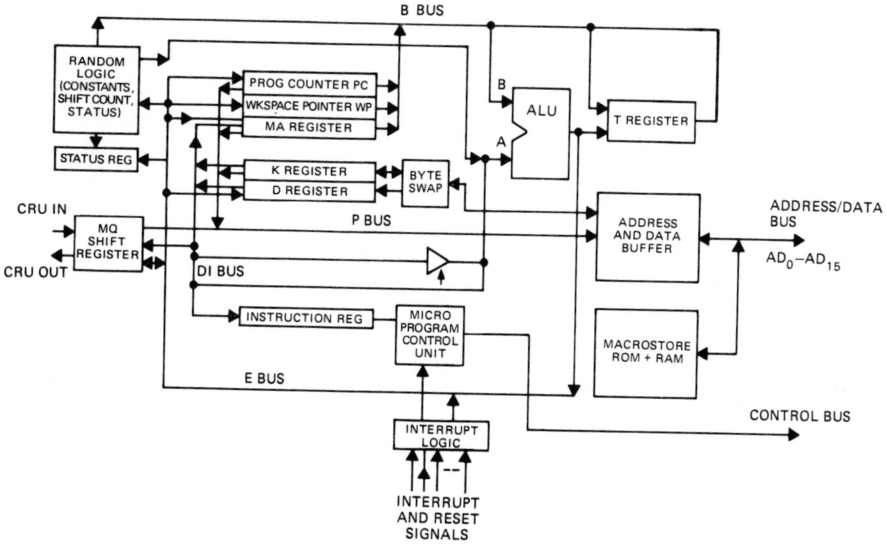

Fig. 4.24 TMS99000 architecture.

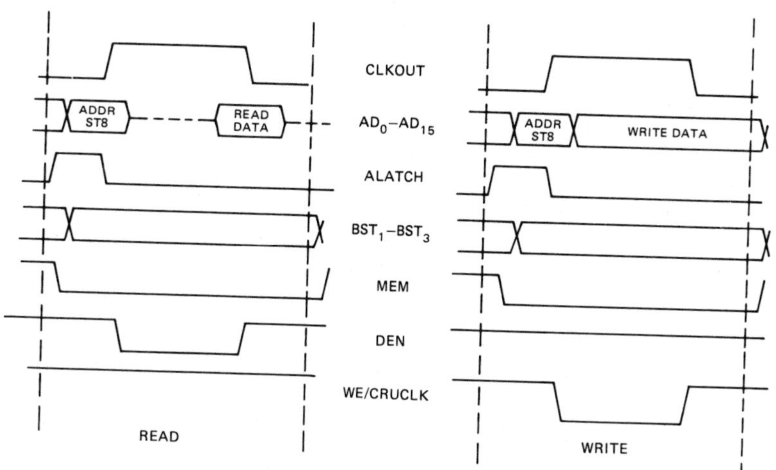

Fig. 4.25 99000 bus cycles (no wait states).

Wait states may be inserted using inputs WAITGEN (generates one wait state) or READY (more than one wait state). The 15-bit address (D15 has no corresponding A15 multiplexed with it but has a status output ST8 used by the memory mapper) allows a direct address of 64 kbytes, but the way in which memory is used overcomes this apparent disadvantage. The TI philosophy is that memory access requires exclusive use of the system bus, and adding more fast memory only makes more sequential functions available, and does not improve system bandwidth. Moreover, system bandwidth is hardly compromised by use of a much larger and cheaper, but slower, main store, with a cache memory. Accordingly, the approach with the 99000 family has been to support a flexible logical memory hierarchy in the order: control ROM workspaces, caches and global memory, and an important support device is the specially designed memory mapper. The memory mapper works by interpreting the four most significant address bits from the microprocessor to designate one of sixteen mapping registers within the SN74LS610 device. These bits specify one of the 4 kbyte 'pages' within a 16 Mbyte memory mapper address space. By moving from this 'system logical address space' to physical memory, different devices can be interpreted as lying within the same virtual memory space.

Table 4.9 Status lines

MEM	BST3-1	Mnemonic	Bus actions
0	000	SOPL	Source-operand transfer (with bus lock)
0	001	SOP	Source-operand transfer
0	010	IOP	Immediate data, second instruction word
0	011	IAQ	First word of instruction fetch
0	100	DOP	Destination-operand transfer
0	101	IACK	Interrupt acknowledge
0	110	WS	Workspace transfer
0	111	GM	General memory transfer
1	000	NOPL	Internal operation (with bus lock)
1	001	NOP	Internal operation or macrostore access
1	010	RESET	Reset
1	011	CRU	CRU transfer
1	100	WP	Workspace pointer update
1	101	ST	Status register update
1	110	MID	Macro-instruction detected
1	111	HOLDA	Hold acknowledge

The real secret of the TMS99000 is called Macrostore, a special memory which is part of a concept which gives a smooth upgrade or migration path for implementation of system functions. In most microprocessors, system functions are implemented in software in main memory ('software emulation'), with coprocessors (floating point arithmetic, operating system primitives) emerging as an alternative, using functions 'cast in silicon'. The problem addressed by Texas with the 99000 family is one of compatibility, and the migration path starts with software emulation, then moves to implementation in fast internal or external Macrostore memory where functions are invoked as macro-instructions. The third step is the implementation of those macro-instructions in a coprocessor or 'attached microprocessor', called an extended instruction set microprocessor which shares the main CPU bus. Finally, the functions may be shifted to an 'attached computer', which has its own local bus system and memory, saving overheads on the CPUs own bus, and executes concurrently with the main CPU, with well-defined communication paths between the two.

Macrostore consists of an internal high speed memory (typically 512 × 16 bits of ROM, 16 × 16 bits of RAM), lying in an address space completely separate from the normal external memory. It may be extended externally to a total of 64 kbytes, and is then accessed using the same timing signals as normal memory. Internal Macrostore will contain system level functions derived from assembly source code but executing much more quickly than with software emulation in main memory, since the internal cycle time is 167 μs, that is, one cycle time of a 6 MHz four-phase internal clock derived from a 24 MHz clock oscillator. Before being committed to internal ROM, the code may be debugged in external Macrostore memory space by forcing the CPU to make all Macrostore accesses over the external bus (this is done by strapping the extended instruction processor present pin, X 1PP or APP, to RESET).

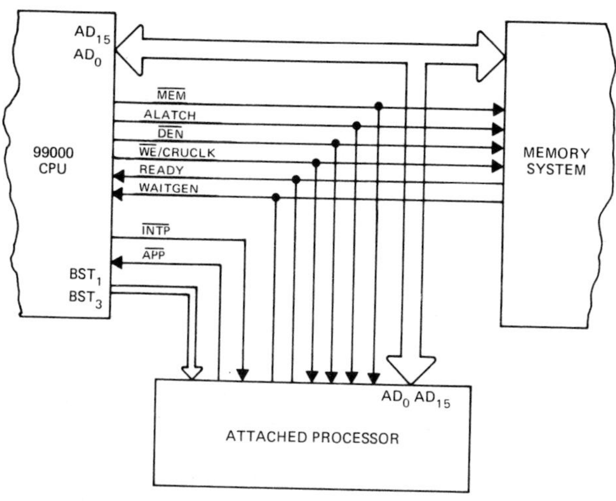

Fig. 4.26 99000 attached microprocessor.

Entry to code in Macrostore is performed using a macro-instruction (MID, XOP or undefined opcode) which causes an interrupt. The macro-instruction will usually be one of a number of user-defined opcodes which can be identified by the CPU. When such a macro opcode is encountered, the method of execution of the macro function is determined as shown in fig. 4.26, where the CPU determines whether an attached computer (autonomous) or an attached microprocessor (shared CPU bus) is present and can execute it; if not, an attempt is made to use Macrostore ROM firmware, then software emulation in main memory, and if none of these elements can execute the macro, an opcode violation exception is raised. The interrupt vector locations of the TMS 99000 are shown in fig. 4.27, occupying the first 128 bytes of main memory space. Included are sixteen extended-operation (XOP) traps, which handle the context switches associated with the user opcodes. Note too, the sixteen levels of external user interrupts.

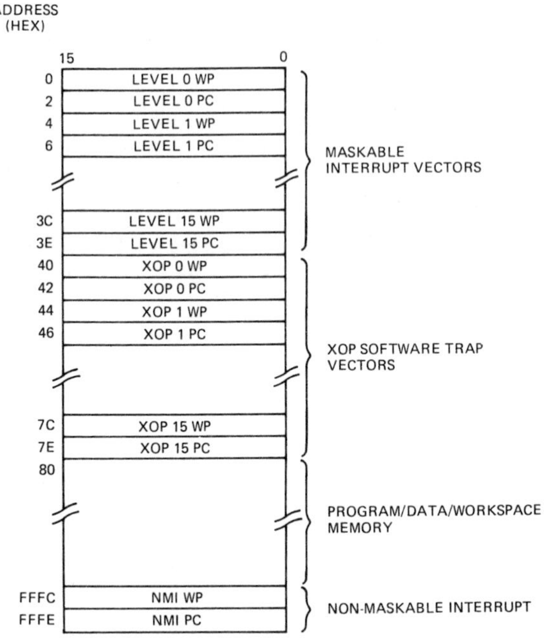

Fig. 4.27 99000 interrupt map.

Other features of the TMS99000 include a bus-lock signal for semaphore manipulation instructions, asserted during various data transfer instructions and internal operations, signed and unsigned multiply-divide on-chip hardware, a number of 32-bit arithmetic operations, and memory-mapper control instructions (usually implemented in part of the Macrostore ROM used in the two pre-programmed Macrostore versions of the 99000, the 99100 and 99120). Like their predecessor, the 9900, the newest Texas family members are unique, and epitomise the unique Texas approach to microcomputers, using memory-memory architecture, and the communications register unit. As a natural consequence of this emphasis on memory operations, the TI method of tackling the problems of very large memory spaces is one which makes use of an off-chip memory mapper (not so sophisticated as a memory management unit) and requires a hierarchical memory involving caches, fast main memory and virtual devices. The accent on modular software, especially systems software, and the strong support that Texas gives to real time operating systems (such as RX), as well as the continuity with the 990 and 9900, make this new family of microprocessors attractive for many real time tasks (where advantage may be taken of the extremely fast context switch mechanism involving workspace switching) and complex memory-intensive ones.

4.5.2 NATIONAL SEMICONDUCTOR NS16032

Another late entry to the 16-bit microprocessor stakes, the 16032[27–30], is at the high end of the National 16000 family of microprocessors. The family consists of three microprocessors, the 16008 (8-bit data bus, 16-bit address bus, with 8080 compatibility), the 16016 (16-bit data bus, 16-bit address bus, with 8080 compatibility), and 16032 (32-bit internal data bus, 23-bit address bus). The 8080 code compatibility of the two lower microprocessors is achieved by the CPU having a dual instruction set, and a 'native' mode of operation and an 8080 emulation mode. Mixed mode operation is possible, allowing 8080 code to be gradually upgraded by supplementing it with native 16000 family code. The native code is upward compatible with the other microprocessors in the family. Supporting the three CPUs are two slave microprocessors, a memory-management unit (MMU) and a floating-point unit (FPU), and a range of interface devices, such as DMA controllers, clock generators, interrupt control units and bus arbiters.

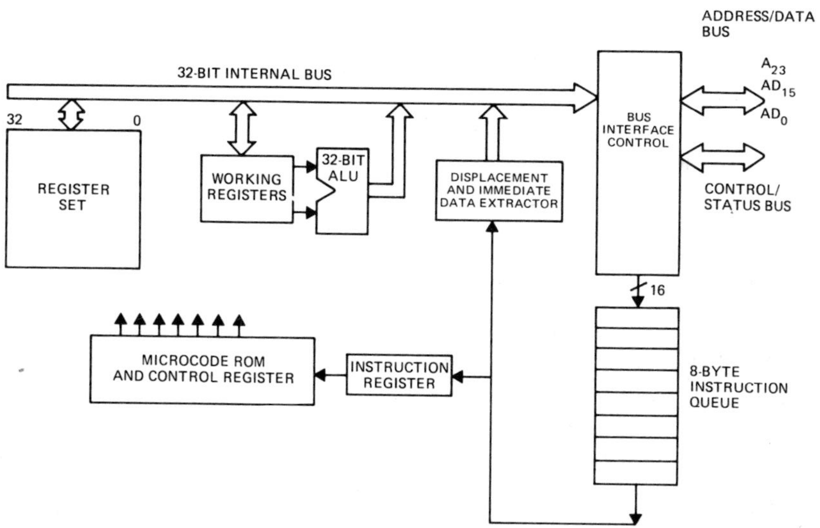

Fig. 4.28 NS16032 architecture.

The CPU block diagram for the NS16032, the top of the range microprocessor, is shown in fig. 4.28. It is microprogrammed, and uses an 8-byte instruction queue and a preprocessor which partly decodes instructions before applying them to the microcode ROM. The internal paths of the CPU are 32-bits wide, as is the arithmetic and logic unit and the register set. The microprocessor occupies a 48-pin package with the low 16 bits of the address bus multiplexed with the data bus AD0-AD15, leaving dedicated pins for the rest of the address bus, A16-A23. Demultiplexing is performed using an address strobe signal $\overline{ADS}$, and bus timing is controlled by data direction in ($\overline{DDIN}$), high byte enable ($\overline{HBE}$) and data strobe ($\overline{DS}$) (data strobe is multiplexed with a float command $\overline{FLT}$, used in conjunction with the slave processor signal $\overline{AT}/\overline{SPC}$). Timing is shown in fig. 4.29. The bus is a synchronous one which possesses a RDY input to stretch bus cycles if required by slow devices and program flow status $\overline{PFS}$ to identify the start of an instruction execution. Bus cycles are identified by four status signals ST0-ST3, detailed in table 4.10.

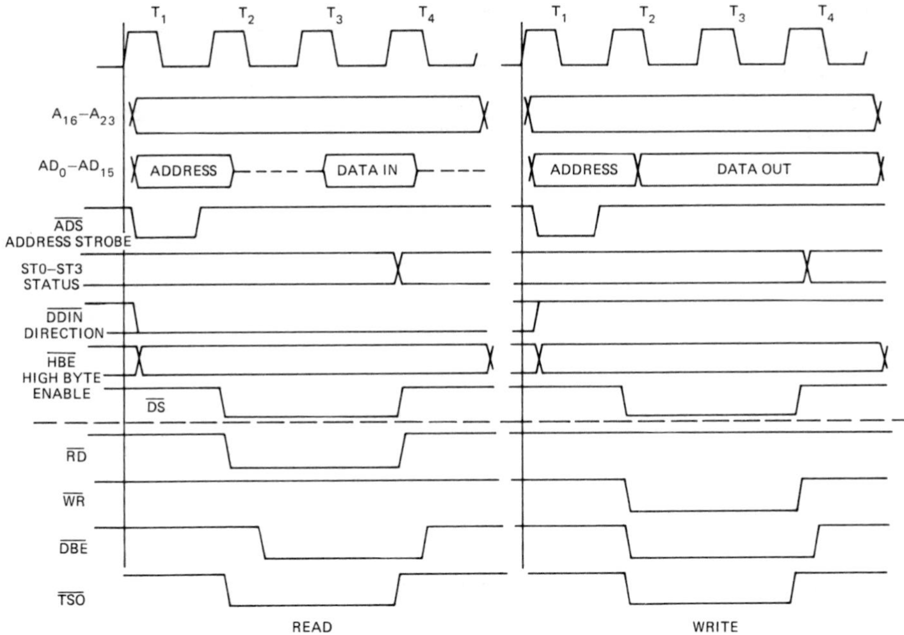

Fig. 4.29 NS16032 bus timing.

Note that separate bus cycles are identified for cascaded or master interrupt controller, and for slave microprocessor interaction. Non-sequential instruction fetch is asserted when the CPU is executing the first instruction fetch after the instruction queue has been cleared as a result of a transfer of program control (e.g. by jump or branch, interrupt or trap). Read for effective address calculation means that the CPU is reading addressing information from memory, as when memory relative or external addressing modes (see later) are used.

DMA cycles are accommodated using $\overline{HOLD}$, $\overline{HLDA}$ (acknowledge), the bus is locked for indivisible operations using $\overline{ILO}$ (interlocked operation).

The register set of the 16032 is shown in detail in fig. 4.30. Eight general-purpose registers, each of 32 bits, are available, as well as a number of specific address pointer registers. The familiar ones are the program counter, and the user

(SPI) and interrupt (SPO) stack pointers. The others are rather special, and contribute to some of the flexible addressing modes of the microprocessor; the frame pointer is used to access parameters and local variables on the stack, and is used in conjunction with the user stack pointer. When a block of data is stored on the stack, SP points to the top of the stack, and FP points to the address which holds the previous FP value, providing a linked list of 'frames', as in the Micro Nova. The static base (SB) register points to the global variables of a software module (to provide a mechanism for relocatable variables), while INTBASE provides a mechanism for relocating the dispatch table for interrupts and traps. The 32-bit microprocessor status and module register has a high word (16 bits) of flags (accessible in both CPU modes) and other status bits (mode switch, trace, stackpointer select and interrupt enable) accessible only in privileged mode. The low word (16 bits) holds the address of the module descriptor of the currently executing process which, since the MOD part of the register is only 16 bits long, must lie in the first 64 kbytes of memory. There is a final register, the configuration CFG register, which records the presence of external devices. It has four bits, labelled C, M, F, I, with meanings

C Custom slave microprocessor present
M Memory management unit present
F Floating point unit present
I External interrupt control unit present

This register can only be referenced in privileged mode during system initialisation following RESET.

Table 4.10 Bus cycle identification

ST3	ST2	ST1	ST0	Bus cycle
0	0	0	0	Idle, bus not in use.
0	0	0	1	Idle, WAIT instruction.
0	0	1	0	(Reserved)
0	0	1	1	Idle, waiting for slave microprocessor
0	1	0	0	Master interrupt acknowledge
0	1	0	1	Cascaded interrupt acknowledge
0	1	1	0	Master end of interrupt
0	1	1	1	Cascaded end of interrupt
1	0	0	0	Sequential instruction fetch
1	0	0	1	Non-sequential instruction fetch
1	0	1	0	Data transfer
1	0	1	1	Read read-modify-write cycle
1	1	0	0	Read for effective address
1	1	0	1	Transfer slave operand
1	1	1	0	Read slave status word
1	1	1	1	Broadcast slave ID

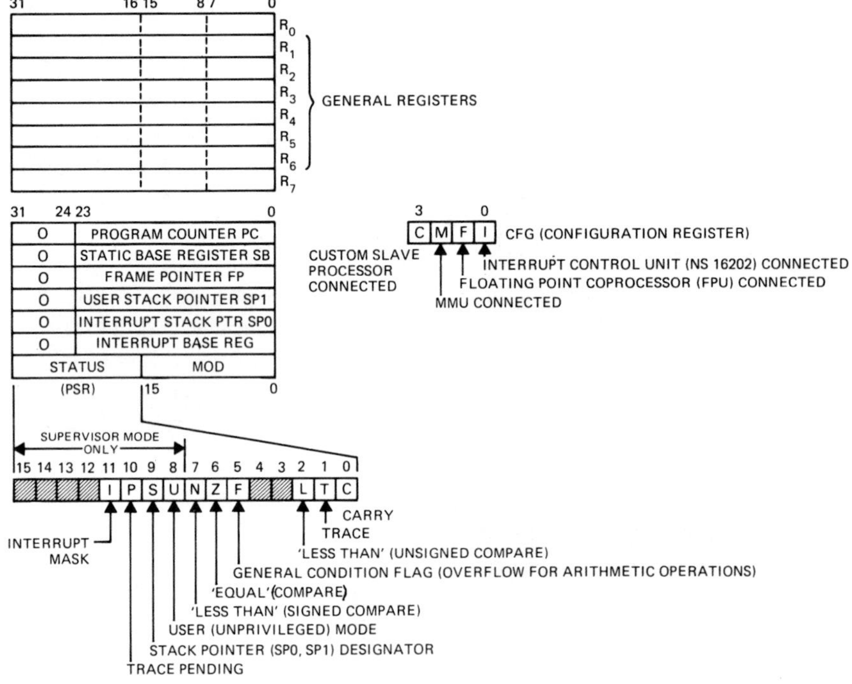

Fig. 4.30 16032 register set.

The interrupt structure of the 16032 is complicated by its use of the interrupt base register INTBASE, which allows the table of interrupt service routine addresses (dispatch table) to be located anywhere in memory. Relative to INTBASE are all the interrupts and traps, as well as the cascade addresses, shown in table 4.11. Non-maskable interrupts are generated at microprocessor pin $\overline{\text{NMI}}$, while maskable interrupts use $\overline{\text{INT}}$. $\overline{\text{INT}}$ may be configured using the configuration register CFG to be either non-vectored (NVI), where there is no external interrupt controller, or vectored, where external circuitry will supply an 8-bit vector number during an interrupt acknowledge cycle. The interrupt, if vectored, may be cascaded (multiple controllers (ICUs) for a possible 256 interrupts) or non-cascaded (single ICU). When multiple ICUs are used, the entries in the cascade address table point to the 16-entry vector registers of each ICU. The interrupt vectors are used to point to entries in the dispatch table, which contain a 32-bit descriptor for the interrupt process. This breaks down into a 16-bit offset and a 16-bit module number. The module number is put into the MOD register which points to an entry in the module table, a data area which provides, for each defined software module, values of static base pointer, link base pointer and program base pointer. The program base pointer is added to the 16-bit offset to give the entry point of the interrupt routine.

Table 4.11 Interrupt dispatch table

Location		Use
	I-16	Cascade address 0
	•	•
	•	•
	•	•
	I-1	Cascade address 15
INTBASE	I	NVI (non-vectored interrupt)
	I+1	NMI (non-maskable interrupt)
	I+2	ABT (abort trap)
	I+3	FPU (FP trap)
	I+4	ILL (illegal instruction trap)
	I+5	SVC (supervisor call trap)
	I+6	DVZ (divide by zero trap)
	I+7	FLG (flag trap)
	I+8	BPT (breakpoint trap)
	I+9	TRC (trace trap)
	I+10	UND (undefined instruction trap)
I+11-15		(Reserved)
	I+16	)
	•	) Vectored interrupts
	•	)

The static base pointer value is put into the SB register, and the link base pointer to address a link table for shared variables. The procedure for interrupt/trap execution and return is illustrated in fig. 4.31. Generally, the sequence of operations is:

(a) Copy program status register (PSR) and set supervisor bit. Possible adjustment of PC, SP.
(b) Save PSR on interrupt stack (but not MOD register).
(c) Acquire vector from data bus or by default.
(d) Use vector to acquire new environment (SB, PB, MOD register and link base pointer).
(e) Save MOD reg, PC on interrupt stack.

The flexibility of the approach makes it a very attractive one, making high-level language supervisor calls and interrupt routines easy to handle.

The slave microprocessors of the 16032 are very closely tied in with the main CPU, and rely not just on the CPUs bus timing signals, but also specially generated status signals which define a variety of slave microprocessor operations. They are described more fully in chapter 5.

The instruction set of the 16032 is notable for its wide range of addressing modes, all accommodating a 24-bit address field, which, like the MC68000, is a linear (non-segmented) one. It is useful to list the modes here to compare them with the three microprocessors discussed in chapter 6:

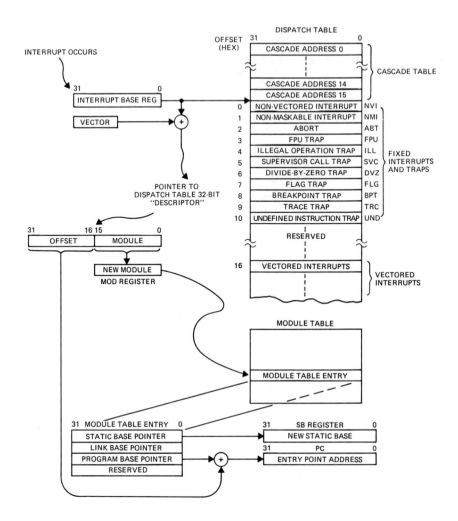

Fig. 4.31 NS16032 interrupt and trap execution.

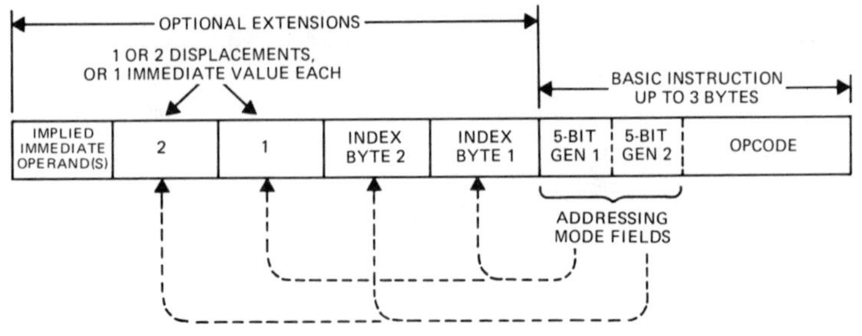

Fig. 4.32 NS16032 instruction format.

(a) Register: contains operand.
(b) Register relative: sum of register contents and displacement gives operand address.
(c) Memory space: register relative using one of PL, SP, SE, or FP.
(d) Memory relative: contents of location addressed by SP, SB or FP added to a displacement to give operand address.
(e) Immediate: operand contained in instruction.
(f) Absolute: address specified by displacement field in instruction.
(g) External: contents of specified link table address added to displacement gives address of operand.
(h) Scaled index: applied as an option on any other addressing mode. The effective address is calculated normally and then added to the contents of a specified register, multiplied by 1, 2, 4 or 8.

A typical instruction format is shown in fig. 4.32. One or two of the addressing modes detailed above may be specified (one per operand) and each may be indexed using mode (h) and have a displacement added to it. Coupled with the adoption of program modules associated with a module descriptor giving BP and program base (PB) values, as well as a link table address value, which points to a link table, used for sharing variables and transferring control between modules, the flexibility of these addressing modes and instruction format makes for a very sophisticated microprocessor indeed. The instruction set itself matches the sophistication of the architecture, extending standard moves and arithmetic instructions, allowing array manipulation, and very comprehensive string handling (comparison, translation, matching) and specific instructions reserved for the existing slave microprocessors (MMU, FPU) and general ones of custom slave microprocessors.

4.6 General comments

The 16-bit microprocessor, a relatively new product, and itself a great advance on the previous 8-bit designs, has itself evolved in its short lifetime. This chapter, describing microprocessors arranged chronologically by date of introduction, charts this progress. The concepts of large address range, segmentation, bus lock and semaphores, large interrupt vector tables, comprehensive addressing modes, user/system modes and others have become commonplace, though a little strange, perhaps, to the 8-bit designer. They are now being joined by the specific high-level language support of link address and base address pointers and added coprocessors and slave microprocessors. It is worth bearing in mind that the introduction time for putting a new device into equipment has been lengthening, and it is only by good software support that implementers can hope to keep pace with the rate of release of new CPU products.

CHAPTER 5
Interfacing

5.1 Introduction

From an interfacing point of view, at the electrical level, 16-bit microprocessors are little different from their 8-bit predecessors; they are faster, of course, with clock rates almost an order of magnitude higher than some 8-bit devices, and they may adopt different local bus conventions. The philosophy, however, has changed little, with most interfaces still needing address, data and control information in the form of both timing and directional information. What has changed in the 16-bit world is the complexity of the devices added to the CPU, and the sophistication of the system or backplane bus it is asked to support.

As an example, take semiconductor random-access memory. To take full advantage of the addressing range of most modern 16-bit microprocessors, memories must be constructed which are comparable in size with the largest mainframe computer memories of just a short while ago. Invariably, dynamic RAM will be used to ensure that physical size and power requirements are kept down, and 64K bit RAMs are in regular use. A large dynamic memory with many integrated RAMs requires a considerable amount of support, needing refresh circuitry which will resolve problems of CPU access contention, and circuitry to provide error detection and correction (EDC). Although semiconductor fabrication process improvements have reduced the alpha particle soft error rate in large memories to manageable proportions, it is nevertheless still present, and sufficient to cause unacceptably frequent errors in very large memory systems. Mainframe manufacturers have long built memories with extra error checking bits built in to each word, extending its length to accommodate these bits, and it is now necessary to provide EDC with large microprocessor memories. With both of these dynamic memory requirements in mind, many manufacturers are providing some integrated circuits which will provide automatic refresh and address multiplexing (most dynamic memories are 16-pin devices, with multiplexed row and column addresses) while interfacing to specific microprocessor buses, and others which will provide EDC. Memory management units, which provide address translation and other facilities between CPU pins and memory, complete the picture. With the increase in size of main memory, bulk storage devices have proportionally increased in storage capacity, with the advent of double and quadruple density diskettes, and the introduction of mini-Winchester (hard) disks. Controllers to interface sophisticated storage devices are also available, as are the DMA (direct memory access) controllers needed to achieve the data transfer rates required.

Adding functions to the basic CPU has been a fruitful area of development, with the introduction of coprocessors or slave microprocessors, of equal complexity to the main CPU, providing autonomous input-output channels, memory management, or floating-point arithmetic. With coprocessors, and in other multiple microprocessor systems, devices such as bus arbiters are necessary, to resolve any contention for use of the system bus. Communications is another area of crucial importance for 16-bit microprocessors, and interfaces in this area have kept pace with developments – not only IEEE-488 general-purpose interface bus (GPIB), but HDLC/SDLC (synchronous data link control), X25 (packet switching standard) and Ethernet are all supported as well as the DES (data encryption standard) algorithm. Lastly, intelligent interfaces (universal peripheral interfaces) based on 8-bit single-chip computers provide flexibility. Of course, virtually all 16-bit microprocessors have been designed to interface simply to all the straightforward interfaces (parallel, serial, timers) designed for their 8-bit predecessors.

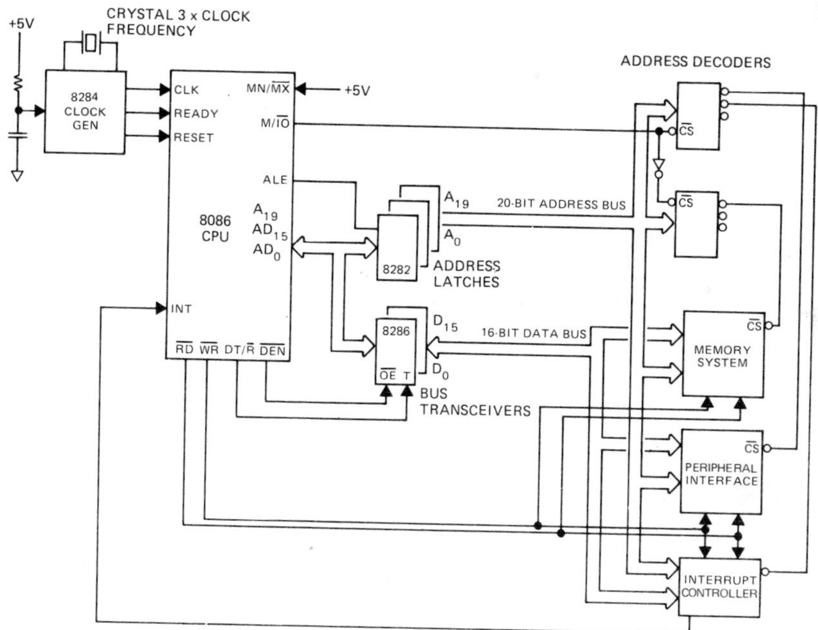

Fig. 5.1 Minimum-mode 8086 system.

5.2 Simple interfaces[1-6]

The three microprocessors concentrated upon in the previous chapter all have signals or modes to make interfacing to standard 8-bit interface parts easy. The 8086, for instance, in minimum mode, generates an equivalent set of control signals to the 8085 (multiplexed address and data, ALE, IO/$\overline{\text{M}}$ and $\overline{\text{RD}}$ and $\overline{\text{WR}}$ can be derived from $\overline{\text{WR}}$, DT/$\overline{\text{R}}$ and $\overline{\text{DEN}}$). A simple minimum mode system is

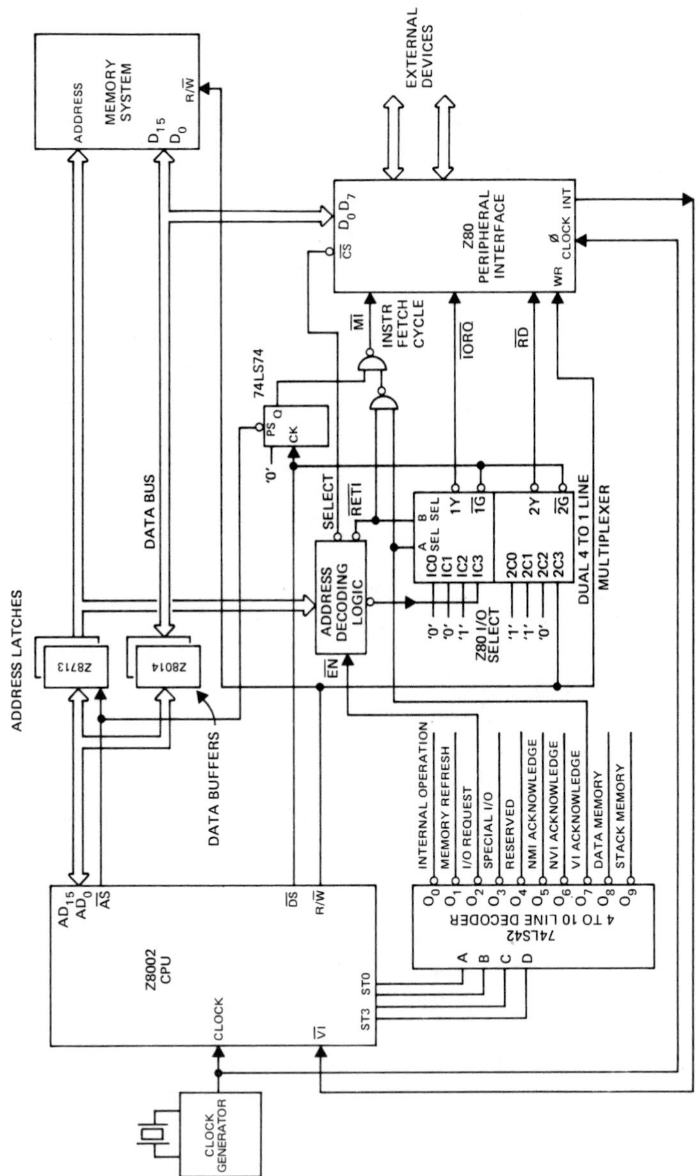

Fig. 5.2 Z8002 simple system (with logic to interface Z80 I/O devices).

shown in fig. 5.1. The Z8000 is a little more tricky to interface to Z80 devices, since many of these require $\overline{\text{MI}}$ (instruction fetch), $\overline{\text{IORQ}}$, and $\overline{\text{RD}}$. Logic necessary to do the conversion is detailed in fig. 5.2, including address demultiplexing and status signal decoding, and wait state generation. The MC68000 uses a signal VPA (valid peripheral address) to give compatibility with 6800 devices. If a 6800 8-bit device returns VPA when its address decoder receives a suitable address, the 68000 will generate 6800 signals E (which it does continuously) and VMA (valid memory address) with the correct timing, but inverted in logic (6800 VMA is active-high, 68000 VMA is active low). These signals may be used by the 6800 device with a minimum of additional logic. Interrupts may be generated using autovectoring (see section 4.4.4, 68000 exceptions). A simple system is shown in fig. 5.3.

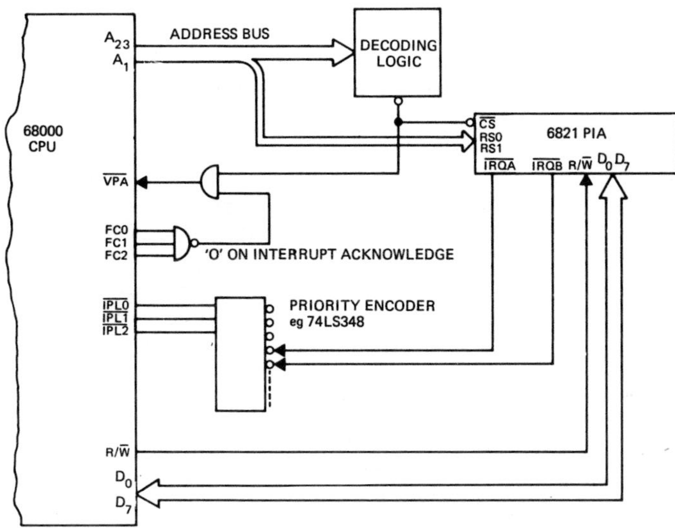

Fig. 5.3 Interfacing to 6800 devices.

5.3 Memory interfaces

The most significant memory device in current use is the dynamic memory, which combines high capacity with low power consumption, but requires special drive circuitry to handle its timing and address signals. Any memory in the megabyte range is likely to use the 64K bit RAM, the largest currently available. The principle of dynamic memory is simple – storage of data is by charge stored on a transistor gate capacitance at each node of an XY matrix of select lines. The multibit array is in the form of a matrix of rows and columns of storage cells, and normally row and column addresses are multiplexed onto the same address pins, to keep the package size to a 16-pin dual-in-line device. The memory will be refreshed a row or a column of cells at a time simply by applying the row or column address and corresponding strobe signal $\overline{\text{RAS}}$ or $\overline{\text{CAS}}$. Since there are 128 rows in many designs, 128 refresh cycles are necessary every 2 ms (total refresh interval) for row refresh. It is usual for these cycles to be distributed through the 2 ms interval; the timing of a particular device (the Motorola 6665) is shown in fig. 5.4. From fig. 5.4(a) and (b), it may be seen that the memory requires a multiplexed 16-bit address (8 upper, 8 lower), with row address applied first, using row address strobe ($\overline{\text{RAS}}$) to clock it into the RAM, and keeping $\overline{\text{RAS}}$ asserted while changing to column address, and asserting column address strobe $\overline{\text{CAS}}$, overlapping with $\overline{\text{RAS}}$. The single R/$\overline{\text{W}}$ line defines the operation, and data must be synchronised to $\overline{\text{CAS}}$ if a write, or, if a read, data appears after a suitable access time following the assertion of $\overline{\text{CAS}}$, and disappears from the bus when $\overline{\text{CAS}}$ is removed. There is an additional timing requirement on $\overline{\text{RAS}}$ – it may be removed before $\overline{\text{CAS}}$ and must not be reasserted for a new cycle until after a minimum precharge time (to allow the memory to be set up to operate on the next cycle). Refresh, shown in fig. 5.4(c), is simple in its timing compared with read and write!

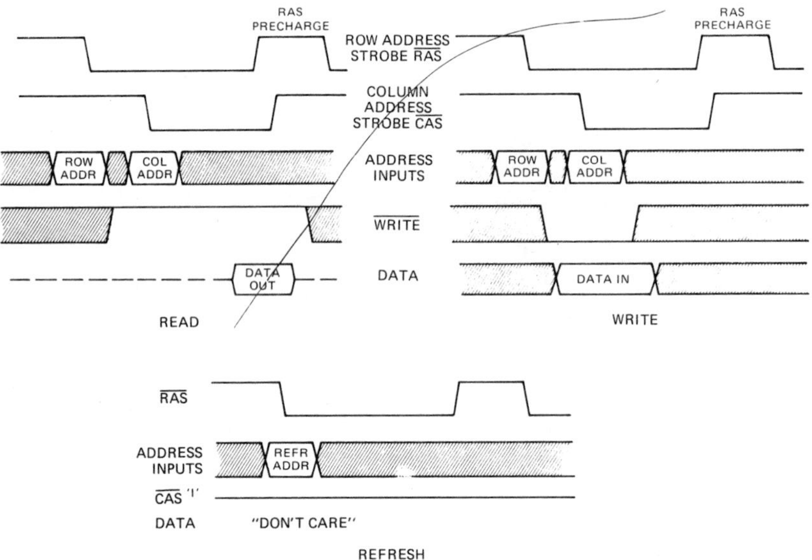

Fig. 5.4 MCM6664 64K bit dynamic RAM timing: (a) read, (b) write, (c) refresh.

The dynamic RAM controller must buffer the memory from the microprocessor address bus, and multiplex the addresses, generate $\overline{\text{CAS}}$ and $\overline{\text{RAS}}$ and refresh cycles, and must maintain a counter to keep track of refresh addresses. In addition, there must be an arbiter on chip to resolve contentions between a refresh operation and the CPU requiring use of the memory.

Error detection and correction requires that more information is stored in the memory array than is actually required, and the additional check bits may be used to correct the wanted ones.

5.3.1 DYNAMIC RAM INTERFACES

The problems with dynamic RAM fall into three categories:

(a) Address multiplexing and $\overline{RAS}$, $\overline{CAS}$ generation.

(b) Addressing banks of RAM using separate $\overline{RAS}$ signals (no chip select $\overline{CS}$ is available, but if only $\overline{CAS}$ is asserted, and not followed by $\overline{RAS}$, output buffers will not be activated).

(c) Refresh, which must be performed 128 times in 2 ms, or 256 times in 4 ms for a large memory, i.e. once every 16 μs, as a $\overline{RAS}$-only operation.

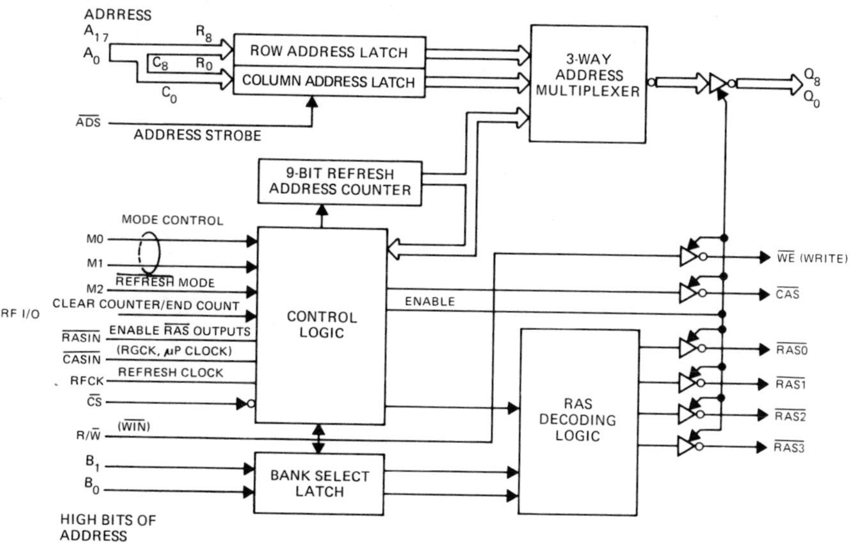

Fig. 5.5 Dynamic RAM controller (DP8409) to 256K.

A typical interface device is shown[7,8,9] in fig. 5.5. The address multiplexer may use as its source address either row or column address, latched using ALE or ADS from a CPU which uses multiplexed address/data buses, or the outputs of a 9-bit counter (allowing RAMs larger than the 64K RAM, such as the 256K ones which are likely to appear in quantity before too long). Bank select logic decodes a bank address input, and selects one $\overline{RAS}$ (out of four) which will be asserted during a normal read or write using $\overline{RAS}$-before-$\overline{CAS}$ RAM operation. During this operation, $\overline{CAS}$ and write enable $\overline{WE}$ are timed from control logic inside the device, using the address strobe and $\overline{RASIN}$, an input to the $\overline{RAS}$ decoder which initiates the cycle timing, starting from $\overline{RAS}$ and then multiplexing row address to column address and asserting $\overline{CAS}$.

Refreshing can occur in a number of ways. A convenient way of timing refreshes to a 16 μs period is to use a divider in the refresh controller which operates from the system clock and generates an output at the required refresh rate and indicates that a refresh is pending. With some microprocessors, bus cycles may be constructed so that there are well-defined times when the CPU is not using its bus (during instruction decoding or other internal operations) and provided these are frequent enough, refreshing can be performed in a 'hidden' manner during these periods. Another way of detecting when a hidden access is possible is to provide logic which will detect read and write strobes (signifying read and write operations) when $\overline{\text{CS}}$ on the memory controller is not asserted, i.e. read or write cycles to other devices, and to use $\overline{\text{RASIN}}$ in the absence of $\overline{\text{CS}}$ to generate refresh $\overline{\text{RAS}}$ without $\overline{\text{CAS}}$. Naturally, the refresh counter must be incremented every time a refresh cycle is performed.

If hidden refreshing has not occurred when the refresh pending signal occurs, forced refreshing must be initiated, using either a bus request-grant sequence, a HOLD/HOLDA sequence, or, if asynchronous bus access is available, allowing the acknowledgement signal of a bus transfer to be delayed if a bus access request and refresh cycle coincide.

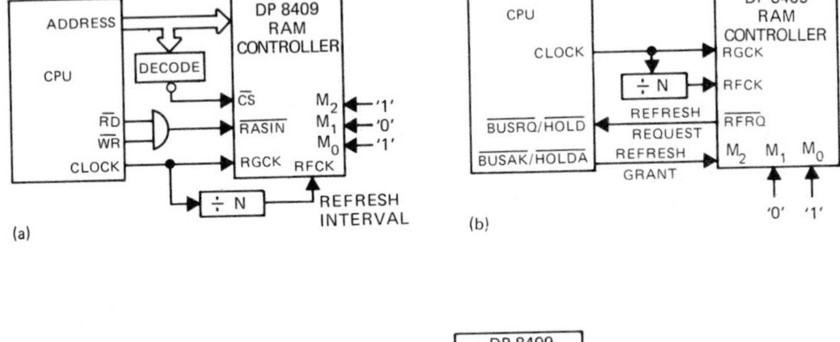

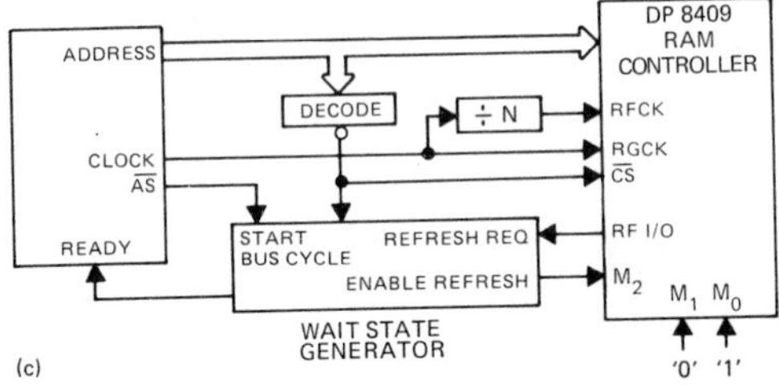

Fig. 5.6 8409 refresh techniques: (a) hidden refresh (while read or write access to other part of system, e.g. ROM), (b) forced refresh by halting the CPU, (c) refreshing using wait states.

A refresh request output and refresh grant input may be provided in the controller logic for forced refresh cycles. The final possibility is burst refresh, where all 128 or 256 refresh cycles are performed together in a fast burst, every 2 ms, and the microprocessor held up while this occurs. Where CPU timing is critical, the 30 μs or so taken for burst refresh may be unacceptably long. Fig. 5.6 illustrates refreshing techniques. Where hidden refresh is backed up by forced refresh if necessary, DMA may be performed with the RAM controller communicating with the DMA controller rather than the microprocessor.

5.3.2 ERROR DETECTION AND CORRECTION (EDC)

To provide EDC capability on memory[10–11], extra bits must be added to each stored word, so that an indication is provided that an error has occurred, and of its bit position in the word. Since binary signals can only be '0' or '1', identifying the bit position of an error is sufficient to correct it. Logic on the input of a memory array must take the incoming data for an addressed location and generate these extra bits which will be stored with the data, and logic on the outputs must check these bits against and correct the data bits as necessary. A block diagram of the structure of an error-correcting memory is shown in fig. 5.7. Design of the check bits so that they correct an optimum number of errors, making an efficient correction scheme, is a problem which has occurred in other areas of technology, notably digital communications, and Hamming code is a standard technique which has been used for many years, and is now being applied to memory design.

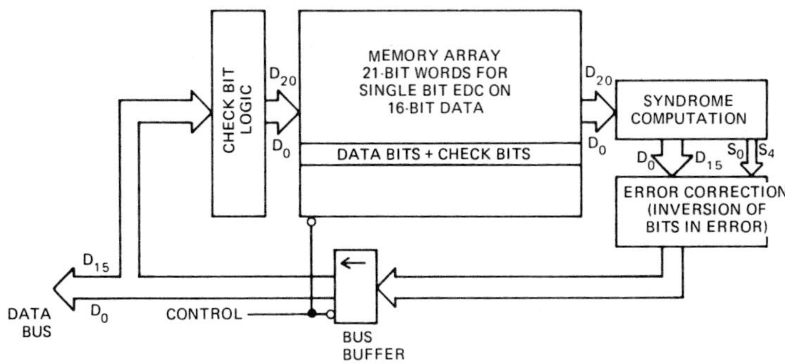

Fig. 5.7 Error-correcting memory structure.

In Hamming code, check bits are arranged which are the modulo-2 sum (exclusive-OR) of a number of data bits, and the secret of the code's efficiency lies in its choice of which data bits are checked by each check or parity bit. An example of an 8-bit word is useful, since practical memory systems are often byte-oriented. Four check bits are added to each 8-bit data word, so the physical memory is 12-bits wide. To illustrate the technique, it is useful to write the 12-bit word with check bits distributed:

Data word	D7 D6 D5 D4 D3 D2 D1 D0
12-bit stored word (Cs are check bits)	D7 D6 D5 D4 C3 D3 D2 D1 C2 D0 C1 C0

Then $C0 = D0 \oplus D1 \oplus D3 \oplus D4 \oplus D6$
$C1 = D0 \oplus D2 \oplus D3 \oplus D5 \oplus D6$
$C2 = D1 \oplus D2 \oplus D3 \oplus D7$
$C3 = D4 \oplus D5 \oplus D6 \oplus D7$

Obviously, it is up to the system designer whether the physical layout of each memory word is like this, but the layout illustrates the way the code progresses in blocks of data which are successive powers of two in the number of consecutive bits involved, and the spacing, if the check bit itself is included. Thus C2 checks groups of $2^2 = 4$ bits grouped C2 D1 D2 D3, D7 (D8 D9 D10), (D15 D16 D17 D18), etc. This progression means that while eight data bits need four check bits, thirty-two data bits need only six check bits to give the same measure of protection, in this case, single error correction. The set of four check bits C3 C2 C1 C0 is stored with the data bits. When encoded data is read from the memory, a new set of check bits can be calculated, C3′ C2′ C1′ C0′, and compared with the first (original) one, by modulo-2 addition. If they are identical, the result should be zero. If there is an error the result will form a syndrome word S3 S2 S1 S0, which indicates the bit position of the error. A numerical example will clarify the procedure:

	D7	D6	D5	D4	D3	D2	D1	D0
Data	0	0	1	0	1	0	1	0

Check bits

$$C0 = 0 \oplus 1 \oplus 1 \oplus 0 \oplus 0 = 0$$
$$C1 = 0 \oplus 0 \oplus 1 \oplus 1 \oplus 0 = 0$$
$$C2 = 1 \oplus 0 \oplus 1 \oplus 0 = 0$$
$$C3 = 0 \oplus 1 \oplus 0 \oplus 0 = 1$$

The word transmitted will be

B12	B11	B10	B9	B8	B7	B6	B5	B4	B3	B2	B1
0	0	1	0	1	1	0	1	0	0	0	0

Suppose an error occurs in bit position B5 (D1), so that the word received on memory access is 0 0 1 0 1 1 0 0 0 0 0 0. When the check bits are calculated

$$C0' = 0 \oplus 0 \oplus 1 \oplus 0 \oplus 0 = 1$$
$$C1' = 0 \oplus 0 \oplus 1 \oplus 1 \oplus 0 = 0$$
$$C2' = 0 \oplus 0 \oplus 1 \oplus 0 = 1$$
$$C3' = 0 \oplus 1 \oplus 0 \oplus 0 = 1$$

When the syndrome is computed S0 = 1, S1 = 0, S2 = 1, S3 = 0 indicating the position in error S3 S2 S1 S0 = 0 1 0 1 = B5. If this bit in the received word is inverted, a correction will have been made. Fig. 5.8 shows circuitry for doing this automatically.

5.4 Memory management devices

As microprocessor direct addressing ranges increase, and memory systems keep pace by becoming larger, the simple linear addressing techniques used by 8-bit microprocessors are no longer efficient or flexible enough in the way in which they permit memory space to be used. Linear addressing, as its name implies, means that an effective (or logical) address used by a program for memory access will correspond directly with a physical memory address, and indeed, the two addresses will often be numerically the same. Such a simple scheme has drawbacks which become evident as system complexity increases; for instance, any shared addresses referred by different programs must be determined at assembly or load time, and the location of the shared addresses in the logical

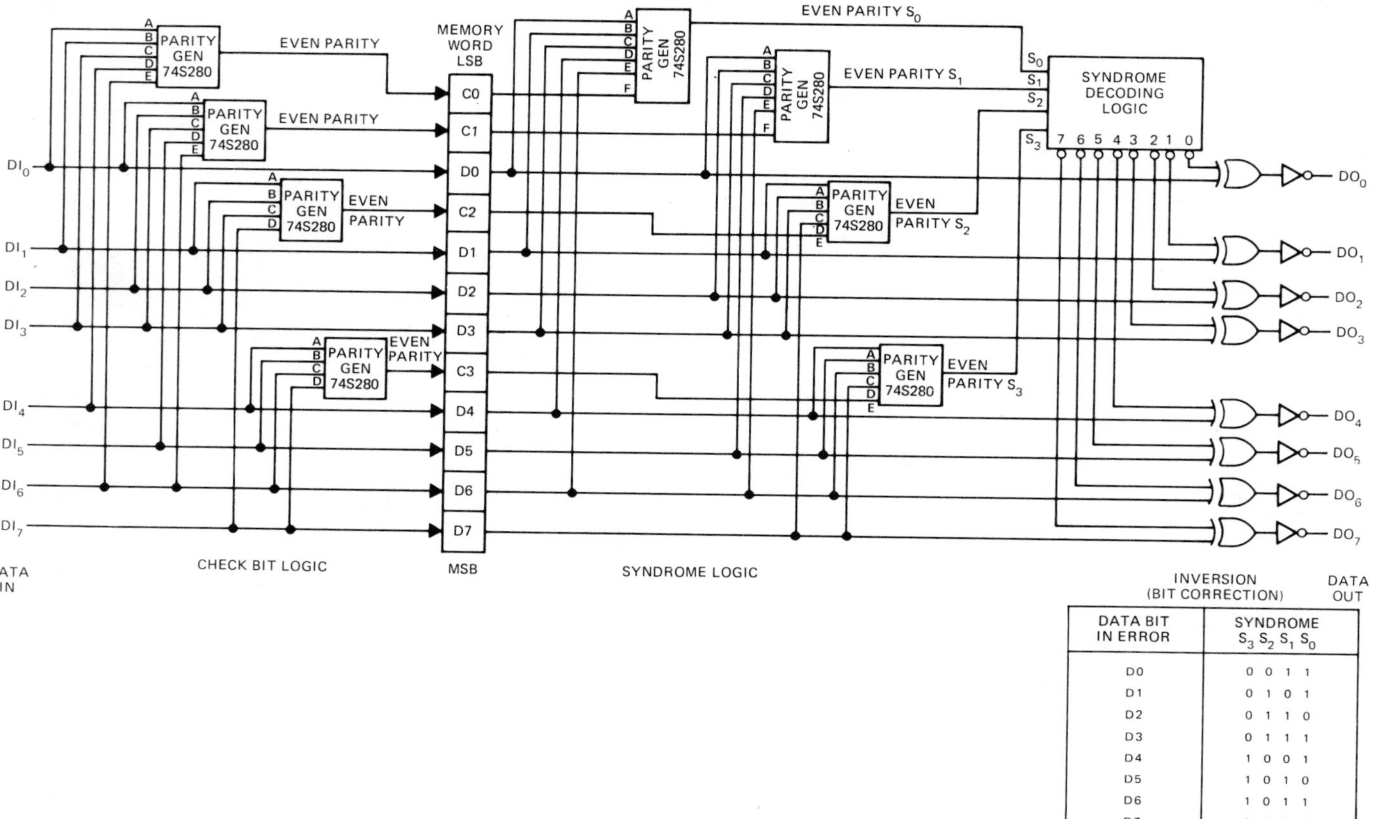

DATA BIT IN ERROR	SYNDROME S_3 S_2 S_1 S_0
D0	0 0 1 1
D1	0 1 0 1
D2	0 1 1 0
D3	0 1 1 1
D4	1 0 0 1
D5	1 0 1 0
D6	1 0 1 1
D7	1 1 0 0

Fig. 5.8 Automatic error correction circuitry.

memory space (addressed by the program) and the physical memory space will be fixed. Loading multiple programs may also present a problem: the logical addresses occupied by a program must be contiguous, and because of the direct relationship, the physical memory addresses must also be contiguous. When programs are loaded and deleted, it is difficult to avoid memory fragmentation, since program and other object sizes vary (an object, in this context, is any memory structure, whether a program, data structure, or stack). Consequently, any unused memory areas created by deletion of an object, and situated between two currently resident objects, may not be compatible in size with any new object which is to be allocated memory, and therefore remain unused. In an extreme case, the total amount of unused memory may be enough to accommodate a new program, but cannot be allocated to that program because it is fragmented into areas that are individually too small. If the relationship between logical and physical addresses can be changed to a more complex one, such problems need not arise, since a contiguous logical memory space may be related to a fragmented physical one.

The major problems with linear addressing may be summarised as follows:

(a) *Memory protection*. With a linear addressing scheme, it is difficult to provide protection against erroneous memory accesses, which may occur as a result of out-of-bounds array addressing, stack overflow into program or data areas, or poor control of shared memory areas accessed by different programs. The usual way of providing protection is to control all memory accesses by software. Instead of using the CPU addressing modes and stack manipulation instructions directly, a program will instead call a subroutine which performs the required function, but first checks the validity of any address supplied against some preset limits and conditions. Such an approach imposes a heavy software overhead (both in memory space and in time) upon any conceptually simple memory access.

(b) *Dynamic relocation*. Any system running different tasks under some operating system must face the problem of relocation. To allow new tasks to become resident in memory, it must be possible to locate them in any available free memory space, and it is desirable to avoid memory fragmentation such as that described earlier. A simple system may use a relocating loader for this task, but such a utility program will only give *static relocation* facilities. Relocation at load time does overcome some of the system management problems associated with multiple-task systems, but is a little inflexible. It is not possible, for instance, for a task to change its location after load time, so that it cannot be moved in response, say, to a stack or other object requiring memory space in the same area. Dynamic relocation will allow a task or object to be moved after load time, and requires a mechanism which will determine actual addresses at run time. Responsibility for relocation may reside either with the task itself ('user-controlled relocation') and use a form of based addressing, or with the system ('system-controlled relocation') and use a memory-mapping hardware device which performs address translation.

(c) *Shared objects.* If an object is to be shared by a number of tasks (e.g. some form of data structure or array), the address of the object must be known to all of the tasks; any relocation of this object must be accompanied by some means of communicating the new address to the tasks.

(d) *Separation of user and system resources.* While a microprocessor mode switch will provide some separation of user and system functions and allow certain instructions to be made privileged, there is not normally a distinction drawn between user and system memory address spaces. Thus a linear addressing scheme may allow a user program to alter system RAM storage areas, with disastrous results. This problem is another aspect of the memory protection one.

All of these problems may be overcome by clever operating system software, and by defining very specific ways in which user programs must access memory (e.g. via a subroutine 'software envelope' which checks validity of access), but program errors may cause problems, and a programmer is still able to bypass this mechanism, and address memory directly, if he chooses. A better way of enforcing memory protection, and of providing facilities to fulfil the other requirements, is to use a hardware address translation or memory management device, which will allow dynamic relocation of tasks by using address translation, and will check access validity[12–19].

5.4.1 MEMORY MANAGEMENT BY SEGMENTATION

The Z8001 is a good example of a CPU which segments memory. Any memory access by the CPU provides a 16-bit 'offset' address on the microprocessor's multiplexed address and data bus, and a 7-bit 'segment number' on appropriate pins SN0-SN6. Both are applied to the memory-management unit (MMU) which is part of the Z8000 family, and from the twenty-three input bits (the 'logical address' generated by the CPU), the MMU produces a 24-bit physical address, and provides access checks against a file of segment descriptor registers, which hold segment attributes (each Z8001 memory request is accompanied by status information which defines the request attributes; if the access check finds that these are incompatible with the addressed segment attributes, an attribute violation trap is invoked).

A block diagram of the MMU is shown in fig. 5.9. There are sixty-four 32-bit segment descriptor registers addressed by the segment number signals, each containing a 16-bit base address field, an 8-bit limit field and an 8-bit attribute field. The seven bits of the segment number will, of course, address a potential 128 segment descriptors, so a single MMU contains half the possible range of segment descriptors ('upper range' or 'lower range'). The most significant bit of the segment number must match the range select input of the MMU. The base address field contains a 16-bit address which is shifted eight places left (multiplied by 256) before being added to the unshifted 16-bit offset address supplied by the CPU. The resulting 24-bit sum is used as the memory physical address. This implies that memory is divided into 256-byte blocks – the segment number specifies a 16-bit address which is then shifted to give a 24-bit address with a

256-byte increment between consecutive addresses, before being added to the 16-bit offset. The 8-bit limit field of the segment descriptor register defines the size of the segment as an integer multiple of 256 bytes, up to a maximum segment size of 64 kbytes. The size of a segment, when the segment descriptor register contains an integer *N*, will be 256 (*N* + 1) bytes. For a stack segment, defined by a bit in the attribute field of the segment descriptor register, the segment size is 64K – 256*N*. This part of the MMU handles address translation, allowing a 23-bit logical address issued by the CPU to be transformed into 24-bit physical addresses. The address translation ensures relocatability of any object in memory, and the operation, since it is carried out by hardware, is both fast and transparent to the user software (fig. 5.10).

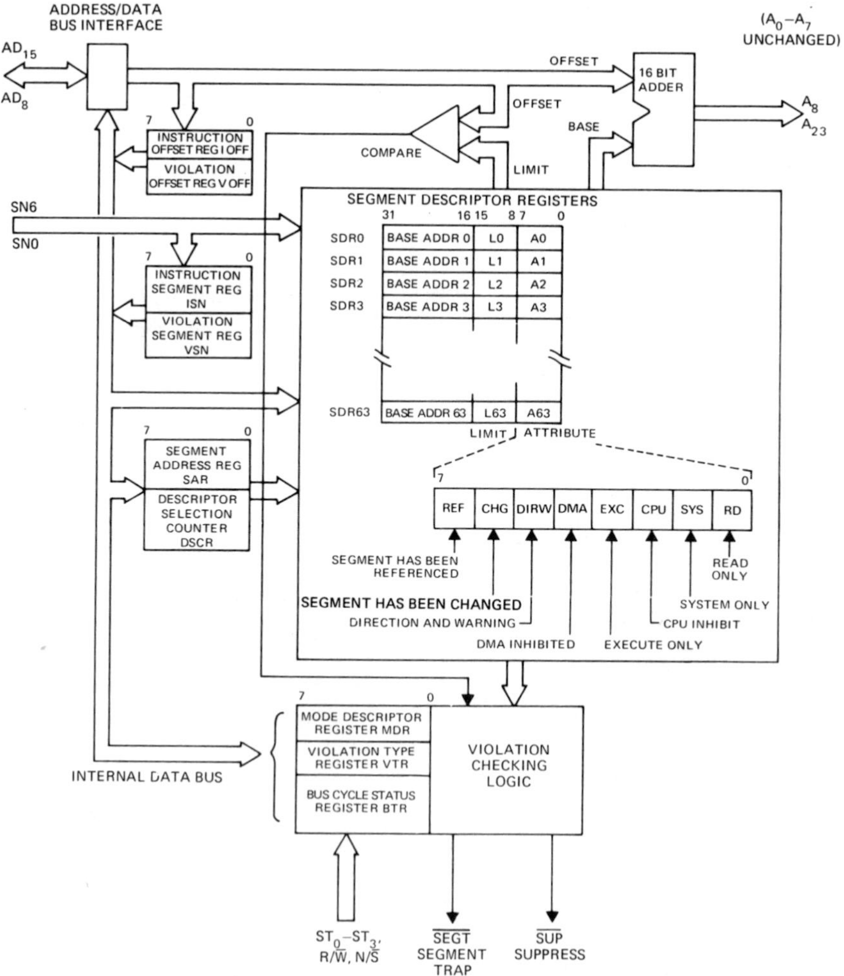

Fig. 5.9 Z8010 memory management unit (MMU).

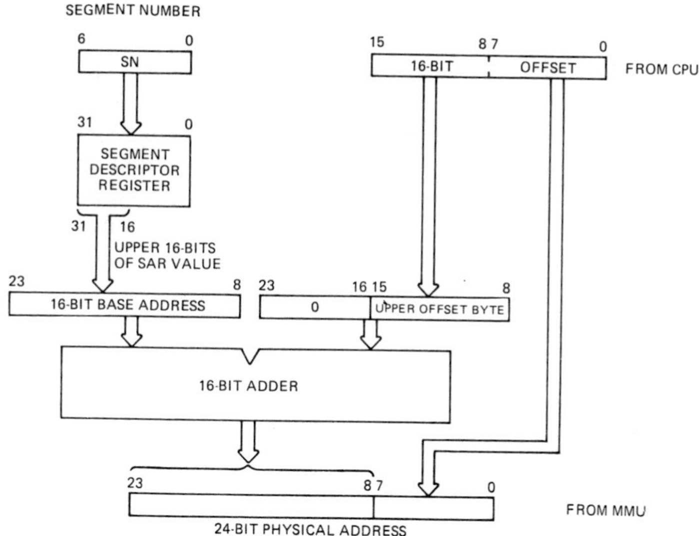

Fig. 5.10 Z8010 MMU address translation.

Like address translation, protection is carried out by segments. The segment attribute field of the descriptor provides eight single-bit flags used to control segment access. These are (least significant bit first):

RD Read only. Set to prevent segment with access.
SYS System mode access only.
CPUI CPU inhibit; the segment cannot be accessed by the CPU and the currently accessible process (though it may be accessible by DMA).
EXC Execute only. The segment may only be accessed during an instruction fetch cycle and is protected against access during any other cycles.
DMAI DMA inhibit. Access only by the CPU.
DIRW Direction and warning. When this flag is set, segment memory locations are assumed to be organised in descending order (as a stack) and each segment write access is checked to see if it is within the last 256-byte block of the segment, indicating impending segment overflow. No action is generated to prevent the write, but a trap is generated if this situation occurs.
CHG Change flag. When set, it indicates that the segment has been altered, and it is set automatically during any valid write access.
REF Referenced. Set automatically during any valid (read or write) access.

The attribute bits of this field (RD, SYS, CPUI, EXC, DMAI) are used to provide memory access protection. The status information which appears on CPU pins ST0-ST3 during a bus cycle indicates the attributes of the memory request. The MMU compares the request attributes with the segment attributes and generates a trap if an attribute violation is present. The MMU output signal $\overline{\text{SEGT}}$ generates the trap directly via a specific pin on the CPU. If the violation is an access violation, the MMU will also generate a signal $\overline{\text{SUP}}$, which can be used to suppress the memory access. Used as an inhibit signal, $\overline{\text{SUP}}$ will prevent invalid memory write operations, and protect data from corruption. One exception to this action is where the segment is defined as a stack segment, growing towards lower memory locations – when the final 256-byte block is encountered, a trap is generated to allow the operating system to allocate more memory to the stack, but no $\overline{\text{SUP}}$ is generated, so that a PUSH cycle will not be inhibited, and no stack data lost.

As well as the file of segment descriptor registers, the MMU has a number of control and status registers. The three control registers allow mode selection and access to the segment descriptor registers. Two of the control registers perform the latter function; the segment descriptor address register (SAR), which contains a 6-bit pointer to the segment descriptor register (DSCR), and the descriptor selection counter, which contains a 2-bit number which indicates which byte field is being accessed as follows:

00 High-order byte of base address field
01 Low-order byte of base address field
10 Limit field
11 Attribute field

The SAR has an autoincrementing feature so that a Z8000 block read or write may be used to access the descriptors. The mode register (MDR) contains a 3-bit MMU identification (ID) field which allows up to eight MMUs to be distinguished in a single system. During a segment trap acknowledge sequence, the ID field is decoded to drive a particular line of the high byte of the address/data bus as an identifier. The remaining 5 bits of the mode register are as follows:

MST Multiple segment table. This flag indicates that multiple segment tables are present in the system, in separate MMUs, and are invoked by either the system or the normal mode of the CPU.

NMS Normal mode select. Used in conjunction with MST. If MST is set, the N/$\overline{\text{S}}$ (normal/system mode indication output by the CPU) must match the logic level at the NMS input for the MMU to operate, and to translate addresses. If there is no match, the MMU outputs are taken to their tristate high-impedance condition, and remain there.

URS Upper range select. Used to indicate which range of segment descriptors is contained in the MMU. The most significant bit of the segment number issued by the CPU must match the URS for the MMU address translation to operate, otherwise the MMU outputs are taken to their tristate high-impedance condition.

TRNS Translate. This flag controls MMU operation directly. Depending upon the state of TRNS, the MMU can either translate logical addresses from the CPU into physical addresses for the memory, or pass through those logical addresses unchanged (and without attribute checking). When the logical addresses are passed through unchanged, the most significant byte of the physical address consists of a leading zero, followed by the 7-bit segment number.

MSEN Master enable. This flag allows the MMU to be disabled, when its outputs will go to their tristate high-impedance condition. It allows the use of multiple MMUs.

The status registers of the MMU may be read by the CPU when a trap occurs, and contain information relevant to the access violation that caused the trap. There are six 8-bit registers, one of which records the type of violation, while the other five contain the state of the CPU when the trap occurred, recorded as violation segment number, violation offset (upper 8 bits), instruction segment number, instruction offset (upper 8 bits), and bus cycle status (CPU status, mode $N/\overline{S}$, operation $R/\overline{W}$).

The violation type register records eight possible types of violation:

FATL Fatal condition flag, set when any other flag in the violation type register is set, and either a violation or a write warning occurs in normal mode (not set for a stack push warning in system mode).

SWW Secondary write warning. Set when a stack write into the last 256 bytes of a system stack segment occurs, and one of the other flags is set. Once set, subsequent similar warnings will not generate a trap.

PWW Primary write warning. Set when access is made to the last 256 bytes of a stack segment (DIRW flag set).

SLV Segment length violation. Set when the offset causes access to fall outside the segment.

EXCV Execute-only violation. Set when access to an EXC segment is made by other than an instruction fetch cycle.

CPUIV CPU inhibit violation.

SYSV System-mode violation. Attempted access to system segment in normal mode.

RDV Read-only violation.

The MMU is set up using special Z8000 I/O (SIO) commands. The Z8000 CPU, when it encounters one of these special commands, generates a normal I/O read or write cycle, but the accompanying status signals indicate the presence of an SIO instruction. The MMU, which accepts the Z8000 status signals, will automatically switch into command mode when it recognises the SIO code.

The facilities of this MMU have been covered in considerable detail to show the degree of sophistication that can be achieved by hardware within a single integrated circuit. The arrangement of memory into segments of variable size is the first obvious departure from a linear addressing scheme; the size increments of 256 bytes have been chosen to suit the degree of complexity of the MMU integrated circuit. The address translation system gives a completely flexible way of relating logical addresses to physical ones, and will allow support of 128 segments directly (using two MMUs), and more if several MMUs are connected in the system. These will then require more complex operating system support, since they must be selectively enabled and disabled. Any memory fragmentation can be completely hidden from the user, and dynamic relocation of objects within logical address space is easy, requiring just a change of segment descriptor register. Moreover, this process is controlled by the operating system, not by the user program. System-controlled relocation is inherently more powerful than user-controlled relocation, since the system may take all user requirements into account, especially access of shared programs or data, and a well-designed system will optimise its efficiency and avoid any conflicts between users. User-controlled relocation performed by the running program, by contrast, will only take local user requirements into account, and can lead to possible conflicts, and does not fully overcome the problem of shared objects.

Access checking using segment attributes is an ideal way to provide memory protection, and, performed by hardware, can operate within the CPU memory cycle timing, providing little or no degradation of speed, unlike a 'software envelope' protection scheme. The memory protection provided fulfils the basic requirements of protecting users against themselves (by allowing separate segments and attributes for code, data and user stack), and protecting the system against user programs. The method of attribute checking is especially useful for shared objects. Different programs may access them in different logical address spaces, and with different attributes. Thus a data structure may be made write accessible by one user program, and read-only by another. In addition, by providing warning signals for impending stack overflow, some potential security against stack failure is provided, allowing the operating system to allocate more memory before the situation becomes irrecoverable. It is worth noting, too, that the MMU for this particular (Z8000) microprocessor is itself protected, since it responds to special I/O instructions which set up its internal registers, and these can only be issued by the CPU when in system mode. Connection of the 8010 MMU in a Z8001 system is shown in fig. 5.11.

5.4.2 MEMORY MANAGEMENT BY PAGING

Closer to linear addressing, but still possessing the advantages of memory address translation and attribute checking, is paging. A paged memory system may be achieved by treating the uppermost bits of a linear address like a segment number, which indicates one of a large number of fixed-length blocks or pages of memory. While segments may be of arbitrary length quantised to some number of bytes and with a maximum size limited by offset length, a program in paged memory will simply be allocated a number of pages. Another difference between segmentation and paging lies in the way in which addresses are computed. With a paged scheme derived from a linear address, the bits used as an effective segment number cannot be used by an MMU until address calculation is complete, so it is likely that such a scheme will be slower than a segmented one, since it cannot achieve the overlap of MMU operation and CPU execution. On the other hand, an advantage which the paged scheme has over the segmented one is that the CPU can deal with objects of unlimited size without having to deal with problems of moving from one segment to another. With an inherently segmented MMU like the 8010, an object over 64 kbytes long needs a small amount of software to deal with it. The paged system, dealing with fixed-length pages making up the total required space, does not.

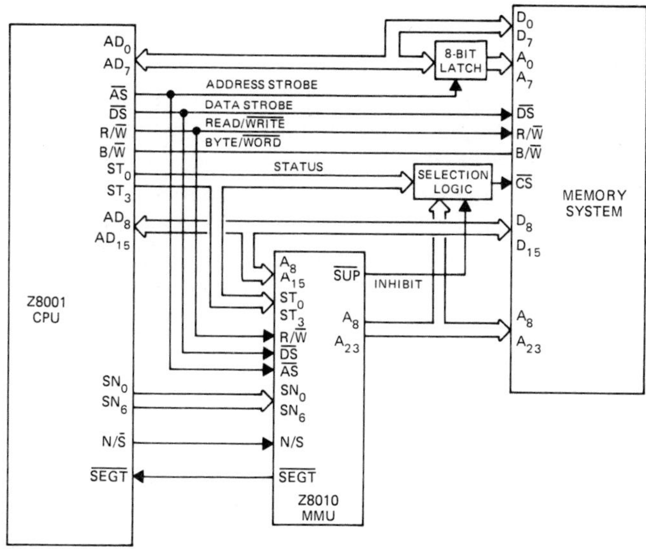

Fig. 5.11 Z8010 MMU in system.

The NS16082 memory management unit is a paged one, which further supports a memory concept usually confined to mainframe computers and large minicomputers: that of virtual memory. The idea of virtual memory is simple – the combination of main microprocessor memory and bulk storage devices is considered to be a single large storage space, and programs and other objects can occupy as much of it as required, without regard for the limitations of microprocessor main memory space. When a program is running, part of the program and data will be in memory, and part stored on a peripheral device. Since the memory is paged, all program and data stored in either medium are organised into pages. When parts of the program are required for execution, a 'page swap' is performed between storage device and main memory. A required page is brought in from the storage device and stored in memory in place of a page not currently in use, which is taken from memory, and returned to the storage device. When a page is brought into memory as a result of a reference request, ideally, other locations which are likely to be referenced should also be swapped into memory, ready for use. From the user's point of view, the process is completely transparent – despite the fact that his program may reside partly in memory, partly on a storage device such as a disk, it will use a consistent set of virtual addresses. The virtual MMU must not only translate a virtual address to a physical one in main memory, but also to recognise a virtual address which corresponds to program or data which is not currently in main memory, and initiate a swap procedure to place it into memory, and access it by translating the virtual address to the appropriate physical one.

The 16082 MMU is shown in block diagram form in fig. 5.12. The structure is similar to that of the previous MMU in so far as it possesses a translation unit which generates physical addresses from virtual ones. The address translation process is illustrated in fig. 5.13. The 24-bit virtual address issued by the CPU are split as follows: the most significant eight bits, 23-16, are an index, Index 1, while the next seven bits, 15-9, are Index 2, and the least significant nine bits, 8-0, are an offset, passed directly through the translation mechanism. The Index 1 selects one of the 32-bit entries in a 256-entry page table. The selected entry points to one of 256 pointer tables each of 128 entries, where Index 2 is used to select a pointer entry which defines the start of one of 32000 512-byte pages in main memory. A unique physical byte address is generated using this page address, combined with the 9-bit offset. The tables are too large to be held entirely within the MMU chip itself and so are held in main memory. To increase the speed of the translation unit, an internal high-speed associative cache memory is maintained from the main tables automatically by the MMU, without CPU involvement. This contains the thirty-two most recently referenced virtual addresses and their translations.

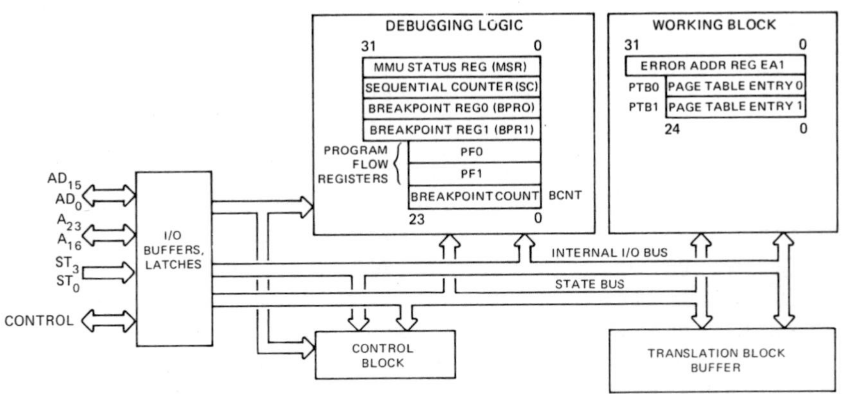

Fig. 5.12 NS16082 memory management unit.

Naturally, this technique for address translation allows dynamic relocation. It also gives protection; each table entry contains a 2-bit protection level code, which is used in conjunction with the mode bit of the program status register (PSR) of the CPU to define access restrictions (no access, read only, full access) which are different for user and supervisor modes. Other bits within each page table entry are used for virtual memory control. A dual-space (DS) control bit in the MMU status register allows user and supervisor modes to have completely independent sets of page tables, and hence completely independent virtual memory spaces of 16 Mbytes each for user and supervisor software. Since the internal MMU page table base address registers (one for user page tables, one for supervisor page tables) PTB0 and PTB1 may be changed by software, there is no limit to the number of users which can be supported, each with his own 16 Mbyte virtual address space.

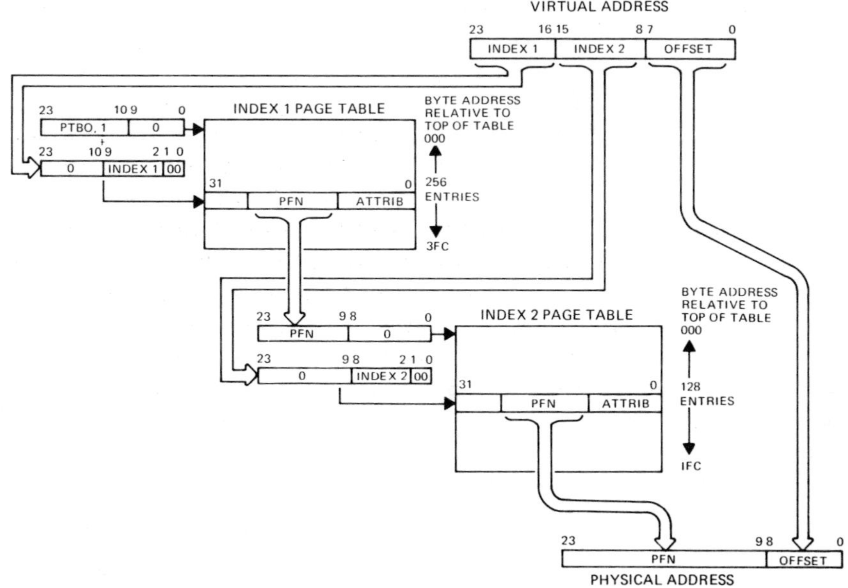

Fig. 5.13 Generation of physical address.

To support the virtual-memory concept described earlier, the 16082 employs a number of other features. For effective page swapping, it is necessary to maintain a lot of information on resident memory page usage which the operating system software can use to decide which pages should be swapped. Often, for instance, a newly-demanded page from a storage device will be loaded in place of the least-used resident page, so a 'page referenced' bit is set in the page table entry each time a reference is made within that 512-byte page. The operating system of the CPU can sample this bit at regular time intervals, and reset it after sampling, and hence collect statistics of page use. Within the swapping process, efficiency can be improved if the operating system can identify whether the page being 'swapped-out' to the storage device has been modified, necessitating a rewriting of that page on the device. A 'modified' flag is included in the Index 2 page table entry for the relevant page. So that the operating system can easily identify which pages are currently resident in main memory, a 'valid' bit is included; if an access is attempted to a non-resident virtual location, the MMU will send a signal to the CPU to abort the instruction execution. The CPU (16032) is designed to stop instruction execution, restore any register contents which have been altered by the instruction, and then invoke the operating system. The operating system action will be to call a memory page load routine, which will handle the page swapping. With a multiprogramming operating system, the CPU can perform another task while the storage device is being accessed. When the load of the demanded page is complete, the aborted instruction which caused the swap can be re-executed. Before this can occur, the operating system must restore the CPU environment to its state prior to the instruction abort. CPU hardware is specifically designed to restore program counter, status register, and stack pointer under these circumstances, and manipulate the instruction pipeline accordingly. Dynamic relocation is achieved by CPU alteration of page tables in memory.

An interesting situation arises because of the pipeline and instruction prefetch of this microprocessor – potentially, a problem could occur if an unnecessary swap were invoked by a never-to-be executed instruction, loaded into the pipeline after a program-flow instruction, such as a jump, call or return. To avoid this, any abort signals are held until the instruction causing them is just about to be executed, and cancelled if it never reaches the state. Similarly, special action is required for aborted string instructions.

To handle updating cache entries, communication with the CPU, and some sophisticated debugging facilities, this virtual memory MMU is itself a CPU, configured as a coprocessor (see section 5.6). This means that it has its own instruction set, consisting of 'slave instructions' which give access to internal registers, and which request address validation, and status information from the MMU. The debugging facilities of the 16082 are impressive; the 'hardware debug block' contains registers and counters which allow program breakpoints to be set, and which permit program flow tracing, allowing debugging software to reconstruct the instructions executed prior to the breakpoint occurrence. The way in which this is achieved is using two 24-bit program-flow registers PF0 and PF1, which store the virtual addresses of the last two non-sequentially executed instructions (PF0 the last one, PF1 the one before it), while a 32-bit sequential counter (SC) register contains two 16-bit counts corresponding to the number of sequentially-executed instructions between PF0 and PF1 instructions, and from PF0 instruction to the breakpoint. Two breakpoint registers, BPR0 and BPR1, are contained within the MMU, allowing either virtual or physical breakpoint addresses to be set and activated, and a single breakpoint counter BCNT may be associated with either BPR0 or BPR1, allowing a 'break after *N* passes' feature. Breakpoints may be designated execution breakpoints (when the instruction at the breakpoint address is executed, a break condition occurs) or data breakpoints, which invoke a break which may be selected to occur on read, write or either read or write to the breakpoint address. Within the MMU status register are bits which control debug operation, as shown in table 5.1.

The rest of the status register is largely concerned with MMU control and error indication, giving a 3-bit error class (ERC) indication of error on address translation, break, or sequential trace interrupt, a 3-bit translation error trace (TET) flag, which distinguishes between protection level errors and invalid page table entries, and a 3-bit error status (EST) flag, set on a translation error to the low 3 bits of the system status bus (of BST). Three separate bits control the translation unit:

Table 5.1

BN	Breakpoint number, set to indicate the breakpoint address of the current break (0 or 1)
BD	Breakpoint direction, which indicates whether a read or write operation caused the break
BST	Breakpoint status, a 3-bit code which reflects the low order three bits of the system status bus, set on an address translation error
BEN	Breakpoint enable
UB	User break; allows the breakpoints to be enabled in user mode and ignored in supervisor mode, or enabled in both modes
FT	Flow trace. Enables PF0, PF1, SC0 and SC1 registers and traces program execution
UT	User trace. Only allows tracing (controlled by FT) in user mode
NT	Non-sequential trace. Enables the non-sequential trace interrupt, a non-maskable interrupt which is invoked by execution of any branch, jump, call or return instruction

TS Translate supervisor. Allows translation of all supervisor mode virtual addresses.

TU Translate user. Allows translation of all user mode virtual addresses.

If either bit is not set, the MMU interprets virtual addresses as physical ones and performs no translation.

DS Dual space bit.

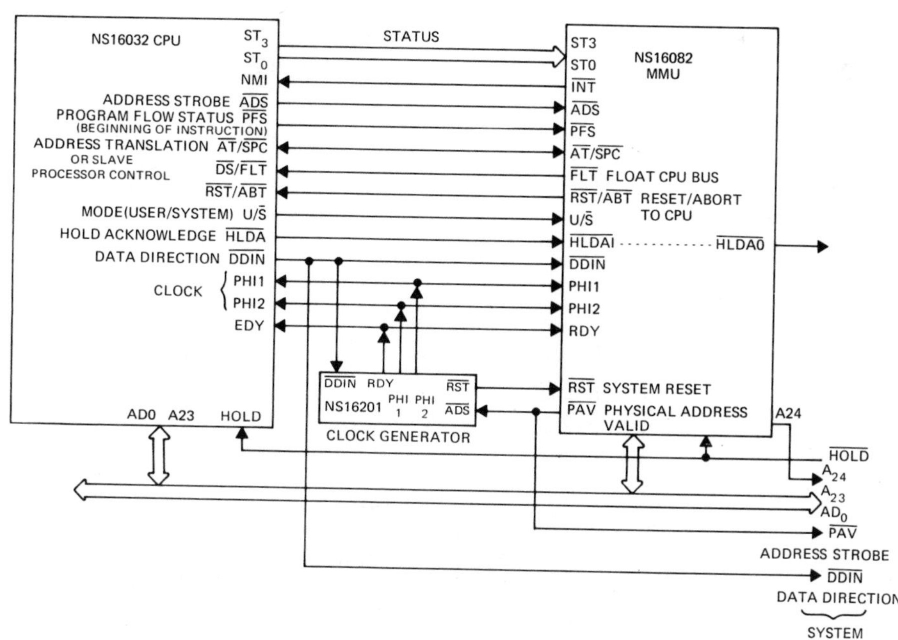

Fig. 5.14 NS16082 MMU connected to NS16032 CPU.

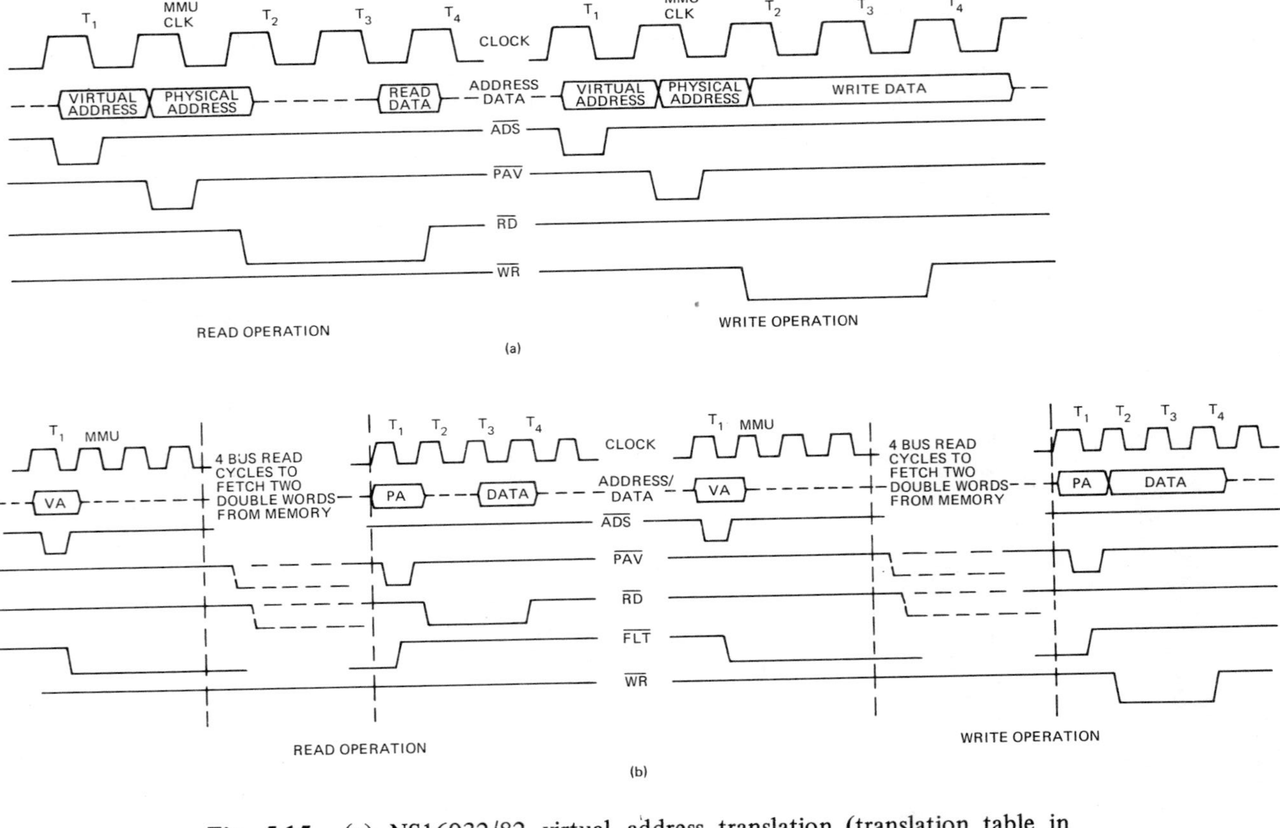

Fig. 5.15 (a) NS16032/82 virtual address translation (translation table in translation cache buffer), (b) NS16032/82 virtual address translation (virtual address not in translation buffer).

The MMU is connected to the 16032 as shown in fig. 5.14, and operates closely with the CPU, to the extent that the multiplexed address/data bus carries sequential virtual (from CPU) and physical (from MMU) addresses, distinguished by address strobe signals $\overline{\text{ADS}}$ (virtual) and $\overline{\text{PAV}}$ (physical). Timing for operation, when the virtual address is in the translation buffer (cache), and when it is not, is shown in fig. 5.15(a) and (b), respectively.

Memory management units like the 16082 are definitely intended for large systems, and, like modern 16-bit microprocessors, are designed to work with sophisticated system software. Virtual memory is a very useful concept for multiple-user systems, and this direction is obviously one in which many of the modern 16-bit systems are looking. The error recovery and debugging aids of this particular MMU reinforce this impression. It is possible to operate a segmented system as a virtual memory machine – the Z8010 MMU may be used with external circuitry which will use segment trap as an indication that a requested segment is not in memory, and use the changed and altered flags in each segment attribute field to implement an efficient virtual management policy. Nevertheless, it is much more difficult to handle variable-length segments than it is to swap fixed-size pages of memory, and generally, a virtual-memory system will be paged.

5.4.3 OTHER MEMORY MANAGEMENT FACILITIES

All of the major manufacturers are now offering, or are likely to offer, memory-management devices, either segmented or paged, with their upper-end 16-bit microprocessors. Both Motorola and Intel are offering enhanced 16-bit microprocessors with built-in memory management units (the MC68010 and iAPX286, respectively, see chapter 12). The same basic concepts discussed earlier still apply to these more recent developments, but facilities may be more sophisticated, using, for instance, virtual input-output, multiple privilege levels (rather than just user and supervisor modes), even wider addressing ranges, with vast virtual ranges (the iAPX286 supports a virtual address space of 10^9 bytes per user) mapping to smaller physical memory and bus error recovery.

5.5 Bus interfaces

Many 16-bit microprocessors will be used in complex systems, based around a standard bus structure, where devices may compete for mastership of the bus, whether they are other CPU devices, coprocessors, or direct memory access (DMA) devices. As a consequence of this requirement, it is advantageous to have an integrated arbitration device which will replace random logic designed to resolve bus request contention. One such device per potential bus master will be required to build a multiple-master system with automatic arbitration. A typical bus arbiter will use the system bus clock for its timing generation, and will accept requests from masters for control of the bus, and issue grant signals to appropriate devices. The block diagram of the 8289 Multibus arbiter for 8086/88 systems is shown in fig. 5.16. The Multibus interface of the arbiter consists of logic which is connected to the bus request and grant lines $\overline{\text{BREQ}}$, $\overline{\text{BPRN}}$ (bus priority input) and BPRO (bus priority output). The other pins of the Multibus interface are connected to the bus clock, BUSY (which is a common open-collector connection used to indicate bus availability), initialisation, and common bus request (see section 11.5). Arbitration logic connected to the Multibus interface resolves any bus request contention, and issues appropriate signals to its associated CPU to indicate that it is now master of the bus, or that the bus must be relinquished. Arbiters in the system are daisy-chained (serial priority resolution) or use external priority encoders (parallel priority resolution), and timing of bus transfers is shown in fig. 5.17.

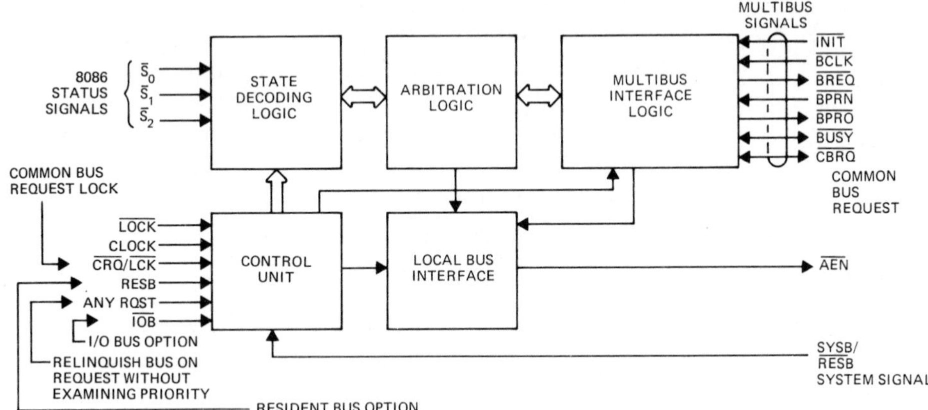

Fig. 5.16 8289 bus arbiter.

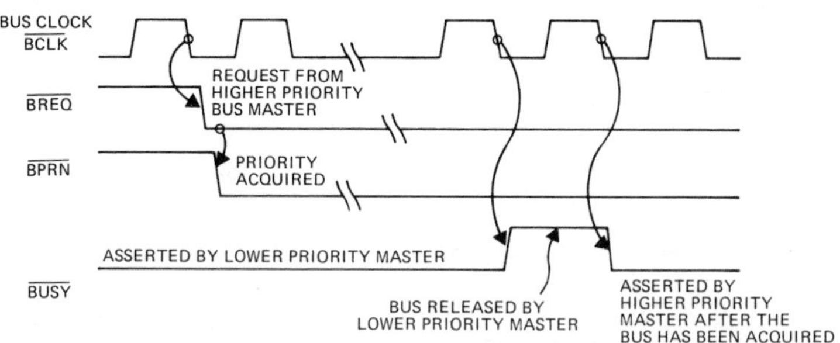

Fig. 5.17 8289 bus arbiter timing.

The usefulness of a bus arbiter such as this one is founded on the compatibility it provides with a standard set of bus signals, and upon the convenience of replacing relatively complex logic with a single device. Its existence emphasises the increase in sophistication of microprocessor systems.

5.6 Coprocessors and slave microprocessors

A feature of modern 16-bit microprocessors is the attempt by their manufacturers to provide them with the means to support additional devices which enhance the basic CPU instruction set, providing floating-point hardware, memory management, or input-output channel management. Such add-on devices have been called coprocessors (Intel), extended processing units or EPU (Zilog), or slave microprocessors (National Semiconductor). A coprocessor is intended to operate closely with its CPU, sharing the same local (component-level) bus. First to introduce the coprocessor idea was Intel; the 8089 I/O microprocessor and 8087 numeric microprocessor have set the pattern for other devices to follow. Both are specialised microprocessors in their own right, of equivalent complexity to the CPU, but they do not possess the bus control structure of a normal microprocessor. Instead, they rely on their associated CPU chip to generate all local bus and memory accesses for them, and they merely take data destined for them as it appears on the bus as a result of CPU bus control; the CPU itself will recognise any coprocessor instruction as one which is not implemented in the main microprocessor, and will ignore it. This is a fundamental concept, allowing the main CPU to generate an instruction stream on the bus which consists of a mixture of CPU instructions and coprocessor instructions, where the coprocessor will automatically select its own instructions from the stream and operate upon them independently of the main CPU. If the CPU has a 'coprocessor present' input, it is possible to make coprocessor instruction codes, which will appear as unimplemented instructions to the CPU when no coprocessor is present, invoke an 'illegal instruction' trap which will transfer control to a routine which will emulate coprocessor functions in software. An assembled program which uses (say) floating-point coprocessor instructions, will then run without modification, on a system with or without a coprocessor, with only a difference (which may be quite significant) in execution speed, hardware functions being much faster than their equivalent software routines.

The advantages of using a coprocessor are that it will execute its instructions in parallel with the main CPU operation and therefore will relieve the CPU of some of its loading, and will increase throughput and processing speed. From the programmer's point of view, the coprocessor is just like an extension of the main CPU – its instructions either occupy codes which are unused by the main CPU, or prefixed by a special pattern to indicate their use. Whereas an improvement to CPU on-chip functions is limited by chip size and complexity, an extension of the CPU instruction set by a coprocessor may be thought of as a doubling of the CPU circuitry! So far, available coprocessors provide:

(a) floating-point hardware[20–22];
(b) independent high-speed I/O channels[23–26];
(c) memory management and virtual memory support (see section 5.4.2);
(d) 'silicon operating system' (see section 8.2.3) microprocessor.

5.6.1 FLOATING-POINT ARITHMETIC COPROCESSOR

Performing arithmetic with real numbers has always been a primary requirement for digital computers, from the earliest mainframe days. With microcomputers, the demands of real time control systems, signal processing systems, and office computers based around the microprocessor CPU all possess this same requirement. For many applications, software routines are sufficient; virtually all of the personal computers, for instance, which run BASIC, implement floating-point mathematics by software. Until recently, each manufacturer had adopted his own floating-point formats (many of them similar, differing only in detail), storage conventions, and error conditioning. As users have become more sophisticated, and more aware of the hazards of poorly-conditioned arithmetic problems and routines, the amount of computation involved within each function of a software arithmetic package has increased, providing better results at the expense of speed and memory usage. Rounding, truncation, handling of indefinite values and exception conditions have become of critical importance, as users have demanded higher accuracy and consistent results. The outcome of all this has been the adoption by the IEEE of a floating-point standard for microprocessors, which is unambiguously defined, and which specifies precisely the formats, and the way in which results and conversions should be handled (see section 7.2.1, arithmetic standards). To implement the IEEE proposals, or an equivalent standard, by software will make computation slow, even with the fastest 16-bit CPU, and the idea of shifting the task onto a special-purpose microprocessor which will operate concurrently with the main CPU is a very attractive one.

The Intel 8087 numeric data processor (NDP) is one such coprocessor, and is useful to review, since it implements the IEEE format. The main features of the 8087 are its accuracy and its speed. Although its external bus connections must match the bus of the 8086 or 8088 in the maximum mode, the internal data paths in the device are extremely wide, and the degree of parallelism in its computation is high. Like a central microprocessor, the 8087 has internal registers which can be considered to be additions to the main CPU register set. The main register stack consists of eight 80-bit-wide registers, which communicate via two internal buses, the fraction bus and the exponent bus, with widths of 68 bits and 16 bits, respectively. A block diagram of the NDP is shown in fig. 5.18. Together with an arithmetic unit, shifter and microcode control unit, the register stack forms the execution unit of the NDP. Notice that, like the 8086, the NDP is microcoded. The bus control unit is part of the NDP which keeps the coprocessor in synchronism with the CPU. Like the CPU control unit, it maintains an instruction queue which tracks that of the 8086 directly, and which accepts instructions from the local data bus as they appear under control of the CPU. The CPU status signals allow instruction fetch bus cycles to be identified and placed in the NDP instruction queue (which is identical to its counterpart in the CPU); to maintain synchronism with the CPU in instruction decoding, the NDP uses the CPU status signals, so that both CPU and NDP fetch and decode instructions in parallel. The distinguishing features of an NDP instruction are the first 5 bits of the instruction, which form a unique pattern called the ESCAPE prefix. This 'coprocessor escape' prefix signals to the CPU that it must merely fetch the instruction, and perform any requested bus cycles (read or write data to memory), but not operate on it. The NDP ignores all instructions without the ESCAPE prefix, since these are directed to the CPU, but upon recognising the prefix, will read the following instruction code into its data buffer, decode it, and execute it. The CPU can identify those prefixed instructions which require a memory reference, and those which do not. If the prefixed instruction does require a memory reference to acquire an operand, the CPU will calculate the operand's effective address, and then performs a 'dummy' read of the word at the addressed location. (By 'dummy' read, it is meant that, from a bus point of view, the read cycle will appear normal, but the CPU ignores any data it receives.) If no memory reference is needed, the CPU will carry on to the next instruction.

A number of situations can arise with memory references:

(a) single word read to the NDP from memory;
(b) single word write to memory from the NDP;
(c) multiple word transfers.

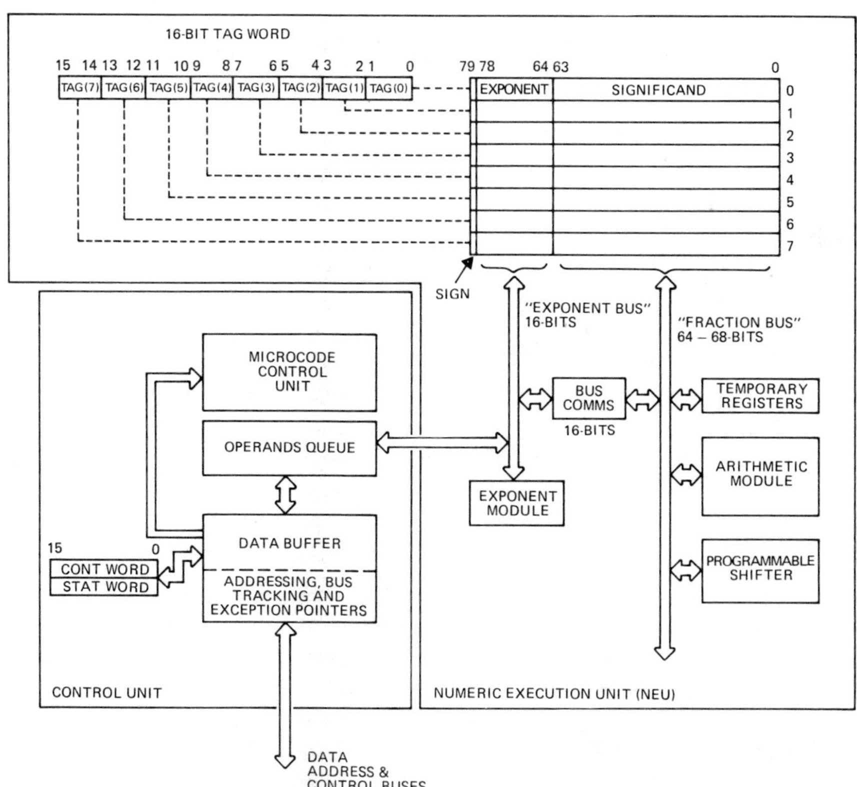

Fig. 5.18 Numeric data microprocessor schematic (8087).

For a single-word read, the NDP uses the 'dummy read' of the CPU, accepting data from the bus at the appropriate time. The control unit of the NDP acquires and saves the address of the operand that the CPU has placed on the bus during the 'dummy read', and if the required operation is a write to memory, it retains the address until it is ready to write the data. The NDP then acquires the bus from the CPU using the bus request lines $\overline{\text{RQ/GT0}}$ or $\overline{\text{RQ/GT1}}$, and writes the operand to the saved address, generating its own bus signals. If the operand requires multiple reads or writes to memory, the NDP acquires the bus from the CPU, and reads the rest of the operand (having read the first word during the 'dummy read' of the CPU) or writes the whole of the operand using consecutive bus cycles, and incrementing its stored address accordingly. When the operand has been read or written, the NDP returns control to the CPU. Because of the way in which the NDP manipulates addresses, it is advantageous from a speed viewpoint, though not mandatory for correct operation, to align NDP operands on even byte address boundaries.

In normal operation, the CPU will execute its ESCAPE instruction upon which the NDP will commence operations, and move on to the next instruction before the NDP completes its operation. The control unit of the NDP will continue to 'track' the CPU instruction stream as before. While the instructions in the stream are all CPU instructions, the CPU and NDP operate in parallel. However, two possible situations may arise which upset this smooth flow of operations:

(a) The control unit of the NDP may recognise a second NDP prefixed instruction while it is still executing the first one. In such a case, the CPU will be held up by the NDP, using the $\overline{\text{TEST}}$ input of the CPU, wired to the NDP BUSY output, asserted during the NDP instruction execution. The CPU instruction WAIT will, when encountered, generate wait states until the NDP BUSY ceases to be asserted. By preceding each NDP ESCAPE prefixed instruction with WAIT – any contention between successive NDP instructions may be avoided, since the CPU will wait for one NDP instruction to be completed before fetching the instruction which constitutes the next one.
(b) The CPU may attempt to access a memory operand which should have previously been referenced by the NDP, when the NDP has not completed its current instruction, and has not yet referenced the operand. Once again, the WAIT instruction should precede the memory reference instruction.

The necessity for the CPU and NDP to be synchronised in these circumstances is a common problem, and the solution described, using WAIT, is an elegant solution. Another interesting feature of this NDP is that it automatically recognises which CPU is present (16-bit 8086, or 16-bit 8088 with 8-bit external data bus) and adjusts its bus handling accordingly.

Connection of the NDP within a system is shown in fig. 5.19, using the CPU local bus. If the linked pair of microprocessors are then to be interfaced to Multibus, a standard bus controller device and bus arbiter can be used. Like the CPU, the NDP can execute wait states if system memory access is slow. Mutual exclusion of a memory location shared between the NDP and a CPU other than the NDP's host CPU, is a problem: the NDP has no bus LOCK facility of its own, and needs the CPU to manipulate the location's access semaphore (using, typically LOCK XCHG, as in section 6.7.1) before the NDP instructions which access that location are executed, and to release the semaphore afterwards.

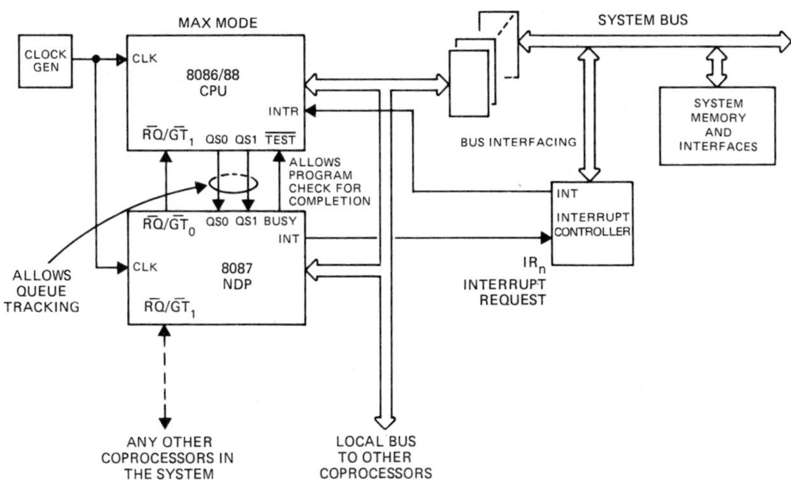

Fig. 5.19 8087 NDP connection to CPU.

The 8087 NDP may use seven data types, shown in fig. 5.20, along with their storage formats. All internal operations are performed in 'temporary real' format, which gives an equivalent precision of nineteen decimal digits, and which gives an internal accuracy greater than that required for the standard. Each of the eight 80-bit registers in the stack has associated with it a 2-bit 'tag', which is part of a 16-bit tag register, and which indicates the contents of the register. The tag values indicate the IEEE conditions:

Tag	Condition
00	Valid normalised or unnormalised number
01	Zero (true representation)
10	Special (not a number, NAN, 'infinity', or too small to be normalised)
11	Empty

Operation of the NDP is stack-oriented; the eight registers form a conventional push-down stack, but they can be addressed individually. Each instruction has one or two operands, which are generally loaded onto the top of the stack from elsewhere on the stack, or from memory. The square root instruction, FSQRT, always takes the square root of the entry at the top of the stack. The simplest and most widely-used of the floating-point operations (add, subtract, multiply, divide and compare) may operate directly on operands which are either in memory or in registers. There are six basic groups of instruction: data transfer; arithmetic; logical; transcendental; constants, and NDP control instructions. Listing them by group, the instructions are shown in table 5.2.

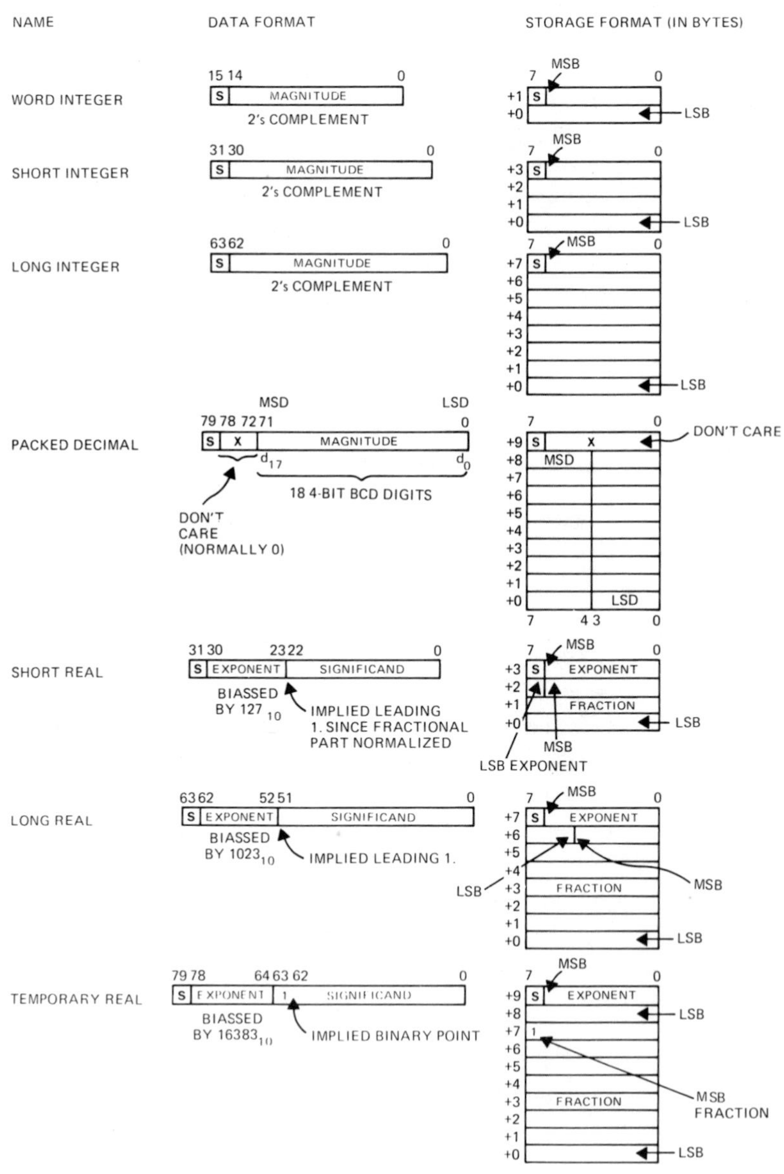

Fig. 5.20 8087 NDP data types and storage formats.

Table 5.2

Class	Mnemonic	Operation
Data transfer	FLD, FST	Read load, store (to, from top of the stack)
	FSTP	Store real and pop
	FXCH	Exchange registers
	FILD, FIST	Integer load, store
	FISTP	Store integer and pop
	FBLD	Packed BCD load
	FBSTP	Store packed BCD and pop
Arithmetic instructions	FADD, FIADD	Add real, integer
	FSUB, FISUB	Subtract real, integer
	FADDP, FSUBP	Add, subtract real and pop
	FSUBR, FISUBR	Subtract real, integer reversed
	FSUBRP	Subtract real reversed, and pop
	FMUL, FIMUL	Multiply real, integer
	FMULP	Multiply real and pop
	FDIV, FIDIV	Divide real, integer
	FDIVP	Divide real and pop
	FDIVR, FIDIVR	Divide real, integer reversed
	FDIVRP	Divide real reversed and pop
	FSQRT	Square root
	FABS, FCHS	Absolute value, change sign
	FSCALE	Scale (rapid multiplication by power of 2 by adjusting exponent)
	FPREM	Partial remainder (performs modulo division of top stack element by next stack element)
	FRNDINT	Round to integer
	FXTRACT	Extract exponent and significand (any integer bit of the mantissa)
Logical (compare)	FCOM, FICOM	Compare real, integer
	FCOMP, FICOMP	Compare real, integer, and pop
	FTST	Compare top of stack with zero and set condition codes
	FXAM	Examine top of stack and return a result as sign, normalised, unnormalised or too small to be normalised.
Transcendental	FPTAN, FPATAN	Partial tangent, arctangent (tangent is computed as a ratio $Y/X = \tan\phi$ where $0 < \phi < \pi/4$ and ϕ is taken from the top of the stack and is replaced by Y, while X is pushed to become the new top of the stack. Arctangent is computed as $\phi = \arctan$

Table 5.2 (contd.)

Class	Mnemonic	Operation
Transcendental (contd.)		Y/X where $0 < Y < X < \infty$. Y is overwritten by ϕ)
	F2XMI	$Y = 2^X - 1$, X real
	FYL2X	$Z = Y \log_2 X$
	FYL2XP1	$Z = Y \log_2(X+1)$
Constants	FLDZ	Load + 0.0
	FLD1	Load + 1.0
	LDPI	Load
	LDL2T	Load $\log_2 10$
	LDL2E	Load $\log_2 e$
	FLDLG2	Load $\log_{10} 2$
	FLDLN2	Load $\log_e 2$
NDP Control N means 'without WAIT on $\overline{\text{TEST}}$'	F1N1T/FN1N1T	Initialise
	FD1S1/FND1S1	Disable interrupts
	FEN1/FNEN1	Enable interrupts
	FLDCW	Load control word
	FSTCW/FNSTCW	Store control word
	FSTSW/FNSTSW	Store status word
	FCLEX/FNCLEX	Clear exceptions
	FSTENV/FNSTENV	Store environment (in main memory, the basic NDP status: control word, status word, tag word, opcode, and instruction and operand pointers)
	FLDENV	Load environment
	FSAVE/FNSAVE	Save state (in main memory, the complete internal stack contents, control word, status, word, tag word, instruction and operand pointers, and opcode)
	FRSTOR	Load state
	FINCSTP	Increment internal stack pointer*
	FDECSTP	Decrement internal stack pointer*
	FFREE	Free register (changes tag to empty)
	FNOP	No operation
	FWAIT	CPU wait

*The internal stack pointer is a modulo-8 register, so an increment when its contents are 07 will change them to 00.

The transcendental functions and constants require some explanation. FPTAN and FPATAN, having a ratio (X/Y) result and arguments, respectively, allow all the other trigonometric functions to be computed, using standard trigonometric identities for SIN, COS, ARCSIN, ARCCOS. F2XMI can be used to give 2^X, by adding one to the result. Remember that X is real, and may be a small value close to zero. Using the constants, common exponentiation functions may be computed, viz:

$10^X = 2^{(X \log_2 10)}$ where $\log_2 10$ can be acquired using FLD2T

$e^X = 2^{(X \log_2 e)}$ where $\log_2 e$ can be acquired using FLD2E

$y^X = 2^{(X \log_2 y)}$ where the exponent may be calculated using instruction FYL2X

$$\left.\begin{aligned} \log_{10} X &= \frac{\log_2 X}{\log_2 10} \\ \log_e X &= \frac{\log_2 X}{\log_2 e} \end{aligned}\right\}$$

$\log_2 X$ can be calculated using FYL2X
$\log_2 10$, $\log_2 e$ may be acquired using FLD2T, FLD2E respectively

Exceptions can occur as a result of a number of circumstances:

(a) Division by zero.
(b) Overflow (exponent of real result too large for destination format).
(c) Underflow (exponent of real result too small for destination format).
(d) Attempt to use a denormalised operand.
(e) Precision – the result is not exactly representable in the required destination formation, and has been rounded accordingly.
(f) Invalid operation, one which causes an indeterminate result, e.g. zero divided by zero, square root of a negative number, if one operand is not a number NaN (see tag description), if an attempt is made to load a register which is not empty (stack overflow), if an attempt is made to pop an operand from an empty register (stack underflow). An invalid operation can generally be traced to a software error.

The status word of the NDP, which records the condition codes of the operation, and the tag words of the operands, are used to detect exceptional conditions, and such a condition will invoke (selectably) either internal action by the NDP or a user-written error handler. Exception flags are set in the status register in either case, and remain set indefinitely (changed only by FCLEX, FRSTOR, FLDENV). If a user exception handler is required, the NDP can generate an interrupt request for its host CPU.

To illustrate the advantages in speed that are gained by using such a sophisticated coprocessor, table 5.3 compares hardware and software implementation of equivalent functions.

The NS16032 has a slave microprocessor for floating point arithmetic, called the NS16081, which is, like the 8087 NDP, closely connected to the host CPU, and relying on the CPU to generate the instruction stream. Connection of the slave microprocessor is shown in fig. 5.21(a) and the slave FPU register set in fig. 5.21(b). ST0 and ST1 are the two lower bits of the CPU status, monitored by the slave microprocessor to determine the type of transfer being made, and to identify instructions. The address translation pin $\overline{\text{AT}}/\overline{\text{SPC}}$ of the NS16032 is used as a data strobe for slave microprocessor transfers, and is driven by the CPU during all slave microprocessor cycles. Slave microprocessor instructions consist of a 3-byte 'basic instruction field', which comprises an identification (ID) byte which is similar to ESCAPE, followed by an operation word. The ID byte is essentially a prefix which identifies the instruction as a slave microprocessor instruction, determines which slave microprocessor the instruction is destined for, and specifies the format of the following operation word. When the CPU fetches a slave microprocessor instruction, it performs the following sequence:

Table 5.3

Instruction	NDP execution time (5 MHz clock) μs	CPU software emulation μs
Multiply (short real)	19	1 600
Multiply (long real)	27	2 100
Add	17	1 600
Divide (short real)	39	3 200
Compare	9	1 300
Load (short real)	9	1 700
Store (short real)	18	1 200
Square root	36	19 600
Tangent	90	13 000
Exponentiation	100	17 100

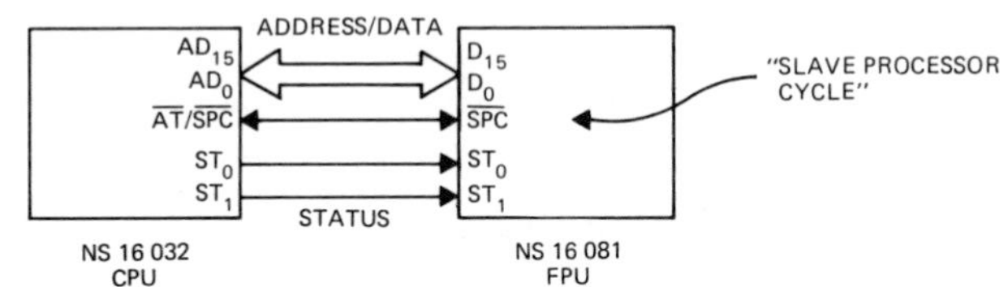

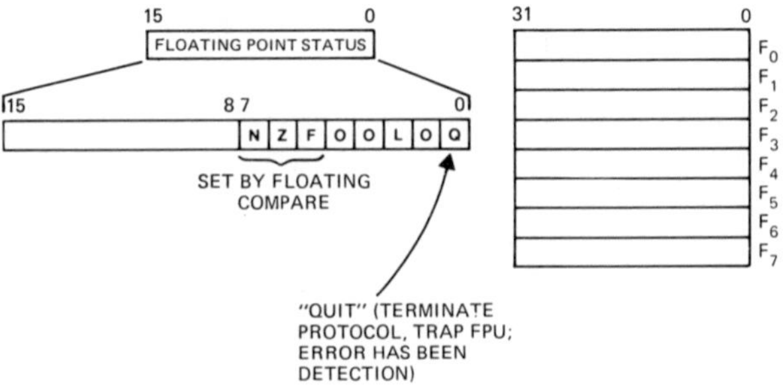

Fig. 5.21 NS16081 floating-point unit (FPU): (a) floating-point unit connection to CPU, (b) FPU registers.

(a) Sets the status output to denote Broadcast ID (code 1111) and transfers the ID byte to all slave microprocessors on the lower half of the data bus using strobe $\overline{\text{SPC}}$. Only the addressed slave microprocessor is activated and takes any further part in the process.
(b) The CPU sets the status output to denote a slave operand transfer (code 1101), and transfers the operation word on the data bus again using strobe $\overline{\text{SPC}}$. Both the CPU and the slave microprocessor decode the operation word to determine the number of operands required (the operation word is byte-swapped on the data bus during its transfer).
(c) The CPU will issue addresses for operands, and transfers them to the slave microprocessor.
(d) When the last operand has been transferred, the slave microprocessor commences execution. The CPU can then continue, and will prefetch instructions into its instruction queue; if it fills the queue before the slave has finished execution, the CPU will signal 'waiting for slave' on its status lines.
(e) When the slave microprocessor has completed its execution, it signals the CPU using $\overline{\text{SPC}}$ (which is bidirectional) and the CPU can then read the slave microprocessor status (using the appropriate status code in conjunction with $\overline{\text{SPC}}$).
(f) The CPU will then, if no slave microprocessor exception or trap has occurred, read the result, if any, and transfer it to memory, using $\overline{\text{SPC}}$ and the transfer slave operand status code.

Notice the difference between this slave microprocessor and the NDP: the slave microprocessor is controlled completely by the CPU using status codes and a strobe signal $\overline{\text{SPC}}$, and although the CPU can prefetch instructions while the NDP is operating, it cannot execute them. By comparison, the NDP can control bus operations, though it relies on its CPU to generate the instruction stream, and can execute concurrently with the CPU, synchronisation being achieved by the WAIT (for $\overline{\text{TEST}}$) instruction preceding the next NDP instruction (or any other instruction which needs to be synchronised with the NDP).

Exceptions, generated by similar conditions to those of the NDP, are transmitted to the CPU via the slave status word, which will immediately cause a CPU FPU trap. Both the NDP and the FPU implement comparable arithmetic operations and extend the instruction set and register set of their respective microprocessors. The NDP implements transcendental functions, as well as the conventional arithmetic operations. Both devices illustrate well the power of the coprocessor or slave microprocessor concept.

5.6.2 I/O COPROCESSOR

The I/O processor (IOP) is a feature of many mainframe and minicomputers. Its function is to handle fast input-output independently of the main CPU, usually organising it into streams or channels, so that input-output devices are transparent to the CPU. The only IOP currently available for microprocessor systems is the Intel 8089, designed to work with the 8086 (or iAPX86) family of 16-bit CPUs. This IOP consists of two independent I/O channels, each of which may be configured as a direct memory access (DMA) channel, supporting very high data transfer rates, and, on the same chip as the two channels of I/O, the IOP possesses a microprocessor capable of handling I/O operations such as peripheral interface device initialisation, I/O transfer, data transformation, error and status checking, and indicating to the CPU that information has been transferred.

Table 5.4 16081 FPU instruction set

Mnemonic	Operation
ADDF, ADDL	Floating point add (single and double precision)
SUBF, SUBL	Floating point subtract
MULF, MULL	Multiply
DIVF, DIVL	Divide
MOVF, MOVL	Move single, double precision
ABSF, ABSL	Absolute value
NEGF, NEGL	Negate
CMPF, CMPL	Compare and set condition codes
FLOORF, FLOORL	Convert to largest integer less than or equal to value
ROUNDF, FOUNDL	Convert to integer by rounding
TRUNCF, TRUNCL	Convert to integer by truncation towards zero
MOVFL	Move and shorten from double to single precision
MOVLF	Move and lengthen from single to double precision
MOVIF, MOVIL	Convert integer to single, double precision floating point
LFSR, SFSR	Load, store status register

Unlike the NDP, the IOP can run programs of its own, concurrently with operation of the main CPU: it may be used in two modes; a local mode where the IOP is closely linked to the CPU, connected to its local bus, and shares its bus interface, and a remote mode, where the IOP and CPU communicate over the system bus, and the IOP maintains its own independent local bus. The two configurations are illustrated in fig. 5.22. The remote solution offers better input-output throughput, since IOP program execution does not require access to the CPU system bus, and can proceed concurrently with that of the CPU. In this configuration, both CPU and IOP only use the system bus to gain access to system memory, and a bus arbiter device is required to manage these references. The local I/O bus is controlled solely by the IOP and is used for all I/O transfers.

A block diagram of the IOP is shown in fig. 5.23. Each channel logic consists of control circuitry for DMA, and a register file which contains details of the transfer. Both channels may operate concurrently, executing channel programs on the same internal CPU by maintaining a separate register set for each channel. A common control unit (CCU) co-ordinates microprocessor activity by allocating clock cycles to internal functions. If the two I/O channels are operating simultaneously, the CCU examines the priority of the two channels, and allows the higher priority channel to run, or if the channels have equal priority, the CCU interleaves their execution. Operation of the microprocessor is controlled

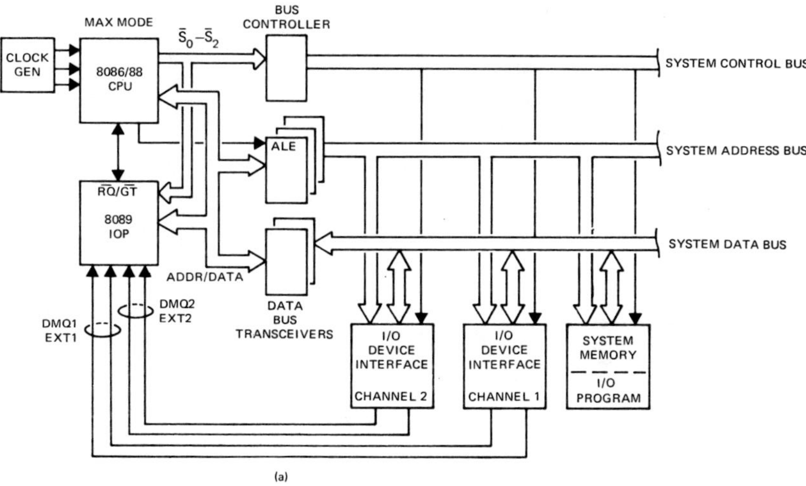

(a)

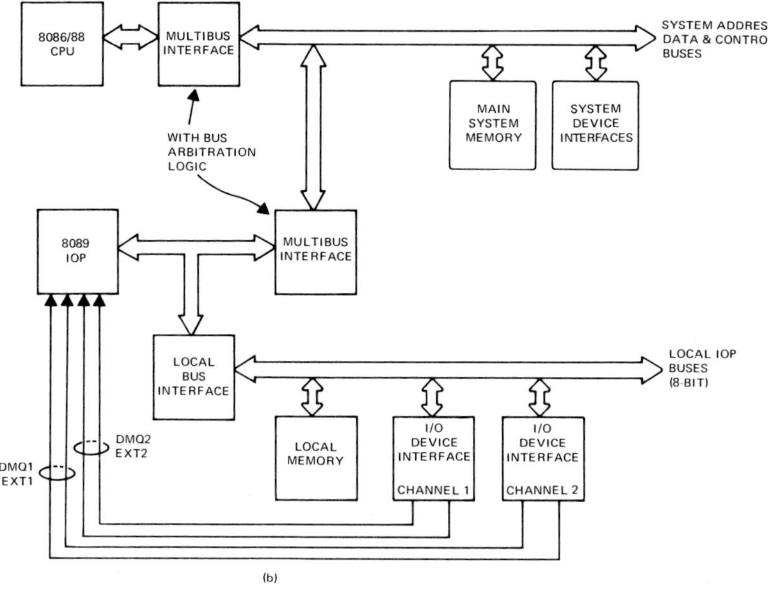

(b)

Fig. 5.22 IOP local and remote configurations: (a) local IOP connection, (b) IOP with its own local bus.

by the instruction fetch and decode unit which fetches instructions for the executing channel, using a separate 1-byte queue for each channel's instruction stream if they are transferred over a 16-bit bus (to reduce bus cycles) and transferring one byte per bus cycle over an 8-bit bus. All data flowing through the IOP, whether destined for DMA transfer, or for the arithmetic and logic unit (ALU), goes via the assembly/disassembly registers, which allow the IOP to transfer data between different width buses in a minimum number of bus cycles (e.g. for DMA transfer between an 8-bit peripheral interface and 16-bit memory, the IOP will perform two bus cycles to read two bytes from the peripheral interface, will assemble them to form a 16-bit word, and write it in one bus cycle to memory). The 8089 IOP does not distinguish separate I/O and memory; I/O devices are all memory-mapped.

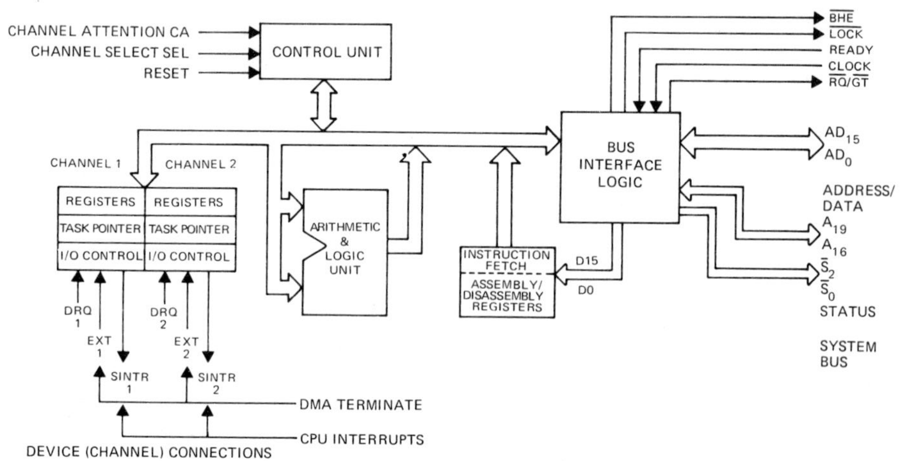

Fig. 5.23 8089 input-output processor (IOP) schematic.

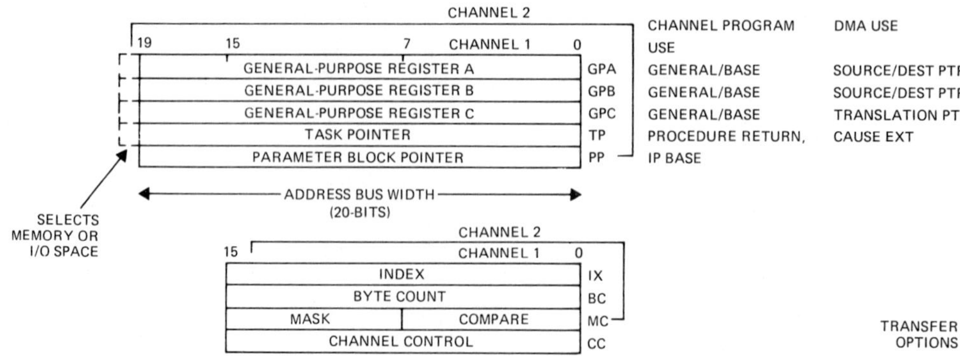

Fig. 5.24 Register set 8089 IOP.

The register set for each channel is shown in fig. 5.24. The four top 21-bit registers in the figure consist of three 'general-purpose' registers GA, GB and GC, and a task pointer register. Each of GA, GB and GC is a 20-bit address register with a tag bit appended to its most significant end; the tag bit is used to distinguish between addresses used to reference IOP channel address space and system memory space. Each register may be used for either – when a register addresses system memory space, its initial contents should contain the start address of the data buffer, and the register will be incremented automatically as the transfer proceeds; when the register is used for addressing I/O space, the upper 4 bits are ignored, giving a 64 kbyte I/O addressing range, compared with a 1 Mbyte memory addressing range.

GA and GB are used as pointers to source and destination locations during any data transfer operations (the register used as source, and the one used as destination address register are programmed by bits in the channel control register). The IOP allows byte data to be translated during the transfer, using a translation table with start address contained in register GC, and with the data byte used as an index to the table. The data byte is replaced by the table entry for the addressed location.

The fourth of the 21-bit registers is the task pointer register, which is used as an instruction pointer for the channel program. It points to the next instruction to be executed, and is loaded from an area of system memory shared by CPU and IOP, called the channel parameter block. The first parameter block location is passed by the main CPU to the IOP during the IOP initialisation sequence, and stored in the 20-bit parameter block pointer of the IOP.

The other registers of fig. 5.24 are all 16-bit ones, the first two consist of an index register IX, which may be used as an index for memory operands but not used for DMA operations, a byte count register BC which may be used either as a general register by the IOP program or as a DMA transfer count register (which is preset with the number of bytes to be transferred, decremented upon each transfer, and used to terminate the DMA transfers if the required flag in the control register has been set). The third, the mask/compare (MC) register may be used either as a general register, or for DMA masked comparison of a byte value. The MC register will then contain an 8-bit comparison value in its low byte, and an 8-bit mask value in its upper byte, which effectively allows 'don't care' bits to be specified for the comparison value. A 'DMA terminate on masked compare' may be specified, which uses this facility. The last register is the channel control register (CCR), which, together with the 8-bit program status word (PSW) register, governs DMA transfers. The two registers are shown in fig. 5.25. Most of the fields require little explanation, but one or two may be unfamiliar; the synchronisation field, for instance, allows 'free-running', or unsynchronised, transfers (memory-to-memory transfers, for example), source synchronisation using the channel DRQ (DMA request) line, or destination synchronisation, using DRQ. The 'lock' field serves the same purpose as the 8086 'lock' instruction prefix, and will cause the IOP to assert the microprocessor bus lock signal, $\overline{\text{LOCK}}$. $\overline{\text{LOCK}}$ is active throughout the channel DMA sequence, and a running channel will retain control of the bus until $\overline{\text{LOCK}}$ is released. The chain bit is a way of altering a CCU program's priority. Programs will normally run at priority three, below the priority of DMA actions, but if the chain bit in the CCR is set, the program will run at priority one, the top priority, and equal to that of DMA transfers. The possible I/O channel activities of the IOP are shown in table 5.5.

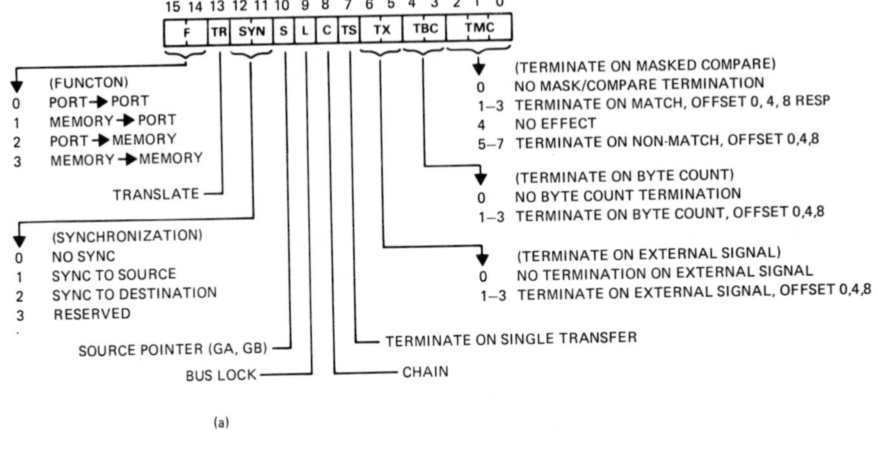

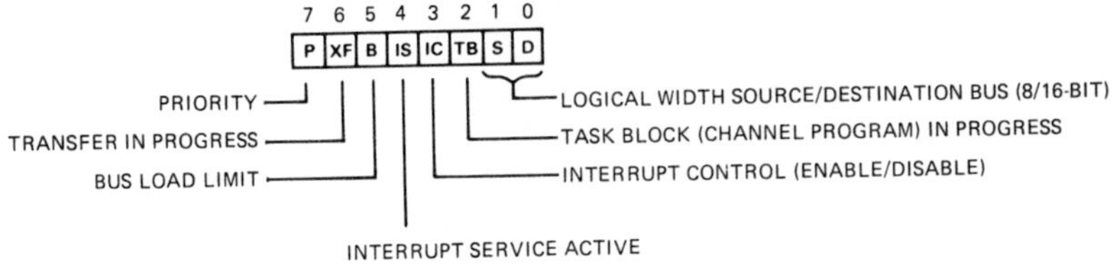

Fig. 5.25 IOP CCR and PSW: (a) channel control register (CCR), (b) program status word (PSW).

Table 5.5

Activity	Priority
DMA transfer	1
DMA termination sequence	1
Channel program (chain bit set)	1
Channel attention sequence	2
Channel program (normal)	3
Idle	4

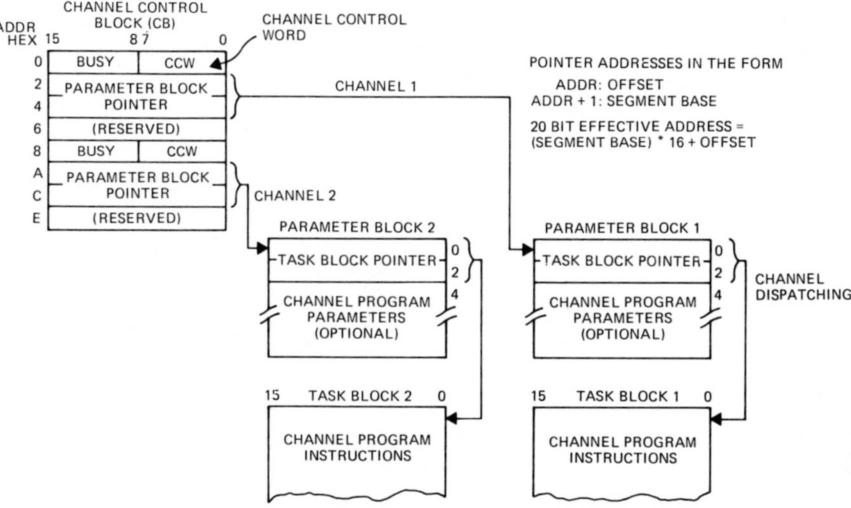

Fig. 5.26 IOP channel control block (CCB).

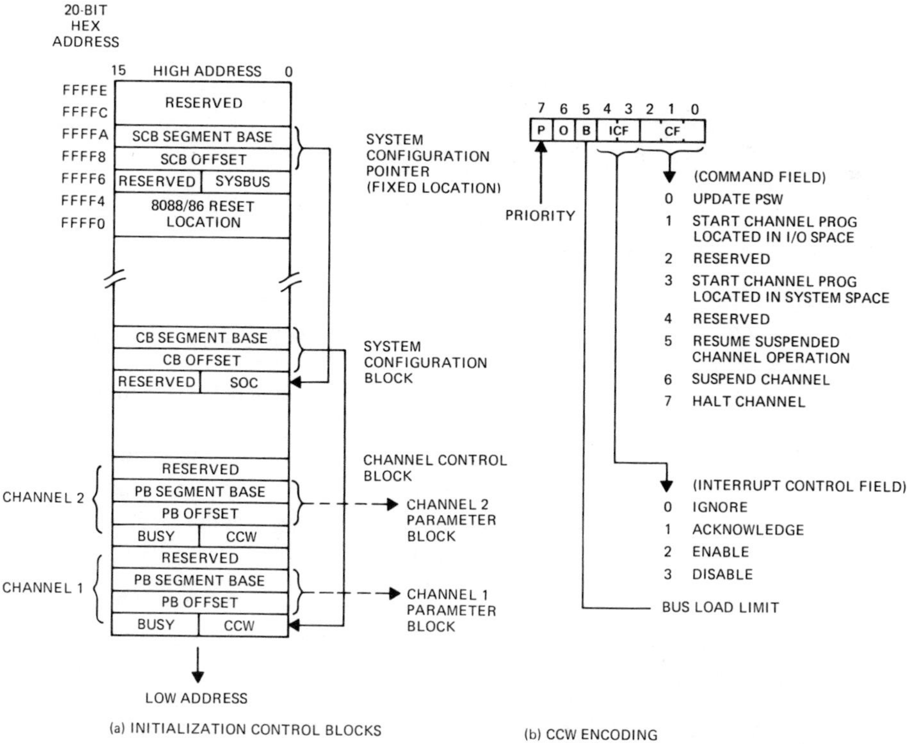

20-BIT HEX ADDRESS
15 HIGH ADDRESS 0
FFFFE RESERVED
FFFFC
FFFFA SCB SEGMENT BASE
FFFF8 SCB OFFSET
FFFF6 RESERVED SYSBUS
FFFF4 8088/86 RESET LOCATION
FFFF0
SYSTEM CONFIGURATION POINTER (FIXED LOCATION)
CB SEGMENT BASE
CB OFFSET
RESERVED SOC
SYSTEM CONFIGURATION BLOCK
CHANNEL 2: RESERVED, PB SEGMENT BASE, PB OFFSET, BUSY CCW
CHANNEL 1: RESERVED, PB SEGMENT BASE, PB OFFSET, BUSY CCW
CHANNEL CONTROL BLOCK
CHANNEL 2 PARAMETER BLOCK
CHANNEL 1 PARAMETER BLOCK
LOW ADDRESS
(a) INITIALIZATION CONTROL BLOCKS

7 6 5 4 3 2 1 0
P O B ICF CF
PRIORITY
(COMMAND FIELD)
0 UPDATE PSW
1 START CHANNEL PROG LOCATED IN I/O SPACE
2 RESERVED
3 START CHANNEL PROG LOCATED IN SYSTEM SPACE
4 RESERVED
5 RESUME SUSPENDED CHANNEL OPERATION
6 SUSPEND CHANNEL
7 HALT CHANNEL
(INTERRUPT CONTROL FIELD)
0 IGNORE
1 ACKNOWLEDGE
2 ENABLE
3 DISABLE
BUS LOAD LIMIT
(b) CCW ENCODING

Fig. 5.27 (a) Initialisation control blocks, (b) CCW encoding.

Control of I/O channel activities (whether the CCU is to execute a DMA transfer, run a program, etc.) is performed by the channel control word (CCW), a bit pattern in memory, and part of the channel control block (CB) of data. The format of the channel control block and its relationship to the individual channel parameter blocks is shown in fig. 5.26. This set of linked data structures forms the primary means of communication between the main CPU and IOP. The main CPU sets up these blocks in memory upon initialisation, and then directs the IOP to the CB using the channel attention (CA) signal, which consists of a write (OUT instruction if the IOP is I/O-mapped, memory reference instruction if it is memory-mapped) to Channel 1 or Channel 2. Upon receipt of the CA signal, the IOP enters an initialisation sequence which starts with bus acquisition; when the IOP has acquired the bus, it assumes a byte-wide system bus, and reads the 8-bit SYSBUS word from preset location FFFF6H in memory. This word controls the IOP recognition of system bus width. The IOP retains control of the system bus, and then reads location FFFF8H, which contains the system configuration block (SCB) address, stored in two 16-bit locations as segment and offset. The three 16-bit locations FFFF6H, FFFF8H, and FFFFAH form the system configuration pointer (SCP). The next word to be read uses the SCB address to acquire the system operation command (SOC) word, an 8-bit word which controls the request/grant (bus control) mode of the IOP and the I/O bus width. The SCB also contains the control block address (segment and offset), and allows access to the CCW. The linked initialisation information is shown in diagrammatic form in fig. 5.27(a), and CCW encoding in fig. 5.27(b).

The instruction set of the 8089 IOP may be divided into five basic groups of CCU instructions: data transfer instructions, arithmetic instructions, logic and bit manipulation instructions, program transfer instructions and microprocessor control instructions. Table 5.6 details the instruction set.

The instruction set can use a number of addressing modes for those instructions which require memory reference. These are:

(a) Based addressing: the effective address is the contents of GA, GB, GC or PP.
(b) Offset addressing: an 8-bit unsigned opcode offset is added to the contents of GA, GB, GC or PP.
(c) Indexed addressing: 16-bit register IX (unsigned) is added to the contents of GA, GB, GC or PP.
(d) Indexed autoincrement addressing: indexed addressing where the index register IX is incremented after the effective address has been calculated (post-increment). The increment size is one for byte addressing, two for word addressing, three for 20-bit pointer load operations.

Using DMA transfers, or independent IOP program transfers, the IOP acts as an autonomous microprocessor, managing data transfers requested by the main CPU via the communication data blocks, and is able to communicate back to the CPU on task completion. BUSY/DONE flags for each channel of the IOP, held in memory, may be examined by the main CPU, or the IOP can request a CPU interrupt upon task termination. The flexibility of the IOP in a large microcomputer system is demonstrated by its application in interfacing a diskette controller to the system. The IOP will automatically handle not only block data transfers to and from the diskette, but also error checking and any necessary retry operations. If necessary, byte-oriented code conversion could also be implemented using the IOP translate capability. A single IOP channel could not only handle this task, but also any others which are required and which need not execute concurrently with the diskette controller task. Any concurrent I/O tasks can use the free IOP channel.

Table 5.6 8089 IOP instruction set

Group	Mnemonic	Description
Data transfer	MOV, MOVB	Move word, byte
	MOVI, MOVBI	Move word, byte immediate
	LDP, LDPI	Load double word pointer, immediate
Arithmetic	ADD, ADDB	Add word, byte
	ADDI, ADDBI	Add word, byte immediate
	INC, INCB	Increment word, byte
	DEC, DECB	Decrement word, byte
Logical	AND, ANDB	AND word, byte
	ANDI, ANDBI	Immediate
	OR, ORB	OR word, byte
	ORI, ORBI	Immediate
	NOT, NOTB	Not word, byte
	SETB	Bit set
	CLR	Bit clear
Program transfer	CALL, LCALL	Short, Long call
	JMP, LJMP	Unconditional jump, short, long
	JZ, LJZ	Jump if word is zero
	JZB, LJZB	Jump if byte is zero
	JNZ, LJNZ	Non-zero
	JMCE, LJMCE	Masked compare equal
	JMCNE, LJMCNE	Masked compare unequal
	JNT, LJBT	Jump if bit true
	JNBT, LJNBT	Jump if bit false
Control	TSL	Test while locked (semaphore operation)
	WID	DMA bus widths
	XFER	Enter DMA mode
	SINTR	Set interrupt service bit
	NOP	No operation
	HLT	Halt

5.7 Communications interfaces and data link controllers

Memory management devices and coprocessors are devices which have been designed specifically for the modern 16-bit microprocessor. The interfaces designed for 8-bit microprocessors will work well with the 16-bit CPU, but the system requirements may demand higher performance parts. In no interfacing area is this more pronounced than that of serial communications. When the 8-bit microprocessor was developed, communications were relatively simple – the CPU would support a small number of terminals, configured as teletypes, running serial asynchronous 20 mA current loop signals or RS-232C standard asynchronous signals. Such simple communications suffer from a number of drawbacks:

(a) Format overheads are high (one start bit and one, one-and-a-half stop bits for every 5, 6, 7 or 8 data bits).
(b) There is no data link control (DLC), so that a serial bus system can be created, with a simple hierarchy, for instance (it is simpler to construct a hierarchical system than a non-hierarchical 'network-type' one).
(c) Error detection is minimal (confined to a single optional parity bit per data word) and correction is non-existent.
(d) Standard speeds are low (typically up to 9600 baud).

Although synchronous communications are available, supported by serial interfaces offered by most manufacturers (8251A, 6851 ACIA, or Z80-SIO), they only support very simple protocols. They allow higher speeds, and reduced format overheads, but still have no line control protocols.

The situation with mainframe computers was somewhat similar until the introduction of the large IBM systems, and led to the development, by IBM, of synchronous data link control (SDLC) standards, which laid down fixed protocols for a hierarchical system of serial communications. SDLC interfaces will allow a simple microcomputer network to be configured, with a single master computer, and a number of slave stations, communicating over a serial 'bus'.

The trend towards hierarchical systems has been a major reason for the introduction of a byte-parallel data communication and control system for digital instrumentation. As such instruments have increased in sophistication, the prospects for their incorporation in automatic test equipment or automatic measurement equipment, controlled by a central computer, have increased. A leading instrument manufacturer, Hewlett-Packard, introduced its 'HP Instrumentation Bus' (HP-IB) in the early 1970s. Now adopted by the IEEE Standards Committee as the 'General-Purpose Interface Bus' (GP-IB), or IEEE-488 Bus, the standard has enjoyed considerable popularity, used not only for its original purpose, but also for computer peripheral interfacing, and has been provided on a number of personal computers. The Commodore PET was the first personal computer to have an IEEE-488 bus port (actually not a full implementation, but a reasonably close approximation), closely followed by Apple Computer and others. The PET uses the interface to communicate with many of its peripherals, and a wide range of interfaces is available with IEEE-488 compatibility.

The most recent development concerned with microcomputer communications has been that of the local-area network (LAN). As a non-hierarchical network, any LAN needs protocols which govern use of its communications media (coaxial cable, twisted pairs or fibre). While large national and international computer networks use packet switching techniques with sophisticated network, host communication, and process communication protocols, simpler protocols devised for microcomputer network use and for small-scale computer networks (local-area networks) are sufficiently straightforward to be suitable for LSI interface circuits. A number of manufacturers have available, or under development, devices which will implement the Ethernet protocols, discussed in chapter 10.

5.7.1 SDLC INTERFACES[27]

The synchronous data link control standards define, with some flexibility, various levels of communication in a system which possesses one master CPU and a number of slave devices, communicating over a loop, point-to-point, or multipoint configuration. The mode of transmission may be either half-duplex or full-duplex, using non-return-to-zero invert (NRZI) encoding, which facilitates clock extraction, usually achieved using phase-locked loop techniques. The SDLC standard is bit-oriented, meaning that no constraints are placed on the user to transmit data in any particular format (e.g. 8-bit characters). The information transmitted using SDLC may use any code or format, and is just treated as a number of bits, bracketted by 'frame' identifiers, address, and control information. The address and control information possesses 'bit significance', that is, it is identified by counting bits from the start of the data block, or frame.

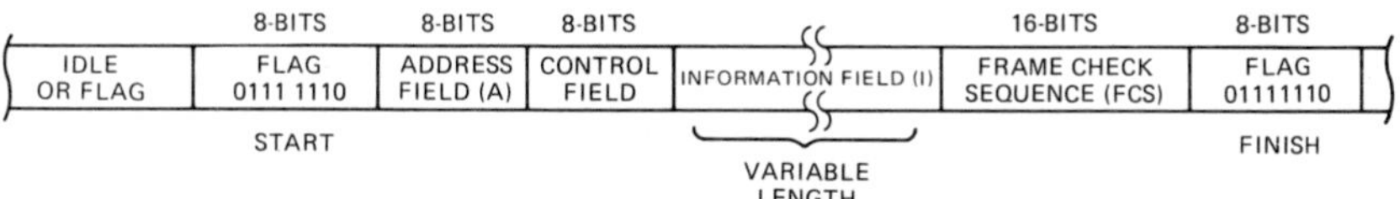

Fig. 5.28 SDLC frame format.

An SDLC frame contains a number of fields, illustrated in fig. 5.28. The flag fields at the beginning and end of the frame serve as delimiters, and should obviously be unique, so there is no possibility of a random data pattern inadvertantly imitating a flag bit pattern, and causing a spurious 'end-of-frame' indication. There are two ways of ensuring flag uniqueness: either data should be restricted so that the only valid data bit patterns cannot imitate the flag pattern, or the data stream must be modified by the transmission circuitry, and restored by the reception circuitry, to ensure the uniqueness of the flag. The latter technique will make the system capable of carrying data in any format, without restriction, i.e. 'code-transparent'. The advantage of code transparency is that the same bit-oriented SDLC may be used to transmit ASCII data in 8-bit characters, binary machine code programs, or any other format.

The way in which the transmission circuitry operates to preserve the unique flag is as follows: the SDLC flag is the bit pattern 01111110, i.e. exactly six consecutive '1's, bracketted by '0's. Whenever the transmitter circuitry encounters five consecutive 1s in a data, address or control bit stream, it automatically inserts a 0 in the stream after the five 1s. This extra 0 ensures that data, address and control information can never have the six consecutive 1s of the flag. Since the 0 is always inserted after five 1s, irrespective of the logic level of the sixth bit, the receiver will recognise the first six bits of a flag, '011111', and then examine the next bit: if the next bit is a 1, the bit pattern is a flag, and the address and control fields follow the trailing zero. If the next bit is a 0, it has been inserted in the data, address or control stream by the transmitter, and must be removed before the data is passed on. The action of the transmitter is called 'bit stuffing', and that of the receiver, 'bit stripping'. Between frames, an SDLC station will transmit either flag or idle (all 1s) characters.

The address and control fields are defined to suit the master-slave protocols of SDLC and are transmitted least-significant bit first. Thus a frame sent by the master CPU to a slave will have the destination (slave) address in its address field, and a command code in its control field, whereas one sent by a slave will contain the originating (slave) address and a response code in the control field. As well as providing access to individual slave devices, the address field may contain a 'broadcast' address, which allows the master station to send data to all slaves simultaneously. The frame check sequence (FCS), defined as the trailing 16 bits of the frame just preceding the termination flag sequence, is a standard block check which covers all the frame bits between the flags. The FCS is similar to a cyclic redundancy check (CRC) word, and like a CRC, uses a generator polynomial, which is usually the CCITT standard polynomial $X^{16} + X^{12} + X^5 + 1$. The 16-bit frame check sequence is the complement of the remainder obtained when the sequence of bits between the end of the leading flag to the beginning of the FCS is divided by the generator polynomial.

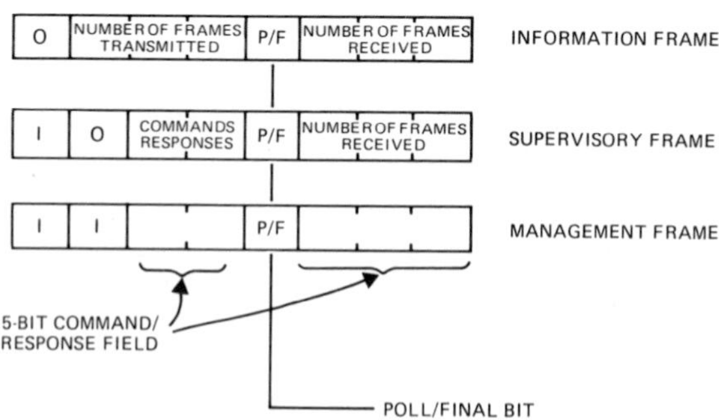

Fig. 5.29 SDLC control field formats.

The control field of SDLC may contain a number of commands, some of which will depend upon the configuration of the network, whether it is point-to-point, multipoint, or loop. In the original definition of the standard, three groups of control field are defined, depending upon whether the associated frame is an information frame (one that carries data), a supervisory frame (for network control) or an unnumbered or non-sequenced frame (for special control purposes). The structure of each type of control field is shown in fig. 5.29. Because SDLC protocol usually uses full-duplex links, successive frames may be transmitted without any pauses for acknowledgement, up to a maximum of seven unacknowledged frames. To keep track of asynchronous acknowledgements, a 3-bit binary sequence number is included in the control field of all information frames, which is incremented with each frame sent, and counts modulo-8 (i.e. 'wraps round' from 7 to 0). The transmit sequence number corresponds to the number of the current frame; the received sequence number corresponds to the number of the last frame for which an acknowledgement has been received. The two should always be different, separated by at least one. The P/F bit (poll/final) is used in polling. The supervisory frame control field is used to control the network, and different uses of the field are distinguished by a 2-bit type field, coded as follows:

Type	Meaning
00	Acknowledgement frame
01	Negative acknowledgement frame (the received sequence number indicates the first incorrectly received frame, and the transmitting station will retransmit this and all subsequent frames).
10	Receiver not ready (typically because buffers are full).
11	Selective reject (only the indicated frame should be transmitted).

The unnumbered frame control field has a 2-bit type field and a 3-bit modifier field, which together will allow thirty-two possible control actions. Typically, not all these may be used, but some that are commonly implemented are:

DISCONNECT	Station is going down, and will no longer be available on the network.
SRNM	Set normal response mode, i.e. a station wishes to be connected to the network.
FRMR	Frame reject. Used to indicate that a frame has been received which has the correct checksum, but is illegal in some other way. A 24-bit data field indicates the reason for the rejection.

The interfaces available which implement some of the basic features of SDLC provide functions which allow a CPU to realise an implementation that is a reasonable subset of the full SDLC definition. In hardware, generation of NRZI full or half-duplex signals, and clock recovery from them, and transmission and recognition of flags is provided, as well as recognition of a unique abort sequence (seven or more ones). Bit stuffing and stripping is also performed by the hardware as is CRC generation and comparison. Address and control fields are generated from registers, loaded with appropriate data from the CPU; the interface receiver will load these fields (both 8 bit) into registers for action by the CPU. Although data is not constrained to be provided in bytes (the protocol is a bit-oriented one), most of the interfaces do handle data in bytes, merely for convenience, using either interrupt-driven or DMA transfers.

The 16-bit microprocessor is likely to be the most widely-used CPU in the burgeoning 'information technology' market, where communications facilities are of paramount importance, and where such communications are required to be more sophisticated than simple asynchronous RS-232C links. SDLC (and the ISO high-level data link control, HDLC, which is similar to SDLC, but does not allow loop-mode operation, and has extended control and address fields) is ideally suited to virtually any such synchronous communications, whether they are centred around a hierarchical network, or a simpler single-link configuration. Indeed, SDLC/HDLC forms part of the CCITT recommendation X25, which defines a set of signals, electrical specifications, and formats for a packet-switched network. SDLC is used for the link specification.

5.7.2 GPIB INTERFACES

GPIB[28-30] is essentially a parallel byte-wide data transmission system standard, arranged around a 24-pin connector, which carries sixteen logic signals, driven by open-collector line drivers, and with resistive terminators. The sixteen signals are as shown in table 5.7; all are active-low.

Table 5.7 GPIB signals

Name	Description
DIO1-DIO8	Data input-output lines (Bus)
NRFD	Not ready for data. Driven by all listener devices as a 'wired-OR' indication that all devices are ready to accept data
DAV	Data valid. Issued by a talker device to indicate that data is available on the bus
NDAC	Not data accepted. Issued by a listener device, and released when data has been read from the bus
ATN	Attention. Issued by the bus controller device to indicate that address or control information has been placed on the bus
EOI	End-or-identify. A talker device uses EOI to notify a listener device that the data byte currently on DOI1-8 is the last one. A controller uses it with ATN to initiate a parallel poll sequence
IFC	Interface clear. Used by a controller to initialise all slave devices to a known state
REN	Remote enable. Used by the controller to assert its bus mastership
SRQ	Service request. Issued by any device requiring service from the controller

Devices are connected to the bus in parallel (the GPIB recommended connector allows piggy-back stacking); each device has a preset primary address, and may have secondary addresses to control its functions. Devices are all under the control of a GPIB controller (normally a CPU), and may be configured as either talker or listener, by hardware or by programming. When the controller causes all devices on the bus to be initialised, it must then set the devices which are required for a particular bus transfer to be talkers or listeners, before initiating any transfers.

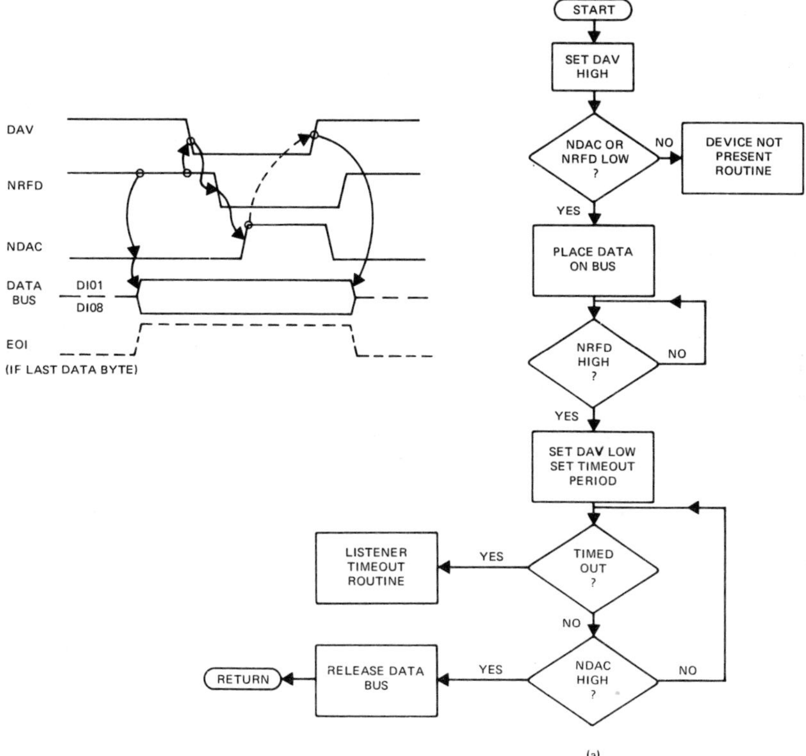

Fig. 5.30(a) GPIB handshaking: talker procedure.

All transfers are carried out over DIO1-8, the data bus lines, using the ground-true signals DAV, NRFD and NDAC to implement handshaking. The basic handshake timing diagram is shown in fig. 5.30(a), which assumes a talker device communicating with a single listener device, with both devices already configured. Initially, NDAC and NRFD are low, indicating that the listener device has not accepted data, and is not ready for data, and DAV is driven high by the talker device, indicating that data is not available on the bus. The transfer sequence starts with the listener indicating its readiness to accept data, by raising NRFD. The talker then responds by putting data onto DIO1-8, and signals that the data is stable on the bus by lowering DAV (data available). The listener, upon receipt of DAV, will immediately lower NRFD to indicate that it cannot accept further data, and will raise NDAC after it has latched the data, indicating that data has been accepted. As soon as the talker detects that NDAC has been raised, it is able to release DAV and remove data from the bus. The listener will respond to DAV going high by asserting NDAC, and when it is able to accept the next data byte on DIO1-8, will raise NRFD, and the cycle repeats. The flowchart shown in fig. 5.30(b) will further clarify the sequence.

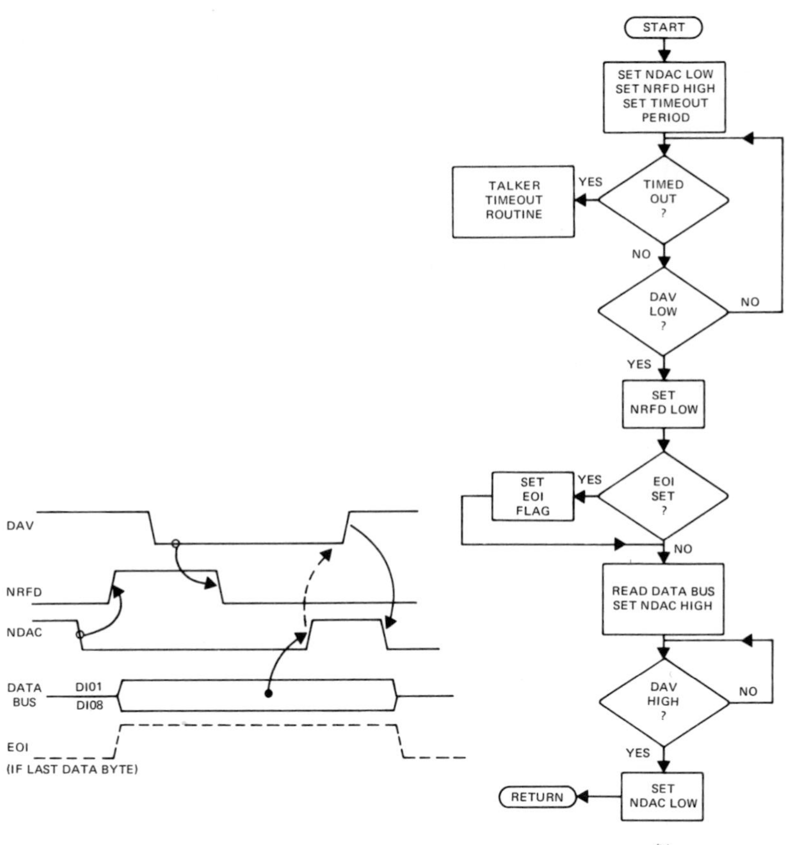

Fig. 5.30(b) GPIB handshaking: listener procedure.

When the controller is setting up other devices as talker or listeners, the same handshake occurs, but the controller asserts ATN for the duration of an address transfer. Since only one talker can be present at any given time, all other devices stop talking when the controller issues a talk address. Each device has a 5-bit address, allowing thirty-one different addresses, with one universal disable address. A secondary 5-bit address may be used, again with thirty-one possible addresses and a universal disable address, as control functions. If both the primary (device) address and the secondary (control) address are used, ATN remains asserted while they are transferred in sequence. As soon as a device has been set up by the controller, it may participate in a data transfer, using the handshaking signals DAV, NRFD and NDAC. Where multiple bytes of data are transferred, the last byte is indicated by the talker asserting EOI. Other signals used by GPIB are detailed in table 5.7.

As mentioned previously, the GPIB is basically an instrumentation bus, and is ideally suited for automatic test equipment (ATE), so its speed of data transfer is not especially high by computer standards. The widespread acceptance of GPIB for all manner of interfacing duties has been due to the simplicity of the bus signals, coupled with their accent on reliability of operation and support of asynchronous transfers. The bus interfaces are ideally suited for integrated circuit implementation, and many manufacturers now offer GPIB interfaces, in the form of chip sets with separate bus drivers, or bipolar single-chip versions with sufficient drive capability to meet bus requirements. The interfaces all contain several control, data and status registers, accessible in microprocessor CPU I/O or memory address space. The CPU may program the GPIB addresses of the interface, including both primary and secondary addresses. Transfers may be handled by DMA or by program control using interrupts, and devices on the bus may be polled automatically. Such devices will certainly find application in many 16-bit systems, especially personal computer systems, where their hardware functions will supersede software implementations like that of the 8-bit Commodore PET. Instruments based on 16-bit microprocessors are already commonplace, and provision of GPIB facilities on such instruments has become virtually mandatory – another obvious niche for the hardware GPIB interface.

5.7.3 OTHER COMMUNICATIONS INTERFACES

As more sophisticated systems are envisaged, and networking becomes more common, integrated interfacing circuits are emerging which will implement their protocols. Obvious contenders for implementation are the X25 standard for packet-switched networks, Ethernet or other CSMA/CD protocols, or Cambridge Ring protocols, and indeed, all are available in integrated form. X25 may form the basis for a large-scale packet-switched network; it defines signals and protocols for the first three layers of the ISO open systems interconnection (OSI) model – the physical (electrical) layer, the data link layer and the network (protocol) layer. Its implementation is an obvious evolutionary step from the integrated SDLC interface, since SDLC is used for the X25 physical and data link layers. Manufacturers backing one or other of the local-area network (LAN) standards have encouraged design of Ethernet and ring-type interfaces. In the light of likely developments in information technology, the next step may be the development of communications interfaces which will allow fibre-optic networks.

5.8 Other interfaces

This chapter has concentrated upon interfaces which have emerged contemporary with, and sometimes specifically to serve the 16-bit microprocessor, and which complement the older interfaces designed for 8-bit systems. Of course, all of the older interfaces can be used with a 16-bit CPU. Devices likely to be of great importance are diskette and Winchester disk controllers, VDU controllers, bubble memory controllers for non-volatile storage, and encryption/decryption devices, for such security-conscious applications as electronic funds transfer. Another device likely to increase in importance as custom interfaces are required for specialist applications is the 'universal peripheral interface (controller)'. This is a device, usually based around an 8-bit CPU, with on-chip ROM which can be programmed to perform any required peripheral control functions, and which communicates with the main (host) CPU via its built-in bus interface.

5.8.1 DISKETTE INTERFACES

Diskette interfaces[31,32,34] are mature devices, which have undergone extensive developments as interfaces for 8-bit systems, the most popular types using soft-sectored diskettes. While 8-bit microprocessors will often be used without diskette drives, it is difficult to imagine any 16-bit personal computer system without them. The available diskette, or floppy-disk controllers (FDCs), handle both diskette drive control and data formatting, usually with selectable recording mode dependent on density. The diskette was originally introduced as a storage device by IBM, and among the most common recording modes and formats for 8 in diskettes are the single-density IBM 3740 format (FM) and IBM System 34 double-density format (MFM). Typically, the diskette controller must be capable of taking an unused diskette intended for soft-sectored use, and must format the diskette. The diskette will be divided into annular concentric 'tracks', defined by radial recording head movement on a stepper-motor driven leadscrew, and the tracks themselves will be divided equally into 'sectors', defined by recording bit patterns at regular intervals as the diskette rotates beneath the read/write head. Sectors are referenced with respect to a single 'index hole', which is punched right through the diskette material, and sensed optically as it passes with the diskette rotation between a lamp and phototransistor pair.

The track format (IBM3740) is shown in fig. 5.31. Tracks are numbered from the outside (00) to the innermost (76), with track 00 reserved by convention for a directory or index of diskette contents. Each sector consists of a leading gap preceding an identification field which itself consists of a synchronisation field of 6 bytes of zeros, followed by an identifier address mark, and fields which include track number, sector number, and sector length, and terminated by a 16-bit CRC word (created using the generator polynomial $X^{16} + X^{12} + X^5 + 1$, the same as that used for SDLC). After another gap, a data field completes the sector; it consists of another synchronisation field of 8 bytes of zeros, a data address mark, 128, 256 or 512 bytes of data, and a final 16-bit CRC word.

With a typical controller, the track format may be programmed, along with the number of sectors/track, the length of each sector, and gap sizes. Any 'bad' tracks which have persistent errors can be flagged by putting a special code in their ID field – when a disk is formatted, it will normally be checked for read/write accuracy, and any bad tracks flagged during this initialisation phase. Tracks 00 to 74 are used for data, and two 'spare' tracks allow bad tracks to be replaced without altering the logical track numbering.

Typical FDC commands are:

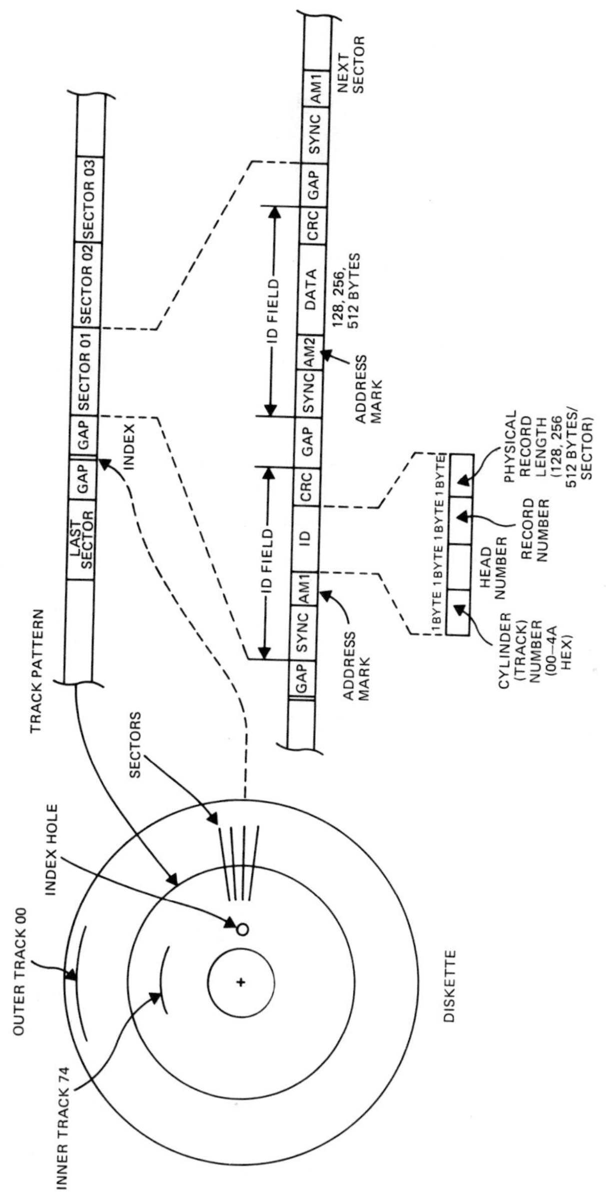

Fig. 5.31 IBM 3740 diskette format.

FORMAT TRACK		as discussed
READ DRIVE STATUS		(write-protected disk, head at track 00, ready, etc.)
SEEK		specified track
SPECIFY		drive characteristics, such as head stepper motor rate, settling time, head load (move into close proximity to disk surface) time
RESET		FDC and diskette interface electronics
READ	DATA DELETED DATA ID	of specified track starting at a specified sector, and continuing for a specified number of sectors
WRITE	DATA DELETED DATA	on specified track, starting at a specified segment
VERIFY	DATA DELETED DATA	using CRC
SCAN	DATA DELETED DATA	for specified pattern

Within these relatively sophisticated commands, the FDC will issue commands to the drive to select the drive, load the head onto the diskette, move the head, identify the diskette index hole, alter the head write current (the read/write head needs less drive on the inner tracks than on the outer ones, where the linear motion of the surface under the head is higher), identify whether the diskette is write-protected, check the ID CRC and the data CRC, and transfer data using DMA. The software making up the disk handler in any CPU operating system may be reduced in complexity and size by relying on these higher level functions. The CPU is relieved of running timing tasks for head motor drive waveforms and settling time delays, by the SPECIFY command, and may be released from the handler task during these periods. The existence of a DMA facility is essential to meet the speed of data transfer in modern diskette systems, and, once again, unburdens the CPU.

5.8.2 BUBBLE MEMORIES AND CONTROLLERS

Much has been said and written about the potential of bubble memory for dense non-volatile storage, but so far, the storage technology has not achieved a high degree of general user acceptance, primarily because of its high cost. Many manufacturers have attempted to enter the bubble memory field with memories of capacity up to 1 Mbit, and all but a handful have dropped out, finding it difficult to handle both magnetic thin film, and semiconductor interface technologies. The material forming the storage medium is a thin film of synthetic garnet, with loops and tracks of permalloy patterns printed on the film surface. The film is uniformly magnetically polarised in one direction, and data is stored as 'bubbles' of micron size, of reverse magnetic polarity to the rest of the film. By convention, the presence of a bubble at a particular point on a loop or track is considered a '1', and the absence of a bubble is considered a '0'. The magnetic environment is formed using a permanent magnet to create a steady bias field, and a pair of orthogonal drive coils which create a rotating magnetic field when driven with alternating current of frequency around 100 kHz. The rotating magnetic field interacts with the permalloy patterns, and drives any bubbles round a continuous loop of the patterns. The loop may be viewed as a shift register with continuously circulating data, so access to a selected bit position in the loop must be achieved serially. Organisation of the complete memory will be as shown in fig. 5.32, and will consist of a number of loops, communicating with an 'input track' of permalloy patterns, and a similar 'output track'. Bubbles are created using a generator which operates by replicating a permanently available 'seed' bubble, which remains at the generator, and the replicated bubbles are fed down the input track. They are transferred, when required, to a storage loop using a magnetic 'swap gate', which is able to transfer bubbles in both directions, allowing old data to be removed from a loop at the same time as new data is transferred to it. Any old data propagates down the input track, and the bubbles are destroyed in a terminator at the end of the track.

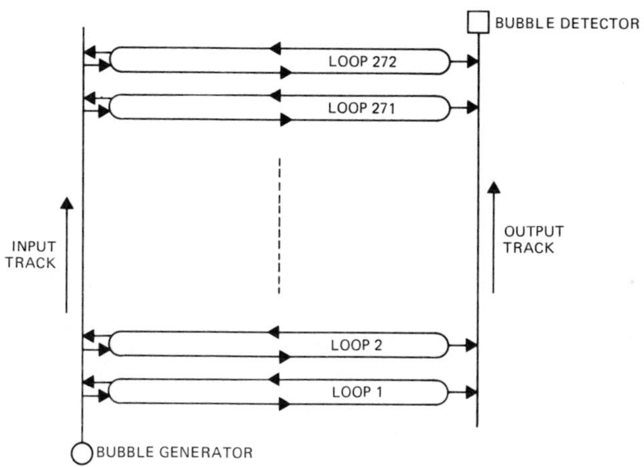

Fig. 5.32 Bubble memory functional organisation.

Bubbles are read non-destructively from a loop onto an output track, using a replicate gate, which splits a bubble into two, one of which is fed back into the storage ring, and the other transferred to the output track. They propagate along the output track to a detector, often a magnetoresistive one, which will generate a few millivolts when a bubble is presented to it. The bubble is then destroyed. As well as the normal storage loops of a bubble memory, a further 'boot loop' is usually provided, which contains a loop mask code which allows faulty loops to be bypassed, and a synchronisation code which identifies the position of locations in the continuously circulating main storage loops. The boot loop is usually initialised by the manufacturer, and used by control circuitry to manipulate the memory.

The interfacing requirements of a bubble memory are:

(a) A coil driver to generate the rotating magnetic field.
(b) A current pulse generator to drive the bubble generator on the memory.
(c) A formatter and sense amplifier (FSA), which interprets the boot loop data, writes data transferred from a main control unit, and reads data. A sophisticated burst error detection and correction system, based on the Fire codes, is necessary.
(d) A control unit which will communicate with the CPU bus system, and which will handle DMA transfers, since although access to a particular data location may be slow, of the order of tens of milliseconds, the transfer rate may be of the order of 100 kbits/s. A first-in, first-out (FIFO) buffer may provide a useful facility, allowing burst DMA.

Chip sets implementing these functions are available[36], and like the diskette controller, they possess a reasonably high level command set:

INITIALIZE
READ, WRITE
READ, WRITE BOOTLOOP
SEEK
READ STATUS
READ CORRECTED DATA
RESET

Although bubble memory devices increase system complexity considerably, bubbles offer the advantages of non-volatility (although electrically erasable PROM, E^2PROM, also gives this facility, with lower system complexity), good environmental tolerance to dust (unlike diskettes and tapes) and to radiation (unlike semiconductor memory) and high density. They are already beginning to be used in high-performance non-cost-sensitive applications, such as those in military systems, aerospace equipment and oilfield instrumentation. Such systems will inevitably require the computing power of the modern 16-bit microprocessor.

5.8.3 ENCRYPTION/DECRYPTION DEVICES

As digital communications becomes more pervasive, more and more sensitive financial and commercial information will be transmitted in this way, and the need for some security devices will increase. To this end, the US National Bureau of Standards (NBS) has issued a Data Encryption Standard (DES) which consists of an algorithm for encoding data using a 56-bit user-defined key to translate a 64-bit block of unencoded data into a 64-bit block of encrypted data. Devices are now available which will implement the DES algorithm in hardware, using data transferred from microprocessor memory via on-chip DMA logic, with a software-written key. Although the absolute security of DES has been a hotly debated issue, it is likely that its use will increase, and microcomputer networks will find DES interfaces useful for passing confidential information over publicly accessible transmission media.

5.8.4 UNIVERSAL PERIPHERAL CONTROLLER (UPC)

While manufacturers are still introducing sophisticated special-purpose dedicated interfaces, the UPC[37-40], which can be programmed and configured by the microprocessor systems designer, is likely to increase in importance. The modern 16-bit microprocessor is very likely to be used in a complex application, with high-performance peripheral devices, and a frequent requirement may be an interface for a non-standard, perhaps new, device. A programmable, EPROM-based UPC can be used to implement specialist low-volume interfaces in an extremely cost-effective way.

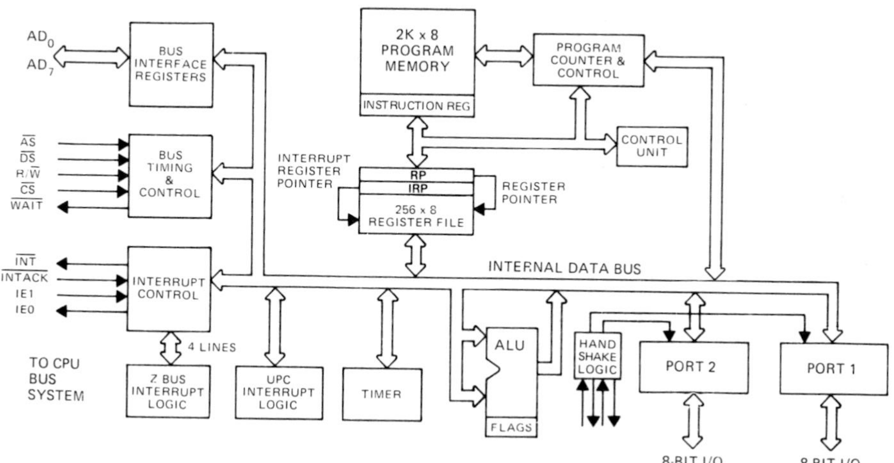

Fig. 5.33 Zilog Z-UPC schematic.

A typical UPC is shown in fig. 5.33. It may be seen that it is very similar to an 8-bit single-chip microcomputer, and indeed, may be derived from one, and share its instruction set (for example, the Zilog Z8034 UPC is compatible with the Z8, and the Intel 8741 UPI is compatible with the 8748 family). The UPC shown is truly a *slave microprocessor*. It possesses an interface to a CPU bus system, with a register file partly configured for dual-port access by the main (master) CPU or the UPC. A number of ports are present (giving up to twenty-four I/O pins on the Z8034), providing input-output lines which may be connected to, and drive, the inputs and outputs of the peripheral device. Like a conventional single-chip microcomputer, this UPC contains an 8-bit arithmetic-and-logic unit (ALU), 2K × 8 program ROM, and RAM, configured as a register file of 256 8-bit registers, organised into sixteen groups of sixteen registers each accessed via a register point (RP). One group of sixteen registers may be designated interface registers, positioned anywhere within the register file, and accessed via a second interface register pointer (IRP). This group of interface registers may be accessed directly by both the main CPU and the UPC for data transfers. Control and status information is transferred between the two microprocessors via an additional four dedicated registers. Facilities for interrupting the main CPU from the UPC are available via four of the UPC I/O lines, and provision is made to support the standard Zilog daisy-chaining peripheral priority scheme. Like the Z8, from which it is derived, the Zilog UPC has two on-chip timers with prescalers.

This brief discussion has outlined the main points of just one universal peripheral interface or controller, but it serves to illustrate the versatility of the concept. While most common interface tasks, or those requiring very high speed, will use dedicated interfaces designed by the semiconductor manufacturer, the UPI or UPC offers an ideal solution to any low volume, non-standard interfacing problems.

CHAPTER 6
Instruction sets

6.1 Introduction

The new 16-bit microprocessors all have instruction sets which are a considerable improvement upon those of their 8-bit predecessors. The flexibility of instructions which have counterparts in third generation 8-bit machines has been greatly enhanced by the removal of many of the apparently arbitrary restrictions on features such as addressing modes and dedicated registers. The architecture of the new generation has influenced instruction set design by allowing microcoded instruction sets, and by providing new hardware features, such as segmentation registers, which need support from the instruction set. Lessons have been learned from the third generation 8-bit microprocessors, and applied to the new 16-bit designs: if we take the two industry-standard microprocessors, 8085 and 6802, their deficiencies in instruction set convenience are well known. Users have long felt the need for better index register facilities, for hardware-multiply-divide instructions, for relocatability of object code and for string handling functions. The Zilog Z80, a well-established 8-bit CPU which does not have such a wide user base as the Intel and Motorola products, has a number of features which have been plagiarised by the designers of the new 16-bit CPUs, and can be properly described as the conceptual link between the third generation 8-bit microprocessors and second generation 8-bit microprocessors and second generation 16-bit ones. The Z80, operating with an instruction set which itself was based on the 8080 set, provides a number of quite sophisticated techniques for block or string handling, uses two index registers (after a criticism that the single MC6800 index register was inadequate), allows several interrupt modes, and both shift and rotate instructions. Following the lead of the Z80, all the second-generation 16-bit machines possess similar features, but have also looked to the 16-bit minicomputer field for improvement ideas.

Relocatability and memory segmentation have been recognised as the major important enhancements. Edsger Dijkstra, inventor of the structured GOTO-less programming style favoured by many mainframe systems analysts and programmers, complained that the early microprocessors put the state of the art computer science 'back 25 years'. In part, this remark can be justified by the inability of the common 8-bit microprocessor to perform any sensible memory management. It is not impossible to write position-independent code for the 8-bit machines, merely somewhat restrictive; their addressing structure can be used to support physical addresses mapped from logical ones, but only by extensive use of machine internal registers, with a time penalty so severe as to make the exercise almost pointless. The 16-bit microprocessor overcomes the practical problem of relocatability by 'segmentation'. In the case of the 8086, memory segments used for code, data, stack and 'extra' data are supported by segment address registers inside the CPU; in the Z8000 and MC68000, the main support lies in 'memory management units' (MMUs), VLSI integrated circuits connected between the microprocessor address bus and memory address inputs. Both styles require special features in the instruction sets of their respective microprocessors. New microprocessor control commands have been developed, to give a minicomputer-like framework for system software and multiple microprocessor systems.

Overall impression of the new 16-bit microprocessors is that all support similar facilities, but that the detailed styles differ considerably. A very evident difference in philosophy may be seen not only in the way in which the new microprocessors each treat memory relocatability but also in their approaches to instruction execution and code compactness. Intel, with the 8086, has opted for a register set based on compatibility with the 8085, and, by using instruction pipelining via its BIU to keep up the execution speed, allows instructions to use variable numbers of bytes, and does not constrain instruction codes to lie at an even byte address or occupy an even number of bytes. Obvious code compaction will result – short offsets, for example, need only occupy one byte, rather than a whole 16-bit word with zeros filling unused bit positions.

Zilog, by contrast, does constrain Z8000 instructions to lie at even byte boundaries, but claims a high code density brought about by careful design of instruction operation codes. Unconstrained by compatibility with the Z80 (unlike Intel, who promised that the 8086 would be compatible with the 8080/8085, and had to design the 8086 structure accordingly), Zilog, or more particularly, the team led by Masatoshi Shima, who designed the Z8000, aimed for an instruction set which coded the statistically most frequency instructions using as few (preferably one) words of memory as possible, increasing both density of code and speed of operation (which in modern microprocessors, may well be limited by memory access time during multiple memory reference instructions). Another of the claims made by Zilog is that of regularity of registers and general architecture, echoed by Motorola with the MC68000, which has internal data paths and registers all arranged to be 32-bits wide. Certainly the existence of a number (sixteen) of general-purpose registers with virtually no restrictions as to their use makes assembly code programming simpler; whether this facility will necessarily lead to few instructions to perform a given task is another matter. The ability to use an arbitrary register as a data stack register will certainly lead to economy of code where first-in, last-out processing predominates.

6.2 Addressing modes

The range and versatility of addressing modes provided by a microprocessor dominates the performance of its instruction set. One of the most successful ranges of minicomputers, the Digital Equipment Corporation PDP-11 series, is

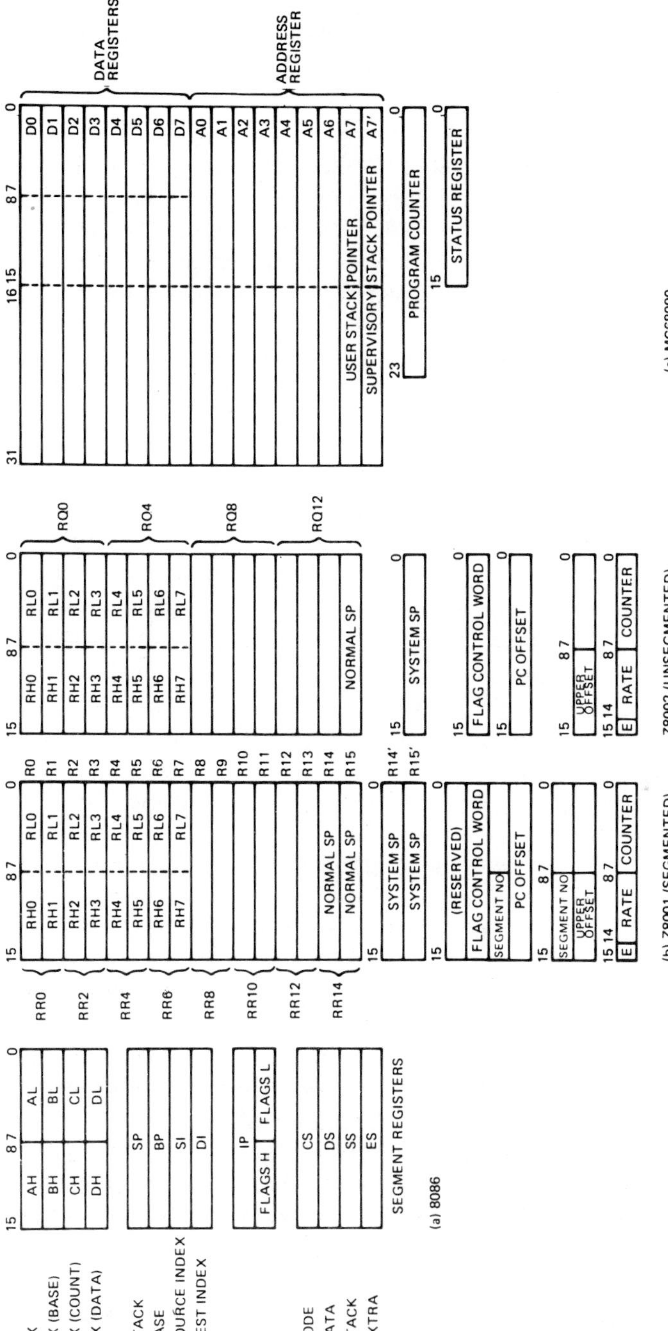

Fig. 6.1 Register models; (a) 8086, (b) Z8001 (segmented), Z8002 (unsegmented), (c) MC68000.

notable for the power of its addressing modes, and the same basic design has served as one of Digital's major product lines for more than a decade. In the following assessment of the three 16-bit microprocessor addressing modes, the influence of the PDP-11 is noticeable, especially in the provision of system support features and facilities for writing re-entrant code.

The register models of the 8086, Z8000 and 68000 have been discussed in chapter 4, but are reproduced in diagram form in fig. 6.1. The need to provide a more diverse range of addressing modes than those of the 'industry-standard' 8-bit microprocessors, coupled with the commitment to supporting an address bus with a range of addressing greater than 64 kbytes, has resulted in microprocessors which have a larger and more general register set than their predecessors. Nevertheless, addressing remains byte-oriented, with the least significant address bit defining upper or lower byte of a 16-bit word. The power of multiple, rather than single index registers, and of base address registers, a common feature in 16-bit minicomputers, has been one motive for the expansion, but so too has been the appreciation that provision of more than one register which can act as a stack pointer can ease the problems of multitask programming. In particular, design of re-entrant subroutines is made easier by the presence of more than a single stack pointer. Autoincrement and autodecrement of addresses are further examples of facilities which the modern microprocessor must provide. It will be seen that the 8086, Z8000 and MC68000 all provide these features in one way or another; although their techniques are noticeably different, it must be remembered that the solutions which look elegant and have won the approval of the purists, do not necessarily lead to the fastest or most economic route to a design, and that software support is worth at least as much as good hardware. The history of computer usage is littered with elegant designs which have not been commercial successes!

The three microprocessors previously named will now have their addressing capabilities considered separately, although a high degree of similarity does exist between them. They are considered on a chronological (in terms of date of launch) basis.

6.2.1 8086 ADDRESSING

The 8086, as mentioned previously, has maintained compatibility with its 8-bit predecessor, the 8080 (8085), and indeed, has spawned an 8-bit offspring, the 8088 (see chapter 2, intermediate microprocessors). Its 'general register file' thus contains four 16-bit general purpose registers, the 'HL group', addressable not only as 4 word registers, but also as 8 byte registers. Coupled with these are a set of four more 16-bit registers, the 'pointer and index (P & I)' group, consisting of two pointer registers, the base pointer and stack pointer, and two index registers, source index and destination index. Although designated, the registers can participate in many of the computational functions of the microprocessor; at first sight they do not appear so regular as the registers of the other two microprocessors, but this does not seem to detract from the capabilities of the 8086. The real departure in philosophy is evident in the provision of internal segment address register. Segmentation of memory, a concept first used with minicomputer memory management systems, is common to all the microprocessors, but the 8086 is the only one to manage it totally internally; both the Z8000 and MC68000 are designed to work with external memory management units or MMUs. Four segment address registers are provided with the 8086, designated 'code segment', 'data segment', 'stack segment' and 'extra segment', and generate 20-bit physical addresses from a 16-bit effective address or offset address (which has a range of 64 kbytes within a segment) as described in chapter 4.

The 8086 has several basic ways of addressing operands within a memory segment, using registers from the general register file. Intel use the term 'displacement', rather than offset, to indicate that a constant contained in the instruction code should be added to other terms to form an effective address. The four memory reference modes are:

(a) Direct, via a 16-bit offset address.
(b) Indirect, through a base address register, with an optional 8 or 16-bit displacement.
(c) Indirect through an index register, again with an optional 8 or 16-bit displacement.
(d) Indirect through the sum of an index and a base register, with an optional 8 or 16-bit displacement.

There are, in addition, some default options which control the segment register used to compare physical addresses. Having assigned segment registers to code, data, stack and extra segments, it is obviously sensible to infer which must be accessed from the addressing mode used. Thus whenever the BP (base pointer) register is used to compute the effective address, the stack segment register is used to compute the physical address. The instruction pointer IP is also invariably used with the code segment register. Any general address operations will use the data segment register; any stack operations which use the stack pointer SP will also automatically use the stack segment (SS) register. There is a further irrevocable default condition concerning string primitive operations, which will be discussed later in the chapter.

Although the default use of segment registers will be acceptable in the majority of memory reference operations, added flexibility will be achieved if the segment registers can be used more generally, and in fact, this is possible. A 'segment override prefix' of a single byte specifying which segment register is to be used, precedes the instruction itself, and will work for most memory reference instructions. A number of instructions exist within the 8086 set which relate specifically to manipulation of the segment registers, and which have no counterparts in the Z8000, MC68000 instruction sets.

It will be noted that there are no autoincrement, autodecrement instruction modifiers; it has been recognised that these facilities are useful mainly during repetitive searching, copying or comparing operations. The string primitives, therefore, implicitly use autoincrement and autodecrement on their source and destination address registers. The 'string primitives' are the only instructions which allow indexed addressing (with autoincrement by an amount appropriate to word or byte operands) on both source and destination addresses. Three of the instructions are of this form, while the other two are accumulator-memory transfer instructions. A repeat prefix may be used to cause repetition of a primitive operation until a count (held in a general register) has been reached; a premature exit from the loop may be programmed to occur, using the zero flag.

Register addressing allows use of any of the general register file registers for 16-bit operands, or any of the HL group for 8-bit operands. The more complex arithmetic operations, such as multiplication and division, use implied register addressing involving only the accumulator; so too do some of the more unusual arithmetic instructions (decimal and ASCII adjustment, translation, etc.). Although the limitations of such implied register addressing may appear to make life awkward for the programmer, forcing him to specifically move data into one particular register prior to instruction execution, there are, nevertheless, some instructions within this group which are not duplicated explicitly in other microprocessors.

Immediate addressing may be used with all two-operand instructions, with the immediate data operands following any other addressing mode displacement constants in the instruction. The immediate addressing mode may be viewed as a restrictive form of implied program-counter relative addressing. A more usual form of relative addressing is reserved for conditional jump instructions, which possess operation codes containing a signed 8-bit displacement (which implies that the destination address must be within ± 128 bytes of the instruction). Unconditional jump and call instructions may cross segment boundaries or move within a segment by specification of a 16-bit displacement, or a 16-bit offset and a 16-bit segment address.

The addressing modes are summarised in fig. 6.2. It will be appreciated that these modes have been designed with a number of objectives in mind:

(a) Upward compatibility with the 8080/8085 family.
(b) Inclusion of non-8085 features popularised by the 8-bit Z80 (seen by many as a significant 'upgrade' to the 8080, although not necessarily offering improved execution speed).
(c) Inclusion of features which aid relocatability and memory management (for example, inter-segment jumps and calls).

What has emerged is a microprocessor with a rather unorthodox set of addressing modes, but one which is nevertheless extremely powerful.

6.2.2 Z8000 ADDRESSING MODES

The Z8000 was designed with the hindsight of experience with 8080 and Z80 microprocessors, and aimed to more closely emulate the mid-range minicomputer (such as the PDP-11) in both instruction set and addressing modes. The register set is more general than that of the 8086, and any specified register in the set of sixteen 16-bit registers may be used as an indirect address register, an index register, or a base address register (with the exception of RØ or RRØ). The eight basic addressing modes are:

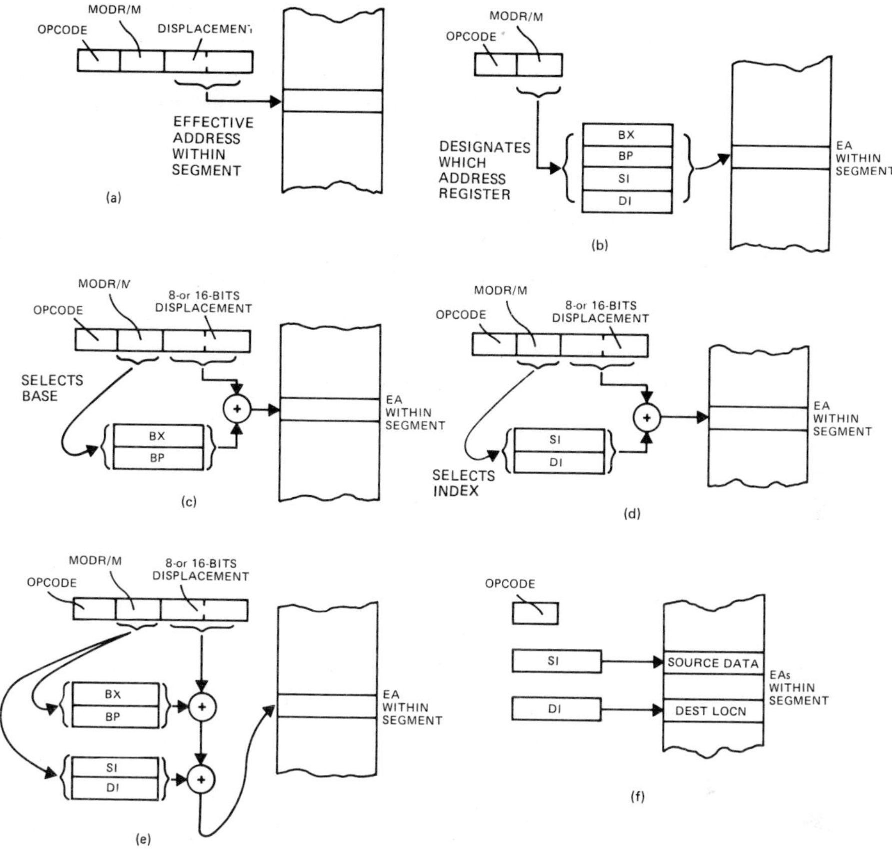

Fig. 6.2 8086 addressing modes: (a) direct addressing, (b) register indirect, (c) based addressing, (d) indexed addressing, (e) based indexed addressing, (f) string addressing.

(a) Register addressing, where the operand(s) are contained in registers specified in the instruction.
(b) Immediate, where the operand is contained within the instruction (following the operation code).
(c) Register indirect, where a register specified in the instruction holds the address of an operand.
(d) Direct, where the address of the operand is specified explicitly in the instruction.
(e) Indexed, where the operand effective address is the sum of the address specified in the instruction and the contents of the specified index register.
(f) Relative, where a displacement contained in the instruction is added to the current value of the program location counter to generate the effective address.

(g) Based, where the effective address is the sum of an offset contained in the instruction, and the contents of a designated base address register.
(h) Based-indexed, where the effective address is the sum of the contents of a specified base address register and the contents (displacement) of a specified index register.

Like the 8086, the Z8000 has no general autoincrement or autodecrement modifiers to allow (for instance) automatic indexing. It has, however, a wide range of what Zilog called 'block transfer and string manipulation' instructions which use automatic increment and decrement specified within the instruction code and a repeat modifier. A condition code may be specified within the instruction to define a termination condition. As with its predecessor, the Z80, and one of its major rivals, the 8086, the Z8000 restricts relative addressing to conditional jump instructions and calls. Based and indexed addressing, too, are largely restricted to the data transfer and arithmetic commands.

6.2.3 MC68000 ADDRESSING MODES

68000 addressing moves even closer to the mid-range minicomputer objective; its register set possesses eight 32-bit data registers, seven 32-bit address registers, and two stack pointers. Any of the registers may be specified as an index register. MC68000 addressing may be divided by mode and by category: while mode defines the way in which the effective address is computed, the category describes the uses to which the addressing mode may be put, in terms of the attributes of the location which may be addressed. Attributes are 'data', 'memory', 'control', 'alterable', and obviously a given location may possess more than one of these attributes.

There are six groups of address mode, defined below:

(a) Register direct: address register direct, data register direct.
(b) Absolute: short (16-bit address) long (32-bit address).
(c) Relative: 16-bit offset relative to program counter with optional inclusion of a specified register as an index register added to PC + offset.
(d) Register indirect: conventional indirect addressing with postincrement or predecrement, with the optional inclusion of an immediate offset value or an immediate offset value and a specified index register.
(e) Immediate: immediate data may be either the next word(s) of the instruction or, in 'quick immediate' mode, may be a byte of data contained in the instruction itself.
(f) Implied: implied addressing is a control form of addressing with an implied control register as source or destination (e.g. status register, user stack pointer, stack pointer, or program counter).

The most powerful modes are in the register indirect group, where post-increment/predecrement facilities remove the need for specific POP/PUSH instructions, and allow user data stacks to be created using any designated register as a stack pointer. The combination of modes (i.e. indirect with index and offset) give the 68000 the 'feel' of a mid-range minicomputer.

6.3 Arithmetic and logical instructions

The move to a 16-bit wordlength confers many advantages, not least the increase in speed for a given precision of operation; multiple precision operations are notoriously time consuming, and the short wordlength of the previous generation 8-bit microprocessors makes them too slow to consider for tasks which involve much arithmetic. A mere duplication of an 8-bit microprocessor instruction set would not have been sufficient to ensure competitiveness with the 16-bit minicomputer CPU, and with this part of the computer market in mind, the designers of all the new 16-bit microprocessors have offered considerable enhancement to their instruction sets. A cursory glance will show the most obvious of the new facilities, provision of hardware multiply and divide with 16-bit signed or unsigned integers. More subtle, however, is the flexibility added by the improved selection of addressing modes available, by the provision of multiple position shifts in a single instruction, and by the provision of support for multiple-precision operations. Better bit manipulation instructions, and bit tests, as well as sign extension (8 to 16 bits and maybe to 32 bits) instructions and more versatile BCD arithmetic instructions all add weight to some very impressive CPU instruction sets. This section considers arithmetic instructions in detail, grouping them as basic arithmetic, basic logical instructions, and finally shifts and rotates.

6.3.1 BASIC ARITHMETIC AND LOGICAL INSTRUCTIONS

The modern 16-bit microprocessor two operand arithmetic and logical instructions will usually be of the form 'result in register = register-operand-operator-operand-from-memory-location or register specified by effective address'. Typical of such instructions are ADD, ADC (add with carry), SUB, SBB (subtract with borrow) AND, OR, XOR (or EOR, exclusive OR); most of the addressing modes discussed in section 6.2 are available, with some minor exceptions. The 8086, for example, permits the result location to be a memory location rather than a register location, but does not allow relative addressing and has no specific 32-bit instructions. The Z8000 does not permit based addressing, but has 32-bit instructions (long word) as well as byte and 16-bit word ones. The Z8000 ADC, SBC instructions are confined to register operands only, presumably because these instructions are most likely to be used in multiple precision operations where register operands are more convenient, otherwise a word count (or precision) would have to be specified, and the total operation would require a string primitive form. Instead, the operation may be performed with indirect load-and-increment instructions, in a loop with a loop . . . while instruction.

The 68000 uses one of its data registers to hold one operand, has specific instructions which allow manipulation of address registers as well as data registers, and like the Z8000, allows operation with long word, 32-bit operands. A small restriction is the one imposed on the address register direct addressing mode, which is not permitted when byte operands are specified.

Comparison operations too, are similar in structure, with only immediate having slight deviations from the structure given at the beginning of the section. The Z8000 compare immediate with memory, for instance, is the only CP operation which does not allow long (32-bit) words as well as 8- and 16-bit ones. The 68000 possessed a unique compare-memory-with-memory command, using register indirect addressing with postincrement, which will allow string comparison when used with a looping primitive such as decrement-and-branch-on-condition (DB_{CC}).

Increment and decrement are available in conventional form in the 8086 (increment/decrement effective address-register or memory operand by one), and in a rather different form in the Z8000, where the specific amount of increment or decrement (a number from 1 to 16, specified in the form 0-15) is included in the instruction word. This Z8000 command will thus replace ADD or SUB immediate by a one-word equivalent, for immediate operands in the range 1 to 16. The immediate operand is unsigned, but the addition or subtraction is carried out in two's complement arithmetic. The 68000 has no explicit INC, DEC instructions but the equivalent operation is provided by ADDQ, SUBQ (add, subtract quick) where the quick operand is represented by 3 bits of data contained within the single instruction word allowing a maximum INC, DEC range of eight per operation.

6.3.2 HARDWARE MULTIPLICATION AND DIVISION

Multiply and divide hardware has become mandatory for any modern 16-bit microprocessor, and is usually provided in signed or unsigned form. Multiply will normally require a 16-bit multiplier and multiplicand, and produce a 32-bit product, whereas divide will normally require a 32-bit dividend and a 16-bit divisor, and produce a 16-bit quotient, and a 16-bit remainder. Because of the complexity of these operations, a register is always used to hold one 16-bit operand (multiplier, multiplicand, or divisor) and will also be used for part of the result. The MC68000 scores heavily on these operations, with its 32-bit internal registers, as a single data register may hold a 32-bit product or 32-bit dividend. Any data register may be specified for this purpose, and the basic size of operands is 16-bit, signed or unsigned. The second operand, addressed by the specified effective address, may be either in another register, or in memory.

The 8086 constrains division and multiplication operations to be performed using the accumulator (with a 16-bit extension register DX where necessary) and a memory operand, once again for signed or unsigned integers. The Z8000, like the 68000, requires a specified register and second register or memory location for its operation. It uses a second or more registers for extension values where double or quadruple-precision products or dividends are used. These other registers are implied by the one specified in the instruction code, and by this means, the Z8000 is able to offer double-precision (32-bit long word) multiplication and division. Only signed operations are allowed, however.

A very basic adjunct to the multiplication and division operations is the ability to extend wordlengths by repeating the sign bit of a short word through each bit of the higher byte or word of the required operand. All microprocessors have some form of sign extend operation, always confined to register operands, with additional extension registers being implied by the register specification in the instruction. The 8086 uses the accumulator with DX as a possible sign extension register, the Z8000 uses any specified register, which then defines a register pair or quadruple where necessary, and the MC68000 need only specify a single data register, which allows 32-bit wordlength without requiring further registers to be dedicated.

6.3.3 BCD ARITHMETIC

A unique feature of the early 8-bit microprocessors, which has been preserved by their successors, is the ability to perform arithmetic on binary-coded decimal (BCD) numbers. The industry-standard (8080/8085, MC6800, Z80) microprocessors all handle BCD numbers by using a half-carry or BCD-carry flag, set during a normal binary arithmetic operation, to provide information for a 'decimal adjust' instruction (DAA in 8-bit mnemonics). The decimal adjust could then operate on the single byte result, to translate it back to two packed BCD numbers in a single byte. The instruction is preserved in the 16-bit microprocessors as a byte mode instruction only. In the MC68000, it has been combined with the ADD, SUB operation to form single ADD decimal with extend (ABCD) or subtract decimal with extend (SBCD), which give the correct packed BCD result of each operation. The Z8000 allows DAB (decimal adjust byte) which is equivalent to the normal 8-bit adjustment. The 8086 places more emphasis on BCD arithmetic than the other two competing microprocessors. To ensure compatibility with the 8080 flag (condition-code) register, two separate adjustment instructions are included in its repertoire for addition and subtraction. Included also are unique correction commands for use with unpacked BCD operations, making direct ASCII arithmetic possible. The unpacked BCD adjustments for addition and subtraction are complemented by two more, for multiplication and division. The idea of operating directly on ASCII data (suitably masked to eliminate the higher 4 bits for 8 bit ASCII) is a powerful one for small scale applications such as measuring instruments, where invariably the display device will require either BCD or ASCII characters. For the minicomputer replacement market, however, its use will not be so widespread.

6.3.4 BIT MANIPULATION AND SHIFTS

Bit manipulation features strongly in the logical group of operations; the usual AND, OR, EOR or XOR are all provided, with word or byte operands, but individual bit test, set, and reset are also provided, with either immediate or register operands. Negate (two's complement) is also invariably provided.

Shifts and rotates, too, are comprehensively provided, both arithmetic and logical shifts, and rotates through carry, and not including carry. An arithmetic shift is one which affects carry, but does not shift explicitly through carry. For an arithmetic left shift, zeros are written to the least significant bits of the word, while the most significant bits are shifted into carry. Any sign change caused by the shift will be indicated by the overflow flag. An arithmetic right shift will maintain the sign bit of the word to the same value, and shift the least significant bits out into carry. A logical left shift will shift ones into the least significant bits of the word, and shift the most significant bits out through carry. A logical right shift will shift zeros into the most significant bits of the word, and shift the least significant bits through carry. The rotates are likewise fairly uniform – they may be specified to rotate a word left or right on its own, or through carry (or in the MC68000 case, through extend). Both carry and overflow flags will be affected for rotates, with sign for the MC68000 and Z8000, and all conditional flags except BCD carry will be affected by the shifts. All shifts and rotates have a count of places shifted and rotated associated with them, which may be specified either in a register or as an immediate operand. Immediate shift operands (Z8000 and MC68000 only) may be of restricted range (1-8) or of range appropriate to the word size, while operands contained in a count register (all 16-bit microprocessors) may simply be interpreted modulo 64, or again of a range appropriate to word size.

6.3.5 OVERALL ASSESSMENT

The 16-bit arithmetic commands may be seen to be a great improvement on those of a typical 8-bit microprocessor, both in flexibility (choice of addressing modes, use of registers) and in performance. For instance, a multiplace shift will not take so many clock cycles as an equivalent number of single bit shift instructions, nor will multiple precision arithmetic be so time-consuming when based around 16- or 32-bit wordlength. Multiplication (especially signed multiplication) is notoriously slow when performed using a software shift and add loop, rather than hardware multiply and divide. A time of around 30 μs for a 16-bit signed multiply (8086 with 5 MHz clock) or around 100 μs for a 32-bit signed multiply (Z8000 with a 4 MHz clock), obviously makes critically timed programs much easier to write than with a software multiply approach. Intel's innovation of ASCII (unpacked BCD) arithmetic is an interesting one, and will obviously be extremely useful in certain areas.

6.4 Move operations

Moves feature prominently in the instruction sets of 8-bit microprocessors, where data shifting was seen as being of prime importance. The lack of power in index registers and automatic increment or decrement of indirect address registers may be shown by observing execution speed for searches and similar operations in personal computer systems based around an 8-bit CPU. The shift to 16-bit wordlength in no way reduces the importance of transfer instructions, and the deficiencies of the 8-bit previous generation microprocessors have been largely corrected in the new 16-bit microprocessors. Multiple moves and more versatile stack movement operations enhance considerably the efficiency of the 16-bit microprocessor, as do the explicit 'load effective address value into register' operations. String primitives are available in one form or another on all microprocessors, largely eliminating any lack of automatic increment and decrement operations.

6.4.1 SIMPLE MOVEMENT INSTRUCTIONS

The simplest of all move instructions are the load and store commands and it is with these that the 16-bit microprocessor demonstrates its full range of addressing modes. Only in its move operations, for example, does the Z8000 allow based addressing. Register-to-register moves and register-to-memory or memory-to-register moves may be generally classified in the form move (or load) from (or to) register to (or from) register (or memory). Apart from immediate moves, a register operand always occupies either source or destination. The exception to this rule is the MC68000, which allows movement from one memory location to another as a 'move data from source to destination'. The other microprocessors have instructions within their string manipulation repertoire which will perform the same function, with autoincrement or autodecrement of source and destination address objects. Immediate move operations are more general, and a 'move immediate data to memory' command is universal. Closely linked with move operations are exchanges, and all 16-bit microprocessors possess fairly general exchange instructions, which allow both register-with-register exchanges and register-with-memory exchanges. Any form of operation which only involves register operands will be fast, as no external references are involved, and with a wider selection of general-purpose registers in which to hold data, efficiency can be improved by using such instructions. Both byte and 16-bit word operands are allowed, so that a byte exchange may be used to swap bytes of a 16-bit register. Motorola has separate instructions for exchanging complete registers and for swapping halves of 32-bit registers, but no explicit byte-swapping command.

The 8086, with its independence of even or odd byte addresses, is not penalised by byte immediate instructions (either arithmetic or move), but both the 68000 and Z8000 require instructions to be a integral number of 16-bit words, and to start on all even byte address boundary. Potentially, this will waste a byte whenever an immediate byte operand is used, as the operand will have to occupy the lower (usually) byte of a complete word, and leave the upper byte unused. To partly overcome this, and to gain some speed advantage, both Motorola and Zilog use 'short' or 'quick' immediate modes, with the immediate operand occupying part of the operation code word. The (normally byte) operand is sign-extended to 16 bits or 32 bits where necessary, and may only have a register as destination. The Z8000 allows a number of consecutive registers to be loaded or stored by a single instruction (load multiple) where consecutive registers are stored or loaded from consecutive memory locations using indirect, direct and indexed addressing modes. The 68000 goes a step further with MOVEM, a multiple register move instruction which allows individual registers to be masked from the move operation. Only those registers selected via bits in a mask word are loaded from or into consecutive locations in memory.

Both Zilog and Motorola allow register moves to use relative addressing. The Z8000 allows a range, relative to program counter of –32768 to +32767 while the MC68000 only allows relative addressing, over the same range, if the memory location is a source operand (destination operands may only be referred to via alterable addressing modes).

Certain categories of moves are allowed to assist operating system support. The 8086 choice of internal segment registers requires that these may be loaded with 16-bit segment addresses using suitable instructions and a variant of the 8086 move instruction is the only instruction allowed to do this. Associated with the 8086 condition code register are two moves which allow byte operands (only to the lower byte of the 16-bit flag register, which contains the 8080-compatible condition codes) to be loaded from or into, the accumulator. Similarly, in the Z8000 we have the privileged load instructions which operate on the CTLR register (load control register from/to one of the general purpose registers), the 68000, too, has a number of privileged moves associated with its status register and stack pointer. Thus we have the unprivileged MOVE to CCR (condition code register) which allows the condition code register to be loaded with data from a memory or register. It is worth noting here that the MC68000 is the only microprocessor in the new 16-bit generation which allows moves to affect its condition code register, eliminating the need for a 'test' or 'OR with self' operation following a move, to set condition codes. The MOVE to CCR operation is unprivileged (i.e. it is available to the application program) since only the arithmetic condition codes (zero, carry, negative, overflow and extension (X)) are affected. The rest of the 68000 status register requires the privileged MOVE to SR (from effective address) instruction; its counterpart MOVE from SR to effective address, is unprivileged. In order that the supervisory state of the MC68000 may access the user stack pointer, to allocate user stack in a position determined by the operating system a MOVE USP instruction is available, again privileged. This is necessary since in the 68000, address register A7 is assigned to be stack pointer, whichever mode (user of supervisory) the CPU is in. Thus in the user mode, a write to A7 will alter the user stack pointer, and in the supervisory mode, the same write will alter the supervisory stack pointer. Ordinarily, there would be no way for the operating system, running in supervisory mode, to set the user stack pointer; MOVE USP overcomes this.

6.4.2 STACK MOVE OPERATIONS

The convenience of maintaining a stack, both for subroutine calls and interrupts, and also as a way of manipulating data, was first appreciated with early minicomputers, and later with 8-bit microprocessors. So essential have stack operations become that it is difficult to imagine any realistically competitive microprocessor being designed without stack features! The most basic stack operations centre around an address register, the stack pointer, initialised to the start location of the stack area. Items are added to the stack with a PUSH operation, after the stack pointer has been decremented to point to the new top of stack. The stack thus grows from high to low memory as items are added. Removal of items is effected with a POP instruction, which removes the item from the top of the stack and increments the stack pointer appropriately. A stack is thus a last-in, first-out queue; the convention that a stack will grow from high-to-low memory is just a convention, but one which is reasonably sensible. It is usually easy to define the highest address of read-write memory, and set the initial value of the stack pointer there, than it is to find an address somewhere within the range of RAM addresses for a stack which would grow in the opposite direction, towards high memory.

All the 16-bit microprocessors use PUSH and POP operations for stack manipulation, not only for register operands, via the stack pointer, but also for memory operands. With the 8086, it is assumed that just one stack will be maintained, using a dedicated stack pointer; with the Z8000, the stack pointer may be any of the general-purpose registers, so that POP and PUSH appear as normal register indirect moves, followed by automatic increment, or preceded by automatic decrement of the contents of the register. The 68000 has no explicit stack operations except PEA (push effective address onto stack), which allows a computed address to be pushed onto the stack. The conventional PUSH and POP operations, however, can easily be implemented with a MOVE which specifies an indirect address via register A7 (user SP when the MC68000 is in its normal mode, supervisory SP when the microprocessor is in supervisory mode) with predecrement or post-increment specified. In Motorola assembly code mnemonics, A7 may be referred to by the notation SP, and PUSH becomes MOVE <source data effective address>, SP@–, and POP becomes MOVE SP@+, <destination effective address>. Any user stack may be operated in a similar manner, by specifying one of A0 to A6 (an address register other than A7).

Movement of status flag and condition code operands to and from the stack is usually performed by separate move instructions; such operations represent an essential part of saving or restoring machine environment, and assume great importance in subroutine and interrupt routine operations. While alteration of individual condition codes is possible, either with discrete SET, RESET operations, or with complete condition code register transfers, saving the complete flag or status register as a 16-bit entity is nevertheless very convenient (all the 16-bit microprocessors possess system control flags which are in the other byte of the status register to the byte occupied by the condition codes). The 8086 operations of PUSHF, POPF implement status register saves directly, whereas the Z8000 only allows the privileged LDCTL already mentioned, and the 68000 allows a privileged autoincremented/autodecremented MOVE to SR, which may perform exactly the same operation.

6.4.3 ADDRESS OBJECT MOVES

A feature not seen in previous microprocessors is that of loading an effective address value to a register. Previous 8-bit microprocessors have allowed address registers to be loaded with a numeric constant address but not the more convenient 'load effective address'. The only restriction placed on this versatile command is that the source must invariably be a memory operand. Thus the 8086 allows LEA, load effective address, into any general, pointer, or index register, and LDS, LES which load 32-bit operands into data or extra segment registers (segment address) and a specified register (offset address). Echoing these instructions, the Z8000 provides 'load address' (LDA) and 'load address relative (LDAR)' instructions which load the effective address (which must be a memory operand) into a designated register. Similarly, the MC68000 employs LEA which will load to any address register. An added feature is the 68000 instruction PEA (push effective address onto stack), already discussed under stack features.

The Z8000 privileged LDCTL, apart from its function in allowing loading of the status word, will also allow loading of the program status area pointer

(PSAP) and its associated segment address register, though with an operand value rather than an address object. It nevertheless can offer a practical way of achieving the same objective as LDS, LES, but by a direct load.

6.4.4 BLOCK OR STRING MOVEMENT

The rise of interest in text handling and record handling computers has emphasised the limitations of the 8-bit microprocessor when dealing with repeated operations on consecutive memory locations, such as copying blocks of data from one area of memory to another, or searching a block of data for the presence or absence of a particular character or bit pattern. The major limitation is speed, and it is easy to see why a conventional 8-bit microprocessor is so slow at such an operation, when memory read, compare, jump on condition, increment or decrement indirect address or index register, test for end of block, and jump on condition, must each be executed as a separate instruction for each target location moved or compared. The Z80 design made the first attempts to streamline the process with its provision of multiple operations, repeated while a condition is true (or false). The Z80 operations made life easy for the assembly code programmer, but used the Z80 available registers rather heavily, making setting up the operation rather difficult.

The new generation of 16-bit microprocessors have been designed specifically with text and string handling in mind, and all possess string primitives (a name used by Intel, less cumbersome than the Zilog term of 'block transfer and string manipulation'). The string primitives fall into four groups: move elements of one string to another string location; compare elements of one string with corresponding elements of another or with a value in a register; fill memory area with specified byte or word, and translate string. All use register indirect addressing to access source and destination operands, and may use an implied or designated register for a count value. Two different approaches are used to accomplish the repeat operation. The Intel approach is to define the basic instruction, which includes autoincrement or autodecrement of address registers, with an operation code which does not include any repeat operation, and which can therefore be used alone as an autoincrement or decrement move or comparison. Repeating the operation for a number of moves or comparison operations, implicitly held in one of the 8086 byte registers, is controlled by prefixing the basic primitive operation with a REP single byte prefix. The Z8000 approach is to define separate instructions for each possible mode. Thus we have, for example, the group of instructions CPD, compare (with value in register) and decrement indirect address register CPDR, compare, decrement and repeat (using a specified count register), CPI compare and increment, CPIR, compare increment and repeat. All are derived from the same basic operation. From a programmer's point of view, it does not matter which approach is used, they are both equivalent, they only differ in the number of repeat operations which may be made – limited to 256 with the 8086 since only a byte count register is used, and 32768 for the Z8000. Only in exceptional circumstances will this difference be significant. Few strings in a real application are likely to be more than 250 bytes or words in length. The string comparison, scan (compare with register value) and move string or copy instructions are obviously useful in a text processing or list processing system. Translation possibly requires some explanation. The idea of translation is simple: using a register or memory operand as an index into a look-up table, the operand may be replaced by the addressed value from the look-up table. This gives the possibility of easy conversion of a variable which has been measured in a non-linear fashion to a corresponding linear scale value, or of direct substitution of one character or byte for another. It is ideal for (to take a practical example) linearising thermocouple measurements, or handling any operation which would previously have been done in a programmed logic array (PLA). Translation of a single byte obviously does not require a repeated operation whereas translation of a string by translating each character separately obviously does, so, again, there are two approaches to the problem: the 8086 uses a single XLAT instruction and relies on the programmer to incorporate it into a software loop where required, whereas the Z8000 defines a whole set of translation instructions covering most possibilities. Thus in the Z8000, instructions implemented are translate and decrement, translate, decrement and repeat, translate and increment, etc.

No mention has been made of the 68000 during this discussion of string primitives. The versatility of the 68000 addressing modes is such that they are scarcely needed as explicit instructions. MOVE, for instance, will perform memory-to-memory moves with autoincrement and autodecrement specified within the addressing mode fields, for byte, word, and long word format. This is virtually identical in execution to the 8086 MOVB, MOVW primitives. Comparison too, features a CMPM variant which compares indirectly addressed memory operands and automatically post-increments both address registers. Using a test condition, decrement-and-branch instruction (DB_{CC}) will perform the same function (with a greater degree of generality) as the Intel REP prefix. It is true to say, therefore, that string and block manipulation are important features of all modern 16-bit microprocessors.

6.5 Program transfer and conditional operations

The simplest program transfer operation, is, of course, the unconditional branch or jump, which immediately replaces the value in the program location counter with its effective address. The power of a microprocessor for many applications depends on the versatility of its conditional jumps, and their implementation. The 8-bit microprocessor designs were divided: the 8080 family, which demanded conditional jumps to absolute locations, and the 6800 family, which recognised that most program transfers would be to locations close to the current program counter value, so invariably used relative addressing for conditional jumps. The Z80 family catered for both schools of thought. With 8-bit microprocessors, the relative jump with only an 8-bit offset (–126 to +129) offers a saving of one byte over an absolute jump. The popularity of the relative jump in 8-bit microprocessors has led to its adoption as the standard addressing mode for the conditional jump in 16-bit microprocessors.

The Z80 possessed another innovation in the form of DJNZ – decrement (register) and jump if non-zero – a simple iteration control which combined three operations into one (decrement register, compare with zero, jump on condition). The flexibility of this conceptually simple instruction has led to the inclusion of iteration control instructions in the instruction sets of all the new 16-bit microprocessors.

Subroutine calls, well established in 8-bit microprocessors, have merely been improved by expanding addressing modes. The inclusion of segmentation and operating system support features in 16-bit architectures has resulted in some new instructions being needed to cater for segment address changes on CALLs, and to allow user programs to call system subroutines.

6.5.1 CONDITIONAL AND UNCONDITIONAL JUMPS

Unconditional transfers have to now take into account the possible segmentation of addresses. The MC68000 does not need to consider segmentation in the CPU, with its 24-bit address structure and 32-bit registers, but the 8086 and Z8000 require the provision of JMP instructions for unconditional jumps within a current segment, and to a piece of code outside the current segment. The 8086 allows direct and indirect jumps, both intersegment and intrasegment, and the Z8000 allows all addressing ranges; non-segmented, segmented with short (8-bit) offset and segmented with full (16-bit) offset.

Conditional jumps are another matter – the 16-bit microprocessors have an extremely wide range of conditions available. Any conditional jumps are of the form JP_{CC} or B_{CC} (on condition) < effective address or offset>. The conditions usually available are: equal; not equal; less than; less than or equal; greater than; greater than or equal; overflow; not overflow; higher than; lower than; plus; minus and perhaps parity odd; parity even. The inclusion of 'condition or equal', avoids the need for two separate conditional operations. The addressing modes available, as well as the relative jumps already discussed, are indirect, direct and indexed (Z8000) while the MC68000, allows relative jumps with two offset sizes, 8- and 16-bits.

Iteration control is provided, almost in the form of direct copies of the Z80 DJNZ instruction. Indeed, in the Z8000, the instructions' similarity extends right down to the assembler mnemonic used! While the size of offset is the same, however, its interpretation is different. The 8-bit offset of the Z80 command is interpreted as a two's complement integer, whereas in the Z8000 it is interpreted as a 7-bit positive integer (the most significant bit of the byte gives a word/byte indication of the size of the specified count register). The integer is doubled and subtracted from the PC value, giving a transfer only in the reverse direction.

The equivalent operations in the 8086 microprocessor are the family of LOOP instructions. LOOP uses a predesignated word register (the CX register) to hold a count which is decremented by one and transfer made on various conditions, in a relative jump with a signed byte offset. The MC68000 uses a modified branch-on-condition instruction (called test condition, decrement and branch) DB_{CC}, which is even more general in the condition which may be specified. Note that none of the flags is affected by the iteration control instruction itself, but that the flags depend only on previous instructions within the loop.

6.5.2 SUBROUTINE CALLS

The subroutine call has not been significantly altered by the transition to higher power, 16-bit microprocessors. As in the 8-bit microprocessor, it performs the minimal requirement of pushing the return address (next instruction following the CALL) onto the stack (either user stack or system/supervisory stack, depending on microprocessor operating mode) and replacing the contents of the program location counter with the effective address contained in the CALL instruction. The 8086 and Z8000, which possess segment registers, must both arrange to store any program counter segment register when the call is made to another segment. Like unconditional jumps, CALLs may use a number of address modes, principally direct address and register indirect. The 68000 offers two CALL instructions: BSR (branch to subroutine) confined to relative jumps, and JSR (jump to subroutine) with a wider range of addressing modes.

Return instructions, too, follow the pattern set by the 8-bit microprocessors. Some minor additions make them slightly more versatile, for instance, Intel provide a facility on the 8086 for automatically adding a constant to the stack pointer after the return, which gives an easy method of discarding stack parameters. The Z8000 allows, like the Z80, a return-on-condition, while the MC68000 gives the option of automatically restoring condition codes on return.

6.6 Interrupt handling

The basic mechanism of interrupt handling has already been discussed from a hardware point of view. The idea of vectored interrupts is a well-established one, and poses no new problems to the hardware designer. From a software point of view, however, the situation with regard to interrupt handling has changed considerably in detail, though not in concept. The restrictions of the typical 8-bit interrupt structure are: transfer of control to fixed locations a few bytes apart (typically eight) or to a single indirect address location, both of which require some software effort just to make a non-trivial interrupt structure viable, and make poor provision for software interrupts. The improved 16-bit structures not only overcome these limitations, but go considerably further towards making real time operating system design much more practical than with the old 8-bit machines. The key to their success has been compromise; a combination of the two approaches of multiple hardware-vectored interrupts and interrupt locations being used for indirect addressing has led to the routing tables of the modern 16-bit microprocessor. The same concept will operate with automatically invoked traps (normally trap-on-specified-error) and software traps or interrupts, and with privileged system calls. Part of the power of such a system when implemented on a microprocessor with user and system or supervisory modes is that all interrupts or traps, whether hardware generated or software generated, or requests to change mode, may be made to automatically change the mode of the CPU to the privileged one. This implies that any of the events mentioned in this section will initiate only a system mode action, and will not necessarily impinge upon operation of a user program. Any asynchronous external events requiring communication with a user program will be forced to channel the communication through the system mode of the microprocessor, and hence, through the operating system. The constraint of invoking action only through the operating system gives a higher degree of integrity to any multiprocess application, and allows system decisions to be taken in a controlled manner. Queueing, running and suspending processes in a multitask environment, using priority, and giving arbitration over contention for shared resources are the major tasks for a real time operating system. Separating user program and system operation is a first step towards achieving a good design, and a major innovation, besides distinguishing two modes of microprocessor operation, is the introduction of separate stacks for the two modes.

6.6.1 DUAL MODE OPERATION

Microprocessors with a dual mode of operation (Z8000 and MC68000) normally support twin stacks; the user stack, which is available to any user program and used during subroutine calls, which do not generally invoke a mode change, and the system stack, used by interrupts and traps which do invoke a mode change. Obviously the system stack cannot be accessed from user programs, but instructions must be included to allow, at least, the system mode programs to set an initial value for the user stack pointer.

Mode switching may be automatic, as in the case of an interrupt or trap, or invoked by a 'system call' or software interrupt. All microprocessors, whether dual mode or not, have this facility for generating a non-maskable software interrupt. The 8086 possesses the INT instruction, and the Z8000 the SC instruction, both with an 8-bit numeric vector specified as an argument. The equivalent 68000 instruction is TRAP, followed by a four-bit argument (allowing sixteen traps). There may also be specific software interrupts or traps for program-referenced conditions, such as trap on overflow (normally the only one implemented).

For a dual-mode microprocessor, the software interrupt is the only mechanism for a programmed change from normal to system mode. Both software interrupts and hardware traps and interrupts will perform the following actions: first, the mode is changed from normal to system mode, then the program location counter value is pushed onto the system stack, followed by the program status register value; the program location counter is then loaded with the address held in the appropriate vector location, so control is transferred to the trap or interrupt routine. Return from interrupt is equally important in the context of a dual-mode microprocessor, since it is almost inevitable that this return will be made while the microprocessor is in system mode, but it is often necessary to have some control over the mode after the return has been made. Usually the original mode must be restored, and this is easily accomplished by a privileged instruction such as RTI, which restores both program counter and status register. Contrast this with the RET from subroutine, a non-privileged instruction which may restore both program counter and the condition codes part of the status register, but will definitely not affect the mode part of the status register.

6.6.2 ENABLE AND DISABLE INTERRUPTS

All microprocessors, whether dual mode or not, have the capability of disabling and enabling maskable interrupts under program control. This action is possible in two ways, either by explicit instructions (privileged in the case of the Z8000) or by manipulating the relevant bits in the status register. The second technique, also privileged, is the only way to enable interrupts in the MC68000 – the enable/disable structure of the MC68000 is somewhat more complex than that of the other 16-bit microprocessors, in that a multiple level of priority is provided by the hardware. The interrupt mask in the status register is a 3-bit binary number which specifies the current microprocessor priority. Three interrupt request lines are provided, on which the interrupting device must place a 3-bit number indicating its own priority. Only if the input priority is greater than the current status register priority will the interrupt be allowed. This mode of operation exactly parallels the operation of many of the priority interrupt controller integrated circuits available for use with 8-bit microprocessor families. With the addition of a single priority encoder circuit, the eight priority levels may be separated, and activated individually (see chapter 5). It is possible to satisfy the priority setting part of the functions of a programmable controller, which would require several writes to its internal registers, with a simple alteration of an internal status register.

6.6.3 HALTS

Wait for interrupt is a well-established instruction available with all microprocessors, 8 or 16 bit. The only small innovation appears with the MC68000 'STOP' which carries an argument in the form of immediate data, transferred to the status register before the halt state is entered. This allows the programmer to set the status of the code which will be executed after an interrupt has transferred control to its service routine, and then returned to the instruction following the halt.

The 8086 has a second WAIT instruction which examines the signal on an external pin, and enters a wait state, or continues, depending on the logic level at the pin. This wait state may be cleared when the pin reverts to its appropriate logic level, or when an interrupt occurs. The difference between this WAIT and a normal HALT instruction lies in the fact that the WAIT will cause the same address as the WAIT to be stored on the stack when an interrupt occurs, so that the return will be to the wait state, rather than the next instruction. The only permanent exit may be effected either by not executing a simple return from an interrupt routine, or by the pin being tested changing its logic level.

6.7 Multiple microprocessor facilities

The significant feature of the new 16-bit microprocessors with regard to multiprocessor systems is the provision of facilities which aid the design of multiple-CPU systems which share resources. The facilities fall into three categories: a test-and-set-semaphore facility to resolve contention for shared resources; a request-grant pair of instructions, and a facility for allowing 'coprocessors' to receive their instructions from the main microprocessor instruction stream.

6.7.1 TEST-AND-SET SEMAPHORE

This instruction is the one which is available with all three of the new microprocessors, in slightly different forms. The basic idea is that use of a shared resource may be indicated using a 1-bit flag, or semaphore, which may simply be the contents of a memory location. Any process which requires use of the resource may examine the semaphore before attempting to use the resource. If the semaphore is set, the resource is being used by another process and is unavailable; if the semaphore is reset, the resource is available, and the instruction may acquire exclusive use of the resource by setting the semaphore itself. Of critical importance is the fact that the test-and-set instruction must not itself be interruptible, and for the duration of the instruction, the CPU must have sole control of the bus (i.e. there must be no bus access by other bus masters). Consequently, some hardware signal must be asserted to prevent other devices gaining bus access during this instruction execution. Such a feature is unique – the test-and-set instruction will normally be the only instruction to possess it. The detailed techniques for providing this system support feature differ between the three microprocessors. The 8086 allows a normal instruction to be used for the test-and-set procedure, but ensures its correct operation by preceding it with a LOCK prefix, which 'locks' the bus to external access for the duration of the succeeding instruction and signals the condition with the $\overline{\text{LOCK}}$ hardware signal. Thus no competing device may alter the semaphore between the 'test' and 'set' operations which will be separated by several machine clock cycles. LOCK may precede any instruction in order to lock out bus access for the duration of the instruction, but the most useful 8086 instruction for test-and-set operations is XCHG. By exchanging the contents of a register with the semaphore location, as a LOCKed instruction, the test for 'already set' may be made after the exchange. The example which Intel give is presented below:

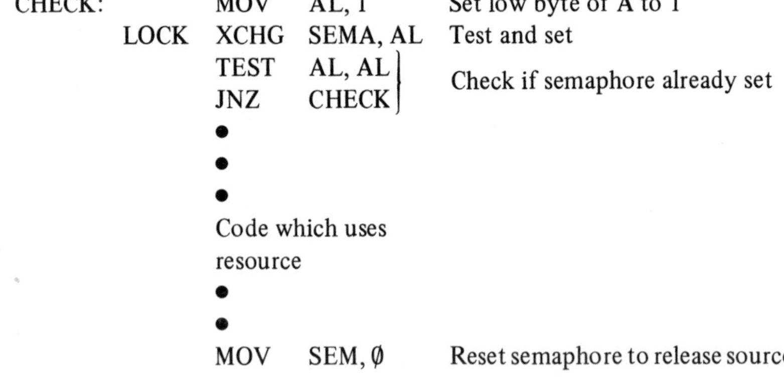

```
CHECK:        MOV   AL, 1       Set low byte of A to 1
        LOCK  XCHG  SEMA, AL    Test and set
              TEST  AL, AL  }   Check if semaphore already set
              JNZ   CHECK   }
              •
              •
              •
              Code which uses
              resource
              •
              •
              MOV   SEM, Ø      Reset semaphore to release source
```

The Z8000 has a specific 'test and set' instruction TSET which copies the most significant bit of the semaphore location into a flag location (the S sign flag) and sets the semaphore location to all logical 1s. For the duration of the instruction, the Z8000 bus is 'locked', and the microprocessor will not respond to any bus requests until after completion. There is no explicit hardware $\overline{\text{LOCK}}$ signal as with the 8086. The code is rather simpler than the 8086 code:

```
CHECK:  TSET     SEMA    Test and set
        JR MI,   CHECK   Check if already set
        •
        •
        Code which uses
        resource
        •
        •
        CLR      SEMA    Clear semaphore
```

The MC68000 equivalent is TAS (test and set an operand), which is almost identical to the Z8000 TSET except that only bit 7 of the destination byte is set, rather than all the bits of the byte. The flag settings are also different, with the Z (zero) flag being used in preference to the sign flag. The code will thus read:

```
CHECK:  TAS      SEMA
        BNE      CHECK
        •
        •
        Code which uses
        resource
        •
        •
        CLR      SEMA
```

6.7.2 MULTIPLE MICROPROCESSOR SIGNALS

In addition to its test-and-set instruction, the Z8000 supports handshaking hardware for multiple microprocessor systems. The hardware, described in chapter 5, has two pins, multimicro in (MI) and multimicro out (MO), which may be used in a daisy-chained manner to link multiple CPUs. The instructions used to drive the hardware are:

MBIT	Test MI and set sign flag accordingly (this determines availability of shared hardware resource).
MREQ	Request shared resource use by testing MI, and, if MI indicates that the resource is potentially available, initiate a request-delay-test-for-access-granted sequence of operations.
MSET	Set MO to 1 to indicate a resources non-availability.
MRES	Reset MO to 0 to indicate a resources availability.

The delay inherent in an MREQ instruction is specified by the contents of a register, which are decremented to produce the delay; its purpose is to allow plenty of time for other microprocessors in the system to respond to the request.

When waiting for a resource to become available, the microprocessor may just loop using MBIT:

```
LOOP:   MBIT
        JR      MI, LOOP
AVAIL:
```

To request use of a resource, the code must allow for three possible outcomes to the test: not available; request not granted; request granted. A typical code section (used by Zilog as an example) is:

```
TRY:          LD RO, #50              Set delay in register 0
              MREQ RO
              JR  MI, AVAIL
              JR  Z, NOTGRANTED
NOTAVAIL:     •
              •
              Code for not available
              condition
              •
NOTGRANTED:   •
              •
              Code for not granted condition
              •
              JR  TRY                 Try again
AVAIL:        •
              •
              Code to use resource
              •
              •
              MRES                    Release resource
```

6.7.3 8086 ESC INSTRUCTION

To facilitate the addition of 'coprocessors', in particular those which provide floating-point arithmetic functions and handle fast and complex input-output functions, Intel provide an instruction called 'escape' (ESC) on the 8086. Escape performs no action within the CPU, but does allow the majority of the 8086 addressing modes, and provides suitable memory control signals. From outside the CPU, the function is merely a memory access which places the memory operand on the bus. The operand is thus made available to another bus device, without a change of bus master. A typical coprocessor is the 8087, which recognises its own instructions within the instruction stream of the 8086, and performs floating point and transcendental mathematical functions.

6.8 Input-output instructions

Like their 8-bit predecessors, not all 16-bit microprocessors possess explicit input-output instructions: the MC68000, like the MC6800, assumes memory-mapped input-output devices. The Z8000 and 8086, however, show a neat contrast in style of input-output appropriate to a double mode (normal and system) and a single mode microprocessor, respectively. The 8086 expands the port structure of the 8080/8085, with either fixed access to ports using an immediate address byte (0-255), or variable access using an indirect address register allowing port addresses 0-65535. Both byte and word transfers are allowed, to and from the accumulator.

The Z8000 has a split set of input-output instructions, for 'normal' and 'special' use. Both obey the same rules for input to or output from a specified register, and may be used in a string primitive form. The special I/O instructions are the interesting ones; they are uniquely identified by an appropriate pattern on the three status pins of the Z8000 and allow access to the memory management unit. It would appear to give a high degree of security making it difficult to misprogram the MMU, since only these specific instructions, not normally used, would give access.

Note that although the MC68000 assumes memory-mapped I/O and has no specific input-output instructions, it has one memory transfer instruction that is well-suited for input-output operations. This instruction is MOVEP (move peripheral data), which transfers packed bytes in a single register as individual bytes in alternate memory byte addresses. Thus a long transfer (32 bits) from a register to a memory even address will result in the 4 bytes being transferred to the high bytes of four successive memory word locations.

6.9 Overall advantages of 16-bit microprocessors

It may be seen from the main discussion of this chapter that the advantages of the new 16-bit microprocessors extend well beyond the obvious ones of addressing range and higher precision. Many of the instruction set enhancements follow the well established minicomputer practices, such as hardware multiply-divide, good selection of addressing modes, provision of instruction traps and system call. Others depart from the minicomputer standard and give unique capabilities – the 8086 unpacked BCD or ASCII instructions for instance, or the wealth of string primitives associated with the Z8000. The net result is a range of new 16-bit microprocessors with capabilities far in excess of their predecessors, which threaten many fields normally confined to mid-range and low-range minicomputers.

CHAPTER 7
Assembly code software and development

7.1 Introduction

Many, if not most, 16-bit applications will be programmed in one or other of the high-level languages discussed in chapter 9. Assembly code, and support of assembly code programs will still be necessary for real time applications, for systems programming (device drivers, various utilities, etc.) and for small embedded systems. The 16-bit assembly-code programmer is faced with a far more difficult task than his 8-bit colleague. All the 16-bit machines have much larger instruction sets than their 8-bit predecessors, and a wider variety of addressing modes and modifiers. Because of the wide choice of instructions, writing efficient assembly code (for minimum space or maximum speed) represents a greater challenge than before. Memory segmentation, exception processing, multiple microprocessor operation and coprocessor software make it necessary for the manufacturers of each microprocessor to provide new development system capabilities and in-circuit emulation features to cater for a possibly high degree of sophistication in the target application. In the area of utilities, especially assembly code arithmetic routines require new standards; the IEEE have a draft Task P754, which defines a 32-bit and 64-bit binary floating-point arithmetic proposed standard, including rounding and truncation conventions and exception conditions. This standard is discussed later in the chapter.

7.2 Macroassemblers

All the major manufacturers provide some assembly capability, to run on their development systems (Intel Series III MDS, Motorola EXORmacs, Zilog System 8000 Z-Lab, Advanced Micro Devices Sys 8/8). Because of the expensive nature of the new systems, many allow multiple users; the System 8000 is particularly strong in this respect, running a Unix-like Zeus operating system. The macroassemblers provided with these systems, and those cross-assemblers provided to run on mainframe host computers, are similar to previous 8-bit ones, though the complexity of the 16-bit microprocessors' instruction set is reflected in their size. In order to cater for the new facilities, some notable enhancements have been made:

(a) Addressing mode specifications. With such a large number of addressing modes available, symbolic specification of addressing modes is almost mandatory, to avoid over-long code lines, and generally follows minicomputer practice. For the Motorola 68000, for instance, effective address specification is as follows:

Register direct	Dn for data register, Am for address register
Address register indirect	(Am)
Postincrement	(Am) + (address register)
Predecrement	–(Aq) (address register)
Displacement	d(Am) (d = displacement value)
Displacement and index	d(An, Dm)
Absolute	$ <number> or <label>
PC relative	<label>
PC relative and index	<label> (An)
Immediate	# $ <number>
Displacement with long word index	d(An, Dm.L)

(b) Symbol specification. Much freer than with 8-bit assemblers, with only the register symbols reserved, and with longer strings allowed.

(c) More flexible macrospecifications, which allow abnormal exit conditions and error actions.

(d) Provision for relocation via segment register or MMU. The assembler directive handling of the segment registers of the 8086 forms a good illustration of the differences between 16-bit and 8-bit assemblers. The 8086 assembler has directives SEGMENT (which may be labelled), and ASSUME (which carries arguments), which may be used by the assembler to initialise the internal segment registers. For example:

```
STACK       SEGMENT
            DW  mm   Reserve nn words for stack use
STACKTOP    LABEL  WORD
STACK       ENDS
DATA        SEGMENT
            DB  mm  + other data reservation statements
DATA        ENDS
CODE        SEGMENT
            ASSUME CS: CODE, DS: DATA, SS: STACK, ES:
            NOTHING <executable code>
CODE        ENDS
```

The code illustrated defines a code, data and stack segments, directs the assembler to set up the appropriate segment registers. Note that if jumps and calls are restricted to one segment (intra-segment calls, jumps), position-independent code is generated.

(e) Conditional assembly directives allow temporary code in the source file, for example, the 68000 assembler will commence conditional code with IFEQ or IFNE, and terminate it with ENDC.

(f) Data reservation may encompass not only bytes and (16-bit) words, but also double (32-bit) and quad (64-bit) words.

Because of the extended development system hardware facilities, such as larger and more varied bulk storage, and more printer options, the assembler directives which control output are appropriately flexible. Error messages, too, are more comprehensive. The coding for 16-bit assembly code routines nevertheless looks similar to that for 8-bit ones. To give the reader the flavour of each of the major machines, small representative programs are given.

7.2.1 8086 BINARY-TO-DECIMAL CONVERSION (UNSIGNED)

```
SEGA     SEGMENT
         ASSUME CS : SEGA, DS : SEGA, ES : SEGA, SS : SEGA
         EXTRN OUTEEE : NEAR (intra-segment call required)
KIOK     DW 10000, 1000, 100, 10, 1 (powers of 10)
CVBTD:   LEA BX, KIOK        (BX is powers of 10 pointer)
         MOV CX, 5           (number of decimal digits)
CVDEC1:  MOV AL, 30H         (ASCII zero)
CVDEC2:  SUB DX, [BX]        (subtract power of 10)
         JB CVDEC3           (jump if result negative)
         INC AL              (no, increment ASCII digit)
         JMP CVDEC2          (loop till transfer to CVDEC3)
CVDEC3:  ADD DX, [BX]        (restore partial sum)
         ADD BX, 2           (increment pointer)
         PUSH DX             (save intermediate result)
         CALL OUTEEE         (print digit)
         POP DX              (restore intermediate result)
         LOOP CVDEC1         (loop till CX = 0)
         RET
SEGA     ENDS
         END
```

This routine takes a binary number in register DX, and converts it to a decimal (ASCII) number printed by routine OUTEEE, which resides in the same segment as the conversion program (hence declaration NEAR within external reference declaration).

7.2.2 Z8002 BINARY-TO-DECIMAL CONVERSION (SIGNED)

```
OUTD     CLRB RH1            (8-bit digit counter)
         TEST R10            (check sign of binary value)
         JR PL, OUT2         (positive)
         LDB RLO, #'–'       (load ASCII minus sign)
         CALL TWR            (print it)
         COM R10             (complement 32-bit value)
         ADDL RR10, #1       (two's complement)
OUTD2    EXSTL RR8           (sign RR10 to RR8)
         DIVL RQ8, #10       (division by 10)
         LD R2, R9           (remainder in R2)
         ADDB RL2, #'0'      (convert remainder to ASCII)
         INCB RH1            (digit counter)
```

```
        PUSH @ R15, R2     (ASCII digit onto stack)
        TESTL RR10         (quotient = 0)
        JR NZ, OUTD2       (relative jump, looping to OUTD2)
OUTD3   POP R0, @ R15      (get ASCII from stack)
        CALL TWR           (print it)
        DBJNZ RH1, OUTD3   (loop till all digits printed)
        RET
```

This routine takes a 32-bit signed binary number in R10, and converts it to a signed decimal one, printed by subroutine TWR (suppressing leading zeros). TWR prints a single ASCII character, passed to it via register RL0.

7.2.3 68000 MEMORY TEST

```
        ORG $0800              (origin)
STACIA  EQU $21EFO             (MAXBUG addresses)
OUTCHR  EQU $21BFA
START   JSR STACIA
        MOVE.B D2, TEMP        (save initial pattern)
        MOVE.A.L LOMEM, A1     (start address)
LOOP1   MOVE.B D2, (A1)+       (store byte)
        ADDQ.B #1, D2          (increment pattern)
        CMPA.L HIMEM, A1       (finish of memory?)
        BCS.S LOOP1            (no, loop till finished)
CHECK   MOVE.B TEMP, D2        (initial pattern)
        MOVE A.L LOMEM, A1     (start address)
LOOP2   CMP.B (A1)+, D2        (match pattern)
        BNE.S ERROR            (no match)
        ADDQ.B #1, D2          (increment pattern)
        CMPA.L HIMEM.A1        (finish of memory)
        BCS.S LOOP2            (loop till finished)
CYCLE   MOVE.B #'.', D0        ('.' is OK character)
        JSR OUTCHR             (print it)
        MOVE.B TEMP, D2        (initial pattern)
        SUBQ.B #1, D2          (new pattern in D2)
        BRA.S START            (short branch)
ERROR   MOVE.B #'X', D0        ('X' is error character)
        JSR OUTCHR             (print it)
        BRA.S START            (try again)
LOMEM   DS.L 1                 (start address)
HIMEM   DS.L 1                 (finish address)
TEMP    DS.B 1                 (initial pattern)
        END
```

This routine interfaces with the MAXBUG monitor program on the 68000 KDM evaluation card. It tests memory between addresses in LOMEM and HIMEM, using a pattern of ascending bytes which are checked after all of memory has been written. At each cycle, the test pattern shifts by one, so after

256 cycles, each byte of the memory has taken on all possible values. At the end of each cycle, a '.' is printed if the pattern check was passed, an 'X' if the check failed. STACIA is a routine to set up the KDM serial interface, OUTCHR prints a single ASCII character, passed in DO.B.

7.3 Standardisation at assembly-code level

Standardisation is an important topic within the microprocessor industry, especially in software, where investments are so heavy. Exchange of data and program code make some degree of uniformity essential, since microprocessor manufacturers, unlike many minicomputer manufacturers, and mainframe builders before them, cannot consider their microprocessors to be isolated data processing entities which need not have any compatibility with other manufacturers' products. The world of personal and business computing demands comparability of systems in various areas:

(a) In hardware, in terms of bus standards (see chapter 11) and compatible use of storage media (such as disk formats).
(b) In operating systems and high level language (see chapters 8 and 9).
(c) At assembly code level:
  (i) industry-wide arithmetic standards (particularly for floating-point arithmetic);
  (ii) throughout all systems using a specific microprocessor CPU, conventions for parameter-passing to subroutines (especially those linked with high-level languages), device drivers and exception handling should be standard;
  (iii) documentation standards.

Documentation standards are those applicable to any engineering project and do not require detailed discussion, but items (i) and (ii) may be usefully explored. In particular, the IEEE proposals mentioned at the beginning of this chapter are likely to achieve considerable success.

7.3.1 ARITHMETIC STANDARDS

The 16-bit microprocessor possesses obvious wordlength advantages when arithmetic operations are considered. For signed integer arithmetic, the basic microprocessor instructions (addition, subtraction, signed multiply, signed divide) provide the basic capabilities and precision may easily be extended using simple routines which provide multiple-word number representation. With multiple register operations ('long word' instructions), integer or fixed-point arithmetic is very straightforward. With two's complement notation, formats are well-defined and no enforced standardisation is necessary.

Floating-point arithmetic software assumes major importance when used to provide support for numeric computation-intensive applications, and for high-level language compilers. Although implementation may be on different machines (with widely different instruction sets) it is important that number formats (in a binary representation) are standard, and also that computation accuracies are

identical in different implementations. Action on exception conditions (the simplest of which is divide-by-zero) should ideally conform to a standard pattern. Draft 8.0 of IEEE Task P754[5] makes proposals for floating-point standards which encompass format of data types, the arithmetic itself, and the exception handling, with the aim of:

(a) Defining a format best suited to user needs, rather than one which corresponds to any existing conventions.
(b) Describing a programming environment, assuming that most implementations 'would rely on software to supply the full functionality of the proposal'.
(c) Encouraging hardware implementations 'that do not preclude an efficient implementation of the total desired functionality'.

The standard achieves its aims, and provides for software which will give direct support for execution time diagnosis of anomalies, smoother handling of exceptions (either by traps or by software examination of exceptional results), and will allow straightforward development of elementary mathematical functions and coupling of numerical and algebraic computation. It defines:

(a) Floating-point number formats.
(b) The results for add, subtract, multiply, divide, square root, remainder, and compare.
(c) Floating-point to integer, and integer to floating-point conversions, and conversions between binary coded decimal numbers and floating point numbers.
(d) Conversions between different floating point formats.
(e) Floating point exceptions and their handling including non-numeric representations in floating point format.

7.3.1.1 Formats

Two basic and two extended floating point formats are defined, illustrated in fig. 5.20. All have three components, which are a 1-bit sign, a biased exponent, and a fractional part. The fractional part is a binary fraction – in the basic fixed-point formats, an integer part of '1' to the right of the binary point is assumed, and in the extended formats, a one-bit integer part is a fourth component of the floating point number. If s is the sign bit (0 = positive, 1 = negative), e is the exponent, biased by an amount b, and f is the fractional part, the value of the number represented will be $(-1)^s 2^{(e-b)}\ (1.f)$ for basic format numbers, and if i is the integer part (= 0 or 1), it will be $(-1)^s 2^{(e-b)}(i.f)$. While these normalised numbers are the fundamentals of the format, various reserved values are used for conventions which allow particularly desirable features. The first of these is the concept of 'not a number' (NaN). This idea of allowing a numeric format to be used for non-numeric information is a very powerful one. It allows any invalid results to be flagged without ambiguity and without the use of hardware-generated exceptions, in a formal machine independent manner. The choice of NaN representation is reasonably arbitrary, but, with a biased exponent, is conveniently the largest exponent value, and this is chosen for the standard (in the case of a single precision number, the exponent is 255 for NaN, and is 2047 in the case of a double-precision one). The condition with the exponent equal to its maximum value and fractional part equal to zero is reserved for representation of infinity $(-1)^S.\infty$, and with a non-zero fractional part, NaN may use the fractional part for any implementation-dependent (not part of this standard) diagnostics. The sign part may be used similarly. NaNs may be used in computations (the notable operation which forms part of the standard is comparison; comparison of an NaN with any other operand, including another NaN, returns a result 'unordered') but will usually result in an invalid operation.

Infinity may be represented, as noted earlier, by a maximum-value exponent and zero fractional part. It is signed, and may result from overflow in an arithmetic operation. Two possible modes for handling infinity are considered in the specification, affine and projective. Briefly, they are defined as follows:

(a) Affine: assumes $-\infty <$ (every finite number) $< +\infty$.
(b) Projective: assumed $-\infty = +\infty$ when compared, and any comparison of ∞ with a finite number will return the result 'unordered'.

Representation of zero, and very small numbers, is a further important part of the standard. A floating-point standard which assumes a one-bit integer part, of value 1, has no natural representation of zero. Its smallest value would, if unaltered, be 2^{-b} (1.0), when the exponent value e = 0, and there would be no unnormalised numbers within the standard. A possible way to represent zero would be to assume that an exponent value of zero meant that the number value was zero – this represents a step change in resolution, since there would be no way of representing any numbers between $2^{(1-b)}$ (1.0) when e = 1 and 0.0 when e = 0. Compare this with the next increment from $2^{(1-b)}$ (1.0) to $2^{(1-b)}$ $(1.0 + 2^{-n})$ (for an n-bit fractional part), and it is easy to see the dramatic change in resolution.

The way in which the IEEE proposed standard provides for a representation of zero, while at the same time avoiding any step change in resolution, is to make the number denormalised at very small values. The smallest normalised value if $2^{(1-b)}$ (1.0) (exponent value e = 1); when e = 0, numbers are assumed to be denormalised, of value $2^{(1-b)}$ $(0.f)$, so increments are equal to those between $2^{(1-b)}$ (1.0) and $2^{(2-b)}$ (1.0). At the limiting value when $f = 0$ and e = 0, the value of the number is zero. The standard defines rules for the sign bit when the number produced as the result of an operation is zero. When a product or quotient is created, its sign is the exclusive-OR of the operand's signs; when a sum or difference is created, the sign of zero result is always positive except in a particular rounding condition.

7.3.1.2 Defined operations

The defined operations for the IEEE standard are as follows (for normalised operands):

(a) Arithmetic (add, subtract, multiply, divide and remainder) implemented using operands of the same or different formats, with the result in a format at least as wide as the widest operand format (remainder is defined by x REM $y = x - y(n)$ where n is the integer nearest x/y, and is even whenever $|n - x/y| = ½$).

(b) Square root: defined for all formats and all normalised operands $\geqslant 0$. The only negative number allowed is -0, and $\sqrt{-0} = -0$.

(c) Format conversions: possible conversions are from one floating point number to another, from floating point to integer and vice versa, and from binary to decimal (BCD) format and vice versa. Rounding may be applied when a result is required in an integer or smaller floating point format. The standard places limits on the decimal digits of precision for each conversion.

(d) Comparison: between operands of the same, and of different floating-point formats. There are four possible results to a comparison operation – less than, equal, greater than, and unordered, which are mutually exclusive. Unordered is the result achieved by a comparison between a finite floating point number and NaN or ∞. The signs of infinity in the projective mode, and zero, are ignored in the comparison.

All operations are to be carried out to an equivalent infinite precision (see section 7.2.1.3) before rounding according to a default or specified mode. Unnormalised and denormalised numbers are more difficult to deal with. (An unnormalised number may only be in an extended format, where the single integer bit is specified. If this bit is zero, with the exponent greater than its minimum value, the number is unnormalised. A denormalised number is a basic format one with $e = 0$ and $f \neq 0$, i.e. between 0 and $2^{(1-b)}(1.0)$). The standard defines a default mode, where at least one operand is not normalised, and an additional mode for extended-format unnormalised numbers, where these are normalised before use. The default mode is as follows:

(a) Arithmetic: basically, if the result can be normalised, it should be, before rounding. Various exception conditions are enumerated.

(b) Square root: invalid if operand not normalised.

(c) Compare: as if both operands had been first normalised.

7.3.1.3 Rounding

Normally, rounding will be performed to fit the fractional part of a result to the required format. The proposed standard requires that all operations be carried out to an equivalent infinite precision before any rounding is carried out. This can be practically done by extending the fractional part of a number by three bits at the least significant end. These bits are:

(a) The guard bit, the first bit beyond rounding precision.

(b) The round bit (necessary, with the guard bit to ensure unbiased rounding to within half a unit in the least significant bit).

(c) The third, or sticky bit, which is the logical OR of all bits beyond round.

The default rounding mode, provides rounding to the nearest floating-point number with rounding to even in the case of a tie (this implies that the rounded result will differ at most from the exact result by one half the least significant bit). Directed rounding modes may provide user-selectable positive- and negative-directed rounding, and truncation. Positive-directed rounding gives a result closest to, and no less than, the exact result; negative-directed rounding will give a result closest to, and no greater than, the exact result, while truncation (or rounding towards zero) will give a result closest to, and no greater than, the magnitude of the exact result. The three bits described allow these directed rounding operations under all circumstances.

7.3.1.4 Exceptions

Five types of exception are defined, each of which may be associated with a microprocessor trap, or with a status flag if trapping is not required. The conditions are:

(a) Invalid operation: one which involves an invalid operand (e.g. square root of a negative non-zero number), or one which returns a result which is invalid for the destination.
(b) Division-by-zero, which will return a default result of a correctly signed ∞.
(c) Overflow: a rounded result which is finite but whose exponent is too large for the chosen format.
(d) Underflow, which occurs when a result before normalising is non-zero, but whose exponent is too small for the normalised format or when an extended-format product or quotient with neither operand zero, returns a result which, before rounding, is indistinguishable from normal zero.
(e) Inexact: if the rounded result of an operation is not exact, or if it overflows without a trap.

If traps are implemented, the trap handler should be able to determine:

(a) Type of exception.
(b) Kind of operation.
(c) Destination format.
(d) In overflow, underflow, inexact and invalid result, the correctly rounded result including information that may not fit into the destination format; in invalid operand, and divide-by-zero, the operand values.

7.2.1.5 Implementation

The intention of the originators of the proposed standard is that operations may be implemented in either hardware (which must support appropriate software) or software. In practice, the provision of floating-point facilities may well be slow (even with modern 16-bit machines) if implemented purely in software, and a combination of hardware and software is the ideal. A coprocessor is the ideal way to implement many of the operations, since it is closely coupled to the CPU, sharing its local bus, and effectively extending its instruction set to include floating-point functions. Its speed may well be almost two orders of magnitude better than with a software implementation. One such coprocessor is already available (see chapter 5).

7.3.2 LINKING CONVENTIONS

Most manufacturers have a convention for linking assembly code programs to high-level languages, and to operating systems. Any such conventions are specific to the particular microprocessor involved, and to the language or system. There can thus be no 'universal' standard, only particular microprocessor implementations. For instance, Intel, with PL/M, defines two microprocessor registers for parameter passing, a 'primary' and a 'secondary' one. Similarly, many of the conventions associated with interrupt control will also affect assembly code software.

7.4 In-circuit emulation

The complexity of in-circuit emulators has risen tremendously with the new generation of 16-bit microprocessors. Apart from the obvious problems of coping with very large addressing ranges, the ways in which an emulator may support the multiple microprocessor facilities, the different microprocessor modes, and complex interrupt structures all add to the sophistication required. A typical example of a modern system is the Zilog EMS 8000. This system, coupled to a System 8000 Z-Lab, which runs a Unix-like operating system called Zeus, provides a particularly comprehensive set of facilities:

(a) An internal local network allows up to eight communication modes in a user's system to be emulated simultaneously, using eight EMS 8000s, allowing direct support of a local network-based multiple microprocessor system. Message sending and reception in the network may be independently monitored with the separate EMS 8000s.
(b) A direct interface with a logic analyser, which can then be synchronised with microprocessor activity. This is almost a necessity for modern high clock rate systems, where timing problems may not be solved by an emulator alone.
(c) Support of multiple microprocessor types by personality card changes (for Z8001, Z8002, and future Z8003 and 4), and in real time.
(d) A large mappable memory of up to 126 kbytes, which can be mapped to anywhere in the target address space. The usual protection and code/stack/data separation facilities are provided.
(e) A large 1K × 64-bit real time trace memory may be used with qualifier functions to record all bus activity; the trace memory may be split to give what Zilog called 'multiple snapshots' of events (including DMA cycles). When the trace memory is split into blocks in this way, each block may be used independently with its own trigger and qualifiers.

The EMS 8000 uses the Unix base of the System 8000 Z-Lab to provide a friendly interface with the user. One of four possible user displays or screens are presented on the system visual display terminal, in an 80 column by 24 line format. Switching between them may be accomplished using the escape (ESC) character on the keyboard followed by a single letter. The four displays are:

(a) default (ESC D) which displays and allows control of target system status, the memory available and the basic state of the EMS;
(b) configuration (ESC C) which allows detailed setting-up of trace qualifier assignment, trigger and breakpoint environments and allows the system to be set up for timing and performance measurements;
(c) programming (ESC P), which details the actual trigger patterns, breakpoint addresses, the number of (say) trigger events before trigger activated, and the number of trace cycles;
(d) SDT (ESC S), which controls the system debugging tool. Most of the debugging functions are incorporated into this display. The screen in this mode has three areas, a command (menu) area which directs the user for keyboard input, a 'watch' area which allows monitoring of selected CPU registers breakpoint locations etc., and a scrollable area, which displays the output of the SDT commands (e.g. trace memory or execution history, displayed with address, instruction mnemonics, and register contents). Cursor control allows easy menu-driven operation, and control of scrolling. SDT may also be used to examine, compare and alter the mappable memory, register contents and input-output locations, to operate with patterns in memory blocks, and to manipulate files created on the host development system. Indirect command files allow easy (repeated) system setup.

It may readily be seen that the combination of system 8000 Z-Lab and EMS 8000 is a very powerful one, and one which goes a long way beyond the previous 8-bit systems. Despite its complexity, the user interface is easy to operate; menu-driven displays have long since proved their worth, and are an obvious approach to making the increasingly large number of emulation and trace choices accessible to the systems engineer. The support of networking and multiple microprocessor systems is particularly necessary – debugging such large interacting systems is a very difficult matter without such support, and such systems will certainly become more commonplace as the modern 16-bit microprocessor becomes more accepted. Besides Zilog, the other manufacturers provide enhanced facilities – Intel with the MDS Series III and ICE-86 and ICE-88, Motorola with EXORMACS (and EXORSET for the 6809). All allow multiple users or networking of the development system, self test and diagnostics, large bulk storage facilities (hard Winchester-type disk drives are options with all of them) and enhanced simulation capabilities.

7.5 Benchmarking

One of the difficulties facing a microprocessor engineer at an early stage of a project is selection of the most appropriate microprocessor for the project. Ideally, there should be some unbiased way of comparing devices which will allow them to be selected objectively, and it is to this problem that the idea of benchmarking is addressed. The concept is simple: by writing a 'representative' selection of programs which will ideally exercise a system in a similar way to the real applications software, these can be coded for various competing microprocessors, which can then be run against one another, and execution times, program sizes and writing or development effort compared. In reality, of course, benchmarks are not nearly so straightforward – they may be chosen by a manufacturer so as to emphasise the strengths of his own microprocessor compared to others (and to mask its weaknesses); it is very difficult for a user to code programs for different microprocessors (when he is more familiar with some than others) equally efficiently, and in any case, the measure of assembly language (or high level language) speed and efficiency is only part of the comparison problem. In reality, other aspects of system development may assume equal importance. For instance, manufacturer's support (software and development system facilities), cost (both of development and final system production) and availability of parts may influence a choice of microprocessor just as much as the comparison of raw speed and memory utilisation.

Nevertheless, when seen in their proper perspective, benchmark programs do have a definite use. Writing (or examining well written) benchmark programs gives the prospective user a useful insight into the operation of the microprocessors he is considering using, and he may well discover features (desirable and undesirable) which will influence his choice. Provided the prospective user takes care to identify any bias in benchmark program choice, he can find out where a particular microprocessor's strengths and weaknesses lie, and decide whether they are important enough in his particular application to eliminate a microprocessor from further consideration.

A major (and controversial) series of benchmarks have been written for the American magazine *EDN*. First published in April 1981 they originally covered the 8086, Z8000, MC68000 and DEC LSI-11/23 microprocessors, and were later updated to allow improved coding (supplied by the manufacturers) for the first three microprocessors. The updated test and results appeared in September 1981[6,7]. The seven programs written for this benchmark were:

(a) An I/O interrupt kernel with four interrupt levels, consisting of disabling interrupts, saving machine context, enabling higher priority interrupts, simulating some processing, disabling interrupts, restoring context, and returning. Some differences in implementation between microprocessors were reflected in unrealistic speed differences which diminished when the program was re-coded.
(b) An interrupt kernel with FIFO (first-in, first-out queue) processing, using four interrupt levels and specifying as test data a set of interrupts as follows: level 1 (once), level 2 (once), level 3 (once), level 4 (once), level 2 (three times), level 3 (five times). These force queueing of interrupts.
(c) Character-string search, using a 120-character long test string with a 15-character long search argument.
(d) Bit set, reset and test, with test data consisting of a 125-bit array consisting of alternating zeros and ones, and starting on a (16-bit) word boundary. Nine tests are run on this data – test bit 10, bit 11 and bit 123; set bits 10, 11 and 123, and reset bits 10, 11 and 123. The objective is to compare the bit manipulation capabilities of the microprocessors.

(e) Linked-list data insertion. A doubly-linked list is created, where each entry possesses a 32-bit integer 'key' field. Each entry in the list has a key and a forward and a backward pointer (the first entry in the list has a backward pointer of zero, the last entry a forward pointer of zero) and new entries must be inserted in ascending order of their keys. A 'list control block' structure contains a pointer to the first entry in the list, a pointer to the last entry in the list, and a count of the number of entries in the list. At the start of the program, the list is emtpy (LCB's pointers are identical, and count is zero), and the timings are taken for the sum of five insertions, whose keys are given (in random order).
(f) Quicksort. The test data consists of 102 records, each 16 bytes long, initialised before program execution. The first and last records hold the lowest and highest key values, respectively, so the sort is actually of 100 records. A key is formed from each records third to ninth bytes inclusive, and this key forms the basis of the sorting procedure.
(g) Bit-matrix transposition. A test array of 49 bits in a 7 X 7 matrix is provided (beginning on a word boundary) and its transposition performed.

These tests are a subset of a Carnegie-Mellon University (CMU) suite of mini-computer and mainframe benchmarks; tests omitted are floating-point mathematics, virtual memory handling and the 'number-crunching' ones such as Fourier transform and Runge-Kutta integration. All these tests would depend heavily on the type of support (numeric coprocessor, memory-management unit) available, and not all 16-bit microprocessors have such support as yet.

Criticism of the benchmarks ranged from highlighting differences in coding (to exploit a particular microprocessor's architecture) which altered test conditions, to use of microprocessors with clock rates which made them slow, when in fact, faster devices were available. Memory space, too, was different for different microprocessors (the Z8000 version restricted to 64K, the 8086 to 1 Mbyte and 68000 to 16 Mbytes). The results of the final (modified) versions are presented in table 7.1.

Table 7.1

Micro-processor	Clock rate (MHz)	Test (bytes/μs) a	b	c	d	e	f	g
8086	10	24/46.4	185/402	44/211	42/119	115/210	276/38254	95/523
Z8002	6	18/42	124/375	66/190	44/124	84/203	334/22211	106/563
68000	10	24/32	130/321	44/225	36/69	100/121	276/17348	74/366
Z8002	10	18/26	124/225	66/114	44/74	84/122	334/13300	106/338
68000	12	24/26.7	130/268	44/188	36/58	100/101	276/14456	74/305

CHAPTER 8
System software and operating systems

Many 8-bit microprocessors are built into microcomputers which support only rudimentary monitor software and BASIC. Their low complexity does not warrant the complex support software of the minicomputer, and their limited speed and addressing puts a constraint on the type of support which can be provided. Although it is possible to write position-independent code on an 8-bit microprocessor, it is cumbersome and not usually necessary. With an embedded 8-bit microprocessor, it is usual for relatively few concurrent tasks to be implemented, and once again, system software may be minimal. Only with disk-based 8-bit microcomputers have some operating systems emerged: CP/M for 8080 and Z80, Flex for 6800. Real time operating systems are confined to simple schedulers with some means for synchronising communications between tasks (e.g. iRMX 80).

With the 16-bit microprocessor, the situation is completely different. When a 16-bit microprocessor is used as the base for a personal or office microcomputer, inevitably floppy- or Winchester-disk based, requirements will dictate some operating system, such as CP/M or Unix. At this early stage, it appears that Unix may well dominate the 16-bit microcomputer software scene as CP/M has done with personal 8-bit machines.

With real time operation, 16-bit microprocessor speeds are such that running many concurrent tasks is possible, and may indeed be desirable. The possibilities opened up by the 16-bit microprocessor (because of its speed, low cost, and small size) are those which are unattainable with 8-bit microprocessors yet not important enough to warrant a minicomputer. Nevertheless most of these 'intermediate' applications require multiple concurrent tasks and hence a suitable real time operating system. (Typical of such applications are engine controllers, which require the speed and precision of a 16-bit microprocessor and have to respond to a number of external stimuli, real time signal microprocessors for sonar and radar systems, and robotics, where small size and weight may be of paramount importance). This chapter discusses two types of operating system designed for 16-bit microprocessors; one, a single-user or time-sharing system suitable for a personal computer system, and the other a real time multitasking system.

8.1 Disk operating systems (DOS) for a microcomputer system

The two systems mentioned in the introduction typify the likely approaches to 16-bit microprocessor operating system design. CP/M, in the guise of 16-bit CP/M-86, has grown up from Digital Research's original 8080-based CP/M. Unix, on the other hand, was originally designed as a small mainframe or large mini-computer time-sharing system by Bell Laboratories in the USA. With support of the Bell System behind it, and its support of the Bell-designed language C, Unix is operating on many installations, providing a friendly software development environment for its users (the original design aim was to provide an in-house Bell operating system for programming research). In its microprocessor realisation, Unix tends to be a subset of the original system. The full operating system requires a very large memory on the host machine. In 1978, the Bell research Unix system ran on a PDP 11/70 computer with 768 kbytes of core memory, with a 90 kbyte system kernel (the permanently resident part of an OS). The same year, Unix was implemented on an LS1-11 16-bit microcomputer with an 8K word (16-bit) kernel. It is instructive to examine each of these systems and to compare their facilities in the light of their different origins.

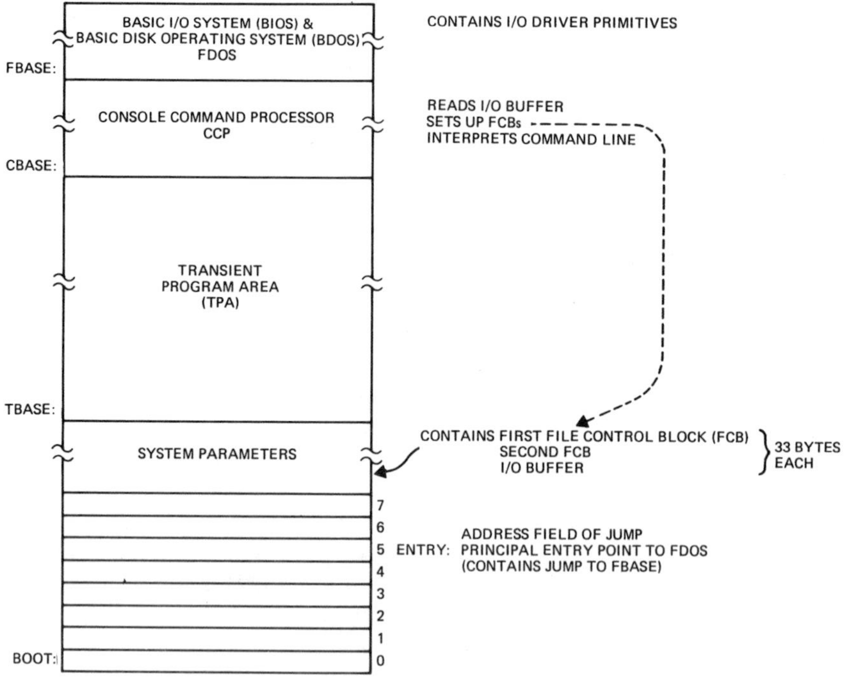

Fig. 8.1 CP/M memory map.

8.1.1 CP/M

CP/M[1] is a single-user, single-task operating system. It provides the user with basic facilities necessary for using a disk-based microcomputer system, giving him control of disk files and I/O devices at a level considerably higher than machine-code, hardware port level. The popularity of CP/M in the 8-bit microcomputer world stems from its early introduction (1976) and its compatibility with Intel and Zilog microprocessors. Indeed, the original development of CP/M was to support an Intel development system (MDS) and PL/M (described in chapter 9): support of a resident PL/M compiler was included in the first version of the operating system. CP/M is small in size, and omits many of the operating-system features found on minicomputers and likely to be required on many 16-bit microprocessor systems. Nevertheless, it is already available for one of the modern 16-bit microprocessors (CP/M-86, for the 8086).

The heart of CP/M is a kernel called BIOS (basic input-output system), whose function is to interact with the hardware facilities of the system, providing input-output handlers and an exception handler, which in many CP/M implementations, will handle only software interrupts. BIOS is used by all the operating-system commands, and other system modules. The other features of CP/M are a command-line interpreter (the console command processor, or CCP), a file manager and basic DOS primitives (BDOS), and a set of utilities invoked by transient commands which run in a shared area of random-access memory known as the transient program area (TPA). A memory map for CP/M is shown in fig. 8.1.

Operation of CP/M revolves around the CCP, which interacts directly, with the user, reading and interpreting commands input via the system I/O device or console. Several disk drives can be supported by CP/M, with the currently 'logged-in' (or active) disk indicated by the CCP prompt of single letter disk identifier (usually A, B, C or D) followed by '>'. On system initialisation, the CP/M system is bootstrapped from disk A (by default), which remains the currently logged-in disk until changed by the user.

The CCP uses one of the BIOS functions to read a line typed on the system keyboard in the form <command> [<filename 1>. <ext 1>] [<file name 2>. <ext 2>], where arguments in square brackets [ ] are optional. If <command> is one of the CP/M built in commands, such as DIR (disk directory), it is executed immediately, otherwise CP/M searches the currently active disk for a file of the form <command>. <COM>, which, if found, is assumed to be of memory image format and loaded into the transient program area for execution. Any arguments following <command> are placed in the name and extension parts of two temporary file control blocks (FCBs) (areas of memory reserved for information concerning files about to be used by CP/M). BDOS is used for reading and writing files on the active disk, and for file creation, directory maintenance, and will use the file control block descriptions of any files required for command execution.

Input-output is supported by BIOS, with software drivers referred using symbolic names TTY:, CRT:, LPT:, etc. CCP and some transient programs use logical devices CON: (console), RDR: (reader, or fast input device), PUN: (punch, or fast output device) and LST: (listing device). Each logical device may be associated with an appropriate driver using an assignment statement which is available as a standard transient command.

The built-in commands of the CCP consist of the basic file handling commands:

ERA Erase specified file.

DIR List disk directory (either of specified disk or defaults to currently logged-in disk).

REN Rename specified file.

SAVE Memory contents in a file. The practical realisation of this command is in the form SAVE *n* <filename>. <filetype> <cr> where *n* is the number of 256-byte blocks of the TPA (which starts at address 1ØØ hex in a standard version of CP/M) stored in the file as an executable machine code memory image. The file may subsequently be loaded into the same memory area and executed.

TYPE Displays the contents of an ASCII source file from the currently logged-in or specified disk on the console device (or list device if required).

CCP uses standard BDOS primitives to access disk files – typically SEARCH (for named file), OPEN, CLOSE, RENAME, READ (a 128-byte record), WRITE (a 128-byte record), SELECT (drive).

In addition to the built in functions of CCP, CP/M possesses various standard transient programs held on disk to facilitate operations. Among these are:

STAT Gives free space on a disk or the size of a file, or logical device assignments.

PIP Peripheral interchange program which allows transfer of files between disks, or between disk and input-output device.

LOAD Creates an executable file (in memory image form, to be loaded into the TPA) from a hex machine code file, produced by an assembler or high-level language compiler. The executable file (of type COM) can be loaded into memory and executed by typing its name in response to the CCP prompt character.

SYSGEN Creates CP/M on a new (blank) diskette. Only CP/M with built-in commands is copied, and all transient command files must be transferred using PIP.

MOVCPM Allows reconfiguration of the CP/M system to suit any memory size between 16 and 64 kbytes (in the 8-bit microprocessor version of CP/M).

SUBMIT Allows creation of an indirect command file.

DUMP Dumps a named file in hexadecimal on the console device.

DDT A dynamic debugging program.

ASM Assembler (optional).

ED Text editor (optional).

A version of CP/M 2.2 is available for the 8086 microprocessor, which allows configuration to support, 1024 kbytes of memory while itself occupying 20 kbytes. Although its facilities are rather more varied than the ones outlined above, the structure is identical. CP/M only allows a single user on a single-processor system to run one task at a time. It has no real time provisions and no networking capabilities. Despite these limitations, and CP/M's adherence to indexed-sequential file structures (a limited form of random access is allowed), the operating system represents a standard which has served the 8-bit microprocessor (in the form of personal and desktop computers) world well.

From a 16-bit microprocessor viewpoint, however, the system is limited. It provides the absolute minimum of support necessary for a viable disk-based system, and takes no account of the extended capabilities of the new generation of microprocessors. The relocatability of code with the 16-bit microprocessors allows more sophisticated memory management, and allows more than one resident transient program at a time, while the resource lockout provisions in hardware resolve any contention problems. Multiple microprocessor operation is likely to become common with the personal computers currently being designed, and networking, too, will rise in prominence. Some enhanced versions of CP/M are available (notably the multi-user MP/M 1.1 and the networking CP/Net 1.0 from the originators of CP/M, Digital Research Inc.) but these rather compromise the original advantages of simplicity and small size. Consequently, CP/M is unlikely to achieve a position of dominance in the 16-bit computer environment; it will have a place, however, in smaller and less expensive systems. Its adoption by a number of companies marketing 16-bit personal computers will prolong its life.

8.1.2 MP/M-86, A MULTIPROCESSING VERSION OF CP/M

The author of the original version of CP/M, Gary Kildall, founded Digital Research to exploit the expanding market for microprocessor systems software. To follow up its success in marketing CP/M, Digital Research has now brought out a multiprocessing operating system (one which supports concurrent processes) for the 8086, called MP/M-86. The organisation of MP/M-86[2] is only very loosely based on CP/M, and the system has been considerably enhanced in two directions, namely to accommodate concurrent multiple processes, multiple users, and resource-sharing (including mutual-exclusion, where processes are competing for use of a shared resource, and inter-process communication), and to include facilities which make better use of 16-bit CPU hardware, such as memory-management.

The heart of MP/M is a 'kernel' which consists of four program modules: the real time monitor (RTM), the basic disk operating system (BDOS), the character input-output system (CIO), and the memory manager (MEM). A supervisor module controls communication between the modules of the kernel and other parts of the system. The other major components of MP/M are the extended input-output system (XIOS), the counterpart of CP/M's BIOS, and the terminal message processor (TMP), which interacts directly with the user, together with various system programs. These system programs include the command-line interpreter (CLI) and parser, a run-time system, and a resident procedure library. Figure 8.2 uses an 'onion-shell' model to illustrate the relationships of various parts of MP/M, starting at the lowest hardware level in the centre, and working outwards through successively higher levels towards the user, on the outside.

Since MP/M is dealing with multiple processes and users, some of its features differ markedly from CP/M. Whereas CP/M supports a transient program area which may be used for a single user's programs, MP/M has a more sophisticated memory manager MEM, which allocates one or more partitions of memory to each user or process. The idea of a process is fundamental to MP/M, as indeed it is to any other multiprocessing or real time operating system. A process is not just a program or static piece of code, but is a dynamic activity which executes both applications and operating-system code. Processes are run in partitioned memory space, with the size of partitions fixed by the system implementer at system generation time. Not all need to be the same size; indeed, they are most often a mixture of sizes, allowing the memory manager to minimise unused memory space (as would be present if a small process were running in a large partition) and at the same time preserve a large contiguous memory space (to avoid fragmentation of large programs).

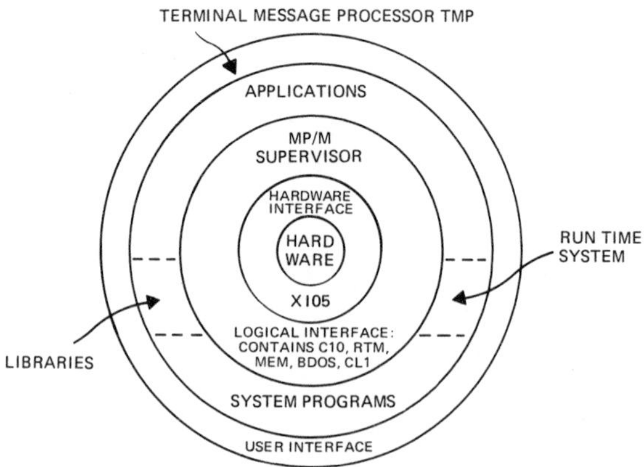

Fig. 8.2 MP/M model.

Each process is represented by a process descriptor which contains status information, register and interrupt-vector addresses, user number, console and password. The process descriptor is used by a process manager in the form of the real-time monitor (RTM), which handles allocation and deallocation of the CPU to a process according to its priority. The RTM of MP/M controls process creation, termination, dispatching and communication, as well as handling logical interrupts and I/O device polling. Like the kernel of a true real time operating system, RTM contains a scheduler (with round-robin priority resolution) and dispatcher, which operate whenever a resource is requested or released by the operating system, or in any case, every 1/60 sec, controlled by a system real time clock. Processes are queued; the ready queue contains the process descriptors of processes awaiting execution, with the descriptor of the currently running process at the top of the queue. The system queue is one of the fundamental data structures of MP/M, and allows not only process scheduling, but also process communication, synchronisation and mutual exclusion from shared resources. A command queue controls command-process scheduling. A queue may contain up to 64K messages, each of a maximum length of 64K bytes (within the constraints of available memory).

Another new feature of MP/M is the idea of a logical interrupt as a means of controlling process allocation. When a process is required to wait for an interrupt, it calls the wait-flag function, with the flag number corresponding to the interrupt it will respond to as an argument, and the process is then suspended by the dispatcher. When an interrupt occurs, the interrupt service routine calls the set-flag function, which places the suspended process on the ready list associated with the dispatcher.

BDOS manages disk areas via the XIOS (hardware driver interface) tables of disk parameter blocks; using tables to relate logical to physical areas means that a single physical disk drive may be related to several logical drives, and indeed, for temporary files, a virtual disk may be defined in memory. Such a device allows fast operation, and since the files are temporary, the volatility of semiconductor memory is no disadvantage.

All the modules which make up MP/M are 'plug compatible' and may be customised by the user; this modular approach allows system development to be carried out on one module without affecting the others. For instance, one of the additions to MP/M is for networking, where a network module may be placed between the supervisor and the kernel (RTM, BDOS, etc.), so as to intercept selected calls, while remaining invisible to the user. A resource-table held in memory indicates whether a requested resource is held locally (where it may be accessed independently of the network), or remotely. A remote request will invoke a resource-requester program which will communicate with the other MP/M network station which contains the resource, using the network I/O system and file server.

From this brief description, it may be seen that MP/M is much more sophisticated than CP/M (which is really just a single-user control program). It allows multiple users and multiple processes using techniques which are similar to those of a real time operating system (see later in this chapter) and possesses a flexibility which makes it much more attractive than CP/M to the 16-bit systems designer.

8.1.3 UNIX

Unix[3] is a disk operating system which has evolved in a rather different manner to CP/M – instead of being designed specifically for a microprocessor environment, Unix was originated by Ken Thompson, of Bell Laboratories, to provide an improved environment in which to write and use programs, based on the PDP-11 range of minicomputers, in particular the PDP11/45 and 11/70. Both of these machines provide comprehensive hardware facilities, including memory management, multiple concurrent users, and a variety of bulk storage and peripheral devices. With the massive support of Bell Laboratories behind it, Unix has become popular in the minicomputer world, where the presence of a standard system has facilitated software exchange among many users, particularly in universities, where its clean and logical command structure and its flexible peripheral management are much appreciated (as well as the fact that Unix was made available to educational users for only the cost of handling). Strictly speaking, Unix itself is not so much an operating system as a time-sharing system, usually built around a more conventional operating system (in the Bell Laboratories PDP-11 System, this 'kernel' operating system was called MERT).

To quote its main authors, Ken Thompson and Dennis Ritchie, Unix '... offers a number of features seldom found even in larger installations, including:

(a) a hierarchical file system incorporating demountable volumes;
(b) compatible file, device, and interprocess I/O;
(c) the ability to initiate asynchronous processes;
(d) system command language available on a per-user basis;
(e) over 100 subsystems including a dozen languages;
(f) high degree of portability.'

Already, it can be seen that Unix is much more sophisticated than CP/M, in terms of its features. In its construction, it reflects this sophistication, and also the author's quest for elegance in an operating system. To satisfy its objectives, Unix has four main parts: its command interpreter, since, like CP/M, the system is interactive; a peripheral management system based on file handling; a scheduling system, and a file security system which allocates system resources (and controls access rights). A MERT operating system, on which a typical Unix system is based, consists of three support layers which allow hardware and software interrupt-driver processes running in segmented memory, provides input-output device drivers, and handles interprocess communications. The MERT kernel runs three processes which must exist for the system to function. These are:

(a) A file manager (since all processes and intercommunications are derived from files).
(b) A 'swap' process (to move segments between secondary storage and memory).
(c) A 'root' process (which handles data transfers between the file manager and the disk).

In addition, it provides trap and interrupt handling, process dispatching (a procedure which consists of saving the current state and setting up the state of and initiating the process) and interprocess communications.

Unix requests will involve running two categories of process: supervisor processes, which run in a privileged system mode and are able to directly affect system operations, and user processes, which may use some of the system facilities, but are unable to execute operations which endanger system integrity. The MERT memory manager processes uses the three processes mentioned earlier to honour Unix requests for running processes. A scheduler process selects the next process to be executed (normally according to some priority allocation algorithm), but it is the memory manager which will load the process, swap segments as required, set those segments into an active state, alter the capability lists of supervisor processes (such lists allow selective access to system facilities, and are maintained in a supervisor process control block, or PCB), and deactivate processes. To actually run the process, the system uses a dispatcher mechanism which uses a number of process lists, each one tied to a different priority. The dispatcher mechanism invokes the scheduler when an appropriate priority software interrupt occurs; the process lists are searched for the highest priority pending process, which, if it is of a higher priority than the currently executing process, will pre-empt the current process.

A number of kernel primitives are available, and may be used by other processes, some solely by supervisor processes, some by any processes. The universally available primitives allow interprocess communications and synchronisation, attaching to and detaching from interrupts, manipulation of segments for I/O resource locking (to avoid contention problems), creating attached timeout events and having access to time-of-day. Those only available to supervisor processes include segment creation, deletion and alteration of segment attributes, and alteration of scheduler parameters.

Using this operating system as a base, Unix implements its time-sharing functions around a universal file system, and a command interpreter called the shell. The Unix shell is a sophisticated interpreter which allows very compact and concise command strings, and, indeed, one of the features of Unix (and a major asset, according to many Unix users) is the brevity of its commands. All commands use the file system which defines structures which may be used as disk or secondary memory files, input-output files, or interprocess messages. They have the structure 'command-name, arg 1, arg 2, etc.', and the first action by the shell is to look for a file name to match 'command-name', which, if found, will be brought into memory and executed, using the arguments arg 1, arg 2, etc. where necessary. When the command has completed execution, it returns to the shell, which delivers a prompt to the user.

File structures are very flexible: ordinary user files have no defined structure and no privileged access, special files are used for input-output (they are read from or written to just like ordinary files, but result in activation of the appropriate peripheral device), and directory files with privileged access for writing to the file provide a structure which allows extreme simplicity of operation together with a sophistication unusual in a relatively small system. For instance, each user has his own directory, and may specify a file either by name or a path name. A system directory called the root directory may be used to point to all the other classes of directory. Whereas a simple file name (which may be up to fourteen characters long) will cause the current directory to be searched for that file, a path name of the form / name one / name two / name three may be used, the first '/' causes the root directory to be searched for a directory file called name one, which is itself searched for entry name two, which is finally searched for entry name three, the required file. The whole directory structure has the form of a 'rooted tree', where, except for special entries, each directory must appear as an entry in exactly one other directory, which is its 'parent'. Manipulation of files is performed by using an index-number pointer to a system table which contains entries pointing to a file description, which controls allocation, creation, opening and closure.

Multiple users are catered for by using images of the execution environment and each process is the execution of an image, which includes a memory image, register values, status of files and current directory, (obviously an image must remain in main memory while its process is executing, and remains there during execution of other processes unless swapped out by a higher priority demand). The user memory part of an image is divided into three logical segments – a write-protected (during execution) code segment, a private writable data segment, and a stack segment separate from the system stack.

Processes are invoked by the system call fork, which splits an executing process into independently executing 'parent' and 'child' processes, which have independent copies of the original memory image, and which share all open files. Execution, termination and synchronisation of processes, as well as interprocess communication, are handled by the system calls execute, exit, wait and pipe. Pipe creates an interprocess channel and returns a file descriptor which allows writing to the channel, and reading from it (with a 'wait till data written' restriction, when the data is written by another process, it is then passed between the two images). The idea of 'fork' is a very powerful one which ensures a large measure of autonomy for users – indeed, fork is used to create independent shells for each user, all children of a parent process created by executing an initialisation program called unit.

The strong points of Unix are its regular command format, and terseness of comments and prompts (although this feature may tend to put off users unfamiliar with it). Its file structure, too, is uniquely simple, with each file considered as a featureless sequence of bytes with no record structure (considered unnecessary by the authors) and an efficient file addressing mechanism. Input-output, too, is regularised by being treated in the same way, but there are possible drawbacks with this approach, which tends to constrain data to blocks when a character-orientated approach may be preferable. Security is good, since the shell has no special privileges, and information and files are well protected, but is poor with regard to system crashes caused by such things as resource exhaustion.

The applicability of the Unix system to microprocessors is easy to imagine. More sophisticated and capable than CP/M, it will give the 16-bit personal and office microcomputers of the future a sound user environment (and a high-level language called 'C', developed at the same time as Unix, with many features similar to Pascal). Moreover, the hardware and systems features of the newer 16-bit microprocessors lend themselves admirably to Unix implementation. Segmentation of memory, and segment protection (either internal protection like the Intel iAPX 286 or external, like the Zilog MMU or Motorola MMU) allow the user segments of Unix to be created very economically and quickly and contention-resolving facilities (such as the Intel 'LOCK' prefix) allow easy resource sharing that is central to the idea of Unix. Powerful interrupt and exception handling facilities ease the Unix scheduler and dispatcher design, and separate user and systems modes in hardware allow the security of the system to be maintained.

Already, Unix is available for the latest 16-bit microprocessor-based systems, and it looks set to become the standard personal or office machine system. Its support of multiple concurrent users makes it especially useful in a business environment, whether for a management information system, a multi-user word processing system, or for financial or stock control. Multiterminal microcomputer systems are likely to become commonplace, and a large body of available software (most of it written for 16-bit microcomputers, notably Xenix (available from Microsoft) and Zeus (Zilog's adopted Z8000 system OS). The popularity of a system which is sold without any software maintenance or support and no warranty (Western Electric conditions) would appear to indicate widespread user acceptance, and in view of the effort required to create a new multi-user interactive operating system, it is unlikely that Unix will have many serious rivals to its becoming *the* standard system for 16-bit microcomputers.

Unix is by no means limited purely to time-sharing, interactive operation, in principle, real time process control could be performed under Unix – the ideas of process scheduling, communication and synchronisation central to process control all exist in a Unix system (indeed, there are system primitives which allow direct access to interrupt and input-output). Some features of the system do somewhat restrict its usefulness in this area, however. Its size, although reduced from the original PDP-11 based system is still relatively large, since features (such as its interactive nature, and maintenance of directories) are included which are unlikely to be required by a control system. Its speed too, may perhaps not be sufficient for some applications – a PDP-11 implementation of Unix has interrupt response times quoted as:

Kernel response 100 ms
Non-swap supervisor process of order milliseconds
Swap processes of order hundreds of milliseconds

The lack of a more general communication or synchronisation scheme may also prove restrictive (Unix contains nothing to parallel, for instance, Dijkstra's P and V semaphores). It seems likely, therefore, that only those control applications which require some of the disk-based file handling or I/O of Unix will use the system, and that most applications will use a simpler specifically real time operating system.

8.2 Real time operating systems

Real time operation has always been a major requirement for many microprocessor applications, and in many cases, where multiple real time tasks are involved, an operating system is necessary to supervise operation of these tasks, and their interaction with the system hardware[4] The task of the system designer is eased considerably by use of an operating system, since all real time tasks are constrained to adopt the same format for communication, for input-output and for synchronisation. This uniformity makes debugging a complex system much easier, allows changes to one task with less risk of compromising the whole system, and lets the system designer concentrate on implementation of applications software.

The major functions of a real time operating system are:

(a) To handle interrupts and input-output drivers.
(b) To schedule concurrent tasks to be run according to some priority scheme.
(c) To handle intertask communications and synchronisation.
(d) To provide controlled access to a shared resource to avoid contention, typically by mutual exclusion.
(e) To provide other time-related functions such as user accessible delays and 'watchdog timing', a technique which allows a user to impose a time limit for a task execution, which allows the system to be forced out of any 'locked-up' state (such as looping).

One manufacturer's approach has been to build a family of operating systems[5–8], starting with iRMX80 8-bit for 8080/5 systems, and growing to iRMX88 and iRMX86 for 16-bit systems (specifically, the 8086). iRMX86 is actually a full multiprogramming operating system while iRMX88 is a small multitasking system, deliberately designed to minimise interrupt response time and context switching. iRMX88 is the direct successor to iRMX80, and employs the same philosophy, and, in many cases, the same program modules.

8.2.1 iRMX88

The philosophy of this real time system relies on the ideas of tasks, messages and exchanges. As defined earlier in this chapter, a task is an independent program which uses resources within the system, in competition with other tasks. A message is the medium through which tasks communicate information, and synchronise with each other, and an exchange is the mechanism (actually a data structure) by which messages are passed from one task to another. The exchange implementation is of crucial importance to the efficiency of the operating system, and an exchange consists of two queues represented by a data structure where messages may be left by one task and picked up by another. A message may be sent to an exchange asynchronously, with any subsequent action determined by the sending task's coding, but will normally be picked up by a task which waits at the exchange until the message arrives. A task which performs an unconditional or untimed wait at an exchange will not run again until it has received the message; one which performs a timed wait may be made ready to run again at the end of the wait period, irrespective of whether it has received the message or not. The iRMX88 exchange data structure consists of two linked lists, one of addresses of messages waiting to be picked up, and the other of identifiers of tasks waiting for messages to arrive. Each item in a list has a 'link address' which points to the next item in the list. One of the powerful features of this approach is that interrupts may be treated just like messages, with their own exchanges. When an interrupt occurs, the operating system creates a special message and sends it to the exchange associated with that interrupt – if a previous message is encountered at the exchange, the message is changed to indicate a missed interrupt. A task waiting at the interrupt exchange may accept the message and be made ready for execution; if the task has a priority corresponding to the interrupt level, it will become the running task (since for the interrupt to be unmasked, its priority must be higher than that of the interrupted task).

The driving element of any real time operating system is the system clock, which provides a basic time increment often called the 'system time unit'. For the original iRMX80, this real time clock was normally of 50 ms period, but for iRMX88, it may be set by the system designer to any value greater than or equal to 1 ms. The system time unit provides for implementation of timed waits, and also allows task scheduling.

Each task may be in one of four states: running (the currently executing task); ready (to start executing when no higher priority task is running); waiting (for a message at an exchange), or suspended (and will not run until it is deliberately resumed). The tasks which are ready form a queue ordered by priority; where the 8-bit iRMX80 had eight software priority levels associated with the 8080/5 hardware interrupts, iRMX88 allows 256 software priority levels. The first 129 software levels are associated with the same eight hardware interrupt levels (level 0 is highest priority, and will cause all interrupts to be masked, and the rest are associated in groups of sixteen consecutive levels with each hardware interrupt) and the remaining 127 may be used purely for software purposes, with the lowest priority (255) task normally used as an 'idle' task which runs when no others are active. All interrupts with priorities lower than that of a currently running task are masked. When a task is interrupted, a context save is performed, and iRMX88 is entered to generate the message which will invoke the higher priority task appropriate to that interrupt. The interrupted task is placed in the ready condition, and will be resumed when its priority permits. Obviously, this way of dealing with interrupts imposes significant software overhead (and hence time overhead) on the system. Where interrupt response time must be minimised, the operating system also allows direct interrupt servicing, where an interrupt vector points to the interrupt service routine itself, which must, of course, manipulate the interrupt control logic and state-saving in the same way as iRMX88 would have done.

Each task has associated with it a task descriptor which contains essential task parameters, for the system, such as task name, start address, stack start address and length (each task has its own stack in RAM), and priority. The initial (or static) task descriptors may be held in ROM and copied into RAM when the system is initialised, and contain initial exchange associated with the task. Three tables are used to initialise a system: one which contains the addresses and number of entries in the initial task table and initial exchange table, the initial task table, which contains each static task descriptor, and the initial exchange table, which contains each exchange address. In operation, the iRMX88 nucleus primitives provide for implementation of various functions which allow most of the real time requirements for small systems. The primitives are:

RQACPT Accept a message from a specified exchange; return with message address or zero if no message is available.

RQCTSK Create a task.

RQCXCH Create an exchange.

RQDLVL Disable specified interrupt level.

RQDTSK	Delete a task.
RQDXCH	Delete an exchange.
RQELVL	Initialise interrupt exchange descriptor and enable specified interrupt level.
RQENDI	User end-of-interrupt.
RQISND	Sends interrupt message to specified interrupt exchange.
RQRESM	Resume a previously suspended task.
RQSEND	Send a message (specified by its address) to a specified exchange.
RQSETV	Set interrupt vector for user-written service routine which bypasses RMX88.
RQSUSP	Suspend specified task.
RQWAIT	Wait at a specified exchange until a message is available or until the specified time limit expires.

Using these primitives, the functions of communication, task synchronisation, and mutual exclusion from a system resource may be constructed. Communication simply consists of task A using RQSEND and task B using RQACPT or RQWAIT, both at the same exchange. Task synchronisation is illustrated in fig. 8.3. Task A uses RQWAIT to generate a specified delay period by waiting at exchange X for a message that will never come (since no task will send a message to exchange X). When task A is invoked at the end of each wait period, it sends a message for task B to exchange Y, (using RQSEND). Task B will acknowledge by sending a message to task A via a third exchange, Z. Involving a 'scheduler task', like task A, means that task B may be synchronised at regular time intervals, independent of its own execution time. Had task B itself waited directly on exchange X, the execution time of B would have to be added to the wait delay to get the time interval between successive operations of task B.

Mutual exclusion may be implemented by an exchange associated with the shared resource (fig. 8.4). At initialisation time, the exchange is created with a single message. As tasks require to use the associated system resource, they wait for a message at the exchange. When the message is received, the receiving task must have sole control of the resource (since there is only one message associated with the exchange). When the task has finished with the resource, it sends the message back to the exchange, allowing the next task waiting at the exchange exclusive access to the associated resource.

The iRMX88 nucleus occupies 3.5 kbytes of ROM, and uses 270 bytes of RAM for stack and temporary storage. Extensions of the nucleus allow minimal terminal handling and an optional command-line interpreter, a free space manager, a disk file system and disk input-output, a disk bootstrap loader and initialiser and some analogue input-output handlers.

The free space manager allows dynamic allocation of RAM, using it as a common resource shared by a number of tasks. Once a task no longer requires the use of its RAM area, the area is freed and made available for other tasks, which must request it through iRMX88. The free space manager maintains a pool of free memory which may be allocated in blocks to a task when requested, and those blocks reclaimed and returned to the pool when no longer required.

The manager does this via an 'allocation' exchange called RQFSAX, where a task requiring memory leaves a message which specifies the length of the required block. If the pool contains sufficient contiguous RAM area, the free space manager sends the requesting task a message of acknowledgement which contains the start address of the allocated RAM block. If insufficient RAM is available, the free space manager sends the requesting task a message indicating how much free RAM can be allocated, and the requesting task may use a message to request a smaller RAM block; alternatively, if the requesting task has made an unconditional request, the free space manager may cause the requesting to wait until sufficient memory is free. Reclamation of RAM is performed by the user task sending a message to the reclamation exchange RQFSRX.

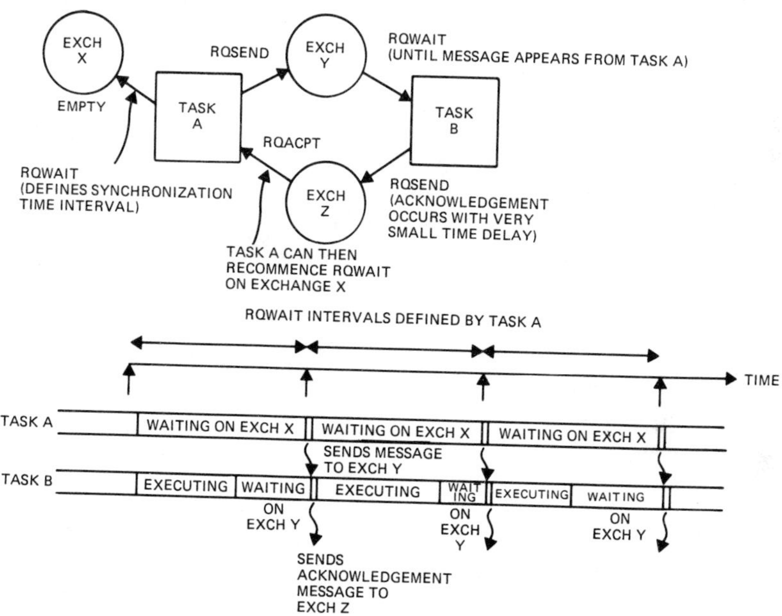

Fig. 8.3 RMX88 task synchronisation.

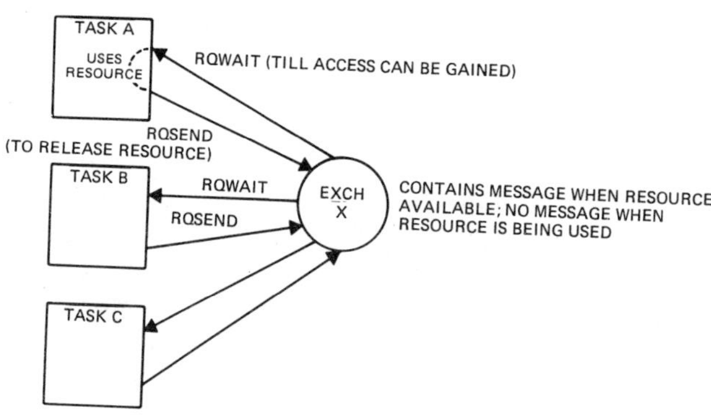

Fig. 8.4 Mutual exclusion.

The disk file system allows sequential and random-access files on both floppy disks and hard disks, and works within the environment created by the iRMX88 nucleus. In conjunction with the terminal handler, it provides basic file maintenance facilities, with the following commands:

OPEN	File ready for processing.
READ	Data from file to memory.
WRITE	Data from memory to file.
CLOSE	Specified open file.
SEEK	Set or return disk file marker.
DELETE	File from directory X release its space on disk.
RENAME	Existing file in the directory.
ATTRIB	Change the attributes of a file in the directory.
FORMAT	Initialise a new disk.
LOAD	A file of executable code into memory.
DISKIO	Fundamental disk sector operations.

In order to facilitate use of a disk system, an extension to iRMX88 in the form of a bootstrap loader is available. This allows a system to be created in RAM from disk to replace one in EPROM. Moreover, iRMX88 may be configured to automatically initialise a system using a coprocessor, creating an area of RAM for the device to use, and accommodating exception conditions raised by the coprocessor.

The terminal handler provided as an extension of the iRMX88 kernel provides real time communication between a serial asynchronous terminal and a running task using two exchanges associated with the handler. Designed to operate with the Intel baud rate timer and programmable communications interface, the handler services read and write requests on a first-in, first-out basis using exchanges RQINPX and RQOUTX, respectively. Each request results in the transmission of one character, line, or set of lines to or from the terminal, with individual characters sent and received in response to interrupts from the programmable communications interface. Associated with the terminal handler and the disk I/O system is a command line interpreter (CLI), which will pass received messages to the appropriate utility routine. While the CLI has a small number of inbuilt commands, others may be added by the user to invoke application system tasks.

Finally, one of the most useful aspects of iRMX88, when developing real time applications, is the existence of an interactive system debugger. This software debugger allows the user to examine an executing task while the system continues to operate, and also allows him to examine and alter items in RAM areas. While this is not, strictly speaking, part of the operating system proper, it is nevertheless a useful facility during program development.

From this brief description, it can be seen that a real time operating system differs considerably from a conventional disk-based system. It is often smaller, provides rather different facilities, and is much more accessible to user software. The utilities provided must be more robust than those of an interactive system since all operations are initiated by the scheduler of the system itself, and any exception conditions must be accommodated by the system itself. The nucleus of any system will perform similar functions to that of iRM88, even though its detailed operation may differ considerably. Microprocessors like the MC68000 or Z8000 require different treatment of interrupts, and any system kernel will run in their privileged 'supervisor mode'. It is likely that a real time OS for either of these microprocessors may be more sophisticated than iRMX88 (and hence larger), but the operating principles remain the same.

8.2.2 iRMX86

Unlike iRMX88, which is specifically designed as a small system, iRMX86 is a larger system, still with real time capabilities, but which supports many more facilities – more than one technique for task communication, for instance. Like iRMX88, this OS has a kernel (or nucleus) which may be configured to suit the application, and with a wide number of extension options. The kernel may be EPROM or disk-based, and besides a real time priority scheduler, has extensive facilities for multiprogramming, critical section management and intertask communication, and in addition, possesses a very powerful error handling system, which will allow reporting of such aspects as excessive system loading and user interaction. To achieve a high degree of uniformity in the way in which different techniques and facilities are manipulated, iRMX86 uses an object-oriented architecture which is more obvious than that of iRMX88 (which may be considered to have task and exchange objects, etc.). Each object is a data structure with a fixed set of attributes, and is manipulated using operating system calls. Using this form of architecture, only four basic techniques are required to accommodate any situation: object management; interrupt management; scheduling, and error management. iRMX86 objects include:

JOBS	with attributes of tasks, memory pool, object directory, and exception handler, used to isolate autonomous programs;
TASKS	with attributes priority, stack address, code address, state, and exception handler, used for program execution;
SEGMENTS	with attributes address and length, used for dynamic buffering (dynamically created RAM area);
MAILBOXES	with attributes in the form of two lists (like the iRMX88 exchange), one of objects and the other of tasks waiting for objects, used for intertask and interprogram data and object transfers;
SEMAPHORES	with attributes of unit value, and a list of tasks waiting for units, used for intertask and interprogram synchronisation and mutual exclusion (stored as a 16-bit integer);
REGIONS	with attributes consisting of a list of tasks waiting for a critical section of code. Typically used to control access to a non-reentrant section of code shared by a number of tasks, or to control access to a shared data structure;
USER OBJECTS	defined for system extension.

Since all objects are dynamic, the iRMX86 free space manager will automatically handle their RAM utilisation.

The nucleus scheduler of iRMX86 performs similar functions to the iRMX88 scheduler, but with extended capabilities – for example, a task can not only specify the time it will wait to receive an object at a mailbox (cf timed wait at an iRMX88 exchange), but also specify a time limit on receiving units from a semaphore, or to look up an object in the directory. A further enhancement allows a task to specify how long it will remain inactive, before continuing instruction execution.

Error management is particularly impressive; a user has the choice of hierarchical error handling within the system, using the error handlers in existence, or may elect to process error conditions using code which is part of the job itself. The iRMX86 terminal handler not only supports real time asynchronous input-output, providing line buffering and character echoing, but also some minimal operator control functions, which will allow an operator to suspend, resume or kill output, abort an applications program, etc. The debugging system too, is more powerful than its iRMX88 counterpart (a real time task breakpoint facility is available, as well as access to operating system lists of jobs, ready tasks, suspended tasks, tasks queued at mailboxes and semaphores, etc.).

It is in the input-output system that much of the power of iRMX86 is evident. Like CP/M, input-output is performed using a system called BIOS, but like Unix, all I/O requests are performed using files. Thus only a single file manager is required to cover all types of input-output requests. In practice, with iRMX86, two file manager support options are provided, to given named file support and physical file support. The named-file manager is essentially used for support of bulk storage devices, such as disk or tape, and, apart from file access protection and control (using password protection and access rights determined at the time of file creation), control over fragmentation is provided (using small blocks of data in a file allows the best use of physical disk space, whereas access is faster if all data is contiguous, and the file manager allows the user to adopt the best compromise between the two). In addition, the named-file manager provides a powerful hierarchical directory support similar to that provided by many more powerful disk-operating systems, giving fast access by logical grouping of files.

The physical file manager gives a direct interface to device drivers, using logical devices names, related to physical device addresses by a routing table. Unlike named files on bulk storage devices, there is no file directory associated with the physical file manager.

Both file managers communicate with individual device drivers – as standard with iRMX86, device drivers are provided for both flexible diskette drives and hard disk drives. Custom drivers may be supported, in the form of random access drivers (where some deblocking of requests may be necessary), drivers for common devices (where it is assumed no deblocking is required, and requests are treated on a first-in, first-out basis), or completely flexible individual drivers, where all queuing and deblocking is the responsibility of the device driver code.

iRMX86 is naturally much larger than iRMX88, and fits neatly between the simpler system and a sophisticated disk OS like Unix. The sophistication of the system naturally means that in real time terms its response is slower, and while the larger system will be the obvious choice for a disk-based system with some real time capabilities, the smaller, specifically real time system is likely to be dominant for such applications as control systems and embedded computers in equipment.

8.2.3 SILICON OPERATING SYSTEMS[9,10]

As systems of all types become more sophisticated, the investment in software becomes more and more important, and the contribution of system software increases. Not only does system software represent significant programming effort, but also imposes a possibly undesirable time overhead on system operation. Although a particular real time operating system may be configurable to suit the needs of any particular application, many of the operating-system primitives will remain the same whatever the system configuration. If these primitives are implemented directly in the hardware of a system, closely connected to the CPU, then the system design and performance will gain on two counts. Firstly, no ROM space need be reserved for these primitives (only a base address allocated), and secondly, execution speed may be increased, since there will no longer be a dependence on ROM or EPROM access times. Obviously the choice of primitives is extremely important – while on one hand, it is desirable for speed to put as much as possible of an operating system into this form, it is manifestly undesirable to restrict the scope of future operating systems by premature integration of primitives which may need to be changed later on.

Following their usual policy of maintaining compatibility with existing products, Intel have developed a kernel control store of 16 kbytes which provides an extension of the 8086 or 8088 instruction set to include operating system primitives, operating in a coprocessor fashion with the CPU. The primitives chosen represent a base set suitable for implementation of either iRMX88 or iRMX86. In addition to its control store, the 80130 device contains some features which will contribute to raising operating system speed – it contains bus-handling logic to support connection to the 8086/8088 bus (allowing direct connection with no external circuitry), address decoders to allow control-store mapping to any 16 kbyte boundary and control registers to any 16 byte boundary in I/O space, and two timers, a bit-rate generator, and some interrupt logic compatible with the standard priority interrupt controller. One timer uses the system clock to generate the system real time clock period (nominally set at 10 ms, but capable of being modified by the system designer), while the other timer acts as a delay timer for the OS kernel; both of these timers are reserved exclusively for the operating system. The timers are connected to one priority level of the eight-level vectored interrupt logic hardware, leaving seven user-available levels, which, with external slave interrupt controllers, can be expanded to a total of fifty-seven user interrupt levels. The interrupt logic possesses further capabilities specific to an Intel Multibus System (allowing localised interrupts on a multicard system) and has individually programmable level- or edge-sensitive inputs. The bit-rate generator is provided purely for the convenience of the system designer; operating from the system clock, it is programmable to give a rate between 75 and 768 kbits/s. A typical system using the 80130 is shown in fig. 8.5.

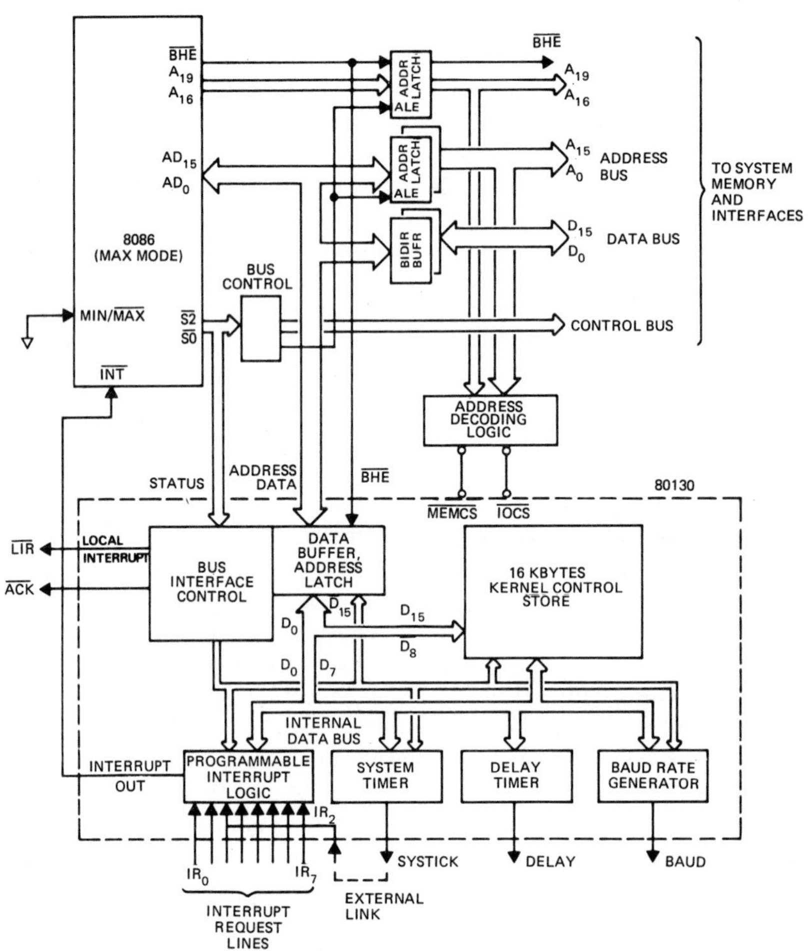

Fig. 8.5 80130 OS microprocessor in use.

The primitives implemented in the control store fall into six groups: job; task; interrupt; segment; mailbox, and region. Like iRMX86, the job concept is used to provide multiprogramming capability, while tasks are the actual executable code. Thus create job, create, delete, suspend and resume task are all provided, together with sleep (puts task in an 'asleep' state for a specified number of system clock periods). Interrupt control occupies a moderate proportion of the control store, with primitives to set, reset, enable, disable, exit, signal, and wait for interrupt, set priority, get level, and to manipulate the exception handler. Segments (used for dynamically allocating memory) may be manipulated with create, delete, enable and disable, while regions (used for mutual exclusion) may be manipulated with create, delete, accept control, receive control and send control. Mailboxes (used for exchange of messages) may similarly be created, deleted, and messages sent to them or received (with optional wait time) from them.

When a system is designed using the 80130, the user must supply only configuration and initialisation information – the 80130 contains a pre-emptive scheduling algorithm. This algorithm ensures that the highest priority ready task will be run, and will only relinquish the microprocessor if a higher-priority interrupt occurs or if the task releases a resource which allows a higher priority task to be brought to the ready state (in which case, the higher priority task will pre-empt the running task). A two-chip set of CPU and 80130, then, gives the user a built-in real time OS of considerable power; the pair may be buffered from the rest of the system as though they were a single CPU. It can be safely anticipated that the other major manufacturers will offer similar, competitive products.

8.3 Future OS developments

The idea of an operating system of microprocessors has come a long way from the simple interactive monitors of the early 8-bit evaluation cards and personal computers. With the emergence of the modern 16-bit microprocessor, two distinct lines of development may be seen – the construction of interactive, possibly multi-user operating systems for 16-bit personal machines, and the use of smaller, faster real time systems for 16-bit microprocessors embedded in equipment. Development in the former area is likely to follow minicomputer practice, but with a higher degree of standardisation, probably on Unix. It is the latter area, however, that presents the most exciting field for development. The trend set by the 80130 for silicon operating systems, with primitives available virtually as an extension of the instruction set of the central microprocessor will continue, as manufacturers and users take advantage of the lower costs and increased performance available with this technique. Indeed, as fabrication technology allows them, increases in complexity and sophistication will occur. From the user point of view, only one disadvantage mars the overwhelming advantages of this approach – the possible lack of flexibility. It is extremely unlikely that any real time OS standard will emerge, adhered to by the major manufacturers. Consequently, there will always be pressure for a user to stick with one manufacturers product to protect his investment in software and knowledge, and any errors or omissions in that manufacturers system may have a more profound effect on the user than in a more competitive area. The rigidity of the system will also be felt more strongly as more and more system software is committed to silicon, and becomes inimitable (except at a great cost). This single drawback may be sufficient to cause users to be wary of this important development, and remain with the traditional software-based OS. With the increasing significance of Ada, however, with its own OS primitives built into the language specification, the silicon OS may regain user confidence.

CHAPTER 9
High-level languages

A 'high-level' computer language is one which allows programming to be performed using constructions which are closer to human language and mathematics than to any particular example of computer hardware. Assembly code programming, mentioned in chapter 7, while ideally producing the most compact and fastest code, is very expensive in terms of time and programmers' effort, and is difficult to fully debug and document. The cost penalty in assembly-code program development time alone is sufficient incentive to adopt an alternative to assembly code.

A high-level language is a compromise between execution speed and programming convenience. Generally, programs written in a high-level language are slower, and sometimes a lot slower, than the speed of equivalent assembly-coded programs. On the other hand, their development time may be much less than their assembly-code equivalent. A rule-of-thumb relating programmer productivity for high-level programs and assembly-code programs claims the same overall effort for writing a line of source code in either. A line of assembly code will assemble into a few hexadecimal bytes in the target machine memory, whereas a single line of high-level language source code may well compile into several (even several tens) of lines of assembly code. The assembly code program will be written in simple mnemonic codes appropriate to the computer used for implementation and not meaningful in terms of program application, with comments which describe elementary machine operations in detail, rather than overall algorithm concepts. In contrast, an appropriate high-level language will have constructions which are meaningful in algorithmic terms (and independent of computer type) and similar style comments. Debugging a program at assembly-code level is both tedious and time consuming, requiring a lot of work in hexadecimal or binary (when examining intermediate results, register contents, etc.) and requires very considerable familiarity with the computer. Combined with the necessarily less than perfect documentation common to assembly code programs, software maintenance becomes a major headache for the system designer. With a suitable high-level language, where perhaps variables can be given appropriate names, mathematical expressions may be written naturally, and programs are split into modules, the software, with comments, may be made almost self-documenting, and is correspondingly easier to maintain. The effect of any software changes can also be more readily assessed.

While the very fastest routines, and any computer-specific programs (such as input-output drivers) may need to be written in assembly code, a good high-level language will allow these short assembly code routines to be incorporated into the main body of its program source code, and integrated with it when the code is translated (compiled or interpreted) to hexadecimal machine code.

The desirability of programming in a high-level language was amply demonstrated in the early days of the mainframe computer. The languages designed for these mainframes were conceived to satisfy the twin objectives of ease of programming and optimum machine use, in either a scientific or a business environment. The hardware costs of early computers pointed the way towards batch and timesharing operation, and the environments pointed towards either numerical-computation intensive, or records-based languages. Algol, FORTRAN, COBOL and later PL/1 typify languages designed for such machines. The advent of the minicomputer in the mid-1960s changed the emphasis somewhat – with cheaper hardware, and better computer architectures, came real time and interactive computing. Languages changed too, as a number of languages specifically designed for real time applications emerged (CORAL, RTL/2, etc.) and teaching languages, notably BASIC, appeared. BASIC has achieved a position as an important language not because of any unique facilities, but because of its extreme ease of use and implementation. Although speed is limited, since many versions of BASIC are purely interpretive (that is, they do not compile source code into machine instructions before execution, but execute source code directly, line-by-line, at run-time, through an interpreter), BASIC has nevertheless become a *de facto* 'standard' (there are so many versions that the concept of standardised BASIC is somewhat elusive). With the introduction of the microprocessor in the form of 8-bit microcomputer systems, the simplicity of BASIC, and the ease with which ROM-based interpreters can be created, has led to its dominance in the personal computer field. Outside this field, new languages have emerged which are appropriate to the new applications and style of software development applicable to the microprocessor. In particular, most manufacturers offer a language on their development systems which is of a type to make structured, real time programming easy. In the rest of this chapter, this family of languages (all are roughly comparable) will be referred to as PL/M-type, from the original Intel product, designed originally for 8-bit use, and now upgraded to match the enhanced facilities of the 16-bit machine. Other teaching languages, notably Pascal have evolved, and seem set to dominate some of the more professional applications, where structured programming and strong data types offer advantages. The US DOD-sponsored language Ada seems set to dominate all Western defence-oriented software, including microprocessor applications, and promises new standards of software reliability.

Many smaller languages have advantages where small to medium sized microprocessor applications are concerned, notably Forth, variants of BASIC (Tiny BASIC, Control BASIC, XYBASIC), and many manufacturers offer modified versions of the popular mainframe languages (FORTRAN, COBOL, etc.). This chapter will examine each of the major microprocessor languages in turn, and then examine the advantages of the modern 16-bit microprocessor architectures for implementation.

9.1 PL/M-type languages

First introduced by Intel to support their 8-bit 8080 via an Intellec development system, PL/M has been introduced, in various guises, by all the major microprocessor manufacturers[1–4]. The original PL/M-80 was conceived as a block-structured language based roughly on PL/1 which would encourage good software practices, such as modularity and top-down design. The statements which form PL/M fall into one of two groups, which may be categorised as declarative and executable. Declarative statements may use the reserved words DECLARE or PROCEDURE. DECLARE allows variables to be defined in attributes and scope, identifiers to be associated with program objects, and storage to be allocated. PROCEDURE declares a block of code or a subprogram, which may be named, between the reserved words PROCEDURE and END. Executable statements are those which generate machine instructions, such as assignment statements, iterative statements, conditional and unconditional transfers etc. Much of the power of PL/M lies in its declarations and its conditional and iteration control statements.

The main features of the original language are:

(a) Its block structure, whereby all source code consists of DO blocks and PROCEDURE blocks, delimited by the reserved words DO ... END and PROCEDURE ... END. All declarations will appear inside a PROCEDURE declaration block. The layout of a typical PL/M program will appear:

```
name: PROCEDURE (arguments) attributes;
        DECLARE variable names and attributes etc;
              <Executable code>
               DO
                .
                .
                .
                .
              END;
        END name
```

A PL/M module, or group of associated procedures, may appear

```
module name:  DO;
                name: Declaration
                         <Executable code>
                          END name;
                name: Declaration
                         <Executable code>
                          END name;
              END module name;
```

Procedures may be nested. This formal structure, coupled with suitable formatting, such as indenting nested loops, makes PL/M source code very easy to read and understand. Modularity is encouraged by the use of PUBLIC and EXTERNAL attributes. A variable declared as PUBLIC is defined in the declaration but referenced outside the module; one declared EXTERNAL is defined outside the module.

(b) The declaration requirements reduce the probability of programming errors inherent in languages which allow default data and procedure types and the declarations allow restriction of scope of variables. Use of restricted scope variables not only eases compiler writing, but also software maintenance and modification.

(c) Well-defined and versatile executable statements. Flow control statements, in particular, are well structured, ranging from the simple DO . . . END; block which delimits the scope of variables used within it, to DO WHILE, DO CASE, DO index = initial expression TO limit-expression BY step-expression, and IF . . . THEN, IF . . . THEN . . . ELSE expressions.

(d) Array manipulation in the form of subscripted arrays and records, parallels developments in mainframe languages. A *structure* allows one identifier to refer to a collection of structure members which may be of different types, each with its own identifier. A declaration with a STRUCTURE attribute allows record construction, for example,

DECLARE name STRUCTURE (variable 1 name BYTE, variable 2 name, ADDRESS)

Where BYTE and ADDRESS define 8-bit and 16-bit quantities, respectively. Arrays of structures allow data structures up to a limit of 'an array of structures which contain arrays'.

(e) Indirect references and based variables. To allow the manipulation of addresses of data elements rather than the elements themselves, based variables may be declared in the form:

DECLARE ITEM BASED ITEM $ POINTER BYTE

where ITEM is a byte variable pointed to by the current value of ITEM $ Pointer (previously declared as ADDRESS). Such a facility not only allows identifiers to be assigned to specific memory locations, but also allows the base to be altered under program control.

(f) Only 16-bit unsigned integer arithmetic allowed.

(g) Interrupt handling (8080 only) for a system with a hardware interrupt controller present, allowing subprograms to be given an attribute INTERRUPT, followed by a number (the 8080 interrupt number). The attribute REENTRANT may be given to a procedure (recommended for all interrupt procedures), and the PL/M compiler will automatically put any variables on the stack, so that recursion is allowable (i.e. the routine may call itself, or be interrupted, and called again before completion of the first entry, without destroying original variables).

Intel have followed up the 8-bit oriented PL/M with an upwards-compatible 16-bit version, PL/M-86, which they now call a 'systems implementation language'.

This description alludes to the fact that PL/M-86 may be used to control hardware directly without requiring the usual assembly-coded I/O drivers. It allows the programmer to write interrupt-handling routines, routines to input or output data directly to CPU ports, and to manipulate memory locations directly. Built-in procedures give access to the hardware stack pointer and CPU flags. In addition, rudimentary multiprocessing facilities are available, which make use of the 8086 hardware grant/request logic and the instruction set 'LOCK' command prefix.

Unlike its predecessor (PL/M-80), PL/M-86 supports a realistic mathematical capability, supporting five data types: BYTE (8-bit unsigned); WORD (16-bit unsigned); INTEGER (16-bit signed); REAL (32-bit floating-point), and POINTER (16-bit or 32-bit address). REAL numbers use a subset of the IEEE Floating-Point Standard (see chapter 8). It also contains string handling functions which utilise the string primitives of the 8086, and may be used to generate code applicable to a coprocessor (in this instance, the 8087 numeric data processor). A code optimiser adds a sophistication appropriate to mid-range minicomputer-based compilers.

While a 16-bit PL/M-type language is available, and strongly supported, for the Intel microprocessors, the other major manufacturers have pinned their main hopes on Pascal for their 16-bit development systems, while still offering their own PL-type languages. MPL for Motorola, and PLZ for Zilog. PLZ[4] is actually a unique family of system languages, based less on PL/M than on Algol and Pascal. Members of the family are PLZ/ASM (which includes assembly language) and PLZ/SYS (which is higher level).

9.2 Pascal

Originally designed to teach good programming principles, Pascal[5–10], like the much less sophisticated BASIC, has achieved 'respectability' as a programming language in its own right. It shares some common features with PL-type languages, but is considerably more general in its scope, with Pascal compilers available on most modern mainframe and minicomputers, as well as on microcomputer systems and development systems. Its popularity stems from its flexibility in source code formatting, its sophistication in data types and structures, and the ease with which compilers may be written for different machines. Pascal is often implemented with a compiler which produces as its output standard intermediate code called 'p-code'. P-code is then interpreted at run time on the target system. Any new implementation of Pascal on a different computer may be written merely by writing a new p-code interpreter specific to the computer instruction set, while the compiler which produces the p-code remains unaltered.

Pascal is a more complex and sophisticated language than those of the PL/M-type. Like PL/M, it is block oriented, but has the facility for the programmer to define his own data types, has easily understood syntax, and more reserved and assigned words. Its basic features are:

(a) Data typing. Four basic data types are allowed – Boolean, integer, real, and character. Supplementing these are scalar types, array types, and record types. A scalar type may be defined by writing TYPE name = (var1, var2, . . .), where the named type has properties similar to one of the four basic types, but variables of this type may only take on the defined values of <var 1>, <var 2>, etc. The values follow the order in which they are declared, and stored internally as a sequence of integers. Once the definition has been made, any variable may be declared to be of the newly defined scalar type in the usual way. Since the values are ordered, numerical comparisons may be made, and functions 'succ' (successor), 'pred' (predecessor), and 'ord' (ordinal or sequence number) are available. Subranges of scalar types may be defined. An array type is an indexed array of elements all of the same type (including scalars, arrays, etc.).

A record type is a collection of items which may be of different types, declared when the record declaration is made. Elements of the record may be referred to individually by <record name> <element name>. A further powerful declaration is 'SET', used to define finite collections of items which may or may not be associated. The base type of a set is an enumeration of the elements that may be in the set. Two dots may be used to indicate all members of an ordered sequence between specified limits. Thus statements

```
TYPE ALPHA = SET OF 'A' . . 'Z'
VAR Q: ALPHA
```

declare ALPHA to be the set type which has all letters of the alphabet as possible members, and declares Q to be a variable of type ALPHA. If now an assignment is made:

```
Q: = ['A' . . 'F', 'Z']
```

Q will contain the members of the set A through F, and Z.

(b) Block structure, not unlike PL/M, but with declarations made without the use of a reserved word DECLARE, with executable code delimited by BEGIN and END, and subprogram declarations PROCEDURE and FUNCTION (a procedure call consists of the procedure name with the parameter list following in brackets, whereas a function call is merely the function name which is assigned a value which is the result of executing the function itself).

BEGIN and END are used to form compound statements, where the whole group of statements between these reserved words is treated as a single statement. The main body of a Pascal program has, in fact, the form of a compound statement. Such clear delimiting contrasts with the vaguely ambiguous DO . . . END; construction in PL/M.

(c) Executable statements, assignment and flow control are again similar to those of PL/M but more extensive. Bit or word group manipulation is particularly easy, using a declaration of a 'variant record' using the reserved word CASE to allow alternative descriptions of the same named record type. (For example, one 32-bit record may be alternatively referred to as one REAL, two 16-bit INTEGERS, 4 BYTES, 4 CHARACTERS etc.). Use of this facility in conjunction with a WITH statement allows the field identifiers of a record variable to be accessed as variable identifiers, instead of using extensions to the field name. CASE may also be used in the form CASE <expression> of <statement-list> END, where the expression is evaluated, and used to point to the next statement to be executed (cf. DO CASE in PL/M).

Input-output statements are easy to use, employing READ and WRITE for character I/O and READLIN, WRITELN for text string (line) I/O. Number format is controlled simply by statement parameters in brackets, and mixed numerics and literals are allowed; a parameter following a literal string and separated from it by a colon indicates the number of character positions occupied by the string – any superfluous ones are interpreted as leading spaces. File handling is approached using extensions of this set of instructions, to open and close files, read and write blocks and buffer contents, etc. To lend simplicity to Pascal's input-output facilities, the only file structure supported in standard ISO Pascal implementation is a sequential one; this may prove restrictive in certain cases (where random-access or indexed-sequential files would be more appropriate).

(d) A very regular statement syntax, summarised in fig. 9.1.
(e) Dynamic allocation, and pointer variables are implemented in most microprocessor versions. Recursion, too, is allowed.

Pascal satisfies the two original goals of its creator, Professor Wirth: 'to be suitable to teach programming as a systematic discipline based on certain fundamental concepts which are naturally reflected in the language ... [and to] develop implementations which are both reliable and efficient on presently available computers.' Its control structures and data types, externally compiled and linked procedures, procedure and function names as parameters, scope rules on declarations (global or local) and allowed recursion all encourage good programming practice. Compared with previous languages such as Algol or PL/1, Pascal's definition is small, so execution of Pascal programs may be fast and implementation of compilers easy. Pascal is much more a general-purpose language than the various versions of PL/M, and lends itself more readily to non-system implementation programs, such as office and personal computer software.

The area where Pascal fails to achieve its aims is in standardisation. IEEE, ISO, BSI, ANSI have all attempted to arrive at a 'standard' definition. While this activity has been going on, user pressure has caused the major microprocessor manufacturers to provide Pascal for their development systems, and has caused software houses to write Pascal implementations for personal computer systems. Many of these versions of Pascal contain extensions to the definition originally published by Jensen and Wirth.[10] Typically, these extensions add facilities such as dynamic arrays, additional standard data types, random access and indexed-sequential file handling, overlays, value-initialisation on declaration, external procedures, and other features present in the older and larger mainframe languages. A proliferation of different versions of Pascal has almost destroyed the potential advantage of portability – the ability to run Pascal programs written for one computer on another installation. A *de facto* standard does exist in the personal computer field, that of UCSD Pascal, available for the widest range of microprocessors, both 8-bit and 16-bit, including the 8086 and MC68000, as well as the older TMS9900 and the Western Digital Pascal MicroEngine (which interprets p-code directly).

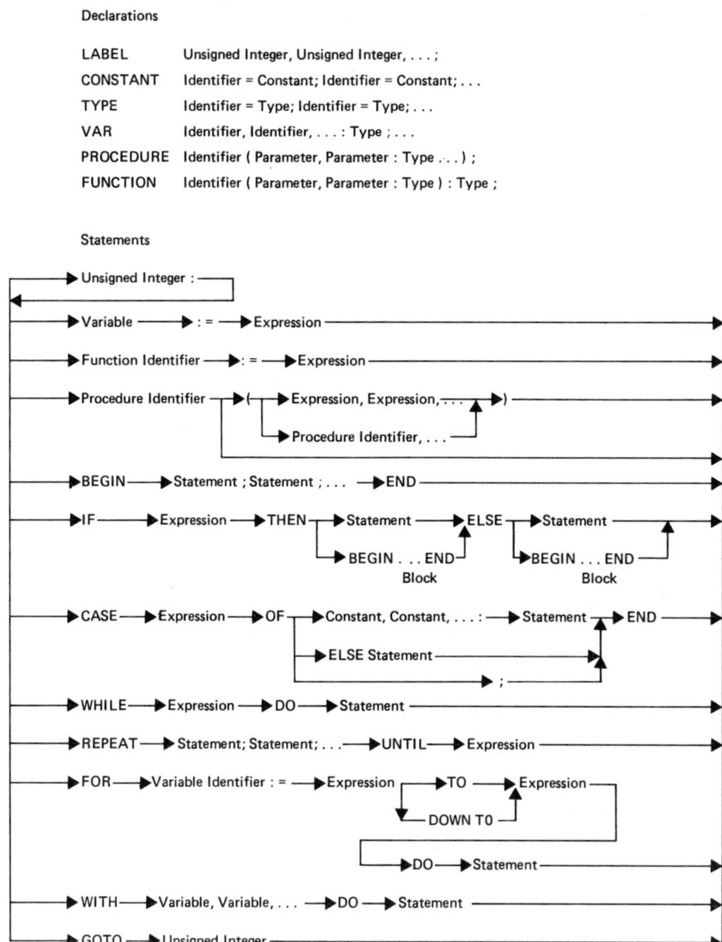

Fig. 9.1 Pascal syntax.

Real time programming, too, is a major problem, since its requirements lie in areas where Pascal may be deficient. Many real time tasks require fast execution which a p-code compiler and interpreter may not give. There are however, compiled versions which compile directly to target machine code which alleviate the speed problem. Other real time requirements are:

(a) The ability to link to assembly code routines (such as device drivers or system routines) and to control devices or memory locations directly.
(b) Resource sharing and multitasking capability.
(c) ROM-able code for stand-alone real time systems.
(d) Octal, hex, or binary constants.

A version of Pascal called Concurrent Pascal makes up the major deficiencies of standard Pascal for real time operation. It does so by allowing procedure declarations with new attributes, which allow resource lockout and task queueing, as well as message exchanges and process synchronisation. Naturally, a suitable real time operating system must also be provided.

Despite the deficiencies mentioned, Pascal has proved to be an advance on previous languages, with its block structure and data typing which assist writing correct and easily maintainable programs, but also because it is a small language, compared with, say, Algol or PL/1. Although an original aim of portability has been somewhat compromised by the number of incompatible extensions to the language, UCSD Pascal, marketed by Softech, has emerged as the most popular microcomputer versions, a situation likely to continue when 16-bit microprocessors are more widely incorporated into personal computer systems. At the same time, all the microprocessor manufacturers offer versions of Pascal with their development systems, usually enhanced with features which aid the design of concurrent programs. A powerful example is Texas Instruments Microprocessor Pascal, designed for the 16-bit TMS9900. With an attendant run-time system, it uses semaphores to synchronise processes (see chapter 8), using procedures WAIT and SIGNAL, with variables given the attribute SEMAPHORE, and it can dynamically allocate memory using procedures NEW and DISPOSE, and maintains both a stack (for declared process variables) and a 'heap' (for dynamically allocated data structures). The combination of stack and heap makes all processes naturally re-entrant. A COMMON declaration allows shared variables with externally compiled modules using statically allocated storage. With such real time extensions, and the promise of better software reliability, Pascal looks set to dominate the microprocessor high-level language scene, at least until the US DOD-sponsored language Ada becomes the required military standard.

9.3 'C'

C is a computer language which is growing in importance, not so much because of the facilities it provides, but because of its association with the Unix operating system. Most of Unix (which now runs to 7 Mbytes of software when all its utilities are included) has been written in C, with only a small amount of assembly code being required. Nevertheless, C is an interesting language in its own right, with its emphasis on allowing the programmer access to all the hardware facilities in a machine, whilst at the same time providing him with a 'moderate-level' (rather than high-level) language. One of the features of C is its generality and absence of restrictions.

Like Pascal, C may have data type declarations: 'char' (byte), 'int' (integer), 'float' (single precision floating-point) and double (double precision floating point); in addition, integer types may be extended to include 'short' (16-bit), 'long' (32-bit) and 'unsigned', whilst 'int' is equivalent to the machine word-length. Arrays (only static allowed, not dynamic) are declared as <type> Array [number of elements], where 'array' points to the first member of the array, whilst structures are aggregates of one or more data objects of different types. Pointer manipulation is a strong feature of C, and a number of operators are defined to aid pointer arithmetic. Thus *<address value> gives the contents of the location indicated by that address, while &<variable name> gives the address associated with the variable. Thus *<array+i> is the value of the ith member of array. Alternatively, this could be written array [i] in more conventional form. Structures may be accessed via address pointers, using '.' to indicate 'element of', i.e., if p is a pointer to a structure containing an array c of three characters, then (*p).c(3) will return the value of the 3rd character. Structures may also be named. A 'union' in C allows a variable name to be used for holding different types of object at different times. A 'function' is C's equivalent of a function or subprogram, and may be declared in terms of the type of the variable it returns.

Statements in C are fairly conventional expressions terminated in a semi-colon with no need for a specific assignment statement. Flow control statements are of the form 'if – else' (conditional alternative), 'switch – case – default' (multiway branch), and there are 3 kinds of loop: 'while' (condition true, execute statement), 'do – while' (execute statement, evaluate expression, repeat if true), 'for' (evaluate first expression, and while second expression is true, execute statement and evaluate third expression). The 'for' loop is rather more general than its namesake in other languages. Many operators are defined in C; the pointer manipulation ones have been described already, and the arithmetic and relational operators are conventional, but to them must be added % (remainder of division), bitwise logical operators AND, OR, exclusive-OR, right- and left-shifts, and ones complement, increment and decrement (used as either prefix or postfix operators) and conditional.

Conversions between variable types may be forced (by statement) or automatic (e.g. character to integer, int or float to double). Data variables may be defined as local or global by simple statements.

Although the language may not seem very comprehensive from this brief description, what may be appreciated is its powerful pointer manipulation and bit manipulation instructions, which all give the programmer complete control over the processor hardware. For systems programming, C has justly achieved a good reputation, and as the number of Unix systems increases, so does the number of C devotees. As a compact high-level language which does not impair access to hardware, it is almost unrivalled.

9.4 Ada

Ada is not specifically a microprocessor language. Its origins lie in a requirement for more reliable, easily maintainable military software, and the language definition, now complete, was designed with the needs of the US DOD, UK MOD, and other interested bodies, in mind. The intention is that all future DOD projects should use a common high-order language 'for programming large-scale and real time defence systems'. The design goals for Ada were:

(a) A recognition of the importance of program reliability and maintenance.
(b) A concern for programming as a human activity (reflected in attempts to keep the language as small as possible, consistent with the intended application).
(c) Efficiency, both in compiler and environment development, and in programming time.

The final version of the language, which is now called Ada[11–13], was selected from four competing languages, all roughly Pascal-based, and all satisfying the common high-order language requirements defined by the Steelman Report. The Pascal base is reflected in Ada's data typing and structure, but the extent of the language is considerably wider than Pascal. The allowed data types of Ada are more extensive, the assignment and control statements similar to Pascal but without some of the shortcomings of the Pascal definition (such as no default in CASE statements), and with added facilities for real time programming. Ada is larger than Pascal, and has been criticised for its size and the complexity of parts of its definition. Despite this, the impact of Ada on microprocessor software is likely to be as great as on mainframe or minicomputer software. Already, two microprocessor manufacturers are offering products (one 16-bit, one 32-bit microprocessor) which are claimed to be particularly suitable for Ada implementation. So far, however, the officially-sanctioned projects to develop compilers and the 'Ada Programming Support Environment (APSE)' have been based on higher-end minicomputers such as the VAX-11/780 and PDP-11/70. APSE will provide not only development tools for Ada programs, but also a run-time package containing a scheduler and other operating system features, to link with the real time task functions of the language.

The main features of Ada may be summarised:

(a) A *program unit* may be defined as a subprogram, which executes algorithms, a package, which is a collection of entities, or a task, which defines concurrent computations. Each program unit consists of two parts: a specification, which contains declarations and information which must be visible to other users, and a body, which defines implementation details which may be kept hidden from other users.

   A *subprogram* may be declared as a procedure or a function, where a procedure defines a series of actions and may have parameters passed to and from it, and a function merely computes a value and returns a result.

   A *package* may define a common pool of data and types, a collection of related subprograms, or a set of type declarations and associated operations. Packages are not active entities in their own right; a package's executable statements are only invoked when one of its visible procedures (declared in its specification part) is invoked by a call – when the procedure is complete, control returns to the calling program, and the package returns to dormancy.

   A *task* is a unit which defines a sequence of statements which may be executed in parallel with those of other tasks. Although in structure, a task appears very similar to a package, operation of a task is invoked by a scheduler or operating system. In addition, certain statements are only applicable to tasks – those which control time dependence (e.g. delay for a specified duration) or control data exchange between tasks (entry call, rendezvous, accept), and give Ada its real time attributes.

(b) Strong data typing, given by four classes of data type:
   (i) Scalar types (both numeric, including delay duration value and enumeration types, i.e. Boolean or character);
   (ii) Composite types (structured objects with related components, such as arrays and records);
   (iii) Access types which allow independent names and objects and ease the problems of referring to one object (contents of an address) by several different names (corresponding to the same address), a process called aliasing.
   (iv) Private types defined in a package which conceals some of its structural details.

(c) Range constraints, associated with data declarations, which place limits on the values taken by the type declared, and allow the creation of subtypes. Ranges may be declared as limits for numeric types, and as beginning and end of lists of indexed names for enumeration types.

(d) Executable statements are similar to those of Pascal, but more robust. (For example, the Ada CASE statement has a 'when others . . .' clause).

(e) Exception handling is explicitly provided for within a program unit using the reserved word 'exception' followed by the condition which causes the exception to occur, and the statements to be executed when the exception condition is true. Reserved word 'raise' followed by the exception name allows a software invoked execution of the exception code.

(f) Real time functions are provided which allow synchronisation of tasks and data exchanges between tasks by a process called rendezvous. Since these functions enhance the usefulness of the language very considerably from a microprocessor point of view, they are explained in more detail below.

The mechanism for a rendezvous between tasks consists of the reserved words entry and accept. A task has named entries declared together with parameters (including if necessary, any range constraints on those parameters) in a similar manner to a normal procedure declaration. These named entries are then used in the task body in conjunction with accept, indicating that the entry will be called from another task, and that any information transfer (specified by the parameter declaration part of the entry declaration) will take place during a rendezvous for which the earlier (whether calling or called) task has to wait. If no parameters are declared by the entry declaration, the two tasks are merely synchronised by the rendezvous.

The calling task merely uses the appropriate entry name to initiate a rendezvous with the called task. Thus a calling and called task may appear:

Called task

```
Task <task-name> is
      entry <entry-name> (<parameter name> ;<attributes>);
end;
task body <task-name> is
      <any declarations>
begin
      accept <entry-name> (<parameter name :> <attributes>) do
            <executable code>
            end <entry name>;
      end <task-name>
```

Calling task

```
task <calling-task-name> is
      <declarations>
end;
task body <calling-task-name> is
      <declarations>
begin
      <entry-name> (<parameters>) (call by name only)
      <executable code>
end <calling-task-name>
```

In operation, the two tasks are synchronised at points corresponding to their calling and accept statements.

```
calling task                          called task
   ↓                                       ↓
entry name;   rendezvous accept   entry-name   do
                                (executable code)
                                end entry-name;
```

The facilities provided by Ada are more sophisticated than this little illustration implies. For instance, it is possible to have alternative entries to a rendezvous with specified conditions using reserved word select accept statement to determine is invoked. In such a conditional list of accept statements, the final one, following an else clause, should be unconditional to avoid an impasse if none of the conditions is true (if the condition were to arise where there were no entry calls honoured, execution of the task would cease – an unacceptable situation in a real time environment).

One way in which multiple entries may be useful is to implement a 'timeout' for a task, to prevent any lack of response causing system failure. The select statement for such a facility would appear:

```
select
      accept <name> do
```

```
            <executable code>
            end;
```

or

```
    delay <number of time periods>
          <executable code>
          end select:
```

Delay invokes a time delay procedure which is part of a package in the Ada support software called CALENDAR, which performs time, date and delay functions.

From the necessarily brief description, it may nevertheless be seen that Ada has the potential to become a very significant language for larger microprocessor-based systems implementation. The combination of Pascal-like structure and code, and real time functions has meant that the language requires a large compiler and support software, and a sophisticated machine environment. Although the Ada sponsors have stated that only complete implementations of the language will be permitted to use the name Ada, already some subsets are being implemented on modern 16-bit microprocessors. With the increasing importance of microprocessors in military hardware, and the US DOD's backing for Ada, the future of the language for 16-bit (and 32-bit) microprocessor systems seems assured, and the familiarity of many engineers with Pascal should speed up the acceptance of this more powerful descendant.

9.5 BASIC

BASIC needs little introduction, since it is used as the main high-level language on the vast majority of 8-bit microcomputer systems. The longer wordlength and higher speed of 16-bit microprocessors should improve the performance of a standard BASIC implementation (such as Microsoft BASIC) and allow source code to be compiled rather than interpreted. The tremendous investment in BASIC software and its great popularity will ensure that the language will be implemented by all the major 16-bit microprocessor manufacturers. Although the language may be criticised for many deficiencies, the main ones are lack of speed, and lack of suitable commands for system implementation. Adding to the proliferation of different versions of BASIC are those which extend the Microsoft BASIC definition to include commands appropriate to 'real time' operation, and which produce ROM-able code. Typified by XYBASIC and Control BASIC, these extended versions of the language are more applicable to control-type applications than earlier implementations, but still preserve the essential simplicity of BASIC. Better mathematical operations, string functions and logical functions are complemented by proper system calls and subroutine calls which allow some useful parameter passing. Time delays and waits are available, and a limited alternative to interrupt handling provided. In XYBASIC, this takes the form of ENABLE/DISABLE; when implemented in a program, enable causes a specified condition to be checked before executing each BASIC statement, and switches context appropriately. The ROM-able nature of such a BASIC allows stand-alone operation, and often a compiled version is available which will increase speed considerably.

So far as 16-bit microprocessors are concerned, the BASIC languages will achieve the same position of dominance in personal systems as with 8-bit microprocessors, but with increased execution speeds and compiled options. In an office or control environment, however, the 16-bit microprocessor is much more likely to be supported by a more powerful and professional high-level language.

9.6 FORTH

FORTH is a language designed for interactive operations with minicomputers, and may be considered a rival to BASIC in the sense that it is interpretive, and suitable for classroom use, or personal computer use. Unlike most versions of BASIC, FORTH can be applied readily to real time applications, and is fast in execution. The structure of FORTH is unlike any of the common languages, since it is based around an open-ended dictionary of words which define operations necessary for a given application. New words may be added to the dictionary using definitions which include words already defined, so a formal language definition can only include the initial 'core' of words common to any FORTH implementation, while the language will be extended in a different way for each application.

In execution, FORTH uses stacks to manipulate parameters and addresses. The parameter stack contains constants, addresses of variables and results, and the return stack contains return addresses for the interpreter. To define arithmetic operations, symbols and words are written in an order similar to reverse-Polish notation, whereby arguments precede operators. This is a natural order for any stack-based system, since it equates directly with the order of items on the parameter stack. Most arithmetic operations in FORTH have been implemented with integers or fixed-point fractions, with few floating-point implementations (new versions, such as polyFORTH, make up this possible deficiency).

FORTH control commands allow structured programming, with IF . . . ELSE . . . THEN statements (stack operation makes it easiest to take the false condition before the true one) which can be nested to arbitrary depth. Iterative commands are flexible, with a basic BEGIN . . . END which relies on the code between the limits placing a Boolean variable on the stack, which terminates the loop if true; if false, looping continues. Similarly BEGIN . . . IF . . . WHILE will loop so long as the IF is true. DO . . . LOOP is a structure which makes use of an operation I, which manipulates an index value left on the stack (along with a termination value equal to the required loop count + 1). Loops with non-unity increment values may be implemented with an instruction + LOOP. Assembly code may be used in FORTH programs, but since the FORTH assembler is stack-based, the format and order may not coincide with that of the computer manufacturer.

Naturally, the FORTH interpreter takes time to look up definitions and to manipulate the threaded list structure that is FORTH's hallmark. Consequently, the speed of FORTH does not rival that of well-written assembly code. In comparison with other languages, however, especially other interpreted ones, FORTH is fast. Because of its structure, it is closely related to the microprocessor on which it runs, and implementation of interrupt handling, multiple task operation and other real time functions is fairly straightforward. FORTH is ideally suited for control system implementation, and most applications of the language have been in this field.

In appearance, FORTH code looks like an amalgam of programmable calculator instructions and function names – indeed, one criticism of the language is its readability. Its dictionary and stack structure impart unrivalled speed and compactness of code compared with BASIC. The designers of FORTH claim that for systems larger than about 2 kbytes, FORTH will produce a program smaller than the equivalent assembly code, and the larger the program, the greater FORTH's memory efficiency becomes. A typical FORTH operating system is 512 bytes, and a complete memory-resident FORTH development and run-time environment may occupy only 6 kbytes (including the compiler, assembler, text editor, input-output drivers, and keyboard interpreter). An extended environment with database manager would require perhaps 10 kbytes.

The structure of modern microprocessors makes them ideally suited to FORTH implementation. Register indirect addressing using post-increment and predecrement facilities with a reasonably sized set of registers makes maintenance of the FORTH stacks very easy. The inner interpreter loop, which works down definitions produced by the outer, or high-level interpreter (which operates on input text), must be coded as tightly as possible in order to make FORTH's execution speed as high as possible. Operation of the inner loop may be expressed as three basic steps:

(a) Using an interpreter pointer I, the address of the entry at I is shifted into a CPU register.
(b) Interpreter pointer I is incremented to the next entry.
(c) An indirect jump is made through the 'code field' of the entry addressed by the CPU register in (a).

Once again, the powerful addressing modes of the 16-bit microprocessor makes implementation of FORTH particularly easy (typically the inner loop may require just two instructions).

The enhanced versions of FORTH, such as polyFORTH, which allow multiple tasks and an improved real time environment, lend themselves even better to 16-bit microprocessor applications. For control applications, for which the language was originally designed, FORTH occupies a niche between assembly code and a large high-level language with real time facilities, which will ensure its survival in a 16-bit microprocessor environment.

9.7 FORTRAN, COBOL and the older languages

Since much of the existing software in the western world is written in FORTRAN or COBOL, it is inevitable that both languages will be offered by the 16-bit microprocessor manufacturers. Used mainly in scientific and business fields, they will take advantage of the speed of the 16-bit microprocessors, and generally be used with large systems with comprehensive bulk storage facilities and input-output and numeric coprocessors (see chapter 5). Since these older languages were based on batch operation in punched-card, paper-tape and printer installations, their original specifications are no longer adequate for any modern computer system with VDUs, disks and interactive operations (including a small office or laboratory computer based on a 16-bit microprocessor). Extensions to older languages are common, and make up for the change in environment. With FORTRAN, for instance, a new ANS I standard was developed (FORTRAN-77). Added to the original FORTRAN-66 specification are implicit data typing, introduction of CHARACTER variables, and more powerful input-output statements (including free-format I/O), and file control. To its execution control statements are added more powerful IF statements, including IF ... THEN ... ELSE and a rationalisation of the FORTRAN DO loop to include the condition of zero iterations. Format specifications may now include binary and hexadecimal in at least one manufacturer's offering of FORTRAN-77.

A SAVE statement for common blocks avoids the previous uncertainty associated with FORTRAN named COMMON blocks once a subprogram return has been executed. Placed immediately before the return, SAVE prevents this.

Although FORTRAN is not naturally recursive (as are Pascal and Ada), FORTRAN-77 may be made recursive and recutrant using a dynamic array structure for subprogram arguments. While these enhancements breathe new life into an old language, they also allow compatibility with FORTRAN software written under the old standard and with most engineers' familiarity with the language, will ensure its provision on all major 16-bit microprocessors, although the influence of FORTRAN, and indeed, the other older languages, on real time systems implementation will diminish in favour of more modern and better-suited languages.

9.8 Suitability of 16-bit microprocessors for high-level language support

Much has been written on this subject, but the central issue is really how well a microprocessor implements a language run-time system and operating systems as well as its efficiency in implementing language constructs, chapter 8 considers operating system support. Generally, for good high-level language performance, a microprocessor should have a set of registers which are matched to language requirements. A study by A. Lunde, admittedly based on scientific high-level language applications on a Digital Equipment Corporation System-10, concluded that only six registers (three of them index registers) were used 90% of the time in this particular environment, and that the full sixteen general-purpose registers of the System-10 were not fully utilised. From the microprocessor manufacturers point of view, a six-register model represents the minimum configuration for efficient high-level language implementation, and all of the major manufacturers exceed this requirement with their 16-bit products. With the Intel 8086, the manufacturer has exceeded the requirement only modestly with eight general-purpose registers, four of which may be used as index registers, while some of the other 16-bit microprocessors exceed it by a comfortable margin (the Z8000 and MC68000 each have sixteen general-purpose registers, while the National NS16000 family has eight). Superficially, it would appear better to over-equip a microprocessor with registers (which need not all be used), but one view is that any general interrupt service program would still have to save all the registers and speed of response would be compromised if there were too many of them.

Addressing modes, too, are important, with stack-oriented modes especially useful (Pascal, for instance, can use multiple stacks to ensure re-entrancy). The autoincrement, autodecrement (with pre- or post- prefixes explicitly or implicitly defined) substantially improve a processors' high-level language operation. Most high-level languages, as has been highlighted earlier in this chapter, operate via declared data structures, which in the case of the more modern languages may possess considerable sophistication (record elements declared as arrays, nested arrays, etc.). Both indexed and based-and-indexed addressing modes dominate handling such structures. All the 16-bit microprocessor manufacturers have recognised the importance of addressing modes which they generally failed to do with their 8-bit microprocessors and have provided more than adequate support in this area. Another area which all manufacturers have excelled with their products is in the design of instruction set so that the most used instructions are the smallest and fastest to execute. The choice as to which instructions are most commonly used differs slightly between manufacturers, although most are based on some benchmarking work done with minicomputers, which has led to the design of a 'standard mix' of instructions.

String primitives are important in two aspects of HLL support – for enhancing compilation speed, and for supporting the previously mentioned complex data structures. Procedure calls, too, can influence the suitability of a microprocessor for HLL implementation. Tannenbaum has suggested that 13-25% of the statements of a well-structured HLL program will consist of procedure calls. For re-entrancy, a typical HLL will store local procedure variables on a stack, so stack handling within procedure calls is of some importance. Once this technique is implemented, however, the system designer will see more efficient memory utilisation, since storage is allocated dynamically during program execution rather than statically during compilation. Return statements in procedures are similarly of importance. Virtually all high-level languages implement floating point arithmetic and mathematical functions, and these will make heavy use of the hardware multiply-divide instructions and multibit shifts of the modern 16-bit microprocessor. A microprocessor with on-chip floating-point hardware (such as one in the NS16000 family) will clearly possess an advantage, as will a microprocessor with a numeric coprocessor (such as the Intel 8087, the Z–EPU, etc.). All the major manufacturers plan either on-chip floating point hardware or floating-point coprocessors to satisfy this HLL demand. For many HLL applications, input-output operations, especially with fast bulk memory devices such as hard disk systems, or fast communications, will place loads on the 16-bit microprocessor which are only seen today on large minicomputers. Once again, the intelligent coprocessor is likely to be the solution adopted to meet this demand.

Memory management is crucial to the efficiency of many high-level languages, where large programs may need overlaying, or where multiple tasks may need protection. Like floating point support, memory management may be implemented internally (e.g. the 8086 segment address registers) or externally (e.g. the Zilog MMU Z8010 or Motorola memory management unit). Such facilities as segment overflow, protection, etc. may be provided in hardware (with most external MMUs) or software (8086). Whichever approach is adopted, the provision of some sort of memory management makes HLL support easier, especially where dynamic memory allocation and overlays may be involved.

In conclusion, all the modern 16-bit microprocessor families provide some useful HLL support. For any specific language, one may possess some advantages over the others. For example, the Western Digital MicroEngine, which implements p-code directly, will obviously support Pascal well. Nevertheless, such advantages may be nullified by other circumstances, such as availability of floating point hardware. Whatever the relative merits of the various processors for HLL implementation, however, it is clear that the dominance of BASIC in the 8-bit microprocessor area will not be repeated with 16-bit microprocessors. The range of available languages will be much larger, and much more 16-bit microprocessor software will be written in a high-level language than in assembly code.

CHAPTER 10
Multiple microprocessor systems

10.1 Introduction

Any system which includes more than one microprocessor CPU, together with some means of communication between microprocessors, may be considered a multiple microprocessor system. Such a system is usually designed to provide an increase in processing power and speed over that of an individual microprocessor, or to allow large and expensive resources, such as large disk storage units or database support, to be shared among individual microprocessors.

A multiple microprocessor system may be organised in a number of ways, which may be grouped into a number of general categories, depending upon any hierarchy created, and upon the degree of coupling between microprocessors. The categories are:

(a) Tightly coupled microprocessors, sharing a clock or equivalent regular synchronisation signals, and also sharing a local bus. Typical of this type of system is the microprocessor-coprocessor pair or trio. Described in chapter 5 (numeric and input-output coprocessors) and chapter 8 (operating system microprocessors), the coprocessor is essentially a slave of the master 16-bit CPU, with a limited degree of autonomy, and relying, in some cases, on the CPU bus control signals, for its operation.

(b) Microprocessors, possibly, though not inevitably, of identical design, each with its own local bus, local memory, and interfaces, communicating with others via a system (backplane) bus, such as Multibus and Versabus, and sharing common system resources. While a system of this design may be hierarchical with a fixed master microprocessor, generally it will be non-hierarchical, with microprocessors of equal status (though not necessarily of equal priority) competing for the system bus, and bus resources using the bus request and grant lines present on all 16-bit backplane buses and suitable arbitration hardware. Competition for resources requires some provision for ensuring exclusive use (in the same way as software semaphores protect single microprocessor resource use). Physically, the microprocessors will all be within a few inches of each other, since the backplane buses are all limited in length.

(c) Hierarchical networks, typically with serial communication, using a standard protocol, such as SDLC/HDLC. While such a system may prove useful in many applications, the problems posed by such a system are similar to the interprocess communication in software, and amenable to similar solution. No resource sharing takes place in most cases.

(d) Local-area networks (LANS), which consist of more widely distributed microprocessor systems, each with its own component-level and system backplane bus, communicating over distances of up to several hundred metres, in a high-speed serial manner. Local area networks represent an increasingly important development, as 16-bit microprocessors make inroads into the office and factory automation fields, themselves heavily dependent upon communications. Almost invariably, local-area networks implement serial data communications using a data packet format, working at baseband or broadband (carrier-based), and using twisted-pair (for the slower baseband networks such as MIL-STD1553[2], an avionics standard) or coaxial cable (for faster baseband networks, such as Ethernet and the Cambridge Ring, and carrier-based networks such as the Wangnet).

Standards for multiple microprocessor systems only exist in limited areas. For instance, the conceptual design of multiple microprocessor systems which are constructed around a data communications network using a packet technique is helped by ISO-OSI (open systems interconnection) which defines seven levels of communication in a message environment. The levels start at the physical connection level and go up to the most sophisticated level of software in a system. They are (summarised from Wallace B. Riley):

Level 1 Electrical and mechanical standards (e.g. RS-232C and 25-way 'D' type connector).

Level 2 Data link level formats, responsible for transmitting frames of data with synchronisation, header, block error detection and correction codes, etc. Typically the synchronous communication will follow the recommendations of HDLC/SDLC, and include within the header both address and control information. Like other data link control standards, HDLC is responsible for initialisation, framing, link management, error control, sequence control, flow control, transparency of transmitted data and system recovery in the presence of error conditions (see chapter 5 for a description of single-chip HDLC interfaces).

Level 3 Network level, which uses the format of level 2 to provide more sophisticated communication and network access. For a packet network, this means packet creation and reassembly, including addition of packet header, control information and error checking. Packet sequencing too, is necessary to avoid out-of-sequence reassembly of repeated packets, and some means of data flow control (which may be left to higher levels). Many of the simpler networks will not require routing control, but those that do will implement it at this level. A packet standard has evolved from the initial experience of national packet networks such as ARPANET in the USA, and EPSS in the UK. Known as CCITT standard X25, this standard covers the first three OSI levels and provides for an extremely flexible network, if a complex one. Many microprocessor systems will adopt a simpler approach, perhaps a compatible subset of X25.

Level 4 Transport level, which handles end-to-end communication, masking the operations of levels 1, 2 and 3 from the user. The mechanics of any transfer of data will be completely invisible to the machines initiating the communication. At this level, messages are transferred and acknowledged, and may use 'virtual circuits', which appear to the user at this level to be just like a direct or circuit-switched physical duplex connection, but in fact are implemented using the packet formats of level 3. For a small network where no routing decisions are necessary, the transport and network layers may be combined into one logical entity.

Level 5 Session layer, where system-to-system connection is established. A necessary layer which performs the system management functions which prevent disruption of individual microprocessor or operation as a result of network problems, such as unfinished and unterminated communication. For a logging or database system, incomplete entries or incomplete modification of entries could be a disaster and the software of the session layer may go some way towards prevention of such a problem, by buffering, for instance. At this level, too, security of a network to protect it from unauthorized use, is established, with logging-in, logging-off, user validation, and, in the case of a commercial network, accounting and statistics.

Level 6 Presentation layer, which supports system utilities and user functions, offering library functions, code conversion (a must for communication between databases of different format), and possibly encryption.

Level 7 Application layer, the one immediately accessible to the user; using all of the lower layers of protocol, it conceals any physical distribution of network resources, making them appear unified to the user.

Other standards rely on operating-system conventions, and for multiple microprocessor systems of type (b) and type (c), resource contention and microprocessor synchronisation may often be tackled using minor extensions to conventional single microprocessor multitasking operating system primitives.

Coprocessors have been covered elsewhere in this book, and other closely-coupled multiple microprocessor systems (array microprocessors and other parallel microprocessor structures in which individual microprocessors have few local resources) are usually special-purpose custom-designed systems, and are outside the scope of this chapter (data-flow computers, which are mentioned in the final chapter, may be implemented as a tightly coupled array). Microprocessors sharing a system bus and certain global resources, and local-area networks, are the two areas of multiple microprocessor implementation which will feature strongly in the design of 16-bit microcomputer systems at card level and complete system level, and will be discussed in depth here[1].

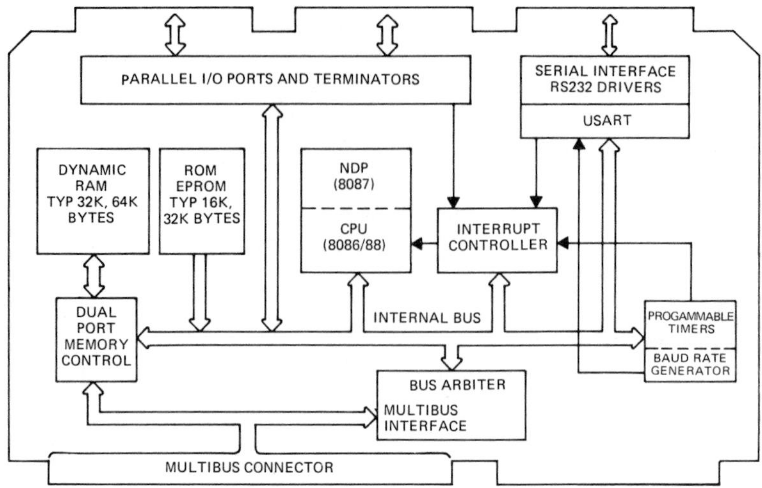

Fig. 10.1 Single-board computer schematic.

10.2 Multiple microprocessors sharing a system bus

As the sophistication of microprocessors and their interface components increases steadily in accordance with the empirical 'Moore's Law' of growth in semiconductor fabrication complexity, the tendency of many original equipment manufacturers to buy their computers at board level will become even more commonplace. Even those manufacturers which buy at component level will be under pressure to adopt one or other of the backplane bus standards which are evolving at the moment. A typical board level product is shown in a functional block diagram form in fig. 10.1. On the card will be sufficient memory and interface devices to support a respectable computer system on just the single board. What is of interest to the manufacturer who needs to construct a multiple microprocessor system is that all the hardware facilities for requesting and relinquishing the system bus are provided on the card, together with arbitration circuitry to resolve contention between requesting microprocessors, and, if required, to prioritise their requests. Most system buses will support hardware daisy-chained requests where a board is fixed in priority by its physical position on the backplane, and will also support parallel priority levels, which may be changed by software.

The requirements for any multiple microprocessor system are:

(a) In hardware, the means to request and gain control of the system bus using the features previously noted, together with some means whereby a microprocessor in control of the bus can lock out further requests (allowing initialisation of shared peripheral interfaces by just one microprocessor, before any of the others are allowed access).
(b) A means of ensuring mutual exclusion to allow a microprocessor to 'lock

out' access to a shared resource. In a software multitasking system, the use of semaphores to provide mutual exclusion, and the indivisible instructions required to check access to a resource shared by several microprocessors running concurrently on the same microprocessor are implemented in software; in a multiple microprocessor system, some hardware assistance helps.

(c) Software support for mutual exclusion, communication between microprocessors (and processes running on them), and synchronisation.

(d) Allied with microprocessor synchronisation, system initialisation is of great importance. With shared resources on the system, one microprocessor must take responsibility for their initialisation.

10.2.1 HARDWARE FEATURES

On each of the modern 16-bit microprocessors, a number of facilities are provided which ease the design of board hardware. Bus request and bus grant signals are supported by all microprocessors (the 8086 has, in maximum mode, two bi-directional pins $\overline{\mathrm{RQ}}/\overline{\mathrm{GT0}}$, $\overline{\mathrm{RQ}}/\overline{\mathrm{GT1}}$, the 68000 has $\overline{\mathrm{BR}}$, $\overline{\mathrm{BG}}$ and $\overline{\mathrm{BGACK}}$, and the Z8000 has $\overline{\mathrm{BRQ}}$ $\overline{\mathrm{BAI}}$, $\overline{\mathrm{BAO}}$). Operation of each microprocessor is as follows.

The 8086 signals operate in a three-phase sequence. The lines are prioritised, with $\overline{\mathrm{RQ}}/\overline{\mathrm{GT0}}$ having a higher priority than $\overline{\mathrm{RQ}}/\overline{\mathrm{GT1}}$. A device requiring use of the bus (either another microprocessor, or DMA device) pulses one of the $\overline{\mathrm{RQ}}/\overline{\mathrm{GT}}$ lines low for a single clock period. During either the final clock cycle of one machine cycle or initial clock cycle of the next, a response will be issued (provided no bus lock instruction prefix is active) on the same line, again persisting for a single clock period. At the same time, the 8086 local bus is floated to a high-impedance state, and the 'hold acknowledge' state will be entered at the next clock pulse – during this state, the bus interface unit (BIU) is disconnected logically from the local bus. When the requesting master wishes to relinquish the bus, it issues a third pulse of one clock period on the $\overline{\mathrm{RQ}}/\overline{\mathrm{GT}}$ line, allowing the CPU in the 'hold acknowledge' state to recover control of the local bus at the next clock. The manufacturers recommend that the $\overline{\mathrm{RQ}}/\overline{\mathrm{GT}}$ pins are only to be used to control multiple microprocessors sharing the same local bus (component-level bus). The recommendation for system bus transfers (in this case, Multibus) is that an external arbitration unit, available as an integrated circuit, be used. Rather than interface with the $\overline{\mathrm{RQ}}/\overline{\mathrm{GT}}$ pins, the Intel bus arbiter decodes the CPU status lines $\overline{\mathrm{S0}}$, $\overline{\mathrm{S1}}$ and $\overline{\mathrm{S2}}$, and handles the Multibus signals $\overline{\mathrm{BREQ}}$, $\overline{\mathrm{BCLK}}$, $\overline{\mathrm{BPRN}}$, $\overline{\mathrm{BPRO}}$, $\overline{\mathrm{CBRQ}}$, and $\overline{\mathrm{BUSY}}$, detailed in chapter 11. The 'Multimaster' bus[3] interface includes not only the bus arbiter, but also a bus controller, and tristate bus buffering. These additional interface devices allow a very flexible Multibus-based multiple microprocessor system. Priority resolution is allowed to be serial (daisy-chained), parallel (requiring the addition of a priority encoder) or a rotating-priority scheme, useful if otherwise high-priority masters would hog the system. A common clock ($\overline{\mathrm{BCLK}}$) is connected to each arbiter in the system. Whenever a microprocessor wishes to gain control of the bus, $\overline{\mathrm{BREQ}}$ is issued, and any current master which will be asserting the $\overline{\mathrm{BUSY}}$ line, if of lower priority (determined using $\overline{\mathrm{BPRN}}$, $\overline{\mathrm{BPRO}}$ lines), will relinquish the bus. The relinquishing master will keep its $\overline{\mathrm{BREQ}}$ signal low to indicate that it requires control of the bus to be restored but will release BUSY, and allow the higher priority master to take control of the bus on the next clock cycle after BUSY has been released. This is illustrated in the timing diagram of fig. 10.2.

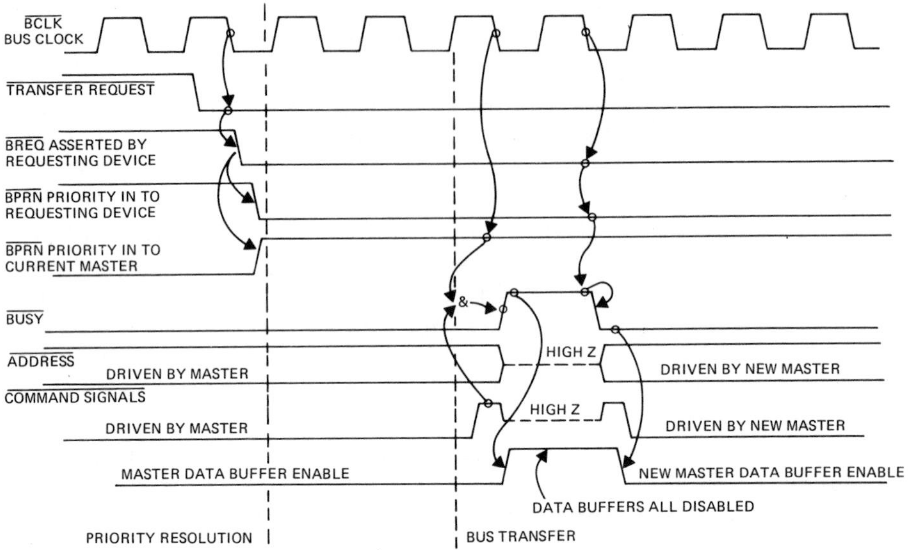

Fig. 10.2 Multibus transfer.

The 68000 signals BR, BG are used in a similar way to allow the CPU and other devices to share the local bus. The wired-OR bus request signal, BR, is issued to indicate that a device requires control of the bus. By inference, the microprocessor which is currently bus master is at a lower priority than the requesting device, and it will relinquish the bus after it has completed the last bus cycle it has started. The microprocessor normally will issue bus grant (BG) immediately after internal synchronisation of BR, and will negate address strobe (AS), data transfer acknowledge (DTACK), and bus grant acknowledge (BGACK), and float its bus lines. The requesting device interprets the negation of AS as an indication that the bus master has completed its bus cycle, and the negation of BGACK as an indication that the bus has been relinquished, and negation of DTACK to indicate that the previous slave device has terminated its connection to the previous master. It is then able to issue its own BGACK signal, and control the bus, removing its BR signal as it does so (if BR is still asserted after BGACK is issued, another arbitration sequence is performed without the microprocessor performing any bus cycles). Bus mastership is terminated upon the negation of BGACK. Like the 8086, the 68000 family also possesses an external bus arbiter device (not released at the time of writing) which will presumably provide Versabus signals. Versabus provides five wired-OR bus request lines BR4 (highest priority) to BR0 (lowest priority). When a bus request line is asserted, a bus arbiter compares priority levels of the new request and the current bus master. If the new request is of higher or equal priority, a bus clear (BCLR) signal is issued by the arbiter, causing the current bus master to stop processing and to clear the bus. As the current bus master enters its last cycle, it negates the bus busy (BBSY) line and this action signals the arbiter to issue a bus grant signal (BG) to the highest priority device requesting use of the bus, and remove BCLR. For each priority level of bus request, there is a daisy-chained bus grant line, so each master device on Versabus has five bus grant in lines (BG0IN to BG4IN) and corresponding bus grant out lines (BG0OUT to BG4OUT). Each level determines grant priority within the level according to the order of devices on the daisy chain. The first device requesting the bus on the chain accepts the bus grant signal, issues a BBSY and removes its request signal. The arbiter responds to the assertion BBSY by the new master by removing its bus grant signal, and it then waits for the next bus request. Data transfer acknowledge (DTACK) and address strobe (AS) must have been removed before the new bus master can start processing. Versabus is very sophisticated in its definition of signals on the bus, and any bus arbiter design must allow for immediate removal of devices (within sixteen clock cycles) using the bus on demand from the bus release signal BREL and must also accept bus error BERR and RETRY signals. Timing for Versabus transfers is shown in fig. 10.3.

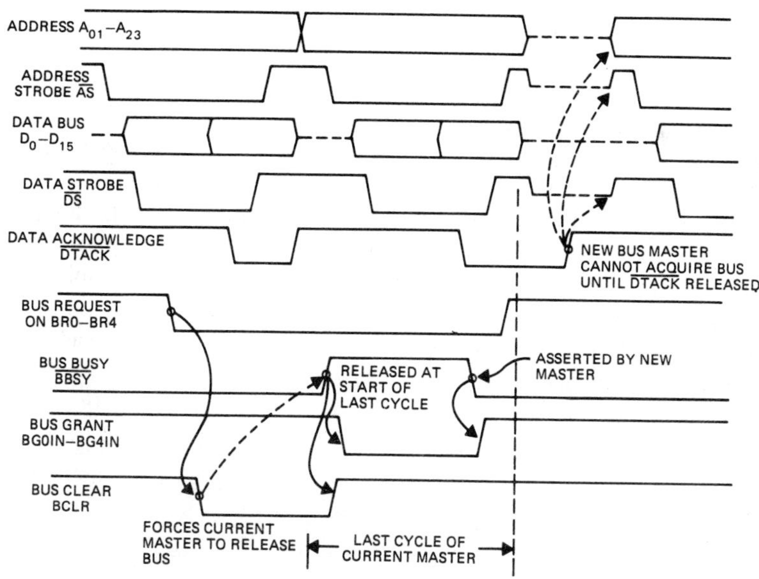

Fig. 10.3 Versabus transfer.

The Z-8000 is a little different from the other mainstream microprocessors, in that the basic microprocessor supports local bus requests and multiprocessor resource requests in a separate way using two distinct sets of signals. The microprocessor bus transfer signals consist of a wired-OR bus request signal $\overline{\text{BUSRQ}}$, a bus acknowledge signal $\overline{\text{BUSACK}}$, and each potential bus requestor possesses a $\overline{\text{BRQ}}$ (bus request) pin, connected to $\overline{\text{BUSRQ}}$, and daisy-chained bus grant signals $\overline{\text{BAI}}$ (bus available input) and $\overline{\text{BAO}}$ (bus available output). Z-bus (the standard Zilog backplane bus system) reflects the microprocessor signals almost exactly, with four lines for request, acknowledgement, and daisy-chain signals. The procedure for bus requests is that a requestor examines the wired-OR bus request connection by examining its own BRQ line (each pin is bidirectional); if the BRQ line is active, the requestor waits (this implements a policy of non-preemption). If the BRQ line is inactive, the requestor activates its BRQ pin and waits for its BAI input to go active, indicating that no higher priority requestor has made a simultaneous request for the bus, when it deactivates its BAO output (stopping the BUSAK ripple-through), and takes control of the bus. The bus transaction is illustrated in fig. 10.4.

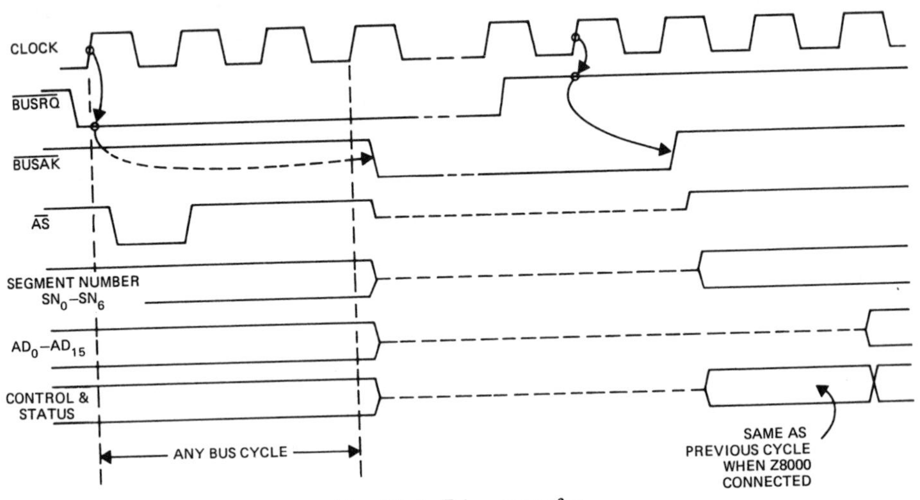

Fig. 10.4 Z-bus transfer.

The Z8000 microprocessor possesses two hardware resource-request lines, multimicro in ($\overline{\text{MI}}$) and multimicro out ($\overline{\text{MO}}$), useful when use of shared resources by multiple microprocessor systems is contemplated. Multimicro out is used to request a shared resource, and multimicro in may be used to recognise or test the state of the resource. Four Z8000 instructions (MBIT, multimicro bit test, MREQ, multimicro request, MRES, multimicro reset, MSET, multimicro set) allow software manipulation of these pins. The Z-bus makes provision for this multiple microprocessor support using four lines, which use the microprocessor $\overline{\text{MI}}$ and $\overline{\text{MO}}$ pins partly as a daisy-chain. The Z-bus lines are:

(a) $\overline{\text{MMRQ}}$, the wired-OR multimicro request line.
(b) $\overline{\text{MMST}}$, multimicro status, which allows a device to examine the $\overline{\text{MMRQ}}$ line.
(c) $\overline{\text{MMAI}}$, multimicro acknowledge input.
(d) $\overline{\text{MMAO}}$, multimicro acknowledge output, used in conjunction with $\overline{\text{MMAI}}$ to form a daisy-chain resource-request line.

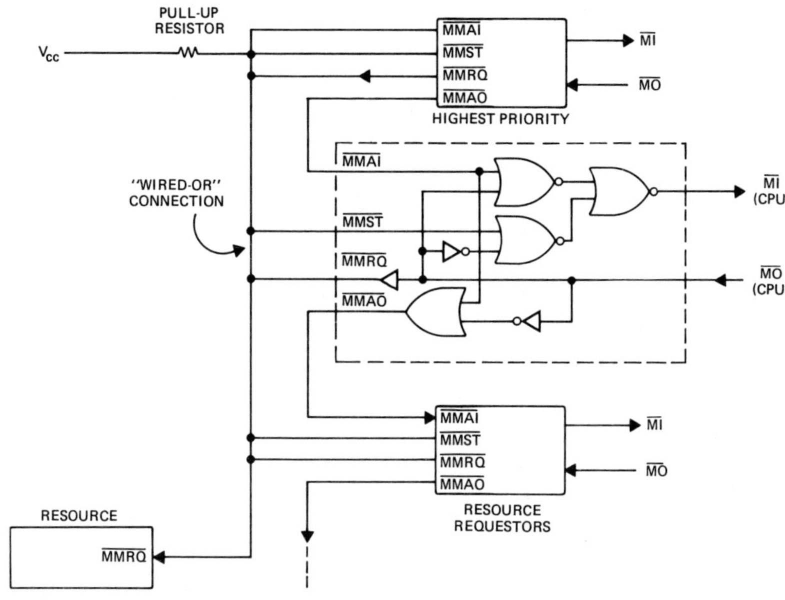

Fig. 10.5 Z-bus daisy-chained resource-request logic.

An arbitration unit associated with each microprocessor will allow the bus signals to be generated from the CPU $\overline{\text{MI}}$ and $\overline{\text{MO}}$, and use the daisy-chained lines to communicate with the arbiters of other microprocessors. A suitable implementation, due to AMD (a second-source Z8000 supplier) is shown in fig. 10.5. No default master exists so no user can be pre-empted. Operation of this system will be as follows: a Z8000 microprocessor requiring use of a resource will check $\overline{\text{MMST}}$ using MBIT to examine its $\overline{\text{MI}}$ line. If $\overline{\text{MMST}}$ is active, another microprocessor is using the resource and the request is terminated. If $\overline{\text{MMST}}$ is inactive, the resource is available, and the requesting processor activates $\overline{\text{MO}}$ (and hence $\overline{\text{MMRQ}}$) and waits for a finite delay before checking the $\overline{\text{MMAI}}$ line (by checking $\overline{\text{MI}}$ again), which, if active, will allow the microprocessor access to the resource. The delay is to allow the daisy-chain of arbiters to resolve any simultaneous requests for use of the resource, and the whole operation may be performed using MREQ, which automatically generates the delay by decrementing the contents of a specified register. Suitable code for requesting use of a resource will be:

```
LOOP:   MBIT            Check MI
        JR MI, LOOP     Repeat until resource is available.

TRY:    LD RO, 50       Load RO with delay
        MREQ RO         Make request
        JR MI, AVAIL    Check flags
        JR Z, NGT
```

```
NAVAIL:                        Resource not available
             :
NGT:                           Resource not granted
             :
             JR TRY            Try again
AVAIL:                         OK, use resource
             :
             MRES              Release resource
```

Other 16-bit microprocessors also support, via their microprocessor local and system buses, the bus arbitration and transfer control necessary for multiple microprocessor operation. While the TMS9900 has only the DMA control pins HOLD and HOLDA, its successor, the TMS99000, has special pins to support attached extended instruction set microprocessors (similar to coprocessors) and both T-bus and E-bus support bus transfers, using HOLD, HOLDA and $\overline{\text{BUSY}}$, with daisy-chained GRANTIN and GRANTOUT signals (T-bus) and using $\overline{\text{BUSY}}$, GRANTIN, GRANTOUT (E-bus). National Semiconductor's NS16000 family too, supports slave coprocessors, which use CPU status signals to synchronise with the CPU and are controlled by SPC (bi-directional slave microprocessor control).

Other hardware functions which are relevant include the 8086 '$\overline{\text{LOCK}}$' output, which allows an instruction with the lock prefix to be executed without other microprocessors being able to request the bus during execution. $\overline{\text{LOCK}}$ remains active only for the duration of a single instruction following the prefix, and does not remain active between the execution of two consecutive lock-prefix instructions or for the duration of a block operation. The $\overline{\text{LOCK}}$ output is an information output which relies on interpretation by other microprocessors on the shared bus so that they do not attempt to obtain the bus while the signal is active.

Note that the bus arbiter designed for the 8086 system accepts $\overline{\text{LOCK}}$ as an input and it will not relinquish the bus when $\overline{\text{LOCK}}$ is active. To co-ordinate access to a common resource (to avoid any contention or data consistency problems, for example) LOCK may be used in conjunction with an instruction such as XCHG (exchange register with memory) to provide an indivisible access to the resource status location, known generally as a test-and-set lock or a locked exchange. The memory location specified must be in global (shared) memory, and accessible by all microprocessors, used as the semaphore for the device being requested. Assuming that hardware on the system will respect the LOCK output, the prefixed LOCK XCHG instruction may be used to write the register contents (set to indicate resource busy) to the resource status location, and return the status in the register. If the new register contents indicate that the resource is busy, writing to the status location will have had no effect, and access will be denied. If they indicate that the resource is available, the exchange will have already set the busy pattern in the status location, and can use the resource knowing that it has exclusive access. The indivisible read-modify-write of the 68000 instruction TAS (test-and-set) serves a similar purpose.

10.2.2 SOFTWARE CONSIDERATIONS

The software considerations for a multiple microprocessor system are very similar to those of a multitasking operating system. In one case concurrent tasks are running on a single microprocessor, in the other, on several microprocessors. The problems are those of mutual exclusion, interprocessor communication, synchronisation and system initialisation.

Mutual exclusion is the fundamental concept behind both real time processing and multiple microprocessor operation. In multiple microprocessor operation, any access to shared resources will be asynchronous with respect to any system clock, and must be controlled to avoid difficulties which arise from simultaneous access by two microprocessors. For instance, any shared data buffers must be protected from simultaneous change by two or more microprocessors, or the data may become inconsistent, half of it originating from one microprocessor, and half from another. The concept of mutual exclusion is simply to 'lock out' all other microprocessors, stopping them gaining access to a resource or shared data area, when it is already being used or its data changed. The lockout process may be realised using a semaphore to control access by critical regions of code (a critical region of code is one that must have exclusive access to ensure consistency). A suitable semaphore is a Boolean variable held in a shared memory location; set when a resource is in use (unavailable) and reset when the resource is available. Obviously, a microprocessor will examine this semaphore before attempting to use a shared resource, and provision must be made to avoid any simultaneous entry, by using the 'test-and-set' type facilities described in the hardware section of this chapter. Test-and-set, an indivisible operation, will test a resource semaphore, allow entry to the resource if the semaphore indicates availability, and set the semaphore to indicate that the resource is now in use, in one operation which cannot be interrupted by other microprocessors, and denies simultaneous access.

Communication between microprocessors in a multiple system will typically be handled via locations in an area of shared (global) memory. This, of course, constitutes just such a situation as that described earlier. Send and receive operations (often termed 'put' and 'get') between producer and consumer processes, running on different CPU cards, can access this buffer storage. In moving blocks of data to and from an area of common memory, it is necessary to ensure data consistency (a consumer process must not be able to receive data until a producer process has completed its transfer, avoiding 'half-changed' data). The buffer access must be performed by a section of critical code and mutual exclusion assured.

Mutual exclusion is also applicable to the problem of synchronising microprocessors. Typically, the way in which synchronisation is performed is for one master to signal to another, while the other is waiting on that signal. A process may 'sleep', and be 'woken up' by this signal, restarting its operation in synchronism with the other microprocessor. The signal may be considered a communication which does not pass data, and mutual exclusion is an appropriate technique for handling it.

System initialisation is a final important technique, essential for multiple microprocessor systems, whereby only one microprocessor must be allowed to initialise any shared resources, whether memory or input-output devices, and to set up the variables that control access to the shared resources. Since all microprocessors will begin executing upon system reset, all but the microprocessor handling the initialisation must be excluded from attempting to access any shared resource before it has been initialised correctly. To implement this very specific mutual exclusion function, a single designated microprocessor must be forced to take control of the shared bus, and set all the resource semaphores, to exclude any access, before running the code which will set up the system correctly.

10.3 Local-area networks

A rather more widely-dispersed multiple microprocessor system is the Local Area Network (LAN)[5–9]. The local-area network has developed naturally from the large national packet-switched computer communications networks, such as ARPANET, and from the requirement that microprocessor-based business computers based in the same area should be able to communicate with each other. The LAN is essentially a data communications system, usually used by a single organisation or company, which allows digital devices, such as microprocessor-based workstations, to communicate over a common transmission medium. Typically, the communications medium is twisted-pair or coaxial cable, supporting high-speed serial transmission, usually in packet format, using smaller packets than a national network, and often at baseband, rather than a carrier system. With limited cable runs, data rates may be considerably faster than with a carrier-based national network using private wires leased from the telephone authority, and a 'standard' rate is 10 Mbits/s for a baseband LAN, though a carrier-based LAN, such as Wangnet, may improve substantially upon this.

As office and factory automation progresses, more and more microprocessor-based pieces of equipment will be installed, and the majority of these will have some provision for networking. In a factory or warehouse environment, for example, there may be a need for inventory control, job progress monitoring and perhaps communication between process control modules. In an office environment, personal desktop computers, word processing equipment, management information systems and other computer-based devices may need to share some centralised resources, such as a database system, some expensive bulk storage devices and similar devices.

Communication in these environments is relatively short-range (up to a few hundred metres perhaps) encompassing only a single site or building, and ideally serial, to minimise wiring costs. To ensure flexibility, such a system must allow easy addition or removal of stations on the network, and require no more than a single cable linking all stations (i.e. stations must communicate via active or passive taps on the cable). In keeping with this concept, any communication protocols in a local area network must match the physical realisation in simplicity and economy of use. Packet communication offers the best facilities in this respect – by their very nature, packets are small 'bundles' of data, and individual packet transmission cannot occupy the shared cable for too long, so hogging of the network by a single user (really pair of users) with a long message is not possible. Although in principle there are a large number of possible configurations for a local area network, in practice, only two types have emerged to dominate the scene: the ring network, where the communications cable is looped back on itself (perhaps via a central ring controller) to form a closed system, and the bus network, where the communications cable is open-ended (physically, of course, it is terminated in its characteristic impedance). In either case, stations are tapped on to the cable – a ring network will often use active taps which physically break the cable and will often carry a power distribution cable alongside the signal cable, whereas a bus network will usually use passive taps. Generally, a ring network will allow simple communications protocols, and is very suitable for optical fibre implementation. A bus network is more easily reconfigured, its distributed control enhances reliability (though a double ring system like Racal's Planet network will be at least as reliable as any other configuration), but the bus suffers from more complex access control and monitoring, and is not suitable for fibres.

Several different *de facto* standards have appeared; baseband (non-carrier) networks align themselves with either the bus structure and protocols of Ethernet (a joint development by Xerox, DEC and Intel) or the ring structure of the Cambridge Ring (a UK development, whose pattern has been repeated elsewhere). An attempt is being made to draft official LAN standards in the shape of IEEE-802, a proposal which defines an Ethernet-like system (though not directly compatible with Ethernet) and which also defines an alternative ring structure and protocols. Broadband (carrier-based) networks are typified by Wangnet, and allow not only packet data, but simultaneous voice and video channels. Much has been made of voice transmission over local-area networks, and obvious advantages rest with any system which will support voice transmission. Claims have been made that Ethernet will support digital packet voice transmission without overloading the network or degrading its performance too much, but for the rest of this discussion, only data transmission will be considered.

10.3.1 IEEE-802 LAN PROPOSALS

Like most of the other local-area network specifications, the proposals cover the physical, data link, and parts of the network levels of ISO-OSI detailed in the introduction. Within a local-area network, since routing is not usually significant (multiple paths between source and destination, so important to national packet-switched networks, do not exist in LANS), the network and transport levels of the OSI model are often combined into a single specification level.

The physical specification of IEEE-802 defines a transmission medium of 50Ω coaxial cable in segments of up to 500 m. Each segment may contain up to a hundred bus transceivers, separated by multiples of 2.5 m (this distance means that impedance mismatch at one bus transceiver, which may cause reflections on the line, will have a minimal effect on other transceivers) and each actual station may be up to 50 m from its transceiver linked by a transceiver cable consisting of five shielded twisted pairs. Segments of cable may be linked using bus repeaters, but an overall limit is imposed of 1500 m between stations. The twisted pair transceiver cables carry power from a station to its transceiver, as well as data and up to ten status signals (such as collision-detection and idle states). Coding for data and control signals is specified as differential Manchester phase encoding, with a speed of 1, 5, 10 or 20 Mbits/s.

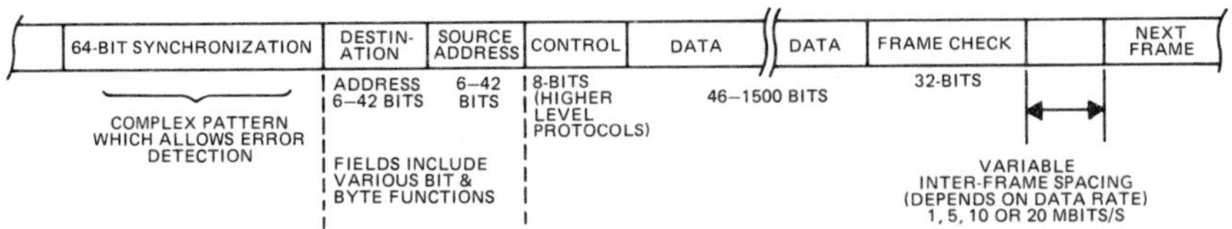

Fig. 10.6 IEEE-802 frame format.

The basic unit of transmission, or frame, is preceded by a synchronising preamble of 64 bits, followed by from 6 to 42 address bits, 8 control bits, 46 to 1500 data bits, and terminated by 32 frame check bits (fig. 10.6). Access to the communications cable is allowed using one of two methods: carrier-sense, multiple-access with collision-detection (CSMA/CD) or token-passing. The CSMA/CD scheme works as follows: when a station wishes to transmit a packet to another, it first of all listens to the communication cable. If another station is transmitting, the station wanting to transmit will wait, and try again. If no other station is transmitting on the cable, the requesting station will initiate transmission of its packet, hence the 'carrier sense' function of the protocol. Allowance must be made for the condition where two stations check the absence of any transmission, and start their own transmissions simultaneously. An overlap of transmitted packets is known as a collision, and can only occur during the initial part of a transmission (the carrier sensing means that if no collision has occurred early on in transmission, the packet will be transmitted without interference). The 'collision window' is approximately the time taken for the transmitted signal to propagate to all parts of the network, since lack of collision cannot be verified before this. Once the collision window has passed, an unaffected transmission will be deemed to have acquired the channel.

If a collision occurs, one of the transmitting stations will detect it, since both transmitting stations will monitor their own transmitted signals. To ensure that all stations on the network have detected the collision, the transmit channel access logic which has first detected the interference due to the collision, will immediately transmit a bit sequence which jams further transmitted bits, extending the collision duration by an extent which allows every station (receivers, as well as would-be transmitters) to identify that a collision has occurred. After the jam sequence has been transmitted, the transmit link management logic terminates further transmission, and waits for a random time interval before attempting to transmit the packet again (the delay is random since if two transmitting stations had their first transmissions collide, and both wait for the same delay time, they will obviously collide again!). If repeated collisions occur, retransmission will be attempted repeatedly, but the random delay generator would back-off (increase the average delay), showing the station's data rate in the presence of heavy network loading. The easiest way to accomplish this backing-off function is to increase the interval from which the random delay time is calculated, at each retransmission attempt ('truncated binary exponential back-off') IEEE-802 allows for a total of sixteen attempts (first plus fifteen retries) to transmit a given packet successfully, after which the transmission is aborted. Efficiency on a CSMA/CD network is good when the network is lightly loaded, but falls off rapidly when the traffic exceeds 30% of the channel capacity.

In order to use a CSMA/CD baseband bus system, the time for a station to transmit a complete frame must be greater than twice the propagation time of the network (otherwise, two stations at opposite ends of the network could transmit pockets which collide, and whose collision is not detected). This gives a relationship between bus length, data rate, and frame length, $2t_p = L/R$, where t_p is the propagation time in seconds, L is the length of the communication cable in terms of the number of bits which may be simultaneously in transit, and R the data rate in bits/second. Once the transmission rate is fixed, and the packet size determined, the overall length of cable is limited.

The CSMA/CD approach exemplified by IEEE-802 suffers from a number of drawbacks. Access logic is relatively complex, in that a given station must transmit and receive (listen for collisions) simultaneously. There is no determinism – successful transmission cannot be guaranteed within a known timescale, and no way of separating errors due to noise on the cable or due to collisions. The lack of determinism means that while the CSMA/CD approach is ideal for office use, it is much less suitable for real time process control applications.

The alternative access scheme is the token-passing one, useful for both bus and ring local-area networks. IEEE-802 defines such a scheme, whereby a single 'token' is passed between stations, and where possession of the token allows a station to transmit a pending packet. Only one station will possess the token at any one time, so there will be no contention between stations wanting to transmit. When the station which holds the token has completed its packet transmission, it will pass the token on to the next station. If there are no pending packets, the token will be passed on immediately. With a ring system, the logical order for token passing will usually correspond to the physical order of stations on the ring. This need not be so for a bus system.

For a ring system too, data frames and tokens transmitted by a station will go only to the next station on the ring, which can either accept the frame or transmit it to the next station, and so on. If a transmitted frame travels completely round the ring, and returns to the originating station, this is taken as a negative acknowledgement. An absence of a returned packet implies that the intended receiving station has received it, but is not a positive acknowledgement, since a break in the ring would have the same effect. A positive acknowledgement must be requested. For a bus system, data frames or tokens transmitted by one station go to all other stations simultaneously, but only the addressed station will accept them. Again, a positive acknowledgement must be requested.

The major advantage possessed by token-passing is its determinancy. The delays in the system are predictable, and the random CSMA/CD delays are avoided, making not only office equipment, but also process control systems possible. The problem, however, with the token system lies in ensuring the integrity of the token. Any undetected loss of the token will halt the whole network, whose function relies on there being a single token permanently in existence. A token-passing scheme must have facilities for detecting the loss if its token, and for recreating it. Since a potential token sender requires a knowledge of which is the next logical station on the network, adding a new station to the network (either ring or bus) may not be straightforward.

In recommending either a CSMA/CD or a token-passing scheme, and, in fact a possible broadband scheme, the proposers of IEEE-802 have hedged their bets, since as yet there is no obvious dominance or overwhelming technical advantage to either of the two baseband protocols. However, it does mean that there will be several IEEE nets; their limitations must be carefully recorded. Like the IEEE-488 instrumentation bus, the network standard will evolve as those parts which are presently optional are hardened by decisions taken by the majority of manufacturers. Despite this vagueness surrounding parts of the specification, IEEE-802 is nevertheless a useful recommendation document, and goes a long way towards a 'manufacturer-independent' standard. The CSMA/CD part of its definition corresponds fairly closely with that of Ethernet, although it differs sufficiently to make IEEE-802 and Ethernet incompatible. Efforts are being made to reconcile these differences, and it is likely that when IEEE-802 is finally published, both it and Ethernet will have changed sufficiently to ensure 100% compatibility.

10.3.2 ETHERNET

Ethernet predates IEEE-802 somewhat, and is based heavily upon work done by Xerox corporation into office automation. 'Experimental Ethernet', designed by Xerox and implemented internally in 1975, has logged many hours of operation, and has supported many users within the Xerox office environment. The 1980 definition of Ethernet combines the Experimental Ethernet experiences of Xerox with the networking ideas of Digital Equipment Corporation and Intel Corporation. It is a CSMA/CD bus-oriented system with an almost identical protocol to IEEE-802, with the following exceptions:

(a) the speed of Ethernet is fixed at 10 Mbits/s;
(b) the total number of stations is 1024 (IEEE-802 puts no limit on the total number of stations);
(c) Ethernet's frame organisation is different (fig. 10.7). The address field is fixed at 47 bits, while 802 uses a variable chained address field of one to seven bytes, and the type field is twice the size of the IEEE-802 control field. The 64-bit synchronisation pattern is one of alternating logical ones and zeros, whereas 802 uses a more complex pattern allowing easier error detection. Ethernet may be more likely to begin frame transmission

prematurely in the event of error;

(d) encoding format in Ethernet is simply Manchester phase encoding, rather than the differential form. The two are illustrated in fig. 10.8;

(e) the transceiver cable in Ethernet uses four screened twisted-pair conductors used for transmit, receive, collision presence, and power;

(f) collision presence in Ethernet is the inverse of the equivalent 802 signal.

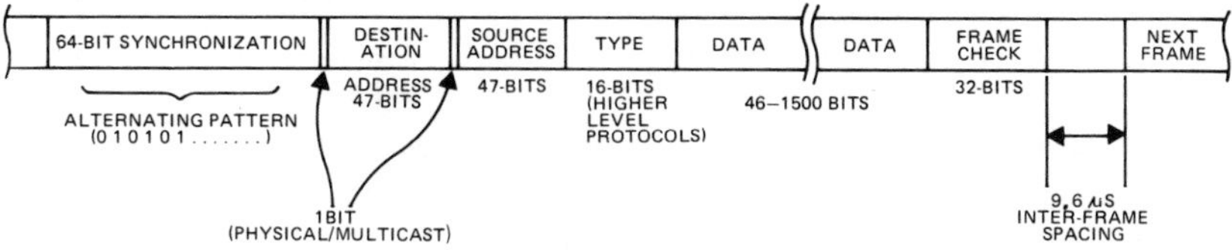

Fig. 10.7 Ethernet format.

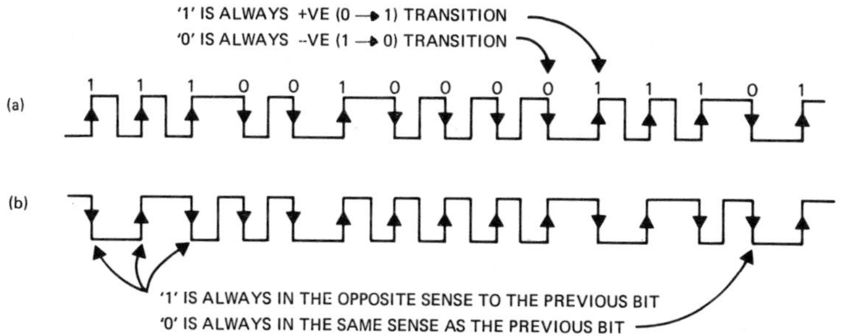

Fig. 10.8 Encoding formats: (a) Manchester phase encoding (Ethernet), (b) differential Manchester phase encoding (IEEE-802).

This list is not complete, but serves to illustrate the areas of incompatibility. Ethernet, however, together with a number of similar systems (Net/One from Ungermann-Bass, a 4 Mbits/s system, and Z-Net from Zilog, an 800 kbits/s system, for instance) has achieved a reasonably high degree of user acceptance, and card-based products supporting Ethernet are available from a number of manufacturers. Although the Ethernet definition only covers the first two layers and possibly part of level 3 of the ISO-IS1 model, Intel has carried things somewhat further by the introduction of iLNA (Intel Local Network Architecture), which uses ROM-based software on a Multibus card to implement the higher levels of the OSI model. Transport, session, presentation and application layers are all provided for, relying on Ethernet to provide the lower layers. The transport layer allows the user to establish virtual circuits between communications 'sockets', which are unique process identifiers, composed of a local network address (to allow multiple network implementation; this network identifier is not used in a single network system), a host address within the network (defining the network node), and the address of a port to a process executing on the host. Using the basic data link packet-handling hardware and firmware, the transport layer virtual circuit allows a variable-length message to be transmitted from one process to another. Any variation in operation of the data link packet delivery service, such as duplicated and out-of-sequence packets will be removed by the transport layer. Flow control is another important function, where slow receivers must be used with fast transmitters. Failure to lower the transmitter data rate will result in frequent packet retransmission, and a reduction in network efficiency.

The transport layer assigns packet sequence numbers, sends acknowledgement packets when correct reception has occurred, and retransmits automatically when no positive acknowledgement has been received within a limited time. Flow control is achieved by using buffer size measurements, and regulating packet transmission rate according to the buffer 'window' size (amount of unused buffer memory available). Using virtual circuits between process sockets allows full-duplex error-controlled and flow-controlled data paths, with multiple virtual connections between processes, using message lengths independent of packet size (and data link protocols). Note that the Ethernet packet format (and also 802) assign one bit to denote broadcast packets, where the 47-bit address then becomes a 'group identifier' for the group of intended recipients. At the end of a communication, the transport layer will clear down the virtual circuit.

The session layer of iLNA performs the important process identification feature which allows location-independent references. The binding function that relates socket addresses and process names and distributes them through the network is the primary function of the layer. Mapping allows the layer to create, or update, translation between a process and a socket identifier. An updating function makes the information network-wide using broadcast packets. The session layer is also responsible for network status information.

The network management layer takes care of network statistical reporting, operational functions and maintenance. Operational functions include bootstrapping a new node onto the network. This can be done by loading the new node's operating system from another already operational node. The new node will initiate its own bootstrap sequence by sending a broadcast packet to any node which has a copy of the operating system and is able to transmit it; normally, more than one node will respond to the request, and the bootstrapping node will accept the first reply. Maintenance consists of keeping a set of error counters which record occurrences of recoverable errors. Error information may be exchanged between nodes, and the network management layer supports an error-logging file. Errors may occur naturally in network operation without implying the presence of a fault on the network. An excessive number of errors, however, may indicate a fault condition. The distribution of errors may help to isolate the fault, and the management layer carries its own diagnostic software, which may be used to examine network devices when a failure has occurred. Test routines exist which apply specifically to each layer in the network, and allow, among other functions, loopback tests, which permit isolated testing to localise any problem. If any problem cannot be corrected by a reinitialisation of each layer by the network layer, the fault is likely to be in hardware, and not repairable by the system itself (faults such as a poor section of cable, or a transceiver permanently jamming the cable, can be found readily).

The addition of this large amount of network support software makes running, in this case, Ethernet, a viable proposition. The top application layer is provided by the user, and all the underlying layers can be virtually invisible to him. Although 8-bit microprocessor networking is possible, LANS such as Ethernet operate much more effectively with the more sophisticated 16-bit devices, which have the speed and functions (such as memory management, protection, etc.) to support the network operating software, and also the type of application software likely to be useful in a networked system (large databases and similar systems).

Net/One, too, uses virtual circuits, creating types used for network management (allowing, as in Ethernet, position-independent station addressing), for session use (set up by the user using network utilities) and a type which may be considered a semipermanent circuits set up at system initialisation time. A non-virtual circuit, or datagram packet, for brief, typically interrogatory, messages, is also provided by Net/One utilities. Z-net provides a simpler datagram service which is directly supported by the Zilog multitasking real time operating system RIO/CP (the CP stands for concurrent processing).

In view of the office automation requirements of a network, which has inspired LANS, such as Ethernet, work has proceeded towards sending digital packet speech (telephone) signals over the same medium as data signals. Normally, the average rate of normal data transmission traffic will be lower than the rate required to sustain a speech link, so it is to be expected that speech transmission will dominate network traffic. An Ethernet study claims that not only local voice, but also voice via the public switched telephone network (PSTN) may be handled on the Ethernet cable. An Ethernet LAN may integrate voice and data services using a telephone network interface module and a gateway module to a PABX. The telephone network interface module connects directly to the 4-wire system via a signalling and control interface and uses a codec which transmits and receives μ-law encoded pulse-code-modulated (PCM) audio signals which employ an 8 kHz sampling rate and where each sample is represented by an 8-bit binary code. This requires a 64 kbits/s transmission rate, not counting any signalling and control protocol signals. The PCM signals are converted to packets by a microprocessor-controlled Ethernet interface, which transmits them using the CSMA/CD protocols of Ethernet. Buffering is necessary at both transmitter and receiver for packet speech signals, to avoid the efforts of delay in gaining access to the network cable (which could create jitter in the timing for reconstruction of the speech signal from its samples). At the receiver, the buffer feeds regular data to the PCM circuitry despite irregular packet deliveries. Buffering creates speech path delays, which may typically be 50 ms in each direction of transmission; because these delays are relatively long, precautions must be taken to avoid echo effects when the system is used with a PABX interface. Typically, the level of service claimed for Ethernet is that if 35% of the 10 MHz bandwidth is reserved for data traffic, and if a 100 ms round-trip delay in speech traffic is acceptable, then about seventy-eight simultaneous telephone calls can be handled by the network (this corresponds to a potential

390 telephone users if only 20% are active at any one time). Trade-offs may be made between the number of telephone users, the maximum acceptable round-trip delay, and the percentage of network capacity devoted to data.

10.3.3 OMNINET

Another CSMA network similar to Ethernet is Corvus Systems Omninet. It is of interest because it uses collision avoidance, by a double carrier sense check, rather than collision detection. The basic medium is a twisted-pair RS422 system supporting a 1 Mbit/s data rate, so it is slower than Ethernet, but has been used with 16-bit LSI-11 computers. Two levels of carrier sense are used:

(a) Sending logic is initiated when no activity has been sensed on the cable for 15 μs (if activity is sensed, a random wait is made before trying again).
(b) A fast gate array checks again just before transmission starts about 20 μs after sending logic has been initiated. No collision detection logic exists.

Every correctly received frame is positively acknowledged within 15 μs of the end of the frame (during the interval in which all other stations will be sensing whether there is activity on the twisted pair). If no positive acknowledgement has been received after 15-20 μs, the transmitting station will wait a random time and attempt to retransmit the frame. The receiver transporter logic automatically checks a received message and positively acknowledges it if it is correct, sending the acknowledgement without any carrier sensing since the line must be free for at least 15 μs after the end of transmission).

The random wait intervals in Omninet are similar to the exponential binary back-off in Ethernet, and generated from a 'wait clock' which only ticks when the network is otherwise idle (this adjustment, depending on the usage of the network, eliminates station queueing). The datagram approach, which does not use transport layer acknowledgement, and the virtual circuit, which requires a relatively complex setup procedure, have both been rejected in favour of a compromise 'micro-virtual circuit', which provides many of the features of a normal virtual connection but does not retain state information for more than a few microseconds. The packet format of Omninet is shown in fig. 10.9.

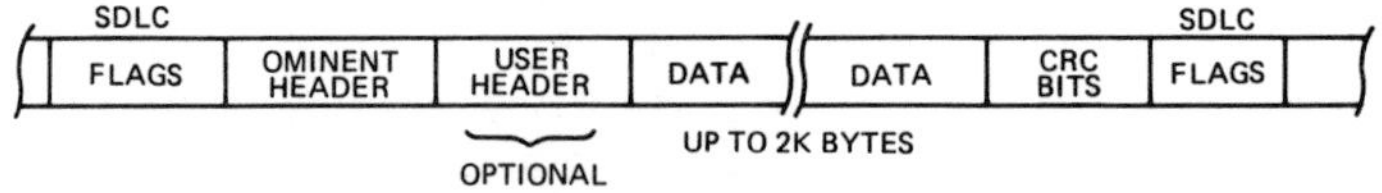

Fig. 10.9 Omninet packet format.

10.3.4 RING NETWORKS – THE CAMBRIDGE RING

One of the first practical data ring networks in the UK was the Cambridge Ring. A packet ring network running at 10 Mbits/s, the Cambridge Ring uses an 'empty slot' technique equivalent to 'multiple token-passing'. The ring consists of a closed loop of two twisted pair cables which carry phase-encoded signals corresponding to data and clock, and also carry power to the ring stations. The ring is broken by each station repeater which regenerates the ring signals, and to this repeater is connected access logic and the station interface. A controller station, called the monitor, is responsible for starting the ring by entering start mode, setting up the standard packet structure and circulating them round the ring with random data as their contents. The packets are passed from station to station round the ring and are finally returned to the monitor, where a bit by bit check on them will allow the overall ring performance to be assessed (and a check to be made on correct synchronisation of individual stations). The start mode is then switched to run mode and the monitor clears the network error counters and maintains the standard framing structure, consisting of a fixed number of packets in transit.

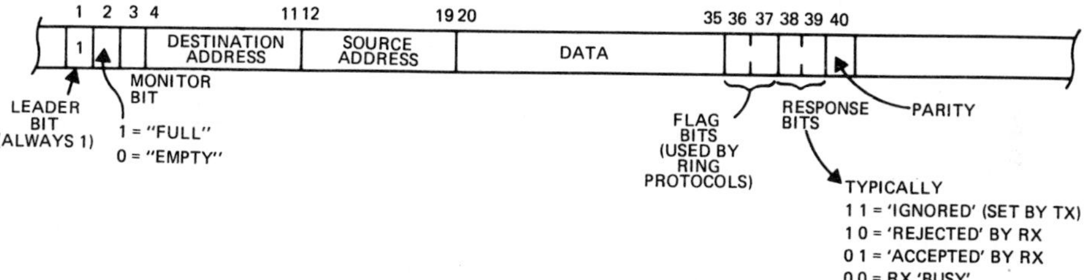

Fig. 10.10 A particular (Toltec) ring implementation.

Packets may be marked as empty, or full, and if full, will contain a source address and a destination address, as well as data, and space for response bits. The packet format is shown in fig. 10.10. When a station wishes to send data, it waits until a packet marked 'empty' passes its repeater. The empty packet is filled with data which has previously been loaded into a shift register, together with source and destination addresses, and passed on to the next station on the ring as a full packet. The full packet proceeds round the ring until it reaches the station marked as the destination address, where its data is loaded into the receiver shift register and used by the receiving station. The packet is marked with its appropriate response bits set, and the receiving station repeater passes it on. The packet travels round the ring until it returns to the original transmitting station repeater, where it is released by being marked empty again.

The traffic is self-regulating with no need for central control except for starting packet circulation and error logging (the monitor can check data error of packets in flight and will correct framing and gap errors). In order to avoid a station hogging the ring, a discipline is imposed whereby a station must release each of its returned packets. It cannot send a packet of data, observe the correct return of the packet and then refill the same packet with new data; it must pass the packet on as an empty packet to the next station on the ring. This enforces a 'round-robin' system for packet access. Each pair of communicating stations may have at most one packet in flight between them round the ring, but in practice, the number of packets in flight round the ring is limited by the user, with switch selection at the monitor.

Unlike Ethernet, the Cambridge Ring is not a contention-based network. There is no need for any arbitration for access – when a station receives an empty packet, it is the only station at that particular time which is able to fill it. Consequently, ring access logic may often be simpler than CSMA/CD logic. The repeater logic of the ring is permanently powered by the monitor via the ring itself, and a repeater will continue to operate when its associated station is switched off. Since the ring is broken by each repeater, expansion is not so easy as with a bus system, but the configuration is ideally suited for optical-fibre implementation, with its attendant safety and interference-free characteristics. Although the packet length is short (40 bits, with 16 bits of data), the maximum data rate from any one station is typically 1 Mbaud. Currently, the availability of ring logic in the UK is better than that of Ethernet interfaces. One possible drawback, however, with this slotted scheme, is its failure in the event of a break in the ring cable, a problem overcome in other token-passing schemes.

Software available to operate the ring using higher levels of ISO-OSI is available. One manufacturer offers BCPL routines which implement functions in the transport layer. The single shot protocol (SSP) is the fundamental method of handling messages in the system, using the basic block protocol to do so. A higher level, file transfer system may be implemented using byte stream protocol, which itself uses SSP to implement operating-system-independent transfers. Machine-independent file servers may be added to the ring with a minimum of effort. Access to a remote file server on the ring may be controlled by a standard file command directory.

10.3.5 TOKEN-PASSING RINGS – PLANET

Both ring and bus systems may be controlled by a technique known as token-passing, which rivals CSMA/CD or the empty slot access techniques. The basic scheme is described with the IEEE-802 definition in section 10.3.1. One UK implementation of a token-passing ring is Racal's Planet. To overcome a ring's vulnerability to breaks in the cable, Planet uses twin coaxial cables as its transmission medium, with packets circulating in opposite directions round the ring structure. If a break occurs in the ring, the cables can be automatically looped back at any access point. It is a much more strictly controlled system than the Cambridge Ring, using a central director station. Like the Cambridge Ring, empty packets circulate continuously round the system. An access node (which interfaces to a station via a V24 connector) can only have access to the ring when it holds the token. Once the token-holding node has dispatched a data packet, it hands the token on to the next node (this means that a single node cannot hog the system). The system runs at 10 Mbits/s, with an effective data rate of 3.5 Mbits/s using 42-bit packets. The V24 interface ports have a speed of 19.2 kbits/s.

The director not only handles monitoring ring integrity, but also handles all call setting-up, and assigns permanent virtual circuits, resource priorities, and network utilities.

10.3.6 A BROADBAND NETWORK – WANGNET

All the local-area networks described so far work at baseband, and are limited in capacity by the speed of baseband drivers. An integrated communications network must provide not only data services, but also voice (which is possible with a baseband system like Ethernet) and possibly video. The bandwidth requirements for such an integrated network are so high as to demand a different approach to time-division multiplexing (TDM), and an obvious solution is to move to a modulated carrier-based system, which will allow a combination of TDM and frequency-division multiplexing (FDM). The approach will be a more expensive one than a baseband one, but considerably more capable. Wangnet illustrates a typical network of this type, currently implemented as a coaxial cable network.

Wangnet uses a 340 MHz bandwidth system covering 10 to 350 MHz, split into three bands:

(a) interconnect, for point-to-point data;
(b) 'Wangband', a 12 Mbits/s timeshared channel;
(c) utility, for video channels.

The interconnect band is itself split into three channel groups (10-12 MHz, containing thirty-two 9.6 kbd duplex RS-232C channels, 12-22 MHz, containing thirty-two RS449 channels up to 64 kbd, 48-82 MHz, containing 256 switched RS-232C channels up to 9.6 kbd) while the Wangband, extending from 217-251 MHz carries packets of variable size HDLC frames containing up to 2 kbytes. Access to this band is by an improved CSMA/CD technique, with virtual circuits, and an exponential back-off algorithm similar to Ethernet, but with full error recovery.

The utility band, from 174-216 MHz, allows for up to seven 6 MHz bandwidth video channels. The gaps in allocation (22-48 MHz, 82-174 MHz, and 251-350 MHz) are reserved for expansion to voice-switched channels. The coaxial cable system is a 75Ω one and each in-line tap gives three user ports and one reserved port.

Wangnet is a very specific product which makes no attempt to compromise in order to allow other manufacturers' products use the system. Indeed, the 'Wangband' is specifically designed for use with Wang systems only. Nevertheless, it is a good example with which to illustrate the high performance of broadband LANS.

10.3.7 IMPACT OF LANS ON 16-BIT SYSTEMS

The 16-bit microprocessor will be widely used in office and personal computer systems, and it is to be anticipated that future products in this area will include facilities for LAN interfacing. As operating system facilities provided by the new 16-bit microprocessors improve, with new protection schemes, and coprocessor systems on silicon, LANS will implement fully the layers of the OSI model (as Intel have already proposed for Ethernet). Gateways between LANS will gradually bring about a complete transformation of data communications, which would not have occurred without the impetus given by the 16-bit machine.

CHAPTER 11
Applications

11.1 Introduction

The 16-bit microprocessor world is much more complex than the 8-bit one; not only are the microprocessors themselves more capable, faster and more versatile, but their whole infrastructure (development systems, languages, system software, operating systems, and board-level devices) is far larger than that of the average 8-bit device. Applications will reflect this in a number of ways; the most obvious one is a shift in the end use, away from stand-alone simple controllers (adequately handled by the modern 8-bit single chip microcomputer, or the quasi-16-bit machines) into the area of distributed computing, with many intelligent interfaces and multiple CPUs, and competing directly with minicomputers, performing more complex control tasks, business and scientific computing, and very strongly affecting what has become known as 'information technology'. Here, their powerful memory management and addressing capabilities, machine integrity provided by privileged and user hardware modes, and their operating system support features, coupled with their size and price advantages over minicomputers, will allow the 16-bit microcomputers to penetrate what has traditionally been a minicomputer or mainframe area. Of great importance to this area will be the adoption of capable backplane bus standards which support board level products and allow systems to be readily expanded; for this reason, a major part of this chapter (section 11.5) is devoted to bus standards, and outlines the latest developments.

The personal computer, too, will benefit, with more languages, faster operation, more versatile displays (the speed of the 16-bit microprocessor, together with new interface devices, will allow high-resolution colour graphics, with animation) and larger memories.

Despite the shift in emphasis away from the 'microprocessor as a component' viewpoint, there will still be many applications which will benefit from the use of 16-bit microprocessors. Control problems which demand a lot of numerical computation will be ideally suited to a 16-bit microprocessor with on-chip floating-point hardware or a mathematical coprocessor. Handling fast mainframe peripheral devices (especially large bulk storage devices with extensive data protection) will also be a natural application for a fast 16-bit microprocessor with intelligent DMA and I/O devices. The field of signal processing, too, is amenable to the 16-bit microprocessor's speed, allowing sampling rates to be increased, and more sophisticated functions to be performed. At present, it is rumoured that the major customers for 16-bit microprocessors are the arcade games' manufacturers, since the increasing sophistication of such electronic games requires ever faster and more powerful microprocessors. Less frivolous applications are being slow to emerge, but will appear as more development software support becomes available, and as the projects started one or two years ago come to fruition. Generally, the average size of 16-bit applications programs is larger than that of their 8-bit counterparts, so development time will also be correspondingly longer.

11.2 General commercial applications

Commercial applications of the 16-bit microprocessor are fairly easy to predict, since in many cases, they will be extensions of existing ideas. Desktop computers, word processors, management information systems, front-end processors for mainframe computers (for database maintenance, private viewdata systems, electronic funds transfer, etc.), and stations on local area networks (LANS). The impact of the 16-bit microprocessor will start with the small personal or business computer. Already, personal computers are available which use the quasi-16-bit microprocessors, for example, Future Technology Systems (8088), IBM Displaywriter (8088) and Sirius One (8088). The full 16-bit microcomputers are being used in such machines as Micro-11 (LSI-11/03), System 8000 (Z8000 with a Unix-like operating system and multiuser and network support), Altos 8600 (8086 with CP/M-86, Oasis-16, Xenix (Unix look alike OS) and with numeric and I/O coprocessors), Apple IV (68000, yet to be released) and various others.

The Sirius One (Victor 9000 in the USA) is a good machine to consider, partly because of its designer, Chuck Peddle, the ex-Commodore engineer who designed the original PET, and partly because preliminary market research has indicated that it will achieve a high degree of user acceptance in the USA. Compared with previous 8-bit personal and business machines, this 'third generation' microcomputer (really a business machine) is impressive for the facilities provided on the standard 'base model'. This is designed as a single card computer housed in the same cabinet as twin 5¼ in diskette drives, and carrying 128 kbytes of RAM, built with 64K dynamic RAM chips. The diskettes are 600 kbytes each, single-sided (1.2 Mbytes total online storage) with optional double-side drives (2.4 Mbytes total) available. (The disk controller is unique to the Sirius, which allows a variable number of sectors per track, and varies the rotational speed of the disk depending on head position. Memory may be expanded to 512 kbytes internally, and to 1 Mbyte externally.)

Interfaces present on the standard card are:

(a) A parallel printer port which supports both Centronics standard and IEEE-488 (interface bus).
(b) An asynchronous RS-232 port with software selectable baud rate (75-9600 baud).
(c) A serial synchronous/asynchronous port which will support a variety of formats.

These ports will cater for most interface requirements for printers and serial data communications. An audio codec is provided on the basic system, which, together with an internal loudspeaker, allows disk storage of digitised speech, which may be 'played back' on command. Although a gimmick, this audio facility does lend some user friendliness to the system, and enables verbal prompts to be made, a useful feature for the unskilled end user. To allow for expansion, four sockets are present in the cabinet, where interfaces or memory may be added internally (to expand to 512 kbytes uses three of these) and an external expansion chassis will be available.

The keyboard, a separately-cased unit, possesses a 17-key 'calculator' pad (which includes functions %, +, –, ×, ÷), cursor and edit control keys, and seven programmable function keys. The display, the third unit in the system, is a 12 in green monitor; in alphanumeric mode, it will display 25 lines of 80 characters, each character displayed as a 9 × 12 dot matrix within a 10 × 16 dot cell. Reverse video, intensity control and split screen operation are all supported. In graphics mode, the Sirius really excels, with a bit-mapped display of 800 × 400 elements (in this mode, it has been pointed out that it is possible to support 132-character columns and up to fifty lines!). A colour display will be available eventually.

While the influence of the new generation of microprocessors is obvious in the hardware of Sirius, the software support is equally impressive. Operating system support is either CP/M-86 or MSDOS. CP/M-86, discussed in chapter 8, is a 16-bit version of the 'industry-standard' 8-bit CP/M. MSDOS is an operating system written for the IBM Personal Computer by Microsoft, and does not suffer from some of the drawbacks of CP/M (this implies that users of Sirius will have access to an extremely large range of software). Supported languages are Microsoft BASIC, compiled BASIC, COBOL, Pascal and FORTRAN, as well as a low-level assembler and future intentions to add PL-1. Software packages available are:

(a) Supercalc, the so-called 'electronic worksheet'.
(b) Micromodeller, the financial modelling package.
(c) Wordstar (and Spellstar) word processing package with built-in spelling checks.
(d) Mailmerge addition to Wordstar.

Future additions include a version of BASIC to support the graphics facilities, software support for user-definable character sets, and colour graphics support. In addition, of course, the wide range of software available elsewhere under CP/M-86 will all run on the Sirius.

This brief review of the facilities available on just one 16-bit system gives some idea of the increase in complexity and capabilities brought about by this new generation of microprocessors. Helped by the rapid erosion of dynamic RAM prices, the cost of this system is little more than many 8-bit systems, and less than some of the more expensive ones. As new designs emerge, using coprocessors and extensive memory management, with networking capabilities, the personal and business computer area will show a further increase in sophistication and in the facilities offered for a given price.

11.3 Control applications

Control, above anything else, has been the area where the microprocessor has found its niche. Early microprocessor-based equipments using 8-bit microprocessors, were limited to elementary controls, such as sequence controllers (replacing relay logic) and single-loop or open-loop digital controllers, implementing simple control or compensation algorithms. Data logging, an activity often related to control system design, has also seen the impact of the 8-bit microprocessor. At the high-complexity end of the control spectrum, where many control loops all interact with complex process dynamics, the minicomputer has reigned supreme in a supervisory role. The supervisory computer will usually work with analogue controllers (often three-term PID controllers) and optimise overall system performance. The theory of sampled-data control systems is well-understood, but the direct digital control (DDC) system is still something of a rarity, and with good reason – a supervisory system can still operate without supervision in many process control environments; loss of the computer will mean a degradation in performance so that the system becomes sub-optimal, but not a total loss of control. With many control loops, too, the sheer computational effort involved will be prohibitive if a single computer were involved, and the precision and speed of the 8-bit microprocessor may be inadequate for multiple-microprocessor implementation.

Nevertheless, there are distinct advantages to be gained if analogue controllers are eliminated, and replaced by digital ones, typically:

(a) Digital systems do not exhibit drift, a common problem with analogue systems including integrators.
(b) It is easier to adjust system parameters, and possible to construct adaptive loops or self-tuning controllers without any increase in hardware complexity.
(c) It may be possible to include front-end filtering and other signal processing in the same unit as the control algorithm.
(d) Arbitrary transfer functions may be realised.
(e) Problems of long transport delays, troublesome with many analogue controllers, and non-linearities, may be overcome.
(f) Supervisory control of a number of simple (say three-term) digital controllers may be easier, since signals are already in digital form prior to transmission to the supervisory system, and supervisory system outputs (controller set points) do not need to be converted back to analogue form. The advantages of a supervisory system, however, may be retained.

The 16-bit microprocessor offers distinct advantages in control applications: it is fast, has good precision, 16-bit hardware multiply and divide, and a good interrupt structure. The quasi-16-bit microprocessors, too, may be equally suitable for many applications, since control functions tend to be limited by computational speed rather than memory or I/O access time. Although capable of very sophisticated operation with large memory systems and complex operating systems, the typical 16-bit (or especially quasi-16-bit) microprocessor is inexpensive enough to be used purely for its speed and precision advantages. Note that at least two of the major manufacturers (Intel and Motorola) have taken pains to make their 16-bit microprocessors compatible with some of the existing multi-function interfaces, to allow a minimal system with a very small parts count.

11.3.1 SEQUENCE CONTROL AND DATA LOGGING

Already a typical application for the 8-bit microprocessor, sequence controllers are unlikely to require the power of the new 16-bit microprocessor. Generally, they take the place of relay logic, cam timers and diode programming boards, and speeds are measured in tens of milliseconds at the fastest. Data logging, however, is another matter; a basic parameter of data logging systems is minimum scan time, the time taken to sample all analogue and digital inputs. The shorter the scan time per input, the faster data can be acquired, or the more inputs than can be accommodated for a given rate. In many applications of data logging, some data conversion and perhaps scaling is necessary (for fluid flow measurement, for instance, most transducers produce a signal which is proportional to the square of the flow rate, so a square root function is required; for other measurements, drift compensation or waveform analysis is required). As previously indicated, the 16-bit hardware multiply-divide and interrupt structure will prove significantly useful. It is interesting to note that for a system which needs the ultimate in speed (and program size), the string primitives and iterative procedures possessed by all the new microprocessors make for a very economical machine code routine!

11.3.2 ANALOGUE CONTROLLER REPLACEMENT

Most of the analogue controllers presently in use implement various versions of the standard three-term (PID) controller. The transfer function algorithm for the ideal linear PID-controller may be expressed in the form:

$$C_O = K\,(e + \frac{1}{T_I} \int e\,dt + T_D \frac{de}{dt}) + C$$

where e is the error between the process variable value and the set point (demanded value of the process variable), i.e.

e = process variable – set point (PV – SP)
T_I = integral term time constant
T_D = derivative term time constant (rate constant)
K = proportional gain
C = constant
C_O = controller output value

By adjustment of T_I, T_D, and the other parameters, the controller may be 'tuned' to optimise its response in any particular application.

In practice, if constant C is omitted, this algorithm may be expressed in the Laplace form:

$$\frac{C_O}{e} = K\,(1 + \frac{1}{T_I s} + T_D s)$$

In a non-ideal, practical analogue PID controller, there is interaction between the three terms, and a realisable transfer function may well be:

$$\frac{C_0}{e} = \frac{K(1 + sT_1)(1 + sT_2)}{(sT_1)(1 + \gamma sT_2)}$$

where T_1 and T_2 are respectively equivalent to integral and derivative time constants, and γ is a rate amplitude constant. To limit high frequency gain and phase, an additional low pass filter (first-order lag) of transfer function $1/(1 + sT_3)$ is usually incorporated. To realise this, or any similarly expressed function in digital form with a microprocessor, the system schematic will be as in fig. 11.1. The analogue-to-digital converter must be preceded by a sample-and-hold circuit (to avoid errors caused by its input changing during the period of conversion) and used to regularly sample the process variable value at the transducer output. If the transducer signal is $X(t)$, then after sampling it will be a set of samples $X(nT)$ where n is an integer, and T the sampling period. Any transfer function may be synthesised in digital form, its implementation using these samples in suitable approximations to the operations performed in the unsampled domain. The most important operations in this respect are integral and derivative ones. Conversion to sampled form may be carried out in a number of ways, which may be classified as time-domain (difference equation) or complex sampled domain (z-plane) methods. Some widely used approximations are:

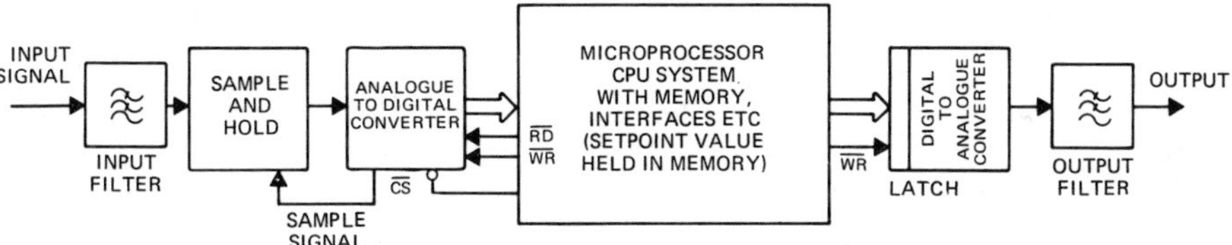

Fig. 11.1 Hardware schematic for control system.

(a) Backward differences for derivative terms (replace $\mathrm{d}x/\mathrm{d}t$ by $(x(nT) - x(n-1)T)/T)$ and simple summation for the integral terms (rectangular summation $\Sigma_{i=0}^{n} x(iT)$). A problem with this naïve approach is the sensitivity of the simple derivative approximation to noise and errors, which implies that some smoothing is required.

(b) Four-point central differences for the derivative terms (replace $\mathrm{d}x/\mathrm{d}t$ with $(1/6T)\ [x(nT) + 3x(n-1)T - 3x(n-2)T - x(n-3T)]$) and trapezoidal rule for integral terms

$$\sum_{i=0}^{n} \frac{[x(nT) + x(n-1)T]}{2}$$

At the expense of speed and complexity of computation, this approach suffers much less from problems of noise.

(c) Tustin's approximation (bilinear transformation) applied to the s-plane transfer function, using a transformation to the z-plane, where z^{-1} may be interpreted as a unit delay. If the transfer function is expressed in the z-plane as the ratio of two polynomials in z^{-1}, the numerator will apply to delayed samples of the input, and the denominator to delayed samples of the output. Complex variable is mapped to the complex z-plane by the relationship

$$s \leftrightarrow K \left[\frac{1 - z^{-1}}{1 + z^{-1}}\right]$$

Constant K is usually taken as $2/T$.

Usually, the sampling period is made much smaller than the smallest time constant in the system, which makes it possible to further simplify some of the approximations. Returning to the realisation of analogue controller replacements, an ideal PID controller may be implemented as

$$C_{\mathrm{O}} = K\, e(nT) + \frac{K}{T_{\mathrm{I}}}\, T \sum_{i=0}^{n} e(iT) + KT_{\mathrm{D}}\, \frac{e(nT) - e(n-1)T}{T}$$

where $e(nT) = PV\,(nT) - SP$.

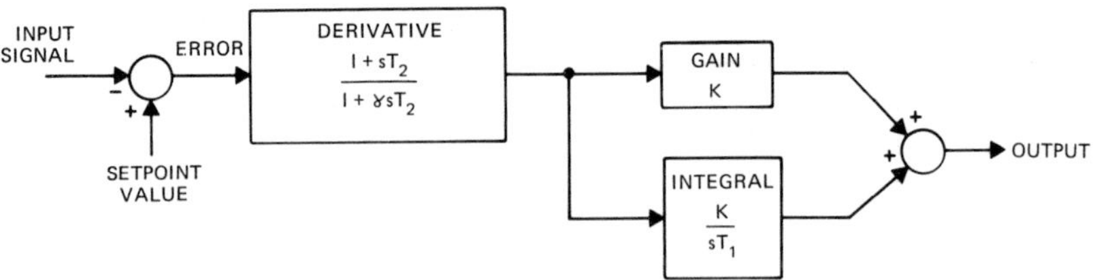

Fig. 11.2 Interactive PID formulation.

A non-ideal (interactive) PID controller may be implemented by the block schematic shown in fig. 11.2, (expressed in s-plane terms). The integral and derivative terms may be implemented by separate algorithms, derived using approximation (a). Thus the derivative term D becomes

$$\mathrm{D}(nT) = \mathrm{D}(n-1)T + \frac{1}{\gamma}\,[e(nT) - e(n-1)T] + \frac{T}{\gamma T_2 + T}\,[e(nT) - \mathrm{D}(n-1)T]$$

Implementation of this or a similar algorithm requires operations where speed and precision is important – multiplication and division, where rounding or truncation is likely to be performed on the result, and subtraction of comparable quantities, where the accuracy of the result is significantly less than the accuracy of the operands. With an 8-bit microprocessor, most control schemes will require multiple-precision arithmetic (reducing speed) and only the pseudo-16-bit microprocessors (such as 6809 or 8088) possess hardware multiply-divide facilities. The 16-bit microprocessor allows much faster operation, and may implement a suitably-designed algorithm without resorting to multiple-precision arithmetic. An important consideration with controller design is dynamic range – often, a control system must cope with a wide range of signal levels, and accommodating the range by increasing precision, while the obvious approach, will increase computation time and possibly lower the sampling rate. A possible compromise may be single-precision block floating-point (where all variables are adjusted by shifting at each stage of the computation so that they all have the same implied exponent value), or, alternatively, it may be necessary to use a true floating-point representation either in software or hardware (as a coprocessor). The improved multibit shifts, hardware multiply-divide, the relative ease with which high precision and wide dynamic range may be achieved, and its low cost make the 16-bit microprocessor ideal for analogue controller replacement. Once the controller algorithm is in digital form, additions may be made to allow 'bumpless' transfer from manual to automatic control, to avoid any integrator saturation problems (if an error persists), and to add further terms (such as feed-forward or deadtime compensation).

For many process control applications, the response times are long enough to allow more than one control loop per microprocessor system. Unlike analogue techniques which would approach the problem of multiple control loops by duplication of hardware, microprocessor realisation may use a standard software routine and requires only multiple interfaces. 16-bit microprocessor capabilities in interrupt handling, memory management and protection and system support lend themselves well to multiple loop implementation. In no way does implementation of multiple control loops by a single microprocessor preclude the construction of a supervisory scheme using a master microprocessor – it is just as easy to read multiple variables and adjust multiple setpoint values and parameters on a single microprocessor as if they were on individual microprocessors.

11.3.3 ADAPTIVE CONTROL AND SELF-TUNING CONTROLLERS

Although it is useful to replace analogue controllers directly by digital ones, allowing easy digital supervisory control, a more important aspect of adopting a microprocessor approach is that it allows those controllers to be made self-tuning, eliminating the need for manual adjustment of controller parameters to match the characteristics of the controlled process. In essence, although a conventional three term controller may be tuned to perform well in the presence of random disturbances to the controlled process, and when process dynamics are poorly defined, a more sophisticated approach may be appropriate where system dynamics may change with time and where frequent set point changes are liable to be made. A fixed parameter controller achieves a compromise between good steady-state performance which minimises disturbances, and good dynamic performance when setpoint changes are made, and this compromise is good only for the system dynamics for which the controller was tuned. A self-tuning controller (fig. 11.3) is considerably more complex than a fixed-parameter one, and consists of three basic elements:

(a) A feedback controller which uses a difference equation algorithm to control to a setpoint value in the same way as a conventional controller.
(b) A parameter estimator which monitors the controlled process responses to

controller outputs, and estimates the process dynamics from these inputs and outputs. Using an internal model of the process, the estimator computes a set of parameters for the model which make it match the process responses most closely. This is usually done using a recursive algorithm.

(c) An algorithm which takes the parameter estimator outputs, and computes coefficients for the feedback controller algorithm which will tune it to the estimated model of the process, and hence to the process itself.

The algorithm which computes coefficients for the controller normally takes no account of the model estimated-parameter uncertainties, and may be combined with the parameter estimator in a single algorithm which performs both functions.

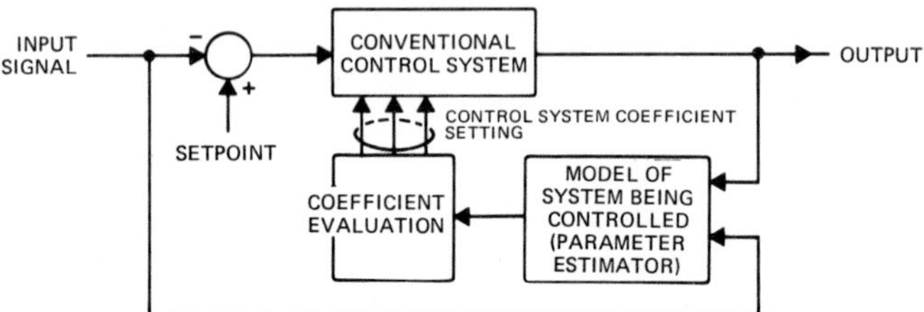

Fig. 11.3 Self-tuning controller.

Unlike the fixed-parameter controller, the self-tuning controller has only become practical with the advent of low cost computing power. The 16-bit microprocessor is an ideal device for implementation so long as the estimator is kept simple (typically, a recursive least-squares approach is used, with the model parameters simply related, by constant factors to the control algorithm coefficients). The requirement on accuracy is more stringent than with a fixed-parameter controller, since inaccuracies in coefficient estimates will increase with the number of computations, and 16 bits is often a minimum acceptable precision. If a minimum acceptable precision is not achieved, poor performance and perhaps instability may result.

11.3.4 DISTRIBUTED CONTROL

When digital or analogue controllers are used in a multiple-loop control system, a distributed system may be created where a supervisory computer is linked to all controllers in the system (whether adaptive or fixed-parameter) and seeks to optimise overall system performance using some cost parameter, by altering controller setpoints according to some optimisation algorithm. By good system design, a hierarchical system such as this one may keep a process running in an optimal manner, and has the advantage that if the supervisory computer fails, the system will continue to be controlled, though in a way which becomes increasingly non-optimal as lack of supervision persists.

Information flow in a hierarchical system implemented using all digital controllers is relatively straightforward, since the individual control loops will already possess the information required in digital form, and this may be transmitted in serial or parallel form to the optimising microprocessor. One potential problem is that of synchronisation; generally, the individual controllers will be asynchronous in operation, and, if they interact, the supervisory computer may require its variable values to be taken at the same instant. Various schemes can overcome problems with synchronisation using:

(a) A common interrupt, and shared memory for parameter passing.
(b) A polling scheme controlled by the supervisory microprocessor.
(c) Running all controllers from a common clock (i.e. synchronously) generated by the supervisory microprocessor.

The optimisation scheme itself may be very complex, and heavily tax the capabilities of any microprocessor, but will often allow much longer response times from the optimisation microprocessor than those of the individual three-term or self-tuning control loops. With a supervisory system, it is often required that the supervisory computer provide a log of process operation, process statistics, and allow manual override, allowing an operator to fix set points in place of the automatic scheme. Unlike individual controllers, the supervisory microprocessor will usually require a reasonably sophisticated real time multitasking operating system to accommodate these requirements, and may well require disk storage and other peripherals.

11.3.5 ROBOTICS

Rather on the fringe of the control field, but an increasingly important microprocessor applications area, is automated assembly and production, test and inspection. Industrial automation is moving towards the general-purpose machine, or robot, capable of performing a wide range of different tasks. Numerical control for machine tools has been well established over the past decade and a half and has proved immensely successful, leading to the development of automatic welders and paint spraying machines. The next logical step has been the design of machines which can be programmed in a learning mode, by human operator example, rather than by laboriously writing down the steps for (for example) three-axis matching platform control, depth of cuts, and all the other parameters for a given task. Many current industrial robots are of this type, and, while they work well when fed with correctly-oriented parts of the expected size and shape, they will not accommodate misaligned parts, and will fail to recognise damaged parts.

The next generation of industrial robots will possess sensors allowing them to identify parts irrespective of orientation and distance, and manipulators with force feedback, allowing them to handle delicate objects with a minimum of damage. Their controllers will require the advanced processing afforded by the 16-bit microprocessor in the following areas:

(a) Image and pattern processing and recognition in real time.
(b) Learning software, which will pave the way towards systems which will be able to tackle problems unforeseen by their designers.

(c) Motor and manipulator controllers.
(d) Multiple microprocessor systems.

Naturally, use of 16-bit machines will carry the usual microcomputer (as opposed to minicomputer) advantages of small size, low weight, low cost and low power consumption, all of which are important considerations with industrial automation.

Image processing requires good numerical manipulation for spatial translation, rotation and scaling as well as feature extraction, all of which may be necessary before recognition algorithms may be applied. Fast multiplication and division are a must, and benefits may be gained by using floating-point hardware (or coprocessors). Because of the large amount of stored data in a typical raster-scan picture (typically, a high-resolution system may be 512 X 512 points X 8 bit colour and luminance; a low resolution system may be 128 X 128 points X 3 bit monochrome), addressing is important, and the large addressing ranges of the modern 16-bit machines are clearly useful. Bit manipulation capabilities, too, may be significant if the information is packed more than one picture point (pixel) to a byte. Recognition algorithms impose a heavy microprocessor load too, especially if a large number of different objects, some similar in appearance, are to be identified. Often, identification will start by finding the optical centre (centroid) of the image of a solid object, rotation and scaling so that its major axis through the centroid is in a known alignment and a known size, followed by comparison of a set of features (edges, corners, internal details) with sets corresponding to the known objects. A popular interactive, keyboard-driven image processing system uses an 8086 as its base, and doubtless the other 16-bit machines may equally well be used in future systems, including those on industrial robots.

Learning software is a subject still in its infancy, but one which promises to become very exciting in the future. The simplest learning program will merely allow a robot to be led through a sequence of operations by a skilled human operator, and will remember and repeat them, editing out any errors but intolerant of environment and other changes. A more sophisticated system, which will adapt to changing conditions and tasks, will require an equally sophisticated software support package, perhaps something like PROLOG, a system programming language well suited to database manipulation and one which, like LISP (the well known list processing mainframe language), is a descriptive language (describing what is required from the machine) rather than a prescriptive or algorithmic one (describing how the machine can compute what is required from it). PROLOG was developed about ten years ago at a French university as a practical tool for formal logic programming, and is widely used in the artificial intelligence research community. The language uses the concepts of a formal logic system called predicate calculus to create a structure whereby a program becomes a description of a set of logical relations (which may define both data retrieval and computation) and mechanisms for pattern matching, record structuring, list manipulation and search strategies. Conventional ideas of GOTO, DO . . ., WHILE, assignment, and reference no longer exist. To quote one of the marketing documents for PROLOG, 'A PROLOG program consists of a clear and concise description of the problem in terms of facts, relationships and rules. The execution of the program corresponds to a controlled deduction through these facts and rules to generate solutions to the problem'. This is just the structure required for a robotic 'expert system' which will go beyond present techniques.

The internal syntax of a PROLOG program regards that program as a list structure (of LISP) which uses sentences (either binary, in the form of two terms or variables linked by a relationship name, or non-binary, simple or conditional) which exist in its workspace or environment. Commands allow adding a new sentence, removing an old one or removing a relationship, definition of rules, query statements and input-output. In most implementations, PROLOG uses an interpreter and is highly interactive, requiring a human operator. While these may not be suitable for some real time applications, the philosophy of this approach is likely to be adopted for future robot development. Naturally, this technique is very intensive in its use of computer resources, especially memory and CPU registers. It is available on minicomputers, and also on an 8-bit (Z80) microprocessor, as Micro-Prolog, as are other advice languages. To realise the full power of the technique, a computer architecture like that of the modern 16-bit microprocessor is necessary, allowing a large addressing space, fast data manipulation, and the sophisticated pattern matching and searching required. The final aspect of robotics (and many other application areas) of interest to 16-bit designers is the likely adoption of multiple microprocessor systems which will allow separate microprocessors for robot sensor processing, manipulator and motor controls, and 'intelligence'. Once again, the new generation of microprocessors is ideally suited, by design, for implementation of multiple microprocessor systems, and will allow the construction of very sophisticated machines.

11.4 Digital signal processing

Many aspects of signal processing are amenable to computer implementation, but some will be inappropriate. For instance, the fast Fourier transform (FFT), is far better performed with a special purpose integrated circuit (made by AMI, or TRW) than in software. Certain types of filtering may be easier with an analogue microprocessor (such as the Intel 2920). Nevertheless, for adaptive processing, for applications which require filtering followed by further digital processing (rather than requiring an immediate analogue output) or for non-standard signal analysis, a general-purpose programmable CPU is an advantage. Image processing (or two-dimensional filtering) is another area where the power of the new 16-bit microprocessors will be useful. A number of features stand out in this respect: 16-bit precision and hardware (on-chip) multiply-divide allow complex filter structures without too many problems with roundoff or truncation errors (which manifest themselves as electrical noise); microprocessor speed allows higher sampling rates than with 8-bit microprocessors; invariably, fast filtering routines will be written in assembly code rather than a high-level language, and the structure of the modern 16-bit microprocessor allows plenty of flexibility with addressing modes and use of subroutines. For many microprocessors it is the multiplications inherent in most filtering schemes that impose most of the time overheads on the algorithm.

Nagle and Nelson[1] have explored digital filter implementation on 16-bit microprocessors, and have written and run a number of representative programs. Their paper examines various digital filter structures, and attempts to arrive at some optimum structure which is a compromise between coefficient sensitivity (since filter coefficients are quantised to a finite precision) and operating speed. To summarise, their paper examines various arrangements for second-order filter sections which may be cascaded or paralleled to form more complex structures with better frequency characteristics, and then goes on to give examples of 8086 programs for each type of second-order section (with approximate timings, assuming a 4 MHz clock), and finally compares other 16-bit microprocessors with the 8086 for realisation of a specific eighth order cascaded filter. The conclusions are that for sampling rates up to a maximum of 1 to 5 kHz (depending on the clock frequency of the particular microprocessor used), a 16-bit microprocessor with on-chip hardware multiply-divide, is a very realistic proposition, and that with appropriate choice of filter structure, good results may be achieved.

11.4.1 DIGITAL FILTER FUNDAMENTALS

A digital filter, like a sampled-data control system, uses (usually) regular time sampling of an analogue signal input, its quantisation (unavoidable when dealing with a digital system of limited wordlength), and the basic operations of adding and multiplying a combination of fixed coefficients and samples. As before, if an analogue signal $y(t)$ is sampled, the result is a set $\sum_{\text{all } n} y(nT)$ samples, where T is the period between successive samples and n is an integer. The idea of a digital filter is a piece of hardware or an algorithm which will manipulate a time-sequence of samples (derived from a continuous waveform) so as to create a desired spectral (frequency response) characteristic. While this may sometimes be a characteristic that could be achieved using analogue passive or active filters, it is also possible to create frequency response characteristics which would be difficult to achieve by analogue means.

In computing this algorithm, the basic operations are those of delay, multiplication and addition. The transfer function may be expressed in the form

$$y(nT) = \sum_{m=0}^{M} a_m X(n-m)T + \sum_{q=1}^{Q} b_q y(n-q)T$$

where $y(nT)$ is the current output value, X are the input values $X(nT)$, $X(n-1)T$ ... $X(n-M)T$, where $X(nT)$ is the current input, and y are the previous outputs $y(n-1)T$ ... $y(n-Q)T$. The coefficients a_m and b_q define the response of the filter.

Realisation of this equation is of major importance; by good choice of the order in which operations are performed, errors in the response and quantisation noise, worsened by round-off effects during calculation, may be minimised. The structure of a filter may be represented in diagrammatic form using delay blocks and indicating data flows. For a hardware realisation, this diagram will indicate the physical structure of the filter, while for a software realisation, it will indicate how the algorithm should be coded.

11.4.2 FILTER STRUCTURES

Digital filter structure invariably rests on the way in which a second-order transfer function is realised; second-order modules (hardware or software may then be combined in series (cascade) or parallel to synthesise the desired response). Although splitting the filter into modules like this is not the only possible way to realise it, it is the most satisfactory practical way, and helps the designer to avoid coefficient sensitivity problems (in addition, it offers some advantages in data handling, when the filter is implemented in software).

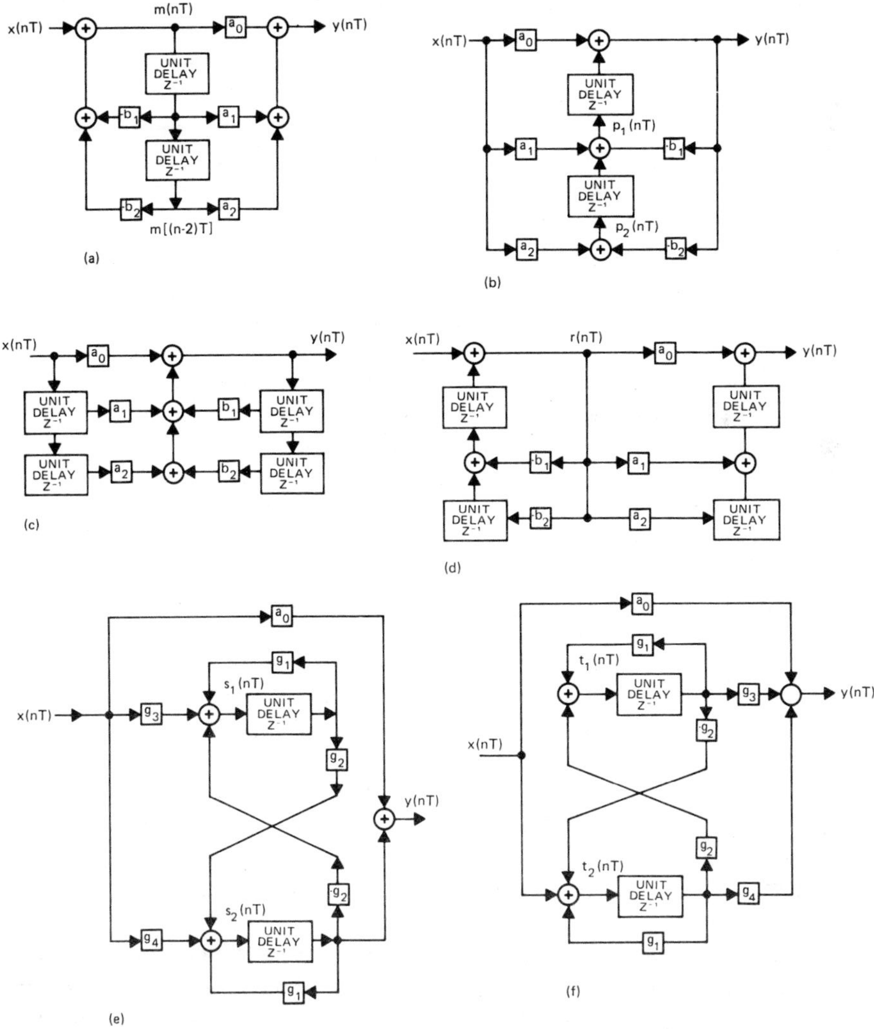

Fig. 11.4 Digital filter structures: (a) Structure 1, (b) Structure 2, (c) Structure 3, (d) Structure 4, (e) Structure 5, (f) Structure 6.

Design of the complete filter and calculation of all its coefficients parallels that of a conventional analogue filter, and is usually expressed in terms of a z-plane transfer function (rather than an s-plane one, which for sampled data would have poles and zeros repeated in the direction of the imaginary axis). In such a transfer function, z^{-1} may be interpreted as a unit sample delay, and generally, the function may be expressed as the ratio of two polynomials in z^{-1}, i.e.

$$H(z) = \frac{a_0 + a_1 z^{-1} + \ldots a_M z^{-M}}{1 + b_1 z^{-1} + \ldots b_Q z^{-Q}}$$

will be the z-plane transfer function corresponding to the sampled time series expression for $y(nT)$. The differences in filter structure correspond to different arrangements of this equation. The four 'direct-form' structures are shown in fig. 11.4; the first two are the 'canonical' forms which possess a minimum number of unit delays (for an nth order transfer function, a minimum of n unit delays is required for realisation). While the canonical forms may be the most economic for a hardware digital filter, they will not necessarily be the preferred forms for a software realisation. The other two structures minimise the number of summing junctions or signal distribution points at the expense of doubling the number of delay elements. By examining each structure in turn, it may be seen that all these direct structures give the same transfer function

$$y(nT) = a_0 x(nT) + a_1 x[(n-1)T] + a_2 x[(n-2)T] - b_1 y[(n-1)T] - b_2 y[(n-2)T]$$

Equivalent to a z-plane second-order response

$$H(z) = \frac{a_0 + a_1 z^{-1} + a_2 z^{-2}}{1 + b_1 z^{-1} + b_2 z^{-2}}$$

Structure 1: (Fig. 11.4(a))

$$m(nT) = x(nT) - b_1 m[(n-1)T] - b_2 m[(n-2)T]$$
$$y(nT) = a_0 m(nT) + a_1 m[(n-1)T] + a_2 m[(n-2)T]$$

Transforming to the z-plane:

$$M(z) = X(z) - b_1 z^{-1} M(z) - b_2 z^{-2} M(z)$$
$$Y(z) = a_0 M(z) + a_1 z^{-1} M(z) + a_2 z^{-2} M(z)$$

and elimination of $M(z)$ gives the correct expression for $H(z)$.

Structure 2: (Fig. 11.4(b))

$$y(nT) = a_0 x(nT) + p_1 [(n-1)T]$$
$$p_1(nT) = a_1 x(nT) - b_1 y(nT) + p_2[(n-1)T]$$
$$p_2(nT) = a_2 x(nT) - b_2 y(nT)$$

Transforming to the z-plane:

$$Y(z) = a_0 X(z) + z^{-1} p_1(z)$$
$$p_1(z) = a_1 X(z) - b_1 Y(z) + z^{-1} p_2(z)$$
$$p_2(z) = a_2 X(z) - b_2 Y(z)$$

Elimination of $p_1(z), p_2(z)$ gives $H(z)$ as before.

Structure 3: (Fig. 11.4(c)) $H(z)$ or $y(nT)$ by inspection.

Structure 4: (Fig. 11.4(d))

$$r(nT) = X(nT) - b_1 r[(n-1)T] - b_2 r[(n-2)T]$$
$$y(nT) = a_0 r(nT) + a_1 r[(n-1)T] + a_2 r[(n-2)T]$$

Transforming to the z-plane:

$$R(z) = X(z) - b_1 z^{-1} R(z) - b_2 z^{-2} R(z)$$
$$Y(z) = a_0 R(z) + a_1 z^{-1} R(z) + a_2 z^{-2} R(z)$$

Once again, eliminate $R(z)$ to give $H(z)$.

'Cross-coupled' second-order structures are also a possibility (Fig. 11.4). The two shown are canonical, and the second is the transpose of the first.

Structure 5: (Fig. 11.4(e))

$$y(nT) = a_0 x(nT) + s_2[(n-1)T]$$
$$s_2(nT) = s_2 s_1[(n-1)T] + g_1 s_2[(n-1)T] + g_4 x(nT)$$
$$s_1(nT) = -g_2 s_2[(n-1)T] + g_1 s_1[(n-1)T] + g_3 x(nT)$$

Taking z-transforms

$$Y(z) = a_0 X(z) + z^{-1} S_2(z)$$
$$S_2(z) = g_2 z^{-1} S_1(z) + g_1 z^{-1} S_2(z) + g_4 X(z)$$
$$S_1(z) = -g_2 z^{-1} S_2(z) + g_1 z^{-1} S_1(z) + g_3 X(z)$$

This can be manipulated to give the same form of $H(z)$, relating $g_1 - g_4$ to $a_0 - a_2$ and b_1, b_2, although this may be done, the structure is derived from an alternative expression

$$H(z) = a_0 + \frac{A}{z+p} + \frac{A^*}{z-p^*}$$

where p is the complex pole position. Then

$$g_1 = -\mathrm{Re}[p]$$
$$g_2 = -\mathrm{Im}[p]$$
$$g_3 = 2\mathrm{Im}\,[A]$$
$$g_4 = 2\mathrm{Re}[A]$$

Structure 6: (Fig. 11.4(f)) As structure 5.

11.4.3 TIMINGS

The Nagle-Nelson paper studies implementation with a 4 MHz 8086. With a 16-bit microprocessor, the integer number range in two's complement form is $-2^{15} \leqslant N \leqslant 2^{15} - 1$; it is usual to consider fractional numbers 'normalised' to the equivalent range $-1 \leqslant N \leqslant 1 - 2^{-15}$. For the filters considered, coefficients exist outside this range (some with magnitudes between 1 and 2) and must be scaled, with scaling to compensate after the operations involving them have been completed. The completion times were measured by writing representative routines, all to the same format. The output processing routine is the minimum possible code between reading the latest sample and computation of the corresponding output value (assuming that as much as possible of the computation has been done during the previous sample interval). This approach minimises the delay between sampling and corresponding output value, the overall computation time, of course, determines the maximum sampling rate. For second-order sections, the Nagle-Nelson results were

Structure	1	2	3	4	5	6
Input-output lag (μs)	177	162	164	177	162	162
Minimum sample period (μs)	793	786	758	779	1044	1056

To give a more convincing demonstration, the authors coded an example of a real fourth-order filter, used in part of the space shuttle control system. For the same 4 MHz 8086, the maximum sampling rate would 1638 Hz, and input-to-output lag 207.5 μs (using parallel type 1 structures).

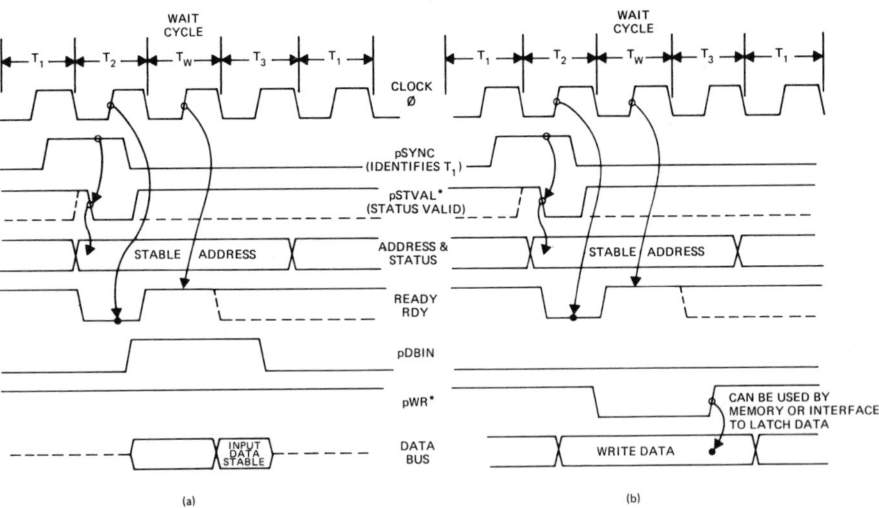

Fig. 11.5

In order to give a comparison between different microprocessor types, the authors designed an eighth-order elliptic low-pass filter (–60 dB stopband and ½ dB passband ripple), implemented using four cascaded type 1 second-order sections. While, like all benchmarks, these timings may be taken merely as rough indicators of performance, they do give some idea of the sampling rates which may be achieved with complex filter implementations.

Microprocessor	8086	Z8000	MC68000	TMS990	9445
Input-output lag (μs)	213	156	82	254	48
Sample period (μs)	856	594	327	1000	194
Microprocessor clock (MHz)	5	4	8	3.3	15

11.4.4 OTHER CONSIDERATIONS

The first parts of this section describe use of microprocessor algorithms for stand-alone fixed-coefficient filtering; it is most likely that in practice any stand-alone filtering will be adaptive, or any fixed-coefficient filtering will be only the first stage of, for example, a complex control algorithm. Since many control functions require only modest sampling rates, filtering input data by digital algorithms is a realistic possibility. Allied to filtering is estimation of time-signal characteristics (spectral characteristics, probability distribution functions, etc.). Such computational requirements as fast Fourier transform, fast Walsh transform, correlation and convolution may routinely be required for data logging, plant characterisation, alarm monitoring (e.g. for vibration resonance within a specific frequency band) and instrumentation. Many characteristics of such signal processing are similar to those of filtering, consisting basically of multiplication, addition, and data movement operations.

A further point to note with signal processing algorithms is the one of precision; while coefficient quantisation problems may be bypassed by choice of filter design and with appropriate scaling, like that used by Nagle and Nelson, a form of block floating-point operation, problems of signal quantisation may be less easily overcome, since not only quantisation noise, but also signal dynamic range, must be considered. Since analogue-to-digital converters with precisions of greater than 16 bits are still rare, the problem may not be a computational one, but a conversion one; nevertheless, there are still occasions when dynamic range considerations will imply the use of floating-point arithmetic, most conveniently implemented in hardware, as a coprocessor or alternative. When a block floating-point approach gives sampling rates in the region 1-5 kHz, software floating-point routines will cause this limit to deteriorate considerably.

Multiple microprocessors have been used for signal processing using 8-bit microprocessors, and will remain an option with 16-bit ones, but such an approach will only be warranted in a very few cases. Image processing by microprocessor is confined to non-real-time applications (so far as fast-scan video is concerned) and may be an extension of the 'one-dimensional' time sequence filtering to a two-dimensional spatial filtering technique. Like simpler digital filters, design of two-dimensional filters is well-documented in the literature, and since the concept of sampling rate does not occur in non-real-time processing, the 16-bit microprocessor, supporting large video display image memories, is ideal for the task. Image enhancement for slow-scan television or facsimile pictures using filtering, simple line-to-line or frame-to-frame correlation, or feature extraction, is ideally suited to the 16-bit microprocessor architecture.

11.5 System bus standards

All of the major manufacturers have issued definitions of system bus standards (mechanical, electrical and logical) for systems built with their own microprocessors and for their own microprocessor-and-interface cards. Quite distinct from the bus at the microprocessor CPU pins (often referred to as a 'component-level' bus), the system bus will normally not simply repeat the component-level signals, but define its own set of signals to give it some independence from a specific CPU[2-4].

Historically, the concept of a system bus standard gained acceptance from the efforts of equipment manufacturers rather than from the semiconductor companies themselves. With the first 8-bit personal computers came the so-called 'hobbyist' S100 bus, which started life as a manufacturer's internal standard, and rapidly became a widely supported system, although lack of a definitive bus description led to incompatibilities between different manufacturers S100 products. When the market for single-board computers and interface cards developed, each semiconductor manufacturer designed his own bus and produced cards to fit it; the manufacturers of card-based systems, too, developed similar buses. As the world of card-based products evolved, so bus standards hardened, and today, in the 8-bit microprocessor field, the dominant systems are Multibus, Exorciser Bus, STD Bus and S100, which has gained respectability by its adoption as a standard by the IEEE. The 16-bit world is much more sophisticated than the 8-bit one, with its emphasis not just on interfacing with peripheral devices and the outside world, but also on multiprocessor operation, working between a local bus and a global system bus, complex interrupt structures, use of memory management devices with a vast physical addressing range, and higher operating speeds. The requirements and design options for a bus structure to satisfy 16-bit microprocessor use may be summarised:

(a) A high data rate should be supported, to allow transfers over the bus without holding up microprocessor operation (typically 10 MHz maximum).
(b) A wide addressing capability, in the megabyte region, is necessary to support the current generation of 16-bit microprocessors, and should extend beyond this to accommodate future expansion.
(c) A data field width of 16-bits, but with the possibility of 8-bit transfers (including byte-swapping) may be desirable.
(d) Data transfers by handshaking (i.e. asynchronous transfers) may be preferable to the synchronous transfers of the 'component-level' bus. Since the adoption of synchronous handshake protocol can cause a system hang-up if no response is received, some provision for a 'watchdog' timer is required,

which will break the potential deadlock, and indicate a bus error.

(e) Bus buffering and termination are desirable, from a speed and system integrity viewpoint, with some allowance in the control signal protocol for buffer propagation delays.

(f) Some form of interrupt handling is essential, and requires consideration of two factors – hardware prioritisation and interrupt management. Hardware prioritisation may be accomplished by daisy-chaining interrupt requests, so that card slots in a bus backplane will have fixed priority, or by parallel lines, each of a fixed priority. Acknowledgement must be arranged so as not to slow down interrupt response more than necessary.

(g) Some form of bus access control to allow multiple bus master devices, any one of which may request, gain, and relinquish access to the bus. This should allow fast DMA via the bus, multiple microprocessor operation, and some form of management protocol for resource sharing (and 'lock-out'). In a multiple busmaster situation, provision must be made to avoid any conflicts between local 'component-level' buses on individual cards, and the system backplane bus.

All of the modern bus standards go some way towards meeting these requirements; ideally, all signals on the system bus should be independent of microprocessor type, but some specific signals are difficult to avoid. Generally, there are two distinct ways to handle read and write operations on a local component-level bus – the first (8080, Z80 style) is to have distinct read and write control signals which signify not only the type of operation, but also its timing. The second (6800, 6502 style) approach is to have a single ($R/\overline{W}$) line to indicate the operation, with a separate strobe or synchronisation signal to fix the timing. These two approaches typified the divisions in the 8-bit microprocessor world, and their influence has extended to the 16-bit one (note that peripheral interface devices designed to work with an 8080 component level bus will normally also operate on a 6800 style bus, but any $R/\overline{W}$ set up time requirement for 6800-style interfaces may not be easily satisfied by signals on an 8080-style bus). Another spill-over from the 8-bit world has been the decision whether to include specific I/O signals on a bus, or to constrain the designer to a memory-mapped architecture.

The buses that are likely to become most popular are those for which there are the largest number and variety of cards available, and an important aspect may be whether current 8-bit cards can operate on a 16-bit bus system (this may involve swapping bytes between upper and lower halves of the data bus) and whether 8-bit and 16-bit microprocessors may be mixed in a single system. Buses like S100 (IEEE Standard 696) and Multibus (formerly Intel, but now the subject of IEEE Standard 796) have grown up from the 8-bit world and have been extended to accommodate the requirements of systems using the new 16-bit microprocessors. In principle, it is possible to use 8-bit cards mixed with 16-bit ones, but for S100, some of the changes made in its adoption by the IEEE have made it difficult to use cards designed before the new standard was issued. The newly-designed buses (Versabus, VME bus, Z-bus and Futurebus), while they will support byte transfers, have as yet no range of 8-bit cards compatible with them.

11.5.1 S100 BUS (IEEE-696)[5]

This bus, derived from a standard evolved in the earliest days of personal computers, is rather a compromise between performance and maintaining some degree of compatibility with the original definition. The bus pins distribute unregulated d.c. power at nominal +8 V and ±16 V levels and each card must provide its own regulation. The bus possesses sixteen bidirectional data lines (used as eight input, eight output for byte operations) and twenty-four address lines, and carry a number (eight) of status signals which identify bus operations, with a disabling control line SDSB(M) and a status-valid strobe pSTVAL(M) (where suffix (M) indicates bus master origin). Other bus lines may be grouped as control output lines (five), control input lines (six), DMA control lines (eight), vectored interrupt lines (eight), and system facilities lines (9). The influence of the 8080 (8-bit) microprocessor signals on the design of this bus is very evident, and in some areas, has compromised bus performance severely. Ground-true signals are indicated with an asterisk (*). The suffix after a signal name indicates its origin: M = master, S = slave, B = bus.

11.5.1.1 S100 bus (IEEE-696) status lines

These are:

(a) sM1(M), which indicates that the current cycle is an instruction fetch;
(b) sOUT(M), which identifies a data transfer bus cycle to an output device;
(c) sINP(M), which identifies a data transfer bus cycle from an input device;
(d) sMEMR(M), which identifies a bus cycle that transfers data from memory to a bus master (other than instruction fetch and interrupt acknowledge cycles);
(e) sHLTA(M), which acknowledges execution of an 8080/8085 HLT instruction (halt acknowledge);
(f) sINTA(M), which identifies any bus cycles which occur in response to an interrupt request signal on INT (interrupt acknowledge);
(g) sWO*(M), which identifies a bus cycle which transfers information from a bus master to a slave (write cycle);
(h) sXTRQ*(M), which requests any 16-bit slaves to assert SIXTN (for identification) (sixteen bit data transfer request).

11.5.1.2 Control signals (Fig. 11.5)

Eleven control lines (six output, five input) carry the following signals:

(a) The control output bus:
  (i) pSYNC*(M), which indicates the start of a new bus cycle.
  (ii) pSTVAL*(M), which, in conjunction with pSYNC indicates that stable address and status may be sampled from the bus, using this signal as a strobe.
  (iii) pDBIN(M), which acts as a generalised read strobe that gates data from

an addressed slave onto the data bus.

(iv) pWR*(M), which acts as a generalised write strobe used to write data from the data bus into an addressed slave device.

(v) pHLDA(M), a hold acknowledge signal that indicates to the highest priority bus temporary master that the permanent master is relinquishing control of the bus. (A system is allowed up to 16 bus master devices, each of which has a priority, plus an additional higher priority device. This highest priority device – normally a CPU – is considered to be the permanent master while all the lower priority devices are considered to be temporary bus masters.)

(b) The input control bus:

(i) RDY(S), used by bus slave devices to synchronise the masters to the response time of the slave. The master CPU is assumed to insert dummy 'wait-state' clock cycles into its operation for the duration of this signal.

(ii) XRDY(S), is a special ready line dedicated to a single slave, such as the front panel of a personal computer, or single instruction step switch.

(iii) INT*(S), is a maskable interrupt request line.

(iv) NMI*(S), is a non-maskable interrupt request line.

(v) HOLD*(M), is a hold request line used by temporary masters to request control of the system bus (may be masked, and has some timing constraints).

(vi) SIXTN*(S), is a response to SXTRQ* and indicates that the request 16-bit transfer is possible.

11.5.1.3 DMA control

DMA (direct memory access) is achieved by using bus control lines HOLD and pHLDA, and additional, specifically DMA control lines, which arbitrate between simultaneous requests, and handle the actual transfers. DMA implies that the bus is transferred from a permanent master (CPU) to a temporary one, and implies that any line drivers associated with address, data, control outputs and status of the permanent master should be disabled during a DMA cycle. The lines are:

(a) DMA 0* to DMA 3*(M), four lines which arbitrate between devices requesting DMA. When requests are made, each requesting device puts its own priority onto these lines, which select the highest priority after a settling time.

(b) ADSB*(M), address bus driver disable.

(c) DODSB*(M), data output disable.

(d) SDSB*(M), status disable.

(e) CDSB*(M), control output disable.

The last four signals allow the permanent master address, data, status, and control signals to be removed from the bus and replaced by signals from a temporary bus master.

11.5.1.4 Vectored interrupt request lines

Eight interrupt lines are provided which are used in conjunction with INT to arbitrate among eight levels of interrupt request priority. They are typically implemented as inputs to a slave priority interrupt controller which masks and priorities the requests, and asserts INT, and will respond to the INTA return signal by making its vectoring data available on the data bus.

11.5.1.5 System facilities

These perform miscellaneous functions for system housekeeping, such as reset, phantom overlayed devices, etc. They are:

(a) System clock Ø(B), generated by the permanent master and from which all bus cycles are derived.
(b) CLOCK (B), a 2 MHz ± 0.5% clock, unrelated to the system clock, for use by timers baud-rate generators, etc.
(c) RESET*(B), resets all bus masters.
(d) SLAVE CLR*(B), resets all slave devices.
(e) POC*(B), power-on reset, which asserts both RESET and SLAVE CLR.
(f) MWRT(B), memory write strobe, must be generated by only one device in the system as a result of pWR.$\overline{\text{sOUT}}$.
(g) PHANTOM*(M/S), allows overlayed bus slaves at the same address. When phantom bus slaves are enabled and normal bus slaves disabled.
(h) ERROR*(S), is used to indicate any sort of error (parity, write protect violation, etc.).
(i) PWRFAIL*(B), indicates impending power failure (allowing the microprocessor just enough time to execute a shutdown procedure.

11.5.1.6 S100 with 16-bit microprocessors

The bus has been much improved by the adoption of a reasonably rigorous definition, and it can certainly offer support to 16-bit microprocessor-based cards. The ability to mix 16-bit and 8-bit cards on a single bus backplane and to swap bytes on the data bus (using SIXTN) is useful, and the mechanical specification is reasonably easy to achieve. However, the influence of the 8080 on the original bus is still very visible. The status lines, the interrupt structure, and some of the control lines are virtual duplicates of signals on the 8080 component-level bus. None of the 16-bit microprocessors generate this strange mix of signals, and may suffer speed degradation because of this constraint. There is no regularity among the signals, which are mixed ground-true and high-true, and no effective grouping physically on the bus connector pins, and no explicit signals for asynchronous (handshaking) operation. Bus exchange is reasonably handled, using a single request line and parallel (coded) arbitration, allowing up to sixteen temporary masters.

Nevertheless, the bus, with its widespread support, will continue to hold its own against the more modern, purpose-designed 16-bit buses. Certainly for personal computer systems and for many business systems, S100 will dominate as a bus standard throughout the introduction of 16-bit microprocessors into such equipment.

11.5.2 MULTIBUS (IEEE-796)

Originally an Intel 'in-house' bus designed for the original Intel 8-bit single-board computer (SBC) family, Multibus has grown to encompass 16-bit microprocessor cards and beyond, and has become the subject of an IEEE standard. It is one of the most widely-supported professional bus standards, with the support of a number of manufacturers in the USA estimated at over 100. Unlike S100, which although now extremely successful, had teething troubles as a standard (due to the initial poor definition of line termination), Multibus has been extremely successful from its original launch in the mid-1970s, and has changed relatively little since. The changes that have occurred have been expansion to assign signals to pins that were reserved for future expansion in the initial definition. Multibus is smaller than S100, but the mechanical card definition includes a second auxiliary connector (P2) to supplement to the 86-way P1 Multibus connector, and many of the 60 pins of this connector have been assigned to optional signals, which include facilities for battery operation under power-fail conditions.

The main connector supplies regulated power to a Multibus card, at levels ±5 V, ±12 V and substantial ground connections. In addition, the signals carried may be categorised into four groups: bus controls; interrupts; address, and data. All signals are defined as ground-true (logic '0' = true).

11.5.2.1 Address and data

Multibus supports 20 bits of address bus and 16 bits of bidirectional data with very well-defined timing and electrical drive characteristics. In the original Intel definition, these pins were numbered in hexadecimal, data DATO/ to DATF/ and address ADRO/ through ADRF/ to AD13/ (where / denotes a ground-true signal). In the IEEE definition, they are numbered in decimal D0* to D15* and A0* to A19*. The definition allows 'both 8- and 16-bit data path products. The 16-bit data path products use byte swapping to allow 8-bit and 16-bit products to work together. The standard designates a 20-bit address path. In many systems a 16-bit address path may be sufficient, though not fully 796-bus compatible. The 796 bus allows for both 8- and 16-bit I/O address paths. The 16-bit path products must also be configurable to act as 8-bit path products'.

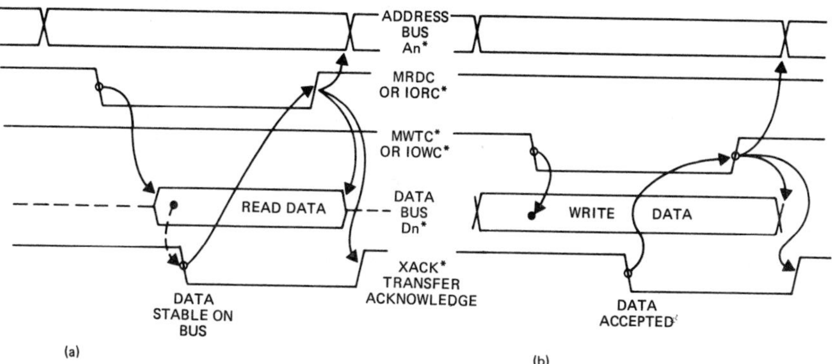

Fig. 11.6

11.5.2.2 Bus controls (Fig. 11.6)

The bus controls are both the master read and write commands and the bus management signals.

Data transfer signals:

(a) MRDC*(M), memory read command.
(b) MWTC*(M), memory write command.
(c) IORC*(M), I/O read command.
(d) IOWC*(M), I/O write command.
(e) XACK*(S), transfer acknowledge, which indicates that data has been placed on, or accepted from, the data lines.
(f) INH1*(S), inhibit 1, (disable RAM). Asserted by one slave (when it detects the specific address during MRDC* or MWTC*) to inhibit another slave's bus activity during the memory read or write operation.
(g) INH2*(S), inhibit 2 (disable ROM or PROM). Asserted as INH1*.

Bus exchange lines:

(h) BCLK*, bus clock (max frequency 10 MHz).
(i) BREQ*, bus request: used by bus masters in a priority resolution circuit to indicate a request for control of the bus.
(j) BPRN*, BPRO*, bus priority. May be daisy-chained throughout the system. As an input, BPRN* indicates that no higher priority master is requesting use of the bus. BPRO* (bus priority out) is an output which, if asserted in a daisy-chained system, will inhibit lower priority masters from requesting control of the bus. They are placed on opposite pins of the double-sided bus connector, to make daisy-chaining easy.
(k) BUSY*, bus busy. Indicates that the bus is in use (and prevents other masters from gaining control of the bus).
(l) CBRQ*, common bus request. A signal which maximises a masters data transfer rate to the bus, by sensing the absence of other bus requests. To the master in control of the bus, it indicates that no other master is requesting control of the bus.

Other signals:

(m) CCLK*, constant clock, a timing source for peripheral devices.
(n) INIT*, initialise, driven by power-on reset, a reset button, or software.
(o) INTA*, interrupt acknowledge.
(p) BHEN*, byte high enable. Used to enable the upper byte of a 16-bit word to drive the data bus. BHEN* may be considered a signal which indicates a 16-bit mode for the bus, whereupon address bit 0 (A0*) indicates an even or odd-byte transfer. When BHEN* is inactive, indicating an 8-bit bus mode, any 16-bit card will swap high bytes onto the low byte of the bus.

11.5.2.3 Interrupts

Eight parallel interrupt request lines INT0* to INT7* are provided. An interrupt is generated by activating one of these level-triggered inputs, and these inputs are prioritised. Interrupts may be of two types: non-bus vectored (where an interrupt vector is transferred over a local bus, rather than Multibus), or bus vectored, where INTA* is used to acquire a vector over the bus, as a byte or sequence of bytes.

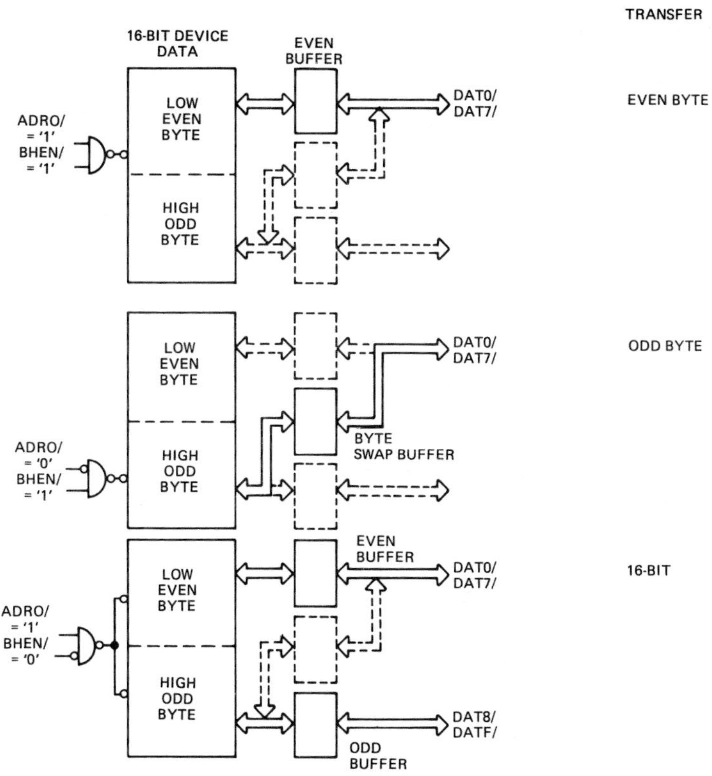

Fig. 11.7

11.5.2.4 Multibus operation

Multibus, while designed for the Intel series of microprocessors, is reasonably microprocessor independent for those microprocessors which have explicit I/O controls and separate read and write controls. Designed for 16-bit operation, the bus has a logical and well-defined set of control signals, well grouped on the physical bus connector. The way in which 16-bit and 8-bit devices can share the bus is illustrated in fig. 11.7 and works well in practice. Asynchronous data transfers allow a mix of master and slave speeds, but to avoid lockout if there is no handshake acknowledge (XACK), a watchdog timer is necessary on each bus master. The interrupt structure is reasonably versatile – non-bus vectored interrupt controller local to the bus master (CPU) will allow most types of microprocessor to use the bus interrupts. Bus vectored interrupts are a little more specific to Intel, using multiple INTA* commands to acquire a vector over the bus. These are defined to be of two types: two successive INTA* commands transfer a single byte interrupt vector, and three successive INTA* commands transfer a two-byte vector (cf. CPU component-level bus). Only one type of bus-vectored interrupt may be serviced by a given bus, but both bus-vectored and non-bus-vectored interrupts may be supported at the same time.

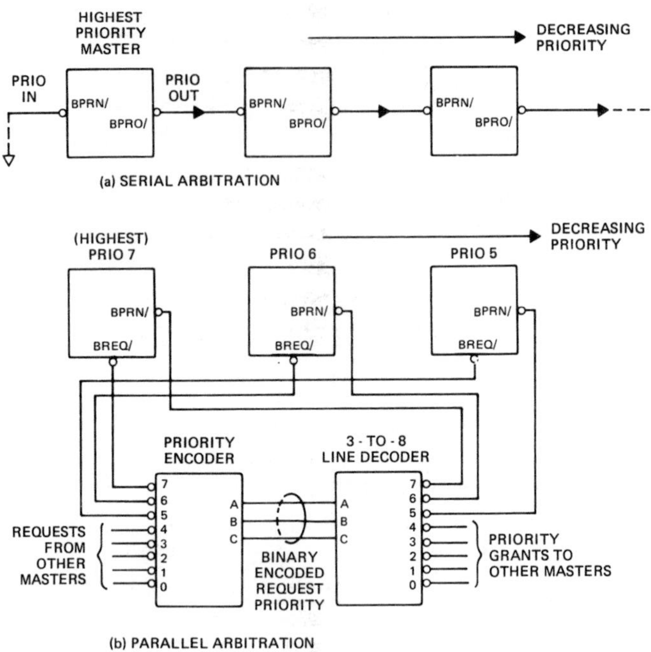

Fig. 11.8

Bus exchange operations (all synchronised by BCLK*), allow both serial (daisy-chained, which, due to timing constraints, limits the number of masters to three) and parallel priority arbitration. Signals BPRO* and BPRN* are used with a parallel bus arbiter (fig. 11.8b). The bus control signals are reasonably general, and can easily be generated by other (non-Intel) microprocessor cards; no specific 'bus grant' signal is generated however – it is inferred from CBRQ* and BPRN* signals.

The maximum bus data rate is 5×10^6 transfers/second, which is easily adequate for today's microprocessors, though it is by no means the fastest bus standard. More likely to restrict its use in the near future, especially for large memory intensive projects, is the limited addressing range of 20 bits (1 Mbyte). Already, there are proposals to extend this to 24 bits (16 Mbytes), and to use auxiliary connector P2 for other signals (not part of 796 standard) such as auxiliary power, power-fail sensing, parity, and memory protection. The number of pins on the two bus connectors (86 on P1, 60 on P2) should ensure adequate expansion, since the majority of P2 pins are undefined as yet. Its wide industry support and heavy backing will ensure the standard's survival for the foreseeable future.

11.5.3 VERSABUS

Designed by Motorola to support the MC68000, Versabus[7] is a relative newcomer to the microcomputer scene. Designed in the light of experience with older bus systems, it is very forward-looking in concept, and will allow up to 32-bit data and address paths. It is specified to the same data rate as Multibus (5 MHz) and is specifically intended to allow local/system buses. More complex than previous bus definitions, it is supported by two backplane connectors, one 140-way (P1) and the other 120-way (P2); a 16-bit data/24-bit address system need only use P1 – P2 is essentially used for expansion to 32 bits. Like the other buses, signals may be grouped as data and address, commands, bus exchange and interrupts.

11.5.3.1 Data and address lines

Like Multibus, all signals are ground-true, but unlike Multibus, a number of parity lines have been added, as have 'data and address valid' signals. With the increase in word and memory sizes and throughput of modern microprocessors, some form of error checking is necessary:

(a) D00* – D15* Bidirectional data lines between master and slave.
(b) DPARITY0* Odd parity for D00* – D07*.
(c) DPARITY1* Odd parity for D08* – D15*.
(d) D16* – D31* Bidirectional lines between master and slave for extended databus.
(e) DPARITY2* Odd parity for data bits D16* – D23*.
(f) DPARITY3* Odd parity for data bits D24* – D31*.
(g) A01* – A23* Address bus.
(h) A24* – A31* Extended address bus.
(i) APARITY0* Odd parity bit for A01* – A23* and LWORD*.
(j) APARITY1* Odd parity bit for A24* – A31*.
(k) LWORD* If the system is using 32-bit words, LWORD* distinguishes between a word (16 bits) and a long word (32 bits). When the system is using 16-bit words, LWORD* distinguishes between a byte and a word.
(l) DS0* Data strobe 0, which indicates a data transfer on 'byte 0' of the data bus (D00 – D07 or D00 – D07 and D16 – D23).
(m) DS1* Data strobe 1, which indicates a data transfer on 'byte 1' of the data bus (D08 – D15 or D08 – D15 and D24 – D31).
(n) DTACK* Data transfer acknowledge, used as a handshaking signal to indicate that valid data has been put onto the bus during a read cycle or that data has been accepted during a write cycle.
(o) WRITE* Read-write indication ($R/\overline{W}$).

11.5.3.2 Command signals

The data transfer strobes, validity and acknowledgement signals grouped in the previous section take care of most bus transactions, with the additional signals noted below added to increase bus flexibility:

(a) ACKIN* Acknowledge input, which forms part of a daisy-chained acknowledge line which signifies that an ACK cycle is in progress.
(b) ACKOUT* Acknowledge output, the continuation of the daisy-chain on other side of the card.
(c) ACFAIL* Mains power failure indication.
(d) SYSFAIL* Exerted when a card fails software diagnostics.
(e) SYSRESET* Global reset control.
(f) SECRESET* Selective reset control, which causes only certain slave cards to be reset (secondary reset).
(g) IRQ1*-IRQ7* Prioritised interrupt request.
(h) SECIEN* Secondary interrupt.

11.5.3.3 Bus exchange commands

The bus exchange commands allow a flexible control structure with facilities for daisy-chaining, and for parallel prioritisation of bus requests. As befits a relatively sophisticated standard like this one, possible bus error conditions can be specified. The signals are:

(a) BBSY* Bus busy (generated by current master).
(b) BERR* Bus error indicated by a slave device, which is unrecoverable.
(c) BCLR* Bus clear, which indicates to the current master that the bus is being requested by a higher priority master, and that the current master must therefore relinquish control.
(d) BG0IN*-BG4IN* Bus grant input, which indicates to a board that it might be next master (daisy-chained).
(e) BG0OUT*-BG4OUT* The other side of the daisy-chained bus grant signals, which allows a board to indicate to the next board that it may be bus master.
(f) BR0*-BR4* Prioritised bus request lines.
(g) BREL* Bus release, a signal which forces the current master to relinquish the bus within sixteen clock cycles.

These bus exchange signals are much more flexible than their counterparts in previously designed buses. The existence of five distinct levels of bus request and daisy-chained grant signals allows a sophisticated arbitration scheme and recognises that the bus masters may need to make requests for control of the bus with different priorities on different occasions. While current multiple microprocessor systems (with probably only a few CPUs present) possess arbitration, operating only on a first-come, first-served basis, this multilevel arbitration is much more suitable for larger systems, with perhaps many functionally dedicated microprocessors.

11.5.3.4 Versabus operation

Versabus forms the basis of the backplane of the Motorola 68000 Exormacs development system, and the design does reflect the 68000 microprocessor to some extent. However, the bus qualifies as an admirable general-purpose, microprocessor-independent bus which possesses expansion possibilities that will enhance its life as a standard. The error detection facilities will be essential for future complex systems with large memories, and many devices connected to the bus. Whereas with microcomputer systems with only moderate memory sizes, the rate of bit errors is small enough to be ignored, this rate rapidly achieves some significance when multimegabyte semiconductor memory is installed. So too does the rate of bit errors induced onto the bus by EMI, as the bus length increases, speeds rise, and more cards are added. Modern memory systems use on-card error detection and correction (EDC), and it is sensible that the rest of the system should offer some detection mechanism. In addition to the parity bits provided on data and address, a bus error return signal allows error exception handling to be implemented by the user, as appropriate.

Another significant feature of Versabus is its potential size: a total of 260 connections in two double-sided edge connectors. In the initial specification, the main bus connector carried all the 16-bit bus signals (with 24-bit address), with several pins reserved for future expansion, and the second connector carried the basic expansion to 32 address and 32 data bits, as well as fifty non-bused input-output signals and some reserved pins. Some of the reserved pins have since been allocated to provide additional facilities:

SYSPAUSE* and SYSPACK*, providing an acknowledged pause.
ROMDIS* and RAMDIS*, providing a 'phantom memory' capability.
TEST* and RETRY*, provide self-diagnostic capability and recovery from transient errors.
PDOWN*, a d.c. power failure signal which complements the original ACFAIL* condition.
IOEN* and EXTDADR*, which allow explicit input-output operations (complementing the 68000 memory-mapped approach on its component-level bus).

Some of these signals occupy part of the memory address modifier space. On the second connector, two more data strobes may be added, giving a unique strobe signal for each byte of the (expanded) 32-bit data bus. Some of the other reserved pins have now been allocated to serial communication lines (non-bused).

Like all the advanced buses, Versabus is asynchronous, so that any speed mix of cards may be used in a system (with a timer associated with the acknowledgement lines, which raises an error indication on the bus if no acknowledgement has been received by the end of the timeout interval, fig. 11.9). The bus exchange facilities are appropriate to an advanced system, allowing five levels of bus arbitration, with daisy-chaining at each level.

Power distribution on Versabus has also been enhanced; aside from the usual logic d.c. supplies, facilities are provided on the main bus connector for +5 V standby (battery) power, and ±15 V analogue circuitry supply rails are provided, with a better supply noise specification, and with an isolated ground return to avoid earth loop currents and induced logic noise. Versabus was introduced by Motorola as recently as 1980 (in their Exormacs development system), with compatible board level products by 1981. As yet, therefore, it has not had the opportunity to establish the sort of wide user base that Multibus, its major competition, enjoys. The bus is an advance on Multibus facilities, and the large number of pins reserved for future expansion should help its acceptance.

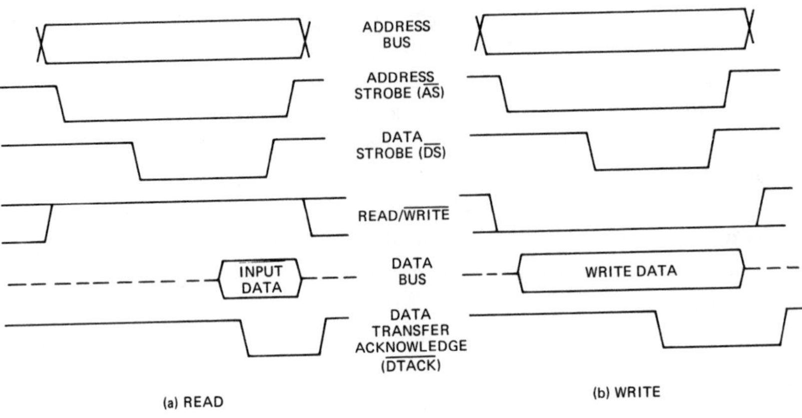

Fig. 11.9

11.5.4 Z-BUS (ZBI)

The Zilog Z-bus[8] backplane interconnect (fig. 11.10) is specifically designed for use with the Z8000 family of microprocessors and components, and will also accommodate the 8-bit Z80 and Z8. Smaller than Versabus, it uses a single 96-way indirect connector (the standard Eurocard connector) with single or double Eurocards. The double card has the option of a second non-bus 96-way connector. The system defines ZCM-1 and ZCM-2 cards corresponding to the two sizes, with parallel power pins on the double Eurocard to double the allowable current. The ZBI signals are grouped as memory bus lines, bus transfer lines, interrupt lines, resource request lines and system control lines. Unlike Multibus and Versabus, not all ZBI signals are active-low; those which are (mainly control lines) are signified by *.

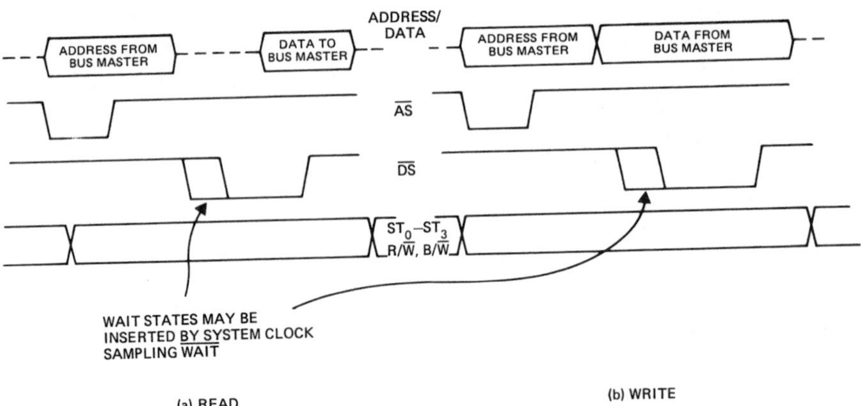

Fig. 11.10

11.5.4.1 Memory bus lines

These lines handle the basic bus transactions, and provide a measure of system integrity by allowing parity checking (by byte) on data and checks on privileged access. The lines are:

(a) AD0-AD31 Multiplexed 32-bit data and address lines; the address and data signals are distinguished by separate strobe signals, and transfers may be asynchronous, or synchronised to the bus transaction clock. For byte data transfers, the low byte of the 4-byte bus is used, and for 16-bit data transfers, the two low bytes are used.
(b) P0-P3 Parity check bits for the address/data bus (1 bit per byte). Use of even parity allows these bits to be used to detect any bus transaction with a non-existent device, since the bus terminators will pull undriven data lines to an odd parity state.
(c) PE* Parity error – a line which indicates to the bus master that parity-check logic on the card receiving any transferred data has detected an error (note that the bus specification does not allow for parity checks on address information).
(d) AS* Address strobe.
(e) DS* Data strobe.
(f) WAIT* A response line whereby the responding card can suspend master operation during a slow operation (cf. Multibus).
(g) STOP* Causes the current bus master microprocessor to halt (provides a synchronisation function).
(h) ST0-ST4 Status line, which define the type of transaction occurring on the bus (typically distinguishing between program and data memory accesses, etc.).
(i) $R/\overline{W}$ Read-write line which determines data direction.
(j) $N/\overline{S}$ Normal-system bus use. When a logic '1', this signal indicates that the CPU is in User mode with no privileged access (e.g. to I/O devices), and when a '0', it indicates that the CPU is in systems mode, and allowed privileged operations.
(k) $B/\overline{W}$ Byte-word select.
(l) $W/\overline{LW}$ Word-long word select. Used with $B/\overline{W}$ to define data-access width.

11.5.4.2 Bus transfer lines

ZBI definition allows a simple (single level) daisy-chained bus arbitration scheme, with additional reserved lines for extending the bus arbitration to multiple microprocessor systems (rather than microprocessor-DMA device systems). The lines are:

(a) BAI* Bus acknowledge in.
(b) BAO* Bus acknowledge out; with BAI*, this signal forms a daisy-chained bus priority system.
(c) BUSREQ* Bus request, requesting that the current master relinquish the bus.

(d) BUSACK* Bus acknowledge, indicating that current master has relinquished the bus.
(e) CAI* CPU acknowledge in.
(f) CAO* CPU acknowledge out.
(g) CPUREQ* CPU request.
(h) CAVAIL CPU available.

The last four lines are the extended bus arbitration lines, which are not fully defined in the original Z-bus specification. BUSACK*, mentioned in the original 1980 specification, appears not to be implemented in later versions of ZBI.

11.5.4.3 Interrupt lines

Three interrupt levels are provided, each one with enable signals daisy-chained through the system. They support the three Z8000 interrupt types, and only those used in a system need be implemented. The types of interrupt supported are (in order of their assumed priority): non-maskable (NMI); vectored (INT); and non-vectored. The lines are:

(a) INT1* Level 1 (highest priority) interrupt request (NMI).
(b) IEI1 Level 1 interrupt enable in.
(c) IEO1 Level 1 interrupt enable out.
(d) INT2* Level 2 interrupt request (vectored interrupts).
(e) IEI2 Level 2 interrupt enable in.
(f) IEO2 Level 2 interrupt enable out.
(g) INT3* Level 3 (lowest priority) interrupt request (non-vectored interrupts).
(h) IEI3 Level 3 interrupt enable in.
(i) IEO3 Level 3 interrupt enable out.

11.5.4.4 Resource request lines

The Z8000 CPU has facilities for multimicroprocessor operation ($\overline{M}_1$ and $\overline{M}_0$) which allow resource sharing and microprocessor synchronisation. These are reflected in ZBI as three lines, a request line and two daisy-chained arbitration lines:

(a) MMREQ* Multimicro request (for software synchronisation). Driven by any device that can use the shared resource.
(b) MMST* (Optional) multimicro status, which allows a device to observe the value of the MMREQ* line.
(c) MMAI* Multimicro acknowledge in.
(d) MMAO* Multimicro acknowledge out; used in conjunction with MMAI* as a daisy-chained line to perform software arbitration.

For different resources, these lines may be replicated, though not on the same connector.

11.5.4.5 System control lines

Really a group of miscellaneous signals generated by the bus system itself.

(a) PWRBAD* Power bad – a d.c. power-fail indication.
(b) MCLK System master clock, a 4 X multiple of BCLK frequency, supplied by the bus controller.
(c) BCLK* Bus transaction clock, derived from MCLK and used by all synchronous devices in the system.
(d) RESET* Global system reset, connected to any 'master reset' switch and power-up reset.

11.5.4.6 ZBI operation

ZBI is a high-performance bus tailored to the Z8000 family of microprocessors. Although defined as a general bus, its signals reflect the Z8000 component-level bus very strongly. Of the three main 16-bit microcomputer bus systems strongly supported by their manufacturers (Multibus, Versabus and Z-bus), Z-bus is the only one to multiplex address and data. Its speed is not compromised by this multiplexing, however, but the standard may require some additional circuitry on a board using another manufacturer's CPU. Like Versabus, the importance of signal integrity has not been lost on Zilog, but parity checking is only applied to data, not to address. Since to apply parity checks to address would require no additional bus signals, it seems surprising that this is not done.

ZBI is a bus well suited to the modern generation of microprocessors (and will support 32-bit devices), but may be considered a little inflexible when more advanced systems (in particular, multiple microprocessor systems) are required. The arbitration applied to bus request, resource request and interrupt request signals is purely one of daisy-chaining enable lines. Only in the case of interrupt requests are multiple parallel priority levels involved, and then under very specific circumstances, appropriate to Z8000 architecture. Despite this, the standard compares well with the older Multibus, but appears less flexible than Versabus. A feature which will improve its popularity (and reliability) relative to both Multibus and Versabus is its adoption of indirect (DIN 41612) connectors for bus connections, and its Eurocard format. Eurocard standards are very well established in the UK and mainland Europe, and in many cases, specified for projects. ZBI will be very well placed to fulfil requirements for a Eurocard-compatible advanced microcomputer bus system, and may well achieve widespread use because of this.

11.5.5 E-BUS AND T-BUS

Less well-known than the other buses, E-bus and T-bus are the formats adopted by Texas Instruments for its 9900-family microprocessor cards. E-bus is a Eurocard format 64-way bus using indirect connectors and T-bus is a 100-way bus using edge connectors.

E-bus uses triple multiplexing on its address/data lines (address, data and interrupts) and multiplexes the top address/data line with the 9900 serial output signal CRUOUT. Its control lines are very 9900-specific, but the bus does have transfer arbitration and some additional signals. Its main advantage is its Eurocard format. Bus signals are:

(a) AD0-AD7; INT0-INT7 Triply multiplexed address/data/interrupt signals.
(b) AD8-AD14 Address/data bus.
(c) AD15/CRUOUT Address/data/serial output.
(d) XA0-XA3 Address extension to 20 bits.
(e) $\overline{\text{MEMEN}}$ Memory access in progress.
(f) $\overline{\text{WE}}$ Enable data on the bus to be written to memory (write strobe).
(g) $\overline{\text{AREADY}}$ Advanced READY (1 clock cycle early).
(h) $\overline{\text{READY}}$ Memory ready this clock cycle.
(i) $\overline{\text{DEN}}$ Data enable (memory read).
(j) ALATCH Address latch (address is present on multiplexed bus).
(k) MEMWIDTH Data transfer width (16-bit word or byte).
(l) CRUIN Serial input (direct to 9900 family CPU).
(m) CRUOUT Serial output (direct to 9900 family CPU).
(n) CRUCLK Communications register unit clock signal generated by the CRU as a strobe signal to indicate serial output data present.
(o) $\overline{\text{BUSY}}$ Bus busy signal (requesting device has taken control of the bus).
(p) GRANTIN Daisy-chained bus arbitration signal which indicates that no higher-priority device is requesting the bus.
(q) GRANTOUT Daisy-chained bus arbitration signal which is generated by a board to indicate that a lower-priority device may request control of the bus.
(r) $\overline{\text{BUSCLK}}$ Bus synchronisation clock (up to 10 MHz) (for bus transfer control).
(s) $\overline{\text{IORST}}$ Input-output reset signal.
(t) $\overline{\text{PRES}}$ Power up signal.
(u) $\overline{\text{NMI}}$ Non-maskable interrupt request.
(v) $\overline{\text{PWRFAIL}}$ Power fail signal.
(w) $\overline{\text{INTEN}}$ Valid interrupt code is on the bus (used in conjunction with requests INT0-INT7).

In addition, E-bus supports an analogue bus: ANAHI, ANALO signal lines and ANACOM ground return path; as well as this, two standby power lines are provided (+5VSTBY and +BATT, for other than 5 V).

Unlike the mainstream buses, E-bus is not intended as a general-purpose bus which is microprocessor-independent, but is very specific, designed solely with the 9900 family in mind. The Eurocard format is useful, but the unique CRU signals and some of the control signals prevent E-bus from achieving the status of an 'industry standard'.

T-bus is a non-multiplexed bus which provides similar facilities to E-bus but with a larger card size and a single 100-way double-sided edge connector. The signals which have been added are:

(a) $\overline{\text{INT8-INT15}}$ Eight additional interrupt lines (giving a total of fifteen, since INT0 is not present).

(b) $\overline{\text{MEMCYC}}$ Indicates a memory cycle is in progress.
(c) $\overline{\text{HOLD}}$ Device is requesting the bus for a (DMA) data transfer.
(d) $\overline{\text{HOLDA}}$ The bus master has relinquished control of the bus.
(e) RESTART Indicates that a load function should be performed.
(f) IAQ Instruction fetch in progress.
(g) REFCLK Peripheral interface device clock.

Since T-bus is non-multiplexed, the multiplex control signals of E-bus are no longer required; ALATCH, MEMWIDTH, $\overline{\text{INTEN}}$ have been omitted, as has $\overline{\text{AREADY}}$. While very effective as a purpose-designed bus, T-bus too is not so suitable as a general-purpose bus standard.

11.5.6 P896 BACKPLANE BUS

With the rapid development of microprocessor-based equipment, and the adoption of two buses (S100 and Multibus) as IEEE standards, the IEEE has recognised that future standards should be more systematically planned. To pre-empt the appearance of another set of manufacturers' bus definitions, an IEEE committee was set up in 1979 to define a manufacturer-independent bus standard capable of supporting up to 32-bit parallel data transfers, multiprocessor operation, and a bus clock of at least 10 MHz. The result has been the draft P896 Advanced Microcomputer System Backplane Bus, or Futurebus. Designed around Eurocard 96-way connectors and multiples of Eurocard standard widths, P896 is potentially capable of becoming an industry standard which has a life of well into the 1990s. The P896 bus consists of a high-speed, high-throughput parallel bus which serves the information transfer functions of a conventional bus, and allows multiple microprocessors, and a serial (2-line) bus which has a lower throughput of interprocessor information, typically to support task handling in an operating system. Because of the multiprocessor requirement, P896 assumes that all boards on the bus are CPU-based, and that the system is non-hierarchical (no master-slave relationship). A group of microprocessors which share the same memory, and which are capable of semaphore operation on a memory location, is called a *node*. Node microprocessors which are interchangeable in terms of each being able to run any one of a number of tasks form a *pool*, and each microprocessor will possess both a microprocessor identifier (PROCID) and a pool identifier (POOLID). A message sent via the serial bus may be addressed to an individual microprocessor, a pool or a node. Microprocessors connected to P896 may have their own local buses, memory and I/O, and will communicate via a sophisticated P896 interface, capable of handling the serial message formats.

The messages, which have a fixed format, may be sent from any source to any destination (microprocessor, pool, broadcast) on the bus, and take the form: <beginning-of-message sync><source><destination><function><arguments> <ACK><end sync>. The function field is designed to define which service is required, and the argument field is used to transmit information or to execute arbitration. The ACK field allows responses in the form of negative acknowledge (NAK) or positive acknowledge (ACK).

Using this facility, it is possible to handle a number of tasks on a number of microprocessors using messages to alter the state of tasks which are running (currently being executed by a microprocessor), ready (waiting for execution, i.e. waiting for a microprocessor) or blocked (waiting for some event in order to make the transition to ready). The term *redispatch* is used to indicate that a microprocessor is changing the task that it is currently running. Reasons for a redispatch operation may be that the current task is finished, that it is blocked (waiting for information), that execution of a new task is required, or that a system interrupt has occurred. A system interrupt is issued by one microprocessor to one or more other microprocessors with the objective of invoking a redispatch operation on another microprocessor. Using a *notify-to-redispatch* message on the P896 serial bus requests execution of a task with a given priority, but is directed at a pool of microprocessors rather than just a single microprocessor. The microprocessor in the pool which is executing the lowest priority task will be selected to redispatch and execute the new task, if the priority is higher than that of the running task. If more than one microprocessor is in the same situation, an arbitration procedure will be necessary. With an appropriate operating system, it is possible to use notify-to-redispatch for a single microprocessor system. To identify the task to be dispatched, P896 defines an 8-bit vector as part of the notify-to-redispatch message, which may be used to indicate a location directly, or as a pointer to an address table.

Other messages passed over the serial link may be notify-to-deactivate, notify-to-ready, may transmit data in the function/arguments field, or the serial line message may be used to give immediate functions such as HALT, RUN or INITIALISE, etc. Their hexadecimal function codes (8-bit) are proposed as follows:

(a) Immediate functions (MSB = 0)

00	INIT (microprocessor reset)
01	HALT
02	ENABLE PROCESSOR
03	DISABLE PROCESSOR
04	POWER UP
05	POWER FAIL
09	Memory parity error
0B	Duplicate memory
10	DISCONNECT microprocessor (halt and remove from parallel bus)
11	CONNECT microprocessor (initialise and connect to parallel bus)
12	Unrecoverable bus error
13	NO ACCESS
14	BUS TIME-OUT (Asynchronous transfer)
20	UNLOCKED LOCKVARIABLE
22	ALIVE
3F	UNDEFINED ERROR
40-7F	User defined

(b) Interrupt messages (MSB = 1)

8Ø-9F System interrupt
AØ-BF Notify-to-redispatch
CØ-DF Notify-to-ready
EØ Notify to deactivate
Messages in the reverse direction are:
CØ Interrupt accept (broadcast)
DØ Redispatch done (broadcast)
FØ Ready done (broadcast)
FF No operation

A microprocessor on a board will see the P896 serial interprocessor link as a peripheral on its local bus, which may involve immediate signals, vectored microprocessor interrupts or internal messages that may be polled by the microprocessor.

Apart from the serial bus, P896 supports a flexible 32-bit multiplexed data and address bus and has two compatible levels of implementation, one based on the 64-way Eurocard connector, and the other on the 96-way connector. In level 1, the lines provided are:

(a) AD0*-AD31* Multiplexed address/data.
(b) C0*-C4* Multiplexed control/status.
(c) AS* Address strobe.
(d) DS* Data strobe.
(e) AK* Acknowledge.
(f) BR* Bus request.
(g) BB* Bus busy.
(h) BP0*-BP5* Bus priority.
(i) SC* Supervisor control.
(j) RZ Reset.
(k) IL* Interprocessor (serial) link.
(l) CK Clock.

In level 2, additional lines are provided:

(a) BP6-BP7 Bus priority.
(b) C5*-C7* Multiplex control/status.
(c) SU* Substitute.
(d) EB0-EB7 Error detection and correction data.
(e) RC0*-RC8* Reserved control lines.
(f) Additional power and ground lines.

The multiplex control/status lines are important, since they may be decoded to give the transfer mode for data on the parallel bus. In keeping with the sophistication of the rest of the bus, they define byte, doublet (16-bit word), quadlet (32-bit word), and potentially possibly octlet (64-bit word) transfers, block transfers, read-modify-write operations on the bus, and are used for acknowledgements, giving details of any error correction applied, invalid addresses, unrecoverable bus errors and other information.

Not all aspects of P896 are defined as yet, and it is not a standard that will become widely used overnight. Level 1 will be the easiest to implement, but level 2 contains those extensions which complex multiple microprocessor systems will demand, such as error detection and correction. The idea of implementing operating system functions on a multiple microprocessor system via the bus is a very powerful idea, and one which is likely to become widely copied as multiple microprocessor systems become the norm for microcomputer installation. Running the communications via a serial bus in a virtual packet format allows a high degree of flexibility, since functions are limited neither by data width nor by sequential word transfer protocols which would have to vie with normal bus data transfers if systems information were transferred as parallel words. With an additional serial bus for system use, system commands may be issued concurrently with normal bus data transfers, without interaction. By multiplexing address and data on its parallel bus, P896 manages to squeeze all its signals onto one 96-way DIN 41612 connector (or one 64-way one if only level 1 is implemented), which allows board sizes from single Eurocard upwards (maintaining compatibility). Since the bus is not designed by a manufacturer, none of the irregularities of earlier standards are present, and it may well become widely accepted in time.

11.5.7 VME BUS

In parallel with the P896 Committee, a consortium of three major manufacturers (Signetics, Motorola and Mostek) has designed a similar standard, capable of bus transfer rates up to 24 Mbytes/second, which also contains a serial 'inter-intelligence bus' (I^2B). VME bus[10] uses a single 96-way connector for 16-bit data, 24-bit address operation and a second 96-way connector for 32-bit data, 32-bit address operation, both with non-multiplexed address and data (the 64 pins of the second 96-way connector not used for bus signals are assigned to user input-output). As a design, VME has taken ideas from earlier standards such as Versabus, and some of the proposals by the P896 Committee, and amalgamated them to form a fully defined bus standard which will outperform virtually all other buses (with the possible exception of the P896 proposals, which are not yet (1981) complete).

Like all of the other advanced buses, VME is an asynchronous bus which has separate data strobes (two) and address strobes, and acknowledgements in the form of DTACK, which terminates a bus cycle normally, and BERR which indicates an unrecoverable error, and terminates the bus cycle to allow the current bus master to repeat or abort the operation. As with other 16- or 32-bit buses, two data strobes are available, DS0 and DS1, which identify byte (on either half of the data bus) and word transfers in a 16-bit system. A signal LWORD identifies a 32-bit transfer. A set of address modifier codes is provided on six bus lines which provide information as to whether the mode of the bus master generating the current address is privileged (supervisory) or non-privileged, whether it is short (16-bits), standard (24-bits) or extended (32-bits), whether it is an input-output address, whether it is for program or data access, or part of a block transfer. With the data and address strobes, and WRITE (defining direction of data flow in the current bus cycle) the address modifiers provide a flexible alternative to earlier buses' transfer control lines, and make for a very general microprocessor-independent bus structure.

The serial data lines of VME bus are used in a similar manner to those contained in P896 proposals. VME packets have the format: <start (1 bit)><priority (5 bits)><source (6 bits)><destination (6 bits)><type (2 bits)><function (16 bits)><ACK (2 bits)>.

Address ranges for source and destination are defined in terms of a few standard system addresses; message types may be user, system, or interrupts (the fourth possible 2-bit code is reserved); function codes allow a variety of operations to be requested – power fail, disconnect, connect (to bus), reset, run diagnostics, manipulate a function table address, set a semaphore, reset a semaphore – they may contain an interrupt vector, or be user-defined. The two acknowledgement bits provide information which signifies a normal acknowledge or a negative acknowledge with one of three reasons: destination disconnected; destination present but unavailable at this time; or (broadcast messages) that only some destinations can accept the message.

Generally, as with P896, the inter-intelligence bus is used for system messages – long messages may be transferred on the VME bus by using a block move. In a block move, it is assumed that the slave device will latch the start-of-block address on the address strobe transition, and thereafter, the address strobe and start address are continuously asserted, and each transfer is signalled using the data strobe signals and DTACK. The slave device is responsible for incrementing the start address on its local address bus at each data strobe transition. This technique allows the slave memory to be pipelined (i.e. it can be reading the next word during bus propagation and handshake time).

Arbitration on the VME serial bus is particularly elegant. Since in the message format, priority follows the sync bit in a ground-true, open-collector, MSB first fashion, any conflict between two masters starting to transmit at the same time is resolved as soon as the bit occurs in which priorities differ; the device which reads a bit of its own transmitted priority in error will be the lower priority one and will stop transmitting immediately, and the other device will automatically continue until its message is complete. Since devices listen before starting to transmit, this is the only collision that can occur. If two devices have the same priority, it is their own (source) addresses which will resolve the conflict in the same way.

11.5.7.1 Data transfer signals

(a) A1-A23 Address bus.
(b) AS Address strobe.
(c) AM0-AM5 Address modifier (see text).
(d) DS0 Data strobe for transfers on D0-D7.
(e) DS1 Data strobe for transfers on D8-D15.
(f) D0-D15 16-bit databus (on single connector).
(g) DTACK Data transfer acknowledge (generated by slave): in read mode, the falling edge indicates that valid data is available on the data bus; in write

mode the falling edge indicates that data has been accepted from the bus.
(h) WRITE Specifies that the data transfer cycle is read (high) or write (low).

11.5.7.2 Interrupt signals

The interrupt facilities on the VME bus follow previous practice, with seven prioritised request lines, and a daisy-chained arbitration signal:

(a) IRQ1-IRQ7 Interrupt request lines (IRQ7 has highest priority).
(b) IACK Interrupt acknowledge (routed to slot 1 IACKIN).
(c) IACKIN Acknowledge in.
(d) IACKOUT Acknowledge out, daisy-chained with IACKIN to indicate an acknowledgement signal is in progress.

11.5.7.3 Bus exchange signals

Following Motorola's Versabus, VME bus exchange signals consist of four levels of bus priority, each individually daisy-chained throughout the boards on the bus. No fixed pre-allocation of priorities is necessary, since each master can reassign its priority as necessary. Normally, it is suggested that three levels would be issued, with the fourth only used in exceptional circumstances:

(a) BR0-BR3 Bus request, indicates that a bus master requires access to the bus.
(b) BG0IN-BG3IN Bus grant input, indicates to the board to which it is input that it may become bus master.
(c) BG0OUT-BG3OUT Bus grant output, indicates to the next board that it may become bus master.
(d) BBSY Bus busy, generated by the current master to indicate that it is using the bus.
(e) BCLR Bus clear, generated by the bus arbiter to request that the current master relinquish control of the bus.
(f) BERR Bus error. Not strictly a bus exchange signal, but one which indicates that an unrecoverable error has occurred and that the current bus cycle must be aborted.

11.5.7.4 System control lines

(a) SYSCLK Constant 16 MHz system clock signal.
(b) SYSFAIL A signal indicating a failure in the system, which may be generated by any board in the system.
(c) SYSRESET System reset.
(d) ACFAIL Power failure signal.

11.5.7.5 Serial bus

Only two lines are required for the serial bus, the data line itself, and a synchronised clock line, SERDAT and SERCLK, respectively. The rising (low-to-high) transition of SERCLK is used to allow a transmitter to put data onto SERDAT, while the trailing (high-to-low) edge is used by a receiver to sample SERDAT bits. SERCLK is nominally 4 MHz.

11.5.7.6 32-bit extensions

The VME bus, when expanded onto its second connector, carries these additional signals:

(a) A24-A31 Address bus.
(b) D18-D31 Data bus.
(c) LWORD Specifies a 32-bit long word data transfer.

11.5.7.7 VME bus operation

Until P896 is finalised, VME bus is easily the most advanced bus standard available. It is unique in its provision of a serial packet bus within the parallel standard (the inter-intelligence bus) and in the facilities this provides for operating system support with multiple microprocessors. As a concept, this built-in serial bus, operating autonomously to the main parallel bus, is likely to be the most significant recent development in bus standards. It represents a departure from the more conventional standards which will be welcomed by system designers, as it makes multiple microprocessor system software so much better defined, with a standard interprocessor communications channel, rather than the *ad hoc* arrangements of current multiple microprocessor systems. Surprisingly, for such an advanced bus design, there are no explicit error detection and correction facilities (like those planned for P896). Nevertheless, the fast bus clock, the flexibility of the address modifiers and other features make up for the apparent omission.

11.5.8 OVERALL ASSESSMENT

Backplane buses are essential for modern microcomputers, and the 8-bit world has already produced many variations on the basic backplane bus concept, originally merely a buffered extension of the microprocessor component-level bus. The 16-bit (and beyond) buses must be more than this, and must provide for multiple microprocessor operation, usually asynchronous data transfers, multilevel interrupt structures and wider address and data paths, as well as higher speed. The future of the buses described in this chapter is linked with different applications areas. Because of its current market position, S100 will continue in enhanced form as a standard in the personal computer field, and in the area of overlap between this field and the small stand-alone business computer. Multibus, too, will continue to flourish in the single-board computer field, for control applications and computer-based instrumentation where the advantages of ready-made board systems outweigh their costs. Already well supported outside the originator Intel, Multibus will continue to develop its range of boards and interfaces. Already, Multibus-compatible boards containing Z8000 and 68000 CPUs are available, and much of the system software for the 8086 family is based on a Multibus environment. Similar comments apply to TI's E-bus and T-bus. Although Multibus will allow distributed computing, its impact in this area may be lessened by the Versabus and Z-bus standards. Versabus in particular, with its error detection and multilevel bus arbitration, is likely to dominate much of the multiple microprocessor system field, while ZBI's Eurocard standard is likely to win popularity because of its use of standard board sizes and more reliable indirect connectors. All of these buses will be used in multiple microprocessor systems in control, instrumentation and general industrial automation, where the advantages of the 16-bit microprocessor are its higher speed, higher precision, and good real time capabilities. Such applications, while they may stretch the capabilities of the microcomputer system, may often handle interprocessor communications in a specialised manner (perhaps synchronously), by exchanging data via the main bus.

With more complex distributed systems, especially office systems and multiuser installations, where operating systems like Unix are used, and access to local area networks (LANs) may be required, the demands made on the backplane bus of a system will increase. Operating system support in the form of arbitration, implementation of resource semaphores, and interprocessor communications independent of the main bus assumes considerable importance, and the newest standards (P896 and VME) will dominate this area once their definitions have been finalised. VME bus is virtually complete, although extensions to improve bus arbitration are already under discussion, whilst P896 is still at the proposal stage. Their contribution to systems design has been the adoption of the serial packet bus incorporated into the main backplane alongside the main parallel bus, and in defining suitable protocols to allow the serial bus to be used to implement multiple microprocessor operating system functions. Like the 'silicon operating system', this merging of software and hardware will improve future microcomputer designs, and achieve a degree of uniformity that has been lacking up to now.

CHAPTER 12
Future developments

Compared with the mature 8-bit microprocessor, the 16-bit microprocessor is just beginning to gain widespread user acceptance. The 8-bit microprocessor is being used in very large quantities in a steadily increasing, predictable market; the more popular devices enjoy an extremely large base of user and system software, and a wealth of applications experience within a wide spectrum of users. By contrast, the 16-bit microprocessor shipments have not yet reached a plateau, and the main manufacturers are still competing in attempts to achieve a dominant position. Even with 16-bit microprocessors, which have claimed compatibility with their 8-bit predecessors, there is not the depth of systems and software knowledge which exists in the 8-bit field. Moreover, potential applications for 16-bit microprocessors are often significantly more complex, and software costs are correspondingly higher.

Despite the relative infancy of the modern 16-bit CPU, and the long time-scales involved in designing it into sophisticated equipment, the main manufacturers have continued to develop enhanced devices and their support chips at an ever increasing rate. As chip densities increase with every advance in fabrication technology (shrinking line widths, scaling, and new processes and materials), costs and die sizes decrease, and it becomes possible to economically integrate more complex devices. Driven by these improvements, the evolutionary development of the 16-bit microprocessor has begun to follow that of 8-bit devices, where more devices are added to the original chip either to enhance it as a general-purpose CPU (by adding on-chip memory management, or hardware arithmetic functions, for instance), or to create a single-chip microcontroller based on the same original CPU. The latter course involves integrating onto a single chip the microprocessor CPU, random-access and read-only memory, and input-output interfaces (usually some parallel digital I/O, some serial asynchronous or synchronous I/O, and one or two timer channels). The input-output interfaces use pins of the microcomputer package which have been made available by the rearrangement of the CPU data, address and control buses, which will be entirely internal to the device, and no longer require external package pins. In the former 'enhanced CPU' category, are the Intel iAPX186 and iAPX286, two derivatives of the 8086 family, and the Motorola virtual memory microprocessor, the 68020, as well as the 8-bit bus versions of existing CPUs, such as the 8088 and 68008. In the 'single chip microcomputer' category are the Intel 8096 microcontroller and the Mostek 68200 single chip computer. The opportunity also exists for more sophisticated interface devices and 'silicon systems software' devices.

Software for 16-bit microprocessors is even more important than for 8-bit ones, and some of the major future developments are likely to occur in this area. The way in which these developments materialise may be significantly different from hardware developments. Whereas hardware developments rely on the semiconductor manufacturers themselves, and are restricted to a single family of microprocessors, software developments are not, and one feature which will feature strongly in any new software will be its portability. Portability of software implies good high-level language support (see chapter 9) and some standardisation of operating systems. To some extent, standardisation of operating systems has begun to occur in the personal computer world, with Unix and CP/M or MP/M, but small, real time operating systems are still specific to one manufacturer's family of devices. So, too, is other special-purpose system software, such as that for 'database microprocessor' implementation. It is anticipated that, eventually, these important systems features will become standardised in the same way as Unix or CP/M. If Ada, and its system APSE (Ada Programming Support Environment) prove suitable for microprocessor use, standardisation of some real time functions will be automatic, since they are defined in the Ada language specification. Into this category fall the functions of process synchronisation and communication.

Two potentially exciting concepts which could alter future microprocessor design are object-oriented programming (which has strongly influenced the design of the 32-bit Intel iAPX432) and dataflow architecture (the subject of many university research programs). Unlike the evolutionary developments outlined above and detailed later in this chapter, designs based on these concepts may be a radical departure from the traditional sequential instruction-execution designs. Other features of these different designs may allow fault-tolerant computing, new multiple microprocessor structures and direct high-level language support, where the native instruction set of the CPU corresponds directly with high-level language constructs.

Although this chapter looks at some of the devices which have already had details released, it is virtually certain that developments will continue at the present alarming rate, and new devices more appropriate to the so-called 'Fifth Generation' of computers will soon appear. Coprocessors or intelligent peripheral interfaces will soon allow reliable speech synthesis and recognition (the former is already a reality), visual pattern recognition (handwriting analysis currently uses a powerful minicomputer and a lot of interface electronics), and 'expert systems' support. The distinction between a mainframe computer and a microprocessor system, already beginning to blur, will disappear altogether.

12.1 Future 16-bit central microprocessors

Intel, first in the field with the 8086 (or iAPX86 as it is now known) has two newer 16-bit microprocessors, the iAPX186[1,2] and iAPX286[3], which offer enhanced performance over the original member of the family. The iAPX186 is designed to minimise parts count in a system, and at the same time, offer higher throughput than the 8086, while the iAPX286 is designed to offer on-chip memory management and virtual memory support. Both devices are instruction-set compatible with the 8086.

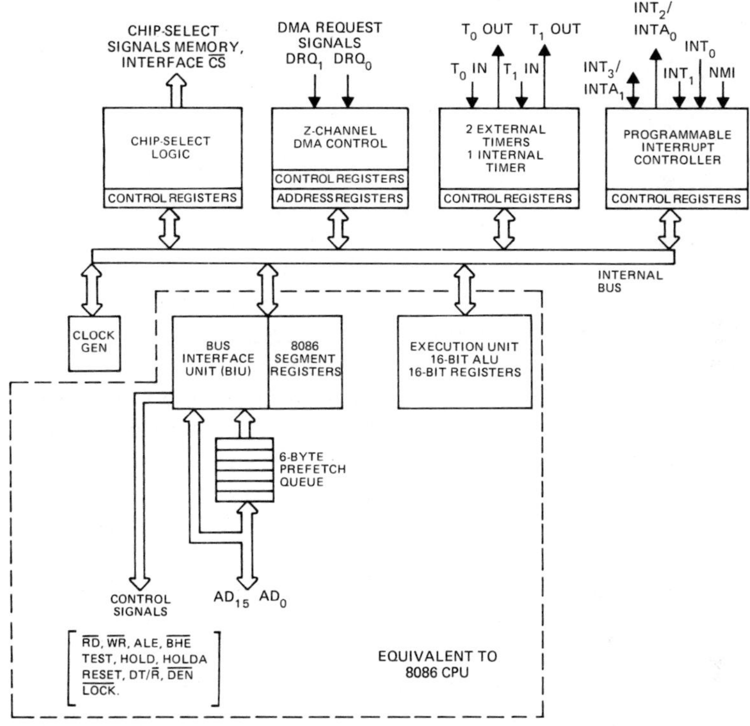

Fig. 12.1 iAPX186 architecture.

12.1.1 80186 or iAPX186

A block diagram of this microprocessor is shown in fig. 12.1. It consists of a number of functional blocks connected via an internal bus, and communicating with the rest of the system via a bus interface unit (BIU). The bus interface unit handles addressing for the system, using the same 6-byte prefetch queue which featured in the 8086, and similar 16-bit segment registers. An improvement in speed has been effected by performing effective address calculation by hardware inside the BIU instead of by microcode. The 16-bit arithmetic-and-logic unit (ALU) has the same 16-bit registers as the 8086, but has a somewhat expanded instruction set, which gives the CPU compatibility with the older members of the family (8086, 8088) and also with the newer iAPX286, which will execute a superset of the 186's instructions. The clock generator, has programmable wait-state generation logic (previously performed using an 8284 clock generator and MSI LSTTL logic) on the chip.

The programmable wait-state generators are actually part of on-chip chip-select logic. For a simple system with only a small number of interfaces, the need for any external address decoding may be eliminated altogether. Within the 80186 address space, four areas are commonly defined:

(a) Top of memory, where systems ROM, accessed via the reset location (in this case at FFFF0H), normally resides.
(b) Bottom of memory, where the 8086 interrupt vector table is located (00000H to 003FFH).
(c) User program area, usually occupying intermediate memory addresses.
(d) Peripheral interface port addresses.

As well as latched address bits A_1 and A_2 and bus buffer control signals DT/$\overline{R}$ and DEN, the 80186 may be programmed to generate chip select (CS) signals for interface devices, eliminating external decoder propagation delays, and generating wait states as required. Top and bottom of memory are each allocated a single $\overline{CS}$ line, but 'mid-range' memory is allowed up to four separate $\overline{CS}$ lines, to retain flexibility in the choice of user ROM and RAM sizes. Peripheral interface devices are allocated up to seven $\overline{CS}$ lines. Although seven interface devices may seem a small number, it may be seen from fig. 12.1 that the 80186 chip contains not only the logic described so far, but also two channels of DMA, three 16-bit programmable timers, and a programmable interrupt controller. With this array of internal interfaces, the provision for seven external devices seems generous!

The DMA controllers allow data transfers between memory and I/O spaces, within memory, or within I/O space. Each supports the full 20-bit 8086 addressing capability, with source and destination pointer registers which may be automatically incremented or decremented after each transfer. Each channel is configured using a channel control word which specifies the type of transfer (byte or 16-bit word), its interrupt logic, number of bytes to be transferred, synchronisation, address space selection (memory or I/O for source and destination), autoincrementing or autodecrementing pointer registers, and priority. A maximum data rate of 2 Mbytes/s is achievable.

The interrupt controller is a dual-mode controller, which can be switched to either a 'normal' mode, or an RMX-86 compatible mode. The former mode allows the user to assign internal and external requests on a priority basis, where internal requests may be masked using the internal device control registers. The interrupts are listed in table 12.1, along with their default priority and 'vector type', a number used in computing interrupt vector locations. The seven hardware interrupt sources may be grouped into seven priority levels (the timers, DMA channel 0, DMA channel 1, and external interrupts 0-3), they may be masked individually or by priority level, and may be extended using an external interrupt controller (8259A) which may itself be used in a master mode to control up to eight other controllers. Cascading like this is achieved using the two interrupt pins (INT0, INT1), with acknowledge signals on the other two pins (INT2/INTA0, INT3/INTA1). The external interrupt pins may be configured to be edge- or level-triggered, and the controller may adopt full nesting, 8259A special nesting, or polling mode, and issue specific or non-specific end-of-interrupt signals (EOI, NSEOI).

Table 12.1 80186 interrupts

Name	Type	Default priority
Type 0 (divide error)	0	–
Type 1 (single step)	1	–
NMI (non-maskable)	2	1
Type 3 (breakpoint)	3	–
INTO (trap on overflow)	4	–
Array bounds (CHECK) trap	5	–
Invalid op code trap	6	–
ESCAPE trap (for 8087 emulation)	7	–
Timer 0	8	2A
Timer 1	18	2B
Timer 2	19	2C
DMA0	10	4
DMA1	11	5
Reserved	9	3
INT0 (external)	12	6
INT1 (external)	13	7
INT2/INTA0 (external)	14	8
INT3/INTA1 (external)	15	9

In the RMX-86 mode of operation, the interrupt controller of the 80186 is configured as a slave controller to an external master priority interrupt controller (one of eight possible slaves), and interrupt vector generation is compatible with that of the 8086. In this mode, no external interrupt sources are recognised by the internal 80186 controller, and all internal sources must be programmed to a predefined priority level. Full nesting, specific-end-of-interrupt commands, individual masking and priority level masking are all supported.

The programmable timers consist of two timers/event counters (TIM0, TIM1) which interface externally to four I/O pins (TIMR OUT 0, 1, TIMR IN 0, 1). Internal or external inputs may be selected for these two timers, and their outputs may be used for waveform generation. The third timer (TIM2) is completely internal, and may be used for a real time clock, a time-delay generator, or as a prescaler for TIM0 or TIM1 inputs. Like the timers of the 8253 interface, the timers TIM0 and TIM1 of the 80186 have several modes of operation – they can be set to halt or continue when a preset terminal count is reached, may use one of two reload register values, may be set to generate an internal interrupt request when the terminal count has been reached, and may retrigger on external events.

The instruction set of the 80186 is an expanded 8086 one; some instructions remain the same, but their execution has been speeded up (MUL, DIV, REP prefix for string moves, shifts and rotates), and some new instructions have been added. Some immediate operations have been added: shift, rotate by immediate, PUSH immediate. Block input-output (string transfers between memory and I/O rather than just memory-to-memory) have been added, CHECK, used to check an array index against array bounds, and PUSH ALL, POP ALL (registers) improve the existing operations. Two significant operations, to support block-structured high-level languages, are ENTER and LEAVE. They provide, as their names imply, high-level procedure calling and restoring functions. The peripheral control information is held in memory or I/O space, in a 256-byte block, addressed by an additional 'relocation register'. This is the register hardware addition to the 8086 structure, as may be seen from the register model of the 80186, shown in fig. 12.2.

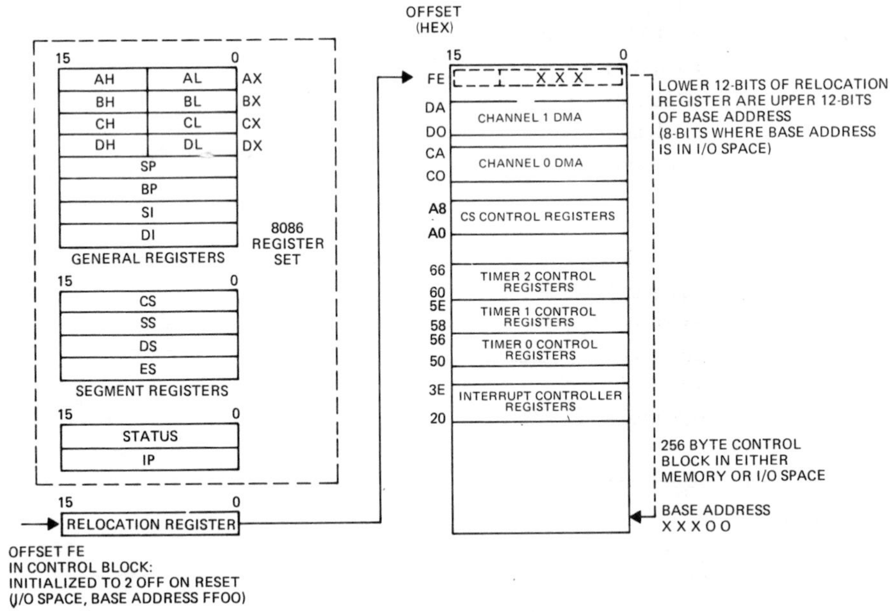

Fig. 12.2 iAPX186 register model.

Overall, the 80186 is a good example of the benefits brought about by increased integration level, on a 1978-vintage 16-bit CPU. More functions and instructions have been added to ensure compatibility with future microprocessors, and support functions which would previously have been implemented using MSI TTL devices or special interface chips (DMA, counter-timers, clock generator, wait-state generator, interrupt controller and address decoders) have now been brought within the CPU package. The estimated saving is perhaps twenty devices. Packaging has been changed away from the conventional dual-in-line package to a 68-pin JEDEC type A hermetic chip carrier. A chip carrier approach allows a smaller package (pins may be taken from all four sides) and allows easier heat sinking. A socket is available for this type A carrier, which has pins on 0.1 in centres and an integral heat sink. Both in its logic and functional enhancements, as well as in its package style, the 80186 indicates one direction in which 16-bit microprocessors generally may evolve. It is targetted at the small stand-alone applications, and may well become inexpensive enough to challenge 8-bit microprocessors in equipment such as stand-alone intelligent terminals, simple process control, and similar applications.

12.1.2 80286 OR iAPX286

At the opposite end of the 16-bit spectrum to the 80186 is the 80286. It is a sophisticated CPU which retains compatibility with the 8086, but which has built-in memory management and virtual memory support. The first obvious enhancement is the addressing range – the 286 will support a 16 Mbyte physical address space (24 bit), and the memory management facilities will provide up to a giga byte (Gbyte = 10^9 bytes or 2^{30} bytes) of virtual address space. The memory management unit (MMU) is operated in conjunction with a pipelining scheme which overlaps MMU, execution unit and bus controller/instruction decoder operation. A block diagram of the 80286 is shown in fig. 12.3. Four processing units operate concurrently to maximise throughput; in particular, the address unit appears transparent to the user program. Two modes of operation of the address unit are possible, the real address mode (equivalent to 8086 operation) and the protected mode (protected virtual address mode). Fig. 12.4 shows the available register sets for the two modes. Like the 8086, the 80286 has four 16-bit segment registers as well as the general-purpose registers. In real address mode, physical address computation is the same as in the 8086, where the 16-bit segment address and 16-bit offset address are combined to form a 20-bit physical byte address. In this mode, the maximum real address space is 1 Mbyte.

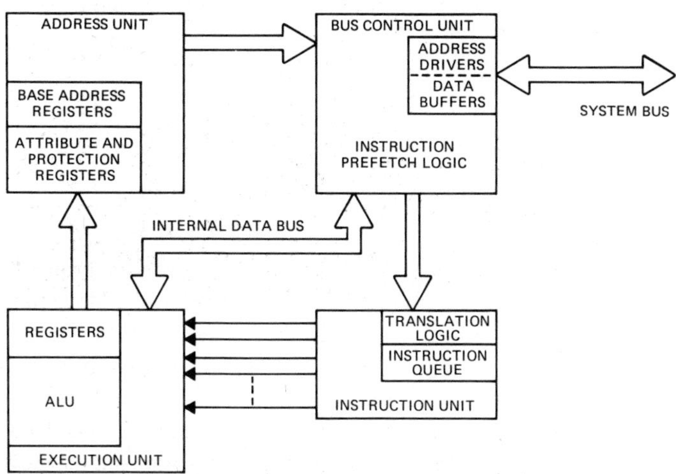

Fig. 12.3 iAPX286 schematic.

In protected mode, the same register set is available, but each of the four segment registers CS, DS, SS and ES is now associated with a segment descriptor register which gives segment size, segment base address and segment access rights. Additional task registers with similar format are available, reserved for operating system use. Protected mode is entered after power-up (which automatically causes the CPU to enter real address mode) by setting a bit in a status register. The only exit mechanism from protected mode is a system reset, which will clear the protected mode flag; the lack of a programmed exit protects the system from any program attempts to circumvent the protection mechanism of protected mode.

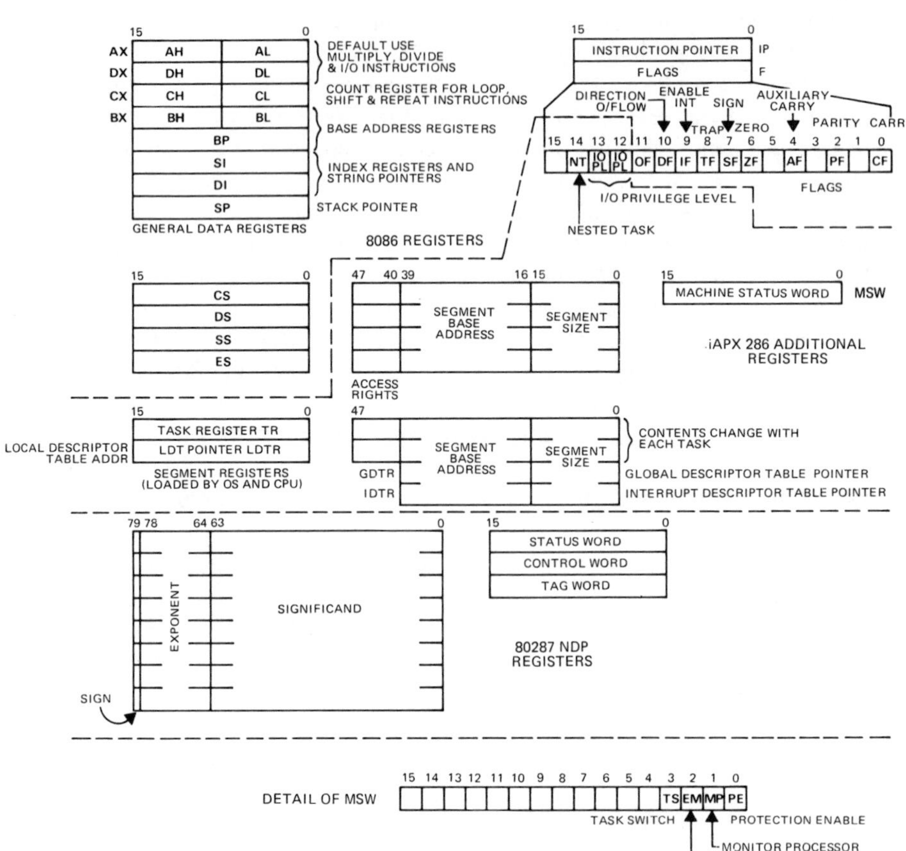

Fig. 12.4 iAPX286 register model.

The segment registers specify one of sixteen thousand (16K) possible 64 kbyte segments of virtual address space. The effective address specifies the offset within the segment, and translation from virtual address to physical address is carried out automatically. The translation process uses memory-based address descriptor tables, which define virtual address space for every task in the system. A segment register is used as an indirect segment address pointer, which indicates a table entry which points to the segment. The segment may be placed anywhere in physical memory, and its position dynamically changed without altering the program address constants. Although the segment registers in protected mode are named the same as the ones in real mode, the interpretation put upon their contents is rather different, being a table index rather than an address. It is nevertheless possible for programs written for the 8086 or real address mode, to be run unaltered in protected mode. The descriptor tables in memory are accessed using the contents of a segment register whenever the program loads that segment register. The CPU automatically copies the addressed descriptor table entry into the associated 48-bit segment extension register, so that the 24-bit segment base address, 16-bit segment size and 8-bit access or protection rights are all stored internally and are updated each time the segment register is changed. The cache memory consisting of the extension registers allows the virtual addressing mechanism to operate using internally-stored information to generate physical addresses.

An enhanced register flag set has fields which denote I/O privilege level and nested tasks, while the machine status word (MSW) contains bits which may be set under program control to control task switching, enable protection, and to cater for coprocessor use and emulation. The descriptor tables which are accessed whenever a segment register is loaded, are themselves pointed to by the contents of the other registers of fig. 12.4: the global descriptor table register (GDTR), which is used by operating system software, the interrupt descriptor table register (IDTR), and the local descriptor table register (LDTR), which is capable of supporting multiple local descriptor tables used by applications software. By changing the LDTR segment register contents, an operating system can effect a switch from one user's address space to another's. The task register (TR) points to the task state segment of the currently active task. Whenever a task switch is made, the CPU saves the state of the microprocessor in this segment before it loads the state of the new task. (The state, in this context, consists of the contents of the task-variable program registers, stack segment selectors and pointers for the three highest privilege levels, the selector for the task LDT, and a link which may point to another nested task.)

Protection in the 80286 consists of four privilege levels, level 0 (most privileged) to level 3 (least privileged). Applications programs normally run at level 3, while the operating system kernel runs at level 0, and other systems programs run at levels 1 and 2. The objective of these privilege levels is to isolate each task in the system from the other tasks. Transfer of control between system modules must be carefully regulated so that a low-privileged program invoking a highly-privileged operating-system service, will not be able to gain privileged access to the operating system. A model of the privilege protection mechanism is shown in fig. 12.5. A separate stack and stack pointer is maintained for each level (this feature prevents an applications program from causing corruption of a system routine's stack), and protection hardware allows a program to access data only at an equal or lower privilege level, and only call routines at the same or higher privilege level. During a call, where necessary, parameters are automatically transferred from the calling program's stack to the called routine's stack, in a manner transparent to the user. To call a procedure in a more-privileged level, a 'call gate' mechanism is used, which restricts access and allows tighter control.

Apart from privilege level control, the 286 also supports segment typing, allowing segments to be defined as execute-only, execute-and-read, read-only, and read-write. When a segment register is loaded, typing is automatically verified by hardware, i.e. the stack segment should be read-write, and the code segment should be executable.

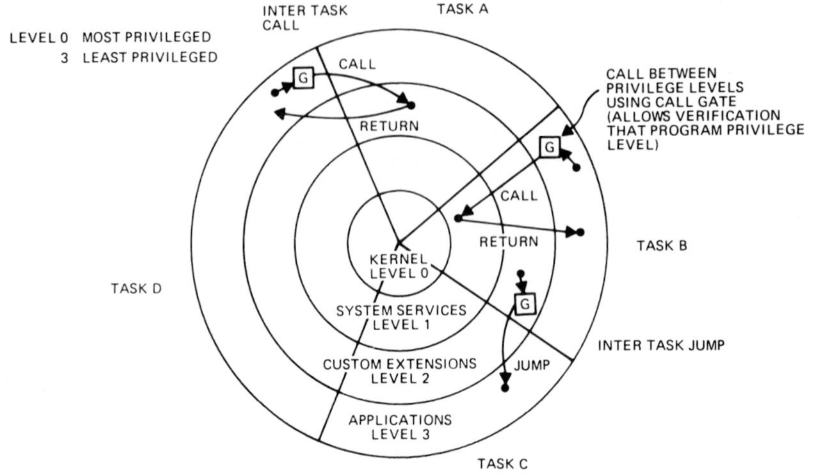

Fig. 12.5 iAPX286 privilege levels.

Operating-system support is provided in the form of a sophisticated interrupt structure which supports two classes of context switch, one which transfers control to service routines which are in the address space of the interrupted task, while the other provides a high-speed switch from the interrupted task to a special isolated interrupt service task (without involving the operating system). Virtual memory support is provided by segment descriptor flags ('used', 'not present in primary memory', 'present', used to aid swapping between secondary and primary memory). Some fault tolerance is provided with restartable instructions (basically segment loading and stack reference instructions) which allow recovery from stack overflow.

As well as these memory-management features, the 286 has an enhanced instruction set, compatible with the 8086. Added are 'procedure implementation instructions' ENTER and LEAVE which use stack 'frames' used by block structured high-level languages, and PUSH ALL, POP ALL multiple register save and restore instructions. A set of protected virtual address mode instructions are available, which allow the descriptor table registers to be loaded, the descriptor table register contents to be stored, and requested privilege level adjusted. In addition, verification instructions for protection parameters are provided, for checking bounds, load access rights, segment limits, read access and write access. They are supported by an extended interrupt vector table (table 12.2).

Those instructions which are the same as 8086 instructions will execute considerably faster than their 8086 counterparts, many implemented directly in hardware rather than using microcode.

Table 12.2

Exception	Description
0	Divide error
1	Single step
2	NMI
3	Breakpoint
4	INTO (overflow)
5	Bounds exceeded
6	Invalid opcode
7	Microprocessor extension not present
8	Double protection
9	Extension segment overrun
10	Task segment format error
11	Segment not present
12	Stack underflow/overflow
13	Protection violation (general)
14-15	Reserved
16	Extension error
17-31	Reserved

The 80286 has significantly improved the 8086 CPU for more sophisticated applications, and provides features which will facilitate multitasking, real time operations, and operating system support, as well as high-level language implementation. All these will feature strongly in other future 16-bit microprocessors.

12.2 Future 16-bit microcomputers

The impetus for producing a 16-bit 'computer-on-a-chip' is really to allow higher-speed processing and better numerical computation facilities (features of a 16-bit CPU) together with on-chip interfaces. At least two manufacturers already have devices ready, and others are likely to follow. Applications include not only the traditional single-chip areas of sequence controllers, simple analogue controller replacement, and intelligent peripheral devices, but also signal processing devices and more sophisticated control systems (both requiring numerically-intensive computation). The Intel 8096[5] is a new microprocessor rather than a derivative of the 8086, while the Mostek 68200[6] claims some compatibility with the Motorola 68000, but is not directly compatible.

12.2.1 8096

The 8096 microcontroller is a superb example of how improved semiconductor fabrication can be used to provide a significantly more powerful design. It is shown in block diagram form in fig. 12.6. As well as a 16-bit CPU, with on-chip

8 kbyte ROM (program memory), 232-byte RAM (data memory and register file) and digital parallel I/O ports, which include bus expansion ports, the 8096 also possesses an eight-channel 10-bit analogue-to-digital converter (ADC), a full-duplex UART (serial universal asynchronous receiver-transmitter), two 16-bit timers, and a programmable pulse-width modulation (PWM) output. The interrupt structure allows eight priority levels.

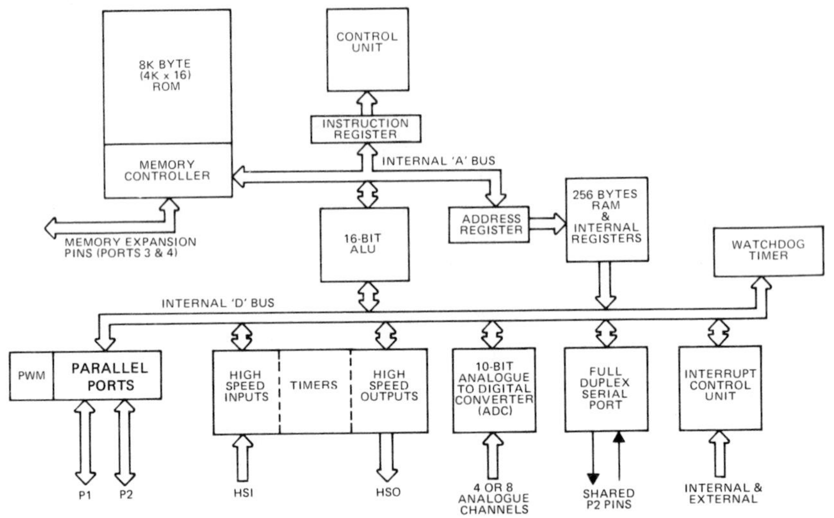

Fig. 12.6 8096 schematic.

The memory map of the 8096 is shown in fig. 12.7 – from this, it may be seen that up to 64 kbytes of memory space may be addressed if external memory is allowed, and I/O is memory-mapped. A significant feature of the internal structure is the use of separate data and instruction buses, a scheme which allows instructions to be executed from external ROM or RAM, but not from internal RAM. The internal on-chip RAM forms an effective large register space, so that commonly-used data held in this space may be accessed quickly, and slower external references need only be generated for infrequently-used data. The 8096 is really the 16-bit equivalent of Intel's successful 8-bit 8048 family of micro-controllers, with vastly expanded input-output capability.

One of the main features of the 8096 is the way in which special input-output is handled, which minimises CPU overheads and increases system flexibility. A high-speed I/O subsystem linked to the 8096 timers is the key to this flexibility. On the input side of the I/O subsystem (fig. 12.8(a)) are four inputs connected to 'change detector' logic which accepts an 8-bit programmable mode word which has two bits dedicated to each input, allowing recognised transitions to be selected as positive, negative, both positive and negative, and positive divided by eight. Each input can be disabled separately by software. A 16-bit timer (timer 0) associated with the input logic is incremented once every eight CPU clock cycles, and counts from 0000H to FFFFH, setting a status bit and generating an interrupt every time overflow (transition from FFFFH to 0000H) occur. The four change detector state outputs and the timer count value (read when an defined input transition has been recognised) are fed as a 20-bit word to a first-in, first-out (FIFO) buffer, which can hold up to seven recorded changes and their associated time values. This input system forms a sophisticated programmable event recorder, which can be used to measure time between events, pulse widths, and frequency and can store up to seven events without CPU intervention. The timer operates as a real time clock.

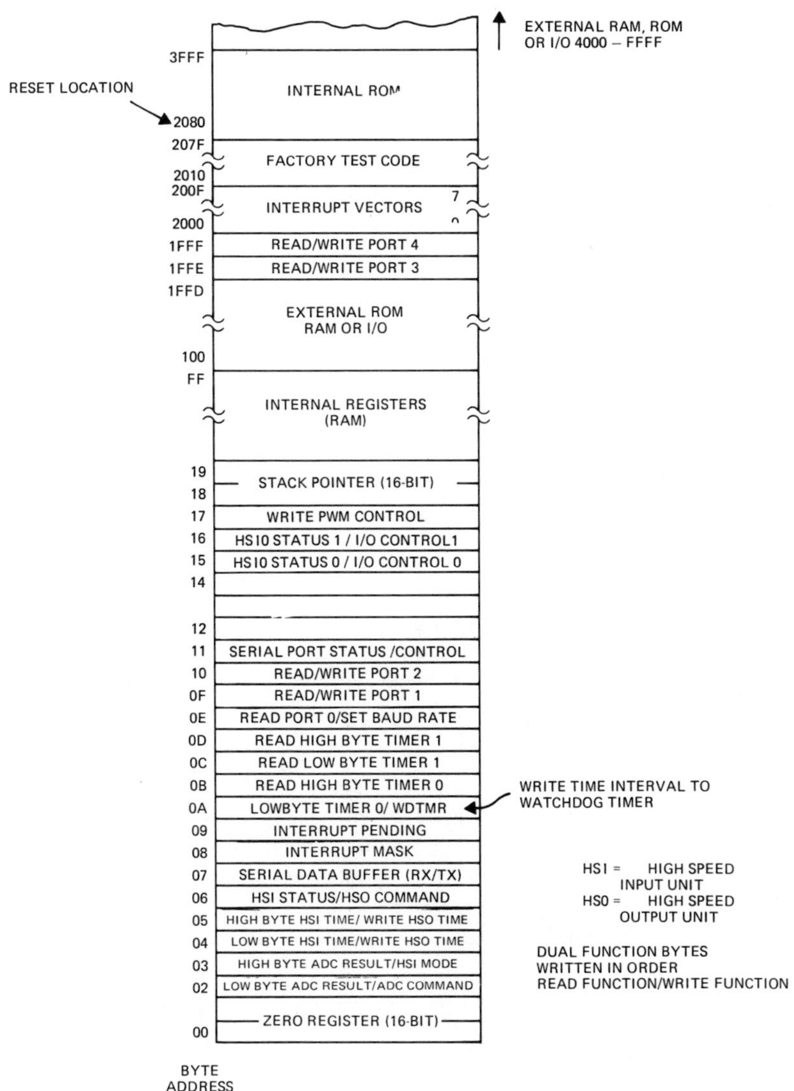

Fig. 12.7 8096 memory map.

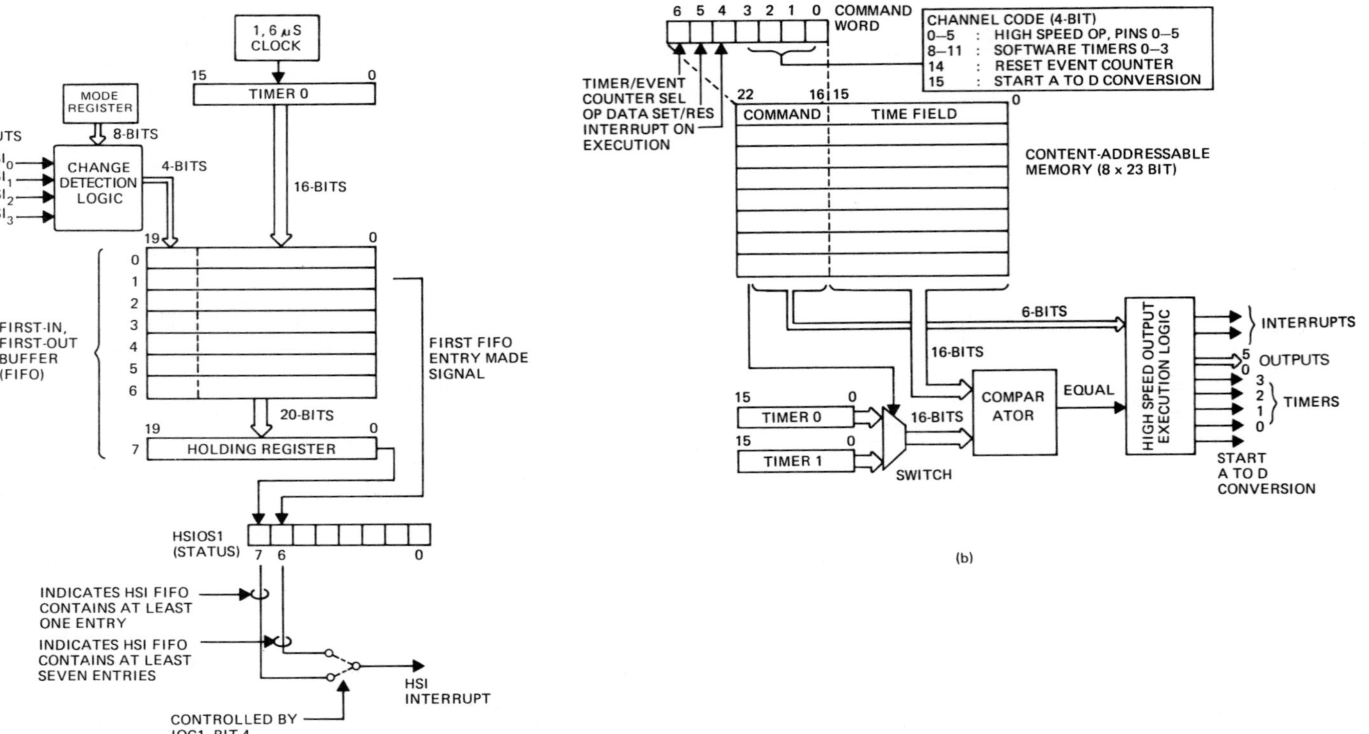

Fig. 12.8 8096 I/O subsystems: (a) high-speed input unit (HSI), (b) high-speed output unit (HSO).

The high-speed output subsystem (fig. 12.8(b)) uses the same timer (timer 0), but in addition, it has an event counter (timer 1). The heart of the output unit is a content-addressable memory consisting of eight 23-bit registers, each of which may be programmed by the CPU with a 7-bit command field, and a 16-bit time field. The command field defines the operation to be performed by the output execution unit; typically this may be high-speed output on one of five pins, either set or reset, start A/D conversion, reset the event counter, control software timers, interrupt on execution, and whether to use the internal timer or the event counter to determine when the command is to be executed. The time (or event) field contains a value which is compared with the contents of either timer 0 or the event counter – when a match occurs, the specified command is executed. This unit provides for sophisticated sequence control; for example, the event counter may be programmed to be reset when a given count is reached, giving a modulo-N divider; the timer-controlled ADC will sample at precisely controlled instants.

As well as the high-speed I/O subsystem, other I/O facilities on the 8096 include a 16-bit 'watchdog' timer connected to the system clock, which must be reset by software at least every 13 ms or so, to avoid overflow. If the counter is not reset before overflow occurs, the 8096 is reset automatically by the overflow condition. Any 8096 software errors, such as one causing infinite looping, will not be able to 'hang-up' the CPU indefinitely, since the forced reset will break the loop condition. The serial interface is similar to one designed originally for the 8-bit microcontroller, the 8051. It includes an internal 15-bit baud rate generator, with a selectable clock input, and has four modes:

(a) A shift register (mode 0), which provides simple synchronous input-output, synchronised by the internally generated, externally available clock.
(b) A 7-bit + parity (8-bit) UART.
(c) An 8-bit + parity (9-bit) UART.
(d) A 9 bit data/address mode used for multiple microprocessor configurations.

An on-chip pulse width modulation (PWM) generator uses logic to provide a simple variable duty cycle oscillator with a fixed repetition rate, with the duty cycle set by an 8-bit word loaded into a control register. The crystal clock frequency is divided by three, and used to clock an 8-bit free-running counter, whose contents are continuously compared with the 8-bit word loaded into the control register. An internal set-reset bistable is set when equality is achieved, and reset when the free-running counter overflows from FFH to 00H. The duty cycle is thus variable in 1/256 increments of the repetition period. The PWM facility can be used as a digital-to-analogue converter, if used with an external integrator.

The analogue-to-digital converter uses 4 bits of an 8-bit command register to specify one of eight channels (3 bits) and method of initiating a conversion, whether immediately following the command register write, or via the high-speed I/O subsystem (1 bit). The result is returned in two 8-bit output data registers, one containing the eight most significant bits, and the other containing the two least significant bits, a 3-bit channel indicator, and a status (conversion in progress) bit. The 10-bit converter uses a successive-approximation conversion technique, which gives a conversion time of 33.6 μs with a 15 MHz CPU clock, for analogue inputs in the range 0 to 5 V.

The instruction set of the 8096 is very much simpler than its mainstream 16-bit CPU counterparts. Because the device is designed as a microcontroller, and needs only a limited (64K) addressing range, the addressing modes of the CPU are relatively simple, made more so by the fact that the internal RAM is a 256-byte register space, which may be addressed as 128 16-bit word registers or 64 32-bit registers occupying the first 256 bytes of memory address space. External RAM is addressed as normal read-write memory, and can occupy byte addresses 0400H to FFFFH. The first 24 bytes of register space are used for on-chip I/O registers, with the 16-bit word register at location 0018H reserved as the stack pointer (note that 16-bit word registers are aligned on even-byte boundaries). The addressing modes are direct, register-indirect, immediate, auto-increment, short (8-bit displacement) indexed, and long (16-bit displacement) indexed. The instruction set contains the conventional mix of arithmetic, logical, and conditional operations. Notably among the arithmetic and logic instructions there are three-operand instructions (ADD, SUBTRACT, MULTIPLY and LOGICAL AND) which eliminate the need for many move instructions. There is an instruction NORMALIZE, which allows fast implementation of floating point data types, and multibit shifts, which allow scaled-integer arithmetic (faster than floating-point), usual for signal processing or control applications. Jumps, both conditional and unconditional, and calls, use program-counter-relative addressing, in a short or long displacement form. Iteration control may be implemented with a decrement-and-jump primitive.

The 8096 is available in both chip carrier (68-pin) and dual-in-line (48-pin) packaging. It represents a real advance in single-chip microcontroller technology, bringing together the combination of 16-bit CPU and 10-bit ADC, and also providing a digital I/O system which itself is a significant departure from existing designs. The I/O subsystem caters for many of the common tasks required of a microcontroller with a minimum of intervention from the main CPU. This approach towards integrating commonly-used functions in hardware is likely to be copied by the other main manufacturers. A further feature, currently supported solely by Intel, is the use, as for the 80186 and 80286, of a chip carrier rather than a dual-in-line package, allowing more connections to be brought out of the chip, and a smaller socket (implying higher component packaging density). For an input-output intensive device such as a microcontroller, the more available I/O pins, the better.

12.2.2 MK68200

The 68200 was designed by Mostek as a single-chip microcontroller with direct bus compatibility with the Motorola 68000, and with a similar instruction set. It can operate either as a stand-alone device, or as a universal peripheral controller (UPC) for 68000-based systems. The system consists of the 16-bit CPU, internal 4 kbyte ROM occupying addresses 0000H to 0FFFH, internal 256-byte RAM occupying addresses FB00H to FBFFH, a serial I/O channel, a number of pins of parallel I/O, an interrupt controller, and three 16-bit timers. In common with 6800, 68000 practice, input-output devices are all memory-mapped, occupying addresses in the MK68200 in the range FC00H to FFFFH.

The three 16-bit timers A, B and C have a number of programmable modes which differ, depending upon which timer is selected:

Timer A: Interval timer, event counter, or pulse width and period measurement.
Timer B: Interval timer, retriggerable or non-retriggerable one-shot (monostable).
Timer C: Interval timer or baud rate generator, for the serial channel.

Timers A and B have associated external input and output connections.

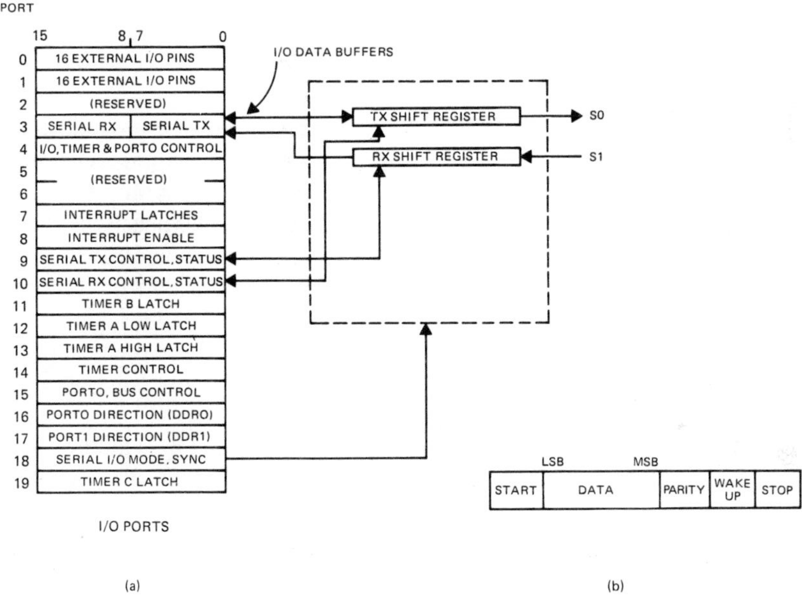

Fig. 12.9 MK68200 serial I/O: (a) serial I/O channel, (b) serial frame with wake-up.

The serial I/O channel is shown in diagrammatic form in fig. 12.9(a). Double buffering is provided on both transmit and receive, with full duplex operation. The format may be asynchronous, with bit rates up to 250 kbits/s, and with programmable wordlength, parity bits and number of stop bits. The byte synchronous mode will support 1 Mbit/s rate. An interesting feature of the serial channel is its ability to add a 'wake-up' bit to a serial frame (fig. 12.9(b)), which allows a distinction to be made between normal data words and special address words. This feature allows the microprocessor to be programmed so that it is interrupted when it receives its own address pattern and can then change mode to receive data. In a multiple microprocessor system which uses a single serial link for communication, and which consists of a number of MK68200s, any single microprocessor may be accessed using its address and the wakeup bit.

The on-chip interrupt controller allows sixteen possible interrupt inputs, each with its own interrupt location: the lowest sixteen words of address space contain the starting addresses of the relevant interrupt service routines. The interrupt types and locations are shown in table 12.3, which lists them in descending order of priority. All maskable interrupts (all except RESET and NMI) may be disabled either by a single bit in the CPU status register, or individually, with unique mask bits.

Table 12.3 MK68200 interrupts

Interrupt		Location
RESET		0000
NMI		0002
S	(spare)	0004
XI2	(external interrupt 2)	0006
STRL	(strobe 'L')	0008
TAOI	(timer A output)	000A
TAI	(timer A input)	000C
STRH	(strobe 'H')	000E
RSCI	(received address data)	0010
RNI	(received normal data)	0012
XI1	(external interrupt 1)	0014
TBOI	(timer B output)	0016
TBI	(timer B input)	0018
XI0	(external interrupt 0)	001A
XMTI	(serial transmit interrupt)	001C
TCI	(timer C interrupt)	001E

Bus outputs of the MK68200 may be configured in a number of ways. Fig. 12.10 shows a connection diagram for the device (48-pin package); for expansion of the RAM, ROM or I/O externally, or DMA access to external memory space, the microprocessor may be put into an external bus mode, using the MODE pin which is automatically examined at RESET time. Port 0 then becomes a 16-bit multiplexed address/data bus, while the upper (most significant) byte of Port 1 becomes a control bus. The 8-bit control bus is available as a general-purpose bus with address and data strobes, R/$\overline{W}$ output and bus request-grant logic, or (with a different chip mask option) as a UPC, which generates 68000-compatible control signals. Using an external address latch to demultiplex data and address, the UPC signals can be connected directly to 68000 bus. In such a configuration, the bus request-grant logic of the UPC will always act as a bus requester, with the 68000 as bus master.

The register set of the 68200 (fig. 12.11) is similar to that of the 68000, but with only one stack pointer, and with only 16-bit wide registers. Addressing modes follow those of the 68000: register, register indirect with no increment or displacement, with postincrement, with predecrement, and with displacement, PC-relative, absolute, and immediate. The instruction set has been defined to minimise code space, by using single-word opcodes for the most used instructions, and to maximise execution speed. Bit operations feature strongly, with not only bit set, clear and test, but also bit change, bit exchange (all linked with bit test) and bit test-and-set semaphore support (this last operation is indivisible). Decrement-and-jump on condition instructions provide iteration control, and as well as normal binary arithmetic, a comprehensive set of decimal operations is supported. It is to be expected that any 16-bit microprocessor will nowadays provide hardware multiply and divide instructions, and the 68200 is no exception. The microprocessor also copies from the 68000 the move multiple registers instruction, and corresponding multiple PUSHes and POPs.

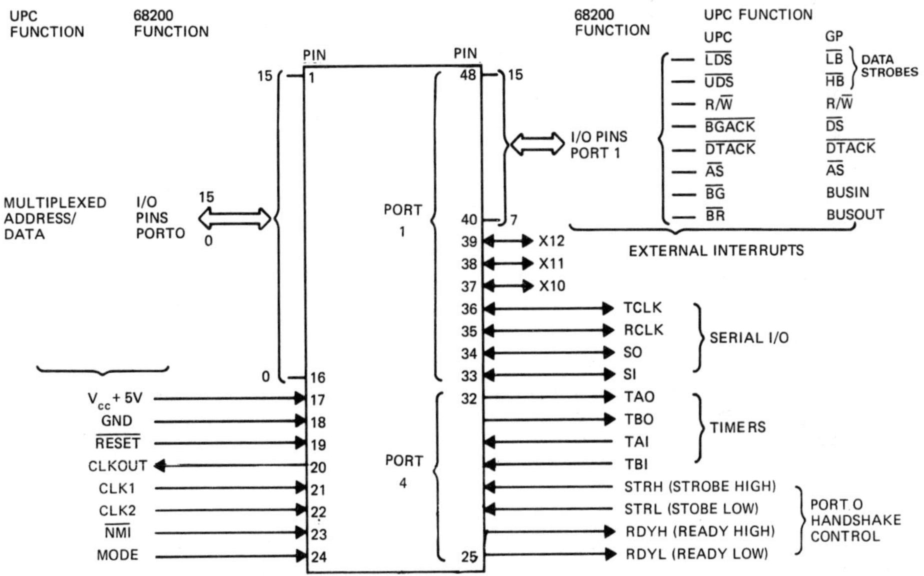

Fig. 12.10 MK68200 pinouts.

The MK68200 is a rather more conventional single chip microcontroller than the 8096, and is aimed at somewhat different applications. It may well more accurately represent the majority of future controllers, since few manufacturers can successfully combine analogue and digital circuitry on the same chip, and most may opt for a similar approach. This automatically implies larger overall systems since any analogue-to-digital conversion must be performed externally, and any sophisticated digital I/O must be performed by software. Because the 68200 is all digital, and sufficiently simple to be accommodated in a dual-in-line package rather than a chip carrier, it promises to be considerably cheaper than the 8096.

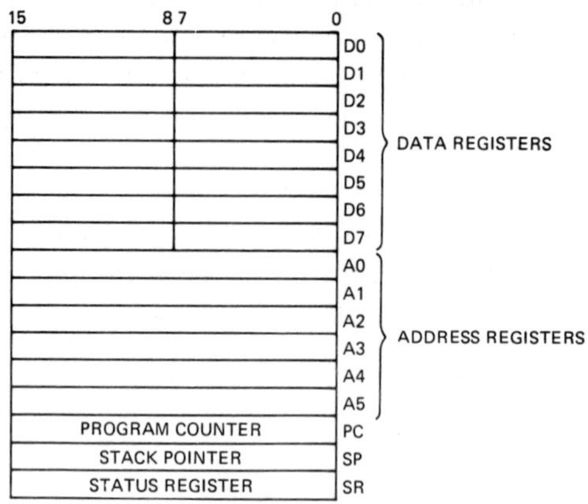

Fig. 12.11 MK68200 register set.

12.3 Special microprocessors

Into this category fall the object-oriented microprocessor, such as the 32-bit iAPX432[7–13], and more unconventional 'data-flow'[14] machines. Such special-purpose machines may show distinct performance advantages over conventional microprocessors which use a normal instruction set, sequential operation and a program counter. Although performance is important, it may not be the only factor governing choice of a microprocessor; indeed the deciding factor may be ease of use, software support, or range of available interfaces. Any radically new microprocessor will most likely not be able to use the existing ranges of interfaces, and will require a large amount of software, and some sort of development system. Because of the complexity of any new design, a large financial investment in support, both hardware and software, will be required, and such systems will take a considerable time to develop. Because of the support factor, and the requirement for user training, it is unlikely that a microprocessor based on a completely new concept will make an immediate impact on microprocessor applications, rather that there will be initial user resistance to it, and that user acceptance will come gradually.

12.3.1 iAPX432

The Intel iAPX432 consists of a three-chip microprocessor set: a two-chip general data processor (GDP) and a single-chip interface processor (IP). The objectives of the device designers were:

(a) To create a microprocessor suitable for complex, software-intensive applications, which would lend itself to multiprocessing and distributed data processing systems.
(b) To ensure a high-degree of fault tolerance (both in hardware and software), and the possibility of 'graceful enhancement', whereby a system can be

increased in power and throughput by adding identical microprocessors, but without the heavy system software overheads often associated with distributed systems.

(c) To support structured, modular software developments by using a high-level language as a 'native language', and discouraging the use of machine code or assembly code.

The final design has a number of unique features which represent a brave attempt to break away from current microprocessor concepts. The iAPX432 microprocessor is 'object-oriented', rather than byte- or word-oriented, so its architecture is arranged so as to facilitate handling different object types as complete entities. The hardware and microcode firmware is designed to recognise and manipulate a number of different objects (or data structures in memory which describe software features):

(a) Data object (simplest) is a structure in memory which contains information in integer, real, character, array or other primitive data types, or combination of types.
(b) Instruction or program object is a defined structure which contains processor instructions and no data. The object is used by the microprocessor as a source of instructions to be fetched and executed.
(c) A context object is a data structure which contains information for executing a given procedure (i.e. for each particular instance of executing an instruction object). It will contain the values of instruction pointer and stack pointer, a return link pointer area, and references for all the objects (usually one instruction object and perhaps several data objects) accessed by the context. The combination of context object, instruction object and data objects provides all the information necessary during one particular execution of a program. A defined 'access environment' for each context provides protection by restricting access to certain objects.
(d) The process object contains information pertaining to the state of each process, or collection of context objects in the system, such as its status (whether it is running, waiting, suspended, etc.), its scheduling information (e.g. priority), and a reference for the currently executing context. The process object consists basically of the data and references necessary for an operating system running on a single CPU, to enable allocation of resources and creation of a machine environment for each particular task or process.
(e) A microprocessor object takes the modular approach typified by the previous objects a stage further. It is a description of a complete microprocessor state, which contains status information, diagnostic information, and references for the current executing process. This logical extension to encompass a complete microprocessor allows easier multiple microprocessor systems management.

The objects defined above have a hierarchy shown in fig. 12.12. The heart of the modular concept is the context object, which, in its access environment specification, more or less requires virtual addressing, with segmentation, including access segments which provide for different protection for different users of the same object. A single operating system can be written which will exercise control over all the objects defined, including microprocessor objects; for the iAPX432, the system is called iMAX, and it embodies all the real time requirements specified in chapter 8.

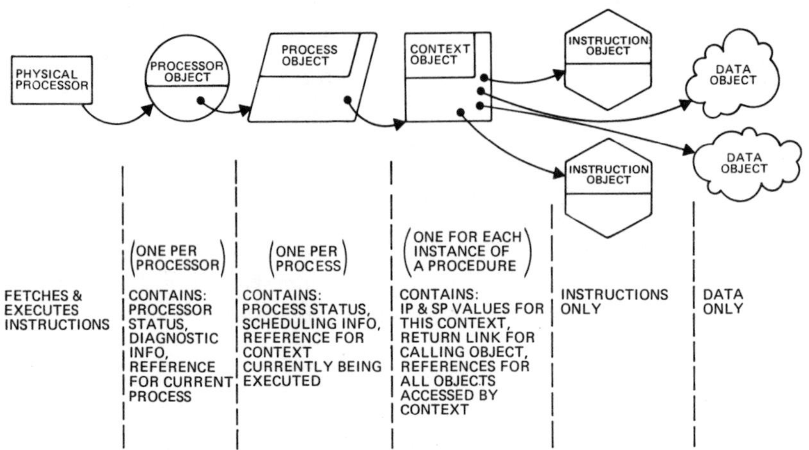

Fig. 12.12 iAPX432 object hierarchy.

For the highest level of the system, which deals with multiple microprocessors, some means of communication must be defined. Conventionally, this takes the form of a hardware bus, but the iAPX432 instead defines a microprocessor connection protocol which is independent of hardware structure, and which allows an individual designer to select an appropriate connection standard. All 432 microprocessors are compatible with the interconnect protocol, which is organised on a *packet* basis, with acknowledgement of a transfer arranged in the same way. Using packets will minimise any hogging of a communications bus by a single microprocessor. The same communications bus is used by microprocessors and by system facilities such as memory and its data width, for instance, is determined by the performance required. A request packet, originated by the microprocessor, may be sent, containing address, byte count and request type information. The packet bus will then be available for other microprocessors, until the recipient of the request packet responds with a reply packet containing data, for instance. The packet protocol allows packets of variable length; a single request or reply packet may contain from 1 to 16 bytes of data. The use of packets also brings flexibility to the logical side of communications. For instance, a microprocessor can send a 'broadcast' packet simultaneously to several other microprocessors in the system, or can send an attention or 'wakeup' signal. A common area of memory called the 'interprocessor message area' is used for passing messages between microprocessors. The originating microprocessor will place its message in the area, and notify the intended recipient of the message's availability using a packet over the communications bus. Typical interprocessor messages in this form are operating system commands to start, stop, or more sophisticated functions like redispatch.

Input-output for the iAPX432 is performed using an attached I/O microprocessor, normally a conventional CPU system (perhaps Multibus based), which contains its own CPU (typically an 8086), memory and specific device interfaces. The GDP communicates with this I/O subsystem via its own interface processor (IP). The IP supports mapping registers which translate the I/O subsystem address space into that of the 432 in a manner completely transparent to the I/O CPU, so that operation of the I/O microprocessor is completely autonomous. Communication betwen the I/O subsystem and the 432 is complicated by the lack of 432 interrupts. The 432 uses messages to communicate; those received by the IP are placed into common I/O subsystem memory, and the IP then generates a 'message interrupt' for the I/O CPU, which can then read the message data. Communication in the reverse direction is implemented by the IP, which appears to the I/O subsystem as a memory-mapped interface device, with direct access to IP registers. The CPU in the I/O subsystem can write to these IP registers, and cause the IP to invoke a 'send message' function, which delivers a 432-format message to the required GDP, communicating in the usual way with packets and the 'interprocessor message area'.

The 432 has a microcode 'silicon operating system', which operates with objects of the form described, implementing virtual memory management, and segment swapping via the I/O subsystem. Part of the microcode (6%) is used in implementing the basic 432 instruction set, and part to implement virtual addressing (7%), but most of the microcode is used for operating system primitives, such as 'send message', etc. Instructions in the 432 are bit-oriented, so any memory organisation will suit the microprocessor, and instructions may be of variable size, and start on any bit boundaries.

The addressing modes are particularly suitable for high-level language support, most being similar to base + displacement, base + index and base + displacement + index, but with no register references (too specific for HLL compiler construction). All operands reside either in memory, or in a hardware managed 'expression evaluation' stack structure. These features, coupled with instructions supporting primitive data types character, short integer (16 bits), short ordinal (16 bits), integer, ordinal and short real (all 32 bits), real (64 bits) and temporary real (80 bits), allow direct translation of many Ada statements into single 432 instructions. Indeed, users will be discouraged from using anything but a high-level language such as Ada for 432 applications. A final hardware feature supporting the 432 operating system, and which can be used to provide graceful failure modes, is the fault-checking mode of the 432 devices. Two devices may be connected in parallel as shown in fig. 12.13, with one of them configured in 'checker mode' and the other as a 'master'. The checker mode device duplicates all operations of the master, and compares its results with those appearing at the corresponding master pins, signalling an error if they are not identical.

The 432 microprocessor set is unique, and represents one of the most advanced microprocessors available today. Naturally it is expensive, but this is hardly surprising when one considers that an 8 MHz clock 432 will out-perform an IBM

370/148 mainframe computer for typical numerically-intensive benchmarks. The approach taken by the 432 means that the very labour-intensive parts of applications software – using and interfacing a sophisticated operating system, and writing applications packages in a high-level language that is well-suited to the computer, reliable, and promotes good programming practice – have been largely taken care of. The relatively high hardware cost is more than offset by the potential savings in software effort and in time to engineer a system. The cost to the semiconductor manufacturer (in this case Intel) of development of such a complex device, its support software and applications information, has been immense. It is difficult to envisage more than one or two other manufacturers having both the capability in resources and effort and the will to implement microprocessors of equivalent sophistication.

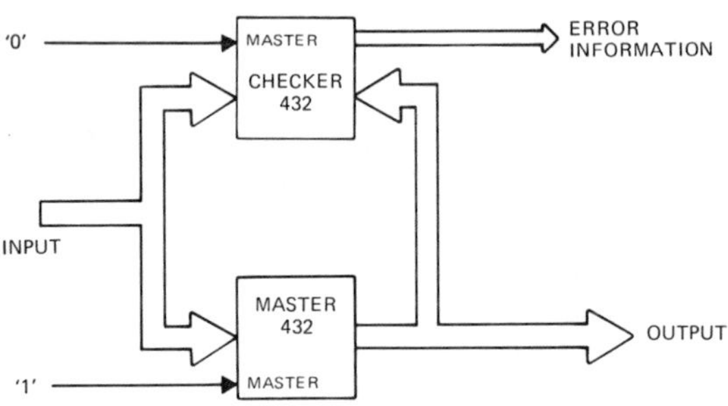

Fig. 12.13 iAPX432 error checking.

12.3.2 DATA FLOW COMPUTERS

In many academic computer science departments, and in many industrial research establishments, the fashionable advanced research topic is 'data flow'. The concept of a computer which would be controlled in its operation by data being available and being required, rather than by a system clock and a sequential list of instructions, is not a new one. Until recently, the requisite hardware for economically implementing such a machine was rather beyond the limits of technology. Several establishments have now recognised that it is now practicable to build such a machine and have started constructional work, coupled with intensive research into the best way of exploiting the inherent parallelism in data-flow computing, and into ways of solving the very difficult software problems posed by the technique.

Data-flow computing can be illustrated using a 'directed graph' similar to one designed for critical path analysis (often called a PERT chart). Operations may be shown in parallel on the chart so long as the information they require is available, and will appear in a sequence when one operation depends upon completion of another for its information. Use of such a technique suggests the maximum number of required operations which can be executed concurrently, the minimum number of sequential ones (which limits the degree of parallelism which can be exploited), and can suggest ways in which a system may be configured to optimise its performance. When used as a management tool, critical path analysis is usually performed manually, but it is possible to define the analysis rules in such a way that they may be executed by a computer; several university groups are working on languages and compilers which will ease the specification of processes to enhance their parallelism and provide for an easy translation from source code to a directed graph, partitioned for the number of available parallel microprocessors in a system.

The design of parallel microprocessors for a data-flow machine is likely to differ somewhat from conventional microprocessors. Instead of executing one operation or primitive at intervals dictated by the clock rate of the microprocessor, a data-flow machine will execute an operation when data and operands are available. While a conventional microprocessor will have a program counter to indicate the next instruction to be performed, the data-flow machine will have a collection of instructions which are executed when possible. In a typical scheme, as it becomes possible to execute an instruction, it will be queued and executed when the CPU is free; once execution is complete, results may be queued in a buffer for access by another CPU, and the next instruction in the queue executed. Efficiency will be high so long as the queue is not empty, and the CPU idle. A hardware configuration to support this non-sequential operation may well take the form of an execution unit supported by a sophisticated stack or first-in, first-out (FIFO) buffer, and could be integrated as a single device. Communication between microprocessors must be defined, and may well take the form of a packet bus.

So many groups are working on data-flow hardware and software, that there is a high probability that a commercially-available data-flow computer, and its support software, will appear in the next few years. An integrated version, supported by one of the major manufacturers, will soon follow. The iAPX432, although not a full data-flow computer, has many aspects of its design which would be well-suited to the task.

12.4 Conclusions

The rate of development of microprocessor hardware and software has been so rapid as to considerably outpace applications, and is continuing unabated. It is difficult to predict the future of an industry only twelve years old, and already an economic force of paramount importance. What is certain, however, is that new developments will bring new opportunities for applications, and that the whole future of microprocessors will be equally as exciting as their brief history. If parallels can be drawn with the minicomputer and mainframe worlds, it would seem that the 16-bit microprocessor represents the best compromise between complexity and precision, cost and speed, and that the computer with 16-bit word length will continue to be a 'standard' workhorse machine for some considerable time, and will not be quickly superseded by 32-bit and other machines. 16-bit microprocessor designs may well find that, despite rapidly changing technology, that it is their longevity as well as their performance that is the key to their importance.

CHAPTER 13
Microprocessor update

The wealth of new microprocessors which have appeared since the original publication of this book have prompted the addition of this new chapter. Already, before many of the 16-bit microprocessors released since 1978 have achieved volume shipments equivalent to their 8-bit counterparts, they have evolved into more advanced devices, and upward-compatible 32-bit devices have been launched. Three terms characterise the evolutionary trend in CPU design – memory management, virtual memory and cache memory. The first two concepts have been described earlier in the book and only examples of them will be given in this chapter.

Cache memory owes its development to the minicomputer world, where its use is widespread. It is justified in the microprocessor area by the fact that CPU on-chip memory can be accessed much faster than external system memory, since no bus cycles are needed. As the CPU executes instructions, they are simultaneously stored in its local on-chip memory. If the instructions are executed again, in a program loop, execution will be much faster from the on-chip memory than with the bus cycles necessary for execution from external memory. To optimise cache benefits it is necessary to achieve a trade-off between the size of the internal cache memory and the likelihood of a cache miss (i.e. execution of an instruction which is not found in the cache). A very practical arrangement, used by many manufacturers, is to organise the cache as a number (perhaps 16) of blocks or lines of perhaps 16 or 32 bytes of successive instructions. Associated with each line is an address field (or tag bits) and one bit for each byte (or word) in the line, to indicate whether the byte or word is valid or not. As an instruction fetch cycle starts, the address of the instruction is compared with the tag bits of each line. If a match is found, the valid bit associated with the addressed word is checked, and if this bit is valid, the instruction is fetched from the cache. (Because the cache is not addressed as a conventional memory, but has addresses stored with their associated data, it is a type of associative memory.) If the valid bit indicates that the addressed word is not in the cache, an external bus cycle is generated, the instruction fetched is loaded into the appropriate part of the cache ready to be used again if required, and its associated bit is set to indicate that the word is now valid. If no tag bits correspond to the address issued, the 'cache miss' causes internal cache logic to allocate a new line for the instruction, set the line tag bits to the new address and reset all the line valid bits, an external bus fetch cycle is generated, and the fetched instruction is stored in the newly-allocated line.

Allocation of lines in the cache requires some form of algorithm built into the cache logic. Perhaps the most common strategy is to overwrite the least-recently-used line. LRU algorithms work well, and optimise cache use, since they allow recently-used lines which have widely-separated addresses to be retained in the cache until their use declines. On a typical mix of program instructions, a cache memory will give a worthwhile increase in processor speed due to the shorter access times and higher speed of internal CPU memory. Examples of new processors which use cache memory and on-chip memory management and virtual memory are given in this chapter.

Applications, too, have developed rapidly. The personal computer market has become dominated, particularly in the USA, by the IBM PC, and its operating system, PC-DOS (or MS-DOS). Consequently, a brief description of this product is given, to supplement the Chapter 11, 'Applications'.

13.1 Virtual memory and the Z8000 family

The original members of the Z8000 family, the Z8001 and Z8002, have already been described in this book. The family has been extended in response to industry trends towards more sophisticated use of memory management devices to include two virtual memory processing units (VMPUs), the Z8003 and Z8004. The two new CPUs are virtual memory counterparts of the Z8001 and Z8002 respectively (the Z8003 Z-VMPU can use both segmented and non-segmented memory addresses, whilst the Z8004 is restricted to non-segmented addressing only). There is a binary code compatibility between the two VMPUs and the original members of the Z8000 family; the VMPUs have some additional features which allow virtual memory operation. Used with the Z8010 memory management unit (MMU), the VMPUs recognise an abort function request from the MMU which indicates that the contents of the virtual address issued by the CPU are not in main memory, but must be loaded into main memory from a secondary bulk storage device (Winchester disk, diskette, or perhaps bubble memory). The abort function request may be originated by the MMU as a segment trap request (typically a CPU-inhibit violation trap, where the CPU-inhibit flag is used to indicate whether a segment is in main memory or not); the action of the VMPU in response to the trap is to stop the currently executing instruction immediately, and to initiate a segment load or segment swap routine. The trap works in a similar way to an interrupt, except that the current instruction being executed (which has caused the access violation) is not completed before a trap acknowledgement occurs. The program which has been interrupted by the trap can be restarted without loss of information once the service routine has loaded the relevant segment from bulk memory.

To aid system management in a virtual memory system, it is useful for the operating system to keep track of those segments or pages in main memory, using the 8-bit attribute field of the relevant segment descriptor registers within the MMU. Two bits of this attribute field are specifically designed to support virtual memory operation; they are the 'Changed' (CHG) bit, and the 'Referenced'

(REF) bit. The CHG bit of a segment descriptor register is set automatically when the segment is accessed by a write instruction, without any access violation, and serves to indicate to the operating system whether the main memory-resident segment or page is identical to its image held in secondary memory, or whether it has been altered, and hence must have its secondary memory image updated if the segment is 'swapped out' or replaced by a newly-loaded segment. The REF bit is automatically set whenever a main memory-resident segment has been accessed (by either a read or a write operation). If this bit is regularly examined and then reset by the operating system, it may be used to establish the amount of use that has been made of the segment. Many virtual memory systems work on the basis of swapping out the least-recently-used segment to make room for a new segment to be loaded.

It is worth noting here that there are two possible schemes for virtual memory operation. The blocks of memory-image data which are swapped between main memory and secondary memory may be variable-length segments, or fixed-length pages. With the Z8003, either approach may be adopted, but the Z8004 may only use paged memory.

Variable-length segments (up to 64K) may allow individual segment sizes to be tailored so as to minimise the number of segment swaps and hence increase the speed of operation, but this is at the expense of complexity within the virtual memory management routines within the operating system. These routines have to determine which segments to swap between main memory and secondary memory on the basis of size as well as least-recently-used criteria. Indeed, a prioritisation scheme may be necessary to ensure adequate performance (implemented perhaps by an approach which will trade off size, number of segments to be swapped, and time since last use).

Fixed-length pages, on the other hand, are easier to swap in and out, but efficiency will depend on page size: too small, and too frequent swaps are needed; too large, and memory utilisation may be poor. The standard Z-VMPU page size is 2048 bytes, which represents an acceptable compromise. The operating system routines involved with paged virtual memory can be made simpler than those for segmented memory since relative segment sizes need no longer be considered.

Page or segment fault signals (access violations) generated by the MMU are connected to the $\overline{\text{SAT}}$ (segment/address translation) input of the Z8003 (or one of the interrupt inputs of the Z8004, which has no $\overline{\text{SAT}}$ input) with input $\overline{\text{ABORT}}$ asserted and $\overline{\text{WAIT}}$ asserted. The combination of signals on these pins is interpreted by the VMPU as the special abort interrupt which is recognised immediately, rather than at the end of the instruction in which it has occurred. In order for the processor operating system to correctly save the current environment when an instruction abort occurs, it is necessary that the system stack access never causes a page fault (an irrecoverable situation), that the I/O instructions never cause a page fault, and that the code which saves the environment is treated as a critical region of code which will not be interrupted by another page fault. Not only must the system stack always be in main memory, but the program status area (PSA) must be permanently resident too. The environment saved is saved partly by external hardware, and partly by software. External hardware must save information that is internal information within the faulted instruction cycle, i.e. the address that caused the fault, the status code (on lines $ST_0 - ST_3$) during the aborted bus cycle, the value of the program counter during the first instruction fetch cycle of the faulted instruction, and, for paged memories, the number of successful data accesses made by the instruction. The fault handler software invoked by the VMPU abort must save the state of the aborted program in the form of the contents of the Program Counter (PC), the Flag and Control Word (FCW) and the general-purpose registers (all performed by a region of critical code). The fault handler must then initiate a routine to load the required segment or page into main memory (the swapping operation). Whilst the new segment or page is being loaded, the fault handler routine can allow the operating system scheduler to ready and run other processes. (Care is needed to avoid too many segment or page faults occurring at the same time in concurrently executing processes.)

When the segment or page has been loaded into main memory, the aborted instruction must be restarted. This is done by invoking an instruction restart routine which will restore the processor environment to its state just prior to the bus cycle which caused the address fault, and then continue the instruction from the point at which it was interrupted.

The Z8004 will only work with paged virtual memory, and in many cases, it is desirable to use the Z8003 with paged memory, too. To complement the segment-oriented Z8010 memory management unit (MMU), Zilog have designed a paged memory management unit (PMMU), the Z8015. The PMMU hardware will automatically save information necessary to restart an aborted instruction, and will give operating system support with its page descriptor registers.

Although the description of the Z8003 and Z8004 has been of their virtual memory support features, since they are otherwise almost identical to the Z8001 and Z8002, it is worth mentioning an additional hardware feature of the two VMPUs. The original test-and-set (TSET) instruction in the Z8000 was an uninterruptible software function, but did not have the hardware bus lock required in a multiple-processor system with shared resources. The Z8003 and Z8004 use one of the previously reserved status codes which appear on $ST_3 - ST_0$ to indicate that TSET is being executed. By decoding $ST_3 - ST_0 = 1111$, a bus lock signal may be generated to prevent preemption of the bus by other processors whilst a resource semaphore operation is in progress.

13.2 The Z800

The Z800 fits into the same class of 'intermediate processors' as the 6809. It is not one, but a whole family of processors based upon the 8-bit Z80 architecture, with some additional 16-bit instructions, with system and user modes, and with two members of the family which are Z80 bus-compatible, and two members which are 16-bit Z-bus compatible. Like the Z80, the Z800 devices have two main register banks, which may be switched by software. As well as an enhanced instruction set, all members of the Z800 family have on-chip memory management including address translation, a paged I/O address space which gives a total of 64K possible I/O addresses, and 256 bytes of on-chip random-access memory which may be used either as a fixed-address local memory, or as a high-speed cache for instructions, data, or both. An on-chip clock oscillator which will support a 10–25 MHz clock and 10-bit dynamic memory refresh counter are also standard features. All members of the family have address ranges greater than 64K. Their bus characteristics are summarised below:

Z8108	8-bit data bus multiplexed with low 8 bits of 19-bit address bus with Z80 control signals.
Z8208	8-bit data bus multiplexed with low 8 bits of 24-bit address bus with Z80 control signals.
Z8116	16-bit data bus multiplexed with low 16 bits of 19-bit address bus with Z-bus control signals.
Z8216	16-bit data bus multiplexed with low 16 bits of 24-bits address bus with Z-bus control signals.

The Z8208 and Z8216, both 64-pin Z800 processors, have some on-chip peripheral devices – four DMA channels, three 16-bit counter-timers, and a serial UART.

13.2.1 Z800 REGISTERS

The programmer-accessible registers in the Z800 are:

(a) The accumulator, flag, and general-purpose 8-bit registers A, F, B, C, D, E, H, L and their alternate set A′, F′, B′, C′, D′, E′, H′, L′, and R.

(b) Program counter (16-bit) contains the logical address of the current instruction. The address is translated to a 19-bit or 24-bit physical address by the on-chip MMU.

(c) IX, IY 16-bit index registers (16-bit).

(d) User and system stack pointers (16-bit) USP, SSP.

(e) The master status register (MSR), which contains information about the currently-executing program. It has seven maskable interrupt enable bits $E_0 - E_6$, a single-step enable bit, a single-step pending bit, a breakpoint-on-halt bit (breakpoint will occur whenever a halt instruction is encountered), and a user/system mode bit. The seven maskable interrupts are INTA, INTB, INTC, Counter-Timer 0/DMA0, Counter-Timer 1/UART receiver/DMA1, Counter-Timer 2/UART transmitter/DMA2, Counter-Timer 3/DMA3. (INTA, INTB, INTC are the external interrupt inputs on the 64-pin Z800 family members.)

(f) The interrupt control registers; these consist of:
(i) The interrupt status register, which contains a request pending bit for each of seven interrupt levels (IP0 – IP7), two bits to set the interrupt mode (0 – 3) and four interrupt Vector Enable bits (one per hardware interrupt source $\overline{INT_A}$, $\overline{INT_B}$, $\overline{INT_C}$ and $\overline{NMI}$) to control which are to be vectored. The four interrupt modes start with the traditional 8-bit 8080

microprocessor mode 0, where a maskable external interrupt supplies a call or restart which is executed as a response to the interrupt. The CPU is automatically set to mode 0 on power up. Interrupt mode 1 causes external interrupts to vector to a fixed location 38H. Interrupt mode 2 is a vectored interrupt mode where an 8-bit vector is supplied by the interrrupting device. The pointer is used to form an index value to a table of 16-bit interrupt routine starting addresses; the table base address is contained in the interrupt, or I register. The interrupt routine starting addresses are obtained from the table, treated as logical addresses and translated by the on-chip MMU. The interrupt mode which allows the user to take advantage of the Z800 facilities is mode 3. In mode 3, acknowledgement of any interrupt request causes the master status register (MSR), the address of the next instruction to be executed (i.e. PC), and a 16-bit 'reason' (cf Z8000), to be pushed onto the system stack. New values of MSR and PC are loaded from the interrupt-trap vector table. The reason code is the bit pattern on the CPU data bus during the interrupt acknowledge cycle; it is supplied by the interrupting device and used as the index to access the interrupt/trap vector table. The 8 internally-generated traps recognised by the CPU are: system call (SC), privileged instruction violation, address access violation (via MMU), system stack overflow warning (S), divide exception, single step, breakpoint-on-halt, and extended-instruction trap (EPA trap). The EPA trap is used to allow software emulation of a coprocessor (or extended processor unit EPU).

(ii) The interrupt/trap vector table register, which contains the upper bits of the interrupt/trap vector table start address, bits $A_{23} - A_{12}$. The lower 12 bits of the address are assumed equal to zero.

(iii) The trap control register, which enables the maskable traps (EPA,S) and enables the I/O instructions to be treated as privileged (inhibit user I/O).

(iv) System Stack Limit Register, which indicates when a system stack overflow warning trap should be generated.

(g) The refresh rate register which allows the programmer to specify via an I/O instruction the refresh interval, and to enable refresh to take place. When the refresh function is enabled, the 6-bit rate value in this register determines the refresh interval and the refresh address counter adjusts the address after each refresh. When a refresh is requested at the end of an interval, the refresh is performed after the last clock cycle of the bus cycle in progress when the request was made, preempting any interrupts pending. When the processor is unable to honour refresh requests (i.e. it has relinquished the bus or is in a wait state), these are stored by the refresh circuitry and issued as a burst of requests when the CPU regains control of the bus or ends its wait state.

(h) The timing control registers. The bus timing and control register allows a specified number of wait states to be automatically inserted in I/O operations and memory operations when certain address conditions are met, and interrupt acknowledge daisy-chain operations. The bus timing and initialisation register controls clock scaling and insertion of wait states when the on-chip memory management unit is used. The register contents also enable the multiprocessor mode of CPU operation and the bootstrap mode (where the on-chip UART is automatically initialised on CPU reset via DMA channel 0).

(i) The I/O page register, which contains the upper 8 bits $A_{23} - A_{16}$ which are added to 16-bit I/O addresses.

(j) The cache control register. The cache memory itself consists of 16 lines, each consisting of 20 tag bits, 16 valid bits, and 16 $\times$ 8 data bits. The cache control register specifies whether the internal Z800 memory is used as cache memory or local user memory, whether the cache is used for data or instructions (or both), and how the cache is to be loaded (burst mode or not).

These registers form a very comprehensive set of registers for an intermediate CPU. Like its full 16-bit counterpart, the 80186, the 16-bit bus compatible Z800 has many peripheral-support facilities, such as on-chip DMA and interrupt control, counter-timers and a UART. All these facilities, together with the bus timing control features, require software programming and hence add to the effective register set of the CPU.

13.2.2 Z800 CACHE MEMORY AND MEMORY MANAGEMENT UNIT

The 256-byte memory contained within the Z800 CPU may be configured either as local user memory or as cache memory, used for instructions, data, or both. It is organised in cache mode as 16 'lines' of 16 bytes each; associated with each line are 20 tag bits (to make a full 24-bit address) and 16 valid bits (one per data byte). The cache is loaded when a cache miss (i.e. the addressed data is not in the cache) on a read operation occurs, detected by the absence of a match of any of the 16 tag words with the upper 20 bits of the address. If the addressed data is not present in the cache, a least-recently-used (LRU) algorithm causes all bytes of the least-recently-accessed line to be flagged as invalid using the 16 valid bits associated with the line. One byte (on an 8-bit bus) or two bytes (on a 16-bit bus) are loaded into the newly-released line, and are then marked valid, with an appropriate 20-bit address placed in the tag register. The cache is only loaded up to the currently-requested address, unless burst mode is used. When the cache is programmed as an instruction-only cache, it is loaded when instruction fetches cause a cache miss. When programmed for data or instructions and data, any writes to data stored in the cache will cause the cache to be updated, and a bus cycle will be generated to update the same location in memory. The cache is updated when DMA cycles are generated, but the least-recently-used algorithm does not recognise a DMA cache update as a 'use' access.

The memory management unit (MMU) contains two sets of page descriptor registers (one set for user mode, one for system mode address translation). Each page descriptor register consists of a 4-bit page attribute field and 12 bits of page frame address. Address translation consists of taking the upper 4 bits of a 16-bit logical address, and using them as an index to the page descriptor register table. The 12-bit page frame address from the table is combined with the remaining 12 bits (or offset) of the logical address, to form a 24-bit physical address. The 4-bit attribute field of the page descriptor register allocates a bit for each of four functions:

(1) V, which indicates whether the page descriptor is valid,
(2) WP, the write-protect bit,
(3) C, which indicates whether the page data is cacheable, and
(4) M, which indicates whether the page has been modified.

The attributes are basically designed to support virtual memory operation and make the Z800 family an interesting choice of CPU for low-cost workstations and similar products.

13.2.3 THE Z800 INSTRUCTION SET

The Z800 has a register set which is directly compatible with the 8-bit Z80, and it maintains object-code (binary) compatibility with the Z80. This basic instruction set has been enhanced in two ways: by adding more instructions (expanding the 16-bit Z80 instructions and adding such things as signed multiply and divide), and by expanding the available addressing modes. The addressing modes available on the Z800 are:

(a) Register addressing (as Z80);
(b) Immediate addressing (as Z80);
(c) Register indirect address via a 16-bit register pair (as Z80);
(d) Direct address (as Z80);
(e) Indexed: 16-bit address contained in bytes following the instruction opcode added to a 2's complement 16-bit index contained in HL, IX, or IY registers to form the effective address;
(f) Short indexed: The 8-bit complement displacement contained in a single byte following the opcode is added to the 16-bit number contained in the IX or IY register to form the effective address (equivalent to Z80 indexed mode);
(g) Relative: Using 8-bit signed displacement (as Z80) or 16-bit signed displacement (which both follow the opcode) relative to the program counter;
(h) Stack pointer relative: A 16-bit signed displacement in HL, IX, IY is added to the stack pointer contents to form the effective address. This facility is useful when parameters are passed via the stack, in frames, by high-level language procedures, and for operating system support.
(i) Base indexed: The contents of IX, IY or HL are added to the contents of another of the 3 16-bit registers to form the effective address.

These addressing modes give the Z800 a 16-bit 'feel', despite the constraints of Z80 compatibility. The instruction set itself has been enhanced by the addition of new instructions to support new CPU hardware facilities:

LDUD(P)	– a privileged instruction to load a byte of data in user data (program space).
LDCTL	– load control (privileged).
PCACHE	– purge cache (invalidate all entries).
EI, DI	– enable, disable specific interrupt levels (privileged).
EPUM	– load extended processor unit (EPU) from memory.
MEPU	– load memory from EPU.
EPUF	– load accumulator from EPU.
EPUI	– EPU internal operation.

As well as these enhancements, many of the basic Z80 instructions have been extended to include 16-bit manipulation capability, using a word (W) suffix to the instruction mnemonic. The range of input-output instructions now has word capability, and the addition of multiply and divide, as both 8-bit and 16-bit operations, signed and unsigned, is a useful one.

13.2.4 Z800 APPLICATIONS

The Z800 family of microprocessors is a useful addition to the Zilog range, and capitalises on the success of the 8-bit Z80, offering an upgrade path which retains upward binary compatibility. The additional features provided, however, would be wasted if only this feature were exploited. By using on-chip memory management with virtual memory support, cache memory, on-chip peripheral support, and system/user modes of operation, the manufacturers have brought the Z800 into direct competition with both true 16-bit and 32-bit microprocessors for many applications. Because the CPU is still based around an 8-bit architecture, it is likely to be most suited for low-cost text handling and workstation environments.

13.3 The Zilog arithmetic processing unit (APU)

The Z8070 APU is designed to operate as a numeric coprocessor (or extended processor unit, EPU) to Zilog's Z800, Z8000 and Z80000 CPU families. Like the Intel coprocessors, it shares the system bus with the CPU, and monitors bus transactions, identifying those instructions which are specific to the APU, and executing them in parallel with main CPU operation. Internally, the APU consists of an interface processor, which is connected to the system bus, and a data processor, which accepts commands and data from the interface processor, but which operates independently, and may use a different clock. The interface processor monitors the main CPU bus activity, including status and control signals, looking for the occurrence of an extended instruction 'template' (cf 8086 ESC prefix). When an EPU instruction has been identified, and has the correct identifier number, the instruction and data will be aligned and read into the instruction queue. The interface processor maintains the instruction queue and may execute instructions which do not involve arithmetic operations, such as APU data movement and control operations. The data processor contains all the arithmetic logic and a set of data registers, and executes the actual arithmetic instructions.

The register set of the APU consists of two groups of registers: the data register file, consisting of eight 80-bit data registers FRO to FR7 and two 80-bit operand registers FOP1 and FOP2, and the status and control registers associated with the interface processor, which consist of three 32-bit status registers, one 32-bit control register, and one 16-bit control register. The three 32-bit status registers consist of two program counter registers, PC1 and PC2, and a flag register, FLAGS. PC1 contains the address of the instruction being executed (whether an arithmetic instruction in the data processor or a control instruction), and PC2 contains the address of any queued instruction. The FLAGS register contains 32 single-bit flags. Eight are used as exception flags, and are called sticky flags since they remain set until explicitly reset by the programmer. Another eight flags are used as previous operation flags – the sticky flags of the previous operation. The remaining flags are used for comparison, with some exception condition flags. The 32-bit control register of the APU is called the System Configuration Register (SCR), which controls interrupt generation and EPU identifiers, EPU and CPU synchronisation. The 16-bit control register, the user control register, allows the user to enable and disable exception traps and to control the arithmetic rounding modes of the APU. The two operand registers FOP1 and FOP2 are used for the APU input operand register and the default result register. Both use floating point format; a 64-bit significand, 15 least significant bits of exponent (the two most significant exponent bits are in the SCR) and a single sign bit. The data registers FRO–FR7 have a similar floating-point format.

The APU supports IEEE standard P754 Draft 10.0 for Binary Floating-Point Arithmetic, and a range of data types which encompasses single (32-bit), double (64-bit) and extended (80-bit) precision floating-points and 32-bit and 64-bit signed (2's complement) integer formats and a signed 18-digit packed binary-coded decimal (BCD) format. The APU instructions fall into three groups: floating-point arithmetic and comparison instructions, 'secondary' arithmetic instructions, and control operations. They are:

(a) Arithmetic instructions

FADD (S) (D) Floating point add extended (single) (double)
FDIV (S) (D) Floating point divide extended (single) (double)
FMUL (S) (D) Floating point multiply extended (single) (double)
FSQR (S) (D) Floating point square root extended (single) (double)
FSUB (S) (D) Floating point subtract extended (single) (double)
FLD (S) (D) Floating point load extended (single) (double)
FLDBCD (IL) (IQ) (M) (TL) (TQ) Floating point load BCD integer (binary long word) (binary quad word) (multiple) (and truncate to integer long word) (and truncate to integer quad word)
FREMSTEP (F) Floating remainder step (and transfer flags to CPU)
FCP (S) (D) Floating compare extended (single) (double)
FCP (F) (FX) Floating compare (transfer flags to CPU) (and raise exception if unordered)

FCPX (S) (D)	Floating compare extended (single) (double) and raise exception if unordered
FCPZ (S) (D)	Floating compare extended (single) (double) with zero
FCPZF (X)	Floating compare with zero, transfer flags to CPU (and raise exception if unordered)
FCPZX (S) (D)	Floating compare with zero and raise exception if unordered.

(b) Secondary arithmetic instructions

FABS (S) (D)	Floating absolute value
FCLR	Floating point clear
FINT (S) (D)	Floating round to floating integer
FNEG (S) (D)	Floating negation

(c) Control operations

FLDCTL	Floating load control
FLDCTLB	Floating load control byte
FRESFLG / FSETFLG	Floating reset (set) flag
FRESTRAP / FSETTRAP	Floating reset (set) trap
FSETMODE	Floating set mode

The Z8070 is unique in that it is compatible with different families of processors and their local buses. Two pins (OPTO and OPT1) are provided on the APU 68-pin chip-carrier package; they define the interface CPU option as 'universal' (non-CPU-specific), Z80000, Z800 and Z8000. The APU will then have direct processor bus compatibility.

13.4 The 32-bit Z80000

Strictly speaking, this 32-bit device is outside the scope of a book on 16-bit microprocessors. However, because it embodies some of the latest techniques of microprocessor CPU design, a brief description is given here. The processor is binary-compatible with the Z8000 family, and supports Z-bus as a subset of its 32-bit multiplexed data and address CPU pins. The 16 internal registers of the Z80000 are 32 bits wide (they are designated RRO – RR30, like the Z8000 double registers) and may be accessed in bytes (RRO – RR6), 16-bit words (RRO – RR14, corresponding to the full Z8000 register set), 32-bit words, or 64-bit words. Addressing modes within the Z80000 operate within three modes of address representation: compact (16-bit), segmented (15-bit segment number and 16-bit offset or 7-bit segment number and 24-bit offset – bit 31 selects which type of segmented addressing), or linear, up to 4 Gbytes.

To support memory management and virtual memory systems, the Z80000 has an internal MMU which operates a paged address translation scheme, taking a logical address with a 22-bit page address and 10-bit offset (i.e. 1K page size) and translating it via the translation lookaside buffer to a 32-bit physical address which consists of a 22-bit frame address and the untranslated 10-bit offset value. The translation tables used by the lookaside buffer are stored in main system memory and are loaded automatically when needed (cf NS16032 and NS16082 MMU). Table access is controlled by one of four table descriptor registers, one for each of the memory spaces for system instructions, system data, normal (user) instructions and normal data. First of all, the 32-bit logical address is split into four fields: an 8-bit 'Level 1' field, an 8-bit 'Level 2' field, a 6-bit 'page number' field, and the 10-bit page offset. The translation table load process proceeds as follows: when the translation lookaside buffer TLB (which itself is an associative memory) does not contain the required translation information, the appropriate table descriptor register is selected. It points to the beginning of the Level 1 table in main memory, and the Level 1 field of the logical address is used as an index into the table. The Level 1 table entry points to the beginning of a Level 2 table, and the Level 2 field of the logical address is used as an index into this table. The Level 2 table entry points to the beginning of a page table in memory, and the page number field of the logical address is used as an index into this third table; the page table entry indicated contains the physical frame address. The immediate translation is performed, and the TLB is loaded (using a least-recently-used algorithm to allocate TLB space) with the logical page address and its correponding physical frame address. The page table entry contains not only the physical frame address, but also four protection level bits associated with the page: a bit to indicate that the frame address is in I/O space (allowing protected access to memory-mapped I/O), bits to support virtual memory (referenced R, valid V, modified M) and a single bit to indicate that instructions and data in the page are non-cacheable. The two other table entries (Level 1 and Level 2) also contain protection and validity bits so that levels of access to the translation hierarchy may be controlled. Because a full set of tables allowing 4 Gbyte address translation would themselves occupy a lot of space, table size and dynamic table control fields (growth direction) are used in the translation table descriptor and Level 1 and Level 2 entries. They allow operating system control over memory allocation and MMU efficiency. Any attempts to use addresses which do not appear in the translation tables are considered invalid and will cause an address violation exception.

In common with other, competing processors, the Z80000 contains a cache memory, used for both instructions and data. The cache consists of 16 blocks, each consisting of 16 bytes of instructions and data. Each block has associated with it an address tag (28 bits) and 16 validity bits (one per byte). A stack mechanism 16 entries deep is used to provide a 'least-recently-used' (LRU) capability. When a memory read is performed by the CPU (either an instruction fetch or data read), the cache tag comparison identifies whether the contents of the addressed location are in the cache, and fetches them from the cache (a fast internal operation) if the addressed location is present. If a cache miss on a read is detected, the action taken by the cache logic depends on the type of read operation. If the read operation is an instruction fetch, the instruction is loaded into the cache, and a burst transfer is used to fill the rest of the block, thereby prefetching the rest of any instruction. If the operation is a data read, only the addressed data is loaded into the cache (by burst mode only if more than one bus transfer is necessary).

A data write (to memory) operation will cause the cache to be simultaneously updated when the address generates a cache hit, otherwise the cache is not affected. Software control of the cache allows the cache to be used for instructions, data, or both, and allows cache loading to be disabled, to lock fixed locations into the cache. This last facility can be used to retain selected, much-used intructions and data in the cache for fast execution, and to prevent them being overwritten on any cache misses.

The rest of the Z80000 architecture is reasonably conventional, but with its 32-bit word length and high clock rate, it offers a considerable increase in throughput over the Z8000. The range of addressing modes has been increased, as has the instruction set, which includes EPU instructions like the Z800, so that the Z8070 APU can be used. The family of Zilog processors (Z800, Z8000 and Z80000) covers the complete spectrum from high-end 8-bit processors to supermini-like 32-bit processors with a range of nine upward-compatible processors. Performance upgrades can be achieved without program code alteration, and standard-bus (Z-bus) systems will accommodate most of the devices. With the ever-rising costs associated with modern microprocessor system development, such a compatible range of devices must appear very attractive indeed to the original equipment manufacturer.

13.5 The Motorola MC68010 virtual memory processor

Motorola's 16-bit microprocessor, the MC68000, has achieved extremely wide user acceptance, and the ease with which software can be developed for this processor, with its very regular register set and its uncluttered instruction set, has made it one of the favourite microprocessors for building Unix-based workstations. In order to implement large software systems, such as Unix, efficiently, good memory management is essential, and virtual memory support is desirable (the latest version of Unix is designed to work in a virtual memory environment). To provide this capability, Motorola have produced a new CPU, the 68010, designed specifically as a virtual memory processor, and a memory management unit which is designed to support either the 68010 or 68000, the 68451.

13.5.1 THE 68010 CPU

The 68010 is fully compatible with the MC68000; it has enhancements which make it particularly suitable for virtual memory operation. The upgrades are:

(a) To accommodate the address or page faulting associated with virtual memory (to indicate that the addressed item is not in main memory, and must be brought in from secondary storage) the 68010 allows a faulted instruction to be continued once the information has been loaded from secondary memory. This requires that the internal state of the CPU is saved completely when a bus error signal ($\overline{\text{BERR}}$) is generated as a result of an address fault. When $\overline{\text{BERR}}$ occurs, the MC68010 immediately suspends execution of the current instruction at the memory reference cycle which produced the bus error, and saves the internal state of the processor on the supervisor stack. The action is that of a special exception which automatically stores on the supervisor stack those registers which would have been stored by the 68000 in a bus error situation:

(i) function code and cycle type
(ii) fault address
(iii) instruction register
(iv) status register
(v) program counter (seven 16-bit words total)

and in addition

(vi) data input and output buffers
(vii) format and vector offset
(viii) some user-invisible data

Overall, 26 words of the supervisor stack are used.

A bus error service routine is then invoked, and this routine will load the required page containing the faulted address data, via the processor operating system.

When the data necessary to continue the instruction is in main memory, a return from exception (RTE) instruction will reload the MC68010 with the internal state stored on the supervisor stack, and re-run the bus cycle which originally caused the fault. This instruction-continuation technique for virtual memory implementation works well, but is not infallible. If a supervisor stack access causes an address fault, the subsequent address faults caused by the bus error exception are irrecoverable.

(b) Virtual machine operation. In order to support virtual input-output, a memory area which is non-resident (i.e. will cause an address fault if accessed) is defined as an I/O device. The operating system must then invoke software drivers when a fault occurs within the I/O address range.
Together with virtual memory, this technique allows both user software facilities and operating system software facilities to be made independent of the CPU used. Both operating system and user software can be run with the CPU in user mode and communicate via traps with a supervisor mode operating system which is privileged.

(c) Movable exception vector table. The 68000 exception vector table is fixed at a starting address of zero, and extended to 3FF (256 exceptions). To improve the flexibility of exception handling, the 68010 vector table can be positioned anywhere in memory. Associated with the vector table is a vector base pointer register (VBR) which contains the start address of the vector table. This register is initialised to zero on CPU reset, but may be altered by privileged instructions. Access to the required program counter value from the table is gained by the effective logical address generated by multiplying the vector number by 4 and adding it to the contents of the VBR.

The 68010 has some further enhancements, such as additional instructions which allow a privileged move of data between operating system address space and user address space, privileged access to the function code register, and others. Relaxed bus timing is also provided to allow memory error detection circuitry to raise a bus error exception after data transfer acknowledge, $\overline{\text{DTACK}}$, has been asserted.

13.5.2 THE 68451 MMU

The 68451 MMU is designed to be used with either the 68000 or 68010 (their bus signals are the same, except for some timing constraints, and their pinouts are identical). This MMU not only supports address translation but also has a technique which will support variably-sized memory segments in a way which will maximise memory utilisation. Internally the 68451 maintains 32 tables of memory blocks ranging in size from 256 bytes to 1 Mbyte in a binary fashion. These 'memory available' lists each contain the address of the start or head of the first 'memory block descriptors' for their particular block size, the address of the tail of the last memory block descriptor, and a count of how many memory blocks are still free. The memory block descriptors form a linked list (each one contains the address of the previous descriptor, and the address of the next descriptor) and are themselves tables in memory which also define the logical-to-physical address mapping for their particular block, whether the block is free or not, and space to record block status and access rights.

When the CPU operating system requires memory to be allocated, the memory available list for the smallest block size that can accommodate the request can be examined. If a block is available, it will be allocated. If no free blocks of that size are available, the memory available list for the next higher block size is examined. If a block is then available, it is removed from that list, partitioned so as to form two blocks of the original size required, one of which is allocated, and the other is added to the memory available list of the original block size as a free block. As blocks are returned to the free memory pool, they are examined to see if one block can be combined with another to form a larger free block (i.e. of contiguous memory, where only one logical-to-physical address translation is necessary). The combination of operating system and MMU is continuously splitting up and recombining memory blocks to give optimum memory space utilisation and fast allocation speed.

The 68451 also maintains an address space correspondence table which relates an 8-bit address reference tag to each of 16 possible combinations of the function codes FC0–FC2 and the bus grant acknowledge signal $\overline{\text{BGACK}}$. These tags can be used to define separate address spaces for user data, user program code, supervisor data, etc. They include DMA access codes, and access by other bus masters. The address translation mechanism demands a match between tag and segment descriptor before valid access is allowed.

The 68451 shows an alternative approach to memory management compared with, say, the paged Z8015 MMU, but one which is equally appropriate to virtual memory operation. The level of protection and efficiency of memory utilisation, as well as the potential for very fast context switching using the address space correspondence table, make it a very attractive device for use with a linearly-addressed processor such as the 68000 or 68010. It is likely that many of the new Unix-based systems which will use virtual memory will be designed around the 68010-68451 pair of devices.

13.6 The 32-bit 68020

The most powerful member of the 68000 family is the 32-bit 68020. Because of its compatibility with the 68000, a brief description is given here. Like the 68010, it is designed for virtual memory operation, but its buses have been expanded to include 32 bits of address and 32 bits of data, non-multiplexed. The register set is similar to that of the 68010, including a vector base register to allow the exception vector table to be located anywhere in main memory. The 68020, like its predecessors, employs an instruction prefetch mechanism, and like the Z80000 and Z800, it uses a cache memory. The instruction cache is 256 bytes, organized as 64 lines of 4 bytes each (4 bytes is a 68000-family long word). The tag field associated with each line consists of the upper 24 address bits; also included are FC2 (user/supervisor mode function signal), and a single valid bit. When an address is generated, if the upper 24 bits match the tag field, the next 6 address bits are used as an index to locate the line in the cache, and the function code FC2 is compared with the required value, before cache data is used. Software control of the cache is achieved using two cache registers, CACR (cache control) and CAAR (cache address).

The instruction set of the 68020 has several important enhancements:

(a) Module support. To improve system integrity and to allow the operating system to control access to program modules, instructions CALLM and RTM (return) are used. CALLM uses a module descriptor which contains module entry control information. It creates a module stack frame (cf. NS16032) and saves the module state in that frame. RTM recovers the module state.

(b) Traps have been made more flexible, with the TRAPV (trap on overflow) being expanded to TRAP on condition, allowance made for trap parameters following the trap instruction, and the addition of a breakpoint trap (BKPT).

(c) Both upper and lower bounds checking. CHK2 and CMP2 have been added to the 68000 CHK (upper bound only). CMP2 sets condition codes after comparison on upper and lower bounds; CHK2 will set condition codes after comparison, and trap if the contents of the register being checked are outside the bounds set.

(d) Call-and-swap, CAS. A more sophisticated multiprocessing indivisible instruction (compare two operands and swap a third).

(e) Additional bit field operations and BCD number packing and unpacking support.

13.7 The MC68881 floating point coprocessor

Like the other numeric coprocessors mentioned, the 68881 is Motorola's hardware for implementing IEEE Task P754 definition. The device will operate as a coprocessor with the 68020 and as a peripheral with 68000 and 68010 (using reserved instruction traps and software to implement CPU – numeric processor communications). In the 68020, communication is via the system bus, using chip selection logic connected to the CPU function code outputs and address lines. Like the other coprocessors, the 68881 has a bank of eight 80-bit internal data registers, FP0–FP7, and also has a control register, a status register, and an instruction address register. The status register records condition codes, exceptions and an accrued exceptions byte, which is set when an exception occurs, and remains set until the user explicitly resets it. The control register gives software control of rounding mode and program flow on exception. The instructions available are:

FABS	Absolute value
FGETEXP, FGETMAN	Get exponent, mantissa
FINT	Integer part
FNOP	No operation
FNEG	Negate
NSCALE	Scale exponent by integer
FTST	Test
FSAVE, FRESTORE	Save and restore
FADD, FSUB	Add, subtract
FMUL, FDIV	Multiply, divide
FSGLMUL, FSGLDIV	Single precision multiply and divide
FMOD, FREM	Modulo remainder, remainder
FCMP	Compare
FSQRT	Square root
FASIN, FACOS, FATAN	Arcsin, arccos, arctan
FSIN, FCOS, FTAN, (FSINCOS)	Sin, cos, tan (both sin and cos together)
FSINH, FCOSH, FTANH	Hyperbolic sin, cos, tan
FATANH	Hyperbolic arc tan
FETOX, FETOXM1	Exp(x), Exp(x) – 1
FLOG10, FLOG2, FLOGN	Logarithms to base 10, 2, e
FLOGNP1	Ln(x + 1)
FTWOTOX, FTENTOX	2^x, 10^x

13.8 Other processors

The NS32032 is a 32-bit bus version of the 16032, but otherwise the same CPU. The Intel iAPX386 is Intel's 32-bit mainstream processor, but insufficient details are available as yet.

13.9 Applications

The 'Applications' chapter (11) discussed under the heading 11.2 (General commercial applications) the likely use of the 16-bit microprocessor in desktop business or personal computers. The Sirius computer discussed in that section has found wide user acceptance in the UK, as has its stablemate, the ACT Apricot, another Intel-based, this time rather more portable, computer. The personal computer which has enjoyed devastating success in the USA, however, is the 8088-based IBM personal computer, or IBM PC. This computer family (there are several models in the range) now dominates the North American personal computer scene, and its success has created an entire industry making IBM PC-compatible clones, add-ons, and writing applications software for the IBM PC. The operating system PC-DOS (almost identical to the Microsoft commercially available operating system MS-DOS) has become the de facto standard operating system for the 16-bit commercial or business application, in the same way as CP/M has dominated the 8-bit world.

13.9.1 IBM PC HARDWARE

The IBM PC includes a basic System Board which contains an 8088 CPU with a 4.77 MHz clock; the relatively conservative choice of a 5 MHz part allows the option of adding an 8087 numeric coprocessor to the CPU. (At the time of writing, the 5 MHz version 8087 is still the only version easily available.) On the same board as the CPU are 16K of read-write memory (RAM) which may be expanded to 64K on the board. The PC case includes expansion slots which allow system memory to be expanded beyond the 64K System Board maximum, up to a total of 544K (480K in the expansion slots, 64K on the System Board). The System Board also contains 40K of read-only memory (ROM), which consists of 32K devoted to the BASIC interpreter (Microsoft BASIC-80 with no diskette functions), 6K to the basic input-output system (BIOS), and 2K for the power-on self-test routines. Basic system input-output facilities include keyboard, loudspeaker and cassette logic, and four channels of direct memory access, as well as support for five System I/O expansion slots. The base level IBM PC will operate using an audio cassette recorder for data storage and without diskette drives, but the vast majority of IBM PCs sold have included diskette drives and interfaces. Three of the four System Board DMA channels are available for use with expansion boards plugged into the I/O slots. Where diskette drives are to be used, a diskette interface, supporting up to four 5¼″ drives (two within the PC case, two external drives), is added to the System Board in one of the I/O expansion slots, and one of the available DMA channels is used for data transfer. Formatted diskette capacity is 163,840 bytes per drive (single-sided) and 327,680 bytes per drive (double-sided).

PC display support is also via an interface card plugged into one of the expansion slots. The IBM PC is supplied with one of two display options. The business option is a monochrome display adapter (interface) which also supports a dot-matrix printer and will allow an 80-character line, 25-line text display. For more general personal computer use, the second option is a colour display interface which will support 40-character lines with standard resolution monitors, with sixteen foreground and eight background colour choices per character. This card also has graphics modes of 320 × 200-point and 640 × 200-point resolution. The lower-resolution graphics mode allows four colours, the higher-resolution mode only two, black and white. The video signal is available as NTSC standard and may be used with an RF modulator. Both monochrome and colour interfaces use the Motorola 6845 CRT controller chip as the basis for their designs, and both include their own video RAM (separate from the main CPU RAM) and use ROM-based character generators for their text modes. Various character fonts and special characters (some Greek characters and some mathematical symbols) are available.

Other adapter cards which may be plugged into the expansion slots are an asynchronous communications interface, a parallel printer adapter (for the IBM 80 cps dot-matrix printer), and a game control adapter which allows joysticks to be used with the computer. Independent vendors offer a very wide range of other interfaces for such devices as colour plotters, more sophisticated colour graphics, HDLC and X25 communications protocols, and networking.

13.9.2 IBM PC SOFTWARE

The basic disk operating system for the IBM PC is PC-DOS, which, as previously mentioned, is almost identical to Microsoft's MS-DOS. Written originally in 1980, PC-DOS started life as a 16-bit operating system similar to Digital Research's CP/M. Like CP/M, PC-DOS (MS-DOS) 1.0 consists of a disk file handling system IBMDOS.COM, a basic input-output system IBMBIO.COM, and a command processor COMMAND.COM. All three parts of PC-DOS reside as files on disk, along with a bookstrap program. The ROM BIOS causes the boot program to be loaded; this program is then run, and it loads the other files.

COMMAND.COM is the equivalent of CP/M's command-line interpreter, but as well as loading and running programs in named files with extensions, .COM or .EXE, it is also responsible for interrupt handling (including keyboard CTRL-BREAK) and 'autoexec'. This last function is a neat feature allowing the processor to automatically load and execute an application program, without the need to have an operator first recognise the system start-up response, and then type in appropriate commands. PC-DOS is structured so that once COMMAND.COM has been loaded from disk and its execution started, one of its first functions is to search the diskette directory for a file, AUTOEXEC.BAT. This file is an indirect command file which contains a series of PC-DOS commands. If found, the file is loaded, and its contents executed. The facility is useful for business applications, where non-technical personnel are required to use the computer with the same program each time (e.g. a word-processor or spreadsheet program, or perhaps one of the 'integrated software' packages such as Lotus 1-2-3).

Like CP/M, PC-DOS contains a number of resident commands which are built into the system, rather than available as separate disk files. These internal commands are loaded with the DOS and are available immediately, without any wait for disk access. They are:

COPY	(Disk files)
DATE	(Enter current date or display current date)
DIR	(Display disk directory)

ERASE	(Files)
PAUSE	(Causes a system wait until a keyboard key is depressed – used with batch files)
REM	(Display remark – used with batch files)
RENAME	(Files)
TIME	(Enter current time or display current time)
TYPE	(Display file contents)

In addition, there is an implicit batch file processing system in PC-DOS. If the name of a file ending in .BAT is typed, the computer will execute the commands in that file. AUTOEXEC.BAT, mentioned previously, is an example of a batch file. Also built into PC-DOS are commands invoked by combinations of 'control' (CTRL) and other keys. CTRL-PrtSc allows a user to switch the printer output (echo of the screen) on and off. Shift-PrtSc performs a screen dump to the printer. Rudimentary command-line editing is also available.

Associated with PC-DOS, but not built into it, are the external commands:

CKDSK <Drive Number>	(Check directory and the file allocation table for the designated drive, and produce a status report)
COMP	(Compare file contents)
DISKCOMP	(Compare diskette contents)
DISKCOPY	(Copy entire diskette)
EXE2BIN	(Converts .EXE file (object code) to .COM format (memory image), starting at 100H)
FORMAT	(Diskette. If /S specified, PC-DOS system files IBMBIO.COM, IBMDOS.COM and COMMAND.COM are copied to the diskette after formatting)
MODE	(Set mode of operation on printer or display/ communications adapter)
SYS	(Transfer system files to diskette)

Also included with the system are a line editor, EDLIN, a linker program, LINK, a debug program, DEBUG. EDLIN uses five of the ten function keys available on the IBM PC keyboard.

13.9.3 EVOLUTION OF THE IBM PC

The IBM PC has evolved both in hardware and software. The first obvious improvements were in hardware, with the addition of a 10Mbyte Winchester hard disk, making the IBM PC the IBM PC-XT. The hard disk replaces one of the diskette drives and requires a minimum of 128K of RAM on the new system board. To accompany the hardware changes is a revised DOS, PC- (or MS-) DOS 2.0. The changes made to the DOS are quite significant, and reflect modern operating system practice. PC-DOS 2.0 is upward-compatible from PC-DOS 1.1, and may be installed on diskette-only systems as well as on the IBM PC-XT. The first change from the earlier operating system is the introduction of tree-structured, rather than linear, directories similar to Unix practice. From a root directory, levels of subdirectories may be created, and files referenced via a pathname. Directory manipulation commands similar to those of Unix are available. Also following Unix, redirected I/O and piping may be used. Whilst PC-DOS 1.0 had a BIOS similar to CP/M which required considerable effort in modification to install new device drivers, PC-DOS 2.0 allows add-on device drivers. A background program for queuing and printing text files is also available. These are just a few of the more significant changes embodied in PC-DOS 2.0. Many other changes have been made to increase the versatility of existing commands, and all reflect the increasing sophistication of the personal computer user.

Whilst the IBM PC has been enjoying huge volume sales, the emphasis for new personal computer designs has moved on from the 8088 to the more advanced 16-bit processors which will allow virtual memory and multi-user operation. For instance, many Unix-based computers already use the 68000, but new designs are beginning to introduce the 68010 virtual memory processor. The obvious upgrade for IBM was to use the 80286 processor, itself a successor to the 8086 family, which supports virtual memory, but will also (without sophisticated memory support) run in a compatibility mode with the 8086, allowing use to be made of existing 8086/88 software. The 8086-compatible real address mode is a compromise which does not allow use of some of the advanced features of the 80286, but for many users, the preservation of their 8088 software base, until it can be superseded by native 80286 software, is of paramount importance.

The new IBM personal computer is the IBM PC-AT, which uses the 80286 with a 6MHz clock and a minimum of 256K of RAM. In its most basic form, a single 5¼″ 1.2Mbyte diskette drive is provided, but usually, this will be accompanied by a 20Mbyte hard disk drive. The hardware and expansion slots are not compatible with all of the IBM PC interfaces, and the keyboard and case have been restyled. The PC-AT has 8 expansion slots which can accept (slots 1 and 7) the display adapters of the IBM PC but not all PC adapters, and battery back-up CMOS memory for time and calendar information. The operating system is PC-DOS 3.0 (similar to 2.0), but Xenix is promised for the future.

Appendix 1

(a) 8086 instruction set

Group	Assembler mnemonics	Description
Data transfer	MOV dest, AX	16-bit move to memory from accumulator. Addressing modes are: direct, indexed, based, and combinations of based and indexed
	MOV dest, AL	8-bit move as above
	MOV AX, src	16-bit move from memory to accumulator
	MOV AL, src	8-bit move as above
	MOV seg reg, src	Move to segment register from memory or a register
	MOV dest, seg reg	Move to memory or a register from segment register
	MOV dest, src	Move from src to dest, where each may be a register or memory
	MOV reg, <immediate data>	Move immediate data to register (8 or 16 bits)
	MOV dest, <immediate data>	Move immediate data to memory
	LEA reg, src	Load effective address into register
	LDS reg, src	Load pointer using data segment
	LES reg, src	Load pointer using extra segt
	XCHG dest, src	Exchange contents of registers, or of register with memory
	XCHG AX (or AL), reg	Exchange register and accumulator
	XLAT	Translate; the contents of AL are used as an 8-bit offset added to the address in the BX register to access a memory byte, which is returned in AL
Arithmetic	ADD dest, src	Add — 8-bit or 16-bit operands may be both in
	ADC dest, src	Add with carry
	SUB dest, src	Subtract
	SBB dest, src	Subtract with borrow

Group	Assembler mnemonic	Description
	AND	AND (registers, both in memory, or one in a register, one in memory)
	TEST	AND with no result returned (registers, both in memory, or one in a register, one in memory)
	OR	OR (registers, both in memory, or one in a register, one in memory)
	XOR	Exclusive-OR (registers, both in memory, or one in a register, one in memory)
	ADD dest, <immediate data>	As above, immediate
	ADC dest, <immediate data>	As above, immediate
	SUB dest, <immediate data>	As above, immediate
	SBB dest, <immediate data>	As above, immediate
	AND dest, <immediate data>	As above, immediate
	TEST dest, <immediate data>	As above, immediate
	OR dest, <immediate data>	As above, immediate
	XOR dest, <immediate data>	As above, immediate
	ADD AX (or AL), <immediate data>	As above, immediate to accumulator
	ADC AX (or AL), <immediate data>	As above, immediate to accumulator
	SUB AX (or AL), <immediate data>	As above, immediate to accumulator
	SBB AX (or AL), <immediate data>	As above, immediate to accumulator
	AND AX (or AL), <immediate data>	As above, immediate to accumulator
	TEST AX (or AL), <immediate data>	As above, immediate to accumulator
	OR AX (or AL), <immediate data>	As above, immediate to accumulator
	XOR AX (or AL), <immediate data>	As above, immediate to accumulator
	INC dest	Increment Register or memory
	DEC dest	Decrement Register or memory
	AAA	ASCII adjust for add
	DAA	Decimal adjust for add
	NEG dest	Negate (2's complement)
	AAS	ASCII adjust for subtract
	DAS	Decimal adjust for subtract
	MUL src	Multiply accumulator by memory or register contents (unsigned, 8 or 16-bit)
	DIV src	Divide accumulator by memory or register contents (unsigned, 8 or 16-bit)
	IMUL src	Signed multiply
	IDIV src	Signed divide
	AAM dest	ASCII adjust for multiply
	AAD dest	ASCII adjust for divide
	CBW	Convert byte to word
	CWD	Convert word to double-word (in AX and DX)
	NOT dest	Invert (1's complement)
Shift and Rotates	SHL (SAL) dest	Shift left by count in CL reg
	SHR dest	Shift logical right by the count in the CL register
	SAR dest	Shift arithmetic right by the count in

Group	Assembler mnemonics	Description	
		the CL register	
	ROL dest	Rotate left by the count in the CL register	
	ROR dest	Rotate right by the count in the CL register	
	RCL dest	Rotate left through carry	
	RCR dest	Rotate right through carry	
String	REP	Repeat string operation, decrementing CX at each repeat until CX becomes zero	
	REPZ/REPNZ	Repeat string operation whilst the zero flag is set/not set	
	REPE/REPNE	Repeat string operation whilst src and dest are equal/unequal	
	MOVSB, MOVSW	Move src string to dest string	src is addressed by SI reg, dest by DI reg, and SI, DI are incremented or decremented by 1 or 2 (byte or word)
	CMPSB, CMPSW	Compare src and dest strings	
	SCASB, SCASW	Scan dest string, set flags after comparison with AL, AX	
	LODSB, LODSW	Load src into AL, AX	
	STDSB, STDSW	Store AL, AX in dest	
Branches and calls	JE/JZ	Jump on equal/zero	<8-bit offset> — Relative to IP, −128 to +127 bytes
	JL/JNGE	Jump on less than/not greater or equal	
	JLE, JNG	Jump on less than or equal/not greater	
	JB/JNAE	Jump on below, equal/not above	
	JP/JPE	Jump on parity (even)	
	JO	Jump on overflow	
	JS	Jump on sign	
	JNE/JNZ	Jump on not equal/nonzero	
	JNL/JGE	Jump on not less/greater or equal	
	JNLE/JG	Jump on not less or equal/greater	
	JNB/JAE	Jump on not below/above or equal	

Group	Assembler mnemonics	Description
	JNBE/JA	Jump on not below or equal/above
	JNP/JPO	Jump on not parity/ parity odd
	JNO	Jump on no overflow
	JNS	Jump on not sign
	JCXZ	Jump on CX = 0
	JMP <16-bit addr>	Unconditional jump, direct within segment
	JMP <8-bit offset>	Unconditional jump, relative to IP, −128 to +127 bytes
	JMP src	Unconditional jump, indirect via register or memory, within segment
	JMP <16-bit IP value>, <16-bit CS value>	Unconditional jump, direct, intersegment
	JMP src	Unconditional jump, indirect, intersegment
	CALL <16-bit addr>	Call, direct within segment
	CALL src	Call, indirect within segment, via register or memory
	CALL <16-bit IP value>, <16-bit CS value>	Call direct, intersegment
	CALL src	Call, indirect intersegment
	RET	Return
	RET <16-bit data>	Return, add immediate data to SP
Iteration Control	LOOP <8-bit offset>	Loop CX times
	LOOPZ, LOOPE <8-bit offset>	Loop whilst CX nonzero and zero flag not set
	LOOPNZ, LOOPNE <8-bit offset>	Loop whilst CX nonzero and zero flag set
Stack	PUSH, POP reg	Push, pop onto stack
	PUSH, POP seg reg	Push, pop segment register
	PUSH, POP src	Push, pop memory value
	PUSHF, POPF	Push, pop flags
Control	LAHF	Load AH with flags
	SAHF	Store AH in flags
	CLC	Clear carry
	CMC	Complement carry
	STC	Set carry
	CLD	Clear direction (increment in string operations)
	STD	Set direction (decrement in string operations)
	INT <8-bit data>	Software interrupt (with type)

Group	Assembler mnemonics	Description
	INTO	Interrupt on overflow
	IRET	Interrupt return
	STI	Set interrupt flag (enable interrupts)
	CLI	Clear interrupt flag (disable interrupts)
	HLT	Halt
	WAIT	Wait until TEST pin asserted
	ESC	Escape prefix; generate address and bus control signals, but take no action
	LOCK	Bus lock prefix; bus locked for the duration of one instruction
	SEGMENT	Override prefix
Input-Output	IN <8-bit port address>	Input from fixed port to AL, AX
	IN	Input from variable port to AL, AX specified in DX
	OUT <8-bit port address>	Output from AL, AX to fixed port
	OUT	Output from AL, AX to variable port specified in DX

(b) 8086 (8088 variations) pinouts

Pin	Signal	Pin	Signal	Max mode variations
1	GND	40	VCC	
2	AD14 (A14)	39	AD15 (A15)	
3	AD13 (A13)	38	A16/S3	
4	AD12 (A12)	37	A17/S4	
5	AD11 (A11)	36	A18/S5	
6	AD10 (A10)	35	A19/S6	
7	AD9 (A9)	34	$\overline{\text{BHE}}$/S7 (SS0)	(HIGH)
8	AD8 (A8)	33	MN/$\overline{\text{MX}}$	
9	AD7	32	$\overline{\text{RD}}$	
10	AD6	31	HOLD	$\overline{\text{RQ}}$/$\overline{\text{GT0}}$
11	AD5	30	HLDA	$\overline{\text{RQ}}$/$\overline{\text{GT1}}$
12	AD4	29	$\overline{\text{WR}}$	$\overline{\text{LOCK}}$
13	AD3	28	M/$\overline{\text{IO}}$ (IO/$\overline{\text{M}}$)	$\overline{\text{S2}}$
14	AD2	27	DT/$\overline{\text{R}}$	$\overline{\text{S1}}$
15	AD1	26	$\overline{\text{DEN}}$	$\overline{\text{S0}}$
16	AD0	25	ALE	QS0
17	NMI	24	$\overline{\text{INTA}}$	QS1
18	INTR	23	$\overline{\text{TEST}}$	
19	CLK	22	READY	
20	GND	21	RESET	

Appendix 2

(a) Z8000 instruction set

Group	Assembler mnemonics	Description
Data transfer	LD LDB reg, src LDL	Load / Load byte / Load long word (32 bits) — into register from register, memory
	LD LDB dest, reg LDL	As above, into memory, register from register
	LD, LDB dest, <16-bit 8-bit data>	Load immediate
	LDA, LDAR reg, src	Load address, Load address relative
	LDK reg, src	Load constant
	LDM reg, src, n	Load multiple; load n words from memory into the registers starting with reg
	LDM dest, reg, n	Load multiple from registers to memory
	LDR, LDRB, LDRL reg, src	Load register relative with word, byte, long word
	LDR, LDRB, LDRL dest, reg	Store relative
	EX, EXB reg, src	Exchange word, byte
	CLR, CLRB dest	Clear word, byte
Arithmetic	ADC, ADCB reg, src	Add with carry
	ADD, ADDB, ADDL reg, src	Add
	SBC, SBCB reg, src	Subtract with borrow
	SUB, SUBB, SUBL reg, src	Subtract
	CP, CPB, CPL reg, src	Compare with register
	CP, CPB dest, <data>	Compare immediate
	MULT, MULTL reg, src	Signed multiply
	DIV, DIVL reg, src	Signed divide
	EXTS, EXTSB, EXTSL	Extend sign

Group	Assembler mnemonics	Description
	dest	
	COM, COMB dest	1's complement
	NEG, NEGB dest	Negate (2's complement)
	INC, INCB dest, n	Increment by n
	DEC, DECB dest, n	Decrement by n
	DAB dest	Decimal adjust
	AND, ANDB	AND
	OR, ORB reg, src	OR
	XOR, XORB	Exclusive-OR
	TEST, TESB, TESTL dest	Test
Bit	BIT, BITB	Test bit
manipulation	RES, RESB dest,	Reset bit static
	<bit no>	
	SET, SETB	Set bit
	BIT, BITB	Test bit dynamic,
	RES, RESB dest, reg	Reset bit bit number
	SET, SETB	Set bit in reg
	TSET, TSETB dest	Test-and-Set (uses most significant bit of dest) Indivisible.
Shifts and	SLA, SLAB,	Shift left arithmetic
rotates	SLAL	
	SLL, SLLB, dest,	Shift left logical
	SLLL <shift	
	SRA, SRAB count>	Shift right arithmetic
	SRAL	
	SRL, SRLB	Shift right logical
	SRLL	
	SDA, SDAB	Shift dynamic, arithmetic;
	SDAL	signed value in reg gives
	dest, reg	count and direction
	SDL, SDLB,	Shift dynamic, logical
	SDLL	
	RL, RLB	Rotate left
	RLC, RLCB dest,	Rotate left through carry
	RR, RRB <shift	Rotate right
	RRC, RRCB count>	Rotate right through carry
	RLDB reg, src	Rotate digit left through both operands
	RRDB	Rotate digit right
Branches	JP <cond>, dest	Conditional jump
	JR <cond>, <8-bit offset>	Conditional jump relative to PC −254 to +256 bytes (8-bit signed value doubled)
	DJNZ, DBJNZ reg, dest	Decrement reg, jump to dest if

Group	Assembler mnemonics		Description
			nonzero
	CALL dest		Call subroutine
	CALR dest		Call subroutine relative
	RET <cond>		Conditional return
Stack	POP, POPL dest, index reg		From stack
	PUSH, PUSHL index reg, src		Onto stack
Control	COMFLG		Complement flag
	SETFLG <flag>		Set flag
	RESFLG		Reset flag
*	LDCTL CTLR, src		Load into Control Register
*	LDCTL dest, CTLR		Load from Control Register
	LDCTLB FLGR, src		Load into Flag Byte Register
	LDCTLB dest, FLGR		Load from Flag Byte Register
*	LDPS src		Load program status
*	EI, DI <int>		Enable, disable vectored and/or nonvectored interrupts
*	HALT		Halt
*	IRET		Interrupt return
	SC src		System Call
	NOP		No operation
*	MBIT		Test Multi-Micro bit
*	MREQ dest		Multi-Micro Request
*	MRES		Multi-Micro Reset
*	MSET		Multi-Micro Set
String and block operations	CPD, CPDB		Compare reg1 with src, set the Z flag if the condition code cond would have been set by the comparison; decrement the src pointer, decrement reg2
	CPDR, CPDRB	reg1, src, reg 2, <cond>	As above, but repeat until cond true or reg2 zero
	CPI, CPIB		Compare and increment
	CPIR, CPRIB		Compare, increment and repeat
	CPSD, SPSDB	dest, src, reg, <cond>	Compare string and decrement; Compare contents of src and dest; set Z flag if cond true; decrement both src and dest pointers, and reg
	CPSDR, CPSDRB		Compare string, decrement and repeat
	CPSI, CPSIB		Compare string and increment
	CPSIR, CPSIRB		Compare string, increment and repeat
	LDD, LDDB		Load and decrement; Load contents of src into dest;

Group	Assembler mnemonics	Description
	dest, src, reg	decrement both src and dest pointers, and reg
	LDDR, LDDRB	Load, decrement and repeat
	LDI, LDIB	Load and increment
	LDIR, LDIRB	Load, increment and repeat
	dest, src, reg	
	TRDB	Translate and decrement; Lower byte of contents of dest is used as an index added to contents of src to access memory byte, which replaces contents of dest; dest pointer decremented, reg decremented
	TRDRB	Translate and repeat
	TRIB	Translate and increment
	TRIRB	Translate, increment and repeat
	src1, src2, reg	
	TRTDB	Translate test and decrement; Contents of src1 used as the index into table of translation bytes accessed via src2; if byte accessed is zero, Z flag set; src1 pointer decremented, reg decremented
	TRTDRB	Translate, test, decrement and repeat.
	TRTIB	Translate, test and increment
	TRTIRB	Translate, test, increment and repeat
Input-Output*	IN, INB reg, src	Input from src to reg
	OUT, OUTB dest, reg	Output from reg to dest
	dest, src, reg	
	IND, INDB	Input from src to dest; decrement reg
	INDR, INDBR	Input, decrement and repeat
	INI, INIB	Input and increment
	INIR, INIRB	Input, increment and repeat
	OUTD, OUTDB	Output and decrement
	OUTDR, OUTDRB	Output, decrement and repeat
	OUTI, OUTIB	Output and increment
	OTIR, OTIRB	Output, increment and repeat
	SIN, SINB	Special input
	SOUT, SOUTB	Special output
	SIND, SINDB	Special input and decrement
	SINDR, SINDRB	Special input, decrement and repeat
	SINI, SINIB	Special input and increment
	SINIR, SINIRB	Special input, increment and repeat
	for MMU	
	SOUTD, SOUTDB	Special output and decrement
	SOTDR, SOTDRB	Special output, decrement and repeat
	SOUTI, SOUTIB	Special output and increment
	SOTIR, SOTIRB	Special output, increment and repeat

*Denotes privileged instructions.

(b) Z8000 pinouts

Pin	Signal Z8001	Z8002	Pin	Signal Z8001	Z8002
1	AD0	AD9	25	SN1	R/$\overline{\mathrm{W}}$
2	AD9	AD10	26	SN0	N/$\overline{\mathrm{S}}$
3	AD10	AD11	27	BUSRQ	B/$\overline{\mathrm{W}}$
4	AD11	AD12	28	WAIT	Reserved
5	AD12	AD13	29	BUSAK	$\overline{\mathrm{AS}}$
6	AD13	$\overline{\mathrm{STOP}}$	30	R/$\overline{\mathrm{W}}$	CLOCK
7	$\overline{\mathrm{STOP}}$	$\overline{\mathrm{MI}}$	31	N/$\overline{\mathrm{S}}$	GND
8	$\overline{\mathrm{MI}}$	AD15	32	B/$\overline{\mathrm{W}}$	AD1
9	AD15	AD14	33	Reserved	AD2
10	AD14	+5V	34	$\overline{\mathrm{AS}}$	AD3
11	+5V	$\overline{\mathrm{VI}}$	35	CLOCK	AD5
12	$\overline{\mathrm{VI}}$	$\overline{\mathrm{NVI}}$	36	GND	AD4
13	$\overline{\mathrm{NVI}}$	$\overline{\mathrm{NMI}}$	37	SN2	AD6
14	$\overline{\mathrm{SEGT}}$	$\overline{\mathrm{RESET}}$	38	AD1	AD7
15	$\overline{\mathrm{NMI}}$	$\overline{\mathrm{MO}}$	39	AD2	AD8
16	$\overline{\mathrm{RESET}}$	$\overline{\mathrm{MREQ}}$	40	AD3	AD0
17	$\overline{\mathrm{MO}}$	$\overline{\mathrm{DS}}$	41	AD5	
18	$\overline{\mathrm{MREQ}}$	ST3	42	SN4	
19	$\overline{\mathrm{DS}}$	ST2	43	AD4	
20	ST3	ST1	44	AD6	
21	ST2	ST0	45	AD7	
22	ST1	$\overline{\mathrm{BUSRQ}}$	46	SN5	
23	ST0	$\overline{\mathrm{WAIT}}$	47	SN6	
24	SN3	$\overline{\mathrm{BUSAK}}$	48	AD8	

Appendix 3

(a) MC68000 instruction set

Group	Assembler mnemonics	Description
Data transfer	MOVE src, dest	Move word, byte or double-word from src to dest; all addressing modes are allowed
	MOVEM <register list>, dest	Move multiple registers; the contents of the specified registers (address or data regs) are moved to dest
	MOVEM src, <register list>	The contents of the locations indicated by src are moved to the registers in the list
	MOVEP data reg, addr reg, <displacement>	Move peripheral data; load alternate bytes of memory, starting at the address specified by the sum of the address register contents and the displacement, from the data register
	MOVEP addr reg, <displacement>, data reg	Move peripheral data into the register
	MOVEQ #<data>, data reg	Move Quick; move immediate 8-bit data sign-extended to 32 bits, into the register
	EXG reg1, reg2	Exchange register contents
	LEA src, addr reg	Load the effective address specified by src, into the address register
	SWAP data reg	Swap the 16-bit halves of the 32-bit data register
Arithmetic	ADD src, data reg	Add binary src data to register
	ADD data reg, dest	Add data reg to dest
	ADDA src, addr reg	Add src data to address register
	ABCD data reg, data reg	Add decimal with extend bit
	ABCD –(addr reg), –(addr reg)	Add decimal contents of two memory locations
	ADDI #<data>, dest	Add immediate to memory or register specified by dest

Group	Assembler mnemonics	Description
	ADDQ #<3-bit data>, dest	Add Quick, immediate data in the range 1 to 8
	ADDX data reg, data reg	Add Extended; extend bit included in the addition
	ADDX –(addr reg), –(addr reg)	Add contents of memory locations, including the extend bit
	SUB src, data reg	Subtract
	SUB data reg, dest	
	SUBA src, addr reg	
	SUBI #<data>, dest	
	SUBQ #<3-bit data>, dest	As Add
	SUBX data reg, data reg	
	SUBX –(addr reg), –(addr reg)	
	CMP src, data reg	Compare src with register contents
	CMPA src, addr reg	Compare address
	CMPI #<data>, dest	Compare immediate
	CMPM (addr reg)+, (addr reg)+	Compare memory
	CLR dest	Clear memory or register
	NEG dest	Negate (2's complement)
	NEGX dest	Negate, including extend bit
	EXT data reg	Sign-extend data register contents to 32 bits from 16, or to 16 from 8
	MULS src, data reg	Signed Multiply
	MULU src, data reg	Unsigned Multiply
	DIVS src, data reg	Signed Divide
	DIVU src, data reg	Unsigned Divide
	TST dest	Test operand (compare with zero) and set flags
	AND src, data reg	Logical AND
	AND data reg, dest	
	ANDI #<data>, dest	AND immediate
	OR src, data reg	Logical inclusive-OR
	OR data reg, dest	
	ORI #<data>, dest	OR Immediate
	EOR data reg, dest	Exclusive-OR
	EORI #<data>, dest	Exclusive-OR Immediate
	NOT dest	1s complement
Shifts and rotates	ASL, LSL data reg,	Arithmetic, logical left shift
	ASR, LSR count reg	Arithmetic, logical right shift
	ROL, ROR #<data>,	Rotate left, right
	ROXL, ROXR data reg	Rotate left, right through extend bit
	dest	Data in a register may be shifted by the number of bits in a count register, or specified in an immediate argument.

Group	Assembler mnemonics	Description
		Data in a memory location (dest) may only be shifted by one place
Bit manipulation	BTST data reg, dest	Bit test. The bit of the destination specified in the register is reflected in the Z condition code
	BTST #<bit no>, dest BSET data reg, dest BSET #<bit no>, dest	Test bit, then set it. Specified bit in dest reflected in the Z condition code and then set
	BCLR data reg, dest BCLR #<bit no>, dest	Test bit, then clear it
	BCHG data reg, dest BCHG #<bit no>, dest	Test bit, then complement it
BCD operations	ABCD data reg, data reg	Add decimal with extend bit
	ABCD –(addr reg), –(addr reg)	Add memory addressed by addr registers, decimal with extend bit
	SBCD data reg, data reg	Subtract decimal with extend bit
	SBCD –(addr reg), –(addr reg)	
	NBCD dest	Negate decimal with extend bit
Branches and calls	B <cond> <displacement>	Branch relative to PC on condition. Displacement may be 8-bit or 16-bit 2s complement. Conditions are: CC carry clear CS carry set EQ equal GE greater or equal GT greater HI high LE less or equal LS low or same LT less MI minus NE not equal PL plus VC no overflow VS overflow
	DB <cond>, data reg, <displacement>	Test condition; perform no operation if true. If not true, decrement contents of data reg; if data reg = –1, count is over, and continues with the next instruction, otherwise performs branch relative to PC

Group	Assembler mnemonics	Description
	S <cond> dest	Set according to condition. Test condition; if true, set byte specified by dest to all 1s; if not true, set byte to all zeros
	BRA <displacement>	Branch always, relative to PC
	JMP dest	Jump unconditional to addr specified by dest
	BSR <displacement>	Call subroutine, relative to PC
	JSR dest	Call subroutine
	RTS	Return from subroutine
	RTR	Return and restore condition codes
Control		
*	RESET	Reset external devices
*	RTE	Return from exception; restores PC and condition codes
*	STOP	Stop
*	ORI #<data>, SR	OR immediate to status reg
*	MOVE USP, addr reg	Contents of the user stack
*	MOVE addr reg, USP	are transferred to or from the specified addr register
*	ANDI #<data>, SR	AND immediate to status register
*	EORI #<data>, SR	Exclusive-OR immediate to status reg
*	MOVE src, SR	Move data to status register
	TRAP #<vector>	Software trap
	TRAPV	Trap on overflow
	CHK src, data reg	Check register against bounds; Lower bound = 0 Upper bound = contents of src
	ANDI #<data>, CCR	AND immediate to condition code register
	ORI #<data>, CCR	OR immediate with CCR
	EORI #<data>, CCR	Exclusive-OR immediate to CCR
	MOVE src, CCR	Load CCR from memory or register
	MOVE CCR, src	Load contents of CCR into memory or register
	TAS dest	Test-and-Set. Indivisible read-modify-write instruction used for shared resource mutual exclusion
	LINK addr reg, #<displacement>	Push the current contents of the addr register onto the stack, load the addr register with the value of the stack pointer, then add the displacement value to the stack pointer
	UNLK addr reg	Load the stack pointer from the addr register with a 32-bit word pulled from the top of the stack

*Denotes privileged instructions.

(b) MC68000 pinouts

Pin	Signal		Pin	Signal	
1	D4		64	D5	
2	D3		63	D6	
3	D2		62	D7	
4	D1		61	D8	
5	D0		60	D9	
6	$\overline{AS}$	Address strobe	59	D10	
7	$\overline{UDS}$	Upper data strobe	58	D11	
8	$\overline{LDS}$	Lower data strobe	57	D12	
9	R/$\overline{W}$		56	D13	
10	$\overline{DTACK}$	Data transfer Ack	55	D14	
11	$\overline{BG}$	Bus grant	54	D15	
12	$\overline{BGACK}$	Bus grant Ack	53	Vss	GND
13	$\overline{BR}$	Bus release	52	A23	
14	Vdd	+5V	51	A22	
15	CLK		50	A21	
16	Vss	GND	49	Vdd	+5V
17	$\overline{HALT}$		48	A20	
18	$\overline{RESET}$		47	A19	
19	$\overline{VMA}$		46	A18	
20	E	6800 Enable	45	A17	
21	$\overline{VPA}$	Valid peripheral addr	44	A16	
22	$\overline{BERR}$	Bus error	43	A15	
23	$\overline{IPL2}$		42	A14	
24	$\overline{IPL1}$	Interrupt priority	41	A13	
25	$\overline{IPL0}$		40	A12	
26	FC2		39	A11	
27	FC1	Function codes	38	A10	
28	FC0		37	A9	
29	A1		36	A8	
30	A2		35	A7	
31	A3		34	A6	
32	A4		33	A5	

Appendix 4

The NS16000 Family instruction set is too complex to describe fully; the majority of instructions are presented here using the following abbreviations to denote addressing modes:

gen	=	any addressing mode
4-bit	=	4-bit 'short' value encoded in the intruction field
reg	=	any general-purpose register
areg	=	any address register
mreg	=	any MMU register
creg	=	any custom slave processor register

Type of operation is indicated by instruction mnemonic suffix:

i = one of B(byte), W(16-bit word), D(32-bit word)
f = one of F(standard length floating-point), L(long floating-point)

NS16000 instruction set (excluding Custom Slave instructions)

Group	Assembler mnemonics	Description
Data transfer	MOVi gen, gen	Move a value
	MOVQi <4-bit data>, gen	Extend and move a 4-bit constant
	MOVMi gen, gen, <byte count>	Move multiple number of bytes
	MOVZBW gen, gen	Move with zero extension
	MOVZiD gen, gen	Move with zero extension
	MOVXBW gen, gen	Move with sign extension
	MOVXiD gen, gen	Move with sign extension
	ADDR gen, gen	Move effective address
Arithmetic and logical	ADDi gen, gen	Add
	ADDCi gen, gen	Add with carry
	SUBi gen, gen	Subtract
	SUBCi gen, gen	Subtract with borrow
	ADDQi <4-bit data>, gen	Add 4-bit constant
	NEGi gen, gen	Negate (2s complement)
	ABSi gen, gen	Take absolute value
	MULi gen, gen	Multiply
	QUOi gen, gen	Divide, rounding towards zero

Group	Assembler mnemonic	Description
	REMi gen, gen	Remainder from QUOi
	DIVi gen, gen	Divide rounding down
	MODi gen, gen	Remainder from DIVi
	MEIi gen, gen	Multiply to extended integer
	DEIi gen, gen	Divide to extended integer
	CMPi gen, gen	Compare
	CMPQi <4-bit data>, gen	Compare with 4-bit constant
	CMPMi gen, gen, <byte count>	Compare Multiple
	ANDi gen, gen	AND
	ORi gen, gen	Inclusive-OR
	BICi gen, gen	Clear selected bits
	XORi gen, gen	Exclusive-OR
	COMi gen, gen	Complement all bits
	NOTi gen, gen	1s complement; least significant byte only
	S <cond> i gen	Save condition code; if cond is 1, integer result is all 1s; if cond is zero, integer result is all zeros
BCD arithmetic	ADDPi gen, gen	Add packed BCD data
	SUBPi gen, gen	Subtract packed BCD data
Shifts and rotates	LSHi gen, gen	Logical shift left or right, depending on sign and value of shift count
	ASHi gen, gen	Arithmetic shift left or right
	ROTi gen, gen	Rotate left or right
Bit manipulation	TBITi gen, gen	Test bit
	SBITi gen, gen	Test and set bit
	SBITIi gen, gen	Test-and-set bit interlocked (indivisible)
	CBITi gen, gen	Test and clear bit
	CBITIi gen, gen	Test-and-clear bit interlocked
	IBITi gen, gen	Test and invert bit
	FFSi gen, gen	Find first set bit
Bit-field manipulation	EXTi reg, gen, gen, <displacement>	Extract bit field
	INSi reg, gen, gen, <displacement>	Insert bit field
	EXTSi gen, gen, <data>, <data>	Extract bit field
	INSSi gen, gen, <data>, <data>	Insert bit field
	CVTP reg, gen, gen	Convert to bit field pointer

Group	Assembler mnemonics	Description
Array manipulation	CHECKi reg, gen, gen	Index bounds check
	INDEXi reg, gen, gen	Recursive indexing step for multiple arrays
String manipulation	MOVSi options	Move string
	MOVST options	Move string, translating bytes
	CMPSi options	Compare strings
	CMPST options	Translate bytes of first string, compare with second string
	SKPSi options	Skip over first string entries
	SKPST options	Skip, translating bytes
Branches and calls	JUMP gen	Unconditional jump
	BR <displacement>	Unconditional jump relative to PC
	B <cond> <displacement>	Conditional branch relative to PC
	CASEi gen	Multiway branch
	ACBi <4-bit data>, gen, <displacement>	Add 4-bit constant value, jump if nonzero
	JSR gen	Jump to subroutine
	BSR <displacement>	Jump to subroutine relative to PC
	CXP <displacement>	Call external procedure
	CXPD <displacement>	Call external procedure using descriptor
	SVC	Supervisor call
	FLAG	Flag Trap
	BPT	Breakpoint Trap
	ENTER reg list, <displacement>	Save registers and allocate stack frame (Enter procedure)
	EXIT reg list	Restore registers and reclaim stack frame (Exit procedure)
	RET <displacement>	Return from subroutine
	RXP <displacement>	Return from external procedure call
*	RETT <displacement>	Return from trap
*	RETI	Return from interrupt
Control	SAVE reg list	Save registers on the stack
	RESTORE reg list	Restore registers from the stack
	LPRi addr reg, gen	Load register
*	LPRD INTBASE, gen	Load INTBASE
*	LPRW PSR, gen	Load program status register
	SPRi addr reg, gen	Store register
*	SPRD INTBASE, gen	
*	SPRW PSR, gen	
	ADJSPi gen	Adjust stack pointer
*	BISPSRW gen	Set bits in PSR
	BISPSRB gen	Set bits in PSR
*	BICPSRW gen	Clear bits in PSR

Group	Assembler mnemonics	Description
	BICPSRB gen	Clear bits in SR
*	SETCFG option list	Set configuration register
Floating-point arithmetic	MOVf gen, gen	Move floating-point value
	MOVLF gen, gen	Move and shorten a long value to standard
	MOVFL gen, gen	Move and lengthen a standard value to long
	MOVif gen, gen	Move and convert any integer to long
	ROUNDfi gen, gen	Convert to integer by rounding
	TRUNCfi gen, gen	Convert to integer by truncation
	FLOORfi gen, gen	Convert to the largest integer less than or equal to
	ADDf gen, gen	Add
	SUBf gen, gen	Subtract
	MULf gen, gen	Multiply
	DIVf gen, gen	Divide
	CMPf gen, gen	Compare
	NEGf gen, gen	Negate
	ABSf gen, gen	Take absolute value
	LFSR gen	Load FSR
	SFSR gen	Store FSR
	NOP	No operation
	WAIT	For interrupt
	DIA	Diagnose. Not for normal programming
MMU		
*	LMR mreg, gen	Load MMU register
*	SMR mreg, gen	Store MMU register
*	RDVAL gen	Validate address for reading
*	WRVAL gen	Validate address for writing
*	MOVSUi gen, gen	Move a value from Supervisor space to user space
*	MOVUSi gen, gen	Move a value from User space to Supervisor space

*Denotes privileged instructions.

References

Chapter 2 references

1. Gooze, M. (1979) 'How a 16-bit microprocessor makes it in an 8-bit world'. *Electronics* (Sept 27), 122-125.
2. Ritter, T. and Boney, J. (1979) 'A microprocessor for the revolution: The 6809'. *Byte* (Part 1 Jan 1979; Part 2 Feb 1979; Part 3 Mar 1979).
3. Motorola Data Sheet AD1-804-R1 MC6809.
4. Thomae, I.H. (1980) '8-bit Microprocessor harbors 16-bit Performance'. *Electronics* (Jan 3), 163-167.
5. Bartlett, J. and Retter, R. (1979) 'CPU brings 16-bit performance to 8-bit systems'. *Electronic Design* **6** (Mar 15), 76-80.
6. Intel 8086 User's Manual (1979).
7. Browne, J. and Moyer, B. (1982) 'µP fits 16-bit performance into 8-bit systems'. *Electronic Design* (Apr 15), 183-187.
8. Texas Instruments (1978) '9900 Family Systems Design' 1st edn. Section 8: TMS9980A/TMS9981.

Chapter 3 references

1. Lynch, F. (1976) 'Keep the PACE up and running'. *Electronic Design* **25** (Dec 6), 64-70.
2. Suri, A. *et al.* (1979) 'Take advantage of bipolar computing power and get mini performance in a micro'. *Electronic Design* **2** (Jan 18), 76-86.
3. Wilnai, D. and Verhofstabt, W.J. (1977) 'One-chip CPU packs power of general-purpose minicomputer'. *Electronics* (June 23), 113-117.
4. Falkoff, D. *et al.* (1977) 'Exploit existing Nova software'. *Electronic Design* **19** (Sept 13), 54-64.
5. Data General Corp (1977) 'MicroNova Integrated Circuits Data Manual.
6. Brown, G. (1979) 'A mini-like memory architecture, flexible I/O and powerful support set the 9900 apart'. *Electronic Design* **14** (July 5), 76-80.
7. Davis, H. (1979) 'Take advantage of the 9900's minicomputer instruction set and separate bus structure'. *Electronic Design* **13** (June 21), 74-81.
8. Texas Instruments Inc. (1977) 'TMS9900 Microprocessor Data Manual'.
9. Loftus, A. (1976) '16-bit microprocessor performs like minicomputer'. *Electronics* (May 27), 99-105.

Chapter 4 references

1. Toong, H.D. and Gupta, A. (1981) 'An architectural comparison of contemporary 16-bit microprocessors'. *IEEE Micro* (May), 26-37.
2. Davis, S. (1979) '16-bit microprocessors'. *EDN Special Report* (EDN August 5), 70-85.
3. Grappel, R. and Hemenway, J. (1980) 'Compare the newest 16-bit μPs to evaluate their potential'. *EDN* (Sept 5), 197-201.
4. Davis, H.A. (1979) 'Comparing the architectures of three 16-bit microprocessors'. *Computer Design* (July), 91-100.
5. Alexy, G. and Kop, H. (1978) 'Get minicomputer features at ten times 8080 speed with the 8086'. *Electronic Design* **20** (Sept 17), 60-66.
6. Katz, B.J. *et al.* (1978) '8086 microcomputer bridges the gap between 8- and 16-bit designs'. *Electronics* (Feb 16), 99-104.
7. Hartmann, A.C. *et al.* (1981) 'A VLSI architecture for software structure: the Intel 8086'. *IEEE Micro* (May), 57-69.
8. Morse, S.P. *et al.* (1980) 'Intel Microprocessors – 8008 to 8086'. *IEEE Computer* (Oct), 42-60.
9. Hartmann, A.C. (1980) 'Architectural issues in the design of the Intel 8086 microcomputer system'. *Electronic Engineering* (Dec), 59-73.
10. Morse, S.P. (1980) *The 8086 Primer*. Hayden Book Co: New Jersey, USA.
11. Intel Corp. (1979) *The 8086 Family User's Manual*. Intel Corporation: Santa Clara, USA.
12. Shima, M. (1978) 'Two versions of 16-bit chip span microprocessor, minicomputer needs'. *Electronics* (Dec 21), 81-88.
13. Shima, M. (1979) 'Demystifying Microprocessor Design'. *IEEE Spectrum* (July), 22-30.
14. Zilog Inc. (1980) *Microcomputer Components Data Book*. Zilog Inc: Cupertino, USA.
15. AMD Inc. (1980) *The AmZ8000 Family Data Book*. Advanced Micro Devices Inc.: Sunnyvale, USA.
16. LeMair, I. and Robis, R. (1978) 'Complex systems are easy to design . . . with the MC68000 μP'. *Electronic Design* **18** (Sept 1), 100-107.
17. Stritter, E.P. and Tredennick, N. (1978) 'Microprogrammed implementation of a single-chip microprocessor'. *SIGMICRO Newsletter* **9**, No 4, Dec 1978.
18. Stritter, E.P. and Gunter, T. (1979) 'A microprocessor architecture for a changing world: the Motorola 68000'. *IEEE Computer* (Feb).
19. Zolnowsky, J. and Tredennick, N. (1979) 'Design and implementation of system features for the MC68000'. *Proc. Compcon Fall.*
20. Hartmann, B. (1979) '16-bit microprocessor camps on 32-bit frontier'. *Electronics* (Oct 11), 118-125.
21. Grappel, R. and Hemenway, J. (1980) 'The MC68000 – A 32-bit μP masquerading as a 16-bit device'. *EDN* (Feb 20), 127-134.
22. Motorola Inc. (1979) *MC68000 16-bit Microprocessor User's Manual.* Motorola Inc: Austin, Texas, USA.
23. Laffitte, D. (1981) 'New-generation 16-bit μPs – fast and function-oriented'. *Electronic Design* (Feb 19), 111-117.
24. Laffitte, D. and Borie, R. (1981) 'Separate address space makes context-switching a snip for μPs'. *Electronic Design* (June 11), 229-232.
25. Laffitte, D. and Guttag, K. (1981) 'Fast on-chip memory extends 16-bit

family's reach'. *Electronics* (Feb 24), 157-161.
26. Laffitte, D. (1981) 'TMS99000: a function-oriented 16-bit μP'. *Electronic Product Design* (June), 49-51.
27. Lavi, Y. *et al.* (1980) '16-bit microprocessor enters virtual-memory domain'. *Electronics* (Apr 24), 123-130.
28. Bal, S. *et al.* 'Bilingual 16-bit μP summons large-scale computer power'. *Electronic Design* **2** (1980) 66-70.
29. Bal, S. *et al.* (1982) 'The NS16000 Family – Advances in Architecture and Hardware'. *IEEE Computer* (June), 58-67.
30. National Semiconductor Inc. (1982) 'NS16032 high-performance microprocessor'. Preliminary Data Sheet (Apr): National Semiconductor Corp., 2900 Semiconductor Drive, Santa Clara CA, 95051.

Chapter 5 references

1. Intel Corp. (1979) Application Note AP-67 '8086 System Design'. (Sept.)
2. Korody, R. and Alfke, P. (1979) 'Learn to apply the power of the Z8002 by studying a small 16-bit computer'. *Electronic Design* **22** (Oct 25), 90-96.
3. Banning, J. (1979) 'Z-Bus and peripheral support packages tie distributed computer systems together'. *Electronic Design* **24** (Nov 22), 144-150.
4. Stockton, J. and Scherer, V. (1979) 'Learn the timing and interfacing of MC68000 peripheral circuits'. *Electronic Design* **23** (Nov 8), 58-63.
5. *Electronic Design* (1980) 'Support chips bring out the MC68000's best'. Editorial comment (June 7), 31-32.
6. Bursky, D. (1980) 'Facile support chips free up the host CPU . . .'. *Electronic Design* (May 10), 133-138.
7. Evans, M. and Carinalli, C. (1982) 'Single-chip controllers cover all RAMs from 16k to 256k'. *Electronic Design* (Feb 4), 119-126.
8. von Glahn, P. (1982) 'Capable support ICs ease dynamic RAM interfacing'. *EDN* (Aug 4), 145-154.
9. Fister, M. (1981) 'Dynamic RAM controller introduces no wait states'. *EDN* (Nov 11), 253-262.
10. *EDN Editorial* (1981) 'Error-checking and correcting ICs see wider use as memory size grows'. *EDN* (Mar 4), 31-40.
11. Korody, R. and Raaum, D. (1980) 'Purge your memory array of pesky error bits'. *EDN* (May 20), 153-158.
12. Hu, J. *et al.* (1980) 'Memory-management units help 16-bit μPs to handle large memory systems'. *Electronic Design* **9** (Apr 26), 128-135.
13. Stevenson, D. (1980) 'Memory management rescues 16-bit μPs from demands of multiple users, tasks'. *Electronic Design* **1** (Jan 4), 112-116.
14. Collins, D.L. and Collins, C.M. (1981) 'Memory-management chip masters large databases'. *Electronic Design* (Aug 20), 115-121.
15. Mateosian, R. (1981) 'Segmentation advances uC memory addressing'. *Electronic Design* (Feb 19), 155-162.
16. Roloff, J.J. (1980) 'Managing memory to unloose the full power of microprocessors'. *Electronics* (Apr 10), 130-134.
17. Stockton, J.F. (1982) 'The M68451 memory management unit'. *Electronic Engineering* (May), 59-73.
18. Zilog Inc. (1980) 'Z8010 MMU memory management unit' (Feb).
19. Nat. Semi. Corp. (1982) 'NS16082 memory management unit (MMU)'. Preliminary Data Sheet (Mar).

20. Intel Corp. (1980) 'The 8086 user's manual numerics supplement' (July).
21. Alexy, G. and Katz, B.J. (1980) 'Multiprocessing increases power of inexpensive μP-based designs'. *EDN* (May 20), 161-166.
22. Palmer, J. *et al.* (1980) 'Making mainframe mathematics accessible to microcomputers'. *Electronics* (May 8), 114-121.
23. El-Ayat, K.A. (1979) 'The Intel 8089: An integrated I/O processor'. *IEEE Computer* (June), 67-78.
24. Staum, D. *et al.* (1979) 'Free the uC's CPU from I/O hassles with a special I/O processor'. *Electronic Design* 7 (Mar 29), 102-106.
25. Intel Corp. (1979) 'The 8086 family user's manual' (Oct.).
26. Bal, S. *et al.* (1980) 'System capabilities get a boost from a high-powered slave'. *Electronic Design* 5 (Mar 1), 77-82.
27. Broussard, T. and Brown, G. (1980) 'Controller plugs SDLC into 16-bit systems'. *Electronic Design* (June 7), 191-197.
28. IEEE STD488 'IEEE Standard Digital Interface for Programmable Instrumentation'. Institution of Electrical and Electronic Engineers, 345 East 47th Street, NY 10017.
29. Hewlett-Packard Inc. (1977) 'Hewlett-Packard Interface Bus (HP-IB)'. Publication 5952-0050 (Mar).
30. Summers, J. (1979) 'IEC interface bus (IEEE–488) simplified'. *Electronic Engineering* (Dec), 45-55.
31. Jaworski, J.V. (1982) 'Floppy-disk control squeezes onto a chip'. *Electronic Design* (June 10), 203-212.
32. Szejnwald, H. and Spears, W.R. (1981) 'Minifloppy controller design minimizes component count'. *EDN* (May 13), 118-123.
33. Leger, G.L. (1979) 'LSI ready to make a mark on packet-switching networks'. *Electronics* (Dec 20), 89-99 (2 Parts).
34. Van Dorsten, D. and Kisner, M. (1981) 'Controller chip simplifies interface to floppy disk drives'. *Electronic Design* (June 25), 145-150.
35. Jaworski, J.V. (1980) 'Controller for hard disks handles 4 drives at once'. *Electronic Design* (Oct 25), 111-115.
36. Intel Corp. (1981) Applications Note AP119. 'Microprocessor Interface for the BPK72' (June).
37. Padda, K.S. (1981) 'Universal peripheral controller frees the CPU for high-level work'. *Electronic Design* (Oct 29), 113-118.
38. Jigour, R. (1979) 'Unload the master with a slave in uC-based sensor monitoring'. *Electronic Design* **4** (Feb 15), 78-84.
39. Zilog Corp. (1980) 'Z8034 UPC Data Sheet'.
40. Banning, J. and Lin, P. (1980) 'Peripheral controller chip ties into 8- and 16-bit systems'. *Electronics* (Aug 14), 143-148.

Chapter 6 references

1. Morse, S.P. (1980) *The 8086 Primer*. Hayden Book Co. Inc., Rochelle Park, NJ.
2. Intel Corp. (1978) *MCS-86 Assembly Language Reference Manual.*
3. Hemenway, J. and Teja, E. (1979) 'As you get to know the 8086, use your 8-bit expertise'. *EDN* (Jan 20), 81-88.
4. Rallapalli, K. (1980) 'Exceptional features of the AmZ8000 instruction

set. *Electronic Engineering* (Sept), 95-104.
5. Starnes, T.W. (1979) 'Compact instructions give the MC68000 power while simplifying its operation'. *Electronic Design* **20** (Sept 27), 70-74.
6. Bryce, H. (1979) 'Microprogramming makes the MC68000 a processor ready for the future'. *Electronic Design* **22** (Oct 25), 98-99.
7. Starnes, T.W. (1980) 'Powerful instructions and flexible registers make MC68000 programming easy'. *Electronic Design* **9** (Apr 26), 171-176.

Chapter 7 references

1. Hemenway, J. and Teja, E. (1979) 'Increase 8086 throughput by using interrupts'. *EDN* (May 20), 179-183.
2. Kister, J.E. and Nangle, R.H. (1979) 'Develop software for the 16-bit uC without making costly commitments'. *Electronic Design* **19** (Sept 13), 112-116.
3. Starnes, T.W. (1980) 'Handling exceptions gracefully enhances software reliability', *Electronics* (Sept 11), 153-157.
4. Hemenway, J. and Grappel, R. (1980) 'Use MC68000 interrupts to supervise a console'. *EDN* (June 5), 183-186.
5. IEEE (1981) Draft 8.0 of IEEE Task P754. 'A proposed standard for binary floating-point arithmetic'.
6. Grappel, R.D. and Hemenway, J.E. (1981) 'A tale of 4 μPs: Benchmarks quantify performance'. *EDN* (Apr 1), 179-265.
7. Patstone, W. (1981) '16-bit benchmarks – an update with explanations'. *EDN* (Sept 16), 169-203.

Chapter 8 references

1. Digital Research Inc. (1978) 'CP/M Interface Guide'. Digital Research Inc., PO Box 579, Pacific Grove, CA 93950, USA.
2. Holsworth, F. (1982) '16-bit operating system supports multitasking'. *Electronic Design* (Apr 15), 171-178.
3. Ritchie, D.M. and Thompson, K. (1978) 'The unix time-sharing system'. *BSTJ* **57** (No 6).
4. Hemenway, J. and Teja, E. (1979) 'EDN advanced software systems design course'. *EDN* (Oct 29), 294-335.
5. Harakal, J. (1980) 'Modular multitasking executive cuts cost of 16-bit OS design'. *Electronic Design* **6** (Mar 15), 245-249.
6. Intel Corp. *RMX86 User's Manual.*
7. Intel Corp. *RMX88 User's Manual.*
8. Irwin, J.M. (1981) 'Multitasking executive speeds 16-bit micros'. *Electronic Design* (Mar 5), 131-135.
9. McMinn, C. *et al.* 'Silicon operating system standardizes software'.
10. Intel Corp. (1982) 'Using operating system firmware components to simplify hardware and software design'. Application Note AP-130.

Chapter 9 references

1. Intel PL/M-86/88 manual.
2. Elmore, M.J. (1980) 'PL/M-86 combines hardware access with high-level

language features'. *Electronic Design* **26**, 181-186.
3. Brown, W. (1978) 'Modular programming in PL/M'. *IEEE Computer*, vol. II, No. 3, 40-46.
4. Bass, C. (1978) 'PLZ: A family of system programming languages for microprocessors'. *IEEE Computer*, Vol. II, No. 3, 34-39.
5. Conway, Gries, Zimmerman, Winthrop (1976) *A Primer on Pascal.* Cambridge, Mass. 1976
6. Krouse, T. (1978) *Electronic Design* series on Pascal Language (six parts): Part 1. *Electronic Design* **19**.
7. Bate, R.R. and Johnson, D.S. (1979) 'Putting Pascal to work', *Electronics*, June 7, 111-121.
8. Isaak, J. (1980) 'A careful evaluation helps avoid Pascal's pitfalls'. *EDN* September 20.
9. Ravenel, B.W. (1979) 'Towards a Pascal standard'. *IEEE Computer*, Vol. 12, No. 4, 68-82.
10. Schneider, G.M. (1979) 'Pascal: an overview'. *IEEE Computer*, Vol. 12, No. 4, 61-66.
11. US DOD (1980) *Reference Manual for the Ada Programming Language.*
12. *Electronic Design* (1980) Series on Ada: Part 1'. *Electronic Design.*
13. Booth, G. (1981) 'ADA promotes software reliability with PASCAL – like simplicity'. *EDN* (Jan 7).

Chapter 10 references

1. Adams, G. and Rolander, T. (1978) 'Design motivations for multiple processor microcomputer systems'. *Computer Design* (Mar).
2. MIL-STD-1553 *Multiplex Applications Handbook.*
3. Intel Corp. (1979) *Intel MULTIBUS Interfacing.* Application Note AP.28A.
4. Riley, W.B. (1981) 'LAN standards controversy looms: Ethernet vs IEEE-802'. *Electronic Design* (Sept 30), SS-25 to SS-29.
5. Kotelly, G. (1982) 'Local-Area Networks: Part 1 – Technology. Part 2 – Low & midrange Products. Part 3 – High-performance Products'. *EDN* (Feb 17), 109-150.
6. Allan, R. (1981) 'Local-area network architecture, protocol issues heating up'. *Electronic Design* (Apr 16), 91-102.
7. Yenchario, L. (1981) 'Local-net communications improves at both ends'. *Electronic Design* (Apr 16), 111-117.
8. Schindler, M. (1981) 'Networks may look alike, but software makes the difference'. *Electronic Design* (Apr 16), 121-126.
9. Hahn, M. and Belanger, P. (1981) 'Network minimizes overhead of small computers'. *Electronics* (Aug 25), 125-128.
10. Dineson, M.A. (1981) 'Broadband local networks enhance communications design'. *EDN* (Mar 4), 77-86.

Chapter 11 references

1. Nagle, H.T. and Nelson, V.P. (1981) 'Digital filter implementation on 16-bit microprocessors'. *IEEE Micro* (Feb), 23-41.
2. Warren, C. (1981) 'Understanding bus basics helps resolve design conflicts'. *EDN* (May 27), 159-173.

3. Warren, C. (1981) 'Compare uC-bus specs to find the bus you need'. *EDN* (June 10), 141-153.
4. Warren, C. (1981) 'High-performance buses clear a path for future μCs'. *EDN* (June 24), 157-187.
5. Elmquist, K.A. *et al.* (1979) 'Standard Specification for S-100 Bus Interface Devices' (IEEE Task 696.1/D2). *IEEE Computer* (July) 28-52.
6. Intel Corp. (1979) 'Intel MULTIBUS Interfacing'. Application Note AP-28A (Jan).
7. Balph, T. and Kister, J. (1980) 'μP bus gears up to a 32-bit future'. *Electronic Design* (Jul 5), 97-103.
8. Zilog Inc. (1980) 'The Zilog Z-Bus'.
9. Allison, A.A. (1981) 'Status report on the P896 backplane bus'. *IEEE Micro* (Feb), 67-82.
10. Kaplinsky, C. (1981) 'Decentralizing μP bus grows easily from 16 to 32 bits'. *Electronic Design* (Nov 12), 173-179.

Chapter 12 references

1. Intel Corp. (1982) 'iAPX186 high integration 16-bit microprocessor'. *Advance Information* (May).
2. Klovstad, J. *et al.* (1982) '16-bit μP crams peripheral support on chip'. *Electronic Design* (June 10), 191-196.
3. Intel Corp. (1982) 'iAPX286/10 high performance microprocessor with memory management and protection'. Advance Information (Sept.).
4. Wiseman, S. *et al.* (1982) 'Controller chip has many industrial, computer uses'. *Electronic Design* (Aug 5), 165-173.
5. Intel Corp. (1982) '8096 16-bit microcontroller architectural information and functional description'.
6. Mostek Corp. (1982) 'MK68200 16-bit single-chip microcomputer'. Advance Information, Mostek Corp, 1215 West Crosby Road, Carrollton, TX 75006, USA.
7. Rattner, J. and Lattin, W. (1981) 'Ada determines architecture of 32-bit microprocessor'. *Electronics* (Feb 24), 119-126.
8. Hemenway, J. and Grappel, R. (1981) 'Understand the newest processor to avoid future shock'. *EDN* (Apr 29), 129-136.
9. Hemenway, J. (1981) 'Object-oriented design manages software complexity'. *EDN* (Aug 19), 141-146.
10. Hemenway, J. (1981) 'Memory segmentation aids object-oriented design'. *EDN* (Sept 30), 131-135.
11. Hemenway, J. (1981) 'Examine programming objects from another viewpoint'. *EDN* (Nov 11), 275-278.
12. Hemenway, J. (1982) 'Understand program structure to fathom 432 operation'. *EDN* (Jan 6), 147-152.
13. Intel Corp. 'iAPX432 GDP Architecture Reference Manual'. 'Introduction to the iAPX432 Architecture'.
14. Johnson, D. (1980) 'Data-flow machines threaten the program counter'. *Electronic Design* (Nov 22), 255-258.

Index